College Learning And Study Skills

Fifth Edition

Debbie Guice Longman
Southeastern Louisiana University

Rhonda Holt Atkinson
Louisiana State University

Wadsworth Publishing Company

I(T)P® An International Thomson Publishing Company

Belmont, CA · Albany, NY · Boston · Cincinnati · Johannesburg · London · Madrid · Melbourne
Mexico City · New York · Pacific Grove, CA · Scottsdale, AZ · Singapore · Tokyo · Toronto

Publisher: Karen Allanson
Senior Editorial Assistant: Godwin Chu
Developmental Editor: Kim Johnson
Marketing Manager: Jennie Burger
Project Editor: Christal Niederer
Print Buyer: Barbara Britton
Permissions Manager: Robert Kauser
Production: Robin Gold, Forbes Mill Press
Cover Design: Bill Stanton
Cover Photo: Tony Stone Images
Compositor: Wolf Creek Press
Printer: Courier, Kendallville, Indiana

Printed in the United States of America
1 2 3 4 5 6 7 8 9 10

For more information, contact Wadsworth Publishing Company, 10 Davis Drive, Belmont, CA 94002, or
electronically at http://www.wadsworth.com

International Thomson Publishing Europe
Berkshire House
168-173 High Holborn
London, WC1V 7AA, United Kingdom

International Thomson Editores
Seneca, 53
Colonia Polanco
11560 México D.F. México

Nelson ITP, Australia
102 Dodds Street
South Melbourne
Victoria 3205 Australia

International Thomson Publishing Asia
60 Albert Street #15-01
Albert Complex
Singapore 189969

Nelson Canada
1120 Birchmount Road
Scarborough, Ontario
Canada M1K 5G4

International Thomson Publishing Japan
Hirakawa-cho Kyowa Building, 3F
2-2-1 Hirakawa-cho, Chiyoda-ku
Tokyo 102, Japan

International Thomson Publishing Southern Africa
Building 18, Constantia Square
138 Sixteenth Road, P.O. Box 2459
Halfway House, 1685 South Africa

Library of Congress Cataloging-in-Publication Data

Longman, Debbie Guice.
    College learning and study skills / Debbie Guice Longman, Rhonda
Holt Atkinson. — 5th ed.
      p.   cm.
    Includes bibliographical references (p.   ) and index.
    ISBN 0-534-54972-1
    1. Study skills—United States.   2. College student orientation—
United States.   3. Active learning—United States.   I. Atkinson,
Rhonda Holt.   II. Title.
LB2395.L58   1999
378.1'70281—dc21   98-48106

To Alden J. Moe and Ray R. Buss
for your friendship and support.

THE WADSWORTH COLLEGE SUCCESS SERIES

Santrock and Halonen, *Your Guide to College Success: Strategies for Achieving Your Goals* (1999). ISBN: 0-534-53354-X

Holkeboer and Walker, *Right from the Start: Taking Charge of Your College Success,* 3rd Ed. (1999). ISBN: 0-534-56412-7

Petrie and Denson, *A Student Athlete's Guide to College Success: Peak Performance in Class and in Life* (1999). ISBN: 0-534-54792-3

Van Blerkom, *Orientation to College Learning,* 2nd Ed. (1999). ISBN: 0-534-52389-7

Wahlstrom and Williams, *Learning Success: Being Your Best at College & Life,* 2nd Ed. (1999). ISBN: 0-534-53424-4

Corey, *Living and Learning* (1997). ISBN: 0-534-50501-5

Campbell, *The Power to Learn: Helping Yourself to College Success,* 2nd Ed. (1997). ISBN: 0-534-26352-6

The Freshman Year Experience™ Series

Gardner and Jewler, *Your College Experience: Strategies for Success*, 3rd Ed. (1997). ISBN: 0-534-51895-8

Concise Third Edition (1998). ISBN: 0-534-53749-9

Expanded Reader Edition (1997). ISBN: 0-534-51898-2

Expanded Workbook Edition (1997). ISBN: 0-534-51897-4

Study Skills/Critical Thinking

Longman and Atkinson, *SMART: Study Methods and Reading Techniques*, 2nd Ed. (1999). ISBN: 0-534-54981-0

Sotiriou, *Integrating College Study Skills: Reasoning in Reading, Listening, and Writing*, 5th Ed. (1999). ISBN: 0-534-54990-X

Smith, Knudsvig, and Walter, *Critical Thinking: Building the Basics* (1998). ISBN: 0-534-19284-X

Van Blerkom, *College Study Skills: Becoming a Strategic Learner*, 2nd Ed. (1997). ISBN: 0-534-51679-3

Kurland, *I Know What It Says . . . What Does It Mean? Critical Skills for Critical Reading* (1995). ISBN: 0-534-24486-6

Contents

CLASS List of Readings

Preface

College Learning and Study Skills (CLASS) was written to help students succeed and prosper in college by developing strategies for time management, study skills, and test taking; by using campus libraries; and writing research papers. To help students refine these skills, this text

- Provides information in a context suitable for postsecondary developmental learners.
- Helps these students become more active learners.
- Explains the mental processes involved in learning.
- Incorporates recent theories and research into reading and study skill instruction.

Major Features

Instructors and students agree that *CLASS* meets these objectives. Written in a respectful and unpretentious writing style, the fifth edition of *CLASS* contains all the best features of the first four editions, including

- Practical exercises that ask students to apply what they've learned to content materials.
- Write to Learn journal activities.
- Group Learning Activities.

New to this Edition

We realized, however, that revisions were necessary to meet the changing needs of the students for whom this book was written. To make these revisions, we relied on information from the people who use the text—both instructors and students. New to this edition are the following:

- Online CLASS: Internet exercises in every chapter.
- Updated CLASSic Critical Thinking exercises that ask students to think and work with related content at high levels of thinking.

- New sample chapters, including content from sociology and criminal justice, biology, and technical communication.
- *CLASS* Action summaries that ask students to synthesize and apply chapter content.
- 75 percent new exercises.

CLASS Supplements

A wide variety of supplements are available with this text to assist you in teaching this course and to promote student involvement and learning.

For Instructors
Print

- *Instructor's Manual* (0-534-54973-X). Revised for this new edition, the Instructor's Manual contains exercise answers, suggestions for instruction and sample exams.
- *The Wadsworth College Success Course Guide* (0-534-22991-3). A wide-ranging guide to the issues and challenges of teaching the college success course.
- *Critical Thinking: Building the Basics,* by Smith, Knudsvig, and Walter (0-534-19284-X). A simple, concise approach for improving one's method of learning through critical thinking.
- *The Keystone College Success Newsletter.* This newsletter of the Wadsworth College Success Series brings you ideas and information about events and resources from your colleagues around the country.
- *Custom Publishing Program.* You can combine your choice of chapters from specific Wadsworth titles with your own materials in a custom-bound book. To place your order, call the ITP Custom Order Center at 1-800-245-6724.

Videos

Wadsworth Study Skills Video Series

- *Volume 1: Improving Your Grades* (0-534-54983-7). Highlights study strategies for college students, such as goal setting, time management, learning styles and SQ3R.
- *Volume 2: Lectures for Notetaking Practice* (0-534-54984-5). Provides academic lectures for notetaking practice on a variety of topics, including anthropology, psychology, economics, health and history.
- *CNN College Success Video Companion* (0-534-53746-4). CNN reports on a variety of topics of student interest, including: The college experience, technology on campus, majors and career choice, values, student

involvement and service learning, diversity, health issues and money management.

- *The Wadsworth College Success Video Series.* These videos cover a wide variety of topics of interest to students, including managing stress, improving grades, maximizing mental performance and more.

- *A World of Diversity,* by David Matsumoto (0-534-23229-9 and 0-534-23230-2). A powerful two-video program designed to help students learn basic skills for interacting effectively with students from different cultural backgrounds.

Internet

- *Success Online.* http://www.success.wadsworth.com Offers a full range of Web-based services.

- *AT&T World Net.* Get your students on the Internet with AT&T—one of the fastest growing Internet access service providers.

For Students

- *Wadsworth College Success Home Page.* http://csuccess.wadsworth.com. Provides updates to URLs in this text as well as a range of free services and information.

- *Franklin-Covey Day Planner Collegiate Edition* (0-534-55836-4). A daily planner to help students manage their college and professional careers.

- *College Success Guide to the Internet,* by Daniel Kurland (0-534-54369-3). Lists sites and activities for topics of interest to students.

Acknowledgments

The completion of any major project requires the assistance of many people. We wish to thank our families who support and assist us in many ways. Second, we gratefully acknowledge our "university" families at SLU and LSU. Our continued appreciation goes to Clark Baxter for his sound advice and constant support during our years at West Publishing. We thank Karen Allanson, Kim Johnson, and Godwin Chu for their patient guidance through our first publishing experiences at Wadsworth. They are the strong ropes on which we firmly (and sometimes frantically) clung during the last two years; we are lucky, indeed, that they didn't "hang" us! We also appreciate the work of the Wadsworth production team, particularly Christal Niederer and Robin Gold whose creative spirits formed *CLASS* 5/e. Finally, we acknowledge and thank our reviewers whose efforts made this manuscript the book it is:

Fifth edition reviewers: Janet Cutshall, Sussex County Community College; Brian A. Richardson, Arizona State University. Previous edition reviewers: Dr. Jim Atkinson, Ottawa University; Dr. Barbara Blaha, Plymouth State University; Jennie L. Brown, Western Kentucky University; Dr. Henry 0. Dixon, Morehouse College; Sharon Freeman, San Jacinto College/Central; Cynthia Golledge-Franz, Cleveland State Community College; Dr. Lynne McRee, Santa Fe Community College; Barbara Moore, Gulf Coast Community College; Patricia Moore, Emmanuel College; Susan J. Nunn, Abraham Baldwin College; Dolly Saulsbury, Wharton County Junior College; Cindy Thompson, Northeast Louisiana University; Suzanne G. Weisar, San Jacinto College/South; Keith B. Wilson, Brewton-Parker College; Donna Wood, State Technical Institute at Memphis; William J. Young, Jr., Wallace State Community College.

Debbie Guice Longman
Rhonda Holt Atkinson

COLLEGE LEARNING AND STUDY SKILLS

Entering the World of Higher Education

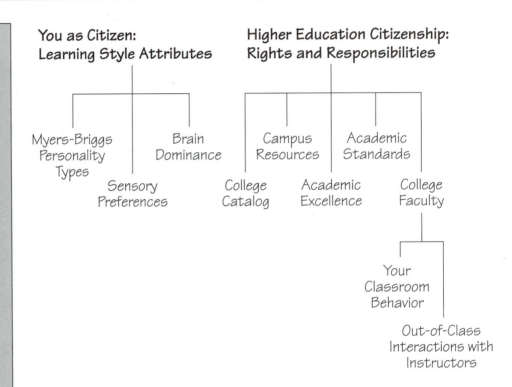

OBJECTIVES

After you finish this chapter, you will be able to do the following:

1. Identify your learning styles.

2. Define the rights and responsibilities of citizenship in higher education.

3. Describe ways to become a part of your college community.

You as Citizen: Learning Style Attributes

- Myers-Briggs Personality Types
- Sensory Preferences
- Brain Dominance

Higher Education Citizenship: Rights and Responsibilities

- Campus Resources
- College Catalog
- Academic Excellence
- Academic Standards
- College Faculty
  - Your Classroom Behavior
  - Out-of-Class Interactions with Instructors

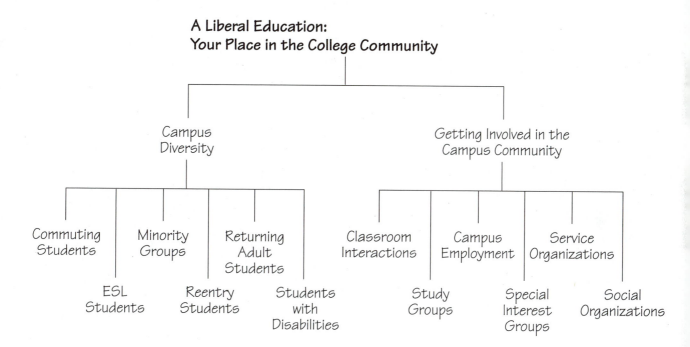

*"Whaddaya mean it's not like bowling?
We don't get practice frames?!"*

> ❝❞
>
> **I am a citizen, not of Athens or Greece, but of the world.**
>
> —Socrates
> *Greek Philosopher*

Higher education changes you in many ways; however, probably the greatest change occurs in the way you perceive yourself and the world around you. Higher education opens to you new vistas of ideas and knowledge.

You enter this world when you become an active participant in your quest for education and interact with others at your institution. You maximize your ability to participate actively in your educational pursuits by understanding the learning traits you possess as a citizen in higher education. Knowledge of your postsecondary institution's policies and programs helps you identify resources in higher education and its expectations of you. And understanding the diversity of experiences available in the world of higher education helps you become assimilated as one of its citizens.

In this chapter, we provide you several ways to assess your learning style and strengths. We identify your rights and responsibilities as a citizen in your higher education institution. Finally, we describe the postsecondary experience through the diversity of individuals with whom you interact and the activities in which you participate.

YOU AS CITIZEN: LEARNING STYLE ATTRIBUTES

As a citizen in the world of higher education, you interact with faculty, staff, and peers on a daily basis. You attend lectures and read course materials. Lab courses offer you hands-on experiences in everything from art to biology and from engineering to music. You'll find you have an almost instant liking for some people on campus. You'll have less in common with others. You'll enjoy some courses and dislike others for their formats as well as their contents.

What you prefer says something about your **style** as well as your interests and goals. Style reveals your temperament—the mix of attributes that defines you. Thus, when you meet people or take courses you enjoy, you feel as if these things somehow fit you. You are in harmony with them. When you do activities contrary to your style, you can feel uncomfortable or dissatisfied. These activities create feelings of discord. As J. Robert Oppenheimer notes, however, style makes it possible to act effectively, but not absolutely. This means that although your style affects how you act, you can modify your style to accommodate others. Thus, you harmonize your style with the styles of others.

Style also reflects the ways you learn. When you study or think in ways that match your style preferences, you learn more effectively. When you engage in study activities contrary to your style, learning takes longer and requires more effort. Modifying learning tasks to match your style helps you maximize learning. Styles that impact learning most involve **personality, sensory preferences,** and **brain dominance.**

Myers-Briggs Personality Types

Based on the work of psychologist Carl Jung, Myers and Briggs developed the **Myers-Briggs Type Indicator (MBTI)** to evaluate personality type. Rather than the eight personality types described by Jung, the research of Myers and Briggs identified sixteen distinct types. Because personality type affects how you interact with people, objects, and situations, you need to know more about your individual preferences. Many college counseling and academic centers administer the MBTI to students, and you would benefit from taking the entire scale. Until you do so, however, the assessment in Exercise 1.1 provides you with a quick and informal estimate of personality type. The results form a starting point for learning more about yourself because the MBTI provides information not only about your preferences, but also about the strengths of these preferences. Your results will consist of a four-letter MBTI type. The type is derived from your dominant preferences in each of the following pairs: extraversion (E) or introversion (I), sensing (S) or intuition (N), thinking (T) or feeling (F), and perceiving (P) or judging (J).

The first letter—the *E* or *I*—indicates whether you get your energy from people (*E* for *extraverted)* or ideas (*I* for *introverted).* This preference comes to you from heredity, while other traits are learned. The second set of letters—*S* or *N*—concerns the information you have an inclination for noticing first. The *S* stands for *sensing.* If you are an *S,* you concentrate on information you acquire through tasting, touching, smelling, hearing, and feeling. The *N* derives from the word *intuition.* You give most importance to information that comes to you through gut feelings or giant leaps in thought if you are an *N.*

> " "
> . . . it is style which makes it possible to act effectively, but not absolutely; it is style which enables us to find harmony between the pursuit of ends essential to us, and the regard for the views, the sensibilities, the aspirations of others . . .
>
> —J. Robert Oppenheimer
> *Twentieth century American physicist*

Exercise 1.1   Circle the letter of the phrase that you prefer. In some cases, both may seem preferable, or neither will be preferable. Still, try to make a choice between the two. Work quickly—first impressions are most likely to be correct. Total your scores for each section and record your type in the blanks below.

I prefer ...

1. A. loud parties   OR   B. quiet gatherings of friends
2. A. working on a project   OR   B. thinking about an idea
3. A. working with others   OR   B. working alone
4. A. managing many projects OR   B. focusing on one project
5. A. talking about an idea   OR   B. writing about an idea
6. A. discussion classes   OR   B. lecture classes
7. A. outgoing people   OR   B. reflective people
8. A. being part of a crowd   OR   B. being alone

Total A responses _____ = EXTRAVERT   Total B responses _____ = INTROVERT

I prefer ...

1. A. practical applications of ideas   OR   B. theoretical considerations of a topic
2. A. lab courses/hands-on projects   OR   B. reading and listening
3. A. factual descriptions   OR   B. metaphorical descriptions
4. A. proven solutions   OR   B. untried solutions
5. A. to go places that I've been   OR   B. to go to new places
      to before
6. A. to attend to details   OR   B. to focus on main ideas
7. A. tasks in which I achieve   OR   B. accomplishing goals over an extended
      goals quickly   period of time
8. A. information derived from logic   OR   B. information that results from conclusions

Total A responses _____ = SENSING   Total B responses _____ = INTUITIVE

I prefer ...

1. A. self-satisfaction in a job   OR   B. appreciation of others for a job
      well done   well done
2. A. multiple-choice tests   OR   B. essay tests
3. A. logical arguments   OR   B. emotional appeals
4. A. impartial people   OR   B. compassionate people

(continues)

Exercise 1.1   *Continued*

5. A. rules and standards   OR   B. negotiation and compromise
6. A. for people to follow the rules OR   B. to allow for exceptions to rules
7. A. professional expertise   OR   B. helpful attitude
8. A. to make decisions based   OR   B. to let my heart influence a decision
        on logic

Total A responses _____= THINKING   Total B responses _____= FEELING

I prefer ...

1. A. to be on time   OR   B. to get places when I get there
2. A. well-thought-out decisions   OR   B. spur-of-the-moment decisions
3. A. organization   OR   B. flexibility
4. A. expected activities   OR   B. improvised activities
5. A. structured assignments   OR   B. unstructured assignments
6. A. step-by-step approaches   OR   B. random approaches
7. A. planned parties   OR   B. surprise parties
8. A. serious people   OR   B. casual people

Total A responses _____= JUDGING   Total B responses _____= PERCEIVING

The next set of letters (*T* and *F*) involves the process you use in making a decision. If *T (thinking)* is your preference, you are logical, fair, objective, and somewhat unemotional in decision making. This lack of emotion sometimes makes you appear aloof. Star Trek's Mr. Spock was a big-time *T*. If *F (feeling)* is your dominant style, you make decisions by considering how your decisions affect people and yourself. The last letter (*J* or *P*) concerns the process by which you make decisions. If your preference is *P (perceiving)*, you like to gather information and delay making decisions. In fact, you'd probably elect not to decide at all. If your propensity is *J (judging)*, you want to make a decision, any decision, quickly and get on with life. Like aptitudes, abilities, interests, needs, and values, each of these traits interact to form your personality. Table 1.1 provides a list of MBTI factors related to learning.

Probably no one type contains all your personality traits, and because both life and stress alter your personality, the personality type you show partiality for might fluctuate as your life does. Nonetheless, knowing your MBTI personality type can aid you in making all sorts of decisions, including those you make as a student.

Table 1.1   MBTI Factors That Relate to Learning

Extraversion (E)

Likes to work with others

Has relatively short attention span

Learns what instructor wants

Acts quickly, but sometimes without completely
   thinking a situation through

Tolerates interruptions

Prefers variety and active learning opportunities

Prefers many activities or ideas to in-depth treatment
   of one idea

Becomes impatient when working on long-term tasks

Introversion (I)

Prefers to work alone

Can concentrate for long periods of time

Sets personal standards

May delay action to think until too late to complete it

Prefers quiet, uninterrupted study site

Prefers in-depth treatment of activities or ideas

Able to follow through until completion of long-
   term tasks

Sensing (S)

Prefers a step-by-step approach

Is oriented to the present

Likes to refine current skills

Prefers realistic application

Is attentive to detail

Is patient

Works steadily

Prefers goal-oriented tasks

Prepares direct experience

Prepares well for tests involving practical application

Likes audio-visuals

Prefers to involve senses (underlining, flash cards,
   recitation)

Needs to know rationale for a task before beginning

Prefers to study from old tests

Intuition (N)

Tends to use a roundabout approach

Is oriented to the future

Becomes bored after mastering a skill

Prefers imaginative application

Is attentive to "big picture"

Is restless

Works in bursts of energy

Prefers open-ended assignments

Prefers reading or thinking

Prepares well for tests involving theoretical
   application

Likes mental visualization and memory activities

Prefers to involve right-brain strategies (mapping,
   drawing, charting)

Is comfortable with incomplete understanding of
   a task

Believes task will "come together" after time

Prefers to make up own questions

Thinking (T)

Prefers objective activities

Seems task-oriented

Tends to be firm

Is motivated by desire for achievement

Applies standard criteria for evaluation

Looks for organizational structure

Feeling (F)

Prefers subjective activities

Considers personal values

Is flexible

Is motivated by desire to be appreciated

Applies personal criteria for evaluation

Looks for personal relevancy

(continues)

Table 1.1   *Continued*

Judging (J)	Perceiving (P)
Is goal-oriented	Is self-directed
Prefers structure of deadlines	Prefers flexibility in completing tasks
Limits commitment	Tends to overcommit
Prefers to work on one task at a time	Starts several tasks at once
Prefers closure to make decisions	Delays closure to gather more information
Persists	Can be distracted
Can seem rigid	Is flexible
Tends to be a perfectionist	Seems more tolerant of imperfection
Prefers to play after work is completed	Prefers to play first and work later (if time permits)
Finds product more important than process	Finds process more important than product
Enjoys planning and organizing	Enjoys thinking and adapting
Likes to know only what is needed to accomplish a task	Likes to know everything before beginning a task

Sensory Preferences

Sensory preferences concern the way or ways in which you like to acquire information—by seeing **(visual),** hearing **(aural),** reading/writing, or through physical experiences **(kinesthetic).** Some learning activities, for example, mapping or charting (see Chapter 6 for additional information), combine visual, reading/writing, and kinesthetic styles. Table 1.2 provides suggestions for using your sensory preferences in classroom, study, and exam situations. If you have no clear preferences for a single type, consider using a **multisensory** approach, one that combines two or more senses (for example, talking yourself through the steps in constructing a model, drawing a diagram for later visual review, or talking yourself through the connections in constructing a map). Exercise 1.2 provides you with an assessment of your sensory preferences.

Table 1.2   Applying Sensory Preferences to Classroom Study, and Exam Situations

	In class	When studying	During exams
Visual	Underline Use different colors Use symbols, charts, arrangements on a page	Use the "In Class" strategies Reconstruct images in different way Redraw pages from memory with symbols and initials	Recall the "pictures of pages" Draw or sketch Use diagrams where appropriate Practice turning visuals back into words
Aural	Attend lectures and tutorials Discuss topics with students Explain new ideas to other people Use a tape recorder Describe overheads, pictures, and visuals to somebody not there Leave space in notes for later recall	Expand your notes Put summarized notes on tape and listen Read summarized notes out loud Explain notes to another A person Compare notes with other students for completeness and clarity	Listen to your inner voices and write down what you say to yourself Speak your answers Practice writing answers to old exam questions
Reading/ Writing	Use lists, headings Use dictionaries and definitions Use handouts and textbooks Read Use lecture notes	Write out the words again and again Reread notes silently Rewrite ideas into other words Organize diagrams into statements	Practice with multiple-choice questions Write out lists Write paragraphs, beginnings, endings
Kinesthetic	Use all your senses Go to lab, take field trips Use trial-and-error methods Listen to real-life examples Use hands-on approach	Put examples in note summaries Use pictures and photos to illustrate Talk about notes with another person Compare notes with other students for completeness and clarity	Write practice answers Role-play the exam situation in your room

SOURCE: From Neil Fleming and Colleen Mills who teach at Lincoln University, New Zealand

Exercise 1.2   Circle the answer or answers that best describe your response for each situation. Note: If a single answer does not match your perception, enter two or more choices. After you answer all questions, total your responses and compute your percentages.

1. You are about to give directions to a friend. She is staying in a hotel in town and wants to visit your house. She has a rental car. Would you
   V. draw a map on paper?
   A. tell her the directions?
   R. write the directions (without a map)?
   K. collect her from the hotel in your car?

2. You are staying in a hotel and have a rental car. You would like to visit a friend whose address or location you do not know. Would you like him to
   V. draw you a map on paper?
   A. tell you the directions by phone?
   R. write the directions (without a map)?
   K. collect you from the hotel in his car?

3. You have just received a copy of your itinerary for a world trip. This is of interest to a friend. Would you
   A. call her immediately and tell her about it?
   R. send her a copy of the printed itinerary?
   V. show her your route on a map of the world?

4. You are going to cook a dessert as a special treat for your family. Do you
   K. cook something familiar without need for directions?
   V. thumb through the cookbook looking for ideas from the pictures?
   R. refer to a specific cookbook that has a good recipe?
   A. ask for advice from others?

5. A group of tourists has been assigned to you to find out about national parks. Would you
   K. drive them to a national park?
   V. show them slides and photographs?
   R. give them a book on national parks?
   A. give a talk to them about national parks?

6. You are about to purchase a car. Other than price, what would most influence your decision?
   A. Talking to a friend about it
   R. Reading the details about it
   K. Driving it
   V. The car's appearance

7. Recall a time in your life when you learned how to do something like playing a new board game. (Try to avoid choosing a very physical skill, for example, riding a bike). How did you learn best?

(continues)

Exercise 1.2   *Continued*

   V. By visual clues—pictures, diagrams, charts
   R. By written instructions
   A. By listening to somebody explaining it
   K. By doing it

8. Which of these games do you prefer?
   V. Pictionary
   R. Scrabble
   K. Charades

9. You are about to learn a new program on a computer. Would you
   K. ask a friend to show you?
   R. read the manual that comes with the program?
   A. telephone a friend and ask questions about it?

10. You are not sure whether a word should be spelled dependent or dependant. Do you
   R. look it up in the dictionary?
   V. see the word in your mind and choose the way that looks best?
   A. sound it out in your mind?
   K. write both versions down?

11. Apart from price, what would most influence your decision to buy a particular book?
   K. Using a friend's copy
   A. Talking to a friend about it
   R. Skimming parts of it
   V. Seeing that it looks OK

12. A new movie has arrived in town. What would most influence your decision to go or not go?
   A. Friends talk about it.
   R. You read a review of it.
   V. You see a preview of it.

13. Do you prefer a lecturer who likes to use
   R. handouts or a textbook?
   K. field trips, labs, practical sessions?
   V. flow diagrams, charts, slides?
   A. discussions or guest speakers?

TOTAL A (auditory) responses _____ / 11 = _____ %

TOTAL V (visual) responses _____ / 12 = _____ %

TOTAL K (kinesthetic) responses _____ / 11 = _____ %

TOTAL R (reading/writing) responses _____ / 13 = _____ %

SOURCE: From Neil Fleming and Colleen Mills who teach at Lincoln University, New Zealand.

WRITE TO LEARN

Read the novel excerpt "Mother" (used as the sample short story on page 534 of this book). Based on what you've learned from this chapter, identify Elizabeth Willard's probable MBTI and sensory preferences. Justify your choices. Write your response on a separate sheet of paper or in your journal.

Brain Dominance

Are you right-handed or left-handed? Scientific researchers report that handedness reflects the brain's division of labor. About 90 percent of the human population is right-handed. If you're right-handed, this means that your brain's left hemisphere is dominant in motor-skills superiority, although you can also perform many physical actions with your left hand.

Brain dominance goes far beyond handedness. In 1981, psychobiologist Roger Sperry won a Nobel Prize for his work on the special abilities of each half of the brain. He specialized in treating individuals with severe and almost constant epileptic seizures. To treat them, he surgically split their brains. As a result, each individual essentially possessed two distinctly separate brains. Sperry conducted a variety of experiments with these persons to see how the surgery affected their thinking.

The results indicated that language appears to be mostly a function of the **left brain.** The left brain also seems more involved in processing math and judging time and rhythm as well as speech and writing. The left brain generally analyzes information by breaking it into parts and tends to process information in sequential, linear, logical ways.

The **right brain** controls different reasoning processes. The right brain processes information in holistic, visual forms. Thus, it prefers to synthesize, rather than analyze. Recognition of patterns, faces, and melodies, as well as other kinds of perceptual understanding, are within the domain of the right brain.

What does Sperry's work have to do with your learning? Although you combine the skills of both sides of the brain in most activities, the ways in which you study affect the two sides of your brain differently. Most information is presented and studied in ways that appeal to the operations of the left brain—linear, verbal, text information. The kinds of formats that appeal to the right brain—visual, holistic, spatial information—are used less often. Learning information in a variety of ways appeals to the multisensory and multifaceted ways in which the brain processes information. A summary of the functions attributed to left and right hemispheres of the brain appears in Table 1.3 with corresponding applications to learning.

Table 1.3   Right and Left Brain Attributes

Left-Brain Processing	Application to Learning
Linear; sequential parts and segments	Ordered detail-by-detail understanding; notes and outlines; analysis of ideas
Symbolic	Formulas, acronyms and acrostics; algebraic and abstract math computation
Logical; serious; verifying, non-fiction; improving on the known; reality-based; replication	Factual, unemotional information; proofs of theorems; grammar; practical application of learning to known situations
Verbal; written	Notes, outlines, lectures, text information; auditory review
Temporal; controlled; planning	Structured management of time, ideas, or resources
Focal thinking	Concentration on a single issue or point of view
Objective; dislikes improvisation	Multiple-choice, true-or-false matching formats

Right-Brain Processing	Application to Learning
Holistic; general overviews	Synthesis of information; mapping; charting
Concrete; spatial	Geometry; math facts; mapping; diagrams
Intuitive; assumptions inventing the unknown; fantasy-based; fictitious	Creative writing; interpreting literature; understanding symbolism or figurative language; drawing conclusions about an issue or idea; use of metaphors and analogies; humor
Nonverbal; kinesthetic; visual	Experimentation; hands-on learning; graphics; photographs; feelings; visualizing notes or situations; drawing; mapping; charting; role playing
Random; nontemporal	Unstructured management of time, ideas, or resources
Diffused thinking	Concentration on a variety of views or issues
Subjective; likes improvising	Essays exams; short-answer questions; creative writing

Just as you have a dominant hand with which you prefer to write, you probably possess a dominant side of the brain with which you prefer to learn. The assessment in Exercise 1.3 helps you determine if you are left- or right-brain dominant.

The closer your scores are to each other, the more easily you can process either kind of information. If your score is higher on one side than the other, try to convert information into formats that your brain prefers. No matter your score, however, incorporating both right-brain and left-brain strategies enhances your learning because it gives you different ways to process and store information.

Exercise 1.3   Respond to the following questions.

1. How do you prefer making decisions?
   a. intuitively
   b. logically

2. Which do you remember more easily?
   a. names
   b. faces

3. Do you prefer
   a. planning your activities in advance?
   b. doing things spontaneously?

4. In social situations, do you prefer being the
   a. listener?
   b. speaker?

5. When listening to a speaker, do you pay more attention to
   a. what the speaker is saying?
   b. the speaker's body language?

6. Do you consider yourself to be a goal-oriented person?
   a. yes
   b. no

7. Is your main study area
   a. messy?
   b. neat and well organized?

8. Are you usually aware of what time it is and how much time has passed?
   a. yes
   b. no

9. When you write papers, do you
   a. let ideas flow freely?
   b. plan the sequence of ideas in advance?

10. After you have heard music, are you more likely to remember the
    a. words?
    b. tunes?

11. Which do you prefer doing?
    a. watching a movie
    b. working a crossword puzzle

12. Do you frequently move your furniture around in your home?
    a. yes
    b. no

13. Are you a good memorizer?
    a. yes
    b. no

14. When you doodle, do you create
    a. shapes?
    b. words?

15. Clasp your hands together. Which thumb is on top?
    a. left
    b. right

16. Which subject do you prefer?
    a. algebra
    b. trigonometry

17. In planning your day, do you
    a. make a list of what you need to accomplish?
    b. just let things happen?

18. Are you good at expressing your feelings?
    a. yes
    b. no

19. If you are in an argument with someone else, do you
    a. listen and consider the point of view of the other person?
    b. insist that you are right?

20. When you use a tube of toothpaste, do you
    a. carefully roll it up from the bottom?
    b. squeeze it in the middle?

(continues)

Exercise 1.3   *Continued*

Transfer your responses to the diagram by shading your responses. The shape with the most shaded pieces indicates your preference.

HIGHER EDUCATION CITIZENSHIP: RIGHTS AND RESPONSIBILITIES

Becoming a citizen in the world of higher education requires that you recognize your citizenship and all that it includes. Citizenship in any new place includes both privileges and responsibilities. It involves understanding of the community's language and expectations as well as the resources that community offers. Your **college catalog** forms a guidebook to the language and expectations of your institution. Your institution staffs a variety of campus offices that provide services and assistance to students. Faculty both teach

ONLINE CLASS

Web Exercise 1.1

A variety of information related to the topics in this chapter is available on the World Wide Web. For this exercise, access Learning Styles Links at http://www.oise.utoronto.ca/~ggay/lstylstd.htm (for the most up-to-date URLs, go to http://csuccess.wadsworth.com) and choose one of the on-line tests or other assessment from the category *Tests*. Complete the test or assessment, then answer the following questions:

1. What test did you take? _____

2. Why did you choose that test? _____

3. Describe how the test compared with the tests in this chapter.

   _____

   _____

   _____

4. Summarize your results.

   _____

   _____

   _____

5. What do your results tell you about the way you learn?

   _____

   _____

   _____

and offer other academic support to you. Your knowledge of what each of these offers and how you can best access these services and information increases your success at your institution.

College Catalog

Your college catalog forms your contract with your institution. The catalog describes courses, degree programs, and other academic information specific to your institution. It lists the academic rules and regulations you must follow. Obviously, you cannot memorize your catalog. You do, however, need to be familiar with it so that you can be prepared for any eventuality—from seeking admission to applying for graduation. Table 1.4 identifies and describes major components of a catalog. Table 1.5 provides a list of common academic terms found in college catalogs. Exercise 1.4 shows you how to find these compenents and terms in your own college catalog.

Table 1.4   College Catalog Components

Academic Calendar	Lists important dates in the academic year, including registration, first and last days to drop classes, midterm and final exam periods, and holidays and vacations.
Student Services	Identifies nonacademic activities and services available to students, including campus organizations, Dean of Students' Office, housing and food service information, and health services.
Admissions Information	Explains criteria for admission to the institution, regulations for the transfer of credits, and availability of special programs.
Tuition and Fees	Lists in-state and out-of-state costs, including tuition, room and board, fee schedules, student health fees, parking fees, and lab fees. Can also identify financial aid opportunities (scholarships, grants, loans, campus jobs.)
Academic Policies and Regulations	Describes certification requirements, academic standards, and registration regulations.
Academic Classification	Describes how the number of completed credit-hours translates into freshman, sophomore, junior, or senior status. Credit-hour value is approximately equal to the number of hours per week of in-class instruction (lab, studio, or performance courses often involve more hours of in-class instruction than are reflected in credit-hour value). Course-load requirements describe the maximum and minimum hours required to be at full-time status.
Academic Standards	Discusses the rules governing student conduct, including disciplinary sanctions, academic disciplinary actions, and appeal procedures. These rules apply in cases of academic dishonesty (cheating or plagiarism) or other institutional infractions.
College Degree Requirements	Identifies the specific and elective courses necessary for completion of a degree. These often divided by semester/quarter or academic year.
Course Descriptions	Summarizes the content of each course, which is usually identified by a number and title.

Table 1.5   Higher Education Terms and Their Definitions

Course Number	Usually indicates the level of difficulty of a course; undergraduate courses range from 100- or 1000-level courses (freshman level) to 400- or 4000-level courses (senior level). Higher numbers indicate graduate courses.
Drop/Withdraw	Resignation from either one course (drop) or from the university (withdrawal); either process requires that you follow the procedures set forth by your institution.
Electives	Courses you choose outside your major from an academic area of interest to you; some electives are required for every major; some majors limit the academic areas from which you can select.
Extracurricular Activities	The nonacademic clubs and pursuits offered by your college; includes intra-mural sports and athletic events for students who aren't members of school-sponsored athletic teams.

(continues)

Table 1.5   *Continued*

Freshman	Classification of first-time college students; students generally remain freshmen until they have successfully completed 30 credit-hours.
Full-Time/Part-Time Courseload	Full-time students enroll for 12 or more credit-hours; part-time students take less than 12 credit-hours.
Juniors	Considered upperclassmen; students generally remain juniors until they have 90 hours of course credit.
Residency	Can have two different meanings: Can refer to whether or not you qualify for in-state tuition or to whether or not you live on campus.
Prerequisites	Courses you must take before you can take a particular course; departments mandate the order in which you take these courses.
Semester/Quarter Systems	Colleges on the semester system have two regular terms (fall and spring) of about 14 weeks each and one or more shorter summer terms; colleges on the quarter system have four terms (fall, winter, spring, and summer) of about 10 weeks each.
Seniors	The final year that leads to an undergraduate degree; considered upperclassmen; students are considered seniors once they have more than 90 credit-hours.
Sophomores	Students maintain sophomore status if they have between 30 and 60 hours of course credit.
Syllabus	An outline of course requirements including assignments and their due dates, exam dates, grading policies, and other information related to a specific course; at many institution, the syllabus is seen as a contact between the professor and the student.
Transcript	Official record of the courses you completed and the grades you made in them.
Transfer Credit	The number of course credits taken by a student at one college that another college accepts for credit.

Campus Resources

Although each institution of higher education has its own campus with its own atmosphere and buildings, all share some common offices and services. Although these resources offer invaluable assistance and a wealth of information, no one will insist that you avail yourself of these opportunities for help. Your institution assumes that you will take advantage of them as needed. Knowing where each office is located and what it can do for you is your responsibility. Making use of available services is your privilege. Table 1.6 provides a list of university offices found on most campuses and describes the functions of each one. You can use Exercise 1.5 to locate resources on your campus.

Exercise 1.4   Locate the following information in your school catalog.

1. If you want to voice a concern, who are the people you need to know? List below the chain of command (the hierarchy of positions or individuals) in the college or department in which you are majoring by name and title. If you are an undecided major, find this information for one of the areas you are considering.

    _____

    _____

2. Locate and record information about two scholarships or loans for which you might be eligible.

    _____

    _____

3. Locate the academic calendar for the current term.
    a. When is the last day to withdraw from courses?

        _____

    b. What holidays occur this term?

        _____

    c. What is the last day of classes?

        _____

    d. When do finals begin? end?

        _____

4. Locate the curriculum in which you plan to major.
    a. Compare and contrast courses suggested for your first term with those suggested for your final term. How do you account for similarities and differences?

        _____

        _____

    b. Examine the curriculum carefully. Locate two courses in your major area and read their descriptions. Which will you find more enjoyable? Why?

        _____

        _____

    c. Read the description for each of the courses in which you are now enrolled. How do the descriptions compare with the actual content of the course? What conclusion(s) might you draw about the courses and their descriptions you identified in b?

        _____

        _____

Table 1.6   Campus Resources and Services

Business Office	Also called Office of the Treasurer or the Bursar's Office. Records student's financial transactions, such as tuition, fees, fines, or other payments.
Campus Bookstore	Sells text materials for course-related topics and recreational reading, including books, magazines, newspapers, journals, and references books. Also offers pens, pencils, notebooks, art supplies, and other materials. Sometimes carries over-the-counter drugs and toiletries and school-related clothing and souvenirs.
Campus Security	Also called Campus Police. Provides parking and traffic guidelines and assistance for improving your personal safety on the campus.
Career Guidance and Placement Office	Administers interest, educational, and aptitude tests to assist you in career decision making. Provides job placement information. Sometimes maintains placement files of transcripts and letters of reference that can be sent to prospective employers at your request.
Correspondence and Extension Division	Administers off-campus and independent study courses that are taken by mail.
Counseling Center	Provides personal counseling on a wide range of problems such as stress, substance abuse, sexually transmitted diseases, depression, and other sources of anxiety. Staffed by trained professional counselors. Sometimes called Wellness or Mental Health Center.
Dean of Students	An administrative unit that serves in an advocacy, advisory, and supervisory capacity for individual students and recognized student organizations. Also serves as a clearinghouse for student concerns and manages the college judicial system and student code of conduct.
Financial Aid Office	Also called Student Aid and Scholarship Office. Provides assistance in locating and distributing supplemental funds such as grants, loans, scholarships, and on-campus employment. Your need for financial assistance is often based on responses you provide in a written application.
Job Placement Office	Maintains listing of full and part-time job openings both on and off campus. Sometimes a part of the Career Planning or Financial Aid Office.
Learning Center	Sometimes called Learning Resource Center, Learning Assistance Center, and Learning Lab, among other names. Offers assistance in study skills or specific content areas through workshops or individualized lessons, tutoring, or taped or computerized instruction.
Library	Contains materials for reference and recreation, including books, magazines, newspapers, journals, reference books, microfilms, and computerized documents. Can also contain a listening room, teacher education materials, and photocopying facilities. Workshops or classes might be available to familiarize you with library services and holdings.
Registrar's Office	Also called Office of Records and Registration. Tracks courses you take and grades you receive. Evaluates advanced, transfer, or correspondence work. Provides transcripts. Can have the responsibility to determine if you meet graduation requirements.
Residential Housing	Concerned with both on-campus living experiences and, in some cases, approved off-campus housing.

(continues)

Table 1.6   *Continued*

Student Center	Also called Student Activities Office or Union. Provides recreational activities, including short courses on crafts and other topics. Sponsors concerts, plays, and other social events. Houses student organizations. Provides meeting places for these and other groups.
Student Health Services	Provides medical assistance for students who become physically ill or injured or who have chronic health problems. Might also offer mental health counseling. Services are usually free for full-time students. Lab work, physical therapy, pharmaceutical drugs, emergency care, and workshops on health-related topics might also be available.

Exercise 1.5   Answer briefly but completely.

1. Complete the following chart by identifying information about resources on your campus.

	Name of office on your campus and phone number	Location	Hours open	Contact person
Career Placement Office				
Learning Center				
Campus Security				
Student Center				
Bookstore				
Library				
Correspondence/Extension Office				
Counseling Center				
Job Placement Center				
Health Services				
Registrar's Office				
Business Office				
Financial Aid Office				
Dean of Students				
Residential Housing				

2. Identify a situation in which you would need help from each of the following resources:

a. Campus Bookstore

_____

_____

b. Learning Center

_____

_____

(continues)

Exercise 1.5   *Continued*

   c. Library

   _____

   _____

   d. Student Center

   _____

   _____

   e. Campus Security

   _____

   _____

   f. Career Office

   _____

   _____

   g. Correspondence/Extension Office

   _____

   _____

   h. Counseling Center

   _____

   _____

   i. Job Placement Office

   _____

   _____

   j. Student Health Services

   _____

   _____

   k. Registrar's Office

   _____

   _____

   l. Business Office

   _____

   _____

   m. Financial Aid Office

   _____

   _____

   n. Dean of Students

   _____

   _____

Academic Excellence

All colleges and universities set certain requirements that must be met before they grant a degree. One of the most important aspects of academia concerns the measure of your accomplishments. Thus, course grades, **grade point average (GPA),** and academic honesty are vital issues for your consideration.

Traditional grading systems consist of the letter grades *A, B, C, D,* and *F.* Other marks include *NC* (no credit), *P* (pass), *W* (withdraw), *W-grade* (withdraw with a grade), and *I* (incomplete). *NC, P, W,* and *I* grades are not used to compute your GPA. Policies about *W-grades* vary. Some institutions use the *W-grade* in computing GPA. Others do not. Check your institution's regulations to be sure.

GPA is a ratio of **quality points** earned to semester hours attempted. Quality points usually use a four-point scale: *A* = 4, *B* = 3, *C* = 2, *D* = 1, and F = 0. Because your courses vary in credit hours, you cannot always assume that the average of an *A,* a *B,* and a *C* equals a 3.0 GPA. See Figure 1.1 for an example of a GPA computation.

A college or university usually places students on **academic probation** whenever their cumulative average is 10 or more quality points below a 2.0 or C average. Once on probation, you remain there until your cumulative average reaches 2.0 or higher.

At the end of the first and each succeeding term, the institution requires that you make a 2.0. If for any reason you fail to do so, **academic action** results. Academic actions differ somewhat from one school to another. However, they generally follow the same guidelines. That is, you might remain on probation for a period of time before suspension results. The first time you get suspended it's usually for one regular term (summers usually don't count). If you have been suspended before, your second suspension spans an entire calendar year. Suspensions for schools other than the one you are currently attending often count in computing this formula. Any additional suspensions will also be for a whole year.

Obviously, you cannot take coursework from the suspending institution during the time you are suspended. Furthermore, any courses you take from another school during the time of your suspension will not count toward your degree at your present institution. Indeed, most colleges and universities will not admit students who are under current suspension from another school.

Once your suspension ends, you need to apply for readmission to your school. Should you be suspended more than two times, however, readmission to the institution holds no guarantee that you will be accepted into all professional, degree-seeking programs, which have their own admission requirements.

Once you let your GPA flounder and fall, it takes more time than you might imagine to get it soaring again. If it can be done at all and how long it will take depends on your current GPA, your future grades, and the number of semester hours you have left. For example, let's suppose you have completed

Figure 1.1   GPA Computation

Course	Grade	Credit Hours		Point Equivalent	Total Quality Points
English 101	C	3	×	(C=)2	6
Math 104	D	4	×	(D=)1	4
Speech 130	B	3	×	(B=)3	9
Music 106	A	1	×	(A=)4	4
Biology 103	W	3			
Totals		11			23

Quality points/semester hours attempted = 23/11 = 2.09 GPA

45 hours and have a 2.0 GPA. You need 83 hours to graduate (including the 15 you are taking this term) and want to graduate with a 3.3 GPA. To reach your goal, you'll need to maintain a 4.0 for each remaining semester you are in school. Figure 1.2 contains the formula for determining this figure and the computations for the preceding example. Exercise 1.6 provides practice for computing GPA. Exercise 1.6 provides practice for computing your GPA.

Academic Standards

Consider the following old joke: A professor comes into the classroom and says, "This exam will be conducted on the honor system. Please take seats three seats apart and in alternate rows."

In all classrooms, and particularly in testing situations, instructors trust you to act honorably. They count on you to value your moral integrity more than any grade in any course. Instructors also expect you to realize at least two other consequences of cheating. First, getting caught means a failing grade, and failing grades lower your GPA. Second, it's embarrassing and troubling for both you and your instructor.

Other than cheating on exams, the most common type of cheating in college is **plagiarism.** Plagiarism is stealing another person's work and presenting it as your own. Plagiarism comes in two forms: unintentional and intentional. Unintentional, or accidental, plagiarism occurs through inaccurate notetaking, by incorrect citing of references, or from poor writing ability. Intentional plagiarism is deliberate, premeditated theft of another person's work or published information. Intentional plagiarism also includes getting a paper from a friend or from a term paper service and results from poor time management, fear of not doing well, and pure laziness. Even though the motives for unintentional and intentional plagiarism differ, the punishment is the same.

Figure 1.2   Formula for and Example of Calculating Needed GPA

$$NGPA = \frac{FGPA\,(TOTHRS) - (CGPA \times CHA)}{SCH}$$

Where NGPA   stands for *Needed* GPA

FGPA   stands for the *Final* GPA you want to attain

CGPA   stands for you *Current* GPA

CHA   stands for the number of *credit hours attempted*; these do not include pass-fail or satisfactory/unsatisfactory hours

SCH   stands for the *sum* of the number of *credit hours* you have left to take plus the number of hours you are currently taking

TOTHRS   stands for the sum of *CHA* and *SCH*; that is, the total number of hours you have taken, are taking, and will take before graduation

Example Calculations

$$NGPA = \frac{(FGPA \times TOTHRS) - (CGPA \times CHA)}{SCH}$$

$$NGPA = \frac{(3.3 \times 128) - (2.0 \times 45)}{83}$$

$$NGPA = \frac{(3.3 \times 128) - (90)}{83}$$

$$NGPA = \frac{(422.4) - (90)}{83}$$

$$NGPA = \frac{(332.4)}{83}$$

$$NGPA = 4.00$$

"Well, you could tell your parents you had a cumulative grade of 3.5 this semester!"

Exercise 1.6   Compute the grade point average for the following:

1. GPA = _____

Course	Grade	Credit Hours	Point Equivalent	Total Quality Points
English 210	A	3	_____	_____
Math 103	F	5	_____	_____
Speech 102	B	3	_____	_____
History 104	C	3	_____	_____
Art 100	W	4	_____	_____

Totals

2. GPA = _____

Course	Credit Grade	Point Hours	Total Quality Equivalent	Points
English 001	NC	3	_____	_____
Math 006	P	5	_____	_____
Physical Education 101	D	1	_____	_____
Word Processing 101	A	1	_____	_____

Totals

3. GPA = _____

Course	Credit Grade	Point Hours	Total Quality Equivalent	Points
English 102	C	3	_____	_____
Math 200	D	3	_____	_____
Music 101	B	3	_____	_____
Nursing 100	A	3	_____	_____
Geography 102	W	3	_____	_____

Totals

4. GPA = _____

Course	Credit Grade	Point Hours	Total Quality Equivalent	Points
English 101	D	3	_____	_____
Math 109	C	3	_____	_____
Geology 107	F	3	_____	_____
Physical Education 107	B	1	_____	_____
ROTC 101	A	2	_____	_____

Totals

(continues)

Exercise 1.6   *Continued*

5. GPA = _____

Course	Grade	Credit Hours	Point Equivalent	Total Quality Points
English 106	F	3	_____	_____
Math 104	D	4	_____	_____
Music 105	B	2	_____	_____
Physical Education 106	A	1	_____	_____
Botany 101	C	4	_____	_____

Totals

List the courses in which you are now enrolled and predict what grade you will receive in each.

6. GPA = _____

Course	Grade	Credit Hours	Point Equivalent	Total Quality Points
_____	_____	_____	_____	_____
_____	_____	_____	_____	_____
_____	_____	_____	_____	_____
_____	_____	_____	_____	_____
_____	_____	_____	_____	_____

Totals

What happens if you're caught? In some cases, charges of plagiarism are kept between you and your instructor. You receive an *F* for the paper or test. However, if your instructor suspects that you cheated on previous papers, assignments, or tests, or if the amount of plagiarism is extreme, he or she could direct your case to a formal committee of other students, professors, or campus administrators. Such a committee possesses the right to suspend you for a semester or more, expel you from the university, place an academic dishonesty clause on your transcript, or refuse you a degree from the department. If you are not certain about the guidelines for plagiarism, you might consider taking your references and a draft of your assignment to your instructor and asking for advice.

The academic standards of your institution concern the rules governing student conduct. The standards include information on the **academic code of student conduct,** disciplinary sanctions, academic disciplinary actions, and **appeals.**

An institution's reputation depends on keeping high standards of intellectual integrity. Breaches of academic integrity consist of cheating and plagiarism. Students accused of such violations receive a hearing through the Dean of Students' Office. In this hearing, an impartial person or panel determines guilt or innocence.

If you are found guilty of academic dishonesty, disciplinary actions include probation, suspension, or expulsion. As a student, you have the right to appeal academic disciplinary actions. You also have the right to know the appeal process. If it is not outlined in your catalog, the Office of Student Affairs or another student advocacy group will assist you in making your appeal.

College Faculty

A popular urban legend (Brunvand, 1989) tells of an instructor whose students changed his behavior. Whenever he walked to the left side of the room, they seemed to lose interest in what he said. They yawned, wrote notes, whispered, and paid little or no attention. When he moved to the right, they sat up straight. They made a point to listen carefully, take notes, and ask questions. The instructor soon began to lecture only from the right side of the class. Like the students in the story, you, too, can influence the behavior of your instructors. Instructors try to be fair and impartial, but they are people, too.

Think about the people you've met in your life. Some had qualities that made you want to know them better. Others had characteristics that made you happy to see them leave. Instructors feel the same way about students. Each semester, they meet a new group of people. They react to and with each one. Your behavior determines if their reactions to you are positive or negative. You control whether or not you are a student your instructor wants to know better.

Your Classroom Behavior

To obtain and maintain an instructor's goodwill, you must be polite and respectful. If you arrive on time and dress appropriately, you make a good first impression. Your prompt and consistent attendance proves your diligence and commitment to the course. The quality of your work also shows your regard for the instructor and the course. Your work is, after all, an extension of

---

WRITE TO LEARN

On a separate sheet of paper or in your journal, explain the irony in the joke that begins the section "Academic Standards." Then identify a situation in which you have seen a student's honesty questioned. Do you feel the situation was handled professionally? Fairly? Why or why not?

SOURCE: Reprinted by permission of Glenn Dines and *Phi Delta Kappan*.

you. Only work of the highest quality in content, form, and appearance should be submitted to an instructor.

Sitting near the front of the room in about the same seat for each class gives the instructor a visual fix on you. Although the instructor might not keep attendance records, he or she will subconsciously look for you and know you are there. Sitting near the front of the room also helps you maintain eye contact with the instructor.

Your apparent interest in the lecture is enhanced when your body language indicates your interest. Facial expressions and movements (smiling, nodding your head, raising your eyebrows) and body language (sitting straight, facing the instructor, arms uncrossed) show your openness and desire to learn.

The opposite of this is also true. Nonverbal responses of skepticism or boredom are evident in body language and facial expressions (yawning, reading the newspaper, sighing, looking out the window, rolling your eyes). Body language is especially important when you read your instructor's comments on returned assignments in class. Constructive criticism is part of the learning process and should be a learning experience, and an instructor's critical comments are not a personal attack. Your body language should reflect your ability to accept those comments in the spirit in which they are given.

Some students fear speaking in class. Often they are afraid that their questions will sound "dumb" to either the instructor or other students. Sometimes the class is a large one with several hundred students. Maybe past experiences in asking questions led to embarrassing results. Generally, however, if something in the lecture confused you, it confused others, too. Many

"Thank you for sharing the story your father told last night, but now I think it best that we return to the lesson."

SOURCE: Val Cheatham

times, others are waiting for someone else to make the first move. That person needs to be you. All you have to fear is fear itself, to paraphrase Franklin Roosevelt, President of the United States during World War II.

Speaking in class is less stressful if you know how to phrase your questions or comments. Questions and comments must be relevant and respectful. Nothing frustrates an instructor more than rude questions; long, unrelated stories; or questions whose answers were just discussed. Preceding your questions with what you understand helps the instructor clarify what confuses you. By briefly stating what you think was just said, you aid the instructor in finding gaps in your knowledge. Another way to help an instructor help you is to be exact about the information you need.

Active participation in class discussions proves your interest. If you ask questions or make comments about the lecture topic, you signal your desire for understanding. If you feel you simply cannot ask a question in class, then see your instructor before or after class or make an appointment with him or her.

WRITE TO LEARN

Do you ask questions or make comments in class? On a separate sheet of paper or in your journal, identify why you are or are not vocal in class. If you tend to be silent on some (or all) occasions, describe how you can overcome or compensate for it.

Out-of-Class Interactions with Instructors

Getting to know an instructor personally involves special effort. Smiling and saying hello when you see an instructor outside of class is a friendly opening gesture. Positive, sincere feedback about lecture topics, the instructor's lecture style, and so on often opens lines of communication. Visiting an instructor's office often and for long time periods also affects how an instructor feels about you—but, unfortunately, the effect is negative. Instructors have office hours so students who have valid problems can contact them. They also use that time to grade papers, complete paperwork, and conduct research. Thus, many instructors resent students who—without valid reasons—constantly visit them.

This does not mean that instructors do not like to talk to you and other students. They do. Talking to you helps them understand your problems and learning needs. It gives them an opportunity to interest you in their content areas.

There are several good reasons to visit an instructor's office. Questions about course content or test items should be asked politely and intelligently. Previous suggestions for asking questions in class also apply here. Appealing a poor grade is another reason for seeing an instructor. Having some viable options to present strengthens your appeal. For example, you could indicate that you are willing to write a research paper, do extra reading, take a makeup exam, or work extra problems. That you have thought of these options proves you realize your grade is your responsibility. Whether or not you are allowed to make up work is at the discretion of the instructor. If your instructor refuses to allow you this concession, you still need to smile, say "Thank you," and take the grade you've earned. Another legitimate reason for seeing an instructor is to ask for an incomplete grade. Usually students who have valid reasons and the proper attitude have few problems with getting extra time to complete work.

*"Well, whatever you do,
never, ever let 'em see you sweat."*

If you discuss your grade with an instructor and feel you have been unfairly treated, you have the right to an appeal. This appeal involves, first, meeting with the instructor and attempting to resolve your problem. During the second step of the appeal process, you write a letter to the head of the department in which the course was taught asking for a meeting with that person and your instructor. If you are not satisfied with the results of this hearing, you may appeal to the dean of the department in which the course was taught. If you are firmly convinced that you are in the right, your final appeal is made to the head of academic affairs at your institution.

There are three "nevers" in getting along with instructors: Never miss class, never be inattentive or impolite, and, if you miss class, never say, "I missed class today. Did we do anything important?" Instructors never feel they are teaching unimportant information.

It is possible to win grades and influence instructors. You can do it by treating your instructors as you want them to treat you.

A Liberal Education: Your Place in the College Community

The word *liberal* comes from the Latin word *liber* meaning *free*. Robert Maynard Hutchins, a staunch supporter of academic freedom and a liberal education, believed that the concept of education was more than learning a trade. Although you might think that your education is confined to the walls of your classrooms or laboratories and prepares you for the world of work, a truly liberal education comes from your interactions with others and the college community. Your education prepares you for life. Your institution offers you a variety of formal and informal opportunities to meet and become part of the college community.

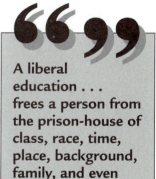

A liberal education . . . frees a person from the prison-house of class, race, time, place, background, family, and even nation.

—Robert Maynard Hutchins
Twentieth century American educator

Campus Diversity

Postsecondary education has changed since the late 1960s. Before then, typical students came from college preparatory schools and had similar economic or social backgrounds.

Today, diversity characterizes the typical postsecondary campus. Students come from a variety of academic backgrounds. Age, ethnic identity, and socioeconomic levels vary. Students with learning and other disabilities all find a place on the college campus. International students from a variety of countries and U.S. students from a variety of states can attend the same institution. Students from rural communities and those from metropolitan areas share classrooms and ideas.

Some groups need additional help during their entry into the confusing realm of higher education. Special programs provide chances for personal enrichment and improvement of learning skills. The campus learning center provides academic assistance, tutoring, and a variety of self-help materials.

Commuting Students

If you are a commuting student, you might not think of yourself as a nontraditional student. However, if you commute to an institution where the majority of students reside on campus, you are a nontraditional student, and you face unique problems. Often you might find that courses are available only at inconvenient times. In addition, schedule conflicts can cause you to miss speeches, study sessions, research opportunities, and other learning experiences that enrich academic life. Next, as a commuting student, you are part of a group often called "suitcase" students. With no dorm room or office to serve as a base, you often find that the materials you need are at home, in your car, or at your job. Finally, traveling back and forth limits your contact with others. This often leads to a feeling of alienation and an inability to find your place in the institution.

Each of these problems requires creative coping. Solving scheduling problems, for example, involves effective time management. Often each minute you stay on campus needs to be stretched to two through careful organization and planning. Having the library run a computer search while you attend a study session is an example of such planning. Another way to cope is to find and use alternative resources. Your neighborhood library or videotaped lectures provide reasonable options to supplement what you miss on campus. Using the time you spend commuting to your advantage is another way you can manage more effectively. Listening to audio tapes,

Rural parking...Urban campus

memorizing and rehearsing information, or discussing information with others in your car pool, for example, help you learn while you travel.

To avoid misplacing important materials, you need to be organized and prepared. You become a suitcase student in fact as well as name. To do so, you use a backpack or a briefcase to hold all the books and papers you use each day. By organizing your pack or case each night, you know you're ready for the next day.

Last, you avoid feeling separated from others on campus by consciously attempting to make yourself a part of the school. Reading the campus newspaper, talking with others before and after class, and exchanging phone numbers with classmates decreases your feelings of alienation.

ESL Students

You, as one of many ESL (English as a Second Language) students, face a unique situation. You are not only learning new subjects, but you also might be learning a new culture and language.

Like other nontraditional students, improving your study skills is important. Some special learning suggestions can aid your understanding. First, preview your text before class to help you predict the information the lecture will contain. This helps you avoid misunderstanding the instructor. Second, watch *successful* American classmates and copy what they do. Your classmates can provide you with models for notetaking and interacting with instructors and other students. Watching other students helps you identify the behaviors American students consider appropriate. Third, study with a native student to practice your English and acquire information. Fourth, many institutions provide special classes and workshops to aid you in perfecting your learning skills. Designed expressly for ESL students, they give you a chance to discuss problems and interact with others who are also new to American culture. These programs are well worth your investigation and time.

Overcoming cultural and language differences involves an open mind and varied experiences. Being here is a novelty for you. Meeting you is a novelty for most Americans. The most valuable way for you and natives to learn from one another is for you to become involved with an American family. Your institution's international office or a local church probably keeps lists of families who will invite you into their homes and their lives. Listening to American radio and television and going to movies are also ways of learning about American customs and language. Visiting shopping centers, museums, and restaurants also increases your knowledge of life and language in the United States. Reading newspapers, magazines, and books is also valuable.

One problem for many ESL students that the English they learned in their native countries is British English. Americans and Britons speak different forms of the English language. Although the grammatical structures are the same, there is sometimes a variation in vowel sounds and word usage. In addition, the rhythm, speed, and slang of American English with its regional differences may be new for you. Your understanding of the language will improve as you hear more of it.

Minority Groups

Minority groups are groups of people who, because of their perceived physical and cultural differences from a dominant group, tend to be treated unequally (Knox, 1990). Minority groups can be defined by race, ethnicity, religion, sex, and age characteristics.

What is college life like if you are a member of a minority group? You might experience some form of prejudice—a learned tendency to think negatively about a group of people—directed toward you. The social outlets available to other students might seem more limited to you. As a result, you might feel isolated and uncomfortable. Involvement, then, is critical for you. Student groups (for example, Society of Women Engineers, Black History Association, Returning Adult Coalition) provide opportunities to network within your minority group.

Membership in other campus groups and associations (for example, music groups, athletics, study groups, dorm groups, professional organizations) provide you with opportunities to become more involved in the campus community, learn more about other cultures, and create new relationships of support. These involvements will help while you are in school and later, when you enter the majority-dominated workforce.

You might also face differences in the academic arena. You may have been actively recruited before enrollment, only to feel virtually alone once you arrive on campus. Such changes in institutional attitude sometimes result in your having increased feelings of isolation. In addition, faculty may expect more—or, perhaps, less—of you if you are a minority student. Both attitudes present problems for achievement. For example, you might feel threatened or insulted. Again, your campus connections and networks should help you resolve such problems. You can also confer with minority faculty members and alumni or departmental counselors and administrators. In addition, you should seek the supports available to all students—library services, career planning and placement, counselors, tutors, campus employment, and so on. These, too, provide insights into academia and assist you in becoming more involved in campus life.

Reentry Students

If you are a reentry student, you are someone who previously entered the institution, left it, and is now returning. The key to your success often lies in the reasons for your previous withdrawal from academic life. You might have run out of money and left school to work until you were once again solvent. Personal problems might have caused you to withdraw. Maybe you weren't ready for college when you first began. Perhaps you lacked the academic goals and desire required for success, and you flunked out. Identifying your reason(s) for "stopping out" is critical in helping you avoid old habits and the same mistakes.

If you previously lacked financial resources, you now have a better idea of what it costs—both in time and effort—to stay in school. If you have not already done so, talk to staff members of the financial aid department. They can help you apply for grants and loans. They also place students in work-study jobs and sometimes maintain lists of off-campus employment opportunities. Second, examine your college catalog for scholarships and requirements for application. Many of these specify degree programs, academic classification, and other criteria required for selection. You might be the person who fits the bill. Finally, look for creative ways to cut expenses and make money. Perhaps a faculty or staff member could use a baby-sitter or chauffeur for their children. Maybe they need a responsible person to house-sit while they're on sabbatical leave. Such services could be exchanged for a salary or for room and board.

The types of personal problems that might have contributed to your previous withdrawal from school span a great range from caring for family members to succumbing to peer pressure. Whatever the cause, determine if the problem is truly resolved, both in your mind and the minds of others. If the problem is not resolved, you must be prepared to handle it, if and when it resurfaces. This can involve examining alternatives personally or with those affected by the problem. You also might need to seek professional counseling or other objective viewpoints to assist you in coping.

Transferring credits from other institution poses another problem for returning students. This procedure is handled by the admissions office. Most problems can be avoided by having transcripts sent to the school you are currently attending as soon as possible. This gives the institution time to evaluate your academic work and make decisions before you register.

Some reentry students are more serious and determined, whereas others seem to fall into the same habits that caused their earlier failures. If you now believe that you are ready for learning and to make commitments for success, you must be especially wary. Examine your previous course loads and content; evaluate how you spent your time. Prepare to readjust. Take advantage of the learning assistance services, workshops, and tutorial programs that are available on your campus. Time management and study strategies will be especially relevant for you this second time around.

Returning Adult Students

How can you be a returning adult student if you've never attended college before? Good question. You are obviously an adult, and you are returning to an academic setting, perhaps after many years. This unique characterization makes you an integral part of a diverse campus.

If you are an older adult student, you possess some advantages over more traditional students. College attendance is your goal, not that of your parents, teachers, or peers. Your life experiences provide a richer background for learning new information. You are sometimes more motivated than younger students. Your maturity and commitment provide you with the will needed to face the problems of an older adult student.

The first problem many adult students face is the red tape that holds together higher education. Particularly trying is registration, a confusing process for anyone. Adults often think that younger students are more experienced and knowledgeable about registration. If registration is computerized, you may feel even more a victim of time. No one is ever totally prepared for registration, however, no matter how it's done. If the registration schedule conflicts with your work or household commitments, you might be able to negotiate night registration or registration by mail. If you still feel confused about the process, have an experienced friend walk through it with you.

As an older adult student, you feel the same pressure to perform that other college students feel. In addition, you face the stress of being in a new situation. Employers, friends, or family can add to this stress by not fully supporting your educational goals. You also might feel the stress of trying to balance academics, work, and personal commitments.

Time probably seems your enemy—an opponent that beats you by moving faster than you feel you can. You combat this problem by being more organized. Like the straw that broke the camel's back, going to school is an overwhelming burden to people who cannot eliminate—without guilt— nonessential responsibilities. Asking friends and family for help involves them in your education. Time is your most valuable resource. You must evaluate each minute you spend. You need to become a careful consumer of it.

A course or workshop in stress management can help you cope with coming to college. Another way to decrease stress is to take a reduced course load during your first term. This acclimates you to academic demands and the concessions and responsibilities they involve. Involvement in extracurricular activities is another way to adjust to higher education. These activities provide new friends and interests. Your interactions with them give you a recreational outlet. They also break barriers between you and traditional students and build ties between you and other nontraditional students.

Your institution probably offers services designed to meet your particular needs. A day-care center, financial aid office, counseling services, and so on might be available to assist you. In addition, most institutions offer educational courses designed to improve academic skills. You need to find out how to locate these services and courses—either through the catalog, from instructors, or from administrative personnel. You need not be afraid or embarrassed to use them.

Working, being part of a family, and going to school are difficult in and of themselves. Doing all three is, at best, a juggling act with bowling balls.

Students with Disabilities

If you are disabled in any way, you know that you encounter challenges usually not faced or even considered by others. You might have a chronic (that is, permanent physical or learning disability) or temporary (because of an illness, accident, or surgery) disability. Whatever the case, federal law protects your rights as a student and mandates that appropriate and reasonable accommodations be made for you. It is your responsibility to determine what services you need for academic success and ensure that you receive them.

To locate services, first contact the admissions office. Its staff should be aware of the services that your institution offers and where to find them. In addition, your college catalog probably lists and describes these services in detail. The academic and student affairs departments, as well as your dean's office, should also provide you with information and assistance.

Getting Involved in the Campus Community

One of your institution's goals is retention. That means your institution wants you to stay in school until you complete your degree or other educational goal. What motivates a person to remain in school? Courses, curricula, and faculty all play a role in whether or not a student stays enrolled. Research indicates, however, that the key to retention is how involved a student is in the institution. The student who feels a part of the campus is more likely to stay than is the student who merely attends classes on the campus. In addition, job recruiters and employers often seek candidates who are well rounded with a variety of interests. Employers want to see students who can handle a diversity of activities while remaining academically successful.

What group should you join? Again, your needs, values, and interests determine which groups suit you best. In general, it really doesn't matter which group you choose, as long as you become involved in campus life.

Classroom Interactions

Each class in which you enroll becomes a group with whom you associate. Your interactions with this group depend on you and your behavior as well as on the other members of the class and how they act. You choose whether simply to come to class, take notes, and leave, or to become an active part of the class through your interactions.

The first impression you make on your classmates often sets the tone for your future interactions with them. Probably the first thing they will notice is your appearance. Although how you dress shouldn't matter, it does. It's true that you can wear almost anything in today's classrooms. However, clothes sometimes form barriers between you and others. Overly expensive or outlandish costumes often alienate or intimidate. Your best bet is clothing that reflects your style and personality but does not draw too much attention to you.

The first day of class is often as unsettling as the first day in a new school or on a new job. You might be eager to meet others but hesitant as well. One step can be taken at any time during the term. It involves smiling and saying hello. Finding out the names of people who sit around you is a second step. To start conversation, you might ask other students if this is their first class, where they're from, or what courses they are taking. In addition to making new friends, knowing the people who sit around you and exchanging phone numbers with them is good insurance for absences. You'll know whom to contact for assignments or notes.

The way you treat your classmates directly corresponds to how they will treat you. Several things can almost guarantee that you will be someone others won't want to know. First, consistent late arrivals or noisiness during lectures distracts people around you. Second, telling numerous personal stories bores everyone. In addition, monopolizing class discussions or asking frequent irrelevant questions annoys others who also wish to contribute. Third, if you show disapproval or voice sarcasm when others make comments, you'll alienate everyone. Your body language often speaks for you, too. What it says might surprise you. The way you sit, move your eyes, or place your arms can signal your disinterest or disapproval.

In every classroom, you are in one of two situations. You either do or do not know about the topic under discussion. If you know, you can make friends by finding classmates who do not know about the topic and helping them learn. Offering help without judging or boasting can be tricky, but it is essential to interaction with others. If you do not know the topic, you need to find someone who does and who is willing to help you. Asking for help gives classmates chances to feel knowledgeable and needed. Sometimes asking for help is just as hard as giving it. You might fear wasting other students' time or making a poor impression. A couple of ways to overcome this fear are to ask several students to join you for coffee to discuss class material or form a study group .

Study Groups

Studying in groups gives you a practical reason to interact with other students on an informal basis. In addition, research indicates that study groups provide optimum learning opportunities. Students who participate regularly in a study group (Shanker, 1988) understand and score better than those who study independently. When independent learners form study groups, their grades improve to the level of those already involved in group study. Work at Harvard University (Light, 1990; 1992) found that in every comparison, working in small groups (three to five people) was superior to another format. Small group learning shows better outcomes than working in large groups, independent study, or—in some cases—one-to-one tutoring from a

GROUP LEARNING ACTIVITY   GUIDELINES FOR ESTABLISHING ACTIVE STUDY GROUPS

A group consists of two or more persons whose contact, proximity, and communication produce changes in each other. As part of the group, you interact with and influence other students. The purpose of your group is the active discussion of information. Therefore, your group needs to have appropriate communication skills, a common purpose, the ability to set tasks, and the skills to accomplish those tasks. Unfortunately, acquiring these is easier said than done. The following guidelines can help you establish an effective study group.

1. *Select group members who have the academic interest and dedication to be successful.* Your friends do not always make the best study partners. Study group members must be prepared to discuss the topic at hand, not what happened at last night's party. You might not know which students in the class are interested in forming a group. Ask your instructor to announce the formation of a study group in class or place a sign-up sheet on a nearby bulletin board.

2. *Seek group members with similar abilities and motivation.* The group functions best when each member of the group contributes to the overall learning of the group, and no one uses the group as a substitute for personally learning the information.

3. *Limit group size to five or fewer students.* You don't want to restructure your entire class into a study group. Five or fewer members is more manageable for arranging schedules and setting goals. Larger groups also decrease the amount of time each member has to actively participate in the group.

4. *Two heads are better than one.* Although a group can consist of as many as five members, it can also contain just two. Lack of interest by other committed members, lack of similar goals, or scheduling problems might preclude your participation in a larger study group. Work or other time commitments also limit the times at which you can

meet on a regular basis. Two schedules generally have more in common than five.

5. *Identify the purpose and lifetime of the group.* Are you looking for a term-length group for in-depth study in a difficult course? Do you need pretest meetings to exchange ideas? Specific goals help prospective members decide if their investments of time will serve their purposes.

6. *If possible, schedule regular meetings at the same place and time.* Group members can plan accordingly if they know that their study group meets every Tuesday afternoon at 2:00. If the group meets less frequently, members might forget which week the group meets. If you meet at different locations, members might forget where to go.

7. *Get acquainted.* You will be investing a great deal of time and effort with these people. Although you don't need to know their life histories, you do need to know something about their level of ability in the course (have they had six chemistry courses and this is your first?), their current time commitments (do they have jobs, family, social, or other activities that affect the times at which they can and cannot meet?), and their expectations of the group. At the very least, you need to exchange names and phone numbers so that you can contact members in case of an emergency.

Application

Form a study group for this class. Establish a purpose for the group and set a schedule for out-of-class meetings. As a group, create a checklist or survey to help you get acquainted with each other. Include questions that help you determine if group members have similar academic interests and levels of dedication. Make copies and exchange your group's checklist or survey with other groups in the class. Compare and determine which features are most appropriate.

faculty member. And, student involvement in a course, enthusiasm for the course, and pursuit of topics to higher levels increase with participation in student groups. Students indicate that working within groups taught them valuable strategies for working with others, strategies that they would have had no other chance to develop.

What is a study group? A study group is a collection of two or more persons whose contact, proximity, and communication produce changes in each other. As part of the group, you interact with and influence other students. The purpose of your group is the active discussion of information. Therefore, your group needs to have appropriate communication skills, a common purpose, the ability to set tasks, and the skills to accomplish those tasks. The creation and maintenance of such a group is often easier said than done. Guidelines for establishing and maintaining a study group appear in the following group learning activity.

What advantages do study groups have over independent study? When you study alone, you have only your skills and strategies at your disposal. Group study allows you to see, hear, and practice a variety of problem-solving, communication, and learning skills. You learn more actively because you participate more fully than in individual study. Group study often helps focus attention and efforts. You have more opportunities to see, hear, verbalize, and otherwise come in contact with the information you study. Group study also increases the ways in which you think about a subject. Other members of the group contribute their perspectives, cognitive processing styles, and insights about a concept. You have not only your own ideas, but the ideas of others from which to draw.

Group study provides psychological as well as cognitive benefits. Your commitment to others in the group enhances your study. You might be prone to break study dates with yourself, but you'll be more likely to prepare if you know others depend on you. In addition, participation in a study group gives you support. Knowing that others are having difficulty or have been successful at a task lessens your anxiety and provides encouragement. Group members provide an empathetic network for the academic, personal, time, and financial problems of the higher education student.

Although group learning certainly has many advantages, study groups have one potential disadvantage. Group study focuses on verbal exchange of information and often fails to provide practice in generating the kinds of answers needed for essay exam questions. And, although some students can explain information verbally, they might not perform as well when asked to provide a written answer. If you have difficulty composing written responses to test items, you need to include writing in your study strategies.

Campus Employment

Campus employment is one of the most lucrative ways for students to get involved in campus life. Even though student wages are often minimal, employment offers many other benefits. First, campus employers understand that a student's real job is school. Such employers are willing to let you work around class schedules and often rearrange work hours to accommodate special projects or tests. Campus employment often offers you an opportunity to work within your field of study in such positions as a lab assistant, office worker, tutor, and so on. Even if your campus job is not in your area of interest, it can provide you with experiences relevant to your career or lead you to an entirely new field of interest. Finally, campus employment gives you additional opportunities to meet and know students, faculty, and staff.

Special Interest Groups

Special interest groups are based on the notion that "birds of a feather flock together." Interest groups develop around a variety of topics from academic interests (for example, Accounting Society, Philosophy Club, College Choir, Pre-Law Association, Marching Band) to those that are simply for fun (Frisbee Club, Chess Club, intramural sports, Science Fiction Association, computer user groups). Groups can reflect political affiliation (College Republicans), sexual orientation (Gay and Lesbian Alliance), ethnic membership (Arab Students' Association), or religious belief (Inter-Varsity Christian Fellowship). Such groups can be formal or informal. Some are honorary and base membership on academic criteria. Joining these groups gives you opportunities to meet others with similar interests or to develop new interests.

Service Organizations

Service organizations provide various opportunities to work for the common good of your institution or community. These groups include any organization in which you volunteer your time for the benefit of others. Student government associations and residence hall associations represent students in a variety of ways. They organize to further the desires and needs of students they represent. The students who staff campus newspapers and yearbook offices often volunteer to gain experience in journalism and production. Many interest groups have a service organization that provides tutoring, advice, and support to its members. Finally, some organizations (for example, Gamma Beta Phi) provide more traditional forms of service (Big Buddy programs, literacy tutors, drives for food or blood banks).

Why should a busy student devote time to service projects? First, some people believe additional education confers additional responsibility as a citizen. Second, service provides valuable experience in working on committees and projects to accomplish specific goals and tasks. Third, experience with such projects can result in leadership positions in which you can develop additional skills. Fourth, employers often look to see the avenues in which you choose to use your free time.

Exercise 1.7   Use Sample Chapter 11 ("Organizing the Police Department") starting on page 482 and respond to the following questions:

1. Read the Review Exercise at the end of Sample Chapter 11. Now, consider that instead of being appointed new commissioner of a police department, you have been named the dean of your college. The former dean provides the same information as the former commissioner's assistant. The Associate Dean (who served under the former dean and now works for you) tells you the same information as provided by the city manager. In view of what you learned in this chapter, how would you reorganize the college?

    _____

    _____

    _____

    _____

2. Read the heading and subheadings beginning with "Police Department Units" and ending with the chapter summary. Describe how specific MBTI attributes relate to preference to work as each of the positions outlined in Table 3-3, "Organizing a Police Department by Function or Purpose."

    _____

    _____

    _____

    _____

    _____

    _____

    _____

    _____

    _____

    _____

    _____

    _____

    _____

    _____

CLASSIC CRITICAL THINKING

If we shrunk the world's population to a village of 100 people, it would look approximately like this:

- In the population of 100, there would be 57 Asians, 21 Europeans, 8 Africans, and 14 people from the Western Hemisphere (North and South America).

- Seventy of the 100 citizens would be nonwhite, and 30 would be white.

- Of the 100 people, 30 would be Christians, 18 Moslems, 13 Hindus, 6 Buddhists, 5 Animists and 28 would be either other religions or atheists.

- Fifty percent of the wealth would be in the hands of six people. These six people would be United States citizens.

- Seventy of the 100 people would be unable to read.

- Fifty percent would suffer from malnutrition.

- Eighty of the 100 would live in substandard housing.

- Only 1 person would have a college education.

What implications does this perspective have for you as a citizen of your hometown, your campus, the United States, and of the world?

SOURCE: School of International Training Newsletter and the SMU MBA Newsletter.

Social Organizations

Some groups form for strictly social reasons. Like many other campus groups, their purpose is to connect you to other people within the institution. Greek groups have national affiliations and a long tradition. Some students join because their parents, grandparents, or siblings were members. Thus, the networks within such groups are often far ranging and well connected. Although Greeks are often known for their ability to party, many also focus on academic standards and community service.

A group need not be affiliated with Greeks to be social in nature. Many other groups provide opportunities for interacting with other students. First, students can join an **intramural sports** group, which organizes athletic events and services for students who are not part of a school-sponsored athletic team. These activities focus on competition that encourages fair play, leadership, health, and fun. Second, students interested in the same subject often form a club through the student affairs office. This helps you develop friendships with others. Third, students might join other clubs on campus that involve individuals with similar interests or hobbies. Membership often depends on grade point average or other criteria. Finally, leisure or other noncredit courses also provide opportunities for you to meet others. Although fun is the immediate goal, the long-range effect is friendship and greater assimilation into the institution.

CHAPTER SUMMARY

1. Studying and thinking in ways that complement and employ your learning style (personality, sensory preferences, and brain dominance) maximizes understanding.

2. The Myers-Briggs Type Indicator provides information about personality for eight factors: extravert/introvert, sensing/intuitive, thinking/feeling, and judging/perceiving.

3. Sensory preferences include learning through visual, aural, kinesthetic, and reading/writing modalities as well as a multisensory approach.

4. Brain dominance reflects differences in right-brain and left-brain processing of information.

5. The rights and responsibilities of higher education citizenship include understanding information in your college catalog, using campus resources and services, striving for academic excellence, maintaining academic standards, and interacting with college faculty.

6. A liberal education involves getting to know members of the diverse groups of individuals found on higher education campuses as well as getting involved in campus life through interactions with other students, employment on campus, and membership in student organizations.

CHAPTER REVIEW

Answer briefly but completely.

1. How does identifying MBTI personality factors, brain dominance, and sensory preferences affect learning? What might be the effect on your learning of a failure to understand these traits?

   _____

   _____

   _____

   _____

   _____

2. Choose any five components of a college catalog as identified in Table 1.4. Describe a specific purpose you might have for using each one you choose.

   _____

   _____

   _____

   _____

   _____

3. Categorize the higher education terms found in Table 1.5 according to the following categories:

Terms related to students	Terms related to courses	Terms related to students and courses
_____	_____	_____
_____	_____	_____
_____	_____	_____
_____	_____	_____

4. What is the relationship between academic standards and academic excellence?

   _____

   _____

   _____

   _____

   _____

TERMS

Terms appear in the order in which they occurred in the chapter.

- style
- personality
- sensory preferences
- brain dominance
- Myers-Briggs Type Indicator (MBTI)
- visual
- aural
- kinesthetic
- multisensory
- left brain
- right brain
- college catalog
- grade point average (GPA)
- quality points
- academic probation
- academic action
- plagiarism
- academic code of student conduct
- appeals
- intramural sports

5. What is the relationship between grade point average and quality points?

    _____

    _____

    _____

    _____

    _____

6. What aspects of classroom behavior also apply to communicating with faculty in out-of-class interactions and office visits?

    _____

    _____

    _____

    _____

    _____

7. Which of the diverse groups discussed in this chapter (for example, ESL students, students with disabilities) do you find to be most prevalent on your campus? What services are available for that group on your campus?

    _____

    _____

    _____

    _____

    _____

8. Compare involvement in campus activities through classroom interactions with involvement in campus activities through study groups.

    _____

    _____

    _____

    _____

    _____

9. Identify five places where students work on your campus and the kinds of work experiences available at each location.

    _____

    _____

    _____

    _____

    _____

10. Compare the number and type of service organizations with the number and type of social organizations on your campus.

_____

_____

_____

_____

_____

VOCABULARY DEVELOPMENT   Terminology: The Language of College Courses

Becoming a citizen in the world of higher education involves setting your own goals, as well as meeting those that your institution sets for you. It means knowing the people who work, teach, live, and study at school with you. Most of all, higher education provides you with opportunities—to assess yourself, enhance current abilities, learn new ideas, and grow in ways you've never even thought of. These changes will require changes in your vocabulary to accommodate the new ways in which you think and communicate. From *academic year* to *astronomy,* from *GPA* to *Greek affairs,* from *provost* to *political science,* from *residential housing* to *religion,* you'll encounter new terminology in the world of higher education.

Since words are the currency of thought, the more words you master,
the richer become your thought processes.

Joseph Bellafiore, 1968

Words are the medium of exchange for the subjects you study. Without them, you can neither buy new ideas nor spend them in the form of written or verbal transactions. Just as sound financing forms the basis of any business, a sound understanding of course vocabulary underlies the business of learning that subject.

Just as your profession affects the terminology you use, the language of the courses in which you enroll varies according to the course. Basically, college courses fall into four categories: humanities, social studies, sciences, and applied or technical courses (see Table V1.1). The kinds of terms you encounter and the way in which you meet them vary according to the course type.

Course vocabulary generally takes three forms: **technical vocabulary, specialized vocabulary,** and **general vocabulary** (see Table V1.2). Your mastery of the vocabulary in a specific course depends on your prior knowledge of the course's content, the stages of your vocabulary development, and the depth of understanding required by the course.

Table V1.1   Academic Disciplines and Subjects of Study

Humanities

Art	Foreign languages	Philosophy
Classical languages	Journalism	Religion
English	Music	Speech

Natural Sciences

Biological	*Mathematical*	*Physical*
Biology	Computer science	Astronomy
Botany	Mathematics	Chemistry
Marine science		Geology
Microbiology		Physical science
Zoology		Physics

Social Sciences

Anthropology	History	Psychology
Economics	Political science	Sociology
Geography		

Technical or Applied

Agriculture	Engineering	ROTC
Business	Physical education	Social work
Education	Psychology	

Table V1.2   Course Vocabulary

Type	Description	Frequent College Contexts	Examples
Technical	Specific to the course	Science Applied/Technical	ion lactose
Specialized	General vocabulary used in new or unfamiliar ways	Humanities Social studies Science	base core cell family rotation
General	Common words unfamiliar to you	Humanities Social studies	euthanasia laconic icon collate

---

Table V1.3   Stages of Vocabulary Development

1. You know that a word is new to you. You have no prior knowledge of the word.
2. You recognize a word but are unsure about its meaning or any general associations with it.
3. You recognize a word but have only vague associations with general concepts.
4. You recognize a word and can use it in the context of the course.

Your knowledge of a word can range from no knowledge to the ability to use the word. Edgar Dale (1958) theorized four progressive stages of vocabulary development (see Table V1.3). In stage one, you have no knowledge of the word's meaning. You only realize that the word you encounter is new. At the second stage, you believe that the word is one you've seen or heard. However, you possess no real knowledge of its meaning. In stage three, you associate the word with a very general concept. For example, suppose you encounter the word *Protista* in biology class. You associate it with classifications of life. Further, you believe it to be a fairly simple form of life. Beyond that general concept, you have no clear understanding. At stage four, you attain an understanding of the word in relation to the course and the manner in which it is used. You know that *Protista* is a kingdom of single-celled organisms of such diversity that they include both plants and animals.

Making an effort to stop and learn the terminology in a course affects the depth of your understanding of the course. One way to estimate your understanding of a course is to identify the levels at which you understand its terms. Such identifications serve several functions. First, when you identify a word that you don't know, you focus your attention on it. This increases your chance of knowing the word in later encounters. Then, by attempting to determine the meaning, you increase your recall through association and active learning. Finally, the more you relate terms and ideas, the more effective you are at making future associations.

Activity 1

An exercise used with high school and college students for a number of years with interesting reactions is included here. The tongue-in-cheek idea is that you may determine your salary level based on your age and the number of words you can identify correctly. The terms come from a wide field.

1. Did you see the *clergy*?   a. funeral   b. dolphin   c. church members   d. monastery   e. bell tower
2. Fine *louvers*.   a. doors   b. radiators   c. slatted vents   d. mouldings   e. bay windows

3. Like an *ellipse*.   a. sunspot   b. oval   c. satellite   d. triangle   e. volume

4. *Dire* thoughts.   a. angry   b. dreadful   c. blissful   d. ugly   e. unclean

5. It was the *affluence*.   a. flow rate   b. pull   c. wealth   d. flood   e. bankruptcy

6. Discussing the *acme*.   a. intersection   b. question   c. birthmark   d. perfection   e. low point

7. How *odious*.   a. burdensome   b. lazy   c. hateful   d. attractive   e. fragrant

8. This is *finite*.   a. limited   b. tiny   c. precise   d. endless   e. difficult

9. Watch for the *inflection*.   a. accent   b. mirror image   c. swelling   d. pendulum swing   e. violation

10. The *connubial* state   a. marriage   b. tribal   c. festive   d. spinsterly   e. primitive

11. See the *nuance*.   a. contrast   b. upstart   c. renewal   d. delinquent   e. shading

12. Where is the *dryad*?   a. water sprite   b. fern   c. dish towel   d. chord   e. wood nymph

13. Will you *garner* it?   a. dispose of   b. store   c. polish   d. thresh   e. trim

14. A sort of *anchorite*.   a. religious service   b. hermit   c. marine deposit   d. mineral   e. promoter

15. *Knurled* edges.   a. twisted   b. weather beaten   c. flattened   d. ridged   e. knitted

16. Is it *bifurcated*?   a. forked   b. hairy   c. two-wheeled   d. mildewed   e. joined

17. Examining the *phthisis*.   a. cell division   b. medicine   c. misstatement   d. dissertation   e. tuberculosis

18. *Preponderance* of the group.   a. majority   b. heaviness   c. small number   d. foresight

19. Ready to *expound*   a. pop   b. confuse   c. interpret   d. dig up   e. imprison

20. Starting at the *relict*.   a. trustee   b. antique table   c. corpse   d. widow   e. excavation

SOURCE: Marian J. Tonjes and Miles V. Zintz, *Teaching Reading Thinking Study Skills in Content Classrooms.* (2E). © 1987, Wm. C. Brown Communications, Inc., Dubuque, Iowa. All rights reserved. Reprinted by permission.

Score your responses using the key following Activity 2. Now, based on your raw score, find your salary level.

Number Correct

Age 17–20		Age 21–29		Age 30 and up	
20–15	$40,000 and up	20–17	$40,000 and up	20–19	$35,500 and up
14–13	32,000–$40,000	16–15	32,000–$35,500	18–17	32,000–$35,500
12–11	28,000–32,000	14–13	28,000–32,000	16–15	28,000–32,000
10–9	25,000–28,000	12–11	25,000–28,000	14–13	25,000–28,000
8–7	20,000–25,000	10–5	20,000–25,000	12–11	20,000–25,000
6–3	15,000–20,000	Below 5	Under 15,000	10–7	15,000–20,000
Below 3	Under 15,000			Below 7	Under 15,000

Activity 2

On a separate sheet of paper or in your journal, copy any 10 of the terms found at the end of Sample Chapter 13 ("Concepts in Human Biology") in this text and from any chapter from a course in which you are now enrolled. Identify which are specialized, technical, and general terms. Then based on Dale's ranking system, identify your level of knowledge of each.

Answers to Activity 1

1.	C	11.	A
2.	C	12.	E
3.	B	13.	B
4.	B	14.	B
5.	C	15.	D
6.	D	16.	A
7.	C	17.	E
8.	A	18.	A
9.	A	19.	C
10.	A	20.	B

Time Management:
Put Yourself to Work

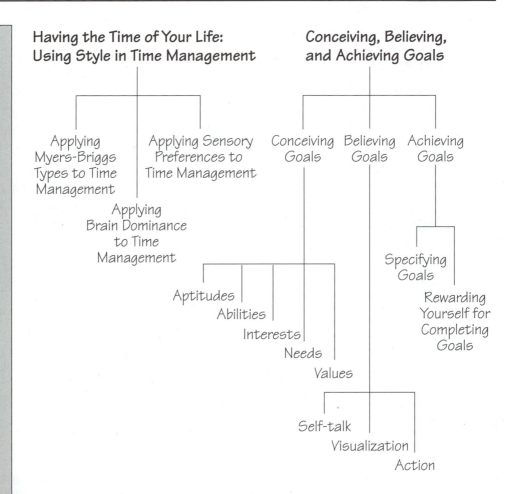

Having the Time of Your Life: Using Style in Time Management

- Applying Myers-Briggs Types to Time Management
- Applying Brain Dominance to Time Management
  - Aptitudes
  - Abilities
  - Interests
  - Needs
  - Values
- Applying Sensory Preferences to Time Management

Conceiving, Believing, and Achieving Goals

- Conceiving Goals
- Believing Goals
  - Self-talk
  - Visualization
  - Action
- Achieving Goals
  - Specifying Goals
  - Rewarding Yourself for Completing Goals

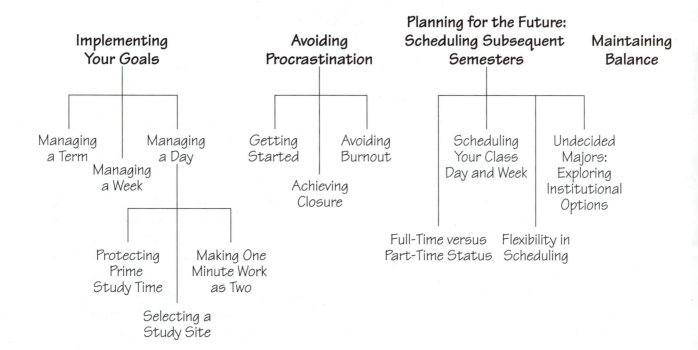

Ziggy's dilemma—things to *do* today versus things *due* today—actually represents differing time-management styles. Some students work methodically on projects and finish them ahead of schedule. They organize papers and other materials and store them in files or other containers. Other students wait until the last minute to begin projects and work in energetic, high-pressure spurts. They place papers and other materials in numerous stacks around a room. Or, a student may fall somewhere in between, carefully organizing some activities and completing others in a more flexible fashion.

Whatever the case, the way you organize time affects the way you work. The same personal attributes that affect your learning style also affect your time-management style. Recognizing how they affect time management helps you make the most of your strengths and, when necessary, modify your style to accomplish what you need to do in a timely fashion. In this chapter we describe how to incorporate personality, brain dominance, and sensory preferences into a time-management system. We show you how to create term, weekly, and daily time-management plans. These help you identify how you can use your goals to maintain your focus on current tasks. This chapter also provides suggestions for overcoming procrastination, scheduling classes for subsequent semesters, and maintaining balance as a postsecondary student.

Having the Time of Your Life: Using Style in Time Management

To have the time of your life means to have a wonderful time. Indeed, it means to have the best experience of your life. When you use your personal style (see Chapter 1) in managing time, every day can be the time of your life . . . as long as what you do in life has the same expectations of time as you have. Unfortunately, life and the demands of life do not always exist on your terms. You must not only understand your time usage style, but you must also accommodate your style to meet the expectations and needs of others.

Applying Myers-Briggs Types to Time Management

Your personality type indicates you tend to have characteristics and behaviors in that type. (See Exercise 1.1 to determine your type.) However, as you solve problems, interact with others, or analyze situations, you use all the dimensions to some degree (Lawrence, 1987). For example, you might use sensing (S) to collect ideas relevant to a paper while remaining open to new angles on the topic (N). At some point, you begin to use logic (T) to analyze the information although you consider your personal priorities (F) as you do so. You could approach your paper in an orderly way (J) and yet retain some flexibility (P). You take time to explore a variety of ideas that interest you (I), yet you keep the deadline for completion of the paper in mind (E). Your personality type determines, to some degree, the level to which you let one dimension override another. For example, if your type includes I rather than E, you might spend so much time exploring ideas that you miss the deadline for completion of the paper.

Applying Brain Dominance to Time Management

If you're a left-brain dominant individual (See Exercise 1.3 and Table 1.3), you'll probably find yourself agreeing with Dr. Bennett. You are the kind of person who favors traditional time-management principles. You feel

---

WRITE TO LEARN

Re-examine Table 1.1 in Chapter 1. On a separate sheet of paper or in your journal, explain how the dimensions of your type affect time management. Then identify ways you can use this information to better manage time.

comfortable with calendars, planners, and lists. You're analytical and detail oriented. You complete tasks on time and in an orderly manner. Your work space is organized with a place for everything and everything in its place. You clean off your desk and put materials away neatly each day. Maintaining a schedule gives you a feeling of control. Interruptions annoy you because they get you off your schedule. You like to get things done. You might already consider yourself a good manager of your time.

If you're a right-brain dominant individual, you probably feel a little less enthusiastic about Dr. Bennett's suggestions. As a right-brain individual, you have the capability to work on a number of tasks, more or less simultaneously. As a result, you feel comfortable shifting from project to project. You feel less comfortable with deadlines and prefer to work in a more self-paced, flexible, and energetic manner. You find interruptions stimulating and interesting. Others might watch you and think you're doing nothing, but you know you are thinking about your project. You tend to organize spatially and like to see everything around you. You prefer to leave projects in progress spread out on your desk until their completion rather than putting things away at the end of each day. When you finish a project, you might find you feel a little unsettled. You might like to use term planners to get an overview of an entire semester and concept maps (see Chapter 6) to organize. Because you don't adhere to traditional time-management plans, you might feel that you lack time-management skills.

Unless you are an extremely unusual individual, you probably find that you have both right- and left-brain attributes rather than only one or the other. The key to time management—like the key to learning—involves balancing the two and using the strengths of one side of the brain to offset the weaknesses in the other. Table 2.1 identifies some right and left-brain problems in time management and provides suggestions for solving each one. Because left-brain individuals possess more attributes compatible with traditional time-management practices, most problems occur when right-brain strengths affect organizational needs.

Applying Sensory Preferences to Time Management

Although sensory preferences have less impact than personality factors and brain dominance, you can still use them to enhance your time-management strategies. For example, if you prefer to learn visually, you could use color coding to indicate task priorities or visualization to sequence activities. Aural learners might use answering machines to their advantage by calling and leaving themselves verbal messages about tasks to accomplish or deadlines to meet. Small tape recorders might also be used for such purposes. Kinesthetic learners might find arranging activities, times, and due dates on a bulletin or magnetic board provides them the physical activity needed to structure time.

Table 2.1   Time-Management Problems Associated with Brain Dominance

Left-Brain Problems	Suggestions for Solution
Overemphasis on detail; spending more time on a project than it warrants; inability to judge when enough is enough.	Set priorities. Determine the grade or amount of effort required. Set time limits for completion.
Impatience with effort or time required to complete a task.	Set realistic expectations.
Inability to handle interruptions.	Determine the best use of your time for a particular moment. You may need to strengthen assertive skills in communicating your needs to others. Consider closing the door to your room or going to a less-distracting place to work.

Right-Brain Problems	Suggestions for Solution
Inability to decide what project to begin first.	Use term and weekly planners to set daily to-do list priorities. Visualize each step of your project from beginning to end before starting the project.
Disorganization of papers and other materials; inability to find things.	Use spatial organizers (for example, boxes, baskets, peg boards, bulletin boards, open shelves). Cluster items by their use (for example, art group, English group, math group). Color-code information and files and store the ones you use most often in a graduated vertical file on your desk or shelf.
Inability to stay on task; boredom and restlessness with concentrated effort.	Allow yourself to take frequent breaks after working for a set period of time; force yourself to return to the task after a specified (short) period of time or switch tasks to maintain concentration.
Inability to meet deadlines.	Break down large jobs into smaller tasks. Set intermediate goals and deadlines for completing projects. Work with a more left-brain individual and follow his or her timetable.

If your preference involves reading and writing, traditional time-management principles probably work well for you with few adaptations.

CONCEIVING, BELIEVING, AND ACHIEVING GOALS

Jesse Jackson's comment applies not only to students but to everyone regardless of age or occupation. The goals you set for yourself determine, in part, where you end up in life. Barbara Sher, author of *I Could Do Anything If I Only Knew What It Was* (1994), believes that goals express only hopeful predictions rather than concrete realities. So, if you might not achieve your goals, why even have any? Sher responds that goal setting and planning for the future

gets you going in a definite direction. If you set a goal and start trying to achieve it, your life will definitely change as a result. Will you reach that goal? Maybe, but maybe not. You might not reach your specific goal, but you could end up someplace better—someplace you never imagined or could have reached if you weren't already on your way to something and somewhere.

Active and enthusiastic pursuit of your goals often puts you in the path of opportunity. To ensure that you head in the right direction, Sher suggests you consider whether a choice will take you closer or farther from what you really want and always choose the action that takes you closer to your goals. For example, your goal might be to become a doctor. You get an opportunity to take a job in sales, which will help you make a lot of money but you must quit school to do it. Or you could take a lesser-paying job as an orderly at a hospital, which would allow you to continue school part time. The first choice has immediate but short-term results. The second choice has more potential for the future because it allows you to stay in college and gain experiences and make connections that could help you get into a medical school.

Conceiving Goals

How do you want to be remembered when you're gone? Loyal friend? Loving spouse/parent/child? Successful business owner? Professional musician? World traveler? Social activist? The list has endless possibilities.

Your goals form the answers to the question, What do you want to do, have, or be at the end of your life? You derive your goals from a combination of factors that contribute to your point of view—your **aptitudes, abilities, interests, needs,** and **values** (see Figure 2.1).

Aptitudes

Aptitudes reflect what you could do—your potential. These natural or inborn traits precede ability. They can be visible or hidden. Visible traits are those you already recognize and have developed. Hidden traits are parts of your personality you have not yet explored. For example, you might have an aptitude for music. If you grew up in a home where you took music lessons or went to concerts, then your aptitude for music is more likely to be developed. If you grew up in a home where music interest was not fostered, then your aptitude for music might be hidden.

WRITE TO LEARN

On a separate sheet of paper or in your journal, explain how you manage your time relative to your MBTI, sensory, and brain preferences. What aspects of your time-management style surprised you? Why? What did not surprise you? Why?

Figure 2.1   Factors That Contribute to Point of View

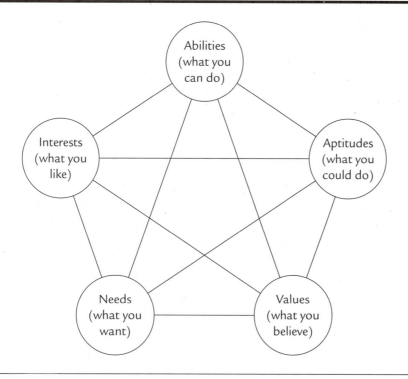

One way to learn more about your hidden aptitudes is to take aptitude tests. General aptitude tests estimate such abilities as verbal skills, numerical skills, spatial skills, motor coordination, and manual dexterity. More specialized aptitudes, such as music and art, are not evaluated by general aptitude tests.

The counseling or placement center at your college probably administers aptitude tests to help you set goals and make career choices. Discovering your aptitudes is important in the goal-setting process because awareness of your visible and hidden traits helps you identify areas of interest and clarify career directions.

Abilities

Abilities are what you can do—your capabilities. They result from aptitude combined with experience. Abilities are not constant. They increase with practice and decrease with disuse.

Unlike aptitude, which is estimated, ability is measured by performance in two ways: formal tests and informal assessment. Formal tests generally do not measure specific skill areas. Instead, they measure generalized areas, such as intelligence and achievement. Because formal tests measure broad skills, they do not identify specific strengths and weaknesses. Thus, informal assessment often results in a more accurate measurement of ability. Informal self-assessment occurs when you look at those areas in which you excel, examine your past performances, and recall comments others have made about your skills.

Such assessments can be misleading, however. First, time is a necessary consideration. In other words, suppose you and a friend each work a set of math problems equally well. However, you finish in one hour while your friend takes all day. Your ability in math, then, is probably greater than your friend's. In addition, ability differs in quality or kind. For example, math ability could mean solving complex equations or simply balancing a checkbook.

How do assessments of ability affect your academic goals? They help you identify your subject-area strengths and weaknesses. Knowing these helps you better determine those courses you're ready for and those in which you might need tutoring or other assistance. In addition, knowledge of your abilities helps you plan time and energy commitments needed for academic success.

Interests

Your interests are what you like. How interests develop has never been completely understood. Your experiences with situations and people create some of your interests. The sources of other interests might not be as easily identified.

Interests can and do change. The things that interested you as a child might not interest you now. The things that interest you now might not interest you in the future. Changes in your life cause changes in your interests. College life, for example, contributes to changes in your interests as you are exposed to new ideas and experiences.

Before college, your academic experiences and interests were probably limited to courses available at your high school (English, math, some science and social science subjects). Part-and full-time employment also might have shaped your interests. Postsecondary education now opens realms of information that were previously unavailable to you—for example, anthropology, philosophy, music history, Japanese, and robotics. And, your first reaction to such courses might be disinterest.

What you perceive as disinterest, however, actually might be unfamiliarity. In contrast, you may find courses that you thought would be interesting are not. You might find such changes in interest frustrating in that you may question your major, your values, and even your reason for being in college. Remember that such changes in interest should be an expected part of the postsecondary education process. Postsecondary education provides you with opportunities to rethink and redefine your interests—and yourself—in the process.

Changing interests do, and should, affect your choice of major and goals. Although it would be nice if these changes occurred in your first semester or two, often they do not. You might find yourself interested in another major in your junior or senior year. Several options should be considered. First, can you pursue this interest as a variation of your current major? If so, completing

Figure 2.2   Maslow's Hierarchy of Needs

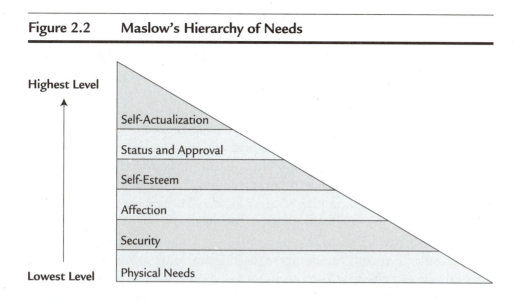

your current degree program with additional electives might suffice. Obtaining advanced degrees or certifications after you complete your undergraduate degree can also help you meet your goal. You might find, however, that only an entirely different course of study will meet your needs. For example, you might pursue a degree in business and later find your interests are in medicine. This change might cause you a loss of applicable credits and require additional time. Although you might wonder if this extra time and effort is worth it, you should consider that time you will spend in your career will be far longer than the additional time you will spend in school.

You determine your interests in several ways. Some of your current interests might be topics you like or activities you enjoy. You discover these by looking at past experiences and preferences. You find other, new interests by trying out new activities and by talking to others. You also might identify new interests by taking a standardized interest inventory. Interest inventories identify your preferences by assessing broad areas of interest or by comparing your responses with those of people in various occupations. Your college counseling center or placement office probably gives vocational interest tests.

High scores in specific areas of an interest inventory should not be the sole factor in academic goal setting. Sometimes an area of interest indicates a hobby, or avocational interest. For example, suppose your score indicates a high interest in art. You may not paint well enough to major in art, but you can enjoy painting as a hobby or you might choose to be an art historian.

Needs

A. H. Maslow (1954) developed a hierarchy of needs (Figure 2.2). He theorized that your lowest needs concern your physical well-being and safety.

Unless these basic needs are met, higher-level needs are never realized. Your need for affection involves interpersonal relationships with others. Self-esteem and independence needs affect your feelings of worth and ability. Your concern for the opinions and approval of others influences your status and approval needs. Self-actualization, the highest level, occurs when you are motivated to be your best for yourself.

Although these needs develop from lowest to highest levels, once developed, they interact. Thus, your needs exist at many levels. They direct and motivate your actions in setting goals. No one level or factor determines what your goals should be. The needs important to you and your choice of goals are unique to you. Thus, the ranking Maslow theorized differs for each person.

Values

Values result from your experiences. You derived some of your values from your family and friends. Your thoughts and reactions to situations and people formed other values. Events and people you learned about through television, literature, and other media also shaped your values.

Just as new courses shape your interests, new ideas shape your values. High school instructors generally hold the same principles and values as the communities in which they teach. Postsecondary faculty represent a greater diversity of geographical regions, ideas, interests, and, therefore, values. In fact, you might feel as though you have stepped into a wind tunnel of contradictory viewpoints and cultures: animal rights, pro-choice, anti-abortion, liberal, conservative, atheist, Christian, Muslim, vegetarian, politically correct, pacifist, pro-union, and so on. Exposure to these perspectives is part of the postsecondary educational process. Indeed, many college instructors see their role as being academically free to pursue intellectual inquiry and research, to ask or stimulate the asking of questions, or to raise controversial issues. As you encounter more and different views, your ability to listen, read, and think critically about information grows. The opinions, attitudes, and influences of others will have less and less impact as you learn to analyze information and judge for yourself. As a result, professors who require you to choose a position and defend it are generally less interested in your opinion than in your ability to logically support your argument in written or oral form. Helping you define your personal values in this way is also a role of the college instructor.

WRITE TO LEARN

On a separate sheet of paper or in your journal, respond to the following: What is your major? How do your interests and values support that choice? How have your postsecondary experiences affected your interests, values, and choice of major?

Why are values important? Values help you rank your needs. Because values vary, you must examine your needs for what you value most. Your academic goals affect study and time commitments, course selection, career orientation, and personal and professional associations. Pursuing your goals—what you value in life—is essential in achieving life satisfaction.

Believing Goals

As Jesse Jackson noted, it's your attitude and not your aptitude that determines your altitude. What you believe about yourself affects your life more than any other factor. You develop your belief in your ability to achieve goals through self-talk, visualization, and action.

Self-Talk

In a variation of Eric Berne's (1966) concept of transactional analysis, Karen Coltharp Catalano at the U.S. Military Academy in West Point, New York, suggests that your inner dialogue affects your beliefs in what you can do. She suggests that when you talk to yourself, you often function in the role of a **child** (the part of you that wants to have fun) or a **critic** (the part of you that denounces you), each of which negatively affects your ability to achieve your goals. Recognizing these roles and the kinds of self-talk each uses are the first steps to controlling them and regaining your ability to think and act in the role of the **adult,** one who thinks analytically and solves problems rationally. Table 2.2 provides some typical comments for each role in terms of goal-setting and achievement.

Visualization

Linda Allred of Conextion Therapeutic Center in Baton Rouge, Louisiana, described the effect of the mind on the body in a recent news report. She said that Dr. Dabney Ewin, a surgeon and clinical hypnotherapist at Turo Hospital in New Orleans, Louisiana, uses visualization to enhance the recovery of burn patients who have second and third degree burns all over their bodies. If Dr. Ewin can work with a patient within the first two to four hours after the burn occurs, he tells them that happy, relaxing, enjoyable thoughts will help release their healing energy. He uses the "laughing place" from the children's story of Brer Rabbit as an example. Using guided imagery, he asks his patients to visualize a place where they feel safe, peaceful, pleasant, happy, and free from responsibility. Once the patients visualize the "laughing place," he tells them that it is also a place where all of their injured areas will feel cool and comfortable. Dr. Ewin helps them go to their "laughing places" frequently in the healing process. The doctor's patients heal within two weeks and experience no pain or scarring.

Visualization has just as much effect on achievement of goals as it has on achievement of physical health. Albert Einstein often thought in images

Table 2.2   Self-talk of the Child, Critic, and Adult

Child Comments	Critics Comments	Adult Comments
I don't see the point of the goal.	This is too hard/too much for me.	This is difficult, but I have a plan.
The things I have to do to reach the goal aren't fun.	I don't know how to get started on something like this.	I didn't do as well as I wanted on that activity, but I know what to do differently next time.
I'm too tired to work toward my goal.	Nobody in my family has succeeded, so why do I think I will?	Other people have succeeded at this and I can too.
I think I'll skip this next class. The professor is dull.	Everyone else can do this. There must be something wrong with me.	This isn't very interesting, but I know I still need to do it to achieve my goals.
I wish I were doing something else.	I didn't think I could succeed at that.	This is hard, but I've learned/accomplished hard things before.
	I'll never make it.	

rather than words and conducted what he called "thought experiments." He sometimes imagined himself riding beams of light. From these imaginings, he eventually developed his theory of relativity. Unfortunately, people often picture the worst. They see themselves failing exams, losing athletic events, and blowing important opportunities. They actually visualize themselves failing to reach their goals. In her book *The Empowered Mind* (1994), Gini Graham Scott suggests that you repeatedly visualize and affirm what you want as if it has already occurred. She recommends that you close your eyes and imagine the future as clearly as if it were projected on a movie screen. You put yourself in the picture as you plan, execute, and realize the success of your goals. Steps to use for visualization appear in Table 2.3.

Action

You might have heard the old adage, "Actions speak louder than words." In other words, what you actually do often overrides what you say you will do. Controlling negative self-talk and visualizing help you focus on the possibility of successfully achieving your goals. Action translates that talk into reality.

What if you aren't sure if you really believe that you can achieve your goals? Gini Graham Scott (1994) and Barbara Sher (1994) both suggest *acting as if* as a mechanism for building confidence when you have personal doubts. *Acting as if* involves pretending that you have the traits or capabilities you need before you have proof of their existence. Thus, if you apply for a job and lack confidence, you act as if you were a confident individual. If you feel nervous

Table 2.3	**Steps for Visualization**

1. **Reduce outside interference.** Find a place where you can be quiet and relaxed. Eliminate outside noise as well as inner distractions and worries. Close your eyes and look through your inner eye.

2. **Create a screen.** As you create images, project them on a movie screen in your mind. You can watch them almost as if you were watching a TV program or movie.

3. **Evolve the image.** Move from the part you see initially to the whole picture, or from the whole to the part. Fill in the details. Picture each step you need to take to reach your goal. Look for logical consequences of your actions. Visualize different options and settle on the one you want to occur. Picture the success of your goal and imagine your feelings of success.

4. **Transfer the image.** Convert your visualization into the reality step by step. Externalize your inner view.

SOURCE: Steps adapted from K. Hanks and J. Parry (1993). *Wake up your creative genius,* (Menlo Park, Calif.: Crisp Publications).

about taking a test, you act as if you were calm. Sher suggests that *acting as if* benefits you in several ways. It helps you think in successful ways, improves your self-image, invites good luck in the form of information or opportunities, and sharpens your instincts.

Achieving Goals

According to time-management consultant Stephen Covey (1994), traditional time-management approaches generally focus on control, independent effort, efficiency, and chronological time. He identifies eight basic approaches to time management. The getting organized approach focuses on order. The warrior approach emphasizes survival and independent production. The goal approach is based on achievement. The ABC approach focuses on values identification and prioritization. The magic tool approach uses planners, calendars, and other technology to organize. The time-management courses approach emphasizes the development of new skills. The go-with-the-flow approach uses harmony and natural rhythms. The recovery approach is based on self-awareness of time-management flaws and dysfunctions. However, the title of Stephen Covey's book—*First Things First*—says it all. Time management isn't a search for a perfect system to run your life. Time management is your life and what you believe is important. Reconsider William Buchanan's quote about obituaries at the beginning of the section on conceiving goals. He said that the focus should be on a person's life, not his or her death. Your goals reflect what you believe is important in life, whether it is making friends, developing personal integrity, supporting a family, completing your education, increasing your professional expertise, and so on.

You've examined your aptitudes, interests, values, abilities, and needs. You've decided what's important to your life—what you want to do, have, or be. You've visualized success. All you need to do now is make it happen. How do you do that? Specifying the steps needed to reach your goal helps you determine how to achieve it. Rewarding yourself for completing these steps helps you maintain your motivation to continue toward your goals.

Specifying Goals

Lifetime goals cannot be achieved overnight. You reach your goals in small steps. Analysis of what you need to do to reach the goal forms your first step. For example, one of your lifetime goals might be to have your own business. The steps toward achieving that goal might include taking economics, accounting, and management courses to prepare you for business ownership; gaining work experiences in similar businesses; and making contacts with individuals who might provide advice, finances, or other support to you in starting a business.

The steps to achieving lifetime goals range from large to small commitments and from **long-term goals** to **short-term goals.** Long-term goals usually extend through a semester (for example, making the dean's list, completing all assignments on schedule) or even through an academic career (for example, finishing a degree with a *B* average). Short-term goals usually span a day or a week (for example, writing an English paper or reading an assigned text). You usually use them to reach long-term goals. Setting achievable goals is no easy task. To be useful, a goal must describe specific measurable outcomes. Your goals need to measure observable, concrete facts, rather than your good intentions. Specific deadlines help you meet your goals and thus avoid procrastination. They offer you the inspiration to get to work.

Consider the following goals:

- Study harder.
- Attend class more regularly.
- Take better notes in class.

Such goals are too abstract to be useful. You have no way of knowing if and when you achieve them. You make these goals achievable by adding measurable outcomes and deadlines as follows:

- Raise my grade point average by 0.2 by the end of the semester.
- Attend class each time it meets for the next quarter.
- Attend a notetaking seminar this term.

Your goals are best when they depend on you alone. "Practice vocal music twice a week with a quartet of singers" and "Complete assigned lab experiments with a partner" sound like achievable goals. Because they rely on others' actions (and inactions), however, your goals can be sabotaged when others fail to do their parts or do not show up.

To know if a goal is achievable, ask the following questions:

- How will I know if I attain this goal?
- When will I attain this goal?
- On whom do I depend to complete this goal?

Evaluation helps you determine where you might have gone wrong and how you can improve future goal setting. To do this, ask the following questions:

- What obstacles delayed the accomplishment of this goal?
- Who or what was responsible for these obstacles?
- How can these obstacles be eliminated in the future?

Exercise 2.1 provides practice in identifying the components of goals.

Rewarding Yourself for Completing Goals

Imagine the following: You stand in a line in the rain for several hours. You pay money for the privilege of pushing your way into a crowded room. For the next two hours, you hear loud sounds and screams that cause possible permanent damage to your hearing. It takes you twice as long as usual to get home because of traffic jams. Would you undergo such an experience? Yes, if the event were a concert you really wanted to attend. What makes you undertake such hardships? Motivation, either internal or external. Motivation is an extension of the needs described by Maslow's hierarchy (see Figure 2.2). Motivation at each level is based on an internal or external reward structure (see Figure 2.3).

Internal motivation comes from within you. It is your desire to accomplish a task. It is more powerful than other forms of motivation. Perhaps your goal is to graduate and attend law school. The good grades you get when you finish a project affect your grade point average. Higher grades improve your chances of getting into law school. Internal motivation, then, corresponds to Maslow's levels of self-esteem or self-actualization.

But what if you're not interested in attending the previously described concert? You might attend to please a date or other friend. Responding to **external motivation** is working for a reason other than yourself. Responding to such needs and desires of others corresponds to Maslow's levels of approval or affection. You might also devise artificial reasons for completing your goals. These might range from getting a candy bar for completing a math assignment to a new car for finishing your degree. These correspond to Maslow's lower physical and security needs.

Exercise 2.1   Use this key to describe each of the following goals. If a goal is **not** satisfactory, more than one letter may apply. Then list five goals of your own and evaluate them.

S—Satisfactory goal
M—Measurable outcomes lacking
D—Deadline lacking
O—Others needed to achieve goal

_____ **1.** Define each biology term by the first exam.

_____ **2.** Know all math formulas by the end of next month.

_____ **3.** Appreciate art more fully as the result of visiting an art gallery.

_____ **4.** Identify the handouts that will be covered on the final exam by Tuesday.

_____ **5.** Learn more about construction engineering.

_____ **6.** Become a better reader.

_____ **7.** Improve my English grade by one quality point by participating in a group study project before the end of the term.

_____ **8.** Complete all assigned history readings by next Wednesday.

_____ **9.** Read geography notes immediately following each class to make additions and corrections.

_____ **10.** Improve my tennis grade by ten points from midterm to final by practicing with another student three days per week for the rest of the quarter.

_____ **11.** _____

_____

_____

_____ **12.** _____

_____

_____

_____ **13.** _____

_____

_____

_____ **14.** _____

_____

_____

_____ **15.** _____

_____

_____

Figure 2.3   Internal and External Rewards in Terms of Maslow's Hierarchy

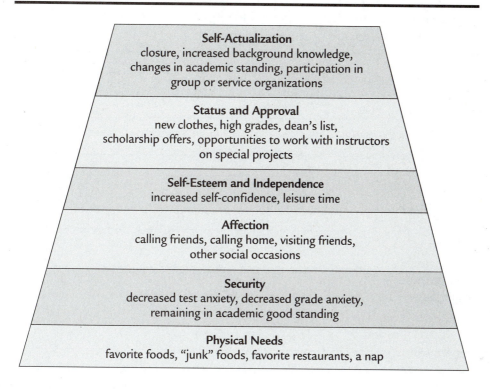

Self-Actualization
closure, increased background knowledge, changes in academic standing, participation in group or service organizations

Status and Approval
new clothes, high grades, dean's list, scholarship offers, opportunities to work with instructors on special projects

Self-Esteem and Independence
increased self-confidence, leisure time

Affection
calling friends, calling home, visiting friends, other social occasions

Security
decreased test anxiety, decreased grade anxiety, remaining in academic good standing

Physical Needs
favorite foods, "junk" foods, favorite restaurants, a nap

Behavior modification is one way to use external motivation in the form of **rewards.** To be effective, the reward should be something you really enjoy or want (for example, an ice cream cone, a movie, a walk). Thus, you substitute desire for the reward for the dread of the task. However, the reward needs to fit the task. For example, if you have a 500-page novel to read for English, your reward should be great enough to make yourself complete the book (for example, a movie). If your task is to summarize a three-page article, an ice cream cone might be sufficient.

Other types of external motivation include **peer pressure** and punishment. By telling a friend you plan to accomplish a certain task by a certain time, you pressure yourself to perform. If you do not complete the task, you face your friend's disapproval, as well as your own. A final form of external motivation is punishment. Here, you take privileges (for example, going out with friends, having dessert, attending a ball game) from yourself if you fail to finish a task. This form of external motivation is generally ineffective and is not recommended. Unless you're a masochist, you won't punish yourself. Exercise 2.2 helps you identify goals, rewards, and motivation.

Exercise 2.2 Decide whether each of the following tasks is a short- or long-term goal. Identify an appropriate reward for each task. Indicate whether the reward is external or internal. Then identify five tasks that you need to complete. Identify an appropriate reward for each task. Indicate whether the reward is external or internal.

Task	Short-/Long-Term Goal	Reward	Internal/External Motivation
1. Read six chapters for a history assignment	_____	_____	_____
2. Make the dean's list	_____	_____	_____
3. Attend a classical concert for extra credit in Music Appreciation	_____	_____	_____
4. Complete half of a math assignment	_____	_____	_____
5. Complete the research for a twenty-page paper for psychology class	_____	_____	_____

Your Tasks

1. _____	_____	_____	_____
2. _____	_____	_____	_____
3. _____	_____	_____	_____
4. _____	_____	_____	_____
5. _____	_____	_____	_____

IMPLEMENTING YOUR GOALS

Examine the following chart. It contains the numbers 1 through 80. Giving yourself one minute, circle in numerical order as many numbers as you can.

76	4	48	28	64	5	77	33	53	45
56	32	16	44	72	17	37	69	29	1
20	36	8	24	52	21	61	13	57	49
68	60	12	80	40	9	41	65	25	73
3	65	47	79	23	70	22	38	14	54
19	31	55	51	71	6	62	2	46	50
59	7	63	27	39	74	10	42	66	26
35	75	15	43	11	78	18	34	30	58

How many numbers did you circle?

Now examine the next figure. It is the same as the preceding figure except that it has been divided into four quadrants. The number *1* can be found in the upper right quadrant, the number *2* in the lower right, the number *3* in the lower left, the number *4* in the upper left, and so on.

Now, giving yourself one minute, circle in numerical order as many numbers as you can.

76	4	48	28	64	5	77	33	53	45
56	32	16	44	72	17	37	69	29	1
20	36	8	24	52	21	61	13	57	49
68	60	12	80	40	9	41	65	25	73
3	65	47	79	23	70	22	38	14	54
19	31	55	51	71	6	62	2	46	50
59	7	63	27	39	74	10	42	66	26
35	75	15	43	11	78	18	34	30	58

How many numbers did you circle? Knowing the plan in which the numbers are arranged aided you in your second attempt. Having a plan and implementing it is equally important in managing a term, a week, or a day.

Managing a Term

The first thing to do to manage a school term is to get a calendar for the months during that term and a college catalog. The purpose of setting up this calendar is to get an overview of long-term goals and commitments. This helps you plan your short-term and daily activities. Your calendar should include recreational as well as serious commitments. Table 2.4 provides steps for constructing a term calendar. Exercise 2.3 helps you construct a calendar to manage a term.

Table 2.4   Steps in Completing a Term Calendar

1. Obtain a college catalog for the current term, a monthly calendar, and course outline.
2. Use the catalog to do the following:
   a. Record any holidays, school vacations, or social commitments.
   b. Record midterm and final exam dates.
   c. Record dates for dropping and adding courses, and so on.
3. Use your course outlines to complete the following:
   a. Record test dates.
   b. Record due dates for papers or other projects.
   c. Set up deadlines for completing phases of lengthy projects.
4. Record important extracurricular and recreational events (for example, athletic events, concerts).

CLASSIC CRITICAL THINKING

Complete the following lifeline by placing your date of birth at point A, today's date at point X, and the estimated date of your death at point Z.

```
_____Z
A           X                                                            Z
```

Consider what you hope to accomplish by the Z point of your life. List below the life events you want to do (for example, complete college, own your own business, sail around the world), what you want to have (for example, children, a nice house, high-paying job, money), a description of the person you want to be (a good friend, president of a company, public official, parent) and the things you want to give to others (friendship, loyalty, time, financial support).

Activities I want to do . . . _____

_____

_____

I want to have . . . _____

_____

_____

Who I want to be . . . _____

_____

_____

I want to give . . . _____

_____

_____

What you choose to do today either takes you toward your goals ... or away from them. As a post-secondary student, describe below what you can do to work toward your goals during this term. What are the implications of these actions? Will they lead you to your goal? If not, what changes do you need to make?

_____

_____

_____

_____

_____

_____

_____

_____

_____

Exercise 2.3   Using a calendar for this year, label the month and days for the term in which you are currently enrolled on the following blank calendars. Using the process outlined in Table 2.4, construct a term calendar.

WRITE TO LEARN

On a separate sheet of paper or in your journal, construct a 24-hour time period in 15-minute increments. Identify the amount of time you spend in each of the following activities:

a. In Commuting

b. In Studying

c. In Class

d. At Work

e. In Rest (sleeping)

f. In Socializing

g. Other

Consider the following: If you were an auditor for an organization similar to the IRS, but for time rather than for money, would you consider yourself a good example of time well spent? Why or why not?

Managing a Week

The span of time covered by a term calendar makes it unwieldy to use on a weekly or day-to-day basis. Thus, you need to review your commitments on a weekly basis. This helps you form weekly plans for managing the term.

A weekly plan consists of a weekly calendar of events and a daily to-do list. As a student, you have much to remember: course information, due dates for assignments, class meetings, appointments, and so on. Your weekly calendar of events helps you keep track of your fixed commitments. It also helps you find the most important items to record on your to-do list. Table 2.5 helps you set up your weekly calendar.

Managing a Day

Within the first few weeks of class, you should have a good idea of how much time it takes you to finish what you need to do. For example, you should know about how many pages you can read, how many problems you can

---

Table 2.5   Steps in Constructing a Weekly Calendar

---

1. List fixed commitments first. This includes classes, meals, sleep, travel time to class, and so on. Allow a realistic amount of time for each activity. For example, daily travel times differ according to time of day, amount of traffic, and route taken. The time it takes to get to campus during rush hour can be very different from the time it takes to get home in the middle of the afternoon.

2. Set aside a few minutes before each class to review your notes and preview that day's topic. Leave a few minutes following each class to correct and add to your notes.

3. Identify blocks of free time.

4. Look for ways to group activities and schedule these in the blocks of free time. For example, if you have two papers to write, you can complete all your library work at once and avoid making two trips.

5. Plan to complete activities before the due date to allow for unexpected delays.

6. Schedule recreational breaks.

7. Schedule time for studying. Two hours of out-of-class study for every hour of in-class time is often advised. However, this rule varies according to your expertise in the subject and the course demands of the subject. Scheduling this much study time may be difficult for someone who works full-time or has family commitments. If you are such a student, you need to be careful not to overburden yourself. If you see you don't have enough time, you might have to drop one or more classes.

---

work, or how many errands you can run in an hour. This helps you determine how much time to allocate reasonably for each activity.

In managing the day, you attempt to accomplish what really needs to get done. After you complete your weekly calendar, construct a to-do list. The items on your to-do list consist of that day's commitments transferred from your weekly calendar, any items left over from the previous day, and any other activities that you think need to be accomplished that day. Some people create time lists and schedule activities for specific times during the day. Other people create task lists and accomplish one job at a time. Either method or a combination of methods works effectively as long as you rank your list in order of importance before scheduling anything. This ensures that you accomplish those activities which are truly priorities.

One way to enhance the effectiveness of your list is by the use of sticky notes to emphasize or supplement an existing list. These handy notes serve as reminders for you (or others) and provide additional information. Their color makes them easy to spot, so they are not often overlooked. Because this is so, putting particularly important tasks or information on them might be a good idea.

Chances are that you won't get to the end of your to-do list by the end of the day. That's okay. If you placed your commitments in their order of importance, then you finished the most important goals first. To obtain closure, you need to update that day's to-do list and construct a new list at the end of the day. When you wake the next morning, you'll be ready to begin.

Finally, keep in mind that your schedule is designed to help you manage your day, not limit it. You don't have to plan every minute of every day to effectively manage your time. Be reasonable. Spur-of-the-moment activities and emergencies will always arise. As long as you realize that you may have to rearrange your schedule to accomplish what you need, you can allow yourself the flexibility to rearrange your priorities and schedule as needed. Exercise 2.4 provides practice in completing weekly and daily plans.

Protecting Prime Study Time

Prime study time is the time of the day when you are at your best for learning and remembering. This time differs from person to person. Your best time might be early in the morning, or you might learn more easily in the afternoon or at night. You determine your prime study time by observing when you get the most accomplished, when your studying results in higher grades, or when you feel most alert and able to concentrate.

Your best time of the day should be spent either in your hardest classes or on the class work that is more important or requires the most effort. Working on the hardest or most urgent task first allows you to work on that problem when you are most alert and fresh. Your one or two most important assignments should be scheduled for this time. By completing the hardest task first, one built-in reward is that you soon get to do an easier task.

Exercise 2.4   Develop a weekly plan for next week and a to-do list for Monday.

Weekly Planner   **Week beginning** _____

Monday _____
A.M. _____
_____
_____

Noon _____
_____
_____
_____

P.M. _____
_____
_____
_____

Tuesday _____
A.M. _____
_____
_____

Noon _____
_____
_____
_____

P.M. _____
_____
_____
_____

Wednesday _____
A.M. _____
_____
_____

Noon _____
_____
_____
_____

P.M. _____
_____
_____
_____

Thursday _____
A.M. _____
_____
_____

Noon _____
_____
_____
_____

P.M. _____
_____
_____
_____

(continues)

Exercise 2.4   *Continued*

Friday _____

A.M. _____

_____

_____

Noon _____

_____

_____

_____

P.M. _____

_____

_____

_____

Saturday _____   Sunday _____

A.M. _____

_____

_____

Noon _____

_____

_____

_____

P.M. _____

_____

_____

_____

TO DO

_____

_____

_____

_____

_____

_____

_____

_____

_____

_____

_____

_____

_____

_____

_____

_____

Threats to prime time include mental distractions. You might find yourself thinking of other tasks you need to do. If so, keep paper and pen handy to make a list of your concerns as you think of them. By doing so, you literally put your problems aside until you are free to think about them. If you find yourself daydreaming, force your mind back to the task at hand.

Physical needs also affect prime study time. If you are too hungry or too full, concentration can be affected. If this occurs, you need to study at a different time. Fatigue is another factor that hinders study. A short nap often restores your stamina and memory. In addition, a well-balanced schedule that provides adequate time for sleep or rest limits fatigue.

Some threats to prime study time are less easily controlled. For example, you might find it difficult to rid yourself of friends concerned with your social life. All too often, invitations to go out with the gang come at prime study times. The solution, although simple, is a hard one to implement. It involves saying "no" in such a way that you offend no one yet make your point clear. Sometimes it's easier just to be unavailable. Taking the phone off the hook or closing the door to your room limits your availability. Another way to solve this problem is to hang a "Do Not Disturb" sign on your door. You can get one from a motel (usually free of charge), buy one at a card or stationery store, or make your own. A final option is to hide in the library or some other out-of-the-way place. You will probably never rid yourself of all interruptions during prime study time, but you can reduce them.

Selecting a Study Site

Managing your day involves more than recognizing your best time of day. You must also manage your surroundings to maximize your study time.

The first thing you do is choose a place to study. Where you study needs to be environmentally comfortable. The temperature, furniture, and lighting should match your physical needs. If they don't, these factors will affect the quality and quantity of your work.

Where you study also should be free of distractions. It should be conducive to work, not relaxation or fun. For example, you might think the student center or your living room is a good place to review. However, if remembering information—not talking to others or watching TV—is your goal, you may be disappointed with the amount you recall later. In addition, the place you study should not hinder your alertness. Studying in bed might be comfortable but make you sleepy. Using music or television as a background for study sometimes affects your recall. If you find yourself singing along with a song or a television commercial, then your concentration leaves something to be desired.

The place you study should be free of clutter but should contain all the materials you need. Clutter affects your concentration because your eyes are drawn away from your notes. It also results in your feeling disorganized and overwhelmed. Your desktop should contain what you are studying, and nothing else. You need to distinguish between clutter and essentials, such as your text,

Table 2.6   Quick Fixes for 5-, 15-, and 30-Minute Time Periods

If you have a spare five minutes, you can
>Review notes.
>Update your schedule or calendar.
>Skim newspaper headlines.
>Make a telephone call.
>Do a few sit-ups or other exercises.

If you have a spare fifteen minutes, you can
>Straighten a room.
>Pay bills.
>Take a walk to relax.
>Survey a chapter.
>Read a magazine.

If you have a spare thirty minutes, you can
>Run errands.
>Begin initial library research.
>Go to the grocery store.
>Brainstorm and/or outline a paper.
>Write a letter.

notes, and so on. All study materials should be organized and within reach to make the best use of your prime study time.

Making One Minute Work as Two

On any one day, you may find yourself with spare minutes before you attack your next major goal. You might be waiting for the library to open, for class to begin, or for the bus to come. These spare minutes seem few when looked at separately. But when you add them up, they total more time than you would guess. Because you can't squeeze these minutes together, you need to do the next best thing. You need to develop a "quick-fix" for your free time. Table 2.6 lists some quick fixes for 5-, 15-, and 30-minute time periods. Once you get the idea, you'll think of others. In Exercise 2.5, you can apply this strategy to your own schedule.

WRITE TO LEARN

Your younger brother is a junior in high school. He almost never completes assignments on time and crams for most of his exams. You think the information you've learned about managing a term and day could benefit him. On a separate sheet of paper or in your journal, explain what suggestions you would give him for getting organized.

Exercise 2.5 Answer briefly but completely. Then categorize each one as 5-, 10-, or 15-minute fixes.

1. List three times you have available for quick fixes.

   _____

   _____

   _____

   _____

2. Identify several tasks you can accomplish during these times.

   _____

   _____

   _____

   _____

   _____

   _____

   _____

AVOIDING PROCRASTINATION

> **Putting off an easy thing makes it hard, and putting off a hard one makes it impossible.**
>
> —George H. Lorimer
> *Twentieth century American magazine journalist*

You've identified your time-management style. You've targeted the goals you want to reach. You've made a term planner, weekly schedule, and daily to-do list. Now is the time, in the words of sports company Nike, to "Just do it!" So, why **procrastinate** (put off activities until later)?

The truth is that everybody—at one time or another—procrastinates, even knowing that doing so only makes things worse. So, why do we procrastinate? What is our motive?

Students—and others—procrastinate for a variety of reasons. One of the most common misconceptions about procrastination is that it is caused by laziness. Generally, if you've had enough drive and ambition to get to a postsecondary institution, laziness is not your problem.

In many cases, the same negative child or inner critic self-talk that influenced your belief in your goals also makes you procrastinate. When the child within you gains control, you avoid those tasks that seem dull, boring, or too difficult. When your inner critic gains control, you doubt your abilities, goals, and yourself. Either way, procrastination results.

The adult in you provides the voice of reason and logic. The adult knows that some tasks are no fun but that they must be completed. The adult then musters the internal motivation to begin dull and distasteful tasks and see them through. The adult must also be able to outtalk the inner critic in a stronger voice. "Yes, this is difficult, but I've been successful before." "I lack experience in this particular area, but I have similar experiences on which I can draw." "I don't have the right background, but I can learn it." "Others have been successful, and I can be, too."

Functioning in the role of the child, the critic, or the adult affects the way you work, as well as the ways in which you perceive problems. The child's primary behavior is lack of productive activity. Conversing with friends, partying, and doing other leisure activities prevent the child from ever getting to the business at hand. Worry is the critic's chief activity. Instead of studying, the critic worries about studying. This includes such self-questioning as "Can I learn this? What if I don't? If I don't, I may fail. What if I fail? What will I do?" and "What will other people think?" Problem-solving is the adult's forte. When the adult must study, the adult thinks, "What do I have to learn? What would be the best way to learn this? Am I learning it? If not, how can I rethink my understanding?"

Finally, the adult may appear to procrastinate at times. Weighing priorities and making choices about when and what to accomplish might seem like procrastination. The difference is in the motive. If your reasoning for putting off something is sound and appropriate, that might be the best plan of action. For example, you might be considering whether or not to drop a course after the first month of class. You've regularly attended class, and you have a good grade in it. However, your financial status indicates that you need to increase your work hours. Logically, you decide that you cannot do justice to the course and work more hours. What appears to be procrastination is actually a logical decision based on the reality of the situation.

Getting Started

Sometimes it is hard to get started on a project or an assignment, and this leads to procrastination. This problem surfaces in several ways, and each way requires its own solution. First, if a project seems too large or complex, you should cut it down to size. For example, you might have to design a school as a project for an architecture class. As a whole, the project might overwhelm you until you divide it into manageable parts. This might consist of researching the needs of the school, determining the price limitations, drawing a bubble diagram, and so on. In other words, use time management to locate the overall goal of the project and the steps needed to complete it. Second, you might not think of yourself as good at thinking of ideas for creative assignments (like speeches, and English themes). Brainstorming with others, asking your instructor for suggestions, or researching several topics to find one of interest often solves this problem. A final reason for procrastination is that the assignment might be beyond your skills in the subject. This occurs for any one of several reasons. You might have been ill or absent from class. Your high school preparation in the subject may have been inadequate. In any case, you can cope with this lack in skills by going to the campus learning lab, arranging for tutoring, or contacting your instructor. Exercise 2.6 helps you idenntify solutions to the problem of getting started.

"I think Harry's taking this concept of closure too literally."

Exercise 2.6   Think of the last major assignment you completed. List below any problems you faced getting started, how you solved these problems, and other solutions you could use in the future when similar problems arise.

Type of assignment:

_____

_____

Problems getting started:

_____

_____

_____

_____

_____

Solutions:

_____

_____

_____

_____

_____

_____

_____

_____

Other alternatives:

_____

_____

_____

_____

_____

_____

_____

_____

WRITE TO LEARN

"25 OR 6 TO 4"

Waiting for the break of day,
Searching for something to say,
Flashing light against the sky,
Giving up, I close my eyes.
Sitting cross-legged on the floor,
Twenty five or six to four.
Staring blindly into space,
Getting up to splash my face,
Wanting just to stay awake,
Wondering how much I can take.
Should I try to do some more,
Twenty five or six to four.
Feeling like I ought to sleep,
Spinning room is sinking deep,
Waiting for the break of day,
Searching for something to say,
Twenty five or six to four;
Twenty five or six to four.

—Robert Lamm

Copyright © 1970 Lamminations Music and Aurelius Music. Printed with permission. All right reserved.

Robert Lamm's song "25 or 6 to 4" tells of the plight of a person facing a deadline for writing music lyrics. The narrator faces a dilemma common to many college students. Should he continue working? Should he give up and get some sleep? Working against the clock often results from poor time management. Effective time management usually prevents a last-minute race with deadlines.

On a separate sheet of paper or in your journal, write a song or poem similar to "25 or 6 to 4" describing a situation in which you are writing a paper or studying for a test. Include information on procrastination, motivation, and closure.

Achieving Closure

Closure is the positive feeling you get when you finish a task. Lack of closure results in the panicked feeling that you still have a million things to do.

One way to obtain closure is to divide a task into manageable goals, list them, and check them off your list as you finish them. For example, suppose your history teacher assigns three chapters to be read. If your goal is to read all three chapters, you might feel discouraged if you don't complete the reading at one time. A more effective way to complete the assignment is to divide the reading into smaller goals by thinking of each chapter as a separate goal. Thus, you experience success as you complete each chapter. Although you failed to complete the overall goal, you know you've progressed toward it.

A second block to obtaining closure is unfinished business. You might have several tasks with the same deadline. Although changing from one task to another serves as a break, changing tasks too often wastes time. Each time you switch, you lose momentum. You may be unable to change mental gears fast enough. You might find yourself thinking about the old project when you should be concentrating on the new one. In addition, when you return to your first task, you have to review where you were and what steps were left for you to finish.

Often you solve this problem by determining how much time you have free to work. If the time available is short (that is, an hour or less), you need to work on only one task. Alternate tasks when you have more time. Completing one task or a large portion of a task contributes to the feeling of closure.

Sometimes, when working on a long-term project, other tasks take precedence before the first one is completed. If this occurs, take time to write a few notes before moving on to the new task. Your notes could include the goal of the task and a list of questions to be answered or objectives to be completed. References, papers, and other materials concerning the task should be stored together, so you know where to begin when you return to it.

"Another classic case of student burnout."

Excerpt 2.1   Overcoming the Deadline Dodge
by Barbara Smalley

- George, a junior at Queens College, rarely takes tests on time. Instead he invents a different excuse for each exam and begs for a second chance.

- Jim, a graduate student at the University of California at Berkeley, hasn't been seen on campus for months. "I'm avoiding my adviser," he explains, "because of all the outstanding commitments to him that I have."

- Kevin, a recent graduate of the City University of New York, is washing dishes because he has postponed making a career choice. "I always thought choosing a career would just happen, and I was having too much fun in school to think about it. One of these days I'll take a career-planning seminar," he vows.

Sound familiar? After teaching and counseling students for more than a decade, William Knaus, psychologist and author of *Do It Now: How to Stop Procrastinating*, estimates that a whopping 95 percent of college students put things off to some degree. And of that number, he says, some 25 percent are *chronic* procrastinators. "These are the ones who end up dropping out. Others finish school but begin postponing assignments when they're out on their own and no longer have the structure of college to rely on."

Procrastination on campus usually means that you delay doing a task that you have agreed to complete. Although the casual procrastinator postpones tasks *sporadically* and the chronic one does so *habitually*, Knaus points out that the differences between the two are not just a matter of degree. "Hard-core procrastinators usually have anxiety problems, may be depressed, or may suffer from acute self-doubt." And though casual delayers may start by putting off tasks now and then, many soon find themselves with a serious procrastination problem. "It's like being on a vicious merry-go-round," he explains, "because postponing tasks, even occasionally, can cause anxiety, self-doubt, and depression, which in turn provide the victim with even greater reasons to procrastinate."

Why You Put Off Projects

Procrastination can be remedied, but the cure often lies in first figuring out exactly why you are unable to complete your projects on time.

Are You Just Plain Afraid?

Fear and anxiety cause many students to dodge deadlines. "Ask me to give a speech, and I'll do fine," says Luann Culbreth, a graduate student at Georgia State University, "but I'm so intimidated by grammar that I can't seem to get started on a writing assignment."

Actually, procrastinators often spend more time worrying about tasks than they would actually use completing them, reports Knaus. Thus the trick to breaking through the anxiety barrier is to stop worrying and start working. Practicing Knaus's "five-minute plan" is a good way to begin. It requires that you commit five minutes to a task that you have been putting off. When the time is up, decide if you can handle another five minutes of it. Chances are that you will have built up enough momentum to forge ahead.

Do You Feel Overwhelmed?

You have to take a biology test, turn in a history paper, and give a speech during the same week, but you are so behind that you don't know where to begin. Knaus advises setting mini-goals and deadlines for each project. "The satisfaction of accomplishing each small step should keep you going." The same principle holds if you are faced with a single but colossal project. First slice the task into more manageable pieces, then set up a schedule of clear and achievable goals.

Are You a Perfectionist?

Surprisingly, perfectionists are especially vulnerable to procrastination. "They are terrified of getting anything less than 100 percent, because the tiniest flaw means an entire assignment is no good," claims Dr. David Burns, author of *Feeling Good: The New Mood Therapy* and *Intimate Connections*. Some perfectionists have trouble starting projects because they have set impossibly high standards. (Their rationale: "If I don't start, I can't fail.") Others refuse to recognize when a task is complete.

Burns concedes that if you are a perfectionist, you may require counseling to change, but he suggests that you try this introspective exercise in an attempt to do so on your own: "Make a list of the pros and cons of behaving flawlessly. Though there may be some pluses to being perfect, those are likely to be outweighed by a host of disadvantages that prevent you from growing and experimenting both with your schoolwork and in

(continues)

Excerpt 2.1 *Continued*

your personal life." The standards you have set for yourself, after all, are *guidelines* and not absolutes.

Are You Unable to Concentrate?

The environment in which you work can have an enormous effect on both your attitude and your productivity. Thus it pays to analyze *where* you typically study. "Students who work on cluttered desks and in areas open to a mass of interruptions are particularly prone to procrastination," says Knaus. He suggests that you choose a quiet workplace with room to spread out, stock it with reference materials you use regularly, and spend a few minutes setting goals. "Most people don't want to waste time getting organized, but spending 10 to 15 minutes a day doing so will save you hours of frustration later."

Do You Feel Indecisive?

Sometimes an uncertainty about your major or a strong desire to do something other than attend college can cause apathy, indecisiveness, and in turn, procrastination. When offered a one-month professional directing job, Natasha Shishkevish quit school 11 credits short of receiving her theater degree from Towson State University. "I fully intended to resume my studies afterward, but I just never got around to it."

Shishkevish has since held enough low-paying and unchallenging jobs to motivate her to return to college. "I'm finally happy with my career choice, and now that I've seen what work is like, I think I can discipline myself to do well in school."

But the transition between college and career may not be that easy for those whose habitual tardiness stems from a desire to be noticed. "I get more attention from professors when I have an excuse for being *late* with assignments than I do when I turn them in on time," admits one student. Although professors who accept excuses from students are merely reinforcing such behavior, students who squeak by on professorial pardons in school won't function well on the job. "Unless a company rides on you and your abilities," reports Knaus, "it simply won't put up with procrastination that causes a work slowdown."

When Postponing Isn't a Problem

Because setting priorities requires postponing activities and assignments, in some cases procrastination makes sense. "If you truly work better in spurts of massed time," admits Knaus, "holding off to do a term paper in the last week of a semester may work fine. Or if you forget things quickly, last-minute cramming rather than studying for days or weeks in advance of an exam may save you time and trouble."

How then can you tell when your stalling is "legit?" Knaus advises that you learn the difference between procrastination and a "strategic delay." Kim Bogert, for example, has purposefully put off taking freshman English in her first year at Northern Virginia Community College. "It's my worst subject," she explains, "and knowing that adjusting to college would be difficult in itself, I figured, why add more pressure up front?"

Because Bogert's postponement is not a cover-up for something like a fear of failure, Knaus, believes her actions qualify as a sound strategy. "In each case you need to apply the definition of procrastination—putting off a relevant activity that *can* be and properly *should* be done today," he says. "Also, since most procrastinators tend to be self-cons, you should always be on the alert for irrational excuses."

New York career counselor and management consultant Janice LaRouche provides another clue. "Procrastination is a problem when you know you'll end up paying a high price as a result." For some, experiencing feelings of guilt for turning in mediocre work is too costly; others balk at receiving "incomplete" or failing grades.

Help Is on the Way

If you're prone to needless procrastination, psychologists and counselors suggest practicing these techniques:

- *Pinpoint where your delays typically start.* "Most procrastinators follow a pattern," Knaus reveals. Determine whether you put off beginning a project, fizzle out at the halfway point, or fade in the homestretch. After examining your behavior, become totally committed to altering it.

- *Discipline yourself to use your time wisely.* "Procrastinators are very bad at telling time," says Dr. Richard Beery, a procrastination workshop leader at the University of California at Berkeley. Most underestimate the time it takes to complete an assignment. Successful time management involves

Excerpt 2.1   *Continued*

setting realistic deadlines, allowing extra hours for the unexpected, learning to use bits of time, and sticking steadfastly to your timetable.

- *Set priorities by making a list.* Force yourself to devote most of your efforts to the number-one task on that list. "Most procrastinators go to the bottom of the list," claims Knaus. "They'll have a history test and study biology instead."

- *Set a deadline and ask someone to hold you accountable for it.* In tight situations, promise to give up something meaningful if you fail to meet your goal. Pledging your front-row concert tickets to your roommate, for instance, might bring newfound motivation.

- *Beware of the inaction-exertion-inaction cycle.* Don't postpone a task and then become so immersed in playing catch-up that you become burned out and postpone your next assignment. Alternate periods of work with stretches of rest and recreation to prevent this vicious circle.

- *Don't wait until you finish a project to reward yourself.* "Most procrastinators value only the finished product," says Dr. Beery. "People need to realize that intermediate steps are also accomplishments."

Most important, says Knaus, procrastinators must learn that it's not terrible to feel uncomfortable. "There are a lot of unpleasant things in life that must be done," he stresses. "The more people are willing to tackle those tasks, the more those jobs become less bothersome-and more routine."

SOURCE: Smalley, Barbara S. (1985, December–January). "Overcoming the Deadline Dodge." *Campus Voice*, pp. 55–56.

WRITE TO LEARN

Read the essay in Excerpt 2.1 by Barbara Smalley entitled "Overcoming the Deadline Dodge." On a separate sheet of paper or in your journal, respond to the following questions. How do Knaus's five reasons for why you put off projects and the six techniques identified in the section "Help is on the Way" relate to Catalono's description of the child, critic, or adult?

Avoiding Burnout

Sometimes you procrastinate because you are burned out. **Burnout** results when you work without breaks. Burnout is unusual in that its causes are the same as its symptoms. Fatigue, boredom, and stress are all signs of burnout.

A balance between break time and work time helps you avoid burnout. Therefore, you need to plan for breaks, as well as study time. A break does not have to be recreational. It simply can be a change from one task to another. For example, switching from working math problems to reading a book for English relieves boredom. Such planning also decreases interruptions during prime study time.

Another way to avoid burnout is to leave flexibility in your daily schedule. If you schedule commitments too tightly, you won't complete your goals and achieve closure. This defeats you psychologically because you fail to do what you planned.

Planning for the Future: Scheduling Subsequent Semesters

If what you want out of life requires postsecondary coursework, certification, or a graduation diploma, you will probably remain in a postsecondary institution for several terms or years. The way you organize your subsequent semesters affects the success you achieve in them. Enrollment as a full- or part-time student, organization of your class day and week, and your need to explore institutional options are factors for you to consider as you make your future scheduling decisions.

Full-Time versus Part-Time Status

You have the choice of being a **full-time student** or a **part-time student.** Full-time enrollment usually means 12 or more hours in a quarter or semester system. This seems like a ridiculously short amount of time to be in class if you're used to a full-time 40-hour work week or a traditional high school schedule. The difference lies in where your work—in this case, your learning—occurs. Most high schools and employers expect you to work during class or on the job. In postsecondary education, most of the work you'll accomplish occurs on your own, after you leave the classroom. Some people say you should spend two hours out of class for every hour you are in class. Thus, for a 15-hour schedule, you spend 30 hours in study. Fifteen plus 30 equals 45 hours per week, more than a full-time job. Of course, such estimates are just that—estimates. Perhaps you love math and finish an assignment in 20 minutes. On the other hand, you might be less proficient in English and spend 6 hours writing a two-page paper. The time you spend in learning must match your strengths and weaknesses, as well as your goals and priorities. Still, a full-time class schedule is generally a full-time job and should be approached in that manner.

Whether you enroll full time or not depends on your other commitments. If you work, have family responsibilities, or are involved in other fixed activities, then the number of courses you can successfully complete might be limited. Course difficulty also affects the total number of hours you schedule. If courses are less difficult, more can be scheduled. Another factor to consider is how experienced you are in a given subject or as a postsecondary student. A French course will be easier for students who have had previous course work in French or other related experience.

ONLINE CLASS

Web Exercise 2.1

A variety of information related to time management are available on the World Wide Web. For this exercise, access any one of the following time management pages (for the most up-to-date URLs, go to http://csuccess.wadsworth.com):

Techniques to Manage Procrastination
> http://128.32.89.153/CalREN/procrastechniques.html

Time Management
> http://ub-counseling.buffalo.edu/Stress/time.html

Procrastination: Problem or Plus?
> http://www.ksu.edu/ucs/procras.html

Overcoming Procrastination
> http://ub-counseling.buffalo.edu/Stress/procrast.html

Use the information you locate to respond to the following questions:

1. On a separate sheet of paper, create a chart that compares the tips in the Web article with the tips in this chapter.

2. Which tip or suggestion in the article is most valuable to you? Why?

   _____

   _____

   _____

3. Which tip or suggestion represents a time management technique that you already use? How did you learn this technique?

   _____

   _____

   _____

4. Why do you think time management is such a great concern for college students?

   _____

   _____

   _____

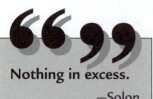

Nothing in excess.

—Solon

Fifth century B.C.E.
lawmaker

Scheduling Your Class Day and Week

Consider that philosophy holds true for many experiences. Overwork leads to exhaustion. Overspending results in high bills. Too much food causes a stomachache. Even too much information is hard to digest at one time.

College classes often cause such information overloads. Because much of your learning occurs outside of class, the time you spend in class is especially valuable. Your professors might highlight only the most important concepts.

They might elaborate on information found in assigned readings. They might shape and refine your understanding. They might focus on application, analysis, and synthesis of ideas. No matter how they approach their courses, your professors generally have one thing in common. They concentrate the information presented in class. The information you add through more reading, study, and thought dilutes it for your understanding. Because the concentration of information is so strong, packing idea on idea often results in your forgetfulness and confusion. After three classes in a row, you might find it hard to recall what occurred in the first. As a result, you spend additional time outside of class trying to figure out just what went on.

Some institutions schedule classes on alternating days so that a class meets two or three days per week. Some students think that by scheduling courses for only two or three days a week, they have time for concentrated study. Often this results in their being overworked and burned out on class days. They spend free days recuperating, rather than studying. If you do not work or have other fixed commitments, you should schedule your classes throughout the week.

A good schedule fills the day as well as the week. Time between classes gives you opportunities to consciously and subconsciously reflect on information. Reviewing information as soon as possible after class provides you with time to think through a lecture while the information is still fresh. Connections among information can be made before you have to go to another class and listen to another concentrated lecture.

Your most difficult courses should be scheduled during the times you are most alert. If you like getting up early, then morning is the time for your most difficult course. If you do your best work after lunch, then schedule your most difficult classes at that time. If you schedule classes on alternating days, consider the level of difficulty or your interest in a course. These factors affect the length of time you can concentrate. If you are very interested in a course or if a course is easy for you, then you can schedule it for longer time periods.

Flexibility in Scheduling

The old adage "First things first" doesn't always apply to choosing your classes. Of course, certain courses must be taken in sequence. Some are prerequisites for courses that you'll need in the future. Few curricula, however, are completely rigid. Generally, the outline of courses in a catalog is just a suggested way to divide coursework into years or terms (semesters or quarters), rather than a requirement. Thus, you have a great deal of flexibility in choosing when to take many of your courses.

Although it would be wonderful if you liked and wanted to take every course in your curriculum, that is rarely the case. No matter what your major, you'll probably take some courses in which you feel you have little initial interest. In addition, based on your aptitudes and abilities, some courses will be more difficult for you than others. Too many difficult courses often overwhelm even the best students. Courses that you perceive as uninteresting might lead you to the conclusion that higher education as a whole is not worth the effort. Scheduling flexibility forms the solution to both problems. Your schedule should include courses that you look forward to attending, as well as those in which you have less interest. You should also balance difficult with easier coursework.

Changes in your personal life can change your scheduling priorities. Perhaps you are an athlete. You might want to schedule more difficult classes during the terms in which your team is less active. Maybe you know that a family member will have surgery during a particular term so you adjust your schedule accordingly. You might have a job, hobby, or other interest with predictable highs and lows in effort during the year. You can accommodate such changes through flexible scheduling and thus affect how well you manage your time during the term.

Finally, flexibility in scheduling helps you choose from whom, as well as when, you will take a course. Interactions with faculty form one of the greatest benefits of a college career. Upper-class students often provide insights into who is considered to be the most outstanding teacher in the field. In addition, many student government associations monitor faculty performance and make the results available to students. These two sources provide you with views of how a professor is seen by other students. Once you decide whom you want for a specific course, you must determine when that person teaches that course. Faculty course loads vary by term. Although a specific instructor might not teach the same courses each term, course assignments are usually made a term, and sometimes a year, in advance. Thus, you can often find out when a specific person will be teaching and take advantage of the best that your institution has to offer.

Undecided Majors: Exploring Institutional Options

If you have not decided on a major, you might fear that your indecision will be costly in both time and money. This does not have to be the case. In most **curricula,** the first year consists of general coursework. Even in more specialized curricula, if you carefully select your courses, you can avoid wasting time. Thus, through careful scheduling you can maintain academic progress while keeping all your options open.

For example, consider Fred. Fred is undecided whether to major in business administration, chemical engineering, or criminal justice. Using the curriculum guides suggested in Table 2.7, Fred plans to take English 101, Math 121, Chemistry 101, Speech 161, and Geography 100. All the courses Fred selected apply to any of the three majors he is considering.

Table 2.7   **Curriculum Guides**

Business Administration	Chemical Engineering	Criminal Justice
Business 101	Chem. 101; 102; 121	Geog. 100 or Hist. 103
English 101; 102	English 101; 102	Crim. Justic 107
Math 121; 122	Math 155; 156***	Math 115 or 121
Science Electives*	Physics 121	Science Electives*
Speech 161 or 162	General Electives**	English 101; 102
General Electives**	Engineering 104	Speech 161

*Choose from Biology, Physics, Botany, Zoology, Chemistry
**Choose from Art, Foreign Language, Geography, History, Music, Speech
***Prerequisite courses are Math 121, 122

All three curricula require English 101. Business administration and criminal justice require Math 121. It is also the prerequisite math course needed in engineering. Engineering requires chemistry, whereas the other two accept any science course. Both business and criminal justice require Speech 161, which is an elective in engineering. Geography is required for criminal justice and is a general elective in the other two.

One way you make more informed choices about a major is to take trial courses. Such introductory courses provide an overview of the subject area. They consist of general information about many related topics. These courses, if in a general field of study, can often be used as **free elective** credits. If more specialized, they can be considered as an investment in your career choice.

Fred can find out more about his chosen fields by taking trial courses such as Business 101, Engineering 104, or Criminal justice 107. However, if Fred takes too long or takes too many trial courses, he will hinder his academic progress. Thus, he should take these courses within the first year or so.

Many undecided students delay making career decisions because they mistakenly think that their majors must exactly match the career they desire. That's true for some careers. If you want to be a druggist, you must major in pharmacy. If you want to be a librarian, you need to major in library science. If you want to be a chemist, you need to major in chemistry. On the other hand, some jobs do not require specific majors. You can major in English or business and still be a lawyer, a journalist, or a secretary. Your career decision then, although important, is not a decision that cannot be changed.

Every day, someone makes a career move—to a different job, to a related career, or to an entirely different field. Changing majors might ultimately result in your spending an additional semester or two in school. In comparison with the 20 to 40 years you will spend in the work force, this time becomes a very brief investment in your future.

If you have not declared your major, you need to learn more about your goals and explore various career options. When you use your time learning about yourself, taking advantage of campus resources, and finalizing a career decision, your time is well spent. Exercises 2.7 and 2.8 provide guidance in making curriculum decisions.

Exercise 2.7   List the courses you want to take next term in the margin and plan a schedule that will allow you to maximize your prime study time.

	Sunday	Monday	Tuesday	Wednesday	Thursday	Friday	Saturday
6–7							
7–8							
8–9							
9–10							
10–11							
11–NOON							
NOON-1							
1–2							
2–3							
3–4							
4–5							
5–6							
6–7							
7–8							
8–9							
9–10							
10–11							
11–Midnight							
Midnight–1							
1–2							
2–3							
3–4							
4–5							
5–6							

Exercise 2.8   Following are curricula guides for the freshman year (fall and spring semesters). Unless otherwise stated, assume that all courses are three-hour credit courses and that specific subject area courses must be taken in sequence (for example, English 101 before 102). Use the curricula to answer the questions that follow.

PRE-MED

English 101, 102

Chemistry 100, 110

Chemistry lab 105, 115 (1 credit hour)

Zoology 101, 102 or Biology 101, 102

3 hours of any foreign language

Any 100-level history course

Math 121, 122

MUSIC

English 101, 102

Approved science electives*

Music Theory 170

Approved math electives* (6 credit hours)

Music History 101, 110

Approved general electives** (6 credit hours)

COMPUTER SCIENCE

English 101, 102

Approved science electives*** (6 credit hours)

Math 121, 122

Approved general electives' (6 credit hours)

6 hours of any foreign language

ELEMENTARY EDUCATION

English 101, 102

Biology 101, 102 or Zoology 101, 102 or Botany 101, 102

History 101, 103

Math 109, 110, or any higher-level course

Education 101

Speech 100

Psychology 105

HOME ECONOMICS

English 101, 102

Chemistry 100, 110

Chemistry lab 105, 115 (1 credit hour)

Home Economics 101, 102

Math 114, 115 or Math 121, 122

Speech 100

Psychology 105

BUSINESS (PRE-LAW OPTION)

English 101, 102

Approved science electives* (6 credit hours)

Math 121, 122

Approved general electives*** (6 credit hours)

Speech 101

History 101, 103

*Approved science electives: Choose from Biology 101, 102; Botany 101, 102; Zoology 101, 102; Chemistry 100, 110; Geology 105, 110; Astronomy 111, 112
**Approved math electives: Choose from Math 109, 110, 121, 122, 155, 157
***Approved general electives: Choose any art, foreign language, music, psychology, sociology, history, geography.

(continues)

Exercise 2.8   *Continued*

1. You want to major in music or computer science. You have a job and will only be taking nine hours this semester. What schedule would give you coursework that will apply toward either major?

_____

_____

_____

_____

2. You are a transfer student with credits in English 101 and 102, Math 121, and Speech 101. You want to take fifteen to sixteen hours this semester. You want a pre-law or a pre-med degree. What should you take?

_____

_____

_____

_____

3. You plan to major in home economics, elementary education, or music. You want to take twelve hours. What could you take that would apply to all three programs?

_____

_____

_____

_____

4. You are completely undecided about a major. Which of these freshman-level courses could apply to any of the curricula?

_____

_____

_____

_____

5. Which of the courses apply only to the curriculum in which they are found?

_____

_____

_____

_____

Excerpt 2.2   Majors Just Don't Matter That Much
by William Raspberry

Soon to every fledgling student comes the moment to decide. But since Angela's a freshman, my advice is: Let it ride.

WASHINGTON—With apologies to James Russell Lowell, that is pretty much my counsel to my daughter, who is about to begin her first year in college. Soon enough, she'll have to face the sophomore necessity of choosing a major whether or not she's decided on a career. In the meantime, I tell her, don't worry about it.

A part of the reason for my advice is the memory of my own struggle to decide on a major. I eventually had four of them, none of them related to what was to become my career.

But the more important reason is my conclusion, regularly reinforced, that majors just don't matter that much.

The latest reinforcement is from John Willson, a history professor at Michigan's Hillsdale College, who, having heard once too often the question "But what do I do with a history major?" has decided to do what he can to put his students at ease.

"Every sophomore has a majoring frenzy," he wrote in a campus publication. "It is typical for sophomores to say, 'I want to be an anchorman. Therefore I will major in journalism. Where do I sign up?.' They act like they have had a blow to the solar plexus when I say, a) Hillsdale has no major in journalism, and b) if we did, it would no more make you an anchorman than a major in English makes you an Englishman."

But rather than simply repeating what professionals already know, or urging colleges to dispense with the requirement for declaring a major, Willson has reduced his advice to a set of rules and principles.

The first, which college students often find incredible, is that aside from such vocational courses as engineering or computer science, any relationship between majors and careers is largely incidental. Physics majors are hardly more likely to become physicists than business majors to become entrepreneurs. The rule that derives from this principle:

If you wanted your major to be practical, you should have gone to the General Motors Institute.

The second principle is that students (and colleges) should delay the necessity of choosing for as long as practicable. "Most students (and even more parents) have rather vague notions of what the subject of any given subject is.... Talk with your parents, but don't let parents, teachers, media experts, television evangelists or fraternity brothers pressure you into a majoring frenzy before you know what the major is all about." In short:

All things being equal, it is best to know what you are talking about, which may even prevent majoring frenzies.

The third is a quote from the Rev. James T. Burtchaell (writing in "Notre Dame" magazine): "Pick your major on the pleasure principle, for what you most enjoy studying will draw your mind in the liveliest way to being educated."

The rule: People do not get educated by hitting themselves over the head with hammers.

It's good advice, and not only for students at small liberal-arts colleges. A few years ago, the University of Virginia published a booklet, "Life after Liberal Arts," based on a survey of 2,000 alumni of its college of arts and sciences.

The finding: 91 percent of the respondents not only believe that liberal arts prepared them for fulfilling careers but would not hesitate to recommend liberal-arts majors to students considering those same careers.

Those who responded to the survey included a biology major who later earned a master's of business administration and became president of a bank, a psychology major who was a well-paid executive, and English majors whose careers embraced television sales, editorial production, systems analysis and law.

The "winning combination" derived from the Virginia survey: a liberal-arts foundation, complemented with career-related experience and personal initiative. Colleges aren't assembly lines that, after four years, automatically deposit students into lucrative careers. What is far likelier is a series of false starts followed by the discovery of a satisfying career. In the Virginia survey, for example, only 16 percent reported being happy with their first jobs.

Willson's advice, the results of the University of Virginia survey, and my advice to Angela come down to the same thing: Major in getting an education.

SOURCE: Reprinted by permission of Washington Post © 1990.

WRITE TO LEARN

Read the essay by William Raspberry. On a separate sheet of paper or in your journal, respond to the following: What three principles does he give for declaring a major? What is your opinion of the validity of these principles? Would you follow them? Why or why not? Explain the meaning of the phrase "major in getting an education." Do you agree? Why or why not?

GROUP LEARNING ACTIVITY   BILL OF RIGHTS FOR GROUP MEMBERS

Time-management strategies make or break study groups. Indefinite goals contribute to group, as well as to individual, procrastination. Although the group should have a long-range purpose, it should also have effective short-term goals that result in members' feelings of accomplishment and closure. The following bill of rights for group members requires commitment of both time and effort by each person.

Bill of Rights for Study Groups

1. You have the right to limit group membership to no more than five and to dismiss members who consistently fail to meet their commitments as group members.

2. You have the right and responsibility to select a study site and time that are mutually beneficial to all members.

3. You have a right to contribute to the formation of group goals that have measurable outcomes and deadlines.

4. You have the responsibility to be an active participant, not a passive receiver, in the group process, and you have a right to expect active participation from other group members.

5. You have the right to have meetings begin and end promptly and to have study session without needless interruptions.

6. You have the right to participate in a group that is free from arguing and competition.

7. You have the right to expect that the group will stay on the task it sets for itself and the responsibility for helping the group do so.

8. You have the right to take a break during an extended study session as long as the group resumes its study after the break.

9. You have the right to ask group members to limit socialization or discussion of off-the-subject topics to before and after study sessions.

10. You have the right to feeling of accomplishment at (1) the end of each study session and (2) the end of the group's life span.

SOURCE: Reprinted by permission of Longman, D. L., and Atkinson, R. H. (August, 1992) *The Teaching Professor*. 2718 Dryden Dr., Madison, WI: Magna Publications.

Application

In your class study group, identify additional rights that you expect in the study group. Are there any occasions for which you might give up your rights? Which ones and why?

Application

Maintain a log of all your academic and nonacademic activities for a week. In your study group, compare logs and identify ways in which group members could use their time more effectively.

MAINTAINING BALANCE

Are you a traditional student who is trying to do it all: full-time student, fraternity member, part-time employee, participant in intramural sports, scholarship student, president of a service organization, and member of the debate team? Or, are you a nontraditional student who is trying to do it all, too: full-time student, full-time parent, part-time employee, active member of a church or synagogue, scholarship student, treasurer of the Spanish Club, and member of a student Union committee? How do you do it all?

Most students feel overwhelmed by the number of roles they hold. The truth is, you can't do it all and do it well. At some point, you must reevaluate your goals and reset priorities according to what's important to you. Your goal is to achieve balance . . . not lose your balance!

Unrealistic expectations can contribute to your situation. Perhaps you plan to finish your coursework in four years or graduate with a 4.0 average. If you are a traditional freshman student who begins college at age 17 or 18, this means that you will finish at age 21 or 22. And then what? You get to work for

---

Exercise 2.9   Use Sample Chapter 11 ("Organizing the Police Department") to respond to the following questions.

---

1. Read the section "Organizing by Time" in its entirety. What aspects of this section reinforce information presented in this chapter about time management? What additional ideas does this section present that you can apply to your personal time management?

   _____

   _____

   _____

   _____

2. Read the section "Organizing by Personnel." What aspects of style (personality, brain dominance, or sensory preferences) would you expect to find in those people who work as quasi-military policemen, police officers, detective/investigators, chief of police/commissioner, and community service officers?

   _____

   _____

   _____

   _____

the rest of your life! If you work until you're 65, this means you will be working for the next 43 or 44 years. If you get involved in a wide range of campus activities, you gain valuable experience though your stay in postsecondary education lengthens. An extra year means you still get to work for the next 42 or 43 years. Some goals (for example, professional postgraduate programs and fellowships) require a show of academic excellence. Although grades are important, many employers prefer to see a prospective employee that can handle a variety of tasks other than academic pursuits. Whatever your goals, consider them in relation to your life goals. If additional postsecondary experiences enhance your life and your chances of gaining employment after you graduate, they might be a trade-off well worth your consideration.

CHAPTER SUMMARY

1. Myers-Briggs type, brain dominance, and sensory preferences interact and affect the ways in which you manage time.

2. Goal achievement is based on first setting goals and then believing those goals are attainable.

3. The goals you set depend on your aptitudes, abilities, interests, needs, and values.

4. You develop your belief in your ability to achieve goals through positive self-talk, visualization, and action.

5. Term calendars, weekly schedules, and daily to-do lists are tools that help you implement your goals.

6. Avoiding procrastination involves positive self-talk as well as strategies for getting started, achieving closure, and avoiding burnout.

7. Factors that affect scheduling in subsequent semesters include full-time versus part-time status, the way you schedule your day and week, flexibility in scheduling, and the degree to which you explore institutional options.

8. Maintaining balance is the key to successfully managing your time and your life.

Class*ACTION*

Respond to the following on a separate sheet of paper or in your journal. Combine the chapter map and chapter summary to form a synthesis map that reflects the main ideas and important details of this chapter. Personalize the map by indicating specifically how you plan to implement this chapter's suggestions.

CHAPTER REVIEW

Answer briefly but completely.

1. Describe how MBTI type, brain-dominance, and sensory preferences interact to affect time-management strategies

   _____

   _____

   _____

2. How do aptitudes, abilities, interests, needs, and values contribute to goal formation?

   _____

   _____

   _____

3. Identify and provide an explanation of the three ways to impact your belief in your ability to achieve goals.

   _____

   _____

   _____

4. What does goal specification involve?

   _____

   _____

   _____

5. What is the relationship between Maslow's Hierarchy of Needs and internal/external motivation?

   _____

   _____

   _____

6. Describe the relationship between goal setting, term calendars, week schedules, and daily to-do lists.

   _____

   _____

   _____

7. How can you avoid procrastination?

   _____

   _____

   _____

TERMS

Terms appear in the order in which they occurred in the chapter.
aptitudes
abilities
interests
needs
values
child
critic
adult
long-term goals
short-term goals
internal motivation
external motivation
behavior modification
rewards
peer pressure
prime study time
procrastinate
closure
burnout
full-time student
part-time student
curricula
free elective

8. How can effective scheduling in subsequent semesters improve your ability to manage time? What time-management problems could arise from an ineffective semester schedule?

_____

_____

_____

9. What are the advantages of being an undecided major? What are the disadvantages?

_____

_____

_____

10. What does it mean to you to maintain balance as a postsecondary student?

_____

_____

_____

VOCABULARY DEVELOPMENT   Learning the Lingo with a Single Flame

The same time-management principles you need for success in higher education aid you in vocabulary development. Modifications of the suggestions for avoiding procrastination and implementing your goals result in vocabulary development without cramming or burnout.

Learning the lingo—the language of the courses you take—can seem like an overwhelming task. You might be tempted to "burn the candle at both ends." Aside from a little more light, you won't accomplish much, and you'll run the risk of burning out twice as fast. How can you learn it all? Consider the following suggestions for managing your vocabulary development. Carrying out each individual suggestion requires relatively little time.

1. **Preview the text glossary before attending the first class.** Invest 10 or 15 minutes in getting a sense of the language of the course. Determine whether the words seem to be general, specialized, or technical terms. (See the Vocabulary Development section in Chapter 1.) Rate your general understanding of the vocabulary. Are the words all new to you? Do you recognize some words? Can you form general associations? Are you able to use any of the words?

2.   **Preview key terms before reading a text assignment.** Texts vary in the way they highlight important terms. These terms may appear in a list at a chapter's beginning or end, in a special typeface (for example, boldface or italics), or as marginal notations (sometimes with definitions). Again, check to see if they seem to be general, specialized, or technical in nature. Consider if you've already heard the terms in a lecture. Do you have any associations with the words? How do you think they will fit into the content of the chapter?

3.   **Review key terms and concepts as soon as possible after each lecture.** After each lecture (and at least within 24 hours), review notes to identify key terms. How do the terms relate to each other? How would you define the terms in your own words? How did they relate to the content of the lecture or reading assignments

4.   **Process terms weekly.** Recognition and memorization provide the raw materials for learning. Learning at these levels often results in a false sense of security because you think you know the information. To understand the language more fully, you must convert information to a form that you can use and understand. Such processing helps you become an owner, rather than a renter, of what you know. Effort forms the key. Such learning involves more than looking at words. It consists of active strategies to integrate information. These include mapping, charting, and creating note cards (see Chapter 6).

"Frankly, aside from a little more light, I don't see what they get out of it."

Source: Reprinted by permission of Bill Maul. *Phi Delta Kappan,* October 1986.

5.   **Use terms in speaking and writing.** The old adage, "If you don't use it, you lose it" applies to vocabulary development. The words you use are those that you will retain.

6.   **Don't be fooled.** Some students get misled by course content. just because you've already had a biology class doesn't necessarily mean you already know the vocabulary as it will be applied to another biology course.

Activity 1

Using the following glossary from a mass communications textbook, preview the terms and determine if they appear to be general, specialized, or technical in nature. How would you evaluate your overall understanding of these terms?

Example of a Glossary

accreditation certification by the government of members of the press to cover wartime action of other official governments.

affiliates broadcast stations that use broadcast network programming but that are owned by companies other than the broadcast networks.

agenda-setting the principle that members of the press do not tell people what to think but do tell people what and whom to think about.

alternative press newspapers that become outlets for the voices of social protest; also called the dissident press.

analog in mass communications, a type of technology used in broadcasting, whereby video and audio information is sent as continuous signals through the air on specific airwave frequencies.

ancillary-rights market the revenue opportunity for a movie beyond its theater audience, including television and videocassette sales.

blanket licensing agreement an arrangement.

blind booking the practice of renting out films to exhibitors without showing the films to the exhibitors first.

block booking the practice of scheduling a large number of movies for a theater, combining a few good movies with many second-rate features.

censorship the practice of suppressing material that is considered morally, politically, or otherwise objectionable.

channel in mass communication, the medium that delivers the message.

concentration of ownership the trend among the media industries to cluster together in groups.

consumer magazines all magazines sold by subscription or at newsstands, supermarkets, and bookstores.

content the multimedia term for information sources and programs that can be digitized for the new communications network.

convergence the blurring of lines between consumer electronics and computers because of advances in technology.

cooperative news gathering a practice first used by the New York Associated Press; whereby member newspapers share the expenses of acquiring news and returning any profits to the members.

CPM is advertising, cost-per-thousand, which is the cost of an ad per one thousand people reached. (M is the roman numeral for 1,000.)

data compression a process that uses software and hardware to squeeze information into a tiny electronic package.

demand programming request radio that is controlled completely by the listener.

demographics the analysis of data used by advertising agencies to target an audience by sex, age, income level, marital status, geographic location, and occupation.

deregulation in broadcasting, the elimination by the Federal Communications Commission in the 1980s of many of the government restrictions on broadcast programming and ownership.

digital a way to store and transmit data by reducing it to electronic signals—digits—and then reassembling them for an exact reproduction.

digital audio broadcast (DAB) a technology that uses computer codes to send music and information, which eliminates the static and hiss of current broadcast signals.

digital audiotape (DAT) a new type of audiotape that uses computer codes to produce recordings.

digital film the electronic manipulation of film images.

direct sponsorship radio and television programming in which the advertiser sponsored an entire show, which often bore the name of the product or company in the title.

disinformation the planting by government sources of inaccurate information.

dissident press see *alternative press*.

duopoly the control by one company owning two AM or two FM radio stations in the same market area. Duopoly ownership was sanctioned by a 1992 FCC ruling.

ethnocentric characterized by the attitude that one's own culture is superior to others.

ethnocentrism the attitude that some cultural and social values, especially American values, are the only correct ones.

false light the charge that what a writer implied in a story about another is incorrect. Federal Communications Commission (FCC) the government agency that regulates broadcasting and cable.

feedback in mass communication, a response sent back to the sender (source) from the receiver.

freelancers in magazine or newspaper publishing, journalists who write for more than one publication and are paid separately for each article they write.

high-definition television (HDTV) a type of television that provides a picture with a clearer resolution than on normal television sets.

interactive a two-way viewer-controlled electronic process that allows the consumer to select among a variety of services.

Internet a web of interconnected computer networks that sprang from a U.S. government effort to connect government and academic locations. It currently links about 15 million people.

LAPS test the local standard of obscenity established in *Miller v. California*: whether a work, taken as a whole, lacks serious *L*iterary, *A*rtistic, *P*olitical, or *S*cientific value.

libel a false statement that damages a person's character or reputation by exposing that person to public ridicule or contempt.

SOURCE: Biagi, Shirley. *Media/Impact: An introduction to mass media,* 3rd ed. (1996). Belmont, CA: Wadsworth.

Activity 2

Copy eight terms from Sample Chapter 13 ("Concepts in Human Biology") (use terms you did not select in the Chapter 1 Vocabulary Activity). What associations do you have with these words? How do you think they fit into the chapter's content?

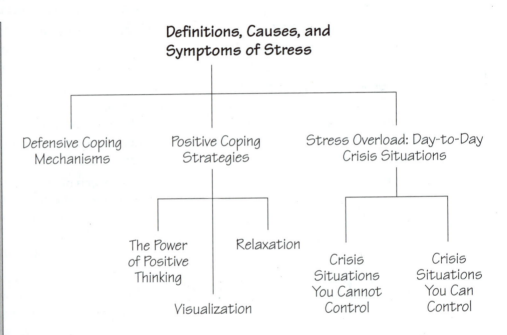

Definitions, Causes, and Symptoms of Stress

Defensive Coping Mechanisms

Positive Coping Strategies

Stress Overload: Day-to-Day Crisis Situations

The Power of Positive Thinking

Relaxation

Visualization

Crisis Situations You Cannot Control

Crisis Situations You Can Control

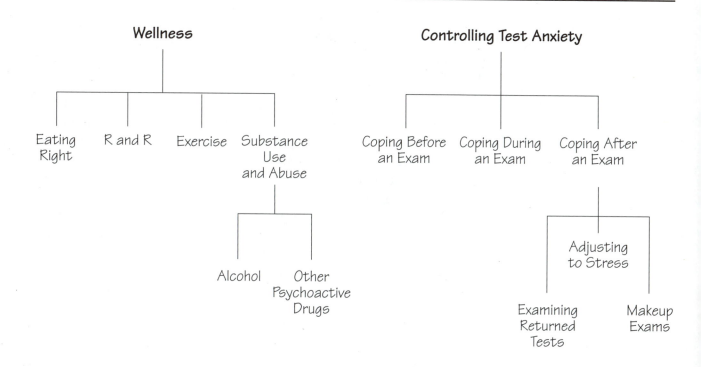

A maiden at college, Ms. Breeze,
Weighted down by B.A.s and Ph.D.s,
Collapsed from the strain.
Said her doctor, "It's plain
You are killing yourself—by degrees!"

If like Ms. Breeze, you feel the stress of college life, you're not alone. Changes in your life, as well as ongoing events and activities, affect the manner in which you manage stress. The strain of getting a college degree affects all students at one time or another. You can determine how stressful your life is by taking the inventory in Exercise 3.1.

DEFINITIONS, CAUSES, AND SYMPTOMS OF STRESS

You know stress by many names—pressure, worry, concern, anxiety, and nervousness, to name a few. These words probably have negative connotations to you. That's because stress hurts more often than it helps. Such stress is called **distress.** It results from many causes and includes many symptoms (see Tables 3.1 and 3.2). Nevertheless, some stress is positive. Positive stress, or **eustress,** is the energy that drives you to be your best. This happens on the playing field, in a performance, or in the classroom. Here, stress motivates and helps you to think clearly and decisively. For example, healthcare professionals face stressful emergency situations as part of their jobs. These professionals use stress to help them perform faster and better. You can harness its power to help you make better grades by using positive **coping strategies** and avoiding defensive coping mechanisms. Coping positively is a more difficult but longer-lasting and more effective solution to stress.

Defensive Coping Mechanisms

Withdrawal tends to block behaviors you need for facing and overcoming stress. You remove yourself from stressful situations by either physically or psychologically withdrawing. You can physically withdraw from school by dropping a class or dropping out of school, and sometimes withdrawal seems the only solution. But because you can't physically withdraw every time you face stress, you might tend to withdraw mentally or emotionally from academic stress. This psychological withdrawal constitutes a normal, and to some degree unconscious, reaction to stress. It is your psyche's attempt to soften the blow of a stressor. Such withdrawal can take place in several ways (see Table 3.3). Blocking the cause of stress from your memory is one way you withdraw from anxiety. Called **repression,** this involves your doing nothing to solve the problem. You think about more pleasant things instead of whatever bothers you.

Exercise 3.1   Have any of the following stressful events happened to you at any time during the last two weeks? If any have, please check the space next to it. If an item has not occurred, then please leave it blank. Scoring instructions appear on the last page of this chapter.

___Death (family member or friend)

___Death of a pet

___Working while in school

___Registration for classes

___Parents getting a divorce

___Trying to decide on major

___Talked with a professor

___Trying to get into your college

___Had a class presentation

___Had projects, research papers due

___Had a lot of tests

___It's finals week

___Applying to graduate school

___You have a hard upcoming week

___Lots of deadlines to meet

___Missed your menstrual period and waiting

___Had an interview

___Applying for a job

___Sat through a boring class

___Can't understand your professor

___Did badly on a test

___Went into a test unprepared

___Crammed for a test

___Used a fake I.D.

___Breaking up with boy/girlfriend

___Holiday

___Bad haircut today

___Victim of a crime

___Can't concentrate

___Coping with addiction

___Found out boy/girlfriend cheated on you

___Did worse than expected on test

___Stayed up late writing a paper

___Problems with your computer

___Favorite sports team lost

___Ran out of typewriter ribbon while typing

___Change of environment (new doctor, dentist, and so on)

___Bothered by not having family's social support

___Arguments, conflict of values with friends

___Had a visit from a relative and entertained him or her

___Noise disturbed you while trying to study

___Maintaining a long distance boy/girlfriend

___Assignments in all classes due the same day

___Dealt with incompetence at the registrar's office

___Someone borrowed something without your permission

___Exposed to upsetting TV show, book, or movie

___Problems getting home when drunk

___Had confrontation with an authority figure

___Got to class late

___Parents controlling with money

___Feel isolated

___Decision to have sex on your mind

___No sex in awhile

___Living with boy/girlfriend

___Felt some peer pressure

___Felt need for transportation

___Couldn't find a parking space

___Property stolen

___Car/bike broke down, flat tire, and so on

___Got a traffic ticket

___No time to eat

___Having roommate conflicts

___Had to ask for money

___Lack money

___Checkbook didn't balance

___You have a hangover

___Someone you expected to call did not

___Lost something (especially wallet)

___Erratic schedule

___Thoughts about future

___Dependent on other people

___No sleep

___Sick, injury

___Fought with boy/girlfriend

___Performed poorly at a task

___Heard bad news

___Thought about unfinished work

___Feel unorganized

___Someone cut ahead of you in line

___Job requirements changed

___Someone broke a promise

___Someone did a "pet peeve" of yours

___Can't finish everything you needed to do

SOURCE: Crandall, C. S., Preisler, J. J. & Aussprung, J., (1992). Measuring life event stress in the lives of college students. The undergraduate stress questionnaire (USQ), *Journal of Behavioral Medicine*, 15(6), 627–662.

Table 3.1   Common Sources of Stress

Classification	Explanation
1. Intrapersonal conflict	The turmoil within you about which paths to take in life includes goals, values, priorities, and decisions.
2. Interpersonal relationships	Interactions between you and friends or peers are common sources of stress as you deal with the differences between you and learn to communicate and compromise.
3. Family	Although a major source of support, the family is also a source of stress because of the strength of the emotional ties among the people involved. Also, interaction among family members is more frequently of a judgmental nature.
4. Work and school demands	Stress resulting from your satisfaction with your work and meeting standards expected of you.
5. Money concerns	Always with you, especially as college students, money problems are usually not a matter of having enough to survive (although it can seem like that at times) but are more how to prioritize how you spend your income.
6. Global instability	In the United States, we are more isolated from the type of regional war that occurs in many other parts of the world, but conflict in another part of the globe can have immediate, deleterious effects here, particularly to students who are immigrants from that area, who are members of the armed forces, or who are related to people in the armed forces.
7. Environmental abuse	Stress can come in the form of pollution (for example, smoking in classrooms, trash in common areas), crowding (for example, in classrooms, cafeterias, and parking lots), crime both on- and off-campus, overstimulation (especially by the media), and ecological damage.
8. Technology	Advances such as the computer are stressful because they require adaptive change and speed up the pace of life.
9. Change	Any sort of change is a source of stress, although certain changes are clearly more stressful than others. College students experience more change than do most other people. The more changes present in your life and the faster these changes come about, the greater the stress you will encounter.
10. Time pressure	Time pressures can cause stress brought on by other factors. Many students are not instinctively effective at time management.
11. Spiritual issues	Coming to terms with discovering meaning in codes of ethical and moral behavior can be stressful, especially if it involves rejecting previously held beliefs.
12. Health patterns	Illness, injury, dietary imbalances, exposure to toxic substances, and the like are fairly obvious forms of stress. The physiological stress response is often more clearly seen in these instances than in situations involving social and psychological stress.

Table 3.2   Symptoms of Stress

Emotional signs	Behavioral signs	Physical signs
Anxiety	Avoidance of responsibilities and relationships	Excessive worry about illness
Apathy		Frequent illness
Irritability	Extreme or self-destructive behavior	Exhaustion
Mental fatigue		Overuse of medicines
	Self-neglect	Physical ailments and complaints
	Poor judgment	

SOURCE: Doctor, R. M. & Doctor, J. N. (1994). Stress. *Encyclopedia of human behavior. Volume 4,* 311–323. San Diego: Academic.

WRITE TO LEARN

Examine the physical and psychological signs of stress in Table 3.2. On a separate sheet of paper or in your journal, respond to the following: Which do you experience? How could you cope better with these in the future? Which have you observed in others? What would be your advice to them?

Table 3.3   Examples of Defensive Withdrawal

Method of Withdrawal	Typical Withdrawal Statements
Repression	"Oh, that test is next week. I'll study after my date Saturday. Where can we go? I know we'll go see that new movie. Then, we'll eat dinner at . . ."
Denial	"I'm not worried about my grade in that course—it's only an elective."
Projection	"Sure, I made a 55 percent! What did you expect? You know my instructor gives the hardest exams in the entire math department—well, she grades the hardest anyway."
Rationalization	"Well, I didn't have time to study for my history exam because I was so busy volunteering at the hospital. My work with disabled children is so much more rewarding than a good grade in one history course."

Denial also provides a way to withdraw. Again, you fail to prepare. By denying the test's existence or its importance to you, you withdraw from the stress it creates within you. Another way to avoid stress is **projection.** Here you blame someone or something else for your failure. You refuse to accept responsibility for your actions and project that responsibility onto someone else. A fourth way to withdraw from stress is to **rationalize** for being unprepared or not making the best grade possible,. Here you identify a reasonable and acceptable excuse for failure and exchange it for the more distasteful truth. Withdrawal techniques work—at best—as only a temporary check on stress.

Positive Coping Strategies

Fast food . . . microwaved meals . . . fax machines . . . faster computers . . . e-mail . . . cellular phones . . . beepers . . . on-line access to libraries. . . . A multitude of services and devices make our lives more efficient and provide us with instant results. Unfortunately, there is no miracle cure for stress that provides instant relief. Stress management requires a combination of effort and time. You must find your personal stressors and figure out which positive coping strategies will help you manage them (see Table 3.4).

The Power of Positive Thinking

Humorist Steven Pearl once joked, "I phoned my dad to tell him I had stopped smoking. He called me a quitter." For some reason, humans most often remember and believe the worst rather than the best about themselves and others. You, too, might find yourself dwelling on past embarrassments, problems, and failures. In similar situations, you think that the same disasters will recur. Your anxiety mounts, you lose confidence, and the cycle repeats itself.

Anxiety about coursework is one of these cyclical processes. When stress begins, you feel pressure from within and without. You lack the confidence to succeed. Voices echo in your mind. Examples of this **self-talk** (see Chapter 2) include statements like "I must pass, or I'll never get into medical school." "What if I freeze up?" "I must, I must, I must." "I can't, I can't, I can't."

The secret to combating anxiety is twofold. First, you figure out what stresses you and why. Is the voice you hear that of your own feelings? Is it a ghost from your past? Can you believe what is being said? Is it true? Have you *never* performed well under pressure? Have you *never* been able to recall dates? What is reality? What is not?

Second, you replace negative messages with positive ones. Consider the coach of a team sport. The coach doesn't say, "Well, our opponent is tough. I don't see any way we can win." No, the coach acknowledges the opponent's worth: "Well, our opponent is tough." Then he or she says, "But, we've practiced hard all week. I know we're prepared. Do your best. That's all I ask, and all we'll need."

Table 3.4   Coping with Personal Stressors

Stressor	Solution
Information overload (class assignments: the number and size of them, workload, spacing of exams, assignment due dates	Reevaluate time-management plan. Consider reducing course load. Form a study group for support and assistance.
Mismatch of instructor/student learning styles	Form a study group.
Stress carriers (peers who are also overstressed)	Find more supportive and positive friends. Seek out counseling services.
Self-doubts (own high expectations, family pressures, concerns about career choices, class presentations, low exam grades, academic competition)	Practice test taking. Avoid cramming. Take stress-management course. Practice relaxation exercises. Seek counseling services. Hire a tutor.
Interpersonal relationships (family conflicts, love decisions, social pressures, family responsibilities, sexual pressures/fears, religious conflicts, job conflicts)	Seek counseling services. Talk to family and friends. Examine values and priorities.
Intrapersonal conflicts (social anonymity, loneliness, depression, anxiety)	Seek counseling services Attend campus activities. Join postsecondary organizations. Volunteer your services.
Financial concerns	Investigate campus loans, grants, and scholarships. Share expenses. Cut current expenses. Seek additional employment.

The coach's talk before a game motivates players to excel even in stressful situations. Table 3.5 contains steps you can follow to fight a negative mindset. The success messages can help you motivate yourself to succeed. Remember, however, the best messages are those you create for yourself. Such statements are personal and, thus, more meaningful. They help you prepare for visualizing success. To be effective, you need to repeat them only once a day—once a day, every day, all day long. Exercises 3.2 through 3.5 help you identify stressors and create positive self-talk messages.

Table 3.5   Self-Talk Success Messages

1. Prepare for an anxiety-producing situation:

    What is the question I have to answer?

    What is the problem I face?

    I know information about it.

    Don't worry. Worry won't help.

2. Confront and handle the situation:

    I can answer this question.

    I can do this.

    One issue at a time, I can handle this.

    I won't think about fear—just what I have to do.

3. Avoid feeling overwhelmed:

    Keep focused. What is the first question I need to answer? What is the major issue I must face?

    This will soon be over.

    This is not a life-and-death issue.

    Life will continue.

4. Reinforce your coping strategy:

    It worked! I answered every question asked of me. I faced the problem with courage.

    It wasn't as bad as I feared!

    Me and my imagination! When I control it, I control my stress.

SOURCE: Reprinted with permission from "The clinical potential of modifying what clients say to themselves," by D. H. Meichenbaum and R. Cameron, in M. J. Mahoney and C. E. Thorensen (Eds.), *Self-control: Power to the person.* Copyright © 1974 by Brooks/Cole.

WRITE TO LEARN

Your best friend is afraid of flying. You think self-talk can help him overcome this fear. On a separate sheet of paper or in your journal, explain self-talk to him. Then provide examples of statements he might use to combat his fear.

Exercise 3.2   Identify one situation in which stress is a problem for you. Then create three self-talk statements you could use to combat this stress.

Situation: _____

_____

_____

Self-Talk Comments:

1. _____

_____

_____

_____

2. _____

_____

_____

_____

3. _____

_____

_____

_____

Exercise 3.3   Think about the ways you view your academic self. What negative messages do you hear? What are their sources? Complete each of the following sentence fragments. Mark the source of each. Then provide examples of messages you tell yourself. Mark their sources.

1. I can't _____

_____

_____

SOURCE: Message comes from me?_____ from others?_____

2. I always _____

_____

_____

SOURCE: Message comes from me? _____ from others? _____

3. I never _____

_____

_____

SOURCE: Message comes from me? _____ from others? _____

(continues)

Exercise 3.3 *Continued*

4. I don't _____

_____

_____

SOURCE: Message comes from me? _____ from others? _____

5. My friends think I _____

_____

_____

SOURCE: Message comes from me? _____ from others? _____

Exercise 3.4 Create three positive messages for each of the following general situations.

1. Writing a paper

a. _____

_____

b. _____

_____

c. _____

_____

2. Solving a problem

a. _____

_____

b. _____

_____

c. _____

_____

3. Taking a final exam

a. _____

_____

b. _____

_____

c. _____

_____

(continues)

Exercise 3.4   *Continued*

4. Taking an unannounced quiz

   a. _____

   b. _____

   c. _____

5. Reading a chapter

   a. _____

   b. _____

   c. _____

6. Taking notes

   a. _____

   b. _____

   c. _____

7. Being called on in class

   a. _____

   b. _____

   c. _____

8. Managing time

   a. _____

   b. _____

   c. _____

(continues)

Exercise 3.4   *Continued*

    9. Choosing a major

        a. _____

            _____

        b. _____

            _____

        c. _____

            _____

    10. Getting back a test with a poor grade

        a. _____

            _____

        b. _____

            _____

        c. _____

            _____

Exercise 3.5   Create a positive message for scenarios 1 through 6. Then provide four examples of situations you have faced or will face this semester. Create a positive message for coping with these.

    1. You enter a class in a subject you know little about. The other students appear much older (or younger) than you.

        MESSAGE: _____

        _____

    2. You have an excellent GPA and plan to go to law school. Now the time has come to take the LSAT (the Law School Admissions Test).

        MESSAGE: _____

        _____

    3. You are a learning-disabled student. You fear explaining to your instructor that you need special accommodations.

        MESSAGE: _____

        _____

    4. You are in a speech class. Your first speech in front of the large class is tomorrow. You are well prepared but afraid.

        MESSAGE: _____

        _____

(continues)

Exercise 3.5   *Continued*

5. Although you have done well on all math homework assignments, a surprise quiz has just been passed to you.

    MESSAGE: _____

    _____

6. You just got back an English paper. There is no grade on it, but the instructor has written a note, asking you to make an appointment to discuss the paper.

    MESSAGE: _____

    _____

7. **Situation**: _____

    MESSAGE: _____

    _____

8. **Situation**: _____

    MESSAGE: _____

9. **Situation**: _____

    MESSAGE: _____

    _____

10. **Situation**: _____

    MESSAGE: _____

    _____

Visualization

As Boorstin noted, our imaginations either free or bind us. **Visualization** takes positive messages one step further. It uses imagination to put positive messages into action. Thus, instead of imagining the worst and seeing yourself fail, you imagine success. Just as you sometimes embellish the worst with all the gory details, you now imagine the best in all its splendor.

We (Americans) suffer primarily not from our vices or our weaknesses, but from our illusions. We are haunted, not by reality, but by those images we have put in place of reality.

—Daniel J. Boorstin
Twentieth century American historian

WRITE TO LEARN

Using any one of the scenarios you created in Exercise 3.5, on a separate sheet of paper or in your journal create a visualization to help you imagine success.

Relaxation

"Relax, you won't feel a thing," many doctors say right before they give you an injection. And, although you're sure to feel the needle going in, it really does hurt less if you can ease the tension in your body. Similarly, relaxation eases stress. Even in the throes of a stressful situation, relaxation occurs. How long it takes for you to relax depends on the time you have available and the way you relax.

Early humans responded to threats by either fighting or fleeing. Contemporary life is not that simple, but people still maintain this fight or flight instinct. As a result, our muscles often respond to stress even when these options are not available. Steps for progressively relaxing your mind and muscles appear in Table 3.6. You can also relax your muscles by doing a physical body check. Whenever you feel tense, stop and see if any muscles are involved that really don't need to be. For example, suppose you feel your shoulders tense as you read. Shoulder muscles play little part in reading, so you should make a conscious effort to relax them. Conscious deep breathing also relaxes the body.

Taking a vacation also relaxes you. Of course, if you're enrolled in school, you can't go to Nassau for the weekend. A mental vacation serves the same purpose as a real one. It's just not as much fun! Mental vacations, however, are fast and inexpensive. To take one, you simply close your eyes. Visualize your favorite vacation spot. Or, see a place where you wish to vacation. You don't always have to picture quiet, relaxing places. You can imagine yourself shopping, sightseeing, playing sports, or whatever you like to do. Simply changing the way you do things can be a kind of vacation. For example, try going to class by a different route, eating in a different location, or shopping at a different grocery. These simple changes of pace are refreshing.

Table 3.6   Steps for Muscular Relaxation

1. Sit or lie in a comfortable position with your eyes closed.

2. Picture yourself in a quiet place in which you felt relaxed in the past (the beach, the forest, a park, your backyard, your room, or elsewhere). Imagine that you're there once more.

3. Breathe deeply, hold for one count, and breathe out. Repeat the word *calm* each time you inhale. Repeat the word *down* each time you exhale.

4. Beginning with your toes, flex, then relax those muscles. Progress to the foot, ankle, leg, and so on.

5. Let your thoughts drift. Allow them to come and go without intervention.

6. Remain calm and quiet. If possible, remain in this state for at least 20 minutes.

7. Open your eyes and remain quiet. Enjoy the feeling of relaxation.

Laughter releases tension, too. It often allows you to put things into perspective. If you have time, you can watch a favorite comedy. If not, listening to a radio station that tells jokes and plays upbeat songs yields the same effect. Print cartoons and funny stories also entertain and relieve stress. Browsing through the greeting card section of a store also relaxes you through humor.

Meditation is yet another form of relaxation. It involves narrowing your conscious mind until anxiety wanes. Several types of meditation exist, but all forms share common features. One form is passive observation. A second is lowering your anxiety levels by focusing on peaceful, repetitive stimuli. A third is repeating **mantras,** which are relaxing words or sounds. The meditation steps are outlined in Table 3.7. Exercises 3.6 and 3.7 help you practice relaxation techniques.

Table 3.7   Steps in Meditation

1. Begin by meditating once or twice daily for 10 to 20 minutes.

2. What you *don't* do is more important than what you *do* do. Adopt a passive, "what happens, happens" attitude.

3. Create a quiet, nondisruptive environment. Don't face direct light.

4. Don't eat for an hour beforehand. Avoid caffeine for at least two hours beforehand.

5. Assume a comfortable position. Change it as needed. It's okay to scratch or yawn.

6. For a concentrative device, focus on your breathing or seat yourself before a calming object such as a plant or burning incense. Benson (1975) suggests "perceiving" (rather than "mentally saying") the word *one* on every outbreath. This means thinking the word but "less actively" than usual (good luck!) You could also think or perceive the word *in* as you inhale and *out* as you exhale.

7. If you are using a mantra, you can prepare for meditation by saying it several times. Enjoy it. Then say it more and more softly. Close your eyes and think only the mantra. Allow the thinking to become passive so that you sort of perceive, rather than actively think, the mantra. Again, adopt a passive, "what happens, happens" attitude. Continue to perceive the mantra. It may grow louder or softer, or disappear for a while and then return.

8. If disruptive thoughts come in as you are meditating, allow them to "pass through." Don't get wrapped up in trying to stop them or you may raise your level of arousal.

9. Above all, take what you get. You cannot force the relaxing effects of mediation. You can only set the stage for it and allow it to happen.

10. Allow yourself to drift. (You won't go far.) What happens, happens.

Exercise 3.6   You need to practice relaxation at least once each day. This is the general order of muscle groups to be relaxed. Do each exercise twice, concentrating on the difference between tension and relaxation. First, tense up muscles in the area mentioned and then relax that area as completely as possible.

1. Relax your hands and arms by
   a. making a fist with your right hand and then releasing it.
   b. making a fist with your left hand and then releasing it.
   c. bending both arms at your elbows, making a muscle, then straightening both arms.

2. Relax your neck, shoulders, and upper back by
   a. wrinkling your forehead and releasing.
   b. frowning and creasing your brows and releasing.
   c. closing your eyes tightly and then opening them.
   d. clenching your jaws, biting your teeth together, and releasing.
   e. pressing your lips tightly together and releasing.
   f. pressing the back of your neck down against a chair and releasing.
   g. pressing your chin against your neck and releasing.
   h. shrugging your shoulders.

3. Relax your chest, stomach, and lower back by
   a. holding your breath for a period of time, then exhaling.
   b. tightening and releasing your stomach muscles.
   c. pulling your stomach muscles in and releasing.

4. Relax your hips, thighs, and calves by
   a. tightening your buttocks and thighs and releasing.
   b. straightening your knees, pointing your feet and toes downward away from your face.
   c. bending your feet toward your face and releasing.

5. Relax as you imagine a calm scene by closing your eyes and visualizing a quiet, relaxed outdoor setting. Pay attention to the sounds and sights in this scene. Try to feel the breeze; try to see the sun, clouds, birds, and trees; try to hear the birds, water, and wind.

Exercise 3.7   Listen as your instructor plays a relaxation tape, and follow the directions it gives. After the tape is completed, record your responses to the following questions on a separate sheet of paper or in your journal.

1. How did you feel as you began listening to this tape?
2. How did you feel at the end of this tape?
3. To what factor(s) do you contribute changes in your feelings, if any?
4. Would you be willing to try this method on your own? Why or why not?
5. Consider your campus. From what sources might relaxation tapes be available?

Stress Overload: Day-to-Day Crisis Situations

As Kissinger noted, there is never a good or convenient time for crisis situations to occur. They always seem to come at the worst possible time, thus causing stress overload. You can't schedule family problems, financial concerns, illnesses, and interpersonal dilemmas when you want. You must be prepared to handle them when they occur.

How do you define crisis? In his April 12, 1959, address, John Kennedy said, "When written in Chinese the word 'crisis' is composed of two characters—one represents danger and the other represents opportunity." The word "crisis" comes from the Greek word *krisis,* which means "decision." A crisis is, then, a juncture—another opportunity for you to make decisions that will affect you both personally and academically. Crises come in two forms, those you cannot control and those you can.

Crisis Situations You Cannot Control

Death . . . illness . . . family problems . . . accidents . . . crimes . . . These are all situations that are outside of your control. How do decision-making skills aid you in coping with such events?

You need to clarify the situation and identify the options available to you. Your goals and values (see Chapter 2) factor into your decision. For example, perhaps, through no fault of your own, you become seriously injured in an accident. You are hospitalized for several weeks and come back to school determined to finish. You discover that you cannot catch up, but you feel that resigning is a cop-out. However, when you reexamine your goals, you realize that your goal is to finish and do well—not finish in a hurry. The death of a close family member can also cause you to focus on family needs. Once the immediate concerns of the funeral arrangements are concluded, you assess your situation. Should you withdraw from school and return home to care for family business? How much of the term remains? Can you delay your return until then, or would it be better to go home now? Again, your goals and values direct your decision. You might choose to compromise and return home on weekends until you straighten things out. Or you might resign with firm intentions to return to school the following term.

You might find that you can't change the problem—your parents divorce, someone steals your car, or you become chronically ill. In such cases, you might have to alter the way you view the problem—your thoughts, attitudes, and resulting behavior. When problems are outside of your control, the most important thing you can do is come to that realization and let go of the problem. Table 3.8 provides some suggestions for doing so.

Crisis Situations You Can Control

Sometimes what seems like a crisis is actually an opportunity to learn and grow. Lack of money, disagreements with others, difficult children or other

> **"**
>
> There cannot be a crisis next week. My schedule is already full.
>
> —Henry Kissinger
> *Twentieth century*
> *American statesman*

Table 3.8   Coping with Problems Outside Your Control

When faced with a problem outside your control, try one or more of the following suggestions:

1. *24-hour rule.* Living each day one day at a time is a first step. Letting go doesn't mean that you don't cope with the problem. You must. Problems that might overwhelm you in a lifetime can be handled for 24 hours.

2. *Talk it out.* Talk to others. Friends, mentors, family, and others can advise you, support you, and listen to you. Problems that seem insurmountable appear less difficult when someone else shares them with you.

3. *Run away.* Although you can't run away forever, you can escape for a while. This takes you away from the problem and helps you regain perspective. If you can't physically leave town for a day or two, then escape to a movie, a new place to eat, a park, or a different place to study.

4. *Act normal.* Do something you normally do. A crisis is an abnormal event. Simple, everyday activities like grocery shopping, taking a walk, or studying can take the edge off and regulate the situation.

5. *Busybody.* Regular physical activity (for example, exercise, building, cleaning, and so on) burns excess energy. Mental activity (for example, reading, studying, solving puzzles) occupies your mind and prevents you from worrying.

6. *Make time for fun.* Schedule time for recreation. Recreation literally means to re-create or renew. Like an escape, it breaks the tension and provides a vacation from the problem at hand. Laughter improves any situation.

7. *Golden Rule.* Do something nice for yourself or for others. You deserve it and they probably do too.

family members, poor performance in courses, job losses, and other problems often seem devastating at the time. Once the issue is resolved, life continues, for the most part, the same as it did before. You may also need to improve your life skills in a variety of ways. Table 3.9 lists some common controllable crisis situations and some ways to solve them.

WELLNESS

How can you keep yourself fit and ready to cope with stress? Baseball pitcher Satchel Paige offers the following suggestions:

- Avoid fried foods, which angry up the blood.
- If your stomach disputes you, lie down and pacify it with cool thoughts.
- Keep the juices flowing by jangling gently as you move.
- Go very light on the vices, such as carrying on in society. The social ramble ain't restful.
- Avoid running at all times.
- Don't look back. Something might be gaining on you.

Table 3.9   Crisis Situations You Can Control

Crisis	Alternatives for Control
Communication problems (for example, assertiveness, parenting skills, personal relationships)	Course in interpersonal communication Counseling Self-help books
Money management	Share expenses Seek financial aid Work part-time Economize Assess priorities Create a budget
Study skills/time management	Counseling Campus learning assistance center Study skills/orientation class Campus seminars
Job loss	Campus career center Retraining Activate network of support (faculty, friends, other employees) to help locate job options

And while Paige's suggestions seem light-hearted, they contain good advice for meeting your physical needs and staying well. Maslow's Hierarchy of Needs (see Figure 2.2) theorizes that physical needs must be satisfied before other needs can be met. Thus, lifestyle factors like nutrition, rest, exercise, sexual activity, and drug use affect how well you cope with stress. They also have bearing on whether or not you reach self-actualization, the top of your mental and emotional health ladder.

Eating Right

Students at Columbia University's College of Physicians and Surgeons try to reduce stress in all the same ways you do. One place they frequent to relax is Coogan's, a beer and sandwich shop on Broadway in Manhattan. To help students cope with the stressors of academic life, Coogan's publishes a brochure that includes a stress diet (see Table 3.10).

Perhaps you've tried diets like Coogan's to cope with stress. Lots of students do, and they find them just as successful as Coogan's expects you to find theirs—which in a word is *NOT.*

Table 3.10   Coogan's Stress Diet: Rules and Sample Menu

1. When you eat something and no one sees you eat it, it has no calories.

2. If you drink a diet soda with a candy bar, the calories in the candy bar are canceled out by the diet soda.

3. When you eat with someone else, calories don't count if you do not eat more than they do.

4. Foods used for medicinal purposes NEVER count, such as hot chocolate, toast, and Sara Lee Cheesecake.

5. If you fatten up everyone around you, then you look thin.

6. Movie-related foods (such as Milk Duds, buttered popcorn, Red-Hots, and Tootsie Rolls) do not have additional calories because they are part of the entire entertainment package and are not part of your personal fuel.

7. Cookie pieces contain NO calories. The process of breaking (cookies into pieces) causes calorie leakage.

8. Things licked off knives and spoons have no calories if you do so in the process of preparing something. Examples: peanut butter knife while making a sandwich and ice cream spoon while making a sundae.

9. Foods that have the same color have the same number of calories. Examples: spinach and pistachio ice cream, mushrooms and white chocolate. Note: Chocolate is a universal color and may be substituted for any other color.

Sample Daily Menu

Breakfast

    1 grapefruit

    1 slice whole wheat toast, dry

    3-oz. skim milk

Lunch

    4-oz. lean broiled chicken breast

    1 cup steamed spinach

    1 cup herb tea

    1 Oreo cookie

Mid-Afternoon Snack

    Rest of Oreos in the bag

    2 pints of rocky-road ice cream

    1 jar hot fudge sauce

    Nuts, cherries, and whipped cream

Dinner

    2 loaves garlic bread with cheese

    Large sausage, mushroom, and cheese pizza

    3 Milky Way candy bars

Late Evening Snack

    Entire frozen cheesecake eaten directly from freezer

Source: Reprinted with permission of Coogan's, New York, NY.

If Coogan's diet relieves any stress, it does so through humor, not by its nutritional suggestions. Nutrition, however, really is a serious subject. Your nutrition affects your physical well-being and your study habits and grades. What you eat affects your stamina and behavior. It's a subject that cannot be avoided, even if you've heard it before. A balanced diet (see Figure 3.1) supplies the nutrients you need, serves as the basis of good health, and helps you store energy. Unfortunately, in college, what and when you eat is not always in your control. Classes, work, and study play havoc with regular mealtimes. Thus, you need a plan for getting good nutrition even when you miss meals.

Figure 3.1   The Food Pyramid

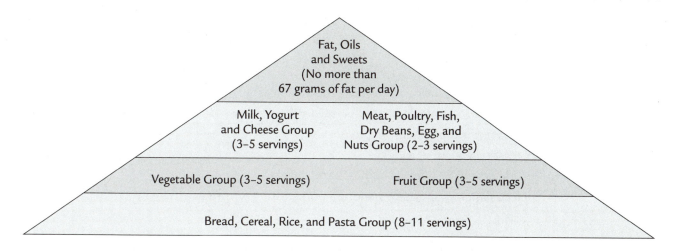

For example, suppose a class extends past the hours the cafeteria serves lunch. Eating a later breakfast or an earlier dinner helps you cope. Or, your college cafeteria might prepare a sack lunch for you. You could carry some fruit or cheese in your backpack for a between-class snack, if all else fails. The Eating Smart Quiz in Exercise 3.8 provides a way for you to measure your own dietary habits.

R and R

In addition to nutritious food, you need adequate R and R—rest and recuperation. What's adequate? It depends on two factors: your physical condition and the tasks you undertake. High degrees of fitness, interest, or skill help you achieve more with less fatigue. Methods of avoiding fatigue vary in quality and effectiveness. Sleep is the most obvious way to become rested. It is, however, not your only choice. Changing activities—for example, studying different subjects—also rests your mind. Recreational activities help you relax.

Exercise 3.8   **Rate Your Plate**. Take a closer look at yourself—your current food decisions and your lifestyle. Think about your typical eating pattern and food decisions. Answer Usually, Sometimes, or Never for each of the following questions:

Do you . . .

- Consider nutrition when you make food choices?
- Try to eat regular meals (including breakfast), rather than skip or skimp on some?
- Choose nutritious snacks?
- Try to eat a variety of foods?
- Include new-to-you foods in meals and snacks?
- Try to balance your energy (calorie) intake with your physical activity?

Now for the basics. Do you . . .

- Eat at least 6 servings of grain products daily?
- Eat at least 3 servings of vegetables daily?
- Eat at least 2 servings of fruits daily?
- Consume at least 2 servings of milk, yogurt, or cheese daily?
- Go easy on higher-fat foods?
- Go easy on sweets?
- Drink 8 or more cups of fluids daily?
- Limit alcoholic beverages (no more than 1 daily for a woman or 2 for a man)?

Score Yourself

Usually = 2 points
Sometimes = 1 point
Never = 0 points

If you scored . . .

24 or more points: Healthful eating seems to be your fitness habit already. Still, look for ways to stick to a healthful eating plan — and to make a "good thing" even better.

16 to 23 points: You're on track. A few easy changes could help you make your overall eating plan healthier.

9 to 15 points: Sometimes you eat smart — but not often enough to be your "fitness best." What might be your first steps to healthier eating?

0 to 8 points: For your good health, you're wise to rethink your overall eating style. Take it gradually — step by step!

Whatever your score, make moves for healthful eating. Gradually turn your "nevers" into "sometimes" and your "sometimes" into "usually."

SOURCE: Adapted from *The American Dietetic Association's Monthly Nutrition Companion: 31 Days to a Healthier Lifestyle,* Chronimed Publishing. Copyright © 1998 The American Dietetic Association, 216 West Jackson Boulevard, Chicago, Illinois 60606-6995. Used by permission.

GROUP LEARNING ACTIVITY   MAKING IT UP

Seeing professors about makeup work is stressful for many students. However, students often give little thought to the feelings of the instructor with whom they're meeting. To help you and fellow group members overcome anxiety, complete the following activity:

1. Write each of the following on a separate, unlined piece of paper:

   a. You are student who has been seriously ill for several weeks. You have a doctor's note and your hospital bill. You meet with your professor to schedule makeup work.

   b. You are student who consistently skips class. It's near final exam time, and you have become worried about your grade. You meet with your instructor to schedule makeup work and exams.

   c. You are student who has missed only one class the entire semester. Your clock battery died in the night, and you overslept. Unfortunately, your instructor assigned a major homework assignment for the next class. You meet with your instructor to get the assignment.

2. Write each of the following on a separate lined piece of paper:

   a. You are a professor who always attempts to be fair. However, it's been a bad semester, and you've given more makeup work than anything else. You are tired of grading late work and hope you never see another student asking for makeup work.

   b. You are professor who never allows student to make up work unless they have documentation from a doctor or a police officer.

   c. You are professor who has no clear-cut makeup policies. As such, it is difficult for students to pin you down as to what work you will let them make up.

3. Fold the pieces of lined and *unlined* paper in fourths and place them in a container.

4. Divide the group into sets of partners.

5. Have each partner select a different kind of paper. (One partner gets lined paper, the other gets unlined paper.) Partners do not tell anyone the role they've drawn.

6. Allow each partner a few minutes to think about his or her role.

7. Have each set of partners role-play a meeting between the two characters they've drawn.

8. After five minutes of role playing, have other group members try to guess what kind of student/instructor pair they just observed.

9. Let the next set of partners begin their role play.

These might include listening to music, talking to friends, or reading a book. Study time is the only price you pay for these activities. This price, however, seems too steep to some students. Such students bypass natural methods of avoiding fatigue. They rely on tranquilizers to relax. They use amphetamines to increase productivity. Other students use alcohol or tobacco to cope with stressful situations. These artificial means are quick, costly, and only temporarily effective (if at all). They can create dependencies and serve as study crutches, not study supports.

Exercise

Exercise also plays a role in reducing stress. You can work off excess adrenaline and energy. You rid your body of these before they make you tired or sick. Paradoxically, exercise also increases your energy level. When this happens, you cope better with stress because you no longer feel exhausted or overwhelmed. It's not surprising, then, that exercise also decreases fatigue. This is particularly true when you use it as an alternative to challenging mental processes. For example, jogging for 30 minutes breaks the intensity of a long study session. Another benefit of exercise is that it tends to have a positive effect on your lifestyle. That is, if you exercise regularly, you'll probably find yourself drinking, smoking, or overeating less often. This, in turn, causes you to feel and look better. If you worry about your appearance often, as do many people, exercise eliminates this potential stressor as well. Exercise affects your long-term health and increases your strength and flexibility while decreasing your chances of cardiovascular or skeletal-muscular problems. Finally, exercise tends to slow the natural aging process.

Substance Use and Abuse

Substance use and abuse alters your attention span, memory, judgment, self-control, emotions, and perceptions of time and events. Why, then, do people use drugs? Table 3.11 provides a classification of drug-taking behaviors.

Alcohol

Which of the following contains the most alcohol?

a. 4-ounce glass of white wine

b. 10-ounce wine cooler

c. 12-ounce draft beer

d. 1 ounce of whiskey

The answer? Each of these contain about the same amount of alcohol, the most widely used drug on any campus. College students use alcohol to celebrate, reduce tension, relieve depression, intensify pleasure, enhance social skills, and change experiences for the better (Brown, 1985). Moderate amounts of alcohol work well in doing all of these. Larger amounts tend to decrease its benefits, however.

How much is moderate? How much is too much? No one really knows. That's because the amount varies from person to person, depending on genetics, health, sex, weight, and age. Nonetheless, most people agree to define moderation as no more than two drinks per day for an

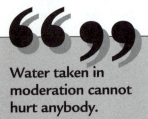

Water taken in moderation cannot hurt anybody.

—Mark Twain
Nineteenth century American author

Table 3.11   Classification of Drug-taking Behaviors

Classification	Reason for Use	Duration	Quote Associated with Classification
Experimental	Curiosity	Short-term	"But I didn't inhale." (Bill Clinton)
Social-recreational	Pleasure, relaxation	Occasional	"I only drink at parties."
Situational	Cope with a problem	Occasional	"Drink today and drown all sorrows." (John Fletcher)
Intensive	Avoid withdrawal; beginning dependence	Daily	"I'm no good until I get my morning coffee."
Compulsive	Avoid withdrawal; dependence	Daily	"Smoking is, if not my life, then at least my hobby. I love to smoke. Smoking is fun. Smoking is cool. Smoking is, as far as I am concerned, the entire point of being an adult." (Fran Lebowitz)

average-sized man or no more than one drink per day for an average-sized woman.

As the drug of choice of most college students, it's not surprising that alcohol takes a direct route (no detours) to your brain. This means that an empty stomach absorbs 20 percent of alcohol molecules almost immediately. One minute after taking a drink, then, and particularly on an empty stomach, you feel the buzz you associate with alcohol.

When alcohol reaches your brain, it first sedates the reasoning part of your brain. Thus, judgment and logic quickly fall prey. This is the reason that when you drink, you find yourself in situations you'd ordinarily avoid or doing things you would not normally do. Next, alcohol affects your speech and vision centers. Third, it attacks your voluntary muscular control, sometimes causing you to stagger or weave as you walk. Loss of vision and voluntary muscular control can cause dire consequences when drinking and driving. Finally, alcohol strikes respiration and cardiac controls. Eventually, the brain is completely conquered, and you pass out before you drink a lethal amount. If you drink so fast that the effects of alcohol continue after you are no longer conscious, you die. This is why you sometimes hear of students dying during drinking contests.

Okay then, suppose you avoid drinking contests. What's the worst that could happen to you? Guilt, shame, poor grades, addiction? Yes, all are possible. And, just as possible, if you drink sensibly, none of these. Table 3.12 contains suggestions for helping you drink intelligently.

Table 3.12   Suggestions for Drinking Sensibly

1. Sip drinks with food or eat a good meal before you drink.
2. Limit your ready (refrigerated) supply of alcohol.
3. Alternate between alcoholic and nonalcoholic beverages.
4. Switch to beverages with a lower-alcohol content.
5. Avoid situations in which you'll be expected to drink heavily.
6. Choose a designated driver.
7. Respect other people's decision not to drink.
8. Act responsibly if you are hosting a party.
9. Set a limit to the amount you will drink and stick to it.
10. Space your drinks—it takes about an hour and a half for your body to metabolize a drink.
11. Sip, don't gulp.
12. Identify your reasons for drinking—get help if you need it.

Other Psychoactive Drugs

Use of **psychoactive drugs** often results in either physical addiction or psychological dependence. Addiction happens most often with drugs that cause withdrawal symptoms like vomiting, diarrhea, chills, sweating, and cramps. In addition to alcohol, such drugs include tobacco, amphetamines, barbiturates, heroin, and cocaine. All psychoactive drugs can lead to psychological dependence, the feeling that you need a drug to stay "normal" or "happy." Table 3.13 lists psychoactive drugs and their classifications, medical uses, dosages, effects, duration of effects, long-term symptoms, and potential for dependence and organic damage.

Table 3.13   **Comparison of Psychoactive Drugs**

Name of Effect	Classification	Medical Use	Usual Dose	Duration
Alcohol	Sedative-hypnotic	Solvent, antiseptic	Varies	1–4 hours
Amphetamines	Stimulant	Relief of mild depression, control of appetite and narcolepsy	2.5–5 milligrams	4 hours
Barbiturates	Sedative-hypnotic	Sedation, relief of high blood pressure, hyperthyroidism	50–100 milligrams	4 hours
Benzodiazepines	Anxiolytic	Tranquilizer	2–100 milligrams	1–8 hours
Caffeine	Stimulant	Counteract depressant drugs, treatment of migraine headaches	Varies	Varies
Cocaine	Stimulant, local anesthetic	Local anesthesia	Varies	Varied, brief periods
Codeine	Narcotic	Ease pain and coughing	30 milligrams	4 hours
Heroin	Narcotic	Pain relief	Varies	4 hours
LSD	Hallucinogen	Experimental study of mental function, alcoholism	100–500 milligrams	10 hours
Marijuana (THC)	Relaxant, euphoriant; in high doses, hallucinogen	Treatment of glaucoma	1–2 cigarettes	4 hours
Mescaline	Hallucinogen	None	350 micrograms	12 hours
Methadone	Narcotic	Pain relief	10 milligrams	4–6 hours
Morphine	Narcotic	Pain relief	15 milligrams	6 hours
PCP	Anesthetic	None	2–10 milligrams	4–6 hours, plus 12 hours recovery
Psilocybin	Hallucinogen	None	25 milligrams	6–8 hours
Tobacco (nicotine)	Stimulant	Emetic (nicotine)	Varies	Varies

SOURCE: Reprinted with permission from *Essentials of Psychology Exploration and Application* by D. Coon. Copyright © 1997 by Brooks/Cole. All rights reserved.

ONLINE CLASS

Web Exercise 3.1

A variety of information related to the topics in this chapter is available on the World Wide Web. For this exercise, access one of the following Web sites (for the most up-to-date URLs, go to http://csuccess.wadsworth.com):

Student Counseling Virtual Pamphlet Collection at the University of Chicago Counseling and Resource Service

> http://uhs.bsd.uchicago.edu/scrs/vpc/vpc.html

Brief Articles about Mental Health Topics at the Manhattan College Center

> http://www.manhattan.edu/stntlife/ccenter/articles/carticle.html

Choose any three articles that relate to the content of this chapter and respond to the following questions:

Identify the articles you choose and respond to the following questions:

ARTICLE 1

Title _____

URL _____

1. How does the article relate to the content of this chapter?

   _____

   _____

   _____

2. Why did you choose this article?

   _____

   _____

   _____

3. What new information did you learn from the article?

   _____

   _____

   _____

4. How will that information help you manage stress effectively?

   _____

   _____

   _____

(continues)

ONLINE CLASS

Web Exercise 3.1 *Continued*

ARTICLE 2

Title _____

URL _____

1. How does the article relate to the content of this chapter?

   _____

   _____

   _____

2. Why did you choose this article?

   _____

   _____

   _____

3. What new information did you learn from the article?

   _____

   _____

   _____

4. How will that information help you manage stress more effectively?

   _____

   _____

   _____

ARTICLE 3

Title _____

URL _____

1. How does the article relate to the content of this chapter?

   _____

   _____

   _____

2. Why did you choose this article?

   _____

   _____

   _____

(continues)

Web Exercise 3.1 *Continued*

3. What new information did you learn from the article?

    _____

    _____

4. How will that information help you manage stress more effectively?

    _____

    _____

    _____

    _____

CONTROLLING TEST ANXIETY

"Just a test" and "only one research paper" don't seem like major stressors. However, they become so when placed in the context of your daily personal and academic life. Two Australian researchers (Sarros and Densten, 1989) identified the causes of stress felt by most college students (see Table 3.14). Do you feel these are still accurate? If so, which ones pose stressors for you?

Coping Before an Exam

Generally speaking, coping before an exam involves keeping yourself physically fit through adequate rest and nutrition. Specifically, this means getting sleep the night before an exam and not skipping meals or eating too much the day of the test. Your body needs to be ready to face whatever an exam has in store for you. Being exhausted from study or partying or hungry or stuffed to oblivion focuses your attention on you rather than the questions whose answers you know. Exercise, too, helps you prepare physically for an exam. After you have tended to your physical needs, you need to consider your emotional needs. Mental preparation takes the forms of study, positive thinking, visualization, and relaxation.

Simply put, coping before an exam involves knowing and practicing the coping strategies discussed in this chapter.

Coping During an Exam

During an exam, you can manage stress by pausing for about 15 seconds and taking a few deep breaths. You need to force your breathing to flow smoothly

---

Table 3.14   Top Ten Stressors of College Students

1.	Number of assignments	6.	Class presentations
2.	Taking course exams	7.	Course work load
3.	Size of assignments	8.	Own expectations
4.	Low grade on the exam	9.	Spacing of exams
5.	Assignment due dates	10.	Class assignments

SOURCE: Sarros and Densten. (1989). Undergraduate student stress and coping strategies *Higher Education Research and Development 8,*P 1.

---

and slowly. Breathe as described in step 3 of Table 3.6. This calms your nerves and steadies your mind. A second way to manage stress while taking a test is to use test-wise strategies. For example, first answering questions you know and making notes of information you're afraid you might forget eases stress. A third way to reduce stress during an exam is to ask your instructor for help if the way a test is constructed or the wording of a question causes you stress. Fourth, the positive self-talk that helped you control stress before the exam works equally well during the test.

Worry about your grade, indecision among possible answers, concern with the physical symptoms of stress, and anxiety about the consequences of failing the test can cause negative self-talk during an exam. To fight a negative mindset during an exam, follow the suggestions outlined in Table 3.5. These suggestions can help free your mind from worry and help you concentrate on test.

Coping After an Exam

Once the test is over, it's over. Waiting for your grade, receiving it, and living with it are the next problems you face. How you manage this time affects your future performance both in your courses and in college.

Examining Returned Tests

What do you do when a test is returned to you? Do you throw it away? Do you file it carefully, never to look at it again? Or do you examine it carefully? Reviewing your test helps you decide which of your study and test-taking strategies work and which do not. You can use this information to improve future test performance and reduce the stress of taking another exam in the same course.

Figure 3.2 provides a form for examining your test paper. To complete this worksheet, list each item you missed in the first column. Then you mark an *X* under the description that best explains why you missed a question.

Figure 3.2   Examining Returned Tests

Test Item Missed	Insufficient Information						Test Anxiety					Lack of Test-Wisdom						Test Skills					Other		
	I did not read the text thoroughly.	The information was not in my notes.	I studied the information but could not remember it.	I knew main ideas but needed details.	I knew the information but could not apply it.	I studied the wrong information	I experienced mental block.	I spent too much time daydreaming.	I was so tired I could not concentrate.	I was so hungry I could not concentrate.	I panicked.	I carelessly marked a wrong choice.	I did not eliminate grammatically incorrect choices.	I did not choose the *best* choice.	I did not notice limiting words.	I did not notice a double negative.	I changed a correct answer to a wrong one.	I misread the directions.	I misread the questions.	I made poor use of the time provided.	I wrote poorly organized responses.	I wrote incomplete responses.			
Number of Items Missed																									

"Let me get this straight. You flunked English because your electric typewriter broke down, you flunked Math because your electric calculator broke down, and you flunked everything else because the electrical system in your car broke down, and you couldn't get to your classes."

Sometimes you will mark more than one reason for a question. Next, add the number of *X*'s under each reason. These numbers indicate the areas of study and test-taking strategies that need more attention.

After you determine or obtain as much information as you can about your study and test-taking habits from the exam, look for information about how your instructor constructs exams. You look for patterns in the types of questions asked. See if your instructor emphasized text or lecture information. Determine grading patterns. This information helps you prepare for the next exam, which will help you reduce stress.

Another way to acquire information after the exam involves asking your instructor for information. You need to make an appointment and ask your instructor to read over your exam with you. This helps you determine why you got credit for some answers and not others.

Adjusting to Stress

Once you've examined your test and learned all you can from it, you need to adjust your thinking to help prepare for future exams in that same course. You can prepare in four ways: First, see your instructor and ask for suggestions. Your instructor can make study recommendations that will aid you in future study. Second, change your appraisal of the situation. All too often the pressure you put on yourself results in the most tension. You can decide that a *B* or *C* is the best you can do in a course, and that your best is the most you can demand of yourself. Removing the self-imposed goal of A-level work lessens

CLASSIC CRITICAL THINKING

WARNING!
THIS MACHINE IS SUBJECT TO BREAKDOWNS
DURING PERIODS OF CRITICAL NEED.

A special circuit on this machine called a "crisis detector" senses the user's emotional state in terms of how desperately he or she needs to use the Machine. The crisis detector then creates a malfunction proportional to the desperation of the user.

Threatening the machine with violence or the use of curses and obscenities may soothe the user, but will not fool the crisis detector and will only aggravate the situation.

Likewise, attempts to use another machine may cause it to malfunction also, because they both belong to the same union.

Keep cool and say nice things to the machine. Nothing else seems to work.

SOURCE: Michael Armstrong. *How to Be an Even Better Manager: Improve Performance, Profits, and Productivity* (1990). Self-Counsel Press, 1481 Charlotte Road, North Vancouver, British Columbia, V7J

When you are in a crisis situation, one alternative is to yell, scream, toss papers about, and otherwise do your temptation of a "machine subject to breakdowns during periods of critical need." A second possibility is the antithesis of such a machine.

Rewrite the preceding warning to reflect actions taken by humans in crisis situations. End it with a description of what "seems to work" in managing stress.

stress. Third, change your response to the situation. This means you avoid stress by replacing anxiety with activity. For example, instead of staying awake and worrying about a grade you made, spend the evening either playing tennis or preparing for the next class meeting. Either way, you gain. If you play tennis, you get needed exercise. You will also probably become physically tired enough to sleep. If you study, you gain the confidence of knowing you're prepared for class. This, too, helps you sleep. That's because you know that whatever happened on the last test, you've taken positive steps toward the future. Fourth, change the situation or take a strategic retreat. This means you can drop a course if it gives you too many problems. A strategic retreat is just that—a logical and temporary step back. Such a maneuver gives you time to reflect on yourself, your goals, and academic realities. This does not mean you won't ever pass the course. It simply means you will take it again at a better time. Exercise 3.9 gives you an opportunity to think about stress from another perspective.

Makeup Exams

As a student, you might feel that instructors do not care how well you do in class. This misconception can prevent you from seeking the help you need to be successful. This is particularly true when it comes to asking for makeup exams.

Excerpt 3.1   Exam Anxiety and Grandma's Health

Every student knows that examination time can be a source of great stress. In the following article, Professor John J. Chiodo of Clarion University describes some truly extraordinary effects of exam-related stress and suggests a variety of ways in which faculty members can help to alleviate the problem.

I entered the ranks of academe as well prepared as the next fellow, but I was still unaware of the threat that midterm exams posed to the health and welfare of students and their relatives. It didn't take long, however, for me to realize that a real problem existed. The onset of midterms seemed to provoke not only a marked increase in the family problems, illnesses, and accidents experienced by my students, but also above-normal death rates among their grandmothers.

In my first semester of teaching, during the week before the midterm exam, I got numerous phone calls and visits from the roommates of many of my students, reporting a series of problems. Mononucleosis seemed to have struck a sizable portion of my class, along with the more common colds and flu.

A call from one young woman awakened me with the news that her roommate's grandmother had died, so she (my student) would be unable to take the exam. I expressed my condolences and assured the caller that her roommate would not be penalized for such an unexpected tragedy.

Over the next few days I received many more calls—informing me of sickness, family problems, and even the death of a beloved cat. But the thought of three grandmothers passing away, all within the short exam period, caused me a good deal of remorse. But the term soon ended and, with the Christmas break and preparations for the new semester, I forgot all about the midterm problem.

Eight weeks into the second semester, however, I was once again faced with a succession of visits or phone calls from roommates about sick students, family problems, and, yes, the deaths of more grandmothers. I was shaken. I could understand that dorm meals and late nights, along with "exam anxiety," might well make some students sick, but what could account for the grandmothers? Once again, though, other things occupied my mind, and before long I had stopped thinking about it.

I moved that summer to a large Midwestern university, where I had to reconstruct my teaching plans to fit the quarter system. I taught three classes. By the end of the first midterm exams two of my students' grandmothers had died; by the time the year was over, a total of five had gone to their reward.

I began to realize the situation was serious. In the two years I had been teaching, 12 grandmothers had passed away; on that basis, if I taught for 30 years 180 grandmothers would no longer be with us. I hated to think what the universitywide number would be.

I tried to figure out the connection. Was it because grandmothers are hypersensitive to a grandchild's problems? When they see their grandchildren suffering from exam anxiety do they become anxious too? Does the increased stress then cause stroke or heart failure? It seemed possible; so it followed that if grandmothers' anxiety levels could be lowered, a good number of their lives might be prolonged. I didn't have much direct contact with grandmothers, but I reasoned that by moderating the anxiety of my students, I could help reduce stress on their grandmothers.

With that in mind, I began my next year of teaching. On the first day of class, while passing out the syllabus, I told my students how concerned I was about the high incidence of grandmother mortality. I also told them what I thought we could do about it.

To make a long story short, the results of my plan to reduce student anxiety were spectacular. At the end of the quarter there had not been one test-related death of a grandmother. In addition, the amount of sickness and family strife had decreased dramatically. The next two quarters proved to be even better. Since then, I have refined my anxiety-reduction system and, in the interest of grandmotherly longevity, would like to share it with my colleagues. Here are the basic rules:

- Review the scope of the exam.
- Use practice tests.
- Be clear about time limits.
- Announce what materials will be needed and what aids will be permitted.
- Review the grading procedure.
- Review the policies on makeup tests and retakes.
- Provide study help.
- Make provision for last-minute questions.
- Allow for breaks during long exams.
- Coach students on test-taking techniques.

I have been following these rules for 13 years now, and during that time have heard of only an occasional mid-term–related death of a grandmother. Such results lead me to believe that if all faculty members did likewise, the health and welfare of students—and their grandmothers—would surely benefit.

SOURCE: Morris, C. G. (1988). *Psychology: An Introduction.* Englewood Cliffs, NJ: Simon & Schuster.

Exercise 3.9   Read "Hispanic Americans" from Sample Chapter 12 ("Women and Ethnic Groups") at the back of this book. Then answer the following questions.

1. Explain the relationship between the information in this section and stress.

_____

_____

_____

_____

_____

_____

2. Create two analogies that compare/contrast *positive coping strategies* and *defensive coping strategies* with information from this section.

_____

_____

_____

_____

_____

_____

3. Identify stressors for Hispanic Americans. Chart the stressors you identified.

CRISES THAT CAN BE CONTROLLED	CRISES THAT CANNOT BE CONTROLLED
_____	_____
_____	_____
_____	_____
_____	_____
_____	_____
_____	_____
_____	_____
_____	_____
_____	_____
_____	_____

(continues)

Exercise 3.9   *Continued*

4. Identify a way Hispanic Americans could cope positively with each of the stressors identified above.

_____

_____

_____

_____

_____

_____

_____

_____

_____

_____

_____

_____

It is true that instructors hear all too often, "I was too ill to take the exam" or "My Great-aunt Wilma is sick, and I have to leave campus immediately." On the other hand, sometimes illness, family, or job pressures cause you to miss an exam. Perhaps your first idea is to simply skip class and confront the instructor later. Contacting the instructor as soon as possible, preferably before the exam, is a better alternative. Making this special effort shows your concern for your grade. It also indicates your respect for the instructor. Arranging for makeup work at this time decreases stress. That's because you'll know if and when you'll be able to make up work. If you are ill for a period of time, you need to talk with your instructor about receiving an incomplete or "I" grade. This enables you to complete the work when you recover.

College instructors care. Give them an opportunity to do so.

WRITE TO LEARN

Your roommate experiences test anxiety. On a separate sheet of paper or in your journal, leave your roommate a note that describes ways to cope with stress before, during, and after an exam.

CHAPTER SUMMARY

1. Stress management involves both defensive and positive coping techniques.

2. Positive coping strategies include positive thinking, visualization, and relaxation.

3. Managing stress also involves knowing what crisis situations you can and cannot control.

4. Physical wellness, mental preparation, exercise, and the avoidance of substance abuse also aid in coping with stress.

5. Controlling test anxiety before, during, and after an exam also alleviates stress.

6. After an exam, you need to examine returned tests, adjust stress levels, and use appropriate mechanisms to schedule makeup exams.

Class*ACTION*

Respond to the following on a separate sheet of paper or in your journal. Combine the chapter map and chapter summary to form a synthesis map which reflects the main ideas and important details of this chapter. Personalize the map by indicating specific ways in which you plan to implement suggestions offered by this chapter.

CHAPTER REVIEW

Answer briefly but completely.

1. Compare and contrast positive and negative ways of coping with stress. Which positive method most benefits you? Which negative method causes you the most grief? How can you increase the positive and lessen the negative?

   _____

   _____

   _____

   _____

   _____

2. Consider the last crisis situation you encountered. Evaluate how well you coped by using information in this chapter. How would you cope with a similar situation if it occurred now?

_____

_____

_____

_____

_____

3. How do you cope with stress before, during, or after an exam? Explain one method you will add to your coping repertoire for handling stress before, during, and after tests.

_____

_____

_____

_____

_____

4. List two specific situations about which you are concerned, and develop three positive messages for each one.

_____

_____

_____

_____

_____

_____

_____

5. Describe in three to five sentences the quiet place you go to relax and ten specific features you plan to use in creating a relaxation visualization of that location.

_____

_____

_____

_____

_____

_____

_____

KEY TERMS

Terms appear in the order in which they occurred in the chapter.

stress
distress
eustress
coping strategies
repression
denial
projection
rationalize
self-talk
visualization
meditation
mantras
psychoactive drugs

6. Perform an after-exam survey of your last test in each of your classes. What is your most common mistake? How can you solve this problem?

_____

_____

_____

_____

_____

7. A student applies for an on-campus job but fails to get it. Create three positive and three negative forms of self-talk that the student might use in this situation.

_____

_____

_____

_____

_____

8. What effect would adjusting to stress after an exam have on future self-talk? Give three examples to illustrate this effect.

_____

_____

_____

_____

_____

9. Consider the stressors discussed in this chapter. Which cause the most trouble for you? Why is this so?

_____

_____

_____

_____

_____

10. Develop a plan for coping with the stressors you identified in the previous question. Use strategies discussed in this chapter.

_____

_____

_____

_____

_____

Scoring for Exercise 3.1

Score the USQ counting the number of items you checked. (Notice that the questionnaire is a mixture of life events and daily hassles.) The following scale is an approximate guide to the meaning of your score.

0–7	Low
8–15	Below average
16–23	Average
24–31	Above average
32–39	High
40+	Very high

VOCABULARY DEVELOPMENT   Structural Analysis: Words in Your Pocket

Test taking requires a calm hand and a cool wit. It calls for strength and perseverance. It takes steady nerves and courage. But, most of all, it requires knowledge and the words that reflect that knowledge. Sometimes knowing a part of a word's meaning allows you to eliminate distractors on exams. Other times, it helps you understand words in questions that seem tricky or ambiguous. Knowledge of word parts, then, aids you in determining correct answers on exams and in showing the knowledge you have gained in a course.

A word is not the same with one writer as with another.
One tears it from his guts. The other pulls it out of his overcoat pocket.

Charles Peguy
Twentieth century French poet

Using the parts of words to determine meaning is called structural analysis. Parts of a word fit together much as parts of a car do. As with a car, some parts are essential to the functioning of a word. Called bases, these word parts give you an overall meaning. Affixes (prefixes and suffixes) accessorize the word and affect the overall meaning. Prefixes occur at the beginning of words. Suffixes are found at their ends.

Affixes sometime help identify the subject area of a word. They can also help determine the part of speech or use. The following charts show common roots (Table V3.1), prefixes (Table V3.2), suffixes (Table V3.3), and math and science roots (Table V3.4). Knowing how word parts fit together saves your guts and puts words in your pocket.

Table V3.1   General Roots

Root	Example	
script (write)	manuscript	_____
vert (turn)	convert	_____
ject (throw)	eject	_____
port (carry)	transport	_____
vis/vid (see)	video	_____
rupt (break)	interrupt	_____
dict (say)	dictionary	_____
aud (hear)	auditory	_____
cede (go)	recede	_____
junct (join)	junction	_____
pseudo (false)	pseudonym	_____
mem (mind)	memory	_____

Table V3.2   Prefixes

Prefix	Example	
be (by)	beloved	_____
pre (before)	prehistoric	_____
de (away, from)	detract	_____
inter (between)	intervene	_____
ob (against)	obstruction	_____
in, il, ir (not)	illegible	_____
a (not)	asexual	_____
un (not)	unconnected	_____
ad (to, toward)	adhere	_____
contra (against)	contraband	_____
en, in (in)	encapsulate	_____
com/col/con/co (together, with)	coauthor	_____
non (not)	nonexistent	_____
auto (self)	autonomy	_____
ex (out of)	exist	_____
re (again)	repeat	_____
pro (forward)	proponent	_____
homo (same)	homogenous	_____
hetero (different)	heterosexual	_____
dis (apart from)	disjointed	_____
over (above)	overwhelm	_____
super (above)	superscript	_____
sub (under)	subscript	_____
mis (bad, wrong)	mistaken	_____
trans (across)	transfer	_____

Table V3.3   Suffixes

Suffixes	Example	
Noun		
ane/ine/ene (forms a name of a chemical)	butane	_____
ade (act of; result or product of)	blockade	_____
age (state or condition of)	blockage	_____

(continues)

Table V3.3   *Continued*

arch/archy (rule)	monarchy	_____
ard/art (one who does something not admirable to excess)	braggart	_____
arian (age, sect, or social belief; occupation)	agrarian	_____
asis/osis/ysis (condition characterized by)	paralysis	_____
tion (state of being)	elation	_____
cide (kill)	homicide	_____
ory (place or state of; ability in)	laboratory	_____
ster (one who is or does)	youngster	_____
wright (one who builds or makes)	playwright	_____
hood (state of being)	statehood	_____
ship (state of being)	leadership	_____
ance/ence/(state of being)	absence	_____
ism (state of being)	communism	_____
ness (state of being)	kindness	_____
sion (act of)	conversion	_____
ation (act of)	jubiliation	_____
ity/ty (state or condition)	creativity	_____
ist (one who does)	journalist	_____
or/er (one who)	inventory	_____
ment (action or state of)	government	_____

Adjective

able (able to/capable of being)	remarkable	_____
ible (able to)	divisible	_____
ful (full of)	beautiful	_____
ous (having)	advantageous	_____
ive (having the quality of)	creative	_____
al (pertaining to)	comical	_____
ic (pertaining to)	academic	_____

Verb

en (belonging to/cause to be)	roughen	_____
ize (to become/to make)	maximize	_____
fy (to make)	unify	_____

Adverb

ly (in the manner of)	carefully	_____

Table V3.4   Math and Science Roots and Affixes

Root	Example	
mono (one)	monograph	_____
aqua (water)	aquatic	_____
hydro (water)	hydrolic	_____
hemi (half)	hemisphere	_____
semi (half)	semicircle	_____
equi (equal)	equidistant	_____
tele (far off)	telescope	_____
some (body)	chromosome	_____
sphere (ball, globe)	biosphere	_____
quad (four)	quadrant	_____
geo (earth)	geology	_____
micro (small)	microscope	_____
onomy (science of)	astronomy	_____
ology (study of)	biology	_____
uni (one)	universe	_____
bi (two)	bisect	_____
tri (three)	triangle	_____
octa (eight)	octagon	_____
dec (ten)	decimal	_____
centi (hundred, hundredth)	millimeter	_____
bio (life)	biology	_____
astro (star)	astronomy	_____
thermo (heat)	thermal	_____
meter (measure)	kilometer	_____
ped/pod (foot)	anthropod	_____
kilo (thousand)	kilogram	_____
botan (plant)	botanist	_____
cyto (cell)	cytoskeleton	_____
lymph (water)	lymph nodes	_____

Structural analysis is an important tool in preparing for and taking a test. Because it is an active process, it stimulates you to use what you know to analyze new words and understand familiar words more fully.

When preparing for a test, you may be struggling with learning the meanings of a large number of words. Structural analysis helps you connect and organize meaning. For example, consider the following words and meanings:

macrophage—a cell derived from the white blood cells called monocytes whose function is to consume foreign particles, such as bacteria and viruses.

monocyte—one type of white blood cells; produces macrophages.

lymphocyte—white blood cell produced by the lymphatic system.

lymphatic system—the system that helps protect the body against infection and returns excess fluid to the blood circulatory system.

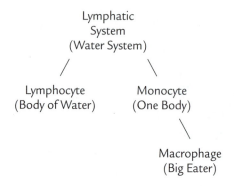

At first glance, they might seem a bit confusing. Consider the following map with meanings (in parenthesis) derived from structural analysis:

Now you see the relationships. The lymphatic system produces both lymphocytes and monocytes. Monocytes produce macrophages, which "eat up" foreign bodies in the body.

How does structural analysis aid you in test taking? Consider the following test questions:

1. Which of the following is a *pseudopod?*

   a. amoeba

   b. horse

   c. spider

   d. anteater

2. Unlike in the aristocracies of Europe, the founders of the United States believed that all humans are of the same worth. As a result of this. philosophy, anyone can rise to power.

   a. egalitarian

   b. diversify

   c. coordinator

   d. unification

Your recall of word parts aids you in answering question 1. But if you cannot think of a specific meaning of a word part, you can attempt to think of other words that contain that particular part. So, if you couldn't think of the meaning of *pseudo* or *pod,* you might think of such words as *pseudonym* or *tripod*. From this, you might generalize that *pseudo* means *false* and that *pod* means *foot*. Thus, *pseudo pod* means "false foot." Since spiders, horses, and anteaters all have some sort of foot, -the answer must be a, amoeba.

In question 2, the correct answer depends on two factors. First, the word that fits in the blank must modify the noun *philosophy*. Thus, it must be an adjective. Second, you must recall how suffixes change part of speech. If you recall that *tion* and *or* indicates nouns and that *ify* indicates verb forms, then answer *a* is the correct choice. This will be verified when you recall that some adjectives end in *ian*.

Activity 1

Fill in the blanks in Tables 1, 2, 3, and 4 with your own examples of words with these parts.

Activity 2

Examine all of the terms from Sample Chapter 13 (Concepts in Human Biology). List below the terms that contain prefixes and/or suffixes. Underline the prefixes and/or suffixes in each word. Then define the term by using word parts.

CHAPTER 4

Listening and Notetaking

OBJECTIVES

After you finish this chapter, you will be able to do the following:

1. Construct a note-taking outline or map through text previewing.

2. Identify factors that affect your ability to listen.

3. Organize notes from various types of lectures.

4. Develop a systematic notetaking approach.

5. Complete notes using an effective postlecture process.

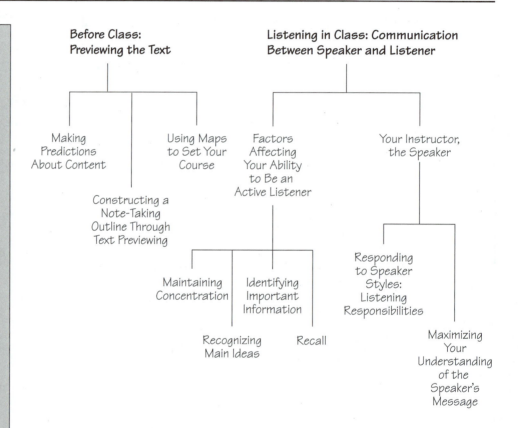

Before Class:
Previewing the Text

- Making Predictions About Content
- Constructing a Note-Taking Outline Through Text Previewing
- Using Maps to Set Your Course

Listening in Class: Communication
Between Speaker and Listener

- Factors Affecting Your Ability to Be an Active Listener
  - Maintaining Concentration
  - Identifying Important Information
    - Recognizing Main Ideas
    - Recall
- Your Instructor, the Speaker
  - Responding to Speaker Styles: Listening Responsibilities
  - Maximizing Your Understanding of the Speaker's Message

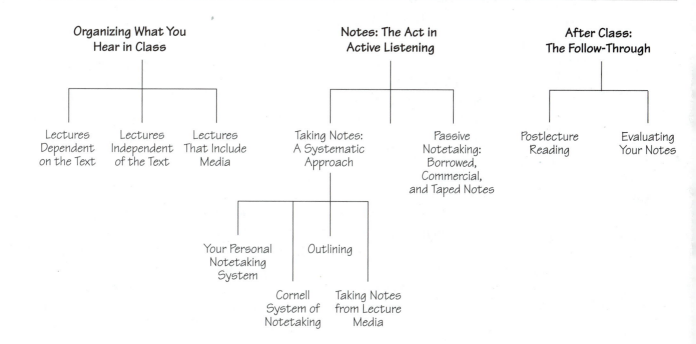

> ❝❞
> There are others who think that the speaker has a function to perform, and the hearer none. They think it only right that the speaker shall come with his lecture carefully thought out and prepared, while they, without consideration or thought of their obligations, rush in and take their seats exactly as if they had come to dinner, to have a good time while others work hard.
>
> —Plutarch,
> *Moralia*, 45.14E
> *First century
> Greek biographer*

Plutarch spoke of a problem your instructors face each day. That problem is students who are not prepared and not ready to learn. Chapter One helped you identify your place in a post-secondary community. Chapter Two showed you ways to manage time, and Chapter Three provided you with specifics for effectively managing stress. You are now ready to confront a college classroom. To do so, you need strategies for studying and learning. Just as an instructor is responsible for preparing a lecture, you are obliged to be ready to process lecture information.

BEFORE CLASS: PREVIEWING THE TEXT

Your enjoyment and understanding of an activity often depend on your **background knowledge.** For example, most people who know nothing about sports fail to enjoy sporting events. Most people who know nothing about music fail to enjoy classical concerts. The same is true of academic activities. If you know nothing of a subject, you often fail to enjoy and understand that subject. On the other hand, the more background knowledge you have, the more easily you will enjoy and learn from lectures. One way to increase your background knowledge is to interact with the text.

Luckily for you, a process exists that helps you predict chapter information and then regulate or control your understanding of lecture content. Just as you examine the sky and check the wind for clues about the weather, **previewing,** or surveying, entails examining text features for clues about content.

Previewing is the first interaction between you and the text. When you survey before class, you think about what you already know about a subject.

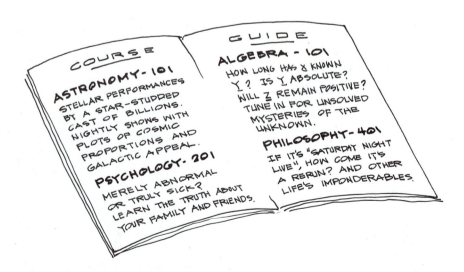

COURSE GUIDE

ASTRONOMY- 101
STELLAR PERFORMANCES BY A STAR-STUDDED CAST OF BILLIONS. NIGHTLY SHOWS WITH PLOTS OF COSMIC PROPORTIONS AND GALACTIC APPEAL.

PSYCHOLOGY- 201
MERELY ABNORMAL OR TRULY SICK? LEARN THE TRUTH ABOUT YOUR FAMILY AND FRIENDS.

ALGEBRA - 101
HOW LONG HAS X KNOWN Y? IS Y ABSOLUTE? WILL Z REMAIN POSITIVE? TUNE IN FOR UNSOLVED MYSTERIES OF THE UNKNOWN.

PHILOSOPHY- 401
IF IT'S "SATURDAY NIGHT LIVE", HOW COME IT'S A RERUN? AND OTHER LIFE'S IMPONDERABLES.

This lets you make the best use of background knowledge in learning and integrating what you hear in class. This information then can be related to what you know about the topic.

Previewing helps you create a mental outline for what the chapter contains. Once you get an overall picture of a chapter, you can see how details relate to major points. Previewing also improves your recall of what you read. This occurs because, rather than reading material that's unfamiliar to you, you read information you've seen before. Finally, previewing helps you set the speed at which you will later read and process information. The steps in previewing appear in Table 4.1.

Making Predictions About Content

The most basic way to begin reading a chapter is to make predictions about what each section contains. This helps you interact more actively with the

---

Table 4.1   Steps in Previewing

1. Read the title. What is the chapter about? Recall what you already know about the topic.

2. Read the introduction or first paragraph. The main idea of the chapter is usually found here.

3. Read the boldfaced headings throughout the chapter.

4. Read the first paragraph or sentence under each heading. This gives you an overview of each section.

5. Look at accompanying graphs, charts, and pictures. Visual aids usually emphasize main points. They also summarize details.

6. Note any typographical aids (boldface, underlining, italics). In the body of the text, these aids highlight important terms. When found in the margins, they can outline important facts.

7. Read the last paragraph or summary. This often gives the main points or conclusions.

8. Read the objectives at the beginning of each chapter. Objectives help you set goals and purposes. Such goals help you determine what you should know or be able to do at the end of each chapter.

9. Read the vocabulary terms at the beginning or end of each chapter. You might recognize some of the terms. They might, however, have specialized meanings for that topic.

10. Read the purpose-setting or review questions that accompany the chapter. These focus on key concepts.

Table 4.2   Questioning Words for Main Ideas and Details

Questioning Words for Main Ideas

If you want to know . . .	*then ask . . .*
a reason	why?
a way or method	how?
a purpose or definition	what?
a fact	what?

Questioning Words for Details

If you want to know . . .	*then ask . . .*
a person	who?
a number or amount	how many/how much?
a choice	which?
a time	when?
a place	where?

---

text. Instead of "just reading," you look for specific information. Predicting chapter content also helps you increase your understanding of lectures.

You can predict content in one of several ways. One way is to examine the chapter objectives provided by the author(s). Objectives specify what you should be able to do or understand after you read the chapter. Examining these objectives helps you set learning goals and compare chapter content to what you already know.

Another method is to preview the chapter summary or review questions. This helps you identify important information that forms the basis of the chapter.

A third method is to change headings and subheadings into questions. Certain questioning words help you identify main ideas, and others help you locate details. Table 4.2 provides a key to these questioning words, and Exercise 4.1 gives you a chance to practice writing purpose-setting questions. In addition, the headings and subheadings guide your understanding of how information fits together. Perhaps in your psychology text, for example, the subheadings "Physical" and "Psychological" come under the heading "Stressors." Already, you know that there are two kinds of stressors, physical and psychological. As such, you know that you can compare and contrast the two. You do not know, however, if one causes the other to occur. You should expect the text to define and describe physical and psychological stressors and give examples of each.

Exercise 4.1   The boldfaced headings from Sample Chapter 12, "Women and Ethnic Groups," follow. Preview Sample Chapter 12, then write a purpose-setting question for each heading. Describe the connections you find for the headings and subheadings.

Heading	Question
I. Women	_____
A. Financial status	_____
B. Middle-aged Displaced Homemakers	_____
C. Single, Widowed, and Divorced Older Women	_____
1. Single Women	_____
2. Widows	_____
3. Divorcees	_____
4. Upgrading the financial status of older women	_____
D. Double Standard of Aging	_____

Connections

_____

_____

_____

_____

_____

_____

II. AFRICAN AMERICANS	_____
A. Income and Housing	_____
B. Health Care and Life Expectancy	_____
C. Family and Social Relationships	_____
D. Future Outlook	_____

Connections

_____

_____

_____

_____

_____

_____

(continues)

Exercise 4.1   *Continued*

Heading	**Question**
III. HISPANIC AMERICANS	_____
A. Demographics	_____
B. Minority Status	_____
C. Migration Patterns	_____
D. The American Experience	_____
E. Utilization of Services	_____
F. Studying Ethnic Variations	_____

Connections

_____

_____

_____

_____

_____

_____

IV. ASIAN AMERICANS   _____

Connections

_____

_____

_____

_____

_____

   A. Japanese Americans   _____

Connections

_____

_____

_____

_____

_____

_____

(continues)

Exercise 4.1   *Continued*

Heading	**Question**
B. Chinese Americans	_____

Connections

_____

_____

_____

_____

_____

_____

| **C.** Southeast Asian Americans | _____ |

Connections

_____

_____

_____

_____

_____

_____

IV. NATIVE AMERICANS _____

    A. Cultural Uniformity and Diversity _____

    B. Population Data _____

    C. Education, Employment, and Income _____

    D. Health Characteristics _____

Connections

_____

_____

_____

_____

_____

_____

V. IMPROVING THE STATUS
OF ETHNIC ELDERS _____

Connections

_____

_____

_____

_____

_____

_____

Constructing a Notetaking Outline Through Text Previewing

Previewing to construct a **notetaking outline** before class (see Table 4.3) also provides you with the basics needed for understanding the lecture. Making a notetaking outline gives you a chance to locate what appear to be important terms, concepts, and dates before the lecture. It helps you predict the content of the lecture. Figure 4.1 shows a notetaking outline, before and after the lecture. Use Exercise 4.2 to practice creating a goal-setting outline.

Some text readings provide general background information, rather than a framework for the lecture information. Notetaking outlines, then, lose effectiveness for lectures that are less dependent on information in your textbook. In these cases, you might have to skim the chapter in its entirety or read it more thoroughly.

Table 4.3   **Constructing a Notetaking Outline Through Text Previews**

Before beginning the previewing process, divide each page for your notes vertically into sections, with one third on the left and two thirds on the right. Record the following in the left-hand section:

1. Survey the physical characteristics of the chapter (that is, length, text structure, visual aids, or term identification).

2. Record the chapter title. Think about what you know about this topic. Summarize in a sentence how you believe this information relates to the course content. Record the sentence below the chapter title.

3. Read the chapter introduction or first paragraph. This gives you the overall main idea of the chapter. Summarize it in one to three sentences. Record these.

4. Read and record each major and minor heading or subheading. Major headings express main ideas. Subheadings provide details to support major headings.

5. Estimate the amount of space for each section and skip lines accordingly.

6. Survey graphs, maps, charts, diagrams, and so on. These summarize details, emphasize main points, and highlight other important information.

7. Look for typographical aids (boldface, underlining, italics). In the body of the text, these highlight important new terms. In the margins, they might outline or indicate important ideas. Record terms.

8. Read the last paragraph or summary. This generally reviews the main points or conclusions of the chapter. Record the main idea of the summary in 1-2 sentences.

Figure 4.1   Example of a Notetaking Outline: Before and After the Lecture

CH1–Human perception
Text Outline   Lecture Notes

P3 Intro
*Chap has 2 purposes

Sees it w/own eyes
Perception/Truth Fallacy

P6 Get what expect:
Perceptual Expectancy
*mental 'set'

CH1–Human perception
Text Outline   Lecture Notes

P3 Intro   1) be more aware of problems in how we
*Chap has 2 purposes   see the world
                              2) deal more effectivly with these
                                  problems

Sees it w/own eyes   Don't accept initial perceptions at face
Perception/Truth Fallacy   value–Know Hoffer Quote P.5

                              Skip Example

P6 Get what expect: mental set causes us to anticipate
Perceptual Expectancy   future behaviors/events
*mental 'set'

                              be able to tell why you see what
                              you think you see from examples
                              (Test questions)

Exercise 4.2   Preview Sample Chapter 13, "Concepts in Human Biology." On a separate sheet of paper or in your journal, create a goal-setting outline based on the headings and subheadings in the sample chapter. Then read the chapter summary points and respond to the goal-setting questions based only on that information.

Using Maps to Set Your Course

Research about how the brain works indicates that its two halves process information differently. The left half of the brain tends to think in analytical, logical, linear, and verbal terms. The right brain prefers holistic, nonverbal, and visual images.

Chapter maps help you set your course with information for both sides of your brain in that they provide verbal information in the context of a visual arrangement of ideas. They show relationships among concepts and express an author's patterns of thought. Each chapter of this text begins with a map for just these reasons.

You construct a chapter map by using headings and subheadings in a family tree–style branching format. Table 4.4 provides the steps you follow to construct a chapter map. After you create your map, formulate some questions that analyze the links between information and synthesize the chapter as a whole. Figure 4.2 shows how these steps would be used to create the map for Sample Chapter 12, and you can analyze the information in Exercise 4.3, then create a chapter map in Exercise 4.4.

Table 4.4   Steps for Constructing a Chapter Map

1. Turn a sheet of paper horizontally.
2. Write the first major heading in the top left corner.
3. Place the next-level headings (if any) underneath the major heading with lines showing their relationship to the major heading. (Use the chapter map at the beginning of this chapter as a model.)
4. Place the next-level heading(s) (if any) underneath the second-level heading(s).
5. Continue the pattern until you come to the next major heading, then add that heading beside the first heading (from step 2).
6. Repeat the process until you finish the chapter.

Figure 4.2   Chapter Map of Sample Chapter 12

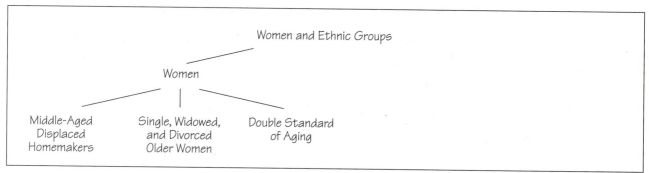

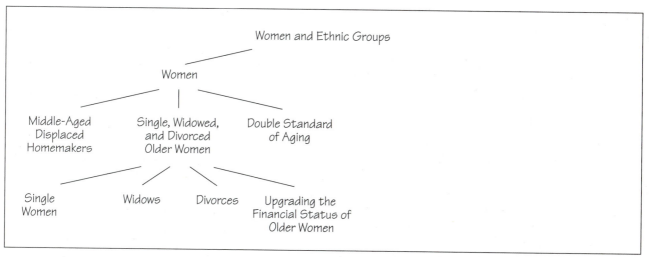

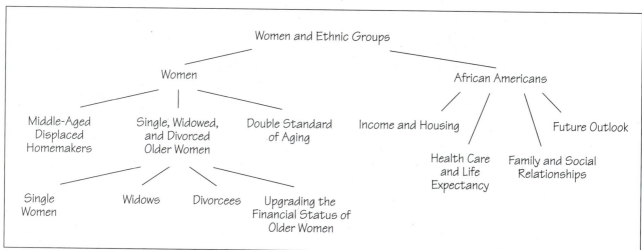

Exercise 4.3   Review Figure 4.2 and Sample Chapter 12 and answer the following questions on a separate sheet of paper or in your journal:

1. How do middle-aged displaced homemakers relate to single, widowed, and divorced women?
2. What is meant by a double standard of aging and how does it affect all women?
3. What is the significance of financial topics to women?

Exercise 4.4   Using Figure 4.2 as a guide, on a separate sheet of paper or in your journal, construct a chapter map of Sample Chapter 11, "Organizing the Police Department." Then create corresponding questions and write them in the following space.

_____

_____

_____

_____

_____

_____

_____

_____

_____

_____

_____

_____

"I think the artist's left brain overpowered his right brain."

LISTENING IN CLASS: COMMUNICATION BETWEEN SPEAKER AND LISTENER

Classroom communication takes place between your instructor, the speaker, and you, the listener. In the first *Doonesbury* cartoon, the cartoon's professor and his students are communicating at opposite ends of the continuum of listening (See Table 4.5). The students apparently are listening at one of the lowest levels of the spectrum, the attention level. The lecturer tries desperately without success to entice them to evaluate what he says. Little communication occurs, no matter how hard the speaker tries.

Listening, then, is more difficult than it looks. It appears easy because it's something you've been doing all your life. It requires only the equipment you have with you, and you can use it in all of your classes and at any time. One problem with learning from verbal information is your lack of training in being a good listener in the classroom. Educators take for granted that you know how to learn from lectures. That, however, is seldom the case. Listening

Table 4.5	Continuum of Listening
Evaluation	Judging information in terms of accuracy and relevance
Application	Applying information to personal experience; using information in new situations
Implication	Drawing conclusions
Interpretation	Synthesizing information; putting information into your own words
Integration	Relating new information to old learning
Definition	Lowest level of active listening; giving meaning to isolated facts and details; no overall organizational plan
Attention	Listening passively; no effort to relate or understand what is being said
Reception	Hearing without thought

WRITE TO LEARN

Examine Table 4.5. Compare your behavior in your favorite and least favorite classes. Consider the amount of time each of these classes lasts. On a separate sheet of paper, or in your journal, determine when and for how long you might be at each level of listening in each of these classes. What factors contribute to the level at which you listen and for how long you remain at a level in each class? Are there any differences?

Doonesbury

BY GARRY TRUDEAU

SOURCE: *Doonesbury*. Copyright © 1985 (1986) G. B. Trudeau. Reprinted with permission of Universal Press Syndicate. All rights reserved.

is a seemingly passive activity, so you can appear to know how to listen even when you don't. You can look like you're listening, even when you aren't. Listening, however, is not an all-or-nothing proposition. The level at which you listen depends on your background knowledge, the difficulty of the concepts, and your purpose in listening.

For most students, listening to lectures involves following a linear sequence of one idea after another. Like the students in the first *Doonesbury* cartoon, they tend to take at face value what is being said. They passively accept any statement, evaluating little of what they hear. What a speaker says should elicit mental comments, if not spoken comments and questions. These comments should question what is said as well as what and how you think about it. In essence, you should always be asking, "What?" "So what?" and "Now what?" Table 4.6 modifies the continuum of listening to include the kind of mental comments that might be appropriate at each level.

Table 4.6	Mental Comments for the Continuum of Listening
Evaluation	Do I agree with . . . ?
	What information supports . . . ?
	Is this true and accurate?
	Why would . . . be so?
Application	How would . . . be used?
	How would . . . differ if one of its components changed?
	What situation would show . . . ?
Implication	What would be the result of . . . ?
	What would cause . . . . ?
	So if . . . is true, then . . . follows.
Interpretation	In other words . . .
	To summarize . . .
	That means . . .
Integration	Then . . . relates to . . .
	. . . is part of . . . process.
	. . . could be organized like . . .
	. . . could be classified as . . .
Definition	The meaning of . . . is . . .
Attention	Sure looks like a nice day outside
Reception	Hmmm?

Doonesbury

BY GARRY TRUDEAU

Factors Affecting Your Ability to Be an Active Listener

The student who spoke in the second *Doonesbury* cartoon demonstrates the alert and active process of listening. He related what the instructor said to what he already knew. He took advantage of this knowledge by communicating with his instructor. He maintained eye contact and gave a thoughtful response. He seemed interested. As a result, the instructor took an interest in him and wanted to get to know him better.

You, too, should be like this *Doonesbury* student. By combining what you learn from the instructor with what you know about yourself and the world, you become an active listener. Active listening occurs when you consciously monitor your listening and use preplanned strategies for improving and maximizing these listening skills.

Are you an effective listener? Do you know what factors affect listening skills? The personal profile found in Exercise 4.5 helps you rate your abilities as a listener.

Maintaining Concentration

Inactive listening results from **distractions.** These draw your attention from the subject being discussed. Some of these factors are beyond your control, and others are not. All prevent you from fully focusing on the topic at hand.

Distractions beyond your control include traffic noises; sounds within the classroom, such as whispering, papers rattling, people moving, or hall noises; and other environmental interruptions. Your instructor's mannerisms pose another distraction you cannot control. Often an instructor's dialect, speech rate, and body language affect your concentration. Because you have no control over these distractions, you must learn to cope with them.

One way to cope is to increase your interest in the subject. You can try to become so interested in what is being said that you ignore what is bothering you. Another way to reduce environmental distractions is to move to a different seat. You might have to move away from a door or window. If you are in a large lecture class, moving closer to the instructor helps you hear better and focuses your attention.

Sometimes distractions are within you. These also prevent you from concentrating on the topic. Such distractions include physical discomforts, personal concerns, and daydreams. It is difficult to think when you are hungry, tired, or sick. Proper nutrition, rest, and exercise get rid of these physical distractions. Personal concerns, no matter how large or small, cannot be solved during a class. If your problem is a large one, consulting a counselor or talking with a friend before or after class might help reduce your anxiety. Worry about small problems (getting your laundry done, meeting a friend, running errands) can be handled by listing them on a page in your notebook. Then you can forget about them until the end of class. Daydreaming is another common distraction. **Self-talk** can be used to force yourself back

Exercise 4.5   Rate yourself as a listener. There are no correct or incorrect answers. Your responses, however, will extend your understanding of yourself as a listener and highlight areas in which improvement might be welcome . . . to you and to those around you.

Classroom Listening Inventory

1. What classroom characteristic interferes most with your listening to a classroom lecture?
   a. temperature
   b. chalkboard and wall colors
   c. outside noise
   d. noise created by other students in class
   e. other

2. What characteristics of the instructor's interfere most with your listening to the classroom lectures?
   a. voice, speech rate, or accent
   b. thought organization
   c. appearance
   d. movement and behavior
   e. vocabulary

3. In the classroom where you listen best, where do you usually sit?
   a. front left
   b. front center
   c. front right
   d. middle
   e. back

4. In the classroom where you listen best, how often does the instructor look at you?
   a. very often
   b. often
   c. sometimes
   d. seldom
   e. very seldom

5. What personal characteristic interferes most with your listening to class lectures?
   a. tired
   b. hungry
   c. daydreaming
   d. preoccupied
   e. not interested in subject
   f. other

6. In the classroom where you listen best, how do you respond to the course?
   a. eye contact with teacher
   b. nod and acknowledge the teacher's comments with facial expressions
   c. take notes
   d. ask questions
   e. anticipate what will be said
   f. other

7. How do you respond to a lecturer
   a. make eye contact
   b. nod and acknowledge my comments with facial expressions
   c. take notes
   d. ask questions
   e. anticipate what I will say next
   f. other

8. At what time of the day do you listen best to classroom lectures?
   a. early morning
   b. mid-morning
   c. around noon
   d. mid-afternoon
   e. evening

9. How do you choose class times for your courses??
   a. only one available
   b. fit my schedule
   c. considered my best time to listen
   d. instructor
   e. other

10. What is the nature of the lecture content to which you listen best?
    a. personally relevant
    b. dynamic
    c. familiar vocabulary and organization
    d. visually aided
    e. well supported with examples and comparisons

(continues)

Exercise 4.5   *Continued*

11. For what purpose do you listen in the class in which you listen best?
    a. to pass a test
    b. to relate to the instructor
    c. to satisfy an interest in the subject
    d. to learn new knowledge
    e. to apply information to self-improvement

12. When you take notes in this class, do you
    a. write down terms?
    b. use a sentence outline?
    c. paraphrase?
    d. use topic outline?
    e. other?

13. What single factor influences your listening behavior most in this lecture?
    a. the room
    b. the instructor
    c. your purpose/attitude
    d. your physical and mental states
    e. other students

SOURCE: Teaching Professor, (January 1993): 3–4.

to attention. Self-talk involves your interrupting your daydream with a strong internal command like, "STOP! Pay attention now. Think about this later." Finally, you must maintain your stamina in listening to lectures. In general, students tend to take fewer and less comprehensive notes as a lecture progresses. Active listening and continued mental questioning help you remain focused and attentive.

Recognizing Main Ideas

Every lecture has a plan, purpose, and structure that indicate the main idea of the talk. Learning to recognize the various patterns that lectures follow helps you distinguish between main ideas and details. This also aids you in recognizing examples and understanding the reasons for anecdotes.

Lectures follow five basic patterns. Instructors either: (1) introduce new topics or summarize information; (2) list or order details; (3) present two (or more) sides of an issue; (4) identify cause(s) and effect(s) or problem(s) and solution(s); or (5) discuss a subject by providing supporting information. These patterns vary as the instructor's purposes change in the course of a lecture. Identifying your instructor's mix of the patterns helps you predict the direction of the lecture. Signal words and other verbal markers help you identify the flow and content of these lecture patterns.

Listening for these signals makes you a kind of word detective. A detective follows a suspect, predicting where he or she will go based on clues left behind. You follow an instructor's lecture and predict the lecture's direction by identifying the **transition words** your instructor uses. These words also mark the end of a lecture. This is important because instructors often restate main ideas in their summaries. Becoming familiar with transition words

Table 4.7   Lecture Patterns and Corresponding Signals

Pattern	Description	Signal Words
Introduction/Summary	Identifies main points	Identified by location, either at the beginning or end of a discussion of a topic; or by such words as: *in summary, in conclusion, as a review, to summarize, to sum up, first, to begin, today we will discuss, in this lecture you will learn*
Enumeration/Sequence	Lists or orders main points or presents a problem and steps for its solution	*First, second, third, next, then, finally, in addition, last, and, furthermore, and then, most important, least important*
Comparison/Contrast	Describes ways in which concepts are alike or different or presents two or more sides of an issue	Comparison—*similarly, both, as well as, likewise, in like manner* Contrast—*however, on the other hand, on the contrary, but, instead of, although, yet, nevertheless*
Cause/Effect or Problem/Solution	Shows the result of action(s) or explains a problem and its solution	*Therefore, thus, as a result, because, in turn, then, hence, for this reason, results in, causes, effects*
Subject Development/Definition	Identifies a major topic and describes or develops it through related details	Identified by terms denoting definition; types or kinds; characteristics, elements, and other kinds of supporting details

WRITE TO LEARN

On a separate sheet of paper or in your journal, identify the lecture pattern in each of your classes today and tomorrow. Also list three to five of the signal words that your instructor(s) used to help you determine this pattern.

helps you organize lecture notes and listen more actively. Table 4.7 compares transition words with **lecture patterns.** Practice determining transition words in Exercise 4.6.

Identifying Important Information

Identifying important information is a third factor that contributes to your ability to be an active listener. Although instructors emphasize main points differently, there are some common ways that they let you know what's important. Instructors often use one or more kinds of emphasis. Careful

Exercise 4.6 Underline the transition words found in each lecture excerpt. Use the following key and write the lecture type in the space below the excerpt.

I/S: Introduction/summary
C/E: Cause/effect
E/S: Enumeration/sequence
C/C: Comparison/contrast
SD/D: Subject development/definition

1. Regardless of cultural or socioeconomic background, socialization has several common goals. The first goal is basic discipline of the individual. This discourages behaviors deemed unwanted by the group. Second, socialization inspires aspiration. In order for the group to prosper, people must continue to grow. Next, socialization forms identities. Who you are is often determined by how you fit into the context of the group. Fourth, social roles are learned from socialization. This includes external actions and internal values. Finally, socialization teaches skills necessary for the person to fit into the group.

   Lecture type: _____

2. In this case, both evaporation and condensation occur in the closed container. Condensation is an exothermic process. This means that it liberates heat. Condensation occurs when a gas or vapor is converted to a liquid or solid. Evaporation is, on the other hand, an endothermic process. In this process, heat is absorbed. Also called vaporization, evaporation occurs when particles leave the surface of a material. Equilibrium exists when two such opposing processes occur at equal rates.

   Lecture type: _____

3. In this problem, we are attempting to show the rate of growth for investments based on five-year intervals. As class ended last meeting, we had completed the majority of this programming example. Today, we will look at how to determine if a year is divisible by five. One way to accomplish this is to use the truncation property of integer division. If an integer is exactly divisible by a second integer—in this case, five—then the quotient times the second integer will produce the first as its value. If the value of the final result is not equal to the first integer, then the year is not divisible by five.

   Lecture type: _____

4. Clinical observation is what most of us think of as the case study method. This model comes from medicine. It is the foundation of the majority of the most popular and influential personality theories. The foremost strength of the clinical observation method is its great depth. The amount of time a clinical observer devotes to each case possibly accounts for this advantage. A second strength is its realism, its lack of artificiality. Despite its popularity, however, clinical observation has its weaknesses. First, there is a possibility of observer bias. A second factor to consider is that clinical observation offers no possibility of replication. Should two observers agree on what they have seen, there is no way to duplicate the same set of circumstances for further study. Finally, there is a problem of sample bias. If observers see a sample of people not representative of the rest of humanity, then the observer finds information not generalizable to others.

   Lecture type: _____

5. How does stress affect you physiologically? When you sense danger, your brain sends a message to the adrenal gland to secrete catecholamines, epinephrine, and norepinephrine into the bloodstream. This causes the liver to release glucose, which gives you more energy. It also decreases blood loss by increasing clotting time. It conserves fluid in the kidneys. Blood moves from the extremities of the body to the vital organs and legs. You breathe faster, which brings in more oxygen and allows you to rid yourself of carbon dioxide more quickly. Your heart rate also increases to provide more nutrients and oxygen to the body via the blood stream.

   Lecture type: _____

6. Money and position affect lifestyles in various ways. Upper-middle class females have more career opportunities. Wealthy women are more likely to

(continues)

Exercise 4.6   *Continued*

combine marriage and work because of a commitment to their careers than are poorer women, who work out of necessity. Poorer families generally maintain the traditional division of labor within their household. Middle-class families exhibit more equal relationships between husbands and wives. Middle-class parents tend to be less strict than working-class parents. Thus, people in higher and lower socioeconomic classes act and react in different ways.

Lecture type: _____

7. Using statistics from law enforcement agencies across the nation, the Uniform Crime Reports (UCR) program provides assessments of crime in the country. Law enforcement agencies make these assessments by measuring the number of crimes that come to the attention of the police. The program's main goal is to generate reliable criminal

statistics for use in law enforcement administration, operation, and management. Criminal justice professors, legislators, and scholars also use this data. The UCR also provides information to the public about levels of crime.

Lecture type: _____

8. Before we begin a discussion of the Basque language, you need to realize how few people actually speak it and why that number is so small. Only one language currently spoken in Europe, the Basque language, came there before the Indo-European invasion. Basque is spoken by about 2 million people in northern Spain and southwestern France. The uniqueness of the language reflects the isolation of the Basque people in their mountainous homeland.

Lecture type: _____

observation of your instructor helps you know when your instructor is stressing a main idea.

First, some instructors write key information on the chalkboard. They often place lecture outlines on the board before class begins. Instructors also write **terms** or key points on the board as they lecture. Copying this outline or list of terms aids your learning in three ways. Initially, you learn as you write. Next, copying the outline gives you an idea of the lecture's topic. Finally, the outline serves as a guide for study.

A second way an instructor stresses a point is by providing "wait time." When an instructor speaks more slowly, you have more time to write what is being said. Hesitations and pauses are forms of "wait time." In addition, you are given "wait time" when your instructor repeats information.

Third, your instructor might change tone of voice when stressing an important point. An instructor's voice could also change in volume or intensity. Listen for these changes.

A fourth way instructors emphasize main points is through body language. If your instructor pounds on the desk, moves closer to the class, or makes some other gesture to stress a point, it is often one essential to your understanding.

The fifth way instructors explain main ideas is by using visual aids. Films, overhead transparencies, videotapes, or other audiovisual materials signal important topics.

_____ **CLASSIC CRITICAL THINKING** _____

Read the "Ten Commandments of Ineffective Listeners." Consider the implications of each of the statements. What are the consequences of not listening? Re-write the Commandments to reflect what effective listeners do. What conclusion(s) do you reach about how effective you are as a listener?

Ten Commandments of Ineffective Listeners

1. **Thou shalt "tune out."** If the subject is uninteresting, find something else to think about.

2. **Thou shalt pretend you are an Olympic judge and rate the speaker's choice of words, speaking style, and mannerisms.** If at all possible, allow this evaluation to take precedence over all other tasks—that is, listening, concentrating, taking notes and so forth.

3. **Thou shalt NOT ask questions.** Questions do nothing to increase understanding; rather, they annoy the instructor and your fellow students by prolonging the lecture. Keep quiet.

4. **Thou shalt note ALL facts.** If the instructor did not want you to know it, he or she wouldn't have said it. Write exactly what the instructor says, syllable-by-syllable.

5. **Thou shalt be easily distracted.** Allow outside noises, instructor's body language, and classroom environment to take your mind from the lecture.

6. **Thou shalt become defensive.** College professors have opinions just like anyone else, and, if you are listening carefully enough, you can find something that offends you. Once you have done so, react immediately. Remember, the best offense is a good defense; so, start an argument or make a rude noise. Your opinions about the subject matter are just as good as the lecturer's, after all.

7. **Thou shalt ignore difficult material.** If an instructor's lecture is unclear, leave the classroom, drop the class, and never return. By doing so, you make your life easier and less stressful. There's always an easier course or instructor out there.

8. **Thou shalt daydream.** Even though instructors speak about 125 words per minute, your brain processes at over 500 words per minute. Purchase a watch that has an alarm. Set it for five minute intervals. Listen for one minute out of every five. Spend the other four daydreaming.

9. **Thou shalt become a distractor.** Daydreaming and becoming defensive have added bonuses. The noise you make during a confrontation and the watch alarm serve as distractions to other students who are also trying to avoid listening. You can also help others by coming to class late, leaving early, rattling papers, or clicking pens.

10. **Thou shalt fake attention.** Whenever possible, make eye contact with your instructor and then nod. Doing so gives the impression you are listening and lessens the likelihood that he or she will call on you to speak. If possible, get the instructor's attention and then quickly write a note on your paper. It will look like you are listening and taking notes. Practice these exercises until you can do them without thought. this enables you to daydream without interruption.

Exercise 4.7   Listen to the instructor on the videotape provided by your instructor. Write down the main points. Following each point, list the cue used to emphasize the information.

> ### WRITE TO LEARN
> On a separate sheet of paper or in your journal, list three ways the instructor for this class emphasizes information. Circle those mentioned in this text.

Sixth, some instructors refer to specific text pages. Information an instructor knows by page number is worth noting and remembering.

Finally, instructors stress information by referring to that information as a possible test question. Your instructor might say, "You may see this again," or "This would make a good test question." Practice your listening skills in Exercise 4.7.

Recall

Sometimes a lecture is like a television movie that's continued for several nights. Often an instructor doesn't finish discussing a topic during one class. He or she begins with that same topic the next class meeting. You need a review, similar to the "scenes from last night's exciting episode." Without this

Figure 4.3   Curve of Forgetting

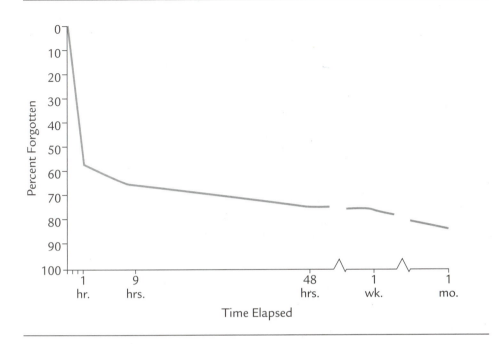

review, you forget what happened in the notes, just as you might forget what happened in the movie. In either case, you lose continuity and interest. Recall is diminished.

Frequent reviews aid recall by transferring information from short-term to long-term memory (see Chapter 7). The more often you hear or read something, the easier it is to remember. The "Ebbinghaus curve" or **curve of forgetting** (Figure 4.3) shows the relationship between recall of information without review and time since presentation. The numbers along the left of the graph indicate the amount of material forgotten. The numbers along the bottom show the number of days since the material was presented. Note that on the basis of one exposure, most information is lost within the first 24 hours. This curve explains why you are sometimes confused by notes that seemed clear when you took them. Reviewing your notes within 24 hours after taking them slows down your curve of forgetting.

Reviewing your notes is your responsibility. After each day's class, reread your notes. Before the next class, review your notes again. Try to anticipate what the instructor will say next. This provides background information for you to use when listening to your class lecture. It helps you relate information and remember more. In addition, it refreshes your memory of content you found confusing. You can begin the class by asking the instructor to clarify this material before he or she continues with the topic.

Your Instructor, the Speaker

The job of your instructor, the speaker, is to provide you, the listener, with information. College faculty spend their lives learning about their areas of expertise so they can share that information with you. As such, they are interested in talking about their topics and hope that you are interested in listening to what they have to say.

Instructors, like any other group, vary in ability. Some are excellent speakers. Others are mediocre at best. Instructors vary in the ways in which they pace information. Some speak very rapidly, others more slowly. Information delivered at breakneck speeds often results in your feeling frustrated and lost. Information delivered too slowly tends to bore and therefore lose you.

Unlike a text, a lecture often shifts between major and minor topics with few cues concerning which is which. Previewing the text chapter, having some ideas about how the content is organized, and recognizing signal words help you determine a lecture's organization.

In general, your ability to distinguish good speakers from poor ones improves with practice. A rating system like the one in Figure 4.4 helps you determine how effective your instructor is and how much you need to work to compensate. The more *A's* your instructor receives, the more effective that instructor is.

Figure 4.4   **Rating Checklist for Instructors**

Indicate how often your instructor does each of the following by marking either A—Always; U—Usually; S—Sometimes; or N—Never.

DOES YOUR INSTRUCTOR	A	U	S	N
1. Explain goals of the lecture?				
2. Review previous lecture materials before beginning the new lecture?				
3. State main ideas in introduction and summary of lecture?				
4. Provide an outline of the lecture?				
5. Provide "wait time" for writing notes?				
6. Speak clearly with appropriate volume?				
7. Answer questions without sarcasm?				
8. Stay on topic?				
9. Refrain from reading directly from the text?				
10. Emphasize main points?				
11. Use transition words?				
12. Give examples to illustrate difficult ideas?				
13. Write important words, dates, and so forth on board?				
14. Define important terms?				
15. Use audio/visual aids to reinforce ideas?				
Totals				

Responding to Speaker Styles: Listening Responsibilities

How determined you need to be as an active listener depends partly on the effectiveness of your instructor. If your instructor is well organized and knows the subject, the amount of work you need to do lessens. Think again of the continuum on which listening takes place. With an effective instructor, you need only focus on the information that's presented. If, however, your instructor is less effective, then your responsibilities as an active listener increase. It becomes necessary for you to define, integrate, and interpret information. In addition, you must draw conclusions for yourself. Finding

Table 4.8   How to Compensate for an Ineffective Lecturer

If your Instructor fails to . . .	Then you . . .
1. Explain goals of the lecture	Use your text and syllabus to set objectives
2. Review previous lecture materials before beginning new lecture	Set aside time before each class to review notes.
3. State main ideas in introduction and summary of lecture	Write short summaries of the day's lecture immediately after class.
4. Provide an outline of the lecture	Preview assigned readings before class or outline notes after class.
5. Provide "wait time" for writing notes	Politely ask the instructor to repeat information or speak more slowly.
6. Speak clearly with appropriate volume	Politely ask the instructor to repeat information or speak more loudly or move closer to him or her.
7. Answer questions without sarcasm	Refrain from taking comments personally.
8. Stay on topic	Discover how anecdotes relate to the topic or use anecdotes as a memory cue.
9. Refrain from reading directly from the text	Mark passages in text as instructor reads or summarize or outline these passages in text margin.
10. Emphasize main points	Supplement lectures through text previews and reading.
11. Use transition words	Supplement lectures through text previews and reading.
12. Give examples to illustrate difficult ideas	Ask instructor for a clarifying example, discuss idea with other students or create an example for yourself.
13. Write important words, dates, etc. on board	Supplement notes with terms listed in text and highlight information contained in lecture or text.
14. Define important terms	Use text glossary or a dictionary.
15. Use audiovisual aids to reinforce ideas	Relate information to what you know about the topic or create a clarifying example for yourself.

> I know that you believe you understood what you think I said, but I am not sure you realize that what you heard is not what I meant.
>
> Anonymous
> 1960s

applications for information and judging its value become your job. The main way that you can cope with ineffective lecturers is to compensate for their deficiencies (see Table 4.8).

Maximizing Your Understanding of the Speaker's Message

The speaker controls what is said and how it is organized. To be sure that you "realize that what you heard is what is actually meant," you need to control the way you listen to get the most from the lecture. You need to use what you know to interpret, organize, and store what you hear. Such information is then available for later retrieval and use. Whatever the lecture ability or style of your instructor, you need a way to understand and remember information. Table 4.9 shows a plan for maximizing your understanding of what you hear.

Table 4.9   Method for Maximizing Your Understanding of the Speaker's Message

1. Have a purpose for listening.
2. Pay careful attention to the instructor's introductory and summary statements. These usually state main points.
3. Take notes.
4. Sit comfortably erect. Slouching makes you sleepy and indicates to your instructor your disinterest.
5. Look attentive. Show you interest by keeping your eyes on your instructor.
6. Concentrate on what the instructor is saying. Try to ignore external distractions. Try to eliminate internal distractions.
7. Think of questions you would like to ask or comments you want to make.
8. Listen for transition words that signal main points.
9. Mark words or references you don't understand. Do not attempt to figure them out now—look them up later.
10. Be flexible—adjust your listening and notetaking to the lecture.
11. If the instructor speaks too quickly or unclearly, then
    a. Ask the instructor to speak more slowly or to repeat information.
    b. Leave plenty of white space and fill in missing details immediately after class.
    c. Exchange copies of notes with fellow classmates.
    d. Ask the instructor for clarification after class.
    e. Be sure to preview lecture topic before class.
12. Avoid being a distraction (keep hands still, wait your turn in discussions, avoid whispering, and so on).

ORGANIZING WHAT YOU HEAR IN CLASS

In learning, it is said that "we hear and we forget; we see and we remember; we do and we understand." Because this is true, you need to apply active listening techniques and take effective notes during class. These processes aid you in collecting information for later learning. They allow you to store data for future recall and use. They provide the oral and visual stimuli you need for remembering and understanding.

The relationship between lectures and textbooks vary. Sometimes, lecture content corresponds closely to assigned textbook chapters. In other lectures, the content of the lecture is not necessarily contained in the text. Rather, the text provides additional information to help you better understand the subject. The third type of lecture can be either text-dependent or text-independent. The lecturer might use media to focus and enhance the delivery of information.

Lectures Dependent on the Text

When lectures are text-based, the way you use your text during the lecture depends on your preclass preparation. If you read the chapter in its entirety before class, you can record notes and instructions emphasized during the lecture directly in your textbook. As your instructor speaks, you can highlight or underline these items. You can cross out information your instructor tells you to omit and note important information in the margins of the chapter.

If you constructed a notetaking outline through text preview, you respond differently during the lecture. Using this method, you record class notes and instructions directly on your outline. You highlight important information and cross out sections that your instructor tells you to omit. You make notes in the larger section of your notetaking outline. When the instructor refers to specific graphics or quotations, you underline or mark these in your text.

Lectures Independent of the Text

When instructors lecture on information not contained in the text, your responsibility for taking notes increases. Because you do not have the text to use as a backup source, you need to be an especially active listener. After the lecture, you need to discover the plan of the lecture and outline or map its content. Your class notes and syllabus aid you in this attempt. Also, setting study objectives for yourself will help you create a purpose for learning and increase recall. To be sure you have fully grasped the content, discuss your notes with another classmate or do supplemental reading. Finally, when lectures are independent of the text, they are based on what your instructor feels is most important about the subject. For this reason, your instructor is a good source for clarifying confusing points. Feel free to ask questions.

Lectures That Include Media

Instructors use a variety of media—handouts, films, slides, models, and so on—to stimulate your visual and auditory senses during lectures. When the instructor selects media from published resources, the information tends to be more general. When an instructor creates the media, the information is more course-specific and more likely to correspond closely to what you need to know for an exam.

Instructors use media to add knowledge and information, arouse emotion or interest, and increase skills and performance. Your responsibility is to recognize your instructor's purpose for using media and judge its worth in meeting your learning needs. For instance, suppose a psychology instructor shows a film introducing the concept of classical conditioning. How carefully you attend to the film depends on your prior knowledge of the topic. If you have extensive knowledge about classical conditioning, then the film serves only as a review for you. If classical conditioning is a new topic for you, then the film builds background knowledge. Table 4.10 is a list of media types and the corresponding purposes for their use. Exercise 4.8 allows you to review media types and their applications.

Table 4.10   Media Types and Corresponding Purposes for Their Use

Purposes for Media	Chalk-board	Trans-parencies	Handouts	Audio-tapes	Films, slides, Television	Models
			Media Types			
Provide examples	X	X	X	X	X	X
List characteristics	X	X	X	X	X	
Describe or define concepts	X	X	X	X	X	
Summarize notes	X	X	X			
Supplement information	X	X	X	X	X	X
Arouse emotion or interest				X	X	X
Document proof			X	X	X	X
Aid recall	X	X	X	X	X	X
Reinforce ideas	X	X	X	X	X	X
Provide back-ground information	X	X	X	X	X	X
Provide a vicarious experience				X	X	X
Demonstrate a process				X	X	X
Introduce new concepts	X	X	X	X	X	X

NOTES: THE ACT IN ACTIVE LISTENING

One of Aesop's fables tells of a blacksmith and his dog. The blacksmith, unhappy about the dog's laziness, said, "When I work, you sleep; but when I stop to eat, you want to eat, too." The moral of the fable is "Those who will not work deserve to starve." This moral holds true for notetaking. While the instructor "works," many students "sleep," passively receiving lecture information. Others actively take notes.

Notetaking supplements **active listening** in several important ways. First, some information in the lecture might not be found in the text or handouts. The lecture might be the only source for certain facts. Second, the information emphasized in a lecture often signals what will be found on exams. Third, class notes serve as a means of external storage. As a busy college student, it is impossible for you to remember everything you hear accurately. Thus, notes serve as an alternative form of memory.

The process of notetaking adds to learning independent of review. Notes often trigger your memory of the lecture or the text. Review, however, is an important part of notetaking. In general, students who review notes achieve more than those who do not (Kiewra, 1985). Researchers found that if important information was contained in notes, it had a 34 percent chance of being

Exercise 4.8   Circle the item that best answers or completes each of the following questions or statements.

1. An English literature professor begins a unit on Shakespeare by showing a film of life in sixteenth-century England. The purpose of this use of media is to
   a. provide contemporary examples of Shakespearean plays.
   b. list characteristics of Shakespearean plays.
   c. summarize notes.
   d. provide background information about life in Shakespearean England.

2. A political science instructor wants to arouse interest in the development of political parties in the United States. Which of the following types of media could be used for this purpose?
   a. Transparencies
   b. Handouts
   c. Chalkboard presentations
   d. Audiotapes

3. A biology professor brings to class a model of the human heart. Which of the following is *least* likely to be a purpose for the use of this lecture media?
   a. To arouse emotion or interest in the processes of the human heart.
   b. To supplement information about the human heart and its processes.
   c. To aid recall of the human heart.
   d. To demonstrate how the human heart processes blood.

4. As a review, a history professor provides a handout of a timeline that includes all important events during the first 20 years of the American colonial period. The purpose of such a handout is most likely to
   a. arouse emotion.
   b. provide a vicarious learning experience.
   c. demonstrate a process.
   d. summarize notes.

5. A mathematics professor shows how to work a complicated algebraic equation using a transparency The purpose of the transparency is to
   a. describe concepts.
   b. list characteristics.

c. provide an example.
d. provide background information.

6. A music history instructor provides tapes of Gregorian chants. The purpose of the tapes is least likely to be to
   a. summarize notes.
   b. aid recall.
   c. provide examples.
   d. supplement information.

7. A chemistry instructor wants to teach a class the properties of solids. To ensure that each student has a complete summary of notes, the instructor provides which of the following?
   a. A film
   b. Models of solids
   c. A simulation of chemical processes
   d. A handout

8. A zoology professor asks students to view a public television special on primates. Which of the following would *not* be a logical purpose for such an assignment?
   a. To aid recall.
   b. To provide background information.
   c. To reinforce ideas.
   d. To summarize notes.

9. An education instructor demonstrates the use of a braillewriter in a class on teaching the visually impaired. The purpose of this activity is to
   a. list characteristics of visually impaired students
   b. document proof.
   c. supplement information.
   d. provide a definition of visually impaired.

10. An astronomy professor wants to provide students with the experience of visiting the moon. Because he can't send them there, his next best opportunity for doing so is
    a. a handout describing the moon's rocks and craters.
    b. an example of a moon rock.
    c. a film of astronauts on the moon.
    d. a transparency of the solar system.

remembered (Howe, 1970). Information not found in notes had only a 5 percent chance of being remembered.

Taking Notes: A Systematic Approach

Peper and Mayer (1978) discuss three theories about notetaking: the attention theory, the effort theory, and the generative theory. The attention theory suggests that, by taking notes, you pay more attention and become more familiar with new material. The effort theory is based on the idea that notetaking requires more effort and thought than reading. The generative theory states that, as you take notes, you paraphrase, organize, and understand information. To do so, you relate this new information to your background knowledge. These three theories regard notetaking as an active process that results in learning. This process requires you to become an active listener. To do so, you need a plan. This plan can be an original creation, or it can be a combination of parts of other plans.

Your Personal Notetaking System

Active listening requires more than passive reception of the speaker's voice. Active learning is enhanced by action. Active listening requires you to recognize important concepts and supporting details. One way to make your listening active is by taking notes (see Table 4.11).

As a knowledgeable notetaker, you need to selectively record only important information. What information is recorded is your choice. You make this decision based on what you know about the lecture topic, what subject you are studying, and what facts your instructor stresses. If you are familiar with a topic, your notes need not be as detailed as when you are less familiar with a subject. Active listening helps you find important information. Now you must get it written down.

Notes are not like a theme you turn in for a grade. They need not be grammatically correct. They don't even have to contain complete words. In fact, as a good notetaker, you need to develop your own system of shorthand to record your notes. In developing your system, limit the number of symbols you use. After you thoroughly learn a few symbols, you can add others. Table 4.12 gives some rules for developing your own shorthand system, and Exercise 4.9 allows you to practice your own system.

Table 4.11   Suggestions for Taking Notes

1. Date each day's notes. The date serves as a reference point if you need to compare notes with someone or ask your instructor for clarification. If you are absent, the missing date(s) identifies which notes you need.

2. Develop a system for taking notes that best fits your learning style and course content.

3. Keep all notes together. You accomplish this in one of two ways. You can purchase a single spiral notebook or ring binder for each class. Or, you can purchase two multiple-subject notebooks or loose-leaf binders, one for your classes on Monday-Wednesday-Friday, and one for your classes on Tuesday-Thursday. This way you carry only one notebook each day. Notebooks with pockets are useful for saving class handouts.

4. Bring all necessary materials (notebooks, pencils and pens, text) to each class.

5. Develop a key for your symbols and abbreviations until you are comfortable using them. Without this, you might be unable to decode your notes.

6. Try to group and label information to aid recall.

7. Write down all terms, dates, diagrams, problems, and so forth written on the board.

8. Use white space. Skip lines to separate important groups of ideas.

9. Write on only the front of your paper. This seems wasteful but makes reading your notes easier.

10. Write legibly. Notes are worthless if you can't read them.

11. If you instructor refers to specific text pages, turn to those pages and mark the information in your text rather than trying to duplicate information in your notes. Record in your notes the corresponding numbers of text pages.

12. Underline or mark important ideas and concepts with a different color ink than the one you used to take notes.

13. Compress your notes as you study. Underline or mark key words and phrases with a different color ink than the one you used to write the shorthand version.

14. Read over notes as soon as possible after class and make connections and additions. If you have any gaps, check with another student, your instructor, or the text.

15. While you wait for class to begin, review notes to set up a framework for new material.

Table 4.12   Rules for Developing a Shorthand System

1. Limit the number of symbols you create.

2. Use the beginning letters of words.

   Examples associated: assoc
   with: w
   geography: geog
   history: hist
   information: info
   introduction: intro

3. Use standard symbols.

   Examples and: &
   number: #
   percent: %
   money, dollars: $
   question: ?
   plus: +
   times, multiply: ×
   less than or greater than: < or >

(continues)

Table 4.12   *Continued*

4. Use traditional abbreviations but omit periods.

   Examples pound: lb
   foot: ft
   weight: wt
   mile: mi
   December: Dec
   United States: US

5. Omit vowels and keep only enough consonants to make the word recognizable.

   Examples background: bkgd
   mixture: mxtr
   develop: dvlp/

6. Drop endings that do not contribute to word meaning.

   Examples ed
   ing
   ment
   er

7. Add "s" to show plurals.

8. Omit *a, an, the,* and unimportant verbs and adjectives.

   Example Write "Cause of CW = slavery" instead of "A cause of the Civil War was the issue of slavery."

9. Write out terms and proper names the first time. Show your abbreviation in parentheses after the term or name. Then use the abbreviation throughout the rest of your notes

10. Indicate dates numerically

   Example 12/7/42 instead of December 7, 1942

11. Use common misspellings of words.

   Examples through: thru
   night: nite
   right: rite

12. Express numbers numerically

   Examples one: 1
   two: 2
   first: 1st
   second: 2nd

Exercise 4.9   On a separate sheet of paper or in your journal, use your personal shorthand system to transcribe the eight paragraphs in Exercise 4.6.

Cornell System of Notetaking

One system of notetaking that works well for students was developed at Cornell University. Because the system is not difficult, it saves time and effort. The step-by-step process brings efficiency to your notetaking. Walter Pauk (1984), director of the Reading Study Center at Cornell, identified five stages in notetaking: record, reduce, recite, reflect, and review. Notes in Figure 4.5 are written according to the Cornell system of notetaking.

Stage 1 is to *record*. You prepare for this stage by drawing a vertical line about 2½ inches from the left edge of your paper. The left column is your recall column. You leave it blank until Stage 2. During the lecture, you listen actively. You write in paragraph or outline form as much information as you think is important in the right, larger column.

Reduce is the key word in Stage 2. As soon after class as you can, condense your notes and write them in the recall column. Your promptness in

Figure 4.5   Notes Written Using the Cornell Notetaking System

	Shelters topic
	Shelters are more efficient made of natural (raw) materials
Tropical shelters list types and quantities	Tropical Dwellers 1) Frequent rainfall 2) Bamboo–made of 3) Roof sloped for run off 4) Floor raised for dryness
Grassland dwellers Types of weather cond. materials	Grassland Dwellers 1) Winds, cold nights, and severe winters 2) Use animal hides stretched over wood 3) These tents are portable
Desert Dwellers Types and quantities of materials	Desert Dwellers 1) Use mud masonry 2) Mud added to wood dries like brick 3) Mud insulates from severe climate changes (Hot day–cool nights) 4) Most are farmers or nomadic 5) Some dried brick shelters have lasted 1000 years
Summary	Shelters are more efficient made of raw materials. There are 3 main types or areas where shelters are built. Tropical, Grassland, and Desert Regions.

SOURCE: Courtesy of Greg Jones, Metropolitan State College, Denver, Colorado.

doing this is important because it helps you decrease your curve of forgetting. To condense notes, omit adjectives and adverbs and leave nouns and verbs intact. It's important to use as few words as possible. If you wish, you can transfer these cues to index cards and carry them with you for quick and efficient review. The reduction stage increases your understanding and recall.

Recitation is Stage 3. During this stage, you cover your notes and try to say what's in them in your own words. You use the recall column to cue your memory. Then, you uncover your notes and check your accuracy. This review also helps you decrease your curve of forgetting.

Stage 4 is to *reflect*. After reciting your notes, you give yourself some "wait time." Then, reread your notes and think about them. Next, read your text to supplement and clarify your notes. Use your text and notes to discover the causes and effects of issues, define terms, and relate concepts.

> **WRITE TO LEARN**
>
> On a separate sheet of paper or in your journal, take notes in your next lecture using the Cornell system. Bring your notes to the next class for evaluation and discussion.

Make generalizations and draw conclusions. This helps you become a more active thinker.

Review is the goal of Stage 5. Briefly reviewing your notes several times a week helps you retain what you have learned. This distributed review keeps information fresh, provides repetition, and decreases your chances of forgetting what you've learned. (Chapter 7 discusses various memory techniques for rehearsing information.)

Outlining

The most common way to organize information you hear is through **outlining.** In this sequential process, record major concepts and supporting details, examples, and other information in the same order as they appear in your text or the lecture. The disadvantage of this system is that you might record information without thought. Because you do not synthesize or relate the information you are writing, your understanding of key concepts remains superficial.

When the lecture is independent of the text, you combat this problem by active listening strategies. If the lecture reflects text content, your notetaking outline gives you a framework for recording information. With this framework, in-class notetaking becomes more active as you listen for details within subheadings.

Outlines use either formal or informal formats (See Figure 4.6). The formal format uses roman numerals (I, II, III, and so on) placed on the left side of the page or margin to note major concepts. You indent ideas that support the major concepts. You indicate these secondary points with capital letters. You show lesser supporting details with indented Arabic numerals (1, 2, 3).

Because notes are for your personal use, they need not be formally outlined. The key to an outline is to visually highlight information in some manner. For the sake of consistency, informal outlines retain the indented format of formal outlines. To make informal outlines clearer, separate major headings and entire sections with a blank line. To construct informal outlines, use symbols, dashes, various print types, or other means of identifying differing levels of information. Practice developing outlines in Exercise 4.10.

Exercise 4.10   On a separate sheet of paper or in your journal, take notes from the videotape shown by your instructor. Use either a formal or informal outline approach to do so.

Figure 4.6   Formal and Informal Outline Formats

Formal Outline
I. Personality theorists
   A. Psychodynamic
      1. Freud
      2. Jung
      3. Erickson
   B. Behavior
      1. Skinner
      2. Bandura

Informal Outline with Dashes
Personality theorists
— Psychodynamic
   — Freud
   — Jung
   — Erickson
— Behavior
   — Skinner
   — Bandura

Informal Outline with Symbols or Print Style Differences
* PERSONALITY THEORISTS
Psychodynamic
   Freud
   Jung
   Erickson
Behavior
   Skinner
   Bandura

Taking Notes from Lecture Media

You take notes from lecture media (for example, handouts, chalkboard, transparencies) in much the same way you take notes from lectures. You can do this because instructors control the pace of presentation and content. Conversely, taking notes from films, slides, or television differs from traditional notetaking in several ways. First, you might associate such formats with entertainment and fail to realize the importance of remembering the information they provide. Second, such media types take place in semidarkened rooms, which sometimes encourage naps, rather than attention. Third, the fast pace and continuous action found in these formats often provide few pauses for taking notes. For this reason, taking notes immediately following the presentation sometimes provides the best alternative for recording new information.

Passive Notetaking: Borrowed, Commercial, and Taped Notes

In his poem "The Courtship of Miles Standish," Henry Wadsworth Longfellow tells of Miles Standish's courtship of a woman named Priscilla. Because Miles was such a shy man, he asked his friend John Alden to talk to Priscilla for him. John did so. During John's attempts to convince Priscilla of Miles's worth, Priscilla fell in love with John. John, however, was unaware of this. One night when he was trying to tell Priscilla of Miles's love of her, she said, "Speak for yourself, John." John did. Soon he and Priscilla were married, much to Standish's dismay.

...and as time passed, technology overtook culture
and culture became extinct.

Longfellow's poem shows that there are some tasks in life a person must do without help from others. For Miles Standish and John Alden, that task was love. For you, it's notetaking. Borrowed or commercial notes reflect the person who took them. They require no effort or action on your part. Thus, they are not part of active listening. The most effective notes are personal and reflect your background knowledge and understanding.

Likewise, using a tape recorder to take notes seems a good solution. After all, a recorder copies every word the instructor says. A recorder doesn't become bored, daydream, or doodle. It appears to be the perfect notetaking solution. On the other hand, using a tape recorder—like letting someone else speak for you—has drawbacks. First, listening to tapes is too time consuming. Transcribing them in their entirety contributes little to understanding the lecture's main ideas. Similar to underlining too much on a text page (see Chapter 5), writing each word the lecturer says decreases your ability to highlight important information. Second, because a tape recorder only records auditory information, your notes lack diagrams, terms, and other information that the instructor might have written on the board. Third, technical difficulties sometimes arise. Problems like dead batteries or missing tapes sometimes prevent you from getting the notes you need. Fourth, the use of tape recorders sometimes offends or intimidates instructors. Therefore, if you want to record notes, you need to get your instructor's permission before recording any lecture. Fifth, your reliance on recorders keeps you from learning good notetaking skills. The sixth and most important drawback is that, as with using borrowed notes, you are a passive listener.

There is a place for borrowed or taped notes, however. If you are ill or unavoidably absent from class, having someone else take or tape notes for you is better than not having notes at all. Another acceptable use of taped notes is to record the lecture while you take notes. Taped information allows you to fill gaps during review. Thus, this method is especially helpful if your instructor speaks rapidly. Like the telephone, taped notes are the next best thing to being there.

AFTER CLASS: THE FOLLOW-THROUGH

It is said that in the classroom there is more teaching than learning. Outside the classroom there is more learning than teaching. In class, you receive information from the instructor. After the lecture, your goal is to process that information. Thus, learning is not simply recording what you've seen or heard during the lecture. It's assimilating what you've seen and heard after the lecture. As a result, what you learn becomes a part of you. Post-lecture reading and evaluating your notes are the follow-through that allows you to truly assimilate course information.

GROUP LEARNING ACTIVITY   EFFECTIVE NOTETAKING—GOOD STUDENTS, TAKE NOTE!

Effective notetaking requires active listening. Active listeners know how to control their attention to avoid classroom daydreaming. Here's a listening/notetaking plan that works for many students. The important steps are summarized by the letters LISAN, pronounced like the word listen (Carman & Adams, 1985).

L = *Lead. Don't follow.* Try to anticipate what the instructor is going to say. Try to set up questions as guides. Questions can come from the instructor's study guides or the reading assignments.

I = *Ideas.* Every lecture is based on a core of important ideas. Usually, an idea is introduced and examples or explanations are given. Ask yourself often, "What is the main idea now? What ideas support it?"

S = *Signal words.* Listen for words that tell you the direction the instructor is taking. For instance, here are some groups of signal words: *There are three reasons why* . . . here come ideas, *most important is* . . . main idea, *on the contrary* . . . opposite idea, *as an example* . . . support for main ideas, *therefore* . . . conclusion.

A = *Actively listen.* Sit where you can hear and where you can be seen if you need to ask a question. Look at the instructor while he or she talks. Bring questions you want answered from the last lecture or from your reading. Raise your hand at the beginning of class or approach your instructor before the lecture begins. Do anything that helps you to be active.

N = *Notetaking.* As you listen, write down only key points. Listen to everything, but be selective and don't try to write everything down. If you are too busy writing, you may not grasp what is being said. Any gaps in your notes can be filled in immediately after class.

Here is something more you should know: A revealing study (Palkovitz & Lore, 1980) found that most students take reasonably good notes—and then don't use them! Most students wait until just before exams to review their notes. By then, the notes have lost much of their meaning. This practice may help explain why students do poorly on test items based on lectures (Thielens, 1987). If you don't want your notes to seem like hieroglyphics or "chicken scratches," it pays to review them *on a regular basis*. And remember, whenever it is important to listen effectively, the letters LISAN are a good guide.

SOURCE: Coon, D. (1997). *Introduction to Psychology, Exploration and Application.* Pacific Grove, CA: Brooks-Cole.

Application

Use LISAN in the next lecture for this class or ask your instructor to give a brief sample lecture. In your study group, compare answers to the following questions:

1. What did you do to lead? What questions did you have? Where did you get your questions?

2. What was the core of the lecture's content? What details supported that idea?

3. What signal words were used in the lecture?

4. What did you do to actively participate in the lecture? Did other group members take note of your active participation?

5. Are you satisfied with your notes? What, if any, gaps occurred? What precipitated these gaps? What could you do differently?

ONLINE CLASS

Web Exercise 4.1

A variety of information related to the topics in this chapter is available on the World Wide Web. For this exercise, access one of the following Web sites (for the most up-to-date URLs, go to http://csuccess.wadsworth.com):

Notetaking from How to Succeed as a Student at Griffith University:

> http://www.gu.edu.au/gwis/stubod/stuadv/stu_advice.html

Notetaking Skills from Sweet Briar College Academic Resource Center:

> http://www.arc.sbc.edu/notes.html

A System for Effective Listening and Notetaking from the Student Learning Center at the University of California at Berkeley:

> http://gbc-178-3.uga.berkeley.edu/CalRen/Listening1.html

Use the information you find to respond to the following:

On a separate sheet of paper or in your journal, create a chart that compares the content of the article with the corresponding information in this chapter. Circle the items as you use them. Then write a paragraph that describes how you could incorporate the items you don't use into your current system for notetaking or listening.

Postlecture Reading

After the lecture, you actually have been exposed to information on the lecture topic twice. First, you either previewed or read the chapter. Your second exposure was during the lecture. Postlecture reading helps you focus on the information emphasized in the lecture. If you previewed the text before the lecture, this final reading provides details, explanations, and examples to support the main ideas of the lecture. If you read the chapter in its entirely before the lecture, you should focus on the areas that confused you or that were emphasized in class. In both cases, post-lecture reading fills the gaps in your understanding.

Evaluating Your Notes

Notes organize the information you hear in a lecture—information that presumably will be the basis of a test. As a result, your notes need to be the best they can be for each course you take. Table 4.13 can be used to evaluate your notes—the higher the number, the better. Assess your notes for each course you take. Notetaking ability varies according to the content and demands of the class. Use Web Exercise 4.1 to find additional notetaking sources.

Table 4.13   Notes Evaluation Criteria

Value points and descriptors of notetaking habits

Format	4	3	2	1	0
Use of ink	I use my pen consistently		I use pen and pencil	I use pencil	
Handwriting	Others can read my notes		Only I can read my notes	I can't read my notes	
Notebook	I use a loose-leaf binder		I use a spiral notebook	I don't use a notebook	
Use of page	I leave enough space for editing		I leave some space for editing	My notes cover the page	

Organization	4	3	2	1	0
Headings	I use new headings for each main idea		I use headings inconsistently	I don't use headings for changes in main ideas	
Subtopics	I group subtopics under headings		I don't indent subtopics under headings	My subtopics are not grouped	
Recall column	I use cue words and symbols to make practice questions		I use cue words in a recall column	I do not use a recall column	
Abbreviation	I abbreviate whenever possible		I use some abbreviation	I don't abbreviate	
Summaries	I summarize lectures in writing		I write a list of summary lecture topics	I don't summarize	

Meaning	4	3	2	1	0
Main points	I identify main points with symbols and underlining		I list main points	I don't list main points	
Supporting details	I show the relationships between main ideas and details		My notes list details	I don't list all details	
Examples	I list examples under main points		I list some examples	I don't record examples	
Restatement	I use my own words		I use some of my own words	I use none of my own words	

SOURCE: Reprinted with permission of Norman A. Stahl and the International Reading Association.

CHAPTER SUMMARY

1. Strategies for previewing the text before class helps you build background knowledge for course content. These include making predictions about content, constructing a notetaking outline through text previewing, and using chapter maps to direct your learning.

2. Several factors affect your ability to listen actively in class and communicate effectively with your instructor, the speaker. These include the abilities to maintain concentration, hear main ideas, identify important information, and recall what you hear. Although your listening responsibilities vary according to the speaker's style, you can develop a plan for maximizing your understanding of the speaker's message. As an active listener, you control the learning process and integrate what you already know with what you hear.

3. Lectures formats vary according to whether they are text-dependent, text-independent, or include media.

4. Taking notes enhances active listening. Your systematic approach to notetaking could be based on your personal system, the Cornell system, or another system. Taking notes from lecture media requires some modification of your notetaking strategy. Passive notetaking methods are less effective because they fail to reflect your own background knowledge and purposes for learning.

5. The follow-through for notetaking occurs after class when you begin to assimilate information through post-lecture reading. Periodic evaluation of your notes for all your classes helps you assess weaknesses and formulate strategies for improvement.

ClassACTION

Respond to the following on a separate sheet of paper or in your journal. Combine the chapter map and chapter summary to form a synthesis map which reflects the main ideas and important details of this chapter. Personalize the map by indicating specific ways in which you plan to implement suggestions offered by this chapter.

CHAPTER REVIEW

Answer briefly but completely.

1. Examine the textbooks you use for each of your classes (or the sample chapters in this text). How do factors within the text impact your choice of previewing strategy for making predictions about content?

   _____

   _____

   _____

   _____

2. Compare and contrast Table 4.1, *Steps in Previewing*, with Table 4.3, *Constructing a Notetaking Outline Through Text Previews*. How are the tables alike? How are they different? What accounts for their similarities and differences?

   _____

   _____

   _____

   _____

   _____

3. Explain how differing lecture formats (text-dependent, text-independent, with media) might affect left-brain and right-brain learning.

   _____

   _____

   _____

   _____

4. How do the listening habits in Exercise 4.5 affect your ability to understand and process a class lecture? Why?

   _____

   _____

   _____

   _____

5. What is the relationship between the factors affecting your ability to be an active listener and the items in Table 4.8, *Rating Checklist for Instructors?*

   _____

   _____

   _____

TERMS

Terms appear in the order in which they occurred in the chapter.

- background knowledge
- previewing
- notetaking outline
- chapter maps
- distractions
- self-talk
- transition words
- lecture patterns
- terms
- curve of forgetting
- active listening
- outlining

6. Which of Peper and Mayer's three theories of notetaking do you feel best supports the Cornell system of notetaking? Why?

_____

_____

_____

7. How do formal and informal outline formats (see Figure 4.5) affect right- and left-brain learning? Why?

_____

_____

_____

8. A notetaking service has just opened near your institution. It sells copies of the entire set of notes for each of the classes in which you are now enrolled. What might be the advantages of having these copies? What would be the disadvantages?

_____

_____

_____

9. How does the after-class follow-through affect the curve of forgetting (Figure 4.3)?

_____

_____

_____

10. Give a specific example of how course content and demands affect note-taking ability.

_____

_____

_____

_____

VOCABULARY DEVELOPMENT   Integrating Listening and Notetaking: Connecting What You Learn with What You Know

Consider Legos. Some people think of college vocabulary development as a building process much as children build with Legos. These people think words are like blocks that can be placed one on top of the other. Words, however, connect to each other in a variety of ways with many connections or only a few. The way you think about information and the connections you make affect what you hear and how you note it. Vocabulary development increases when you connect what you learn with what you know.

Background knowledge forms your personal set of mental Legos for connecting new information with what you already know. You make these connections as you listen to a lecture. You use the words you hear to cue the information you know. The information you know helps you make sense of and learn more about the topic. Vocabulary development is more efficient because learning something you already know about is easier than learning something you know nothing about. Notes that reflect your reactions, feelings, and connections, as well as lecture content, help you integrate new information more fully.

Background knowledge consists of everything you know about a topic. It is your knowledge of language and the world. Your knowledge of language consists of two areas: vocabulary and grammar.

Your vocabulary contributes to your knowledge of language. Your personal vocabulary consists of four subsets: listening, speaking, writing, and reading. Your listening vocabulary consists of words you understand when you hear them. Your speaking vocabulary includes words you use in talking, just as your writing vocabulary contains words you use in writing. Finally, the words you know when you see them constitute your reading vocabulary.

These four types of vocabulary can be divided into two groups, according to their use. The first group consists of those words you deposit in memory through listening and reading. The second group encompasses those words you use in speaking and writing (see Figure V4.1). You increase your listening vocabulary, the largest of the four types, with the least effort. Anything you hear (television, radio, teachers, friends, and so forth) enlarges your listening vocabulary. Similarly, your reading vocabulary increases each time you find the meanings of new words. Both reading and listening involve actively receiving new information. Speaking and writing are the ways you use the words you learn. If you make no deposits, you have no words to use.

The second area of language knowledge is grammar. Even if English isn't your favorite subject, you possess much knowledge about the English language. Your knowledge of words and their functions in sentences allows you to find meaning.

Figure V4.1   Four Types of Vocabulary

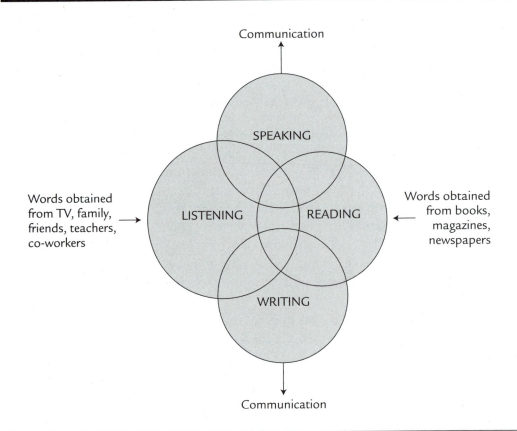

Communication

SPEAKING

Words obtained from TV, family, friends, teachers, co-workers →

LISTENING   READING

← Words obtained from books, magazines, newspapers

WRITING

Communication

Your knowledge of punctuation also helps you find meaning. This process is cyclical. The more you know about how language functions, the more you are able to learn. The more you are able to learn, the more you know. Knowledge of language aids you in becoming a more active listener. Active listening, in turn, helps you increase your language knowledge.

World knowledge comes from the sum of your experiences. It consists of what you know about the way people, places, things, and concepts work and relate to each other. It includes facts, opinions, inferences, and other information you get through direct experience or through vicarious learning.

For example, it's one thing to go to France. It's another to read about going to France. Although both provide you with information about the country, the direct experience of traveling to France provides you with more complete and direct information. The sights, sounds, and feelings you experience are your own. However, time, money, or other factors can keep you from taking such a trip. You can still learn about France vicariously through reading, television, Web sites, movies, travel brochures, conversations with people who have been there, and so on. The quantity and quality of the information you get depends on the viewpoints, experiences, and perceptions of your sources. Active listening also increases your store of world knowledge.

Activity

In the space following the quote, list the things you associate with the phrase

"Every man a king but no one wears a crown."

Now read the following passage from a biography of Huey Long, Louisiana governor in the 1930s (Williams, 1969). After reading, add to your list in a different color ink. On a separate sheet of paper, respond to the following question: How did the passage affect your consideration of the topic? What accounts for the differences in before and after reading? What happens when you connect what you learn with what you know? What happens if you fail to connect what you learn with what you know?

Above the platform stretched banners proclaiming the Long slogan: "Every Man a King, But No One Wears a Crown." John H. Overton presided and introduced the dignitaries on the platform, among whom were John P. Sullivan and Swords Lee, and the candidate who was also the speaker of the evening. Huey gave the same kind of speech that he had given in launching his campaign four years before.... He wanted to make Louisiana into "a progressive, educated and modern commonwealth." He promised free textbooks, free bridges, surfaced roads ("practically every public road" should be surfaced), improved state hospitals and other institutions, natural gas for New Orleans and other cities, state warehouses to aid farmers in marketing their crops, vocational training for the deaf, dumb, and blind, and an expanded court system. He strongly implied that the state should supply financial assistance to local school units (every boy and girl should be able to live at home and have access to an education) and to students of poor families who wished to attend higher institutions. He denied that he was hostile to corporations. He had opposed only the evil ones, but he thought that all the big ones should bear a higher and fairer burden of taxation.

CHAPTER 5

SQ3R: A Systematic Plan for Reading Text Chapters

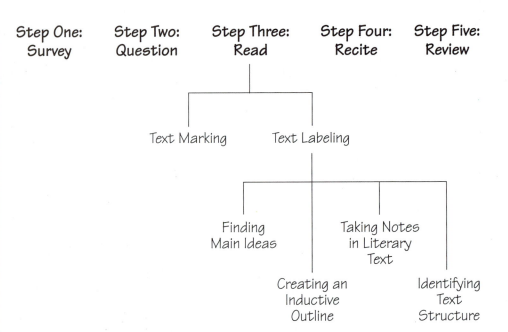

Step One: Survey

Step Two: Question

Step Three: Read

Step Four: Recite

Step Five: Review

Text Marking

Text Labeling

Finding Main Ideas

Creating an Inductive Outline

Taking Notes in Literary Text

Identifying Text Structure

The president was introducing the commencement speaker and Kate forced herself to concentrate. A plump woman in her fifties took the podium, her plain, stern-lipped face was hazily familiar as that which in photographs of feminist rallies, usually appeared just behind that of Friedan or Steinem.

"I envy you women," she was saying. "The path is so clearly marked for you. There will be no need for you to repeat the mistakes of my generation. The obstacles that blocked us now exist only for you to hurdle. You will be free to go out and have anything and everything you want!"

Kate listened attentively. The message was clear: Go out and do something and be sure that it is creative and meaningful, that it gives you power and above all makes you a success. But now the speaker was retiring from the podium. Wait! Kate shrieked silently. Don't go yet! You haven't told us what that something is, nor shown us how to get it. The path isn't clear . . . no, not clear at all.

SOURCE: Reprinted with permission from *Everything We Wanted* by Lindsay Marcotta. Copyright © 1984 by Lindsay Marcotta.

As a student, you face a challenge in each class you take. Like Kate, you know what is expected of you—good grades, a degree, a new job. You probably have a general idea of what you need to do to meet your goals. You know that studying and preparing for class lead to success. Also like Kate, you might feel that you have no specific plan to help you accomplish the necessary tasks (reading texts, reviewing information) for achieving your goal.

Such a plan exists for using information from texts. Developed by Frances Robinson, the SQ3R study system has been used by countless students to help them read and recall text information. SQ3R involves five steps: *survey, question, read, recite,* and *review.* Table 5.1 defines all steps of the SQ3R process and also provides a quick index of where additional information about each step is found.

STEP ONE: SURVEY

Surveying, or previewing, is the first step in your interaction with the text. Surveying before reading accomplishes two goals. First, it makes reading an active, rather than a passive, process. Surveying requires you to think about the topic of the chapter before you begin reading. Second, it provides you with an opportunity to connect what you already know about the topic, your background knowledge, with the new information you will be learning. How does your background knowledge affect your understanding? Read the passage below and answer the accompanying questions.

Table 5.1   Steps in SQ3R

SQ3R Step	Definition	Process Used
Survey	Previewing to find main ideas or get the gist of chapter.	Previewing. See Table 4.1.
Question	Predicting chapter content or setting purposes for reading.	Making predictions about content. See Table 4.2.
Read	Checking your predictions through literal and inferential comprehension.	Reading or processing text and scanning. See Tables 5.3, 5.4, 5.5, and 5.6 and Figure 5.3.
Recite	Checking your understanding of the text.	Monitoring understanding. See Table 5.9.
Review	Transferring information from short-term to long-term memory.	Rehearsal through practice, organization, and association. See Chapter 7.

The procedure is actually quite simple. First you arrange things into different groups. Of course, one pile may be sufficient depending on how much there is to do. If you have to go somewhere else due to lack of facilities that is the next step; otherwise, you are pretty well set. It is important not to overdo things. That is, it is better to do too few things at once than too many. In the short run this may not seem important but complications can easily arise. A mistake can be expensive as well. At first the whole procedure will seem complicated. Soon, however, it will become just another facet of life. It is difficult to foresee any end to the necessity for this task in the immediate future, but then one can never tell. After the procedure is completed one arranges the materials into different groups again. Then they can be put into their appropriate places. Eventually they will be used once more and the whole cycle will then have to be repeated. However, that is part of life.

Source: Reprinted with permission from Contextual Prerequisites for Understanding: Some Investigations of Comprehension and Recall. By Bransford, J. D., and Johnson, M. K. Copyright © 1972 by *Journal of Verbal Learning and Verbal Behavior* 2:6. All rights reserved.

1. What is the topic of this passage?
2. What do you know about this topic?
3. In the first sentence, what procedure is being referred to?
4. How did you identify this procedure?
5. The passage states that after putting things into different groups, you might have to go somewhere else due to lack of facilities. What place does "somewhere else" refer to?

6. How do you recognize the location of "somewhere else?"

7. The passage states that mistakes could be expensive. What does that mean?

8. Why is there no foreseeable end to this procedure?

The topic of the passage is identified on the bottom of the last page in this chapter. After you have checked the topic, answer questions 2 through 8 again.

How was your understanding improved by knowing the topic? Although the passage contained no more information than when you first read it, you—the learner—provided the details needed to understand it. Before you knew the topic, you had no way to interact with the information. Without information supplied by you, it made little sense.

When you learn, information comes from two sources: one external, the other internal. The text is an external source of information. You, the learner, are the internal source.

Many students learn without making the most of the interaction of internal and external sources. Because you are a less obvious source of information, you might not have thought of yourself as a source.

The survey step in SQ3R allows you to maximize yourself as a source of information in learning. Surveying usually is part of your before-lecture preparation. As such, surveying, or previewing, was described in Chapter 4, Table 4.1. Creating a chapter map (see Table 4.4) also provides a means of previewing chapter content.

STEP TWO: QUESTION

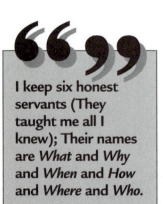

I keep six honest servants (They taught me all I knew); Their names are *What* and *Why* and *When* and *How* and *Where* and *Who.*

—Rudyard Kipling
*Nineteenth century
English author*

For many students, the goal of reading is to finish. Whether or not they learn anything is beside the point as long as they meet their goal.

Your goals for learning should be part of a quest for knowledge. Employing Kipling's six servants assists you in your quest by helping you set goals for understanding what you read. Although you set your goals by asking questions as part of the before-lecture process as described on in Chapter 4, you find the answers to your questions through reading—Step 3 of the SQ3R process. Table 5.2 summarizes the kinds of information that each of your "honest servants" helps you find.

STEP THREE: READ

If you have ever bought a product marked "Some Assembly Required," you know how vital it is to preview the diagrams and read carefully all of the directions before beginning. This thorough reading, in combination with your preview, provides you with all available information before you tackle your task.

Table 5.2   Question Words and Corresponding Indicators

If your question begins . . .	Look for . . . when you read.
Why?	Words such as *because, for that reason, consequently, as a result*
How?	A sequence; a list; or words such as *by, through, as a result of*
What?	Nouns; linking verbs; punctuation symbols (commas, dashes, parentheses); words such as *involves, consists, includes*
Who?	Capitalized words or names of groups; nouns
How many? How much?	Numbers (written or Arabic)
Which?	Nouns and adjectives
When?	Capitalized words such as days, months, or other time periods; time of the day (written or Arabic); numerical symbols for months, days, and years; words like *before, during, after, soon, later, prior*
Where?	Capitalized places (cities, states, countries); addresses; words such as *behind, across, near, next to*

Similarly, reading a chapter in its entirety before class helps you glean all important details and main ideas for use during class. Rather than encountering new ideas in the lecture, you affirm what you read and clarify misconceptions. Your background knowledge enables you to grasp new ideas more quickly and firmly.

To get the most from reading you must do more than simply sit and stare at a text. In the second step of SQ3R, you posed questions. Now you need to actively seek their answers. This means that you look for patterns, or connections, among information. You consider the meanings of terms in their surroundings. You try to summarize main ideas. You draw conclusions. You attend critically to the information in the text. One way to ensure that you read actively is to mark your text as you read. Table 5.3 summarizes the reading process.

Text Marking

Text marking sounds simple. You find important information and mark it. You highlight or underline what you want to remember. But what exactly do you mark? How do you know what is really important? How do you know what to "overlook?"

Table 5.3   Steps in the Reading Process

1. Keeping your purpose-setting question in mind, read the paragraph or passage.

2. Identify the topic by looking for the repetition of key words and phrases. If the main idea is unstated, identify the topic by retrieving background knowledge that seems appropriate until details confirm or disprove your choice.

3. Retrieve the background knowledge necessary to understand the text.

4. Based on elements in the text and your background knowledge, identify stated details and make inferences about new terms or concepts.

5. Make inferences about unstated details or the text pattern of the main idea.

6. Restate the main idea through paraphrasing, summarizing, or synthesizing.

7. Determine if the main idea answers your purpose-setting question.

The art of becoming wise is the art of knowing what to overlook.

—William James
Nineteenth century American psychologist

First, what you mark depends on how much you already know about the topic. Consider what might happen if you were studying about the settlement of Salt Lake City. If you're from Salt Lake City, you'd probably mark less. This is because you might already know some of the information. In contrast, if you know little about Salt Lake City, you'll probably mark more. In general, the less you know, the more you mark. The more you know, the less you mark.

Second, if you previewed and asked content-predicting questions, what you mark should answer your questions. As a result, you mark the information that highlights terms and main ideas.

You might also include other details that support your answers to your questions. These could be the steps in a sequence or other kinds of lists, reasons, conclusions, and so on. Knowing which and what kind of details your instructor deems most important helps you choose what to mark.

The difficulty of text language is a third factor to consider in text marking. Although how difficult you find a topic to be depends on your familiarity with that topic, its difficulty also depends on how it is written or presented. Such factors as subject depth, number of details. and vocabulary affect the ease with which you understand.

As you read the following excerpts, note their differing lengths. Although both passages concern the same topic, their content differs. The second passage includes more details and provides more information about the subject. In addition, the vocabulary (see bold-faced italicized words) is much more difficult.

PASSAGE 1

Babbage did not give up, however. In 1833 he developed a plan for building an *analytical engine*. This machine was to be capable of addition, subtraction, multiplication, division, and storage of intermediate results in a memory unit. Unfortunately, the analytical engine was also too advanced for its time. It was Babbage's concept of the analytical engine, though, that led to the computer more than a hundred years later. This earned him the title of "the father of modern computers."

PASSAGE 2

One reason Babbage *abandoned* the Difference Engine was that he had been struck by a much better idea. Inspired by Jacquard's punched-card-controlled loom, Babbage wanted to build a punched-card-controlled calculator. He called his proposed automatic calculator the *Analytical Engine*.

The Difference Engine could only compute tables (and only those tables that could be computed by successive additions). But the Analytical Engine could carry out any calculation, just as Jacquard's loom could weave any pattern. All one had to do was to punch the cards with the instructions for the desired calculations. If the Analytical Engine had been completed, it would have been a nineteenth-century computer.

But, alas, that was not to be. The British government had already sunk thousands of pounds into the Difference Engine and had received nothing in return. It had no intention of making the same mistake with the Analytical Engine. And Babbage's *eccentricities* and *abrasive* personality did not help his cause.

Looking back, the government may have even been right. If it had *financed* the new invention, it might well have received nothing in return. For, as usual, Babbage's idea was far ahead of existing mechanical technology. This was particularly true because the design for the Analytical Engine was *grandiose*. For example, Babbage wanted his machine to do calculations with fifty-digit accuracy, an accuracy far greater than that found in most modem computers and far more than is needed for most calculations.

What's more, Babbage often changed his plans in the middle of a project, so that everything done previously had to be abandoned and the work started anew. How *ironic* that the founder of operations research, the science of industrial management, could not manage the development of his own inventions.

Babbage's *contemporaries* would have considered him more successful if, he had stayed with his original plan and constructed the Difference Engine. If he had done this, however, he would have earned only a footnote in history. It is for the Analytical Engine he never completed that we honor Babbage as "the father of the computer."

Your goal should be to mark amounts of information that are "just right." Consider the two examples of text marking found in Examples 5.1 and 5.2. In Example 5.1, the student marked too much information to be useful for study. Remember that the purpose of text marking is to tell the difference between important and unimportant information. Here, there is no difference. Even if you know nothing about a subject, you should be marking half or less of the information.

In Example 5.2, the student marked too little information. This could mean that the student already felt confident about understanding the information. It also could signal a lack of attention, poor understanding, or a lack of knowledge about what to mark.

Now consider the text marked in Example 5.3. It shows the "just right" amount of text marking. Remember, although the amount you mark depends on what you know about the topic, the difficulty of the text, the goal-setting questions you posed, and what you think your instructor will ask questions about, overmarking results in nothing gained but a neon-colored page.

Text Labeling

Imagine that you take a trip and have gotten lost. When you ask for directions, a friendly citizen gets a map and highlights the route you should take. Thanking your new friend, you start off once more. When you look at the map, however, you find no names for streets, buildings, or other locations. Although you might be able to reach your destination, it will take more effort to get there.

Much the same problem occurs in text marking. Many students read and mark information, just to find themselves somewhat "lost" when they have to study. Only with effort can they reconstruct why they marked their texts as they did.

Consider again the marked text in Example 5.3. Most students would agree that, just by looking, it appears to be appropriately marked. However, reviewing for a test several weeks later, you might forget how the information relates. You would need to reread most of what you marked to reconstruct your thoughts.

Example 5.1   Overmarking Text

Organizing Course Content to Set Reading Goals

Think again about how you best learn information (see Chapter 1). Outlines and maps help you predict and organize information while surveying. This is particularly true if you rephrase headings and subheadings into questions or connect chapter titles with headings and subheadings to questions. Questions require you to look for answers and thus, make reading more active. You read to answer *what, how, when, who, which, where,* and *why.* (see Table 2.3). When previewing, you will normally be looking for main ideas. Thus, *why, how,* and *what* questions will form the basis of your previewing outline. Question outlines and maps make previewing less covert and more concrete. They help set goals for reading.

Organizing Through Outlining

An outline consists of a written collection of ideas ranked according to importance. Every idea is subordinate to or summarized by another idea. Thus, an outline forms an ordered picture of information. You determine importance based on the ways in which ideas fit together.

One way of organizing information in a chapter is outlining it. The subject of the chapter serves as the subject of your outline. The question you created from each major heading in the chapter is a major heading in your outline. Each question you formed from a subheading becomes a minor heading. Information found under subheadings becomes questions about supporting details.

Outlines can be formal or informal formats (see Table 2.4). The formal format uses Roman numerals (I, II, III) placed on the left side of the page or margin to note major concepts. You indent ideas that support the major concepts. You indicate these secondary points by capitalizing them. You show lesser supporting details by indented Arabic numerals (1, 2, 3). You note details that refer to these third-level facts with lowercase letters (a, b, c).

Informal outlines look much like formal outlines. The key difference is that they don't follow the Roman and Arabic numeral format. Instead, white space or other symbols identify major and minor points. The purpose of the outline is to organize ideas and the structure of the outline adds little to understanding. Informal outlines are just as useful as formal outlines.

Organizing Through Mapping

Maps provide a quick means for determining the plan of a chapter. They form pictures that show relationships among concepts. In addition, they express patterns of thought. You sketch a map by using headings and subheadings in a combination boxed-branching format (see Table 2.5 and Figure 2.1). You place each question you created from major headings in separate boxes horizontally (from left to right) in the order in which they appear in the chapter. You then arrange questions about subheadings in a branching formation within the box.

Example 5.2   Undermarking Text

Organizing Course Content to Set Reading Goals

Think again about how you best learn information (see Chapter 1). Outlines and maps help you predict and organize information while surveying. This is particularly true if you rephrase headings and subheadings into questions or connect chapter titles with headings and subheadings to questions. Questions require you to look for answers and thus, make reading more active. You read to answer *what, how, when, who, which, where,* and *why.* (see Table 2.3). When previewing, you will normally be looking for main ideas. Thus, *why, how,* and *what* questions will form the basis of your previewing outline. Question outlines and maps make previewing less covert and more concrete. They help set goals for reading.

Organizing Through Outlining

An outline consists of a written collection of ideas ranked according to importance. Every idea is subordinate to or summarized by another idea. Thus, an outline forms an ordered picture of information. You determine importance based on the ways in which ideas fit together.

One way of organizing information in a chapter is outlining it. The subject of the chapter serves as the subject of your outline. The question you created from each major heading in the chapter is a major heading in your outline. Each question you formed from a subheading becomes a minor heading. Information found under subheadings becomes questions about supporting details.

Outlines can be formal or informal formats (see Table 2.4). The formal format uses Roman numerals (I, II, III) placed on the left side of the page or margin to note major concepts. You indent ideas that support the major concepts. You indicate these secondary points by capitalizing them. You show lesser supporting details by indented Arabic numerals (1, 2, 3). You note details that refer to these third-level facts with lowercase letters (a, b, c).

Informal outlines look much like formal outlines. The key difference is that they don't follow the Roman and Arabic numeral format. Instead, white space or other symbols identify major and minor points. The purpose of the outline is to organize ideas and the structure of the outline adds little to understanding. Informal outlines are just as useful as formal outlines.

Organizing Through Mapping

Maps provide a quick means for determining the plan of a chapter. They form pictures that show relationships among concepts. In addition, they express patterns of thought. You sketch a map by using headings and subheadings in a combination boxed-branching format (see Table 2.5 and Figure 2.1). You place each question you created from major headings in separate boxes horizontally (from left to right) in the order in which they appear in the chapter. You then arrange questions about subheadings in a branching formation within the box.

Example 5.3 Text Marking

Organizing Course Content to Set Reading Goals

Think again about how you best learn information (see Chapter 1). Outlines and maps help you predict and organize information while surveying. This is particularly true if you rephrase headings and subheadings into questions or connect chapter titles with headings and subheadings to questions. Questions require you to look for answers and thus, make reading more active. You read to answer *what, how, when, who, which, where,* and *why.* (see Table 2.3). When previewing, you will normally be looking for main ideas. Thus, *why, how,* and *what* questions will form the basis of your previewing outline. Question outlines and maps make previewing less covert and more concrete. They help set goals for reading.

Organizing Through Outlining

An outline consists of a written collection of ideas ranked according to importance. Every idea is subordinate to or summarized by another idea. Thus, an outline forms an ordered picture of information. You determine importance based on the ways in which ideas fit together.

One way of organizing information in a chapter is outlining it. The subject of the chapter serves as the subject of your outline. The question you created from each major heading in the chapter is a major heading in your outline. Each question you formed from a subheading becomes a minor heading. Information found under subheadings becomes questions about supporting details.

Outlines can be formal or informal formats (see Table 2.4). The formal format uses Roman numerals (I, II, III) placed on the left side of the page or margin to note major concepts. You indent ideas that support the major concepts. You indicate these secondary points by capitalizing them. You show lesser supporting details by indented Arabic numerals (1, 2, 3). You note details that refer to these third-level facts with lowercase letters (a, b, c).

Informal outlines look much like formal outlines. The key difference is that they don't follow the Roman and Arabic numeral format. Instead, white space or other symbols identify major and minor points. The purpose of the outline is to organize ideas and the structure of the outline adds little to understanding. Informal outlines are just as useful as formal outlines.

Organizing Through Mapping

Maps provide a quick means for determining the plan of a chapter. They form pictures that show relationships among concepts. In addition, they express patterns of thought. You sketch a map by using headings and subheadings in a combination boxed-branching format (see Table 2.5 and Figure 2.1). You place each question you created from major headings in separate boxes horizontally (from left to right) in the order in which they appear in the chapter. You then arrange questions about subheadings in a branching formation within the box.

Text labeling helps you identify relationships and summarize information. It does not replace text marking. Instead, you use it in addition to text marking. Text labeling forms a kind of index to help you locate information more quickly. You also use it to write yourself notes for later review.

Text marking and labeling require several steps (see Table 5.4). First, you read and mark your text. Then you look for patterns, main ideas, and ways to summarize information. Once you've thought of one or two summary words, you write them in the column next to that information. Finally, you include any notes to yourself about how and what to study (see Example 5.4).

Finding Main Ideas

Every chapter and every paragraph of a text has a main idea, a central thought. The main ideas and supporting details of each paragraph support the key concept of the chapter. Sometimes, but not always, a topic sentence tells you the main idea; this sentence usually appears at the beginning or end of the reading but can appear anywhere. To answer your goal-setting questions and understand how information in a section relates to the chapter, you must locate and label main ideas.

Table 5.4   Guidelines for Marking and Labeling Text

1. Read a paragraph or section completely before marking anything.

2. Mark those points that comprise the answer to your purpose-setting question.

3. Number lists, reasons, or other items that occur in a series or sequence.

4. Identify important terms, dates, places, names, and so on.

5. Be selective in marking. If you identify every line as important, you lose the benefit of text marking. If you are not good at being selective, mark your textbook in pencil first. Then, go back with a colored pen or highlighter and selectively mark important information.

6. Write main idea summaries, questions, or other comments in the margins.

7. Put a question mark beside unclear or confusing information.

8. Put a star or exclamation point beside information your instructor emphasizes in class, possible test questions, or what seems to be extremely important information.

9. Write comments on the table of contents or make your own table of contents of important topics inside the front cover or on the title page of the text.

10. When buying a used text, never choose one that's been underlined by another student.

Example 5.4 Text Labeling

Stated Information:
  Outlines/Maps = ways to
  organize info

Organizing Course Content to Set Reading Goals

Think again about how you best learn information (see Chapter 1). Outlines and maps help you predict and organize information while surveying. This is particularly true if you rephrase headings and subheadings into questions or connect chapter titles with headings and subheadings to questions. Questions require you to look for answers and thus, make reading more active. You read to answer *what, how, when, who, which, where,* and *why.* (see Table 2.3). When previewing, you will normally be looking for main ideas. Thus, *why, how,* and *what* questions will form the basis of your previewing outline. Question outlines and maps make previewing less covert and more concrete. They help set goals for reading.

Translation:
  Main Ideas = why, how,
  what

Application:
  maps/outlines also used
  for test preparation??

Organizing Through Outlining

An outline consists of a written collection of ideas ranked according to importance. Every idea is subordinate to or summarized by another idea. Thus, an outline forms an ordered picture of information. You determine importance based on the ways in which ideas fit together.

Conclusion:
  Heading questions: focus
  attention

One way of organizing information in a chapter is outlining it. The subject of the chapter serves as the subject of your outline. The question you created from each major heading in the chapter is a major heading in your outline. Each question you formed from a subheading becomes a minor heading. Information found under subheadings becomes questions about supporting details.

Analysis:
  comparison/contrast of
  outline formats

Outlines can be formal or informal formats (see Table 2.4). The formal format uses Roman numerals (I, II, III) placed on the left side of the page or margin to note major concepts. You indent ideas that support the major concepts. You indicate these secondary points by capitalizing them. You show lesser supporting details by indented Arabic numerals (1, 2, 3). You note details that refer to these third-level facts with lowercase letters (a, b, c).

Informal outlines look much like formal outlines. The key difference is that they don't follow the Roman and Arabic numeral format. Instead, white space or other symbols identify major and minor points. The purpose of the outline is to organize ideas and the structure of the outline adds little to understanding. Informal outlines are just as useful as formal outlines.

Comment:
  Good idea!

Organizing Through Mapping

Stated Information:
  Mapping process

Synthesis:
  Maps: right-brain learning
  Outlines: left-brain
  learning

Maps provide a quick means for determining the plan of a chapter. They form pictures that show relationships among concepts. In addition, they express patterns of thought. You sketch a map by using headings and subheadings in a combination boxed-branching format (see Table 2.5 and Figure 2.1). You place each question you created from major headings in separate boxes horizontally (from left to right) in the order in which they appear in the chapter. You then arrange questions about subheadings in a branching formation within the box.

Look at the following paragraph.

TWO THEORIES OF POWER

The two major theories of power are *pluralism* and *elitism*. According to the *theory of pluralism,* decision-making is the result of competition, bargaining, and compromise among diverse *special interest groups*. In this view, *power* is widely distributed throughout a *society* or *community*. On the other hand, according to the theory of *elitism,* a *community* or *society* is controlled from the top by a few individuals or organizations. *Power* is said to be concentrated in the hands of an *elite* group with common interests and background.

SOURCE: Reprinted with permission from *Sociology,* 2d ed., by Shepard. © 1984 by West Publishing Company. All rights reserved.

To find the main idea of the preceding paragraph, first create a purpose-setting question from the heading. Here, the question might be "What are two theories of power?" Then read the paragraph to identify key words and phrases. (Italics highlight key words for you in the example.) You now look to see what idea the sentences share (that is, two theories of power—elitism and pluralism—affect societies and communities). Next, you decide if the key concept answers your purpose-setting question. Yes, your prediction is verified. Now, create a label that states the key concept. In this case, your label might read *Two theories of power—elitism and pluralism—affect societies and communities.*

Now consider the following paragraph:

THE FIRST BUG

The first "bug" was found in the summer of 1945. The Mark II computer used by the Department of Defense suddenly stopped functioning. Routine checks found no problems. The search continued until a moth, which became stuck in one of the computer's relays, was located. Since then, the term has come to mean any hardware malfunction or software error which affects the ability of the computer to run.

Before reading, your purpose-setting question probably was "What was the first bug?" Perhaps you then inferred that the paragraph would have something to do with insects. Thus, you chose that background to use in understanding the text. As you read, you quickly found that you lacked details to support that topic. The second sentence probably led you to retrieve knowledge related to computers. Based on text elements and your knowledge about computers, you understood references to terms such as *hardware, software, computer relays,* and *run*. You inferred that the people who located the moth coined the term bug, filling that element by default. Therefore, you conclude that the main idea is that the first bug in computer technology was a moth and that the term bug became synonymous with a computer malfunction. This inferred main idea answers the question "What was the first bug?" Your label for this paragraph might

---

Table 5.5   **Shorthand Symbols for Text Labeling**

Symbol	Meaning
Ex	Example or Experiment
FORM	Formula
Conc	Conclusion
MI	Main Idea
! or *	Important Information
→	Results, Leads to, Steps in a Sequence
(1), (2), (3)	Numbered Points—Label What Points Are Important
circled word	Summarizes Process
?	Disagree or Unclear
TERM	Important TERM
SUM	Summary
{	Indicates that Certain Pieces of Information Relate
OPIN	Author's Opinion, Rather than Fact

---

read: *The first computer bug was a moth that caused trouble; now* bug *refers to a part of the computer process that causes trouble.*

The examples of labels for these paragraphs are complete sentences. When you label your text, often there is not room in the text or time in your life to write complete sentences. Then, you identify the main idea and abbreviate your main idea statement. For example, an abbreviation of the last example could be as follows: 1st computer bug = moth → TROUBLE—now "computer bug" = TROUBLE.

A list of some simple shorthand symbols and their meanings appears in Table 5.5. This list changes depending on your needs and the course you take. Be careful not to abbreviate too much. You need to be able to decode your labels when studying. Practice labeling in Exercise 5.1, using Sample Chapter 11 at the back of this book.

WRITE TO LEARN

Consider again the quote by William James that accompanies the section on text marking: "The art of becoming wise is the art of knowing what to overlook." On a separate sheet of paper or in your journal, explain this quote in light of what you have learned about text marking and labeling.

Exercise 5.1   Read, mark, and label each paragraph of Sample Chapter 11 ("Organizing the Police Department") in the margins of the sample chapter.

Exercise 5.2   Create an inductive outline for Sample Chapter 13 ("Concepts in Human Biology") on a separate sheet of paper or in your journal.

Creating an Inductive Outline

Have you ever heard the expression, "He's on a fishing expedition?" It dates back to 1682 and literally refers to a long sea voyage. Today, it implies someone who possesses little information that a wrongdoing has occurred but who still looks carefully for evidence of it. When you create an **inductive outline** to locate main ideas, you go on a fishing expedition, with one notable difference. You know there's a main idea lurking in the content from which you fish.

When you make an inductive outline, you reduce information from major concepts to specific main ideas. To do so, you follow the steps outlined in Table 5.6. An example of an inductive outline is found in Table 5.7. Notice that if you read from right to left, you see a traditional outline form. The difference is that instead of outlining major concepts first (and then finding supporting details), you outline supporting details and generalize major concepts. Use Exercise 5.2 to practice making an inductive outline.

Taking Notes in Literary Text

Reading narrative text or poetry in a literature class demands a specialized notetaking process. This process allows you to go beyond simple recall of details to a more complex level of understanding, a dimension where you compare, contrast, synthesize, and evaluate text for word choice, figurative language, theme, plot, character, tone, setting, and literary type.

When an instructor assigns literary selections as part of course requirements, he or she usually outlines the purpose for your reading. Such tasks might include summarizing the reading, analyzing character development, or delineating plot. On the other hand, sometimes instructors make assignments without providing needed instructions. When this happens, you can feel lost in setting goals for yourself. After all, narrative text, like nontraditional texts, contains no special features to guide your reading. Thus, the strategies you use for creating reading goals, marking, and labeling for nontraditional text work equally well for narrative text. Furthermore, Table 5.8 provides guidelines for previewing, reading, and evaluating narrative text.

Table 5.6   Steps in Creating an Inductive Outline

1. Write the title of the chapter in the center of your notebook page.

2. Indicate the page number of the piece of text you are summarizing. Be sure to show when this page number changes on your outline.

3. Create three vertical columns in your notebook. Label the first column, *What are the facts?* Label the second column, *What is their immediate significance?* Label the third column, *What is their larger significance?*

4. Take notes *in your own words* on the first paragraph of the text, noting italicized words and definitions, lists, steps, and so forth. Be sure to number each paragraph in consecutive order.

5. Complete the entire section of text before you proceed to the second column.

6. Reread your notes in the first column. What do you see as the overall significance of these notes? Do you detect a trend? Are any concepts repeated? Can you group any of the notes together? Summarize and record these labeling them consecutively as *A, B, C,* and so forth.

7. Complete the entire section of text before you proceed to the third column.

8. Reread your notes in the second column. Locate and summarize related concepts to find their overall significance of the big picture. Label your summary statements consecutively as *I, II, III,* and so forth. This completes your inductive outline.

Table 5.7   Example of an Inductive Outline

Chapter IV. "Reading Effectively"

What are the facts?	What is their immediate significance?	What is their larger significance?
1. Mathematics Chemistry History English	A. Different courses require varying amounts of reading.	
2. Arnold reports 7% of college group below 8th-grade norm in reading comprehension.		
3. Pressey reports 20% of freshman class were less efficient than 8th-grade-pupils.	B. Ability in reading varies with individuals	I. Reading ability is an important factor in academic success.
4. U. of M. "How to Study" classes; less than half of 272 students equaled median of high school seniors in reading comprehension.		

SOURCE: Byrd, C. (1927) *Effective Study Habits.*

Table 5.8   Guidelines for Previewing, Reading, and Evaluating Narrative Text

Previewing

1. What kind of literature is this? How is it representative of the time period in which it is written? How is it representative of its genre?
2. What can I determine from the title, size of print, illustrations, chapter headings, and opening pages?
3. For what age range is this literary selection appropriate?
4. What interests are reflected in this literary selection?

Reading and Evaluating

5. Does the selection tell a good story? Will I enjoy it? Will others?
6. Is the plot original and fresh?
7. It is plausible and credible? Is there preparation for the events? Is there a logical series of happenings? Is there a basis of cause and effect in the happenings?
8. Is there an identifiable climax?
9. How do events build to a climax?
10. Is the plot well constructed?

Setting

11. Where does the action take place?
12. How does the author indicate time?
13. How does the setting affect the action, characters, or theme?
14. Does the action transcend the setting and have universal implications?

Theme

15. Does the selection have a theme? What is the theme?
16. Is the theme a worthy one?
17. Does the theme emerge naturally form the action or is it stated too obviously?
18. Does the theme overpower the action?
19. Does it avoid moralizing?

Characterization

20. How does the author reveal characters? Through narration? In conversation? By thoughts of others? By thoughts of the character? Through action?
21. Are the characters convincing and credible?
22. Are their strengths and their weaknesses shown?
23. Does the author avoid stereotyping?
24. Is the behavior of the characters consistent with their ages and backgrounds?
25. Has the author shown the causes of character behavior or development?

Style

26. Is the style of writing appropriate to the subject?
27. Is the style straightforward or figurative?
28. Is the dialogue natural and suited to the characters?
29. Does the author balance narration and dialogue?
30. What are the main characteristics of the sentence patterns?
31. How did the author create a mood? Is the overall impression one of mystery, gloom, evil, joy, security?
32. What symbols has the author used to communicate meaning?
33. Is the point of view from which the action is told appropriate to the purpose of the selection?

Format

34. Does the selection contain illustrations? If so, do they enhance the action? Are they consistent with the action?
35. How is the format of the selection related to the text?

Other Considerations

36. How does the selection compare with others on the same subject?
37. How does the selection compare with other selections by the same author?
38. How have other reviewers evaluated this selection?

Tomlinson (1997) created a six-step process for taking notes from literature. Step one suggests that you assign a code letter to each theme, character, or concept you need to follow throughout the text. Your second step is to create a directory of your codes either in the front of your book or in your notebook. Consistently using a code to denote a particular concept makes the process simpler and easier. Step three involves your listing the code letters in your notebook, leaving space between the letters. In step four, you read your text, placing the appropriate code letter beside relevant information. Your fifth step is to list the page number next to the code number you have already written in your notebook. Step six, the final one, suggests you keep a notebook page for each major theme, character, or concept, and write a brief summary or make notes about important details. You should also note text page numbers. Example 5.5 contains an example of a coding system, and you can practice your own coding in Exercise 5.3.

Identifying Text Structure

Text structure consists of how the vocabulary and topic of a text are organized. The patterns in which ideas, or details, are structured include introduction/summary, subject development/definition, enumeration/ sequence, comparison/contrast, and cause/effect. Recognizing how ideas fit together helps you relate information more easily. Instead of having to recall isolated details, you fit them into an organized pattern. This helps you recall categories or blocks of information more easily within paragraphs, sections, and entire chapters.

Because text structure varies according to the topic and the author's purpose, there is seldom one single pattern. Features of various types of text structure usually are combined, with one predominant type. For example, a cause/effect passage might enumerate causes or effects. Nonetheless, patterns of text structure do exist, and identifying them aids you in reading and understanding texts. Special words signal the way the text is structured. These words show the direction and organization of the ideas being presented. Signal words within the passage, if present, help you draw conclusions and find

WRITE TO LEARN

On a separate sheet of paper or in your journal, use Tomlinson's process and create a list of steps for taking notes from literary text.

Exercise 5.3   Use the six-step process created by Tomlinson (1997) to take notes from "Mother," the short story at the back of this book (page 534).

Example 5.5   Coding System Applied to Characters in *After the First Death*

Code Directory Inside Front Cover

I – innocence

B – bravery

L – love

P – physical

I – intellectual

E – emotional

S – social

Code Directory Inside Back Cover

I   129, 144, 183
B   146, 211,
L   145,

Kate
P – 68, 144
I – 68, 69
E – 68, 69, 99, 105, 123,
S – 69, 129–130

Miro
. . .
Ben
. . .

Page 68 Coded

P   . . . She was blond, fair skinned, slender, no
     weight problems, had managed to avoid
P   adolescent acne. A healthy body with one
     exception: the weak bladder. . . . cheer-
P   leader, prom queen, captain of the girls'
     swimming team, budding actress in the
     Drama Club. . . . But there were other Kate
     Forresters, and she wondered about them
     sometimes. The Kate Forrester who awoke
E   suddenly at four in the morning and for no
     reason at all couldn't fall back to sleep. The
     Kate Forrester who couldn't stand the sight
     of blood. . . .

Page 69 Coded

She wanted to find somebody to love, to love
forever . . . That question brought up another   E
Kate Forrester disguise. Kate the manipulator
. . . Getting straight A's from Mr. Kelliher in   E
math and barely lifting a finger to do so but
knowing how to smile at him, feign interest . . .
She'd always been an excellent student in math.   I
She didn't know why she'd gone out of her
way to charm Mr. Kelliher. Just as she didn't
know why she used the same charm to win the
role of Emily in the Drama Club's presentation of *Our Town*. She knew she could play the
part, she was certain of her talent. . . . Gene
Sherman. Kate had been enthralled by him . . .   S
until they sat together during a lunch break

---

main ideas. Table 5.9 gives a short description of each of the text structure types and lists examples of signal words. If no signal words are present, you determine structure by examining how the information is discussed.

Introduction/summary text structures differ from other text structures in that they are identified by their physical placement in a chapter or by headings such as "Introduction" or "Summary." Introduction/summary text paragraphs also can be found at the beginning or end of major sections. Once you have discovered the placement and identification of these passages in a

Table 5.9   Text Structure Patterns and Signal Words

Pattern	Description	Examples of Signal Words
Introduction/Summary	Identifies main points	Identified by location, either the beginning or end of a discussion of a topic, and by such words as *in summary, in conclusion, as a review, to summarize, to sum up*
Subject Development/ Definition	Identifies a concept and de-scribes, develops, or explains it	Linking verbs, lists of facts related to the topic but unrelated to each other
Enumeration/Sequence	Lists or orders main points or presents a problem and steps for its solution	*First, second, third ... first, next, then, finally, in addition, last, and furthermore, and then, most important, least important*
Comparison/contrast	Describes ways in which con-cepts are alike or different or presents two or more sides of an issue	Comparison—*similarly, both, as well as, likewise, in like manner* Contrast—*however, on the other hand, on the contrary, but, instead of, although, yet, nevertheless, distinguish, alternative*
Cause/Effect	Shows the result of action(s) or explains a problem and its solution	*Therefore, thus, as a result, because, in turn, then, hence, for this reason, results in, causes, effects, leads to, consequently*

textbook chapter, you probably will find them in the same place with the same identification throughout the other chapters of that text.

The content of an introduction or summary contains features of other structure types and aids you in choosing the information you need to retrieve from memory. Many readers skip these sections, but they often concisely iden-tify the main points of a chapter. To use an introduction/summary text struc-ture, you identify the placement of introductory and summary passages and the major points in the chapter or section. Example 5.6 shows this structure type.

Subject development/definition text structure identifies a concept and lists its supporting details. Such paragraphs are usually found at the be-ginning of major sections.

A subject development/definition passage describes or explains a topic by providing a definition or listing characteristics. Often these facts relate to the topic but have little or no relationship to each other. To locate subject de-velopment/definition passages, look for a key concept and details that de-scribe, develop, or explain it. Example 5.7 exemplifies this structure.

Enumeration/sequence text structure lists major points. Although you might not be told initially how many points will be discussed, words such as "first, . . . second, . . . third" or "first, . . . next, . . . finally" often signal the num-ber of points under discussion. The points are a list of equivalent items (enu-meration structure) or a list of items in a progression (sequence structure).

Example 5.6   Examples of Introduction and Summary Structures

---

Introduction Passage

The way anthropologists approach the study of humanity has undergone many changes since the discipline originated in the nineteenth century. Some ideas held by most scholars a century ago have been discarded today; others are still with us. In this chapter, we discuss some of the important scholars and schools of thought that shaped the way modern anthropologists approach their studies. For each approach, we emphasize its assumptions, its basic questions, its errors, and its contributions to the theoretical ideas of modern anthropology.

Summary Passage

In this chapter we have reviewed the functions of society, the ways in which societies are organized around food, the basis of social structure, and the process of social interaction. We have learned that society is an exceedingly complex phenomenon with its inner workings hidden from the casual view.

Individuals in every society must be socialized to behave in ways that are beneficial for that society. In the next chapter, we examine the process of socialization and consider how both the individual and society benefit from such socialization.

Example 5.7   Example of Subject Development Structure

SLUMP. A slump is the intermittent movement of a mass of earth or rock along a curved slip-plane. It is characterized by the backward rotation of the slump block so that its surface may eventually tilt in the direction opposite the slope from which it became detached. Slumps are most likely to occur on steep slopes with deep, clay-rich soils after a period of saturation by heavy rains. The movement generally takes place over a period of days or weeks and is nearly impossible to control or halt once it has begun.

Slumps are common along the California coast, where slopes have frequently been oversteepened by wave undercutting. They also occur along the sideslopes of river gorges in various parts of the western United States. Small slumps capable of blocking traffic frequently occur on steep roadcuts following heavy rains.

Such lists include information arranged alphabetically or in order of importance, direction, size, time, or other criteria. This structure also describes solutions to problems, answers to questions, or proofs of thesis statements. To use the enumeration/sequence text structure, look for the overall concept, procedure, or problem; the total number of items in the list or steps in the sequence, whenever possible; the signal words that indicate the points in the list; and the relationship of items in the list or steps in the sequence. Example 5.8 shows this structure.

Example 5.8   Examples of Enumeration and Sequence Structures

---

Enumeration Passage

Nerve cells can be categorized by structure or function. For our purposes, a functional classification is more useful. According to this system, nerve cells fall into three distinct groupings: (1) sensory neurons, (2) interneurons, and (3) motor neurons.

Sensory neurons carry impulses from body parts to the central nervous system, transmitting impulses from sensory receptors located in the body. Sensory receptors come in many shapes and sizes and respond to a variety of stimuli, such as pressure, pain, heat, and movement.

Motor neurons carry impulses from the brain and spinal cord to effectors, the muscles and glands of the body. Sensory information entering the brain and spinal cord via sensory neurons often stimulates a response. A response is brought about by impulses transmitted via motor neurons to muscles and glands of the body. In some cases, intervening neurons—called interneurons or associated neurons—are present. Interneurons transmit impulses from the sensory neurons directly to motor neurons and may also transmit impulses to other parts of the central nervous system.

SOURCE: Reprinted with permission from *Human Biology* by Chiras. Copyright © 1991 by West Publishing Company. All rights reserved.

Sequence Passage

OUTPUT

Once processing is complete, the results are available for output. There are three steps involved in the output phase of data flow. In retrieving information, the computer pulls information from storage devices for use by the decision maker. By converting information, the computer translates information from the form used to store it to a form understandable by the user (such as a printed report). Finally, communication occurs when the right information is in the right place at the right time.

SOURCE: Reprinted with permission from *Introduction to Computers* by Brenan and Mandell. Copyright © 1984 by West Publishing Company. All rights reserved.

Comparison/contrast text structures express relationships between two or more ideas. Comparisons show how ideas are alike, whereas contrasts show how ideas differ. Signal words indicate whether likenesses or differences are being shown. Both comparisons and contrasts can be included, or the structure can consist of only comparisons or only contrasts. To use this type, you look for the items that are related and the signal words that indicate comparison or contrast. Example 5.9 exemplifies this structure.

The **cause/effect** text structure shows an idea or event resulting from another idea or event. It describes what happens (the effect) and why it happens (the cause). To use this type of text structure, look for the effect and the cause(s) of the effect. Example 5.10 shows the cause/effect structure.

Practice identifying text structure in Exercises 5.4, 5.5, and 5.6. Then use Exercises 5.4 and 5.5 to practice text labeling in Exercise 5.7.

Example 5.9   Example of Comparison/Contrast Structure

A fault takes the form of a two-dimensional plane that typically extends from the earth's surface downward to a variable but often considerable depth. The trace of the fault on the surface is termed the fault line. Fault lines may extend for hundreds of miles, but lengths of a few tens of miles are more common. Most faults are nearly straight. This linearity, which results from the tendency of rock to fracture along straight lines, contrasts markedly with the irregularity of the features produced by most other geomorphic processes.

Geologists recognize four general categories of faults according to the nature of the displacements that occur; these are termed normal, reverse, transcurrent, and thrust faults. Relative motion is more vertical than horizontal, and an expansionary component is present, so the opposing sides also move apart, resulting in crystal extension. Normal faults are usually produced by broad regional arching in areas of tetonic stress.

Reverse faults are so-named because the movement of the opposing sides is reversed from that of normal faults. Like normal faults, reverse faults have deeply dipping fault planes and undergo predominantly vertical motion. Unlike normal faults, though, reverse faults are produced by regional compression. Crystal shortening results, and a net uplift of the surface normally occurs.

Transcurrent faults undergo a predominantly horizontal offsetting of their opposing sides. They are most frequently located along transform plate boundaries, where the relative motions of the opposing plate boundaries are essentially parallel. Most transcurrent faults are located on the floors of oceanic plates and are produced by seafloor spreading movements, but some, like California's San Andreas Fault, occur on land.

Thrust faults result from the extreme compression of rock strata produced by lisopheric plate collisions. The relative movements of the opposing sides is similar to that of a reverse fault. Relative motion, however, is predominantly horizontal, as one side is thrust over the other, sometimes for considerable distances.

Source: Reprinted with permission from *Essentials of Physical Geography* by Scott. Copyright © 1991 by West Publishing Company. All rights reserved.

Example 5.10   Example of a Cause/Effect Structure

Chemical weathering processes are considerably hampered by a lack of water in arid regions. As a result, the aridsols are shallow, stony, and mineralogically immature, with poorly developed horizons. Soil textures are generally coarse and sandy, leading to water retention ability even when water is available. The humus content is low to completely absent because of the sparseness of vegetation.

An important characteristic of the *aridsols* is their high alkalinity. Evapotranspiration exceeds precipitation, producing a surfaceward movement of ground water and dissolved minerals. Well-drained soils typically experience an accumulation of calcium carbonate and other soluble bases at the site of water evaporation, normally a few inches below the surface. Frequently, this produces a duricrust layer. In poorly drained depressions, the salinization process results in conditions toxic for most vegetables.

Source: Reprinted with permission from *Essentials of Physical Geography* by Scott. Copyright © 1991 by West Publishing Company. All rights reserved.

Exercise 5.4   Circle the signal words, if any, in the following paragraphs. Then identify the predominant text structure (introduction/summary, subject development/definition, enumeration/sequence, comparison/contrast, cause/effect) of each passage. Write your answer in the corresponding blanks.

1. _____
2. _____
3. _____
4. _____
5. _____
6. _____
7. _____
8. _____

1. The duties of the bailiff vary. As sergeant-at-arms within the courtroom, he or she keeps watch over defendants and suppresses disorderly behavior among spectators. He or she summons witnesses when they are called to testify and maintains the legal proprieties pertaining to the actions of jurors and witnesses. When the jury is sequestered on the order of the judge, the bailiff accompanies the jurors and guards to prevent violations of trial secrecy—such as making unauthorized phone calls, reading an unedited newspaper, or listening to accounts of the trial on the radio or television. It is also the bailiff's job to see that the jury is suitably housed and fed during a trial.

2. But today's union member seeks satisfaction on a wider range. Money or safety is no longer the dominant reason for joining a union. Most people earn a livable wage and work under reasonable conditions. Today, the need to join a union often stems from a higher level. Labor relations professors Arthur A. Sloane and Fred Witney tell us that "research suggests that dissatisfaction with the extent of gratification of (1) safety, (2) social, (3) self-esteem needs—in approximately that order—has motivated many workers to join unions. To a lesser extent, status and self-fulfillment needs have also led to union membership."

3. Let us start with the religion most familiar to North American readers, Christianity. Christianity has approximately 1 billion adherents in the world, more than any other religion, and is the predominant religion in North America, South America, Europe, and Australia. In addition, countries with a Christian majority can be identified on every other continent. No other religion has such a widespread distribution.

4. Whether using the topical or regional approach, geographers can select either a descriptive or systematic method. Again, the distinction is one of emphasis, not on absolute separation. The descriptive method emphasizes the collection of a variety of details about the characteristics of a particular location. This method has been used primarily by regional geographers to illustrate the uniqueness of a particular location on the earth's surface. The systematic method emphasizes

(continues)

Exercise 5.4   *Continued*

the identification of several basic theories or techniques developed by geographers to explain the distribution of activities.

5. Victims of crime and their relationships with criminals were briefly explored in this chapter. Beginning with a historical sketch of the ways in which various societies in the past have dealt with the victim of crime, the pioneering work of Hentig and Mendelsohn in the development of victim typologies was discussed and some consideration was given to the issue of victim compensation and restitution. Models for the delivery of victim services were also examined briefly. Victimization surveys and their significance for the assessment of crime were treated in some detail, and the chapter concluded with several observations on the bystander who remains a passive witness to someone else's victimization.

6. Three major aspects of communication must be understood for anyone to be an effective communicator: (1) people, (2) messages, and (3) the environment. In communication, the person, or both *people,* is the focus of understanding. Communication really represents people in transaction. Second, although the people are of primary importance in a study of communication, *messages* mediate their transactions. Through sending or receiving messages, people make sense of one another. Third, communication takes place in a social environment. An organization where one works can be a major environment in which one communicates.

7. Fear is a basic ingredient of any psychological or social reaction to crime. It is a gut reaction that produces marked changes in individual behavior. The most intense fear is of the crimes least likely to occur: murder, assault, and forcible rape. Ironically, the perpetrator in such crimes is often a family member, close friend, or personal acquaintance. Nevertheless, what people fear most is violence at the hands of a stranger. Fear of an unknown assailant is prominent in both individual and collective responses to crime. Fear of strangers generalizes to fear of strange places, and people eventually see even public streets as unsafe. When fear of public places peaks, people avoid areas perceived as potentially hazardous. Consequently, normal activity is interrupted in various areas, removing one deterrent to criminal activity. Areas thus avoided are then increasingly frequented by persons bent upon crime.

8. **Modem Romance Languages.** The five most important contemporary Romance languages are Spanish, Portuguese, French, Italian, and Romanian. A reasonably close fit exists between the boundaries of these languages and the modern states of Spain, Portugal, France, Italy and Romania. An examination of a physical map of Europe provides ample evidence for the development of separate Romance languages, because the Spanish, Portuguese, French, and Italian language regions are separated from each other by mountains—the Pyrenees between France and Spain and the Alps between France and Italy. Romania is isolated from the other Romance language regions by Slavic-speaking people. Mountains serve as a strong barrier to communications between people living on opposite sides. Languages evolve over time. The distinct Romance languages did not suddenly appear. Instead, numerous dialects existed within each province, many of which still exist today. The creation of standard national languages, such as French and Spanish, was relatively recent.

Exercise 5.5   Read each of the following paragraphs and identify their text structures. (Note: page numbers in this exercise refer to the page numbers in this book for Sample Chapter 12 and Sample Chapter 14, both of which appear at the back of this book.)

1. First full paragraph, page 510, of Chapter 12 ("Women and Ethnic Groups") and under the major heading "Widows," beginning with the words "Widows constitute. . . ."
    Text Structure _____

2. First paragraph, under the heading "Income and Housing" on page 514 in Sample Chapter 12 ("Women and Ethnic Groups"), beginning with the words "Compared with. . . ."
    Text Structure _____

3. First full paragraph, page 517, of Chapter 12 ("Women and Ethnic Groups"), under the major heading "Family and Social Relationships," beginning with the words "Despite racism . . ."
    Text Structure _____

4. First paragraph, page 518 of Chapter 12 ("Women and Ethnic Groups"), under the major heading "Future Outlook," beginning with the words "Studies of. . . ."
    Text Structure _____

5. Last paragraph, page 524, of Chapter 12 ("Women and Ethnic Groups"), under the major heading "Chinese Americans," beginning with the words "Chinese elders. . . ."
    Text Structure _____

6. First full paragraph, page 529, of Chapter 12 ("Women and Ethnic Groups"), under the major heading "Improving the Status of Ethnic Elders," beginning with the words "Upgrading the. . . ."
    Text Structure _____

7. Third paragraph, page 560, of Sample Chapter 14 ("Organization of Information") and under the heading "Outlining," beginning with the words "Figure 7.2 shows. . . ."
    Text Structure _____

8. First paragraph, page 565, of Sample Chapter 14 ("Organization of Information"), under the heading "Organizing Information," beginning with the words "Does every. . . ."
    Text Structure _____

9. First paragraph, page 568, of Sample Chapter 14 ("Organization of Information"), under the heading "Spatial Order," beginning with the words "Spatial order. . . ."
    Text Structure _____

Exercise 5.6   Examine the text structures in Examples 5.6, 5.7, 5.8, 5.9 and 5.10. Identify the words that signal each particular type of text structure by circling them.

Exercise 5.7   Reread each paragraph in Exercises 5.4 and 5.5. Mark and label each one.

CLASSIC CRITICAL THINKING

Respond to the following:

A. What factors do you infer contribute to the ease or difficulty with which you read? Think of a text, novel, or magazine that you either enjoyed or disliked. List the factors that you think have affected your ability to comprehend the information. Circle the number of those that you feel are areas you need to strengthen.

1. _____

2. _____

3. _____

4. _____

5. _____

B. Consider the following titles. *Romeo and Juliet, Time* magazine, *Reader's Digest, Popular Mechanics, Psychology Today, The New York Times,* your hometown newspaper, your campus newspaper. Make an inference about the overall average readability levels of the materials these titles represent by ranking them form easiest to most difficult. (A readability level is the assignment of a grade level based on what an average student should be able to read at each grade or the lowest grade level at which at least half the students can read and understand 75 percent of the material.) Identify those factors that you used in determining the relative ease or difficulty of the text.

1. (easiest) _____

Factors contributing to readability:

_____

_____

2. _____

Factors contributing to readability:

_____

_____

3. _____

Factors contributing to readability:

_____

_____

4. _____

Factors contributing to readability:

_____

_____

(continues)

CLASSIC CRITICAL THINKING *(Continued)*

5. (most difficult) _____

Factors contributing to readability:

_____

_____

6. _____

Factors contributing to readability:

_____

_____

7. (most difficult) _____

Factors contributing to readability:

_____

_____

C. Consider the following sections of the newspaper: *Front page, sports page, financial page, editorial page, comics page.* Make an inference about the overall average readability levels of the materials represent by ranking them from easiest to most difficult. Identify those factors that you used in determining the relative ease or difficulty of the text.

1. (easiest) _____

Factors contributing to readability:

_____

_____

2. _____

Factors contributing to readability:

_____

_____

3. _____

Factors contributing to readability:

_____

_____

4. _____

Factors contributing to readability:

_____

_____

(continues)

CLASSIC CRITICAL THINKING *(Continued)*

5. (most difficult) _____

Factors contributing to readability:

_____

_____

D. Consider Sample Chapters 11, 12, 13, and 14, at the back of this book. Make an inference about the overall average readability levels of the chapters by ranking them from easiest to most difficult. Identify those factors that you used in determining the relative ease or difficulty of the text.

1. (easiest) _____

Factors contributing to readability:

_____

_____

2. _____

Factors contributing to readability:

_____

_____

3. _____

Factors contributing to readability:

_____

_____

4. (most difficult) _____

Factors contributing to readability:

_____

_____

E. Review your answers in this exercise and respond to the following on a separate sheet of paper or in your journal. What contributes to *your* ease of reading? What makes reading difficult for you? What can you do to increase your ability to read "with ease?"

STEP FOUR: RECITE

If, at the end of each section of a chapter, you can recite correct answers to your purpose-setting questions, then you continue reading.

What if you cannot completely answer your questions? One of two things has happened. Either you have asked the wrong questions, or you have not understood what you read.

GROUP LEARNING ACTIVITY   READING STRATEGIES FOR GROUPS

An important phase of reading and learning information is monitoring. This stage helps you determine when you know information or when you need to reflect and review. Many students, however, lack the self-awareness to differentiate between when they know information from when they don't know it. The following group reading strategy helps you learn to monitor learning as well as practice summarization and memory skills. The group's goal is to master text information. This strategy incorporates visual, verbal, and aural components and provides group members with opportunities to see how others identify, organize, and learn important information.

The following steps, based on cooperative learning instructions (Larson and Dansereau, 1986), can be used in your in-class study group:

1. Select and study a limited amount of text information. Initially, or when reading complex or unfamiliar information, this might be as little as a section in a chapter introduced by a minor subheading. Don't select more than two or three pages.

2. Each group member should practice appropriate marking and labeling strategies in reading the information.

3. Members continue to study and reflect on the information until everyone has completed the task.

4. Select one person to recall and summarize the information *without looking at the text*. That person should include important terms and ideas in the summary, and describe mnemonic devices, analogies, charts, drawings, or other visuals which reinforce or clarify information.

5. As the recaller summarizes information, group members *using their texts* check the accuracy and completeness of the summary. Group members correct errors and supply or elaborate on information following the summary, again using any mnemonic devices (see Chapter 7), analogies, charts, drawings, or other visuals to reinforce or clarify information.

6. The group then discusses the information, continues to clarify information, and suggests ways to consider and remember concepts.

7. During discussion, each person should note important information, terms, visuals, or other information for later individual study.

8. Repeat the process with another member of the group serving as the recaller until all the information has been studied or all the members have had the opportunity to serve as recallers. To be most effective, group members need to actively facilitate the understanding of the recaller and themselves through questioning, elaborating, or otherwise amplifying information.

Application

Using the first section in the next chapter, apply the cooperative learning instructions with you in-class study group.

Application

Using the same text material, use the cooperative learning activity in your group. Then, compare notes with other groups in the class, focusing on how others identify important information and facilitate learning.

You decide where the problem lies by looking at your questions given the content of the passage. Does the content answer your questions? If not, you asked the wrong ones. Your skill in developing purpose-setting questions improves with practice.

Recitation becomes easier and more active when you study with someone. This helps you see how others develop questions and find answers. You can also practice by using a tape recorder. First, record your purpose-setting questions. Then read and record your answers. When you play your tape, see if your questions were appropriate and if your responses answered the questions correctly. Another way to practice involves writing your questions on index cards. Again, after reading, determine if your questions were appropriate. Then, write your answers on the back of the card.

If you find your questions are inappropriate, form new questions and reread. If you still have problems understanding, you need to assess your reading relative to the passage at hand. Do you know the terminology? Are you confused by the author's writing style? Table 5.10 provides a list of common comprehension obstacles and solutions.

Evaluating your text marking also helps you increase your understanding. If you marked too much, you might not be able to separate important from unimportant information. If this is a common problem for you, use a pencil while marking and labeling. This allows you the freedom to rethink your notations. If you overmark only on occasion, you can remark text with a contrasting ink or highlighter. If you marked too little, you might not have enough information to comprehend fully. Thus, you need to reexamine the text and make more explicit notations. You need to be sure you have labeled all text markings. If you have done so, you can see at a glance where important information lies. If your labels are vague, then reread and relabel your text. Labels should concisely, yet completely, summarize what you've marked.

STEP FIVE: REVIEW

At this point in the SQ3R process, review seems redundant. You've already seen the information four times. You previewed the chapter to get the big picture. You began your analysis of content by asking questions. You examined each section by reading. You checked understanding. The review stage, however, brings you full circle by allowing you to synthesize the chapter's meaning as a whole, to see how information relates, and to begin studying information for recall.

Although Chapter 7 will provide many memory and study techniques, three strategies are immediately available to you as part of SQ3R. First, many chapters begin with objectives; you surveyed them during the first step of SQ3R. One way to review is to determine if you met all the objectives. A second way to review involves answering, without referring back to the text, any pre-chapter or postchapter questions posed by your author; these, too, should have been identified during your initial survey of the chapter. Both of these review strategies rely on the good graces of the text's author. Chapter objectives and questions might or might not be part of the text you are reading.

Table 5.10   Reasons and Solutions for Comprehension Failure

Reasons	Solutions
Failure to Ask Right Question	
Lack of experience in questioning	Practice with index cards by putting a question on one side and the answer on the other.
	Practice with tape recorder.
	Practice with study partner.
	Review types of questioning words.
Failure to Understand Text	
Lack of concentration	Avoid external distractions.
	Study in short blocks of time over a longer period.
	Use a study system.
	Set learning goals.
	Keep a "worry list."
Unfamiliar terms	Use context and structural analysis to decode unknown terms.
	Use the text's glossary.
	Find the word in a dictionary or thesaurus.
	Actively consider new terms in context.
Lack of understanding	Reread or skim for main ideas.
	Scan for specific information.
	Verbalize confusing points.
	Paraphrase, summarize, or outline main ideas.
	Consult an alternate source.
	Reset learning goals.
Speed	Adjust speed to purpose.
	Take a speed-reading course.
	Use a study-system.
	Practice with a variety of materials.
	Read recreationally.
Failure to identify text structure.	Examine transition words as you reread.
	Outline the paragraph or passage.
Failure to locate main idea.	Label the main idea of each paragraph.
	Identify text structure.
	Outline details.
	Summarize the main idea in your own words.
Insufficient background knowledge for understanding.	Find alternative sources of information.
	Obtain tutoring.
Inability to set appropriate purpose-setting questions	Practice with a tape recorder.
	Practice with a friend.
	Reset learning goals.

The third review strategy depends solely on you. For this review, you return to the outline or map you created during the second stage of SQ3R and answer your goal-setting questions.

Any of these three study strategies—indeed, all three—allow you to test your recall and determine where you have memory deficits. This provides you with information about what and how much you need to study to complete the learning process. Practice your skills in Exercise 5.8.

ONLINE CLASS

Web Exercise 5.1

A variety of information related to the topics in this chapter is available on the World Wide Web. For this exercise, access one of the following Web sites (for the most up-to-date ULRLs, go to http://csuccess.wadsworth.com)

Dartmouth's Six Reading Myths from the Academic Skills Center at Dartmouth College:
    http://www.dartmouth.edu/admin/acskills/reading.html

Efficient Reading from the University of Melbourne, Australia:
    http://www.services.unimelb.edu.au/lsu/reading.html

Increasing Reading Efficiency: Rate and Comprehension from Purdue University Liberal Arts Learning Center:
    http://www.sla.purdue.edu/studentserv/learningcenter/handouts/speedrd.htm

How can I Organize my Textbook Reading? Or Unraveling the Textbook Maze from Purdue University Liberal Arts Learning Center:
    http://www.sla.purdue.edu/studentserv/learningcenter/handouts/txtvid94.htm

P-R-R: How to Read Your Textbook from Our Favorite Handouts at the University of Texas:
    http://www.utexas.edu/student/lsc/handouts/1422.html

1. Which Web site did you choose?

   _____

2. Why did you choose this site?

   _____

   _____

3. How did the title of the Web site relate to the content of the Web site?

   _____

   _____

   _____

4. Using one of the sample chapters as your example, what did you learn from this Web site that you can incorporate into your process of reading that information?

   _____

   _____

   _____

Exercise 5.8   Survey, question, read, recite, and review Sample Chapter 12 at the back of this book. You can use either text marking and labeling or an inductive outline to do so. Record your notes on a separate sheet of paper or in your journal.

CHAPTER SUMMARY

1. SQ3R is a systematic reading plan for studying text chapters. Its steps include survey, question, read, recite, and review.

2. Surveying, or previewing, is a strategy often used before attending a lecture. It helps you be an active learner and connect what you know with what you are learning.

3. The questioning stage concerns setting goals for reading.

4. Reading a chapter involves finding and recording main ideas.

5. When you recite information, you check your understanding and use strategies to solve comprehension problems, if they exist.

6. In the review stage, you attempt to see and remember how all information in the chapter relates. Additional strategies for learning information are included in Chapter 7.

Class*ACTION*

Respond to the following on a separate sheet of paper or in your journal. Combine the chapter map and chapter summary to form a synthesis map that reflects the main ideas and important details of this chapter. Personalize the map by indicating specific ways in which you plan to implement suggestions offered by this chapter.

CHAPTER REVIEW

Answer briefly but completely.

1. Complete the following analogy:

   goal: objective :: survey: _____

2. Which of Kipling's questioning words (*What, Why, When, How, Where,* and *Who*) might elicit main idea responses? Which would require details for answers?

_____

_____

_____

_____

_____

3. Create a drawing that shows the role of topic, main ideas, and details in a paragraph or passage.

4. Think of the following subjects in light of the factors to be considered when marking text. Which factor might be most important to you in each area?

   a. Freshman-level chemistry _____

   b. Music appreciation _____

   c. European history _____

   d. Junior-level trigonometry _____

   e. Introduction to computer science _____

5. Create a cardinal rule for text marking that explains how much information should be marked.

_____

_____

_____

_____

6. Locate examples from the running text in this chapter for any three different types of text structure.

    a. Type: _____

       Page: _____ Paragraph: _____

    b. Type: _____

       Page: _____ Paragraph: _____

    c. Type: _____

       Page: _____ Paragraph: _____

7. What are the functions of signal words?

    _____

    _____

8. Compare/contrast inductive and deductive outlines.

    _____

9. Examine Table 5.9. Which of these comprehension obstacles, if any, do you feel you experience most often and why?

    _____

    _____

    _____

    _____

10. How do the three review strategies discussed in this chapter allow you to evaluate recall? What might you do if you find your recall failing in a given area?

    _____

    _____

    _____

    _____

VOCABULARY DEVELOPMENT   Context: Time Flies versus Fruit Flies

Look around you. Are you in your room? Your car? A bus? A classroom? Outside? Your surroundings are your current context. What you see in that context often depends on those surroundings to make sense. The kind of seat you find in a car or bus differs from that found in a classroom or living area. Similarly, words differ according to the context in which they are found. Context helps you make sense of the new words you encounter when you read and forms a means of developing vocabulary.

Time flies like an arrow.
Fruit flies like a banana.

—Lewis Grizzard
Twentieth century American humorist

What does *flies* mean in each of the sentences above? The meaning of many words changes according to the words that surround them. These words—called context—give you the meaning and usage of the word in a realistic setting. For example, in psychology, the word *set* means orientation, as "mind set." In math, *set* refers to a group of things. *Set* refers to scenery in drama. As a result, context forms one of the most valuable aids to vocabulary development. Context consists of both stated and unstated clues to meaning.

Although context is your first best choice in defining words you do not know, it is not foolproof. Sometimes authors embed words in weak context. That means they provide too little information for you to identify the meaning of a new term. When that happens, your only alternative is to consult a dictionary or glossary. Then you need to reconsider the word in its original context.

"Sure I've seen a good play . . .
in the game on Sunday."

Stated Context Clues

Stated context clues consist of various punctuation marks and key words that signal meaning (see Table V5.1). In addition, stated context clues rely on your language knowledge to help you define unknown words. For example, punctuation clues actually identify appositives, words, or phrases that restate or modify an immediately preceding term. Definition clues link nouns with describing or renaming words. Other clues indicate both synonymous (comparison and example) and antonymous (contrast) relationships among ideas within a sentence or paragraph. Finally, meanings can be located in other sentences.

Table V5.1   Types of Stated Context Clues

Stated Types	Stated Clues	Examples
Punctuation	commas,, parentheses () brackets { } dashes –	He also distinguished between *social statics*—the study of stability and order—and *social dynamics*—the study of change.
Definition	*is, was, are, means, involves, seems, is called, that is, i.e., which means, resembles*	One of his enduring contributions is the idea that sociology should rely on *positivism*; that is, it should use observation and experimentation, methods of physical sciences, in the study of social life.
Comparison	*similarly, both, as well as, likewise*	Similar in function to the parity bit is the *check digit*. Like a parity bit, a check digit is used to catch errors.
Example	*such as, such, like, for example, e.g., other*	Have you ever watched people's eyes closely when they read? Their eyes don't flow smoothly over the words; instead they skitter or jump across the letters. Such motion is called *visual saccade*.
Contrast	*however, on the other hand, on the contrary, while, but, instead of, although, nevertheless, yet*	Participants in an artificially created situation in a laboratory may not behave as they would in a real-life situation. In contrast, the *natural* experiment takes place in a real-life situation that is not totally created or controlled by the experimenter.

Unstated Context Clues

Unstated context clues require the use of your background knowledge to infer meaning. Key words and phrases identified within the text provide you with the clues necessary for decoding meanings. For example, consider the word *elite* in the following paragraph:

> The existence of a surplus food supply explains why cities were able to develop but does not explain why people were attracted to them. Cities tended to attract four basic types of people: *elites*, functionaries (officials), craftsmen, and the poor and destitute. For elites, the city provided a setting for consolidating political,

military, or religious power. The jewelry and other luxury items found in the tombs of these elites symbolize the benefits that this small segment of the population gained from their consolidation of power and control. Those who lived in cities as political or religious officials received considerably fewer benefits, but their lives were undoubtedly easier than those of the peasant-farmers in the countryside. Craftsmen, still lower on the stratification structure, came to the city to work and sell their products to the elites and functionaries. The poor and destitute, who were lured to the city for economic relief, were seldom able to improve their condition (Gist and Fava, 1974).

SOURCE: Reprinted with permission from *Sociology,* 2nd ed., by Shepard. Copyright © 1984 by West Publishing Company. All rights reserved.

The text does not define *elite* for you or provide stated clues. The words *power, jewelry, luxury,* and *benefits* help you know that *elite* describes a wealthy class of people. In addition, by process of elimination, you may realize that a wealthy class of people is the only class that the text fails to mention.

Activity 1

Define any ten of the following words in context from Sample Chapter 13 "Concepts in Human Biology." Then identify the type of context clue that helps you determine the word's meaning. Words appear in boldface in the chapter in the same order as they appear in the activity.

1. evolution

Definition: _____

_____

2. vertebrates

Definition: _____

_____

3. Homo sapiens

Definition: _____

_____

4. energy

Definition: _____

_____

5. DNA

Definition: _____

_____

6. cell

Definition: _____

_____

7. metabolism

Definition: _____

_____

8. ATP

Definition: _____

_____

9. homeostasis

Definition: _____

_____

10. inheritance

Definition: _____

_____

11. mutations

Definition: _____

_____

12. adaptive trait

Definition: _____

_____

13. hypothesis

Definition: _____

_____

14. prediction

Definition: _____

_____

15. experiment

Definition: _____

_____

16. control group

Definition: _____

_____

17. theory

Definition: _____

_____

Activity 2

Provide a definition for each of the following words before reading the chapter. Then identify the meanings of these words from context from Sample Chapter 13, the section entitled "Defining Death." The words appear in the boldface typeface in the same order as they appear in the activity.

1. stem

Your definition: _____

Definition in context: _____

2. bit

Your definition: _____

Definition in context: _____

3. course

Your definition: _____

Definition in context: _____

4. adopted

Your definition: _____

Definition in context: _____

5. strict

Your definition: _____

Definition in context: _____

6. beat

Your definition: _____

Definition in context: _____

7. pump

Your definition: _____

Definition in context: _____

8. grapple

Your definition: _____

Definition in context: _____

Answer Key

The topic of the passage on page 209 is "Washing Clothes."

Seeing What You Mean: Learning from and with Graphics

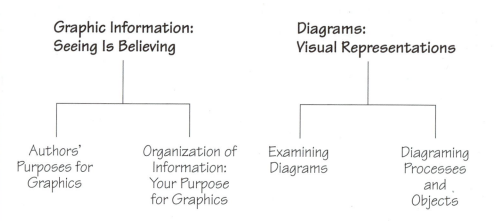

Graphic Information:
Seeing Is Believing

— Authors' Purposes for Graphics

— Organization of Information: Your Purpose for Graphics

Diagrams:
Visual Representations

— Examining Diagrams

— Diagraming Processes and Objects

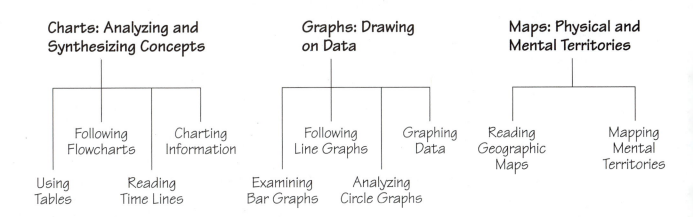

Before the development of written language, ancient people communicated through pictures they carved or painted. These pictures helped Egyptians, Aztecs, Native Americans, and other early societies express ideas and concepts. Today, both words and pictures express and relate ideas and concepts.

Graphics organize written forms, or try to explain them, or try to relate them to other pieces of information. This chapter provides information about different kinds of graphics and shows you how to apply them to learning situations.

GRAPHIC INFORMATION: SEEING IS BELIEVING

In 1918, sports cartoonist Robert Ripley published his first sketches of "Believe It or Not!" in the *New York Globe*. This feature depicted such unlikely events as men who won races by running backward or fish that walked on land. Encouraged by an enthusiastic readership, Ripley pursued his quest for oddities. "Believe It or Not!" was eventually carried by more than 300 newspapers in 38 countries. His readers evidently subscribed to the notion that seeing is believing.

Graphics provide ways to see what you or an author believe about information. Graphics refer to visual representations such as diagrams, charts (tables, flowcharts, and time lines), graphs (bar, line, and circle), and maps (general reference, special purpose, and idea). The type of information determines the graphic format to some degree. For example, a chart or graph summarizes or classifies data whereas diagrams illustrate complex ideas. You and authors use graphics, therefore, to exemplify, clarify, organize, and illustrate key ideas.

Authors' Purposes for Graphics

Authors often use graphics to illustrate complex information. Many students conclude that the graphics, too, must be complex—probably too complex to understand. Once you learn how to decipher graphics, you will find that reading them is actually faster and easier than understanding written information. This is because graphics focus your attention and provide visual reinforcement. Graphics give authors ways to make abstractions more real. Table 6.1 summarizes purposes of graphics by type.

As a reader, you should examine graphics carefully in an attempt to see why the author included them. Your goal is to find their main ideas. Your success depends on the information in them and your store of background knowledge. Much like the title, headings, and subheadings of a

Table 6.1   **Purposes of Text Graphics**

	Diagram	Table	Flow chart	Time Line	Bar or Line Graph	Circle Graph	Map
Summarize	X	X	X	X	X	X	
Organize		X	X		X	X	
Illustrate	X		X	X	X	X	
Demonstrate	X		X				
Compare		X	X	X	X	X	
Contrast		X	X	X	X	X	
Show parts of a whole	X		X	X		X	
Sequence	X		X	X			
Depict location	X						X

chapter, the title of a graphic identifies its subject and, thus, the information you need to draw from your background to understand it. Authors usually identify the purpose and subject of untitled graphics in the text. Because you must recognize and evaluate this information for yourself, processing untitled graphics requires higher-level thinking and the ability to draw conclusions.

Understanding graphics helps you learn information in another way. Your brain consists of two halves. The left side processes text and data in a logical, systematic fashion. The right side processes information that has a more artistic, visual nature. Graphics appeal to the right side of your brain. By attending to both text and graphic information, you use both sides of your brain to aid learning and memory. (See Chapter 1 for more information about brain dominance and learning style.)

You process graphic information through an overt action—writing. Taking notes from text graphics involves six steps. First, decide why you think the author included a graphic. Because publishers pay illustrators or others for permission to print graphics, if it's there, it's there for a reason. Second, identify important details or features of the graphic. From these, you can determine the graphic's main idea. In other words, summarize the information the graphic includes. Third, note your summary in the margin beside the graphic. Fourth, draw conclusions about the importance of the graphic to your overall understanding. Fifth, check your understanding of the graphic with information presented in the text or emphasized in class. Sixth, record in your notes where important text graphics are located.

Organization of Information: Your Purpose for Graphics

Picasso, Monet, Rembrandt, Michelangelo
Posh, Baby, Ginger, Scary, Sporty
Matthew, Mark, Luke, John
Cecil, Katy, Isaac, Regina

Everything is organized in some way. Each of the previous four lines contains members of specific sets of information. The sense you make of each line depends on whether you can discern what concept organizes that set. Your ability to do so depends on your background knowledge. In analyzing line 1 you might recognize that Picasso, Monet, Rembrandt, and Michelangelo were all artists. Posh, Baby, Ginger, Scary, and Sporty were members of a musical group called the Spice Girls. Matthew, Mark, Luke, and John were apostles in the New Testament. Your analysis of the last line might not provide you with a single organizational format that includes all the names. Nothing in your background knowledge seems to fit. Indeed, the last line consists of names of pets of the authors of this text. So background knowledge forms one key to organizing information for learning. When you lack sufficient background knowledge, analysis of text organization or lecture content often provides you with the connections you need to categorize and organize new information.

Lecture notes, text chapters, and other materials provide a variety of details about new information you need to learn. Deciding what information you have forms the first step in creating your own graphics. Once you identify the information, you organize it by analyzing how the details relate to each other. For example, your details might consist of dates in history, ways to solve a physics problem, or processes in cell replication. You then decide which graphic fits your needs. The arrangement that best suits your needs depends on learning goals, course emphasis, and course content. Sometimes an instructor suggests organizational structures by identifying types of information to remember (dates, names, places). An instructor might also provide the general categories of information you need to know. Other times, you need to do this for yourself. Like many other memory aids, the most effective organizational structures are those you make for yourself. A time line could depict historical sequences of events, a chart could be used to compare ways to solve problems, and a diagram or flowchart could be used to show cellular processes. With the exception of mapping, you use the same purposes for text graphics that authors use (see Table 6.1). Although maps enable you to show relationships among physical locations, they also help you visually represent mental relationships.

Just as understanding graphics requires both right- and left-brain processing, creating graphics that represent text information uses both sides of the brain. This, too, aids your learning and memory.

DIAGRAMS: VISUAL REPRESENTATIONS

> A dignified old lady, attending a contemporary art exhibition, was caught staring at a painting by its artist. "What *is* it?" she inquired. The artist smiled condescendingly.
>
> "That, my dear woman, is supposed to be a mother and her child."
>
> "Well, then," asked the lady, "why isn't it?"

Often you encounter **diagrams** in texts that make you, like the woman in the story, wonder, "What is it?" That's because diagrams often depict complex concepts. They explain as well as represent relationships. Authors use them to help you picture events, processes, structures, relationships, or sequences described in the text.

Examining Diagrams

Diagrams often require both the written description and the visual picture for understanding. The written description often explains the connections and relationships among the parts shown on the diagram. The title of the diagram and labels on it help you identify concepts important to your understanding. Consider the following description of the visual cliff:

> The visual cliff—a tool for studying depth perception—consists of a center board on top of a glass table. On one half of the board, a patterned surface is directly below the glass, whereas on the other half of the board the patterned surface is several feet below the glass table. This gives the illusion of a cliff.

This somewhat confusing description makes it difficult to understand the concept of the visual cliff (unless you are already familiar with it). Now, consider the diagram in Figure 6.1. The precision with which the diagram has been drawn and labeled allows you to better understand the concept of the visual cliff. Analyze a diagram from Sample Chapter 14 (at the back of this book) in Exercise 6.1.

Diagramming Processes and Objects

If you like to doodle, you probably like to diagram ideas. You use diagrams for the same purposes as authors do—to represent and explain complex text concepts. You can also use diagrams as right-brain mnemonic devices (see Chapter 7).

To create a diagram, first identify the concept you want to depict. Second, list the parts of the concept you want to include. Third, identify relationships among the parts. Finally, create a drawing that represents and explains the concept. In diagramming information, artistic ability is helpful,

> "
>
> If you can describe clearly without a diagram the proper way of making this or that knot, then you are a master of the English tongue.
>
> —Hilaire Belloc
> *Twentieth century*
> *English author*

Figure 6.1   Example of the Use of a Diagram

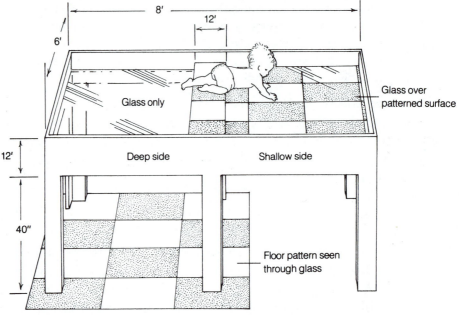

but not necessary. The key to understanding the process of the diagram comes from your analysis of the relationships and from the cognitive rather than from the aesthetic quality of your conceptual synthesis.

CHARTS: ANALYZING AND SYNTHESIZING CONCEPTS

Like diagrams, **charts** show information too complex to be easily understood in written or oral forms. Charts condense and simplify information. They help you compare like and different attributes. They organize information by order or time. They emphasize important points. Common types of charts include **tables, flowcharts,** and **time lines.** Examples of common charts include class schedules and academic calendars.

Using Tables

Tables indicate relationships among pieces of information. To permit direct comparisons, tables organize information into rows and columns. A row runs horizontally across the page (left to right). A column runs vertically down the page (up to down). Headings or labels identify rows or columns.

Exercise 6.1   Use Figure 7.9 (page 569) from Sample Chapter 14 ("Organization of Information") to answer the following questions.

1. What object is diagrammed in Figure 7.9?

    _____

    _____

    _____

2. What is the initial step in the process? The final step?

    _____

    _____

    _____

3. If a chip is rejected, what happens?

    _____

    _____

    _____

4. How many chips arrive from a supplier to the test facility? Describe them as they arrive.

    _____

    _____

    _____

5. What is the function of the MCT handler? Where is it housed?

    _____

    _____

    _____

6. What is the function of the operator once a chip has been tested and found to be "good?"

    _____

    _____

    _____

A special type of table shows the presence or absence of common features for the items being analyzed (see Figure 6.2). If a feature is possessed by an item, a mark fills the box or space where the item and feature intersect or meet. If the feature is not possessed by that item, the box or space is left blank. This type of table is called a **feature analysis table.** This chart allows you to find details related to the items being compared, infer unstated information, and summarize.

Figure 6.2   Example of a Feature Analysis Table

Three Views of Human Developmental Challenges

	Erikson	Gould	Levinson
Childhood	•		
Adolescence	•	•	•
Early Adulthood	•	•	•
Middle Adulthood	•	•	•
Late Adulthood			•
Old Age	•		

Figure 6.3   Example of a Quality Table

COST OF FINANCING $1,000 ON AN INSTALLMENT PLAN

Percentage Rate (Annual)	Length of Loan (Months)	Monthly Payments	Finance Charge	Total Cost of Loan
9.25%	6	$171.19	$ 27.14	$1,027.14
	12	87.57	50.84	1,050.84
	24	45.80	99.20	1,099.20
	36	31.92	149.12	1,149.12
10.5	6	171.81	30.86	1,030.86
	12	88.15	57.80	1,057.80
	24	46.38	113.12	1,113.12
	36	32.50	170.00	1,170.00
12	6	172.55	35.30	1,035.30
	12	88.85	66.20	1,066.20
	24	47.07	129.68	1,129.68
	36	33.21	195.56	1,195.56
13	6	173.04	38.24	1,038.24
	12	89.32	71.84	1,071.84
	24	47.54	140.96	1,140.96
	36	33.69	212.84	1,212.84
15	6	174.03	44.18	1,044.18
	12	90.26	83.12	1,083.12
	24	48.49	163.76	1,163.76
	36	34.67	248.12	1,248.12
18	6	175.53	53.18	1,053.18
	12	91.68	100.16	1,100.16
	24	49.92	198.08	1,198.08
	36	36.15	301.40	1,301.40

SOURCE: Miller, R. L., and Stafford, A. D. (1997). *Economic Issues for Consumers.* Wadsworth Publishing Company.

Table 6.2   Steps in Reading Tables

1. Read the title. This tells you the subject or general content of the table.

2. Identify the type of table. This helps you determine the kind(s) of information given. A table shows the presence or absence of a feature, or it shows the quantity or quality of a feature.

3. Look at the labels or headings in the table. These tell you what items are being compared and what features are being used to compare them. You need to keep the items and features in mind so you can recognize when and how the relationships change.

4. Note any general trends.

5. If you are looking at a table as part of a chapter survey, stop your examination of this graphic. Continue previewing the chapter.

6. When you reach the section of the text that refers to the table, identify the purpose before turning to the table. Does the author want you to note specific facts, generalizations, or trends?

7. Turn back to the table. Use the purpose set in the text to look at specific areas of the table.

8. Reread the section of the text that referred to the table. Make sure you understand the points and relationships noted by the author.

A second kind of table shows the amount or quality of the items being compared (see Figure 6.3). This table allows you to locate details about each item or feature, infer unstated information, and identify **trends** (directions in which features change). Such a chart is called a **quality table.**

Table 6.2 lists steps in reading both feature analysis and quality tables. Use Exercises 6.2 and 6.3 to practice analyzing tables.

Following Flowcharts

Flowcharts diagram the sequence of steps in a complex process. Arrows show the route through the procedure. Circles, boxes, or other shapes tell what should be done at each step. Flowcharts also depict ordered associations among elements. In such an arrangement, a ranking of information shows superior, equal, and lesser relationships. Some flowcharts show both sequence and hierarchical relationships. The flowchart in Figure 6.4 indicates the process for the movement of water through a watershed. Table 6.3 depicts the steps in following a flowchart. Practice reading flowcharts by answering the questions in Exercise 6.4.

Exercise 6.2   Examine Table 3-1 (Sample of Police Departments Allowing Lateral Transfers) and the section entitled "Lateral Transfers" on page 493 of Sample Chapter 11 ("Organizing the Police Department") at the back of this book and answer the following questions.

1. What is a lateral transfer?

_____

_____

_____

2. Why wouldn't all states/cities allow lateral transfers?

_____

_____

_____

3. From what source does the information in Table 3–1 come? What can you determine about its reliability?

_____

_____

_____

4. Which three departments allow in- and out-of-state lateral transfers?

_____

_____

_____

5. Which department nearest your home (city or state) allows lateral transfers?

_____

_____

_____

_____

_____

Exercise 6.3   Use Table 3-4 (Staffing of a Police Department by Function and Time) on page 503 of Sample Chapter 11 ("Organizing the Police Department") at the back of this book to answer the following questions.

1. List the people who are paid by the police department.

_____

_____

_____

2. List the three major divisions under the police department. Now list the bureaus and units under each division.

_____

_____

_____

(continues)

Exercise 6.3   *Continued*

3. At which time do the largest number of police officers work?

_____

_____

_____

4. In which position are there no full-time employees?

_____

_____

_____

5. Examine the heading labeled "Civilian." How can ½ a person work?

_____

_____

_____

6. Examine the heading labeled "Sergeant." What trend can you identify from the information here?

_____

_____

_____

7. Which bureau has the most employees? Why would this be so?

_____

_____

_____

8. How many employees work for the police department?

_____

_____

_____

9. Who is the most powerful person in the departmental hierarchy? Explain your answer using Table 3-4.

_____

_____

_____

10. What role might a civilian police chief fill?

_____

_____

_____

Figure 6.4   Example of a Flowchart

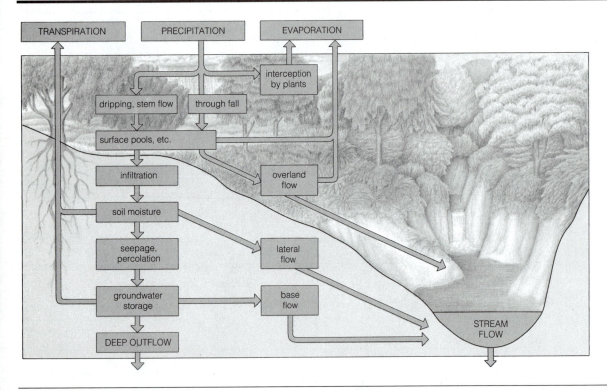

SOURCE: *Human Biology* by Cecie Starr and Beverly McMillan, 2nd ed. 1997. Wadsworth Publishing Company.

Table 6.3   Steps in Reading a Flowchart

1. Look at the title to determine the subject of the flowchart.

2. Note the beginning and ending points on the flowchart.

3. Infer trends or any breaks in trends by identifying the regularity or irregularity of steps.

4. If you are looking at a flowchart as part of a chapter preview, stop your examination of this graphic. Continue previewing the chapter.

5. When you reach the section of the text that refers to the flowchart, determine the author's purpose before turning to the flowchart. Does the author want to emphasize specific facts, generalizations, or trends?

6. Turn to the flowchart. Use the purpose set by the author to look at specific areas of the chart.

7. Reread the section of the text that referred to the flowchart. Make sure you understand the information noted by the author.

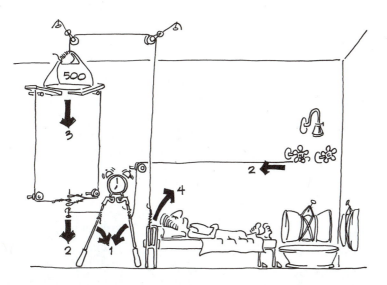

Exercise 6.4   Use Figure 1.4 on page 548 from Sample Chapter 13 ("Concepts in Human Biology") at the back of this book to answer the following questions.

1. What serves as the basis of all organisms?

2. How many steps are there before an atom becomes a cell?

3. What is a *tissue*?

4. Of the 13 levels of organization listed in Figure 1.4, to which level does one human belong? A group of humans? (*Hint*: There is more than one correct answer)

5. What is an *ecosystem*?

6. What is the significance of the arrow that connects *cell* to *population*?

7. Identify a part of the atmosphere and the earth that is NOT a part of the biosphere?

Reading Time Lines

Suppose that a local radio station intends to spotlight musical acts from the 1950s, 1960s, and 1970s—one act per night. Its advertisement of this musical revival is a series of posters, each with a rebus indicating the band that will be featured that night. Because the posters appear in chronological order, they form a sort of time line of music. Can you decipher the rebuses in the cartoon to determine who has been chosen to perform? (The answers appear on the last page of this chapter.)

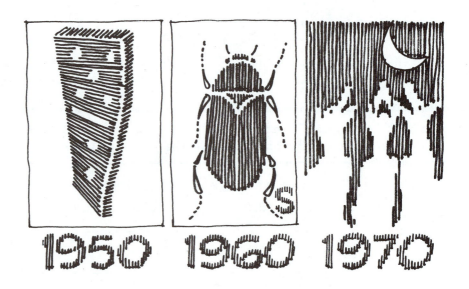

Table 6.4   Steps in Reading a Time Line

1. Look at the title to determine what time period is being covered.

2. Note the beginning and ending points on the line.

3. Infer trends or any breaks in trends by identifying the regularity or irregularity of events.

4. If you are looking at a time line as part of a chapter preview, stop your examination of this graphic. Continue previewing the chapter.

5. When you reach the section of the text that refers to the time line, determine the author's purpose before turning to the time line. Does the author want to emphasize specific facts, generalizations, or trends?

6. Turn to the time line. Use the purpose set by the author to look at specific areas of the chart.

7. Reread the section of the text that referred to the time line. Make sure you understand the points and relationships noted by the author.

A time line is a graphic **chronology** (time-ordered sequence) or outline of important dates or events that relates these features to the overall time frame in which they occur. Thus, time lines indicate order. Table 6.4 lists the steps in reading a time line. A time line, like the one in Figure 6.5, describes the history of a topic or the sequence in which things happen. Exercise 6.5 provides practice creating time lines.

Charting Information

What you understand about the relationships among ideas can be indicated by charting. Thus, charting organizes information. It helps you compare

Figure 6.5	**Example of a Time Line**

SIGNIFICANT DATES

1643	Counties and quarter courts established in Massachusetts
1645	William Berkeley becomes governor of Virginia
	Thomas Mayhew, Jr. begins Martha's Vineyard mission
1646	Child protest
	John Eliot first preaches to Indians
1651–1674	Massachusetts Indian praying towns established
1656	First Quakers arrive in Massachusetts
1660	Execution of Mary Dyer
	Berkeley restored as Virginia governor
1662	Half-way covenant adopted
1666	Viceroy de Tracy attacks Mohawks
1670s	"Covenant Chain" established between English and Iroquois
1675	King Philip's War
1675–1676	Bacon's Rebellion
1679	General Court calls the Reforming Synod
1680	New Hampshire becomes a royal colony
1683	Crown institutes *quo warranto* proceedings against Massachusetts charter
1685	James II accedes to English throne
	Dominion of New England created
1686	Sir Edmund Andros arrives in Boston as dominion governor
1688	Glorious Revolution; William III invades England
1689	Revolts in Massachusetts, New York, Maryland
	War of League of Augsburg begins
1690	Attack on Schenectady
	Governor. William Phips attempts to invade Canada
1692	Salem witchcraft trials
1697	Peace of Ryswick
1701	Grand Settlement between Iroquois and French
	Iroquois-English agreement signed at Albany
1705	Virginia slave code

SOURCE: Ronald P. Dufour. 1996. *Colonial America*. West Publishing Company.

Exercise 6.5   Use the information in "Dempsey's Law: Making Rank," page 490 in Sample Chapter 11 ("Organizing the Police Department") at the back of this book to construct a timeline that represents Professor Dempsey's career as a policeman.

information according to specific factors or traits. It allows you to classify information and look for trends across time. It enables you to sequence processes, events, and ideas.

Listing the information you have forms the first step in creating a chart. Once you create a list, you analyze it to identify relationships within it. For example, information could relate according to time, common traits, spatial proximity, causation, result, order, or other attributes.

Once you determine how ideas relate, you determine which kind of chart best fits your needs. Time lines are most suitable for information that occurs in a linear time order or sequence. Flowcharts apply to processes that flow in more than one direction or that have multiple simultaneous steps. Tables best organize like information that compares in more than one way. Table 6.5 provides steps in creating time lines and flowcharts. Table 6.6 lists the steps involved in creating tables. Figure 6.6 gives examples of organizational formats for tables.

Table 6.5   Steps in Creating Timelines and Flowcharts

---

1. Make a vertical list of the items you want to show.
2. Determine if the list follows a linear or multilevel order.
3. If items are linear, arrange them according to time or order.
4. If items are multilevel, organize them by levels before arranging according to time or order.

Table 6.6   Steps in Charting Information

---

1. Make a vertical list of the items you want to compare.
2. List horizontally the factors you want to know about each item.
3. Draw a grid by sketching lines between each element and each factor.
4. Locate and record the information that fills each box of the grid.

Figure 6.6   Synthesis Charts

CHARTS FOR TERMS IN ANY SUBJECT

Term	Definition	Connotation	Personal Example/Association

CHART FOR ARTISTS AND AUTHORS IN HUMANITIES CLASSES

Title	Author/Artists	Theme	Setting	Description of Action	Main Characters

CHART FOR DISCOVERIES IN APPLIED AND SOCIAL SCIENCES

Who?	From Where?	What?	When?	How?

GRAPHS: DRAWING ON DATA

Painting can illustrate but it cannot inform.

—Samuel Johnson
*Eighteenth century
English author*

Graphs both illustrate and inform. They allow large amounts of information to be organized into a more manageable form. **Graphs** show quantitative comparisons between two or more sets of information. By looking at comparable amounts or numbers, you determine relationships. The most common types of graphs are **bar graphs** (or **histograms**), **circle graphs,** and **line graphs.** Table 6.7 lists the steps in analyzing graphs.

Examining Bar Graphs

Bar graphs (see Figure 6.7) compare and contrast quantitative values. They show the amount or quantity of an item. Although the units in which the items are measured must be equal, they can be of any size and can start at any value. If the units are large, the bar graph might show approximate rather than exact amounts.

Following Line Graphs

Line graphs (see Figure 6.8) show quantitative trends for an item over time. Each line on the graph represents one item. When one or more lines are shown,

---

Table 6.7   Steps in Analyzing Graphs

1. Read the title, heading, or caption to identify the general group of objects being compared.

2. Note labels or headings for each item or unit to identify the specific objects being compared or contrasted in a line or bar graph. Look at the labels for each part of the circle.

3. Determine the units used to measure the items in a bar or line graph. Identify the general sizes for each part of the circle graph. Note relationships between and among the parts.

4. Note any general trends.

5. If you are looking at a graph as part of previewing a chapter, stop your examination of this graphic. Continue previewing the chapter.

6. When you reach the section of the text that refers to the graph, identify the text's purpose before turning to it. Does the author want you to note specific facts, generalizations, or trends?

7. Turn to the graph. Use the purpose set by the author to look at specific areas of the graph.

8. Reread the section of the text that referred to the graph. Make sure you understand the points and relationships noted by the author.

Figure 6.7   Example of a Bar Graph

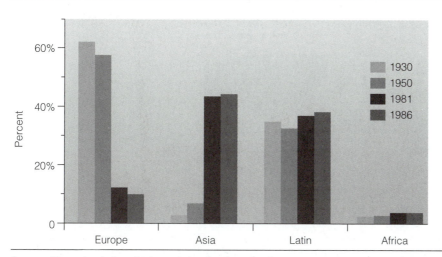

SOURCE: *Humanity: An Introduction to Cultural Anthropology* by James Peoples and Garrick Bailey. 1997. 4th ed., Figure 17.4, page 344. Wadsworth Publishing Company.

Figure 6.8   Example of a Line Graph

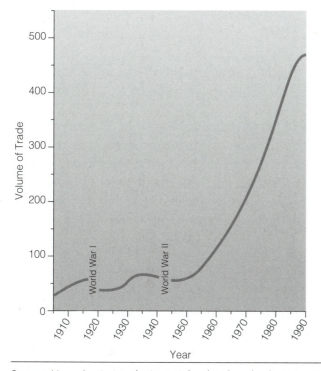

SOURCE: *Humanity: An Introduction to Cultural Anthropology* by James Peoples and Garrick Bailey. 1997. 4th ed., Figure 17.3, page 340. Wadsworth Publishing Company.

Figure 6.9   Example of a Circle Graph

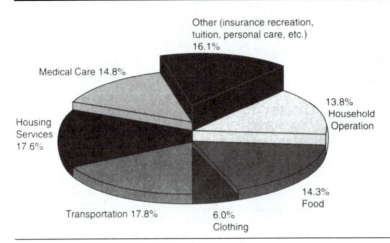

SOURCE: *Economic Issues for Consumers* by Roger LeRoy Miller and Alan D. Stafford. 1997. 8th ed., Exhibit 8.2, page 175. Wadsworth Publishing Company.

a **key** or **legend** tells what each line represents. Lines show increases, decreases, or no directional changes. Line graphs often are thought to be more accurate than bar graphs because they represent amounts more precisely.

Analyzing Circle Graphs

Probably the most common circle graph resembles something you might have had for lunch today—a pizza. Because circle graphs so closely resemble pies, they often are called pie charts.

A circle graph (see Figure 6.9) represents only one unit. It shows the relationship of parts of one unit to the whole of that unit. Because all the parts equal the whole unit, or 100 percent of the unit, percentages or fractions measure the parts of the graph. Contrasting colors or shading often denote these components in pie-shaped wedges. Circle graphs deal with fractions of a whole, instead of units on a continuum. Practice reviewing circle graphs in Exercises 6.6 and 6.7.

Graphing Data

Graphing allows you to organize quantitative information to visually show relationships and trends. Like creating a chart, graphing begins with a collection of information. Although you can use charts to organize quantitative information (for example, grades in a gradebook), the resulting table often contains too much data for quick analysis. Graphing forms a synthesis in that it allows you to show numerical changes for individual items. Each line,

Exercise 6.6   Use Figure 13.1 (Percentage by Race of Persons . . .) on page 515 from Sample Chapter 12 ("Women and Ethnic Groups") at the back of this book to answer the following questions:

1. What group represented the largest number of people living below poverty in 1992?

    _____

2. What group represented the smallest number of people living below poverty in 1992?

    _____

3. What is greater: the difference in the percentages of whites to Hispanics living below the poverty or the difference in the percentages of Hispanics to African Americans?

    _____

4. What could you infer about these percentages today? Are they similar or different? If the same, why? If different, how and why?

    _____

    _____

    _____

    _____

    _____

    _____

bar, or circle represents quantitative changes for a particular item or class of items. Thus, when you want to show what happens to a class of quantitative information as well as organize it, graphs are a better choice than charts.

Once you collect data, you organize according to the attributes of the data that you want to examine. For example, your data might consist of scores on tests for students in a class. You might arrange the data by students, by

Exercise 6.7   Use Figure 13.2 (Hispanic Population by Nation of Origin), page 519, and the two paragraphs that precede the heading "Minority Status" in Sample Chapter 12 ("Women and Ethnic Groups") at the back of this book to answer the following questions:

1. From what country does the largest percentage of the Hispanic population come?

   _____

2. What might explain this number?

   _____

3. From what country does the smallest percentage of the Hispanic population come?

   _____

4. What might explain this number?

   _____

5. What countries comprise Central/South America?

   _____

6. Examine the text information about censuses taken in 1970, 1980, and 1990. Now compare this information with that given in Figure 13.2. What do you note?

   _____

7. Assuming that information given in the text is accurate, what can you infer about these percentages?

   _____

range of grades (for example, number of people whose scores fall between 90 and 100), by exam, and so on. Once you choose the attributes, you select the upper and lower limits for comparison. For example, 0 to 100 is the range for most exam grades. Using appropriate labels, scale the range along the horizontal or vertical side of your graph (for example, 10, 20, 30, and so on). Again, using labels, list the items being compared across the remaining side of the graph. Finally, plot the score for each item on the graph. If you construct a bar graph, you create bars that extend from the lower limit of your range to the point you plot. If you construct a line graph, you connect the points as they change. The result is a jagged or smooth curve.

Just as reading circle graphs differs from reading line or bar graphs, creating circle graphs differs from creating line or bar graphs. Because circle graphs represent segments of a whole, the first step in creating a circle graph is determining what unit represents the entire circle. The second step is converting the data to fractions or percentages. The final step is sketching the parts and labeling accordingly. Exercise 6.8 provides practice in graphing data.

Exercise 6.8   Read the following information from Sample Chapter 11 ("Organizing the Police Department"). Then answer the following questions.

Many departments now distribute patrol officers according to a work load formula based on reported crimes and calls for service. The Dallas Police Department, for example, assigns 43 percent of its officers to the tour from 4 P.M. to midnight, 25 percent to the tour from midnight to 8 A.M., and 32 percent to the tour from 8 A.M. to 4 P.M.

However, a survey by the Police Executive Research Forum found that some cities still routinely distribute one-third of all patrol officers to each shift.

1. Construct a line graph that shows the distribution of patrol officers in the Dallas Police Department by time of tour of duty.

2. What percentage is ⅓? _____

3. Now add a second line to your graph that corresponds to information from the Police Executive Research Forum.

4. Construct a key so that a reader could tell what each line on your graph represents.

5. What advantages, if any, do you see in the Dallas system compared with that used by the cities survey by the research forum?

    _____

    _____

    _____

6. What advantages, if any, do you see in the system used by the cities surveyed by the research forum as opposed to the Dallas system?

    _____

    _____

    _____

CLASSIC CRITICAL THINKING

A variety of information related to the topics in this chapter is available on the World Wide Web. For this exercise, access Longview Community College's Critical Thinking Across the Curriculum Project, *Charts and Graphs: Traps and Tricks used in Showing Statistical Data Visually.*

http://www.kcmetro.cc.mo.us/longview/ctac/GRAPHS.HTM

Read the information from this Web site. For each of the following graphics in the Web site, identify the source of the graphic and summarize what you think the purpose of the graphic is. Then, identify the trick that alters it's meaning and describe the effect of the trick on meaning.

1. Death rate from home fires by age group

   Source _____

   Purpose _____

   Trick _____

   Effect _____

2. Teacher vacation time

   Source _____

   Purpose _____

   Trick _____

   Effect _____

3. Richest U.S. zip codes

   Source _____

   Purpose _____

   Trick _____

   Effect _____

4. Projected media use

   Source _____

   Purpose _____

   Trick _____

   Effect _____

5. Fewest/most students per computer

   Source _____

   Purpose _____

   Trick _____

   Effect _____

How does the text information support or fail to support the information in this graphic?

WRITE TO LEARN

On a separate sheet of paper or in your journal, use the following information to construct a line graph, a bar graph, and a circle graph. Students at Northeast College:

Freshmen	3500
Sophomores	2500
Juniors	2000
Seniors	<u>1500</u>
Total	9500

MAPS: PHYSICAL AND MENTAL TERRITORIES

> "You want to know how to get to the library? Well, first you go past Jones Hall, or is it Smith? Anyway, then you pass three, or maybe four more buildings, turn right, go straight for another two buildings, and turn left. You can't miss it."

If you've ever received directions like these, you probably wished you had a map. **Maps** provide information about places and their characteristics in two-dimensional formats. Because they often depict places you haven't physically seen, maps often—as Lawrence notes—appear more real to us than the lands they show.

Most commonly found in geography or history texts, maps are sometimes found in science, math, or literature texts and recreational leading books. Map-reading skills add to your understanding of the text by giving you visual representations of what's been written.

Unless you're giving directions to someone, mapmaking might seem like an unlikely study strategy. For learning, however, maps refer to physical representations of connections among mental concepts. Like geographical maps, these maps show the location of ideas in relation to one another. They provide an overview of mental territory and help you analyze and synthesize relationships.

The map appears to us more real than the land.

—D. H. Lawrence
Twentieth century American author

WRITE TO LEARN

On a separate sheet of paper or in your journal, select a graph type of your choice and use it to demonstrate a feature of your class (for example, number of males to females, students by major, hair color, eye color, and so forth).

Reading Geographic Maps

The **general reference map** and the **special purpose map** (also known as a **thematic map**) are the most common types found in texts. The general reference map (see Figure 6.10) gives general geographical information. This includes surface features (rivers, plains, mountains), places and their distances from each other, political data such as boundaries between states or countries, and urban population data. Special purpose or thematic maps (see Figure 6.11) highlight a particular feature of a geographical region. They show variations among other regions relative to this feature. Such maps include information on scientific data (for example, ocean currents and climate), social or cultural data (people and customs), political data (boundaries, governments), and economic data (expenditures and finances).

General reference and thematic maps come in two types: physical—showing the natural features of an area—and political—indicating human-made features of an area. City, state, or national boundaries comprise the only political information found on physical maps. Mountains or major bodies of water (rivers, oceans) comprise the only physical information found on political maps.

Special characteristics of maps include a **scale of distance,** symbols, and keys or legends. Although these might seem to add to the complexity of maps, such devices let authors provide vast amounts of information concisely. They also help you recognize the features highlighted by maps and make comparisons among these.

Because it would be unrealistic to make a map the actual size of the area it represents, **cartographers** (mapmakers) draw maps according to a set scale.

"I think it's a bad omen to take a test on Friday the thirteenth on a chapter whose map looks like this!"

A scale of distance, found on most maps, shows the relationship between distances on a map and distances in real life. Scales can be shown in the following three ways:

Fraction	1″ : 50 miles
Written Statement	1 inch equals 50 miles
Graphic Scale	/ / / /

0	50	100	150

Symbols, contrasting colors, or shading represent natural or human-made details. Thorough reading of a map depends on a thorough understanding of the ways in which features are represented. This understanding is

---

Figure 6.10   Example of a General Reference Map (Political)

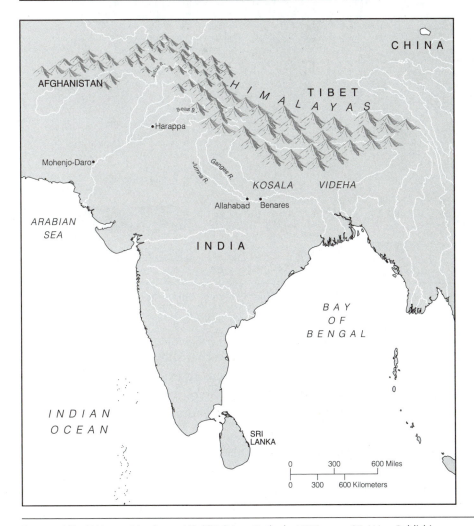

SOURCE: Alfred Warren Matthews. *World Religions,* 2nd ed., 1995, page 85. West Publishing Company.

Figure 6.11   Example of a Special or Thematic Map (Physical)

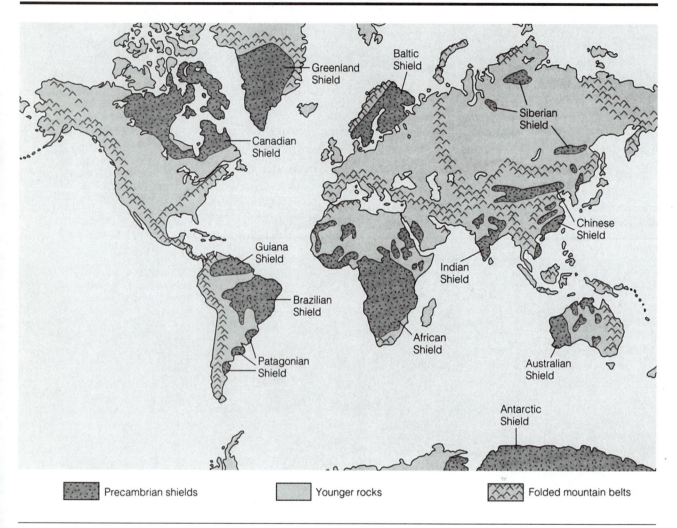

SOURCE: Reed Wicander and James S. Monroe. *Essentials of Geology,* 1995, page 132. West Publishing Company.

accomplished with the aid of a key or legend that shows each symbol, color, or shade used on a map and its corresponding explanation. Figure 6.11 shows a key ("Shields") on a thematic map. Steps for reading maps appears in Table 6.8. Exercise 6.9 provides practice in reading maps.

Mapping Mental Territories

Throughout history, individuals explored new territories. As they did so, they created maps to show where they had been. Their maps represented the synthesis of their background knowledge about a particular place. Mapping mental territories serves somewhat the same purpose as mapping physical

Table 6.8   Steps for Reading Maps

1. Locate and read the title, heading, or caption. This identifies the geographical area represented by the map.

2. Read the key or legend to identify symbols that are used on the map. Check the scale to get an idea of how much area the map covers.

3. If you are looking at a map as part of a chapter preview, stop your examination of the map. Continue previewing the chapter.

4. When you reach the section of the text that refers to the map, identify the text's purpose before turning to the map. What information does the map illustrate?

5. Turn to the map. Use the purpose set by the text to look at specific features of the map.

6. Reread the section of the text that referred to the map. Make inferences about information provided by the map and the text.

WRITE TO LEARN

A friend of yours needs directions from your house to the nearest grocery store. On a separate sheet of paper or in your journal, provide the following: (1) written directions and (2) a map (including landmarks, scale of distance, and key). Compare the two. Which provides the clearest instruction? Why? Which type of map did you draw? How is this type different from the other type?

---

territories. Visual representations, often called maps, represent the synthesis of relationships about a topic in graphic form. Because the visual representation of ideas affect a different area of the brain than do words (see Chapter 1), visual representations provide another way for you to encode and recall information. Taking an active part in organizing and creating visual representations helps you remember more with less effort.

Visual representations of information include **idea** or **concept maps** and word maps. Some kinds of representations are more appropriate for certain kinds of information than others. Determining the graphic you need depends on the content of the information and your skill in representing ideas visually.

Idea or concept maps are pictures that show relationships among concepts. They express patterns of thought. Idea maps can be used to organize or condense text chapters or lecture notes. Because concepts and ideas are related in various ways, maps differ. Thus, you can be somewhat creative in your mapmaking. The text structure you've identified from the lecture or text

---

Table 6.9   **Structure Patterns and Corresponding Elements in Idea Maps**

Pattern	Examples of Elements	
Introduction/Summary	main ideas supporting details	
Subject Development/Definition	characteristics elements supporting details	definitions examples types or kinds
Enumeration/Sequence	details main points steps	elements procedures
Comparison/Contrast	differences and similarities pros and cons	
Cause/Effect	elements procedures solutions	problems reasons

(See Chapter 4 and 5) helps you decide what concepts to map (see Table 6.9). In addition, if your instructor or text specifies elements or relationships, your map should reflect these.

Idea maps relate information to a central topic. They indicate major, minor, and equal relationships among details. Such maps show rankings of details by branching out from the central topic (see Figure 6.12). This text uses idea maps at the beginning of each chapter to show the relationship between chapter headings and subheadings. Another way idea maps show how details relate to a topic is by showing a progression of steps or chronological order of events or historical periods. Such maps show the logical flow of information (see Figure 6.13). The idea map you choose to use depends on the type of information you diagram and your preference (see Figure 6.14). Table 6.10 explains the steps in drawing an idea map.

WRITE TO LEARN

On a separate sheet of paper or in your journal, briefly explain the differences between outlines and graphic representations of information. Which appeal to you? Why?

Exercise 6.9   Use Figure 3-3 (Map Dividing Precinct into Sectors), page 495, of Sample Chapter 11 ("Organizing the Police Department") at the back of this book to answer the following questions:

1. What Brooklyn precinct covers the most streets?

   _____

2. What Brooklyn precinct covers the most distance?

   _____

3. The Long Island Railroad seems to run parallel to what two streets?

   _____

4. Identify the names of the two parks located in Brooklyn. List the streets that border each of them.

   _____

   _____

5. Which precinct is triangular in shape? Which precinct(s) is rectangular in shape?

   _____

6. In which precinct would you find Chauncey Street?

   _____

7. In which precinct would you find Summer Housing? What streets border it?

   _____

8. Suppose you are at the high school in precinct G. You have a friend who lives at the corner of Howard Avenue and Madison Street. Identify the route you will take to visit your friend after school. Approximately how far will you have to walk or ride?

   _____

   _____

   _____

9. On what street is the playground located?

   _____

10. What two facts are unusual about Utica Avenue (compared with other streets and avenues on the map)?

   _____

   _____

Figure 6.12   Example of a Web Idea Map

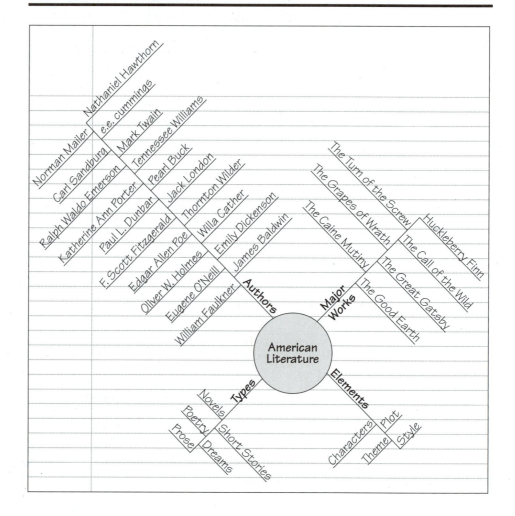

Another way to map concepts is to draw or map the terms in a particular chapter. These form a word map. You do this by identifying general headings under which terms might fall. Then you draw a map showing these headings. Under each heading, you list the appropriate terms. Draw two lines under each term. On the first line, create a picture that you associate with the term or its meaning. On the second line, write the term's meaning in your own words. Figure 6.15 provides an example of a word map.

When studying terms, cover the information below the term. Then try to remember the term's meaning. If you are not successful, you reveal the picture. Seeing your drawing should cue recall. If not, uncover the definition. Your final step in using this memory technique is to spend a few seconds studying the term and recalling why you drew the picture you did. You can apply mapping strategies in Exercise 6.10.

Figure 6.13   Example of a Branching Idea Map

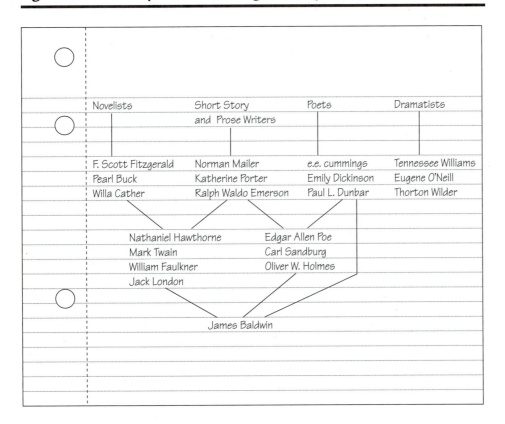

Table 6.10   Steps in Constructing Idea Maps

1. Choose a word or phrase that represents the topic you want your map to cover. This word could be the chapter title, a purpose-setting question, a heading, an objective, a term, or any other major concept.

2. Write this concept at the top of your notebook page.

3. List information about the concept. This could include descriptive details, definitions, functions, reasons, or any other listing of facts.

4. Examine the elements to determine how they relate to one another. Identify any associations between elements (least to most, largest to smallest, nonequivalent or nonsequential details, cause-to-effect, problem-to-solution, and so on).

5. Choose the type of idea map that can best represent the relationships you've identified.

6. Sketch the map.

7. Draw lines or arrows to indicate relationships among details and between the topic and details.

8. Judge the usefulness of your map by answering the following questions:

    a. Does the word or words you used to label the map accurately define the concept?

    b. Do the terms and ideas adequately support and describe the concept?

    c. Is the map logically organized?

    d. Is the map easy to read?

Figure 6.14   Map Structures

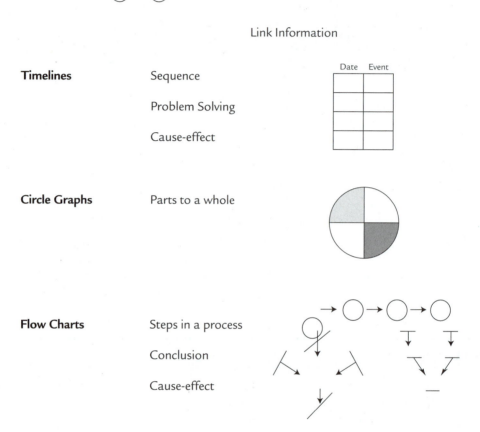

Webs

Link Information

Timelines   Sequence

Problem Solving

Cause-effect

Circle Graphs   Parts to a whole

Flow Charts   Steps in a process

Conclusion

Cause-effect

ONLINE CLASS   Web Exercise 6.1

A wealth of information related to the topics in this chapter is available on the World Wide Web. For this exercise, access the Inspiration Web site at http://www.inspiration.com/ and download a demo copy of the program. Type in the outline from Sample Chapter 14 and convert to it a map. Explore how you can modify or rearrange the pieces of the map. On a separate sheet of paper or in your journal, describe the version you prefer—outline or map. Explain how the version you chose supports the results of your learning style preferences.

Figure 6.15   Example of a Word Map

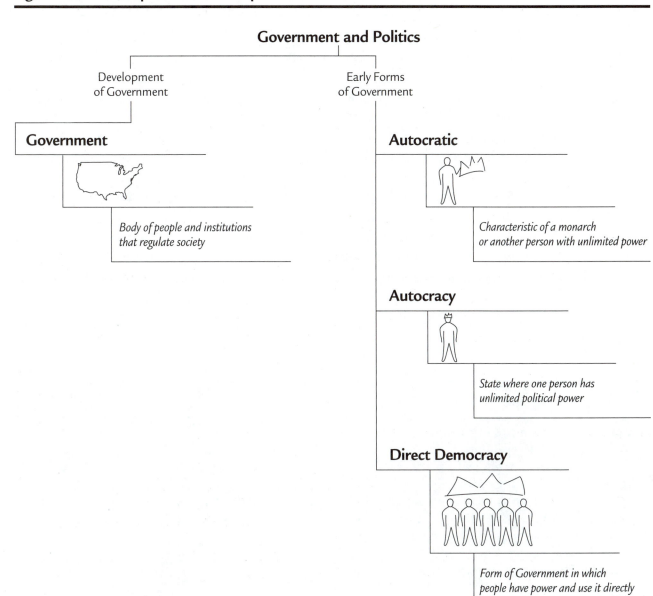

Exercise 6.10   On a separate sheet of paper or in your journal, answer the following questions completely.

1. Create a feature analysis chart that compares and contrasts the types of text structure discussed in this chapter with that discussed in Sample Chapter 14 ("Organization of Information").

2. Which chapter (this one or Sample Chapter 14) contains the more comprehensive information?

3. According to the *In Brief* that begins Sample Chapter 14 ("Organization of Information") at the end of this book, "The organization of a document affects the meaning your readers construct. Changing the organization of information can change your readers' understanding." Explain these statements. Do you agree or disagree? Why or why not?

4. Use Figure 7.3 of Sample Chapter 14 ("Organization of Information") at the end of this book to evaluate the goal-setting outline you created in Exercise 4.2 of Chapter 4.

5. After evaluating your outline, make corrections. Then on a separate sheet of paper or in your journal, create a map based on your corrected outline. If you want, you can use the Inspiration Web site discussed in *Online Class* (Web Exercise 6.1).

GROUP LEARNING ACTIVITY   A PICTURE OR 1,000 WORDS

Consider again the job of cartographers. They observe, plot, survey, photograph, and otherwise describe the locations of places by measuring distances, directions, and elevations. The maps they draw contain lines, words, symbols, and colors that describe new places to us or help us move from place to place.

In the following activity, you will create a map and interpret both written and graphic information.

Application

Step one: Create a map of a mythical country. Include information about the size and shape of the country; number and location of large cities; descriptions of natural formations; and names, sizes, and shapes of border countries and their locations. Select your own symbols for major highways, cities, natural formations, and so forth.

Step two: Pass your map to the person on your left and take the map from the person on your right. Write a one- to two-paragraph description of the mythical country based on this map.

Step three: Give this description to the person on your left and take the description from the person on your right. Now draw a map of the country that person has described.

Step four: Return the maps and accompanying descriptions to the original owners. Provide time for each person to compare his or her map with the corresponding description and map.

Step five: Discuss as a group how people interpret written and graphic material.

CHAPTER SUMMARY

1. Graphics provide ways to see what you or an author believes about information and how each of you organizes it to exemplify, sort, and clarify key concepts.

2. Graphic information helps you process and remember information more effectively because it involves both sides of the brain.

3. Diagrams provide visual representations of events, processes, structures, relationships, or sequences.

4. Charts (time lines, flowcharts, and tables) organize, condense, and simplify information so that you can analyze and synthesize concepts more easily.

5. Graphics (bar graphs, circle graphs, and line graphs) enable you to interpret or organize two or more sets of quantitative information.

6. Maps provide information about physical locations or mental relationships in visual form.

Class*ACTION*

Respond to the following on a separate sheet of paper or in your journal. Combine the chapter map and chapter summary to form a synthesis map that reflects the main ideas and important details of this chapter. Personalize the map by indicating specifically how you plan to implement suggestions offered by this chapter.

CHAPTER REVIEW

Answer briefly but completely.

1. Examine Table 6.1. Which type of text graphic is most versatile? Least versatile? Why is this so?

    _____

    _____

    _____

    _____

    _____

2. How do graphics enhance your ability to process and recall information?

_____

_____

_____

_____

_____

3. What is the process for taking notes from text graphics?

_____

_____

_____

_____

4. How do feature analysis tables differ from quality tables? How are they alike? How can you use purpose to identify the type you need?

_____

_____

_____

_____

_____

5. In what ways are tables, flowcharts, and time lines alike? How do they differ? How can you use purpose to identify the type you need?

_____

_____

_____

_____

6. In what ways are bar graphs and line graphs alike? How do they differ? How can you use purpose to identify the type you need?

_____

_____

_____

_____

_____

7. How do circle graphs differ from bar or line graphs?

_____

_____

_____

_____

_____

8. What is the difference between general reference and special purpose maps?

_____

_____

_____

_____

_____

9. Compare physical and political maps.

_____

_____

_____

_____

_____

10. What is the purpose of keys or legends in reading graphs or maps?

_____

_____

_____

_____

_____

VOCABULARY DEVELOPMENT   Right-Brain Note Cards: Picture This!

Think of your instructor for this course. Did you think of a name or a face? Authors know that verbal and visual information affects learning and memory differently. A combination of text and graphic information provides you with stimuli for both kinds of understanding, Similarly, vocabulary development can be enhanced through the use of visual as well as verbal information.

One picture is worth ten thousand words.

—Frederick R. Barnard

In many ways, Barnard's view of pictures has been scientifically validated by the work of Nobel prize winner Roger Sperry (See Chapter 1).

Wittrock (1977) put Sperry's findings to work in a study of memory and learning. He found that students remembered vocabulary words better when they drew pictures to represent them than when they read and wrote the words and the definitions. Tracing a picture of a definition resulted in better recall than writing the definition. Creating a personal visual image for the word proved to be more effective than tracing.

The work of Sperry and Wittrock has clear implications for college vocabulary development. Pictures capture the attention of the right brain. Like text graphics, pictures affect your brain, your learning, and your memory differently than do words alone. Using both sides of the brain—instead of relying only on the left side—increases your potential for learning. Although your pictures might not be worth ten thousand words, they will help you picture—and learn—the words you need.

Use the following suggestions and Figure 6.16 to picture words with note cards that appeal to the right brain.

1. Write the word on the front of the card.

2. On the front of the card, draw a picture that represents its meaning: Form personal associations. Use humorous or outrageous images. Use common symbols.

3. Write the word's meaning on the back of the card.

4. Use the front of the card for recall. If you cannot recall the meaning, look at your drawing. Try to remember why you drew what you did. If you still cannot recall the meaning, refer to the definition.

Activity

Choose any five of the terms on page 504 in Sample Chapter 11, "Organizing the Police Department" from the back of this book and create right-brain note cards for them.

Figure 6.16   Example of a Right-Brain Note Card

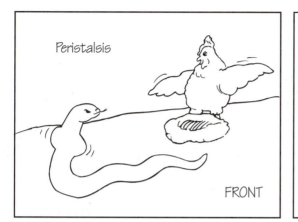

Peristalsis

FRONT

Involuntary contraction of the muscular wall of the esophagus to force food to the stomach and propel waste through the rest of the digestive tract.

BACK

Key to the cartoon on page 264

The singers and groups in the time line are Fats Domino, the Beatles, and Three Dog Night.

OBJECTIVES

After you finish this chapter, you should be able to do the following:

1. Identify the stages in processing information.

2. Apply association techniques for recall.

3. Compare practice strategies.

4. Identify ways information is lost from long-term memory.

5. Use general suggestions for taking exams.

6. Apply strategies for preparing for and taking subjective exams.

7. Apply strategies for preparing for and taking objective exams.

8. Apply strategies for preparing for and taking specialized exams.

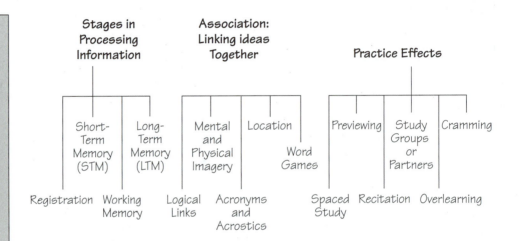

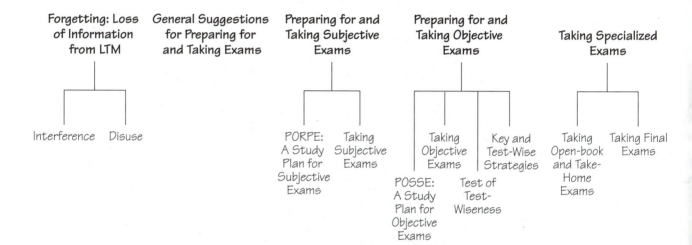

> A learned fool is one who has read everything and simply remembered it.
>
> —Josh Billings
> *Nineteenth century American humorist*

The process of learning is far more than memorization. Memorization, or recall, is the lowest level of understanding in Bloom's taxonomy, a system developed in 1956 to describe levels of difficulty, sophistication, and thoroughness in thinking and reading (see Figure 7.1). Indeed, you can memorize information and not understand it at all. In memorization, what you "learn" is all there is. In general, you have no way to use the information other than in the form in which you learned it.

That's why many students who had very good high school grades discover that the learning and memory strategies they used in high school often result in less-than-satisfactory grades in college courses. After studying for tests, they can define or recite almost any fact from the text or lecture; however, they often lack the ability to make important connections among information. This is a problem of depth. How deeply you process information affects how well you understand it. The more you know about a concept, the better you can relate it to other ideas. This requires a deeper understanding. In high school, you are most often asked to think in words; in college, you must think in concepts.

Processing depth varies for a number of reasons. The strength of your interest in a subject and the amount of desire you have for learning affect how deeply you process information about the subject. Intense interest or desire causes you to process more thoroughly. Negative attitudes often result in superficial processing. Purpose and intention also influence depth of processing. Like setting purposes for reading, determining the level of understanding you need gives you a goal. In addition, how well you concentrate affects how deeply you process information. When you concentrate well, you make stronger and more numerous links among facts and ideas in the information for future applications. Finally, relating information to what you know—your background knowledge—affects processing. It allows you to form more connections between new information and what you already know.

For instance, consider what you know about Abraham Lincoln (sixteenth president of the United States) and Andrew Johnson (seventeenth president of the United States). If you are like most people, you can visualize Abraham Lincoln (tall, thin, bearded, black top hat). You associate several ideas with him (Civil War, Gettysburg Address, assassination, lawyer, log cabin). Like most people, however, you might find that you recall little about Andrew Johnson, other than his name and that he succeeded Lincoln as president. What you recall about each man reflects, to some extent, depth of processing. Because you know more about Lincoln and connect him to other concepts, you possess a deeper understanding of him. In contrast, if you know few details about Andrew Johnson, you make few connections between him and what you know. Your understanding of Andrew Johnson is shallowly processed.

As you use the various rehearsal techniques in this chapter to help you process information, you also must consider how you associate and organize

Figure 7.1   Bloom's Taxonomy of Thinking

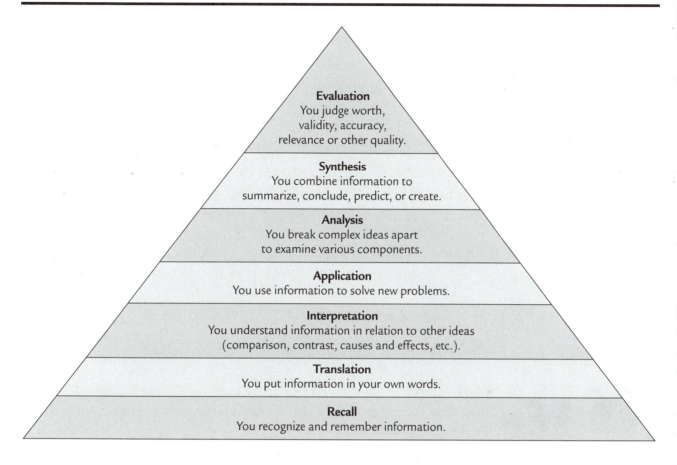

information. Doing this allows you to develop the necessary links among information, thus increasing your ability to apply what you've learned.

For example, in a psychology course, you might be learning about the biological bases of behavior. As you study, you memorize the parts of the forebrain—thalamus, hypothalamus, limbic system, corpus callosum, cerebrum. You also learn a definition for each and can identify its function. With this information stored, you can answer questions, such as the following:

1. What is the thalamus?
2. What part of the brain regulates autonomic functions?

However, on the test you find the following questions:

1. A classmate experiences memory lapses. Which part of the forebrain is most likely to contribute to this problem and why?
2. Hypothesize a time line for the development of forebrain structures and provide a rationale for the order of development.

3. As a research psychologist, devise a research question that you want to investigate for each of the components of the forebrain.
4. Which of the components of the forebrain have the most impact on the acquisition of knowledge for elementary school students?

To answer the second set of questions, you must not only know the information but also be able to apply that knowledge to different situations. This requires you to have a deeper understanding of the biological bases of behavior.

Processing depth varies from person to person and from subject to subject. The way you practice, organize, or associate information depends on your personal learning preferences and goals, what your instructor emphasizes, and the content information and requirements.

Learning, then, involves a process or action that results in a product—knowledge. This process depends on your prior knowledge of the material, your reason for learning, and the level of understanding you need as well as the kind of material to be learned. You, the learner, control the process by understanding how memory enables you to select, assimilate, retrieve and use information.

STAGES IN PROCESSING INFORMATION

Do you remember . . . your first birthday? your first kiss? where you found your keys the last time you lost them?

Do you ever wonder why you remember some things and not others? Because you store memories in different ways and forms, you remember some things more easily or clearly.

You probably cannot recall your first birthday. Two factors account for this lapse of memory. First, the brain structures used for remembering don't fully develop until you are about two-years old. Second, because you had not learned to speak at one-year old, you could not store information in words the way you do now. Thus, although that information is still stored in your brain, you cannot access it.

You might remember your first kiss, but not your fifth, tenth, and twelfth kisses, because the first kiss was a new event that caused a new category to be formed in your memory. With each subsequent kiss, more information was added to that category, and kisses became less unique.

You probably don't recall where you found your keys the last time you lost them because you have no single specific place where lost keys are found. Because you have no general category for "lost keys" in memory for you to search, you don't recall where you found them.

Thus, how our memories work determines what we remember and what we forget. Because school courses require you to remember vast amounts of information, you need to understand the stages involved in processing information. These stages are **registration, short-term memory, working memory,** and **long-term memory** (see Figure 7.2).

Figure 7.2   A Model of Memory

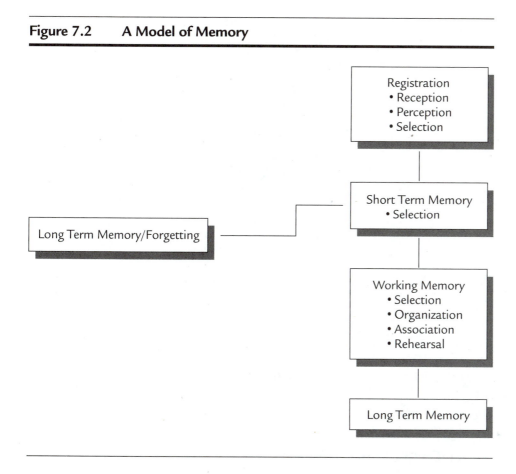

Registration

Just as your first interaction with college classes is registration, your first interaction with information involves its registration. In this initial stage, you receive information but do not necessarily understand it.

Next, depending on your background knowledge, you perceive information. For example, suppose you visit a foreign country whose language you do not speak. When you see signs and billboards there, you receive stimuli and recognize the symbols on them as words. However, you do not understand their meanings. This is similar to what happens when you first encounter information. If you do speak that country's language, however, you understand their meanings. Thus, **reception** leads to **perception.**

The final phase of registration involves **selection.** What you select depends on you and the material at hand. Your purpose for learning and your background knowledge help you decide what to select. The content and difficulty of the information, as well as the way it is organized, also play a part in what you select. For example, suppose you need a place to sleep in the country you're visiting. As you look at the signs and billboards, you ignore ones advertising restaurants, tours, or shops. You concentrate on those for hotels.

"Come on, Harold! The sign says 'Girls! Girls! Girls!'
but it's not the bathroom!"

You selectively ignore or process depending on your purpose. You quickly forget what's ignored. The information you choose is transferred into your short-term memory—the second stage of memory processing.

Short-Term Memory (STM)

All information you plan to remember goes through short-term memory (STM). When you try to remember a telephone number until you dial it, you use your STM. Its stay there is brief, lasting perhaps as little as fifteen seconds. This short duration results from the limited capacity of STM. This capacity resembles a library shelf that holds only a certain number of books. Miller (1956) found that STM could hold seven plus or minus two **chunks** of information. This varying capacity depends on how well or how poorly you "chunk," or group information for easier recall. The meaningfulness of the information chunks also affects capacity. For example, suppose you try to remember the numbers 1 - 8 - 6 - 0 - 1 - 8 - 6 - 4. If you chunk those numbers into dates (1860–1864) the numbers are easier to recall. This allows more memory space for other information. Factors such as age, maturation, practice, and the complexity of information also affect the size of STM. From its short stay in STM, information is either forgotten or moved to working memory.

Working Memory

Thinking takes place in working memory—the third stage of memory processing—through selection, association, organization, and rehearsal.

Learning about working memory, then, helps you understand how and what you think about information.

Working memory is like a worktable on whose surface are the tools and materials you need. The tools and materials in your working memory include your intent for learning, your skills in processing information, relevant STM and background data, and the choices you make concerning how to process information. Thus, you take STM and background information, decide what you want from it, inventory your choices about how you could process the information, and choose the most appropriate one.

For example, you might have to evaluate various perspectives on U.S. foreign policy since World War II. You get your notes, text, and so on for reference and consider the background knowledge you already have. Then, you consider the ways in which you might process the information through association or organization. You decide to organize information so that you can identify the patterns of the perspectives and their effects to judge their worth. Rehearsal strategies help you encode the information—or place it in memory—more fully. How rehearsal takes place depends on the type of information to be learned and your strategies for organizing and associating it with other information. The amount of time you spend rehearsing information is less important than what you do during that time.

Like any worktable, working memory has a limited amount of space. Just as you clear table space to work on a project, you clear memory space to process information. And just as you lose items on an overloaded table, memory processing becomes confused and information is lost when you think about too many ideas at one time or fail to clear memory space. For example, in learning a poem or in understanding U.S. foreign policy, you might find

---

WRITE TO LEARN

Two actors of the sixteenth century, Samuel Foote and Charles Macklin, reportedly argued about who had the better facility for learning lines. Macklin boasted that he could learn a speech after hearing it once. Foote then asked Macklin to repeat the following, "So she went into the garden to cut a cabbage leaf to make an apple pie; and at the same time a great she-bear, coming up the street, pops its head into the shop—What! No soap? So he died and she very imprudently married the barber; and there were present the Picninnies, the Joblillies, and the Garyalies, and the grand Panjandrum himself, with the little round button at top." Macklin could not remember the speech and was defeated. On a separate sheet of paper or in your journal, explain how the factors that contribute to the process of learning—prior knowledge, intent, level at which information is to be learned—affected Macklin's inability to remember the speech.

the information as a whole too complicated or unwieldy to think about at once. You need to divide the information and process a bit at a time.

Long-Term Memory (LTM)

If a library shelf represents STM, then the entire library corresponds to LTM. Following rehearsal, information enters LTM. It stays there until it is consciously or unconsciously recalled to working memory. Information in LTM is organized and stored for long periods of time. How long information remains there depends on how deeply you processed or learned it and factors relating to forgetting. The apparent permanence of LTM is somewhat misleading, although the actual loss of information is slow. This loss results from variations in processing depth or forgetting.

ASSOCIATION: LINKING IDEAS TOGETHER

John Gilbert, an early twentieth-century actor, was once called on at the last minute to play the role of the heroine's father. He succeeded in learning his lines but had great difficulty in remembering the name of the character he played—Numitorius. A fellow actor helpfully suggested that he associate the name with the Book of Numbers in the Bible. Confidence renewed, Gilbert rushed on stage and delivered his opening line, "Hold, 'tis I, her father—Deuteronomy."

Association forms links between familiar items and the items you want to remember. Once established, the links become automatic. Recalling a familiar item cues recall of the other item. Unfortunately for John Gilbert, he associated what he had to learn with the wrong book of the Bible.

This familiar mechanism is one you use every day. For example, perhaps you associate a certain song with a particular time, event, or person in your life. Hearing the song cues that memory. In much the same way, you form conscious associations between something familiar to you and the information you need to recall. Thus, to be effective, associations must be personal.

Logical links, mental imagery, physical imagery, acronyms and acrostics, and word games connect information. The effectiveness of the various techniques depends on the type of information you need to learn and, most important, on you. Table 7.1 lists questions to help you choose the most appropriate technique.

Logical Links

Sometimes the logic or meaning of the information lends itself to memory. In this case, the whole might, indeed, be greater than the sum of its parts. For example, you might have to learn about the following aspects of aging:

Table 7.1   Questions for Developing Associations

1. Does the item remind you of anything?
2. Does the item sound like or rhyme with a familiar word?
3. Can you visualize something when you think of the item?
4. Can you rearrange any letters to form an acronym?
5. Do you know of any gimmicks to associate with the item?
6. Can you draw a picture (mnemonigraph) to associate with the item?
7. Can you associate the item with any familiar locations?
8. Can you form logical connections among concepts?

nutritional implications of aging, the effect of loneliness on nutrition, financial worries associated with aging and nutrition, assistance programs, and preparing for the later years. Such concepts would be difficult to learn in isolated parts. The sense of the concept as a whole forms the key. Consider the logic that links these ideas: What one eats (nutrition) affects aging. Loneliness and lack of finances affect nutrition. Assistance programs provide adequate nutrition. One can prepare for aging if one knows what to expect and what assistance is available.

Understanding how concepts connect facilitates learning through the elaboration of ideas. Elaboration allows you to reframe information through what you already know from experience. You provide the logic from your background knowledge of how information fits together.

Mental and Physical Imagery

When you picture something in your mind, you experience mental imagery. Mental imagery is a natural occurrence because you often think in pictures, rather than words. For instance, think of an ice cream cone. Do you think i-c-e / c-r-e-a-m / c-o-n-e, or do you picture how an ice cream cone looks, smells, or tastes? This use of your visual and other senses aids your recall of both the familiar and unfamiliar. In addition, pictures are stored differently in the brain than words (See Chapter 1). Imagery provides an additional way to encode information. Table 7.2 lists suggestions for creating effective mental images.

Such mental associations link concrete objects with their images (for example, a picture of an apple with the word *apple*) or abstract concepts with their symbols (for example, a picture of a heart with the word *love*). Mental imagery also links unrelated objects, concepts, and ideas through visualization. For example, suppose you want to remember the name of the twenty-first president of the United States, Chester Arthur. You visualize an author

---

Table 7.2   Suggestions for Maximizing Mental Imagery and Examples

---

Goal: To remember the four food groups: milk, meat, fruit and vegetables, and breads and cereals.

	Suggestion	Example
1.	Use common symbols, such as a heart for *love* or a dove for *peace*.	A cornucopia overflowing with cheese (*milk*), sausages (*meat*), fruits, and breads
2.	Use the clearest and closest image.	Your family sitting at your dining table and eating fully loaded *cheeseburgers* (bread, meat, cheese, lettuce, tomatoes, onions, and so forth)
3.	Think of outrageous or humorous images.	A *milk* cow (*meat*) eating a banana (*fruit*) sandwich (*bread*)
4.	Create action-filled images.	See 2 and 3

---

writing the number 21 on a wooden chest. This mental picture helps you associate chest, author, and 21 to recall that Chester Arthur was the twenty-first president.

If you draw your mental image on paper, you make use of another sense, your **kinesthetic perception.** This type of memory aid is called a **mnemonigraph.** By actually making your mental image a physical one, you provide yourself with a form of repetition that reinforces your memory. Drawing or diagramming information also helps in another way. Rather than learning a list of details, you sketch a picture that includes all the details you need to learn. For instance, suppose you need to remember the parts of an eye. Drawing and labeling the parts aid your recall.

Acronyms and Acrostics

Forming **acronyms** or **acrostics** is most helpful for recalling lists of information (for example, the bones in the body). Acronyms are words created from the first letter or the first few letters of the items on the list. *Roy G. Biv,* one of the most commonly used acronyms, helps you recall the colors of the rainbow in order (red, orange, yellow, green, blue, indigo, and violet). *HOMES,* another common acronym, cues your memory of the names of the Great Lakes (Huron, Ontario, Michigan, Erie, and Superior). Another acronym that aids your recall of the Great Lakes might be "Sho' me." Acronyms, then, need not be real words. Like others mnemonics, they work best when you create them for yourself.

"If only the test were just ten questions long!"

Acrostics are phrases or sentences created from the first letter or first few letter of items on a list you need to remember. For example, "George eats old gray rat at Paul's house yesterday" helps you spell "geography" correctly. Note that to be used as an acrostic, sentences need not be grammatically correct. They need only make sense to you. Thus, an acrostic ("Hot oatmeal makes eating sensational") cues your memory for the Great Lakes just as the acronym *HOMES* does.

Location

The location method of mnemonics dates back to a gruesome event in ancient Greece. According to Cicero (Bower, 1970), Simonides, a Greek poet, had just finished reciting a poem when a messenger asked him to step outside the building. Just as he left the building, the roof collapsed. Everyone inside was killed. The guests' bodies were so mangled that they could not be identified. Simonides identified the corpses by remembering where each guest sat. Similarly, location memory occurs when you associate a concept with a place. This includes where you were when you heard the concept, how it looked in your notes, which graphics were on the page containing the information, and so on.

You can create location memory artificially as well. To create a memory map, think of a familiar place. You associate the facts you need to know with features of that location. Then, visualize yourself either walking around the place or looking at each feature of it. As you "see" the features, you recall the topic you've associated with it. For instance, suppose you want to learn a list of chemical elements. You choose a familiar route, like the route from the college bookstore to your math class. As you pass each building along the way, you assign it a chemical element. Later, in your class, you visualize your route. As you "see" each place, you recall the element it represents.

This same type of system works by visualizing a closet that contains many pegs or hooks for clothes. You "hang" information on each hook and then recall what's on each one.

Word Games

Some memory aids involve what amounts to playing games with information. Such techniques aid your memory in two ways. First, they require you to actively think about the information to create the game. Second, they provide clues that entertain you and stimulate your recall. Diverse in nature, word games can be both easy and difficult to create.

Advertisers realize the value of rhymes and jingles in making their products memorable. Rhymes and jingles can make what you need to learn memorable as well. A common rhyme or jingle that aids recall of a spelling rule is "*I* before *E* except after *C* or when sounded like *A*, as in *neighbor* or *weigh.*"

Puns and **parodies** are humorously copied common words, poems, stories, or songs. A pun is the humorous use of a word or phrase to suggest more than one meaning. Parodies copy serious works or phrases through satire or burlesque. The humor of puns and parodies also brings cognitive benefits. Like other mnemonics, they make studying more imaginative and entertaining. For instance, suppose you want to learn the meaning of *numismatist* (a coin collector). You might parody the children's nursery rhyme "Four and Twenty Blackbirds." Instead of the king being in his counting house, counting all his money, you change the rhyme to "The numismatist was in his counting house, counting all his money." Or, you might make a pun to help you recall the definition. This could be something like "two numismatists getting together for old 'dime's' sake."

Many people create other memory tricks to aid recall. Many such tricks have been created to teach the basics of common concepts. A good example of this is a trick for remembering the multiplication tables for nine (Table 7.3). Others you devise for yourself. For example, one student—needing to know the difference between *skimming* and *scanning*—decided to use the letters in the word to signal its purpose. The *mi* in *skimming* cued the purpose of finding main ideas. The *an* in *scanning* cued the purpose of finding specific answers. Exercise 7.1 provides practice in different methods of associating ideas.

Table 7.3   **Memory Trick for Multiplying by Nine**

---

1. List the numbers 0 to 9 in a column.

    0
    1
    2
    3
    4
    5
    6
    7
    8
    9

2. List the numbers 0 to 9 in a column starting from the *bottom* beside the numbers you've already listed. Your combined columns form the products derived from multiplying 9 times 0, 1, 2, 3 . . . 9. (that is, $9 \times 0 = 00$, $9 \times 1 = 09$, $9 \times 2 = 18$ . . .)

    0**9**
    1**8**
    2**7**
    3**6**
    4**5**
    5**4**
    6**3**
    7**2**
    8**1**
    9**0**

3. Note also that if you add the two digits in each product, you get 9. For example,

    $9 \times 1 = 09 \ (0 + 9 = 9)$
    $9 \times 2 = 18 \ (1 + 8 = 9)$
    $9 \times 3 = 27 \ (2 + 7 = 9)$

WRITE TO LEARN

On a separate sheet of paper or in your journal, select one of the association techniques to help you remember the names of each of your instructors. Explain how and why the technique cues your memory.

Exercise 7.1   Respond to each of the following:

1. Create an acronym or acrostic to help you remember the chain of command in Figure 3-2 of Sample Chapter 11 ("Organizing the Police Department").

_____

_____

_____

_____

_____

_____

2. Create a word game to help you remember the difference between time or function/purpose management as described on pages 496–502 of Sample Chapter 11.

_____

_____

_____

_____

_____

3. Create and draw physical images to help you recall the concepts of the three-tour conditions as described on pages 496–498 of Sample Chapter 11.

4. Create an acronym or acrostic to help you recall how quasi-military police differ from civil police as described on pages 486–487 of Sample Chapter 11.

_____

_____

_____

_____

_____

_____

PRACTICE EFFECTS

When the Polish pianist Ignacy Paderewski played before Queen Victoria, she said, "Mr. Paderewski, you are a genius!" Paderewski replied, "Perhaps, Your Majesty, but before that I was a drudge."

Learning is less genius and more drudgery. But rather than practice making perfect, as it does in music, practice makes permanent in learning. Practice aids storage in LTM. In addition, practice helps make retrieval from LTM into working memory more automatic.

You practice information visually, auditorily, or semantically. **Visual practice** usually involves the silent reading of information. Such practice often takes place in frantic, last-minute cramming sessions. **Auditory practice** occurs when you repeat information aloud or discuss it with another student. You practice information semantically when you write or diagram it. Both auditory and **semantic practice** yield better results because they involve active processes. And, as with any learning process, the more actively you are involved, the more learning takes place.

Practice methods assume many forms. They vary in amount of time involved, depth of learning, and manner in which information is learned. When you choose a practice method, you should consider your purpose for learning the information and the way you learn most effectively. No matter which method you choose, you will be repeating information in some way.

Spaced Study

Spaced study consists of alternating short study sessions with breaks. This method is also known as **distributed practice.** You set study goals by time (for example, 15 minutes) or task (for example, three pages) limits. After reaching these goals, you allow yourself a short amount of free time. You

"A score of 7.5 isn't earth shattering unless I grade it on the Richter scale."

could take a walk, have a soft drink, or call a friend. This method helps you process information into LTM.

Spaced study works for many reasons. First, spaced study rewards hard work. This form of study involves **behavior modification.** This type of learning is based on research by B. F. Skinner, an American psychologist. In his studies with animals, Skinner found that they respond best when rewarded with food. The breaks in spaced study serve as your reward for completing a set amount of study. Second, because you work under a deadline of time or task limits, you complete quality work. Knowing you have a certain amount of time or work to study motivates you. Third, because working memory has limited capacity, breaks provide time for information to be absorbed into LTM. Fourth, when you study complex, related information, study breaks keep you from confusing similar details. Avoiding this **interference** is best accomplished by sleeping between study sessions. This is why cramming seldom works well as a form of practice.

Previewing

As discussed in Chapters 4 and 5, many study strategies suggest that you preview information before reading a text or hearing a lecture. The primary purpose of previewing is to access what you already know about a topic. Previewing also provides a form of practice because it requires you to analyze information before you read or study it. As a result, you increase the amount of details you can later recall.

Recitation

Recitation involves silent, oral, or written repetition of the answers to study questions. These questions can come from the text, the instructor, or yourself.

Thus, the first step of recitation is to locate or create study questions. Next, you read or study information to answer these questions. Third, you recite answers. Fourth, you use your text or notes to check the accuracy of your answers. This process keeps information in your working memory. Repeated recitation transfers information to LTM.

Study Groups or Partners

The old saying "Two heads are better than one" describes the purpose of study groups or partners. The purpose of such groups is discussion of information. Therefore, learning becomes an active, rather than passive, process. In a group, members explain and listen to explanations from each other, which allows them to use their auditory, visual, and physical senses. Combining these sensory impressions not only enhances the active learning process but also helps transfer information to LTM. Finally, group discussions motivate members. This happens because members make commitments to prepare for and come to study sessions.

Study groups learn a variety of information. Group members provide drill in learning **verbatim information,** such as definitions of terms or lists of names or dates. In addition, group members practice skills, such as solving math problems or learning foreign languages. Analysis and organization of complex or confusing information enhances the understanding of group members. Finally, creating and discussing test questions provides practice of test-taking skills and reduces test anxiety.

One note of caution concerns the way in which groups practice. Because most groups discuss information orally, members might neglect practicing their writing skills. If you have difficulty composing written responses to test items, you also need to practice your skills in putting information on paper.

> The more we study, the more we know.
>
> The more we know, the more we forget.
>
> The more we forget the less we know.
>
> The less we know, the less we forget.
>
> The less we forget, the more we know.
>
> So why study?

Overlearning

Overlearning, most appropriate for verbatim information, consists of overlapping study. This form of practice continues to reinforce information after you've first seen it (Tenney, 1986). For example, suppose you need to learn a list of forty terms for a history course. You can overlearn the list in one of two ways as described in Table 7.4.

Cramming

It's the night before the test. You have 12 chapters left to read. You missed the last week of classes but borrowed a friend's notes. Unfortunately, your friend doesn't take very good notes.

What to do? Cram for the exam! **Cramming** involves frantic, last minute (and sometimes all-night) memorization. Such learning rarely results

Table 7.4   Methods of Overlearning

Method I	Method II
1. List each item separately on note cards.	1. Divide the list into manageable units (three to five items per unit, depending on the difficulty of the material).
2. Learn the first three cards.	2. Learn one set by practicing it orally.
3. Add one card.	3. Add another set.
4. Practice all four cards orally.	4. Practice all sets orally.
5. Add one card.	5. Repeat steps 3 and 4 until you know all the items.
6. Practice all five cards orally.	
7. Delete the card from the original set that you know the best and add one new card.	
8. Practice with all five cards.	
9. Repeat steps 7 and 8 until you know all the items.	

in complete success because there is not enough time to learn information. Crammers simply try to memorize everything. As a result, they become renters, rather than owners, of information. Short-term benefits rarely translate into long-term results. Since crammers fail to really learn the information, they must memorize it over and over. Cramming, then, is one of the least effective means of study.

But, what if it *is* the night before the exam and you really do have 12 chapters left to read? Your best bet is to use parts of the SQ3R process to maximize your efforts. You begin by reading all chapter introductions and summaries. These provide you with the most basic condensation of information. Then you construct chapter maps or outlines. These show you the connections among ideas. Finally, you examine the terms to see how they support chapter concepts. These measures will not ensure a good grade. They only represent a more informed means of cramming.

FORGETTING: LOSS OF INFORMATION FROM LTM

Once information is processed, it might or might not remain in LTM. You, too, might wonder "why study?" When you lose information from LTM, more commonly known as forgetting, you do so because of interference or disuse.

*"If she can remember our credit card number,
seems like she could remember our phone number."*

Which of these two occurs more often depends on four factors: your interest in learning, your purpose for learning, the frequency you use information, and the number of connections you make with other information. For instance, suppose you hear a funeral home ad the same day you meet an attractive member of the opposite sex. Whose name are you more likely to recall? Because you have greater interest in meeting new people than in visiting funeral homes, your recall of the person's name is stronger. If you plan to contact the person at a later date, your purpose for remembering also strengthens recall. If you date the person often, remembering the person's name becomes automatic. This is because you use it so frequently. As you learn more about the person, you associate these additional bits of information in your background knowledge with the person. This, too, strengthens recall.

Interference

Have you ever been listening to your favorite radio station when another station broke into your station's frequency? That's called interference. This happens in your memory, too. Interference occurs because new, conflicting information affects background knowledge. Interference hinders memory for specific details more often than it does memory for main ideas.

Interference occurs for two reasons. Either new information confuses existing knowledge or existing knowledge confuses new learning. For example, suppose you are taking courses in both sociology and psychology. Because the content of these courses is somewhat alike, interference is more likely to occur. Interference is best avoided by alternating study periods with at least a short nap.

Disuse

"Who was President Carter's vice-president?" "What does M*A*S*H* mean?" "How do you write 51 in Roman numerals?" Part of the fun and frustration in answering these and other trivia questions is remembering information learned long ago. The answers to such questions depend on your ability to recall seldom-used information. Such information is sometimes difficult (or even impossible) to locate in memory because you have not used it for a long time. Because of its disuse, you no longer remember where the information is stored. Or you forgot many of the details concerning it. In a way, "use it or lose it" applies to memory.

General Suggestions for Preparing for and Taking Exams

Successful test taking involves what someone once called "that old *ABC*— ability, breaks, and courage." Luckily, you can acquire these. Successful test-taking abilities include knowing about kinds of tests, various memory strategies, and how to alter your studying to make the most of the two. Being test-wise means that you take advantage of breaks and avoid any pitfalls you might encounter during a test. Having the courage you need to be a successful test-taker means identifying and effectively managing the stress that comes with exams. just as the *ABCs* are the basics of language, these *ABCs* are the basics you need to maximize your test performances.

Tests consist of two types: **subjective** and **objective.** Subjective tests require you to supply the answers in your own words. They measure your recall of information, your skills in organizing and expressing yourself, and your ability to relate ideas. Types of subjective test questions include short-answer, essay, and fill-in-the-blank (see Table 7.5). Objective tests involve your choosing among provided answers. Instructors frequently give objective exams because they allow the quick testing of a large amount of material and are easy to grade. Types of objective test questions include multiple-choice, matching, and true-false (see Table 7.6). Some students think objective tests are a fairer judge of their abilities because these exams are free from grader bias.

To prepare for a test, you need to know what to expect from it. Because most exams are written by the instructor, the instructor is a prime source of information about them. Most instructors want you to do well. Thus, they are willing to answer questions about test content and format. Instructors can tell you if a test is **comprehensive** (covering all material presented since the beginning of the term) or **noncomprehensive** (covering only that information presented since the last exam).

Extensive preparation alone is not all you need to pass an exam. Special test-taking skills enhance your carefully acquired knowledge. No matter how

---

Table 7.5   Subjective Test Formats

Example of an essay question:
Compare and contrast Emily Dickinson's "Because I Could Not Stop for Death" with Hilda Doolittle's "Evening."

Example of a short-answer question:
Briefly describe the hydrologic cycle.

Example of a fill-in-the-blank question:
A _____ is a form of figurative language in which two dissimilar objects are compared using the words *like* or *as*.

Table 7.6   Objective Test Formats

Example of a true-false question:
T   F   Soil fertility depends upon relative amounts of gravel, sand, silt, and clay.

Example of a multiple-choice question:
Sources of vitamin A include all of the following except
a. dark green leafy vegetables.
b. yeast.
c. fish liver oils.
d. yellow and orange fruits.

Example of matching questions:

1. Johannes Gutenberg	a. Electric self-starter
2. Guglielmo Marconi	b. Mimeograph machine
3. Charles F. Kettering	c. Printing press
4. Thomas Edison	d. Wireless telegraph

---

well you are prepared, you should use the following general suggestions for taking exams (see Table 7.7).

All exams test the way you process information. Some questions ask you to define or remember information exactly as it was presented in your text or the lecture. Other questions demand you link information to form conclusions about a topic. You might also be asked to use information in a new way. Questions that ask you to think critically require you to analyze, synthesize, and evaluate information. Both subjective and objective exams often test your ability to remember and manipulate concepts in a variety of ways. The kinds of knowledge required for different kinds of questions appear in Figure 7.1, Bloom's Taxonomy at the beginning of this chapter.

Table 7.7   Steps in Taking Exams

1. Bring the appropriate materials for the test (pencil, paper, blue book, calculator).
2. Arrive at the test on time.
   a. If you are early, do not discuss the test with other students. Their concerns and worries will increase any anxieties you have.
   b. If you are late, you might miss important verbal directions. Arriving late also makes you feel rushed and anxious. If you do arrive late, take a minute to relax and organize your thoughts. Ask your instructor for clarification if you feel confused.
3. If you are trying to keep a difficult formula or process in mind, jot it down after you get your test paper.
4. Preview the test. Note the total number of items. Identify variations in point values. Estimate the amount of time to spend on each item. Spend the most time on questions receiving the most credit.
5. Read all directions slowly and carefully. When given a test, many students ignore the directions. However, directions often state information you need to receive full credit. They also provide information about the way answers should be marked. Although you might have all the right answers, selective instructors might not give full credit when responses are not correctly marked.
6. Underline key terms and steps in the directions.
7. Answer the easiest questions first. This builds your confidence and triggers your memory for other information. Also, if you run out of time before you complete the test, you will have answered the questions you knew.
8. Expect memory blocks. Mark difficult questions, but skip them and go on. Return to these questions, if time permits.
9. Answer every question, if possible. If incorrect answers are not penalized, guess at all objective and subjective questions.
10. Make your responses as neat and legible as possible.
11. Work at your own pace. Do not be concerned when other students finish and leave before you.
12. If time permits, review questions and answers. Be sure you understand the question and marked the correct response. Some students think it is better to always stay with their first answer. You can determine what's best for you by examining some of your old tests. Count the number of questions you changed to correct answers. Compare that total with the number of those you changed to incorrect answers.

Preparing for and Taking Subjective Exams

"Writing is hell," someone once said. This certainly seems true to many students who face subjective exams. These exams require you to understand major concepts and describe them in a coherent written form. Your essay must state main points and contain the facts that support the ideas you express. You must show your analysis or synthesis of ideas and application of knowledge. Taking such exams requires careful preparation and confidence in your test-taking skills.

Web Exercise 7.1

A variety of information related to the topics in this chapter is available on the World Wide Web. For this exercise, access one of the following Web sites and respond to the questions which follow (for the most up-to-date URLs, go to http://csuccess.wadsworth.com):

Mind Tools: Memory Techniques and Mnemonics:
  http://www.www.mindtools.com

Preparing for Tests and Exams at the Counseling and Development Center at York University (choose one of the 6 articles):
  http://www.yorku.ca/admin/cdc/lsp/ep/exam.htm

Test-Taking Strategies: Preparing for Tests Before Your Final Review at Academic Advising Services at the College of St. Benedict/St. John's University:
  http://www.csbsju.edu/advising/help/teststrt.html

Studying for Tests and Quizzes from An English Teacher's Home Page at Delta College:
  http://www.delta.edu/~anburke/test.html

1. Which site did you choose? _____

2. Why? _____

_____

_____

3. Respond to the following on a separate sheet of paper or in your journal. Select one of the sample chapters and describe how the information at the Web site you chose could help you prepare for a test on the content. Give specific examples.

PORPE: **A Study Plan for Subjective Exams**

Often students fear subjective exams because they are uncertain of their writing skills. A study plan exists that helps you become a better writer by asking you to practice writing. This plan, PORPE, consists of five stages: Predict, Organize, Rehearse, Practice, and Evaluate (Simpson, 1986). When put into motion at least three days before an exam, PORPE helps you predict possible essay questions, organize your thoughts, and find strategies for recalling information.

Even if your predicted questions never appear on the test, PORPE will not be a waste of time for several reasons. First, your predicted questions will probably reflect the content, if not the wording, of the test. Second, you often can use the information you rehearsed and practiced in answering questions you might not have predicted. Third, the practice you give yourself in writing increases not only your self-confidence but also your writing ability. According to Epictetus, "If you wish to be a writer, write." To follow the stages in PORPE, you answer a series of questions and complete the steps at each stage (Table 7.8).

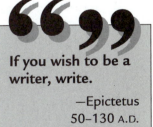

If you wish to be a writer, write.

—Epictetus
50–130 A.D.
First century Roman philosopher

Table 7.8   Stages of PORPE

Three days before the exam:

Predict

Predict information about the test by answering these questions:

> What does the test cover?
>
> Is the test comprehensive or noncomprehensive?
>
> How many questions will the test contain?
>
> Will the test require me to apply information?
>
> How much does this test count in my final course grade?
>
> When is the test?
>
> Where will the test be given?
>
> What special material(s) will I need to take the test?

Predict essay test questions by answering the following questions:

> What information did the instructor stress during the lectures?
>
> What information did the text emphasize?
>
> What questions appeared in both my initial preview and the chapter's review or study guide?
>
> What terms did the instructor emphasize during the lectures?

Predict at least three times as many questions as your instructor has indicated will be on the exam.

Two days before the exam:

Organize

Organize information by answering the following questions:

> What type of text structure will best answer the questions I set (cause/effect, subject development, enumeration/sequence, or comparison/contrast)?
>
> What is the best way to organize this information (outline, idea map, note cards, chart)?
>
> What information is essential for answering this question?
>
> What information adds relevant, supporting details or examples?
>
> What is the source of this information:
> textbook?
> handouts?
> lecture notes?
> supplemental readings?

Rehearse

Lock information into your memory by answering these questions:

> What mnemonic techniques (acronyms, acrostics, word games, and so on) can I use to practice this information?
>
> How much time each day will I study?
>
> When will I study?
>
> How will I distribute my study time?
>
> Where will I study?
>
> If necessary, when will my study group/partner and I meet?
>
> What obligations do I have that might interfere with this study time?

Construct mnemonic aids.

Use overlearning to help you practice mnemonic aids overtly (writing or speaking them).

One day before the exam:

Practice

Practice writing your answers from memory.

Evaluate

Judge the quality of your answer as objectively as possible by answering the following questions.

> Did I answer the question that was asked?
>
> Did my answer begin with an introduction?
>
> Did my answer end with a conclusion?
>
> Was my answer well organized?
>
> Did I include all essential information?
>
> Did I include any relevant details or examples?
>
> Did I use transition words?
>
> Is my writing neat and easily read?
>
> Did I check spelling and grammar?

If you answered any of these questions negatively, you need to continue practicing your answers. Repeat the final four stages of PORPE until you answer all of these questions positively.

After the exam has been returned, read your instructor's comments and compare them with the last evaluation you made during your study sessions. Look for negative trends you can avoid or positive trends you can stress when you study for your next exam. File your PORPE plan, course materials, study aids, and evaluation data for future reference.

Taking Subjective Exams

> Freshmen who are preppies have a great advantage.... They ... arrive at college well-versed in the techniques of the essay question, and could pad their paragraph with such useful phrases as "from a theoretical point of view," or "on first inspection we may seem to discern a certain attitude which may well survive even closer scrutiny," and so forth. This sort of wind can sail you halfway through an hour test before you have to lay a single fact on paper.

SOURCE: Reprinted with permission from *The Class* by Erich Segal. Copyright © by Bantam Publishers. All rights reserved.

The great advantage that Segal describes is part of what preppies learn at college-preparatory schools. They learn the art of taking subjective tests—a skill you, too, can learn.

Essay exams require special test-taking considerations. Because answering them is much like writing short papers on assigned topics, there is more work involved. The procedure outlined in Table 7.7 is important to follow, but other steps are also necessary (see Table 7.9). The wording of essay questions helps you organize and write your answers (see Table 7.10).

The wording you use to answer the questions determines the quality of the responses. Example 7.3 shows examples of good and poor responses to an essay question. How do they differ?

The good response begins with an introductory sentence that identifies the three symptoms of Parkinson's disease. The second sentence identifies early symptoms of the disease. Sentences 3 and 4 identify and describe the

---

Table 7.9   **Taking Essay Exams**

1. Choose a title. Even though you won't necessarily entitle your paper, a title helps you focus your thoughts and narrow your subject.

2. Outline your response or list main points before you begin. This keeps you from omitting important details.

3. Have a beginning, a middle, and an end. Topic and summary sentences are important in making your answer seem organized and complete.

4. Use transitional words. The key words in each question help you identify the transitions you need for clarity.

5. Attempt every question. If you run out of time, outline the remaining questions. This shows your knowledge of the content. Partial responses often result in partial credit.

6. Proofread your answers. Check spelling, grammar, and content.

Table 7.10   Key Terms in Essay Questions

If You Are Asked To . . .	Then . . .
compare or match,	identify similarities.
contrast or distinguish,	identify differences.
discuss or describe,	provide details or features.
enumerate, name, outline, or list,	identify major points.
sequence, arrange, trace, or rank,	list information in order.
explain, defend, or document,	give reasons for support.
relate or associate,	show connections.
summarize, paraphrase, or compile,	provide a short synopsis.
outline,	list major points.
apply,	show use for.
construct, develop, or devise,	create.
criticize or analyze,	review features or components.
demonstrate, illustrate, or show,	provide examples.

Example 7.1   Examples of an Essay Question and Responses

Question: Identify and describe the symptoms of Parkinson's disease.

Response I

Parkinson's disease is a neurological disease characterized by gradual changes in three fundamental symptoms: tremor, rigidity, and bradykinesia. Although the onset of this disease is so gradual that neither the patients nor the people close to them notice it, early symptoms include fatigue and complaints of mild muscular aches. Tremor is often the first real symptom to appear. Conspicuous, but rarely disabling, tremor usually begins in one hand and occurs when the limb is at rest. Rigidity, the second major symptom, is muscular stiffness. This results in slow movement, muscle cramps, and resistance against passive movement. The most disabling symptom is bradykinesia. This describes slowness and poverty of voluntary movements. It also leads to difficulty in performing rapid or repeated movements. It underlies facial masking and involuntary hesitations. Variations in these three symptoms cause the variety of disabilities associated with Parkinson's disease.

Response 2

Parkinson's disease was first described by Dr. James Parkinson, an English physician. Parkinson wrote an essay entitled, "Essay on the Shaking Palsy," which described the symptoms he saw in six patients. He described the three primary symptoms as involuntary shaking movements of the limbs, muscular stiffness, and slowness and poverty of movement. Because the entire body was involved, Dr. Parkinson theorized that it was a mental illness resulting from a dysfunction in the brain. Parkinson's disease can affect anyone—men, women, children. Various theories account for the symptoms, including genetic links, viral causation, stress, neurotransmitter damage, and environmental causes.

Response 3

Parkinson's disease is a terrible disease. It affects millions of people. Parkinson's disease has many symptoms. One symptom is shakiness. Some people become very shaky. Their hands shake most. This makes it difficult to pick up things or hold things. Another symptom is that you can't move very well anymore. You have difficulty climbing stairs or walking. So, these symptoms are very terrible.

first major symptom. Sentences 5 and 6 identify and describe the second major symptom. The next three sentences identify and describe the third major symptom. The last sentence summarizes the effects of variations in these symptoms.

At first glance, the second response appears to be a good one. It is well written and appropriate in length. It appears to be the work of a student who knows something about Parkinson's disease, but it lacks the specific information required for a correct response to this question. Closer inspection reveals several weaknesses. Sentences 1 and 2 could be considered introductory sentences; however, sentence 3 is the only sentence that identifies (and not by correct terminology) and describes the three major symptoms of Parkinson's disease. Sentence 4 incorrectly identifies the disease as a mental, rather than a neurological, illness. Sentence 5 describes who is affected by Parkinson's disease. The last sentence—an attempt at a summary—actually lists the theories that account for the symptoms.

The last example, another poor response, is more clearly identifiable as such. The writer uses the word *symptom* frequently to disguise the fact that he or she really has little understanding of what the symptoms are. Sentences 1, 2, and 3 are feeble introductory attempts. Sentence 4 identifies one symptom as shakiness, without using the appropriate terminology. Although the writer apparently knows that the hands are often affected, he or she does not realize that this occurs most often when the limb is at rest. Sentences 8 and 9 identify mobility impairments and their effects. The reader cannot tell if this refers to the symptom of rigidity or that of bradykinesia. The last sentence attempts to conclude the paragraph by restating the main idea of sentence 1.

PREPARING FOR AND TAKING OBJECTIVE EXAMS

Find a perfect star in the pattern at the top of the next page. As you look for it, try to be aware of the search strategies you use.

Did you find the star? If not, reexamine the lower-right quadrant. If you did, how did you go about finding it? (A key appears after the chapter review.) According to Roger von Oech, who originated this exercise in his book *A Kick in the Seat of the Pants,* the point of the exercise is that you have to know what you're looking for before you can find it. To locate the star, you first have to determine what kind of star you're seeking. The star could be a regular five-pointed star, a Star of David, a seven-pointed sheriff's star, or the Chrysler star. It could be large or small. It could be composed entirely of white pieces, black pieces, or a combination of both. In other words, to locate the star, you need the ability to recognize it when you see it. You also need a strategy for finding it.

The same is true when you prepare for and take objective exams. When you take an objective exam, your job is to search among the answers provided

SOURCE: Reprinted with permission from *A Kick in the Seat of the Pants* by Roger von Oech. Copyright © 1986 by Roger von Oech. Reprinted by permission of HarperCollins Publishers. All rights reserved.

by the instructor for the correct one. If you've studied carefully and are more than familiar with the information covered on the exam, you can focus on the one or two choices that are most appropriate. Test-wise strategies aid you in making the best choice possible.

POSSE: **A Study Plan for Objective Exams**

In preparing for an objective test, you need to know the harbor you are making for and how you intend to get there. POSSE (Plan, Organize, Schedule, Study, and Evaluate) is a system that helps you identify your study goals and make plans for achieving them. To follow the stages of POSSE, you answer a series of questions and complete the steps at each level (Table 7.11). Responding to the questions in written form forces you to concentrate on each question. It also keeps you from inadvertently omitting one. You will obtain many answers from either your syllabus, your instructor, or your experience in the class. Other questions, however, will force you to examine your study strengths and weaknesses. Your success on your upcoming test depends on your honesty in dealing with such issues. It is also important that you begin the POSSE process at least a week before the test is scheduled. If you work through POSSE with care and determination, you will make the best of your study time and efforts.

> **Our plans miscarry because they have no aim. When a man does not know what harbor he is making for, no wind is the right wind.**
>
> —Seneca
> *First century Roman philosopher and dramatist*

Table 7.11   Stages of POSSE: Questions to Be Answered

Plan

Answer these questions:

> What does the test cover?
>
> Is the test comprehensive or noncomprehensive?
>
> Will the test questions be multiple-choice, true-false, and/or matching?
>
> How many questions (of each type) will the test contain?
>
> In what ways will the test require me to apply information or think critically?
>
> How much does this test count in my final grade?
>
> When is the test?
>
> Where will the test be given?
>
> What special material(s) will I need to take the test?

Organize

Answer these questions:

> What information do I predict will be on the test?
>
> What materials do I need to study:
>
> > textbook?
> >
> > handouts?
> >
> > lecture notes?
> >
> > supplemental readings?
> >
> > old exams?
>
> What study and memory methods will work best with this material?
>
> Can I find a partner or group to study with?

Gather materials together.

Construct study and memory aids.

Schedule

Answer these questions:

> How much time do I have before the exam?
>
> How much time will I need to study for this test?
>
> How much time each day will I study?
>
> When will I study?
>
> How will I distribute my study time?
>
> Where will I study?
>
> When will my study group/partner and I meet?
>
> What obligations do I have that might interfere with this study time?

Construct a time schedule.

Study

At the end of each study session, answer these questions:

> Am I studying actively, that is, through writing or speaking?
>
> Am I distributing my study time to avoid memory interference and physical fatigue?
>
> Am I following my schedule? Why or why not? What adjustments do I need to make?
>
> Am I learning efficiently? Why or why not? What adjustments do I need to make?

Evaluate

After the test has been returned, complete the worksheet in Table 3.15.

Answer these questions:

> What pattern(s) emerge(s) from the worksheet?
>
> What type of questions did I miss most often?
>
> What changes can I make to my study plan to avoid these trends in the future?

File your POSSE plan, course materials, study aids, exam, worksheet, and evaluation for future reference.

WRITE TO LEARN

On a separate sheet of paper or in your journal, compare and contrast PORPE and POSSE.

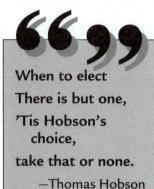

Taking Objective Exams

"Hobson's choice" refers to Tobias Hobson, a stablekeeper who made his customers take whatever horse was nearest the door when they came into his stable. Hobson's choice, then, refers to the only choice possible. In taking objective exams, your goal is to find Hobson's choice among the answers provided by the instructor. You seek to locate the one alternative that answers the question completely. Even when you've adequately prepared for the test, finding Hobson's choice isn't always easy. You need test-taking tips to help you find the correct answer among the alternatives. The following Test of Test-Wiseness shows you these strategies.

Test of Test-Wiseness

The test below measures your test-wiseness. Little content knowledge is required and the answers to all questions can be determined through test-taking skill.

After finishing the exam, score it using the key that follows. Specific test-taking strategies are explained there. Follow specific directions given for each section.

Multiple-Choice Questions

Credit: 2 points each

Circle the correct answer for each multiple-choice question.

1. SQ3R is
    a. a study plan.
    b. a kind of test.
    c. a course number.
    d. none of the above.

2. The first thing you should do when taking a test is
    a. have a sharpened pencil.
    b. look over all questions.
    c. read the directions.
    d. ask the teacher for clarification of directions.

3. Which of the following is true of standardized reading exams?
    a. Standardized reading tests require no special test-taking skills.
    b. A score on a standardized reading test may equal the number of right answers minus a percentage of the number of wrong answers.
    c. Always guess on standardized tests.
    d. Standardized tests are never timed tests.

4. If you do not understand a question during a test, you should
   a. ask a friend to explain it to you.
   b. skip that question.
   c. look it up in your textbook.
   d. ask the instructor for clarification.

5. Response choices are found on
   a. an objective test.
   b. a multiple-choice test.
   c. an essay test.
   d. all of the above.
   e. a and b only.

6. All of the following are parts of a study plan except
   a. reviewing information frequently.
   b. copying another person's notes.
   c. surveying a chapter.
   d. reading assignments.

7. Which of the following should not be done before taking a final exam?
   a. Review study notes.
   b. Find out when and where the test will be given.
   c. Determine if the test will be comprehensive or noncomprehensive.
   d. Become anxious.

8. An illusion is
   a. something that is not really there.
   b. an allusion.
   c. the same as elusive.
   d. another word for illustration.

9. The capital of Canada is
   a. New York City.
   b. Paris.
   c. Ottawa.
   d. Dallas.

10. The SQ3R study plan was developed in the 1940s by
    a. Francis Robinson.
    b. George Washington.
    c. Michael Jackson.
    d. Christopher Columbus.

11. The chemically inactive substances used in experiments to determine drug effectiveness are

    a. prescription medications.

    b. federally controlled pharmaceutical products.

    c. similar to physician-prescribed drugs.

    d. placebos.

12. Who was the third president of the United States?

    a. Lyndon Baines Johnson

    b. Franklin Delano Roosevelt

    c. Rutherford B. Hayes

    d. Thomas Jefferson

True-False Questions

Credit: 5 points each

Respond to each question by writing the word True or False in the blank.

_____ 1. You should always answer every question on every test.

_____ 2. All exams are comprehensive.

_____ 3. Never study with a partner.

_____ 4. Some tests are too lengthy to complete in the allotted time.

_____ 5. A test may not be without poorly worded questions.

_____ 6. Following directions is not unimportant.

Matching Questions

Credit: 4 points each

Write the letter of the correct answer in the blanks. Answers may be used more than once.

_____ 1. George Washington   a. a study plan

_____ 2. SQ3R   b. multiple-choice

_____ 3. example of an objective test   c. essay

_____ 4. example of a subjective test   d. president

_____ 5. a written theme

Math Questions

Credit: 10 points each

Write your answers in the blanks.

_____ 1. A container holds 20 gallons. It is 3/5 full. How many gallons do you need to fill the container?

_____ **2.** 20,819 + 74,864 =

      a. 10,993

      b. 95,683

      c. 95,666

      d. 85,333

Key and Test-Wise Strategies

The Test of Test-Wiseness helps you examine your test-taking skills. When taking any test, it is important that you preview the test and carefully follow directions. If you previewed this test, you probably realized that the test contained more multiple-choice questions than any other type. However, the multiple-choice questions received the least amount of credit. If you spent too much time on these questions, you might have failed to complete questions with higher point values.

Directions had to be followed exactly. If you failed to underline answers to the multiple-choice section, count them as incorrect. If you responded to the true-false questions with letters instead of the entire word, count them as incorrect. All other answers should have been written in the blanks to the left of the questions for you to receive credit.

Responses on any test often are designed to be similar and confusing. Whenever possible, after you read the question, you should answer it in your own words without looking at the responses given. Then, you should search for a response that matches your answer.

The following test-wise principles are no substitute for study and preparation. They can, however, help you eliminate choices and make educated guesses. The principle to remember is italicized.

Multiple-Choice Questions

Question 1

If you don't know an answer, skip it and go on. Don't waste time mulling over an answer. Go on to the questions you know. Sometimes a clue to the answer you need is found elsewhere in the test. In this case, the clue is in question 10. The answer is *a*.

Question 2

Eliminate grammatically incorrect responses. Sometimes, questions are poorly worded. The only grammatically correct choice in this question is answer *c*. Misuse of *a* or *an* is also a common grammatical error found in test questions.

Question 3

Often the longest choice is correct. For a correct answer to be absolutely clear, a response might have to be lengthy. The correct answer is *b*.

"You may be wise to the test, but is this test-wise?"

Questions 4 and 5
Be sure the right choice is the best choice. At first glance, answer *b* seems correct for question 4; however, further examination of choices reveals that answer *d* is a better choice. Watch for "all of the above," "none of the above," and paired choices. Answer *d* is the correct answer for question 5.

Questions 6 and 7
Read questions carefully. *Not* and *except* are small words, but they completely change the meaning. The careless reader might interpret question 6 as asking for a part of a study plan. Such a reader might also interpret question 7 as asking for a procedure to be done before taking a final exam. The correct response for question 6 is *b*. The correct response for question 7 is *d*.

Question 8
Responses that look like the word to be defined are usually incorrect. *Allusion, elusive,* and *illustration* all resemble the word *illusion*. These are called "attractive distractors" because they look so appealing. Attractive distractors are almost always poor choices. The answer, therefore, is *a*.

Questions 9 and 10
If you do not know what the answer is, determine what the answer is not. Eliminate silly choices and use common sense. You may not know the capital of Canada. However, you should realize that New York City and Dallas are in the United States and Paris is in France. Only answer c remains. For question 10, answer *c* is silly. Answers *b* and *d* are wrong because neither Christopher Columbus nor George Washington was alive in the 1940s. Answer *a* is correct.

Question 11

Watch for responses that are essentially the same. A careful reading of choices *a*, *b*, and *c* reveals that they restate the same idea in a variety of ways. In this case, a physician-prescribed drug is a prescription medication. It is also federally controlled and a pharmaceutical product. Because these answers are synonymous, none of them can be the correct answer. The correct answer is answer *d*.

Question 12

Use what you know to analyze and make decisions about information. At first glance, you might not recall who the third U.S. president was. And, unlike the responses in questions 9 and 10, all the men identified in the responses have served as president of the United States. But when were their terms of office? You reflect on what you know about each man. You might think of Lyndon Baines Johnson as a recent president, perhaps recalling that he took office after the assassination of John F. Kennedy and that the nation was involved in the Vietnam War during his presidency. Clearly a president of the twentieth century, he could not have been the third president. You might associate Franklin Delano Roosevelt with the Great Depression and World War II. Thus, he, too, was also a relatively modern president. You might have little knowledge about Rutherford B. Hayes, so you go on to Thomas Jefferson. You recall that he signed the Declaration of Independence and visualize him in colonial-era clothing. Logically, then, *d* is the correct choice.

True-False Questions

Questions 1, 2, 3, and 4

Look for words that determine limits. Words such as *always, never, none, every,* and *all* place no limitations on meaning. Words such as *some, few, often, many,* and *frequently* limit meaning and are better choices. If you can think of one example that contradicts an unlimited meaning, then it is false. For example, the answer to question 1 is false. This is because you wouldn't answer every question if a percentage of wrong responses were to be subtracted from the total of correct choices. The answers to questions 2 and 3 are also false. The answer to question 4 is true.

Questions 5 and 6

Watch for double negatives. Just as multiplying two negative numbers equals a positive number, two negative words in a sentence indicate a positive relationship in standard English usage. In question 5, *not* and *without* cancel each other. The gist of the sentence is that a test can have poorly worded questions. The answer to question 5, then, is true. In question 6, the word *not* and the prefix *un-* cancel each other. The gist indicates that following directions is important. The answer to question 6 is true.

Matching Questions

Matching sections are somewhat like multiple-choice tests. Thus, the same principles apply. However, there are some special strategies for matching sections.

Often the two items being matched rely on an implied rather than a stated association. These relationships include a word and its definition, a person and a noted accomplishment, a step in a process and the process from which it comes, and so on. As with other test questions, complete items you know first. Use the side with the longer responses as your question side. This keeps you from repeatedly reading through numerous lengthy responses. When responses are used only once, do not blindly fill in the last question with the only remaining choice. Check to make sure it fits. If not, recheck all answers.

The answers to the matching section are as follows: question 1, *d;* question 2, *a;* question 3, *b;* question 4, *c;* and question 5, *c.*

Math Questions

Many good math students have difficulty with word problems. Panic prevents them from translating a word problem into a numerical one. Thus, the first step in solving math problems is to remain calm and avoid negative thinking. Second, visualize the problem. This allows you to determine what the question asks. Next, identify your facts and the processes required. If possible, estimate the response. Work the problem and check it against your estimate. Recheck if necessary.

Problem 1
Picturing the problem reveals an everyday situation. You have a container that is partially filled, and you want to know how much more is needed to fill it. You have the following facts: a 20-gallon container that is $\frac{3}{5}$ filled. You will need to multiply $\frac{3}{5}$ and 20 to find out how much is in the container. Then you subtract that amount from 20 to find out how much more can be put in the container. You know that the container is more than half full but less than $\frac{3}{4}$ full; $\frac{1}{2}$ of 20 is 10 and $\frac{3}{4}$ of 20 is 15. The container holds between 10 and 15 gallons now. Subtracting those amounts from the total results in an estimate of 5 to 10 gallons. The problem is worked in the following manner:

$$\frac{3}{5} \times 20 = 12$$
$$20 - 12 = 8$$

The answer is 8; 8 is within the estimated range.

Problem 2
Standardized math tests provide a choice of answers. You can save time by estimating answers and eliminating responses. In this problem, adding the final digits (9 + 4 = 13) indicates that the response must end in 3. This eliminates answer *c.* Rounding off the two figures results in 21,000 and 75,000. The sum of the rounded figures is 96,000. The answer that is closest to the estimate is answer *b.*

CLASSIC CRITICAL THINKING

Because of your ability to think critically, you can "know" information that you have really never learned. Sound impossible? Answer the following question by choosing the answer that you think is the closest.

What ingredient of cakes comes from beans?
A. Coconut B. Vanilla
C. Vermilion D. Chamomile

You probably chose *B*. And, even if you answered accurately, chances are you didn't really know the answer. How, then, did you manage to select the correct answer?

You arrived at your answer by connecting different facts in your mind; making judgments about these facts; eliminating and retaining data; checking and double-checking the possible answers; relating new, additional information; and checking your assumptions and inferences against the possible answers. You, in fact, thought critically about the question and arrived at a logical answer.

In determining your answer, you probably thought along these lines:

"Let's see. Not all cakes are coconut, so the answer can't be coconut. Chamomile is a kind of tea my grandmother drank as a kind of medicine, so the answer is not chamomile. Hmm, vanilla or vermilion. . . . *vermilion* is answer *C*. I've heard when in doubt, pick *C*. But I think *vermilion* means *red;* it seems like I remember something about Santa's suit being *vermilion* in color. And, since I know teachers sometimes put answers together that look similar to make sure students

know their stuff, I am going to pick *B, vanilla,* as my answer."

The sources of the information you used in selecting your answer were myriad and varied. You used your knowledge of cakes to know that not all of them are coconut. Your grandmother's medicinal tea helped you eliminate another possible answer. At this point, you had a 50 percent chance of making a correct choice. Next, you accessed your childhood memory of Santa and correctly recalled that *vermilion* meant red. You used your knowledge of instructors and exams to double-check your reasoning and ultimately inferred that *B* was the correct answer.

Thus, it was not your memory of *vanilla beans* that resulted in your selecting the correct answer. Rather, it was your ability to make unconscious links or, rather, your ability to think critically about memories that rescues you when you are faced with questions for which you have not learned answers.

Examine the following questions. Choose any one and indicate on a separate sheet of paper or in your notebook the thought processes you used to determine your answer.

1. How many months of the year don't share their first letter with another month?
   A. 7 B. 4 C. 6 D. 5

2. Which domestic animal often wears man-made apparel?
   A. Hog B. Horse C. Cat D. Canary

3. Which southern city of the United States is named after an ocean?
   A. Atlanta B. Ithaca C. Augusta
   D. Indianapolis

WRITE TO LEARN

On a separate sheet of paper or in your journal, create five subjective questions and five objective questions that cover information discussed in Sample Chapter 13, "Concepts in Human Biology" at the back of this book.

TAKING SPECIALIZED EXAMS

Marathon runners often talk about "hitting the wall." This happens when runners get to the point where they feel they can no longer keep going. Although some runners can routinely cover several miles each day with ease, the length or difficulty of some race routes can sometimes seem insurmountable.

You, too, might feel like you've "hit the wall" when it comes to taking specialized exams. The strategies you successfully use in subjective and objective tests are not sufficient. Just as runners develop specialized techniques to help them pass "the wall," you need special strategies for specialized tests, open-book, take-home, and final exams.

Taking Open-Book and Take-Home Exams

Open-book and take-home tests are types of finals that sound too good to be true. You might think that these tests require no study at all. In fact, they require as much studying as any other exam. Such tests are easier when you have the appropriate strategies for taking them (see Table 7.12).

An open-book exam tests your ability to locate, organize, and relate information quickly. Such tests also measure how quickly you can read and process information. Thus, the open-book test might be biased toward well-prepared students. This is another reason why you need to study thoroughly before taking this type of exam. Insufficient studying results in your wasting test time while you decide what the question means or where to find the answer.

A take-home exam also evaluates your ability to locate, organize, and relate information. Because you are not expected to take the test during class, it measures your knowledge more fairly, although spelling and neatness generally count more. In most cases, a take-home test allows you to

---

Table 7.12   Steps in Taking Open-Book and Take-Home Exams

1. Familiarize yourself with your text. Tab sections of the text that deal with major topics or contain important formulas or definitions.
2. Organize your notes. Mark them in the same way you tabbed your text.
3. Highlight important details in both your text and notes.
4. Know how to use the table of contents and index to locate information quickly.
5. Paraphrase information. Unless you are quoting a specific source, do not copy word-for-word from your text.
6. Use other applicable test-taking strategies.

avoid the stress associated with in-class exams. On the other hand, setting your own pace has drawbacks, particularly if you tend to procrastinate. Waiting until the last minute to begin working on such a test results in the same stressful feelings you get during an in-class test. Such scheduling also results in work of lesser quality.

Taking Final Exams

You might not believe it, but in many ways a final exam is just like all the other tests you take. However, finals usually are longer than regular exams. In

---

GROUP LEARNING ACTIVITY   MEMORY DETECTIVES

You might not think of yourself as a "memory detective," but active probing often helps improve recall. A case in point is the *cognitive interview,* a technique used to jog the memory of eyewitnesses. The cognitive interview was created by R. Edward Geiselman and Ron Fisher to help police detectives. When used properly, the cognitive interview produces 35 percent more correct information than does standard questioning (Geiselman, Fisher, MacKinnon, and Holland, 1986).

By following four simple steps, you can apply cognitive principles to your own memory. The next time you are searching for a "lost" memory—one that you know is in there somewhere—try the following search strategies.

1. Say or write down everything you can remember that relates to the information you are seeking. Don't worry about how trivial any of it seems; each bit of information you remember can serve as a cue to bring back others.

2. Try to recall events or information in different orders. Let your memories flow out backward or out of order, or start with whatever impressed you the most.

3. Recall from different viewpoints. Review events by mentally standing in a different place. Or try to view information as another person would remember it. When

taking a test, for instance, ask yourself what other students or your professor would remember about the topic.

4. Mentally put yourself back in the situation where you learned the information. Try to mentally re-create the learning environment or relive the event. As you do, include sounds, smells, details of weather, nearby objects, other people present, what you said or thought, and how you felt as you learned the information (Fisher & Geiselman, 1987).

These strategies help re-create the context in which information was learned, and they provide multiple memory cues. If you think of remembering as a sort of "treasure hunt," you might even learn to enjoy the detective work.

Application

As a pre-exam activity, use the preceding strategies to assist recall when you or another member of your study group becomes stumped on a question. Compare memories among group members. Once you learn to use these strategies, you can use them to aid recall on exams.

SOURCE: Reprinted with permission from *Introduction to Psychology, Exploration and Application* by Coon. Copyright © 1997 Brooks/Cole Publishing Company. All rights reserved.

WRITE TO LEARN

On a separate sheet of paper or in your journal, explain the logic in the poem on page 309 ("The more we study . . ."). What is illogical about it?

a way, this works to your advantage. Longer exams cover more information. You get a better chance to get answers correct because there are more questions to attempt. The same strategies and suggestions for taking other tests apply to final exams (see Table 7.7).

Finals are often given in places and at times that differ from your regular class schedule. Final exam locations and schedules are printed in campus newspapers, posted in each department, and announced by your instructor. If more than two of your exams occur on the same day, you can sometimes ask to reschedule one of them. Procedures for such requests vary. Seeing your advisor is the first step in the process.

SUMMARY

1. The process of learning includes the ability to evaluate, synthesize, analyze, apply, interpret, and translate, as well as recall, information.

2. The stages of processing information are registration of information, transference to short-term memory, manipulation in working memory, and transference to long-term memory.

3. Logical links, mental and physical imagery, acronyms and acrostics, location, and word games are associational techniques for linking ideas.

4. Information can be organized into lists or visual representations, such as idea maps, charts, and word maps.

5. Rehearsal occurs through practice strategies, such as spaced study, previewing, recitation, study groups or partners, and overlearning. Cramming is also a way of rehearsing information, but it is not as effective as other means.

6. Forgetting, or the loss of information from long-term memory, results from interference or disuse.

7. All exams require certain test-taking strategies (getting to the test on time, reading the directions, and so on).

8. Because subjective exams require you to provide your own answers, you need to be well-versed in the subject matter and skilled in writing.

9. Objective exams force you to select an answer from a set of instructor-made choices. Your selection needs to be based on both your knowledge of content and test-wise strategies.

10. Finals are longer forms of subjective and objective exams; they require no special test-taking strategies, unless they are open-book or take-home exams.

ClassACTION

Respond to the following on a separate sheet of paper or in your journal. Combine the chapter map and chapter summary to form a synthesis map that reflects the main ideas and important details of this chapter. Personalize the map by indicating specific ways in which you plan to implement suggestions offered by this chapter.

CHAPTER REVIEW

Answer briefly but completely.

1. Using the levels of understanding in Bloom's taxonomy (Figure 7.1), determine the level for each of the following sample questions:

   a. State exactly the meaning of *secondary reinforcer*.

   _____

   b. Compare your text definition of visual thinking with that of the supplemental reading.

   _____

   c. You are an advisor to the president. After considering the four futures of U.S. foreign policy identified in my lecture, what other future would you conceptualize?

   _____

2. Choose any two courses in which you are now enrolled. Compare the depth at which you have processed information for each. How do you account for these differences?

   _____

   _____

   _____

   _____

   _____

3. Organize the following list of locations for recall: Las Vegas, Brazil, Alabama, Utah, Canada, Greenland, Connecticut, London, and Munich.

_____

_____

_____

_____

4. Locate a list of information you need to remember for a course you are taking. Devise and show an acronym or acrostic to aid you in recalling this list.

_____

_____

_____

_____

_____

5. In what ways are visual representations of ideas improvements on lists?

_____

_____

_____

_____

_____

6. Describe the differences between objective and subjective tests. Which kind do you personally find easier to prepare for and take? Why?

_____

_____

_____

_____

_____

7. Create a chart for practice strategies (spaced study, previewing, recitation, study groups or partners, overlearning, and cramming) and give examples of how they can include visual, auditory, and semantic practice.

_____

_____

_____

_____

_____

_____

_____

_____

8. Identify the reason why each of the following people forgot information:

a. Meguami cannot remember the name of the person who sat behind her in first grade.

_____

b. Mrs. Johnson cannot recall if the education department's number is 757–0349 or 759–0346.

_____

c. Kate has difficulty remembering the difference between inductive and deductive reasoning.

_____

d. Lee failed to remember what he received as graduation gifts.

_____

9. Relate time management to the use of PORPE and POSSE.

_____

_____

_____

_____

_____

10. Identify what the text describes as the *ABC*s of successful test taking. Which one(s) do you possess? Which one(s) do you need to improve? Give examples of each for a specific course in which you are enrolled.

_____

_____

_____

_____

Key to Star Puzzle on page 320

VOCABULARY DEVELOPMENT   Word Histories: Using the Results of Reasoning, Belief, Action, and Passion

Numerous supermarket tabloids appeal to the public's desire for gossip. "Is Elvis still alive?" "Was there a conspiracy to assassinate Kennedy?" "Are aliens living and working in the United States?" The stories are often more interesting, and therefore memorable, than the people they describe. And so it goes with words. Word histories provide you with many of the some sort of stories. They whet your interest and help you remember the meanings of the words you encounter.

What is all knowledge too but recorded experience,
and a product of history; of which, therefore,
reasoning and belief, no less than action and passion,
are essential materials.

Thomas Carlyle
Nineteenth century Scottish essayist

Knowledge springs from a variety of sources. According to Carlyle, reasoning, belief, action, and passion form the essential materials for its development. The words that define and describe that knowledge also find their roots in these essential materials. And just how do these materials create words? *The Mother Tongue: English and How It Got That Way* (1990) provides some answers. According to Danish linguist Otto Jespersen, people form words by adding or subtracting from current words, by making them up, or by attaching new meanings to them. Bill Bryson, the book's author, adds two other ways words are developed: we borrow them from other languages and create them by accident.

And so it goes throughout history. People acted and reacted according to their thoughts, beliefs, and passions. The names of some of these people became so intertwined with their actions that they now refer to that action. For example, Vidkun Quisling was a leader of Norway in 1940. He undermined his country by collaborating with the Nazis during World War II. Today, *quisling* means "traitor." Josh Billings, a humorist in the 1800s, popularized a bantering comedy style now known as joshing.

Words from other countries also contribute to the English language. For example, the meaning of *calculate* dates back to ancient Rome. Romans often hired carts to take them where they wanted to go. The cart was equipped with a kind of taxi meter. A cylinder filled with pebbles was attached to the wheel. Each time the wheel turned, a pebble dropped through a slot into a separate container. The fare was computed based on the number of pebbles that fell into the container. The Roman word for pebble was *calculus*. Thus, calculate means to count. As a second example, in the 1812 campaign against Napoleon's armies, Russian soldiers got as far as Paris. They patronized sidewalk cafes and shouted "Bistro!"—or "hurry up"—to the slow-moving waiters. Today, *bistro* is a synonym for a sidewalk cafe.

Words often reflect current interests, trends, and innovations. These include such words as *feminist, New Wave, planned parenthood,* and *rap music.* New products of technology also result in new words. These include *astronaut, lunar module, user-friendly, byte, nylon, yo-yo,* and *trampoline.*

Words also come from abbreviations when the abbreviation is commonly used as the word itself. These include *IQ* (intelligence quotient), *TV* (television), and *CD* (compact disk). Words also come from acronyms (words formed from the first letter or first few letters of several words). The word *posh* originally stood for "port outbound, starboard home." Passengers traveling through the Suez Canal in the 1800s ordered cabins on the left side of the ship for the trip out and ones on the right for the return trip. This kept their staterooms in the shade both ways. Records for these very desirable accommodations noted them as "P.O.S.H."

The creation and development of a word is its etymology—the word's history. Found in dictionary entries, etymologies tell information about a word's evolution, how it was first used, and how it is used now. Knowing a word's etymology serves as another mechanism to expand your connections with and understanding of that word.

Activity

Look up the etymology of the boldface words in a large collegiate dictionary. Describe the history or origin of each. Then define it. In the sample dictionary entry, the history of the word has been underlined.

---

hip-po-pot-a-mus (hip -a -pat'-a mas) n. a very large pachydermstous African quadruped frequenting rivers. -pl. -es or hippopotami (hip a pat' a mi) (Gr. hippos, a horse; potamos, a river)

---

1. Convert 45° on the Celsius scale to its **Fahrenheit** equivalent.

   etymology _____

   definition _____

2. **Gremlins** are fictitious creatures.

   etymology _____

   definition _____

3. Prisoners who **escape** are generally recaptured within a short period of time.

   etymology _____

   definition _____

4. **Radar** enables ships to navigate treacherous seas.

   etymology _____

   definition _____

5. Few people know what **RSVP** means.

etymology _____

definition _____

6. **Luscious** fruits come from tropical regions.

etymology _____

definition _____

7. The owner of the company was a **shyster.**

etymology _____

definition _____

8. The **Miranda warning** must be given to each suspect.

etymology _____

definition _____

9. **Sequoia** forests flourish in California.

etymology _____

definition _____

10. Oil **derricks** dotted the countryside.

etymology _____

definition _____

Activity

Read the following essay, "A Few Famous Trips of the Tongue," by Jack Smith. On a separate sheet of paper, describe the histories of each of the following words: *spoonerism, sandwich, boycott, Wellington, cardigan, raglan,* and *bowdlerize.* Identify the dictionary definition and check the history for each one. Give one of Smith's examples of a spoonerism. Create a spoonerism of your own to help you remember any concept from one of the sample chapters.

Excerpt 7.1   A Few Famous Trips of the Tongue
by Jack Smith

For no discernible reason other than sheer whimsy, John Liddle of San Diego has sent me a London-dateline story from the Los Angeles Times of Sept. 11, 1977, about the inimitable Rev. William Archibald Spooner (1884–1930).

No reason other than whimsy prompts me to recall that otherwise extraordinarily dull man's one endearing service—his gift to the English language of that slip of the tongue known, in his honor, as a spoonerism.

Thus, Spooner joins the small company whose names, usually because of some personal quirk or invention, have become common nouns. It was John Montagu, 4th Earl of Sandwich (1718–1792), who invented the sandwich to avoid having to leave the gaming tables, and hence gave his name to that handy meal.

Boycott comes from Capt. C. C. Boycott (1832–1897), an Irish land agent who was boycotted by his tenants when he refused to lower their rents in 1880.

Wellingtons are the boots named after Arthur Wellesley, 1st Duke of Wellington (1769–1852), who bested Napoleon at Waterloo and wore that type of boot.

Cardigan—a long-sleeved, collarless knitted sweater that buttons down the front—was named after James Thomas Brudenell, 7th Earl of Cardigan (1797–1868), a vainglorious martinet who led the foolhardy charge of the Light Brigade at Balaklava, in which Errol Flynn was a film hero. A notorious dandy, Cardigan evidently favored that garment.

Raglan, an overcoat or topcoat with sleeves that continue in one piece to the collar, was named after FitzRoy James Henry Somerset, 1st Baron Raglan (1788–1855). He was the British commander-in-chief during the Crimean War who issued the ambiguous order sending Cardigan on his disastrous charge.

And a verb:

Bowdlerize, to damage a literary work by censoring lines that one finds offensive, comes from an English editor, Thomas Bowdler (1754–1825), who had the effrontery to publish an expurgated Shakespeare.

Spooner's gift was his habit of transposing the initial or other sounds of words. For instance, it is said that Spooner once referred to Queen Victoria as "the queer old dean," when he meant to say "the dear old Queen."

Spooner's slips were never deliberate, though they brought him a strange sort of fame. He lived in dread of making the next error and remained modest about his accomplishment.

Finding his name in a newspaper, he noted, "But of course they thought me most famous for my spoonerisms, so I was not greatly puffed up."

For 60 years Spooner was a member of New College, Oxford, and served as its warden from 1903 to 1924. He was a small man and colorless, in fact an albino, and had cruelly been called "this shrimp-like creature."

That this remarkably unprepossessing Anglican clergyman should be remembered with such reverence today is owed entirely to his oral lapses.

He was likely to drop them in church and once assured his flock that "the Lord is a shoving leopard." Also, he once announced that the next hymn would be "Kinkering Kongs Their Titles Take."

It is said that he once told a lady, "Mardon me, padam; this pie is occupied; allow me to sew you to another sheet," but that sounds too contrived to be authentic.

Perhaps his most famous was a quadrupled prodigious accomplishment even for the gifted Spooner. While lecturing a delinquent undergraduate, he is said to have told him: "You have tasted a whole worm. You have hissed my mystery lectures. You were fighting a liar in the quadrangle. You will leave by the town drain."

The complexity of that quadruple suggests that it was invented by one of Spooner's contemporaries or perhaps even put together from remarks Spooner made to different students at different times. But there is evidence that Spooner himself was capable of such an achievement.

This is one of my favorite spoonerisms, perhaps because it was spoken during World War I, when the dean was getting on in years, and it suggests that age had not diminished his powers.

When Brits were fighting across the channel, he told the Home Front: "When the boys come back from France, we'll have the hags flung out." Typical of the kind of British spunk that helped them survive the deaths and mutilations of two world wars.

Perhaps Spooner hoped wistfully to be eulogized for a more scholarly skill. "We all know what it is," he once told his flock, "to have a half-warmed fish within us."

8 Thinking Critically

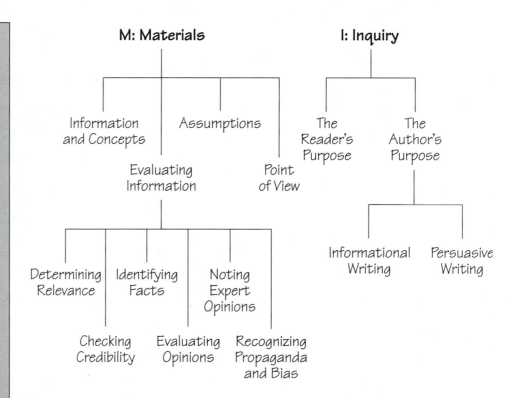

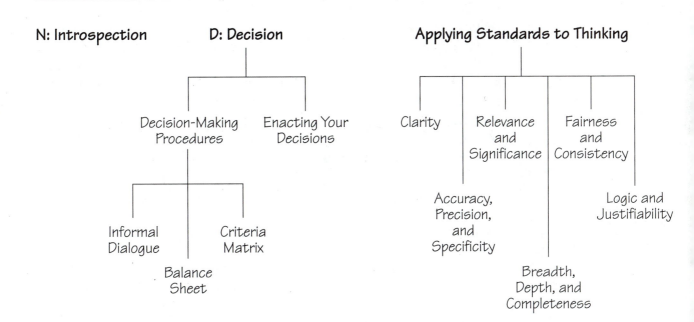

Imagine yourself sitting in an introductory zoology class. Your instructor's first lecture concerns the cattywampus. She describes it as an ill-adapted and nocturnal animal that became extinct during the Ice Age. She notes that no traces of it remain. Using an overhead projector, she shows a diagram of the animal's skull. Dutifully, you—and the rest of your classmates—take notes. At the end of the class, your instructor gives you a quiz. Confidently, you record your answers. To your surprise and dismay, you—and the rest of your classmates—fail the test.

What happened? Your experience was the same as that of David Owen (1990). The best teacher he ever had, Mr. Whitson, fabricated the preceding information about the cattywampus to make a point; that is, neither teachers nor textbooks are perfect. Mr. Whitson wanted his class to avoid uncritical acceptance of spoken or printed information. In the case of the cattywampus, if no trace of the extinct animal remained, there could be no physical evidence of its skull nor could its behavior be characterized. What made David Owen describe Mr. Whitson as the best teacher he ever had? Mr. Whitson introduced the class to **critical thinking,** the ability to discipline and take control of your thinking so that you can process information more easily (Paul, 1990). How you discipline and control your mind depends on your purpose and subject.

Your professors expect you to think at higher levels and in new ways in college. Each course you take requires thinking that is specific to that discipline. For example, rather than simply memorizing facts in a history course, you need to think like a historian: to look for causes that led to events, effects of those events, implications of one person's influence over another, what-if situations, and ways to prevent repetitions of disastrous historical events. Although the prospect of thinking like a historian, biologist, mathematician, or professional in whatever subject you take might seem overwhelming, you possess a wealth of personal background for doing just those kinds of thinking. When you decide not to invite someone to a party because that person ruined the last party you gave, you think historically to avoid repeating a disastrous event. Likewise, you think historically when you try to predict how your relationship with someone would change if you got married by considering the implications of your influence over one another. When you develop your ability to discipline and take control of thinking, you think more effectively and efficiently. The discipline involved in thinking critically requires an orderly and careful way of thinking about issues, people, and problems. However, the control you exert over the process depends on your ability to think about your own thinking. Using the acronym **MIND** helps you systematically work through the process of critical thinking. Figure 8.1 identifies the components in the MIND process. The circle reminds you that there is no one magical starting or ending place to ensure critical thinking. Indeed, you can examine your thinking by starting at any point as long as you cover all components. For example, if you are a college student in California considering a job offer in West Virginia, you might start by examining your assumptions about the people and climate of that state. Or, you might

Figure 8.1   MIND Components

Purpose

Questions

I

N

Interpretation

Inferences

Concepts

Information

Assumptions

Point of View

M

D

Conclusion

Implications

Consequences

start with the information on salaries in that state or the cost of living there. Your conclusion could even be to get more information or to test the validity of your assumptions. Regardless of where you begin the critical thinking process, you fail to logically cover the issue unless you consider all components.

Some aspects of critical thinking fit together because of their relationships to each other. For example, if your purpose for thinking about a possible job change is to decide how you feel about it, you will almost immediately identify a question that you want to answer about that topic. That question might be, "Should I take the job?" or "Will my family be better off in another state?"

M: MATERIALS

Quick, can you trace the following spiral to the center of the whirlpool? (Answer appears after the chapter review on page 388.)

The results of your thinking depend on the materials you use. You get materials from two sources. First, materials come from outside of you in the form of **information** and **concepts.** These include things you see (for example, words and pictures), things you hear (for example, words, music, or other sounds), and things you experience (for example, situations, activities, experiences). The materials with which you work also come from within you—your **assumptions** and **point of view.**

The preceding figure provided you with information in the form of a visual figure and the verbal concepts of *spiral, center,* and *whirlpool.* Your point of view was probably that of a learner or competitor—one who was to follow directions quickly to complete a task. If you checked the answer at the end of the chapter, you found that the design and wording of the information and concepts affected your assumptions about the figure. You assumed that the figure was as stated—a spiral—and responded accordingly.

Information and Concepts

Information comes from the data you acquire from life—what you see, hear, smell, taste, touch, and feel. As you gather information, you categorize and organize it to form concepts or ideas. This forms the basis of your background knowledge and the concepts you understand. You might think of a concept as a connected and organized network or web of information. For example, as a resident of the United States, your concept of money includes information like penny, dime, dollar, and so on. Although you might understand the concept of money relative to foreign currency, you probably lack detailed information for a specific country (for example, Japan and the yen). In other words, even though you understand that other countries have units of money with which you buy and sell merchandise, you probably don't know the names of the units or their worth.

When you think critically about a subject, you consider the information and concepts that concern that subject. A different subject might or might not result in different concepts. For instance, choosing the right major requires that you consider the concepts of *interest, marketability,* and *personal aptitude.* Without considering these concepts, you might choose a major because your best friend likes it or because your parents urge you to select it. Concepts form interconnected, organized webs or networks, but they are empty terms without data or information to fill and support them.

Evaluating Information

Gathering and evaluating information often seems like the easiest aspect of thinking critically about an issue. However, inaccurate, incorrect, insufficient, or irrelevant information affects your ability to think critically about its content. Think about the effects of trash being dumped next to the river. Suppose organic insecticide in the trash kills only mosquito larvae. In this case, dumping might do area residents a service rather than harm. Normally, however, dumping trash supports the concepts of toxicity and environmental imbalance and is considered a problem, not a benefit.

What information is relevant? What do lager-beer and pumpkins have to do with a doctor's case? What's credible? Can doctors who discuss such things instead of patients be trusted? What information is provided without bias? As twentieth-century novelist Anthony Burgess once said, there is as much sense in nonsense as there is nonsense in sense. For the critical thinker, separating the nonsense from the sense is sometimes difficult.

Determining Relevance

Relevance involves determining what you need to solve a particular problem or answer a particular question. Your role in determining relevance is to separate similar pieces of information into those you need and those you do not need. The way you think of the problem determines what you perceive to be relevant. In addition, what is relevant in one situation might or might not be relevant in another.

Anderson and Pichert (1978) examined the effect of point of view on recall. They asked students to read a passage about what two boys did at one boy's home when playing hooky from school. Some readers were asked to read as if they were burglars. Others were asked to read as if they were home buyers. A third group read from no particular point of view. Researchers found that the reader's point of view affected what was relevant and later recalled. For example, those who read as burglars were more likely to recall where the money was kept. That's what was relevant to them. Readers who read as home buyers recalled more about the home's landscaping. That's what was relevant to them. Determining the relevance of information, then, depends on your purpose, the question at issue, and your point of view. Exercise 8.1 helps you find relevance in reading.

Checking Credibility

What is truth? What is real? Who can you trust? P. T. Barnum, owner of a circus show he billed as "The Greatest Show on Earth" is often thought to have said, "There's a sucker born every minute." He often used exaggeration and deception to create interest in his circus shows; thus, logically, he might have thought and even said that a sucker is born every minute. In reality, however, no record exists of Barnum making this statement. In fact, in Barnum's time, the word *sucker* was not used in this context. And so, what is truth? What is real? Who can you trust?

In a free country like ours, almost anything anyone thinks can be spoken or printed. Whether those thoughts begin as fact or not, distortions

> Now when a doctor's patients are perplexed,
>
> A consultation comes in order next—
>
> You know what that is?
>
> In a certain place Meet certain doctors
>
> To discuss a case And other matters,
>
> Such as weather, crops,
>
> Potatoes, pumpkins, lager-beer, and hops.
>
> —Oliver Wendell Holmes
> *Nineteenth century American author*

Exercise 8.1   Respond to the following using Sample Chapters 11, 12, and 13 from the back of this book as sources.

1. You must write a paper on the ageism. Which chapter or chapters are relevant to this purpose? What specific sections within the chapter(s) could you use? Why do you think so?

    _____

    _____

2. You are preparing for midterm exams and want to review terms in assigned materials. Which chapter or chapters are relevant to this purpose? Where would you find that information within the chapter(s)? Why do you think so?

    _____

    _____

3. You are writing a paper on inheritance. Which chapter or chapters are relevant to this purpose? What specific sections within the chapter(s) could you use? Why do you think so?

    _____

    _____

4. You are making a speech on the unions. Which chapter or chapters are relevant to this purpose? What specific sections within the chapter(s) could you use? Why do you think so?

    _____

    _____

5. You want to compare family practices in the Japanese and Chinese cultures. Which chapter or chapters are relevant to this purpose? What specific sections within the chapter(s) could you use? Why do you think so?

    _____

    _____

occur. You are responsible for determining if information is fact or opinion, and, if opinion, whether or not to give credence to that opinion. You evaluate **credibility.** You control whether you exist as a critical judge of information or just another sucker.

Identifying Facts

Witnesses sworn in during trials promise to tell all the **facts** they know about a crime. Their opinions are immaterial, or not important. The judge wants to

hear what the witnesses know to be true. Thus, they describe what they actually saw or heard. They cannot add to, subtract from, or change the facts in any way. It is the judge and jury's job to determine how closely each witness sticks to the facts.

What are facts? A fact is a statement of reality. For example, there are seven days in a week. That's a fact. Canada is north of most of the United States. That's also a fact. Facts also exist in the form of events known to have occurred. For instance, George Washington was the first president of the United States. The bombing of Pearl Harbor occurred on December 7, 1941. These are facts. Facts are truth.

When you evaluate information, you act as judge and jury to decide if the information is factual. Facts are based on direct evidence or on actual observation or experience. The sources of this information are called **primary sources.** Primary sources consist of original documents or first-person accounts of an event.

Secondary sources also provide facts. They interpret, evaluate, describe, or otherwise restate the work of primary sources. Because information can be altered or lost in translation, primary sources provide more accurate information.

Qualitative words describe facts. They give details but are not judgmental. They express absolutes and represent concepts that can be generally agreed upon. Words like *dead, freezing,* and *wet* are examples of such words.

Other words, sometimes called **weasel words,** limit a statement of fact. Weasels are animals with keen sight and smell that are known for their

"But, how will we footnote this source?!"

quickness and slyness. Because of these characteristics, words that show the possibility of other options and lack exactness are called weasel words. Information is given but not guaranteed. For example, look at the difference between these two statements: "I make *A*'s and *B*s." "In some courses, I make *A*'s and *B*'s." The words *in some courses* limit the truth of the first sentence. Words like *frequently, occasionally,* and *seldom* are examples of such words.

Evaluating Opinions

Like facts, **opinions** are also a form of truth. The difference between the two lies in whose reality is being represented. Facts belong to everyone; they are the same for everyone; they are universally held. An opinion belongs to one person.

An opinion is what you think about a subject. It is a belief or judgment. Opinions reflect attitudes or feelings. Words describing opinions are interpretive.

Consider again the topic of grades. Suppose instead of saying "I make *A*'s and *B*'s," you say, "I make *good* grades." How is *good* defined? What you consider to be "good grades," someone else might consider to be inferior grades. Other students might consider them to be excellent grades, ones they could not achieve in a lifetime of effort. *Good* is a qualitative descriptor and, as such, depends on what you think for its definition. Its meaning is strictly your opinion. When you assume everyone defines qualitative words the same way you do, you make a **definitional assumption.**

Because opinion is biased, you need to be objective as you consider it. Objectivity refers to your skill in reporting facts without including personal opinions, definitional assumptions, feelings, or beliefs. Inclusion of such material in critical thinking undermines the validity and value of the conclusions you reach.

Noting Expert Opinions

The background of the person giving an opinion affects the value of the opinion. Anyone can give an opinion, but some people have the qualifications necessary to give **expert opinions.** For example, suppose a freshman tells you, "Take Sociology 421—my friend Jana said it's a great course." Now suppose your academic advisor says, "Take Sociology 421—with your background, you'd really enjoy it and learn a lot!" Which person would you trust to know more about Sociology 421?

An expert opinion depends on many factors. First, you need to evaluate an author's or speaker's educational and professional background. An author's or speaker's background affects point of view, what is said about a topic, and the way in which facts are reported. You find background information about an author in the preliminary or concluding statements of an article or book. A biographical dictionary or an encyclopedia also contains such information about authorities in a vast number of fields. You also gain knowledge though discussions with others in the same area of expertise. You judge where the author or speaker works and the reputation of that institution.

You also judge the reputation of the author or speaker. This works both as an advantage and disadvantage. People who are well-known authorities in one field might write or speak below their standards in another. As a critical thinker, you need to know the difference.

Sometimes information about the author's or speaker's credentials is missing. You then need another way to judge information. For example, suppose an article in *Today's Science* compares the incidence of cancer in the United States with that of France. The author, who is unknown to you, concludes that the air in France is cleaner than the air here and that this keeps the French in better health. You have no information about the author's background, so you cannot evaluate his or her qualifications or **bias.** In this case, you judge the standards and credibility of the journal containing the article.

WRITE TO LEARN

On a separate sheet of paper or in your journal, respond to the following: In your American history class, a graduate student in history guest lectures. She asserts that Grover Cleveland was the most effective president. Do you consider hers an expert opinion? Justify your answer.

Recognizing Propaganda and Bias

The magnificent promises and sublime and pathetic words advertisers use to sway our minds are forms of **propaganda.** Propaganda provides faulty information in that it is one-sided; it tells only one side of an issue to make you believe that side is the right one. It is used to try to make you think a certain way or believe or desire a certain thing.

Advertisers have used propaganda to convince you to buy their products since perhaps even before the eighteenth century. Politicians often use propaganda to convince voters to vote for them. Even authors and speakers slant the meaning of text, or bias it, both knowingly and unknowingly, through propaganda. Likewise, people around you use propaganda, both consciously and unconsciously, to persuade you to form opinions that conform with their own; that is, to bias your beliefs. Exercise 8.2 provides practice in finding facts and opinions.

Propaganda and bias affects the accuracy and objectivity of information. You can be wary of its effect by knowing what it is (see Table 8.1).

In addition to propaganda, authors and speakers use **euphemisms** and **loaded words** to sway beliefs. The word *euphemism* comes from two Greek word parts—*eu,* which means *good,* and *pheme,* which means *voice*—which

Table 8.1   Types of Propaganda and Bias, and Definitions

Types of Propaganda	Definitions
Image advertising	Associates a person, product, or concept with certain places, sounds, activities, symbols, or people in order to create a positive mental image of the initial person, product, or concept.
Bandwagoning	Implies that you must conform to the wishes or beliefs of a particular group to be right; suppresses individual rights.
Testimonial	Suggests that when a famous person or authority on a subject says a product, person, or idea is good, you must believe it.
Plain folks	Attempts to make you feel that ordinary, everyday people like yourself approve of the person, product, or idea.
Ad hominem (name-calling)	Forms unfair comparisons between two persons, products, or ideas by using unpopular or unflattering language about the competition.
Strawman	Shows an opposing person, product, or idea in its weakest form.

Exercise 8.2   Locate 10 facts and 10 opinions from "You Are There: What Cops Do as Told by Cops" on page 500 of Sample Chapter 11 ("Organizing the Police Department").

FACTS   OPINIONS

1. _____   _____
   _____   _____

2. _____   _____
   _____   _____

3. _____   _____
   _____   _____

4. _____   _____
   _____   _____

5. _____   _____
   _____   _____

6. _____   _____
   _____   _____

7. _____   _____
   _____   _____

8. _____   _____
   _____   _____

9. _____   _____
   _____   _____

10. _____   _____
    _____   _____

11. How do you recognize facts? How do you recognize opinions? What makes one different from the other?

   _____
   _____
   _____
   _____
   _____
   _____
   _____

WRITE TO LEARN

On a separate sheet of paper or in your journal, create or think of an example for each of the types of propaganda listed in Table 8.1.

---

translate literally into "good voice." Euphemisms substitute "good" or pleasant phrases for "bad" or unpleasant phrases. Authors and speakers use them to soften the reality of negative statements or to disguise the truth. For example, describing a fellow instructor as being *careful with details* sounds better than saying the person is *picky.*

Loaded words, on the other hand, make people, issues, and things appear worse than they might really be. Because of the definitional assumptions carried by loaded words, a word that seems okay to you might trigger an emotional response in another. For example, examine these terms from criminal justice class, *accused murderer* and *convicted felon. Accused murderer* has a different impact than *convicted felon* because you have more definite feelings about murder and less definite ideas about felonies. Because the way speakers and authors use words affects what you hear and believe, you need to be a critical evaluator of all you read and hear. Practice finding euphemisms and loaded words in Exercise 8.3.

Exercise 8.3 Read the following selections from the indicated sample chapters. Examine each of the italicized words or groups of italicized words that come from these selections. Determine if each is used as a euphemism or a loaded word(s). Identify why the author chose to use the word(s) in this way.

From the "Police Unions" section of Sample Chapter 11:

   1. Police Unions have a long and *colorful* history.

   Meaning: _____

   Image evoked: _____

   Euphemism or loaded word(s)? _____

   Why word(s) is used this way: _____

   _____

   2. The Boston Police Strike of 1919 . . . was *triggered* by the refusal of the city of Boston to recognize the AFL-affiliated union.

   Meaning: _____

   Image evoked: _____

(continues)

Exercise 8.3   *Continued*

Euphemism or loaded word(s)? _____

Why word(s) is used this way: _____

_____

3. Unions exist in order to *harness* the *individual power* of each worker into *one* group, the union, which can then speak with *one* voice of all the members.

Meaning: _____

Image evoked: _____

Euphemism or loaded word(s)? _____

Why word(s) is used this way: _____

_____

_____

From the "Double Standard of Aging" section of Sample Chapter 12:

4. Older women were concerned with *wrinkles, "saggy" jowls,* and *"droopy" eyelids.* These concerns led to face- and neck-lifts and to chemical peels to "smooth" the skin.

Meaning: _____

Image evoked: _____

Euphemism or loaded word(s)? _____

Why word(s) is used this way: _____

_____

5. The successful *exploitation* of women's fears of growing older has been called age *terrorism.*

Meaning: _____

Image evoked: _____

Euphemism or loaded word(s)? _____

Why word(s) is used this way: _____

_____

6. Women are so frightened of being *rejected* or *abandoned* at home by *romantic* partners and in the workplace that they will buy any product to prolong a youthful look (Pearlman, 1993).

Meaning: _____

Image evoked: _____

Euphemism or loaded word(s)? _____

Why word(s) is used this way: _____

_____

(continues)

Exercise 8.3   *Continued*

7. Women *suffer* a loss of self-esteem, depression, and feelings of shame and self consciousness. . . . Brown . . . referred to age as the *great destroyer.*

   Meaning: _____

   Image evoked: _____

   Euphemism or loaded word(s)? _____

   Why word(s) is used this way: _____

   _____

8. [Brown] says: "I'm afraid of losing my sexuality. I'm desperately afraid of retirement. I fear that with age, I'll cease being a woman, that I'll be *neuter*. I fear losing my looks and ending up looking like . . . like an *old crumb* . . ."

   Meaning: _____

   Image evoked: _____

   Euphemism or loaded word(s)? _____

   Why word(s) is used this way: _____

   _____

From the "Utilization of Services" section of Chapter 12:

9. One example is *nursing home* care, where Hispanic *elders* are greatly underrepresented . . .

   Meaning: _____

   Image evoked: _____

   Euphemism or loaded word(s)? _____

   Why word(s) is used this way: _____

   _____

10. Popular beliefs characterize Mexican Americans as living in *extended families* and, in fact, Hispanic families do tend to be larger than white families in the United States.

    Meaning: _____

    Image evoked: _____

    Euphemism or loaded word(s)? _____

    Why word(s) is used this way: _____

    _____

WRITE TO LEARN

On a separate sheet of paper or in your journal, discuss the role of propaganda in national and international politics. Is it ever appropriate to use propaganda? Why or why not?

Assumptions

As detailed in Ann Lander's advice column on August 22, 1994, Morty Storm of Brooklyn, New York, wrote a humorous story called "A Dog Named Sex." In this story, the narrator describes several ways in which his dog's name, Sex, resulted in confusion. For example, when he went to get the dog a license, he said, "I want a license for Sex." The clerk replied that she wanted the same thing. He told the clerk that he had had Sex since he was nine years old, and the clerk said, "You must have been quite a kid!" When he took the dog on his honeymoon, he told the manager that Sex kept him awake at night, and the manager said he had the same problem. After a number of similar experiences, the narrator said that Sex ran away from home one evening, and he spent several hours looking for him. When a cop asked him what he was doing on the streets at four o'clock in the morning, he said that he was looking for Sex. The narrator concluded the story by saying that his court case was coming up next Friday.

The humor of the preceding story depends on assumptions embedded in the concept of *sex*. Assumptions consist of the beliefs and expectations you take for granted about a situation. They come from your actual and/or vicarious background experiences. Identifying your assumptions helps you analyze your interpretation of a situation. In this story, the people the narrator met assumed that Sex referred to something other than a dog; however, the narrator assumed that people understood he was talking about a dog when he talked about Sex. These assumptions resulted in a variety of misunderstandings.

Identifying assumptions in your own thinking as well as in the thoughts of others is no easy task for several reasons. First, assumptions are somewhat hidden. They reside below the surface of any thought or argument. Second, because assumptions arise from background knowledge, they are second nature to you. You unconsciously think them. Third, you might have held certain assumptions for so long that you do not recognize them as assumptions—you see them as truth or fact.

Ironically, actively attacking or defending an alternative argument helps you identify the underlying assumptions in any situation. For example, suppose, in discussing a psychology chapter your instructor says, "To remove the burden from a family of a terminally ill patient, euthanasia is the best course of action." How can you recognize the assumptions your instructor is making? If you can identify and defend another alternative, like hospices, you will recognize the instructor's assumption—the patient's death will help the family.

Another way of identifying the assumptions of others involves identifying qualitative terms, those words whose definitions vary from one person to another. Likewise, these words seem most persuasive in leading you toward one idea over another. Think again of your instructor's statement: "To remove the burden from a family of a terminally ill patient, euthanasia is the best course of action." Which words seem less clear in definition and, thus,

Exercise 8.4   In each of the following situations, identify the common assumption that led the individuals to react the way they did.

1. Gerald is going out with his friends. He tells his parents he will be home about midnight. His friends want to stop by a club where a new band is performing. The band will not perform until 11:45 P.M.. One of Gerald's friends offers to take him home before the performance. Gerald's response: "No problem. I won't be more than one hour late."

    Assumption: _____

    _____

    _____

2. Several of Jennifer's professors will be absent next Friday because of a professional conference. Her professors have asked graduate assistants to cover their classes. Jennifer decides to go home for the weekend on Thursday.

    Assumption: _____

    _____

    _____

3. Jack is driving down the highway. As he glances in the rear-view mirror, he sees a highway patrol car rapidly approaching. Jack curses and pulls over.

    Assumption: _____

    _____

    _____

4. Sue sees a dog running across a busy highway. The dog has a collar and tag. She captures the dog and calls the vet.

    Assumption: _____

    _____

    _____

_____

leave room for argument? *Terminally ill, patient,* and *euthanasia* seem exact enough, but what about the words *burden* and *best?* Their definitions differ qualitatively from one person to another, one situation to another. Locating these words helps you identify and clarify definitional assumptions. You can practice identifying common assumptions in Exercise 8.4.

Point of View

Point of view involves perspective—the position from which you view or evaluate things. Just as an astronaut's view of earth from the space shuttle differs from your view of earth from your window, your perspective affects how you see things. Gender, ethnicity, educational background, personal experience, or other concepts form perspective, which affects a person's point of view. For example, a Hispanic male who graduated from Harvard 10 years ago probably has a different point of view of the university experience than does a Hispanic female high school student who is applying for admission to Harvard this year. Recognizing point of view helps you understand why you or someone else takes a particular position about an issue. Exercise 8.5 helps you determine your point of view.

Consider the story about the dog named Sex again. It contains several points of view. First, the narrator's point of view was that of a typical dog owner. Everything he tried to do was perfectly normal. The clerk's perspective was sympathetic because she assumed a license for "Sex" sounded like a good idea. According to this clerk's point of view, the narrator must have been quite a kid because he had had "Sex" since he was nine. Another clerk with a different point of view might have been horrified at such an idea. The hotel manager also had a sympathetic point of view because he thought that he and the narrator shared common sleepless experiences with "Sex." Finally, from the cop's point of view, anyone who was looking for "Sex" at 4 A.M. probably ought to be arrested for something.

I: *INQUIRY*

A popular supermarket tabloid uses "Inquiring minds want to know" as their slogan. Why? Their writers know that people want the scoop on a story: what happened and why. As a critical thinker, you, too, need the scoop on the subjects about which you think. Identifying a **purpose** for thinking and **questions** to answer helps you achieve that goal.

Consider the following example. You are reading the newspaper. You turn to the sports page and begin to read an article about your favorite professional basketball team. Your *purpose* is to find out what happened at the game. The primary *question* at issue for you might be, "Did they win?" Your roommate, who heard the score on the radio, enters the room and reads over your shoulder to answer the *question, "Who* scored the winning basket?" At this point, you should realize that two people could have the same purpose but a slightly different question at issue.

Thus, your goal for thinking or reading is the same as your purpose. To benefit from thinking or reading you must have a reason for doing it. If no reason exists, you probably won't get any results or satisfaction from the activity. What you want to know about the topic results in the question at issue. When you read or think critically, you need to clarify or refine your purpose by identifying a problem you need to solve or question you want to answer.

Exercise 8.5   On a separate sheet of paper or in your journal, answer the following.

1. I am _____ years old.

2. My ethnic background is _____.

3. I am _____.
   a. male
   b. female

4. My political views would best be described as _____.
   a. conservative
   b. moderate
   c. liberal

5. I would characterize my religious beliefs in the following way:
   a. devoutly _____ (religious affiliation)
   b. _____ (religious affiliation)
   c. agnostic
   d. atheist

6. The place I grew up would best be characterized as which of the following?
   a. rural
   b. urban

7. What is your MBTI personality style? (see Chapter 1)

8. Based on your responses to questions 1-7, describe your point of view.

9. Locate someone in your class that has a similar point of view. Why is it similar?

10. Locate someone in your class that has a different point of view.

WRITE TO LEARN

On a separate sheet of paper or in your journal, explain the factors in your background that most affect your point of view. Your assumptions about any given topic form the remainder of your perspective and, thus, vary from subject to subject. From what source(s) do most of your assumptions about life originate?

The Reader's Purpose

Just as you have a purpose for the thinking that you do, you also have a purpose for the reading that you do. For all too many students, that purpose is to finish as quickly as possible. This purpose requires no critical thought and results in little

---

Table 8.2   **Purposes for Reading**

1. To answer questions
2. To confirm data
3. To get an overview of a topic
4. To identify an author's point of view
5. To check predictions
6. To enjoy reading by reading recreationally

---

understanding. In fact, one basic difference between critical and uncritical readers is that critical readers delineate a clear and specific purpose for their reading.

The actual purpose of your reading varies from one situation and its materials to another (see Table 8.2). Whatever your purpose, knowing it helps you become a more active and involved reader. Reading that's active is far more interesting and results in critical thinking and efficient learning. Asking questions, making predictions, and identifying problems to be solved all are ways to set purposes in thinking and reading.

Questions for reading arise from a variety of sources. Instructor questions often help you set purposes for your reading. You might find these questions written on an overhead transparency or chalkboard or as part of your course syllabus or other course materials. Whatever the case, they provide you with a means for identifying information you need to know. Questions also come from the author of the text itself. How? Authors often provide pre- or postchapter exams for your use in evaluating your understanding (see Chapter 4). Questions also occur as a result of your interactions with author-provided information. For example, the use of a study system like SQ3R mandates that you set your own questions as part of an initial skimming of the title, headings, subheadings, and terms (see Chapter 5). If the title, headings, or subheadings are ambiguous or missing, then the first sentences of sections often provide information on which you can base your questions.

Making predictions goes hand-in-hand with asking questions. That is because when you ask a question, you are in fact predicting that its answer appears in the section or chapter you are about to read. Thus, asking questions is one way to make predictions. Another way involves examining illustrations and guessing their importance to the information in the text. Based on the extent of your background knowledge, you might be able to make predictions by summarizing what you already know about a chapter before reading it. Corrections to or elaborations on the content of this summary after reading provides an effective study aid. Making predictions increases your curiosity, a kind of motivating force, and provides an additional purpose for reading: learning how accurate your predictions are.

A final way to set purposes for reading involves your linking text information with yourself. If you identify how the text relates to a problem you or someone you know faces or how information in it connects with what you wish to do when you graduate, You have identified a purpose for reading.

Creating and pursuing questions are both the rigor and the passion of critical thinking and reading. Making predictions allows you—the critical reader or thinker—to be curious and creative in approaching information. Linking the text with yourself encourages individuality.

The Author's Purpose

Every term, college instructors ask the routine question: "Why did you come to college?" Traditionally, the answers seem as cliché as the question itself. Nonetheless, the question remains a valid one. That's because everyone has a purpose, a goal they mean to achieve, for everything they do.

Authors are no different. In most cases, they consciously decide to write with a specific objective or purpose in mind. Although some, like poets, artists, or composers create for the joy of artistic expression, other authors write to influence your understanding, emotions, beliefs, and actions.

Because writing is purposeful, an author seeks to obtain a desired response from you. For example, if an author writes to inform, then you should expect to acquire information you have not known before or review knowledge you already possess. If an author writes to persuade, then you should expect to examine your beliefs in light of the information the author provides. If an author writes to entertain, you should expect to feel amused or interested. These, then, comprise the three purposes authors have when writing: to inform, persuade, or entertain.

Although one purpose might be foremost in mind, an author sometimes mixes in the other two. For example, consider the following sentence from a college anthropology text.

> Anthropologists ... want to understand the rules that you know unconsciously that instruct you when to bow your head and speak reverently, when to sound smart, when to act dumb, and when to cuss like a sailor.

WRITE TO LEARN

On a separate sheet of paper or in your journal, write a short paragraph about a homework assignment that you recently completed. What questions do you have about that assignment? What questions do you think your instructor had that led to making the assignment? Were you able to answer all of your questions before you completed the assignment? How did the questions and the answers affect the quality of your completion of the assignment?

Here the author has added humor to informative writing. Or, an author might support a persuasive writing with information. For example, consider this sentence from the same anthropology text:

> Anthropology has practical value in the modern world, and it is not as esoteric as many people think . . . The value of inculcating understanding and tolerance between citizens of different nations is another practical lesson of anthropology . . . The information that ethnographers have collected about alternative ways of being human allows us to judge the benefits against the costs of industrialization and progress. The comparative perspective of anthropology helps us to see which elements of societies are amenable to change and what the consequences of this change might be. . . .

Here the author attempts to persuade you to believe that anthropology is a practical, day-to-day science by providing examples of how it affects your life. Finally, even writing whose sole purpose is to entertain contains information; however, because such writing exists strictly for your recreational pleasure, you do not have to explore it with as much critical thought as you do persuasive and informative writing. Thus, the remainder of this section focuses on only informational and persuasive writing.

Informational Writing

Informational passages seek to educate. Usually, an author tries to present material in a way that readers will easily understand. Such writing often consists of explanations, analyses, descriptions, demonstrations, and definitions. It also includes examples, statistics, comparisons, contrasts, and expert opinions. Although it is most often found in textbooks, newspapers and magazines also include informational writing.

Persuasive Writing

An author writes a persuasive passage to bring about a change in either your opinion or your behavior. Authors change your opinion by convincing you to agree with what they think. Such writing seeks to make you believe the author's point of view. For example, an author might try to convince you that survival depends on conservation of resources. This author can try to change your behavior in two ways. First, he changes your beliefs. Then, he asks for a promise of action by you. For example, the author might convince you that conservation is necessary. Then, you'd be asked to recycle waste products in order to conserve resources.

You find persuasive writing in educational, cultural, or historical documents. Like informational writing, it includes examples, statistics, comparisons, contrasts, and expert opinions. Practice determining purposes in Exercise 8.6.

Exercise 8.6   Answer briefly but completely.

Create a purpose and question at issue for your thinking about the following situations:

1. Choosing a major

    Purpose _____

    Question at issue _____

2. Your grades in a class

    Purpose _____

    Question at issue _____

3. Your summer plans

    Purpose _____

    Question at issue _____

Identify the purpose for reading about the following topics:

4. An article about an upcoming election

    Purpose _____

    Question at issue _____

5. An article about AIDS research

    Purpose _____

    Question at issue _____

6. A chapter in a history text about the Vietnam War

    Purpose _____

    Question at issue _____

7. A chapter in a biology text about plant cells

    Purpose _____

    Question at issue _____

Identify the writer's purpose in writing about the following situations:

8. A writer who states "Some scientists believed that the accumulation of carbon dioxide and other human-generated gases were creating a 'greenhouse effect.' These gases, according to the theory, were preventing the escape of the sun's heat from the earth's atmosphere, causing the earth to heat up in much the same way an automobile with closed windows does on a summer day . . . Geological records indicate that the earth goes through many cyclic changes of temperature and rainfall over time. We do not know what precise factors are most significant. . . . How much modern industrial practices have contributed is not clearly known."

Exercise 8.6   *Continued*

Purpose _____

Question at issue _____

9. A writer who states, "Within a few weeks after first exposure, some HIV-infected persons develop a seven-to-fourteen-day illness with enlargement of the lymph glands, sore throat, fever, muscle aching, headache, and a skin rash that often looks like measles. HIV can be detected in circulating blood lymphocytes at this time, but tests for antibodies to HIV seldom become positive until six weeks to six months later. This early form of illness usually disappears or is so mild that it is not even remembered."

Purpose _____

Question at issue _____

10. A writer who states, "The relationship between the experience of past stress and current stress tolerance suggests that confidence in your ability to handle stress is an important factor in how much tolerance you have. The greater your confidence that you can handle such threats to your adjustment as they come along, the less likely you are to experience events and changes as stressful. To put it another way, your past experience affects your cognitive evaluation of a situation."

Purpose _____

Question at issue _____

WRITE TO LEARN

Choose an editorial from your school paper or local paper. After reading the editorial, on a separate sheet of paper or in your journal write a short paragraph in which you identify what the writer would like you to believe and the question at issue. Were the purpose and question actually stated? If so, include the quote. If they were not, how did you know what the purpose and question were? Give examples of any information the author adds to back up the persuasion. Does the author attempt to use humor to convince you? If so, give examples.

N: INTROSPECTION

The word *introspection* comes from the Latin word *introspectus,* meaning to look inward. Introspection means using what you already know to think about and process new materials under consideration. This combination of old and new knowledge results in **inferences** and **interpretations.**

An inference can be defined as a statement or prediction about the unknown based on the known. The process of inferring involves interpreting information or occurrences to make predictions about the present or future or a guess about the past.

Making accurate predictions or educated guesses often poses problems because people who get identical information about a topic do not necessarily "see" or interpret the information in the same way. As a result, completely different predictions about what that information suggests could result. In other words, you form guesses and inferences by interpreting the information at hand in light of your background knowledge, assumptions, and point of view.

A particularly tragic example of differing inferences and interpretations using the same information involves the death of a Japanese exchange student in Baton Rouge, Louisiana, in October 1992. Invited to a Halloween costume party, the student and his American friend attempted to find the home where

---

Exercise 8.7   Respond to the following using Sample Chapter 12 ("Women and Ethnic Groups"):

1. Refer to pp. 523–528, "Asian Americans" and "Native Americans." What questions should you ask so you can compare these two groups?

   _____

   _____

   _____

   _____

2. Refer to pp. 517–518, "Future Outlook." What are the implications of considering or not considering the future of African-American elders?

   _____

   _____

   _____

   _____

3. Refer to pp. 509–512, "Single, Widowed, and Divorced Older Women." What are the implications of being single as an elderly woman? Widowed? Divorced?

   _____

   _____

   _____

   _____

a party was being held. By mistake, they went to the wrong address in a neighborhood that had recently experienced several burglaries. The homeowners who answered the knock were frightened, so the man at the house came to the door with a gun. As the exchange student moved toward him saying, "We're here for the party," the man yelled "Freeze." The student, new to the United States and unfamiliar with that expression, continued to advance. The man inferred that only someone who intended harm would continue to move toward him. The man also inferred that since the intruder failed to "freeze," his intentions were to rob the home. Acting on his incorrect inference, the man shot the student, fatally wounding him. Consider the role of background knowledge in introspection. Because burglary and homicide are not societal problems in Japan, the exchange student failed to infer that he was at risk. For the same reason, he did not interpret the command to freeze as a warning statement. The homeowner used his own background and new information to interpret the actions of the student as threatening. Ironically, the non-threatening student was at risk, whereas the threatening homeowner was not.

Reconsider the example regarding reading a the newspaper article about a basketball game. Suppose one of your favorite players often scores 20 to 30 points per game. As you read the article, you notice that he scored only 20 percent of his shots resulting in 10 points. Based on your knowledge of his past performance, you infer that he has some sort of problem—an illness, a worry, or an injury, perhaps. Someone who knew little of this player's background might read the same information and infer that he's not a very strong player. The information remains the same, but the interpretations result in very different inferences.

D: Decision

You gathered the information you needed. You identified your purpose and questions. You analyzed your interpretations and inferences. Now it's time to make a decision and do it—in the words of the American proverb: to fish or to cut bait!

All critical thinking is done for a purpose, so it must end in a **conclusion** concerning the situation or a solution to the question at issue. In a way, the conclusion often brings you full circle in your thinking. You might reach a decision about the question at issue, but that decision might be to examine another question or gather more information before reaching a decision. A student who critically examines possible majors as a freshman might not reach a conclusion about the perfect major. Instead, that student might eliminate certain majors and begin the thinking process again as new courses and information become available. In some cases, two people begin with the same purpose and question and use the same information, but their individual points of view, assumptions, and inferences lead them to different decisions.

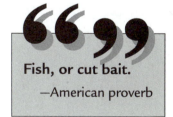

Fish, or cut bait.
—American proverb

For example, rational people armed with the same information about the death penalty often come to separate and different conclusions.

Whenever you reach conclusions, **implications,** or **consequences,** follow. Conclusions and implications/consequences are analogous to causes and effects. They form chain reactions; that is, a conclusion sets into motion a series of possible outcomes, or implications, and given outcomes, or consequences. For example, the implications and consequences of living in an apartment rather than at home or in a residence hall might include the need for transportation to and from your institution, the cost of turning on utilities, monthly bills, and cooking for yourself. Problems occur when conclusions are reached with little or no consideration of possible implications and probable consequences. Perhaps you rented an apartment within walking distance from the campus because you don't own a car, and your city provides no public transportation system; however, you failed to think about the need for transportation to a supermarket so that you could cook for yourself. Thus, reaching a conclusion or solving a problem requires that you carefully consider the implications and consequences of each available alternative before making a final decision.

Think again about the report of the basketball game. You had a purpose—to locate information—and a question at issue—who won the game. After reading the article, you found the information that answered your question. You might make inferences, but no decision needs to be made based on your original question. In other words, although you were thinking, you were not thinking critically.

Have you ever heard the phrase, "He met his Waterloo"? It means that the person in question suffered a crushing defeat. The etymology of the phrase alludes to the critical battle at Waterloo in which Napoleon Bonaparte lost the war to England and Prussia and, thus, lost his title as Emperor of France. Napoleon probably carefully considered his options and weighed the possible implications of victory or defeat before choosing to attack at Waterloo. Changing his mind might have changed the outcome of the war and its consequences on his career.

The outcome of most decisions can be rethought. Even decisions that appear monumental in scope can be altered. For example, perhaps you decided to live off campus because it offered you more privacy, more independence, and a change from living at home or on campus. However, you discovered your expenses were greater, you hated walking to campus in bad weather, you didn't like to cook for yourself, and you got lonely. At this point, you might feel compelled to stick to your decision. But, why? If you made a decision that isn't working, what's a better choice—being miserable or rethinking the situation and making another decision?

The notion of assessing and rethinking is, for some people, a new idea. Some people think that once you decide, you stick with that decision, no matter what. Assessing a decision gives you the power and the freedom to change your mind, your situation, and your life.

Decision-Making Procedures

It's been said that the only exercise some people get is jumping to conclusions, sidestepping responsibility, and pushing their luck. These same people exercise this way because they do not think critically. Hence, the decisions they make often involve hasty leaps, tricky stepping, and what they would probably call bad luck. You, the critical thinker, can label these conclusions as what they really are—faulty. You recognize that without a decision-making process, logical conclusions are difficult to make. You know the importance of considering assumptions, point of view, information, concepts, purpose, and the central question at issue in decision making. You also understand the importance of knowing about ways of thinking; having several plans for weighing implications; reaching a final conclusion; and assessing the consequences. In this process, **informal dialogues, balance sheets,** and **criteria matrices** are tools that can help you reach your final inference, your conclusion.

Informal Dialogue

Informal dialogue refutes the suggestion that the people who talk their heads off aren't losing much. That's because informal dialogue involves your talking about your possible decision and its implications both to others and to yourself. Speaking with others just makes sense. Informal dialogue with others allows you to explore new points of view, acquire new information, and hear what others see as the implications of various issues. Placing possible solutions on the worksheet found in Table 8.3 provides you with an active way to see possibilities concretely.

Table 8.3   Possible Solutions Worksheet

Possible Solutions Worksheet

Problem to Solve/Decision to Make _____

Possible Solutions	Positive Implications	Negative Implications

How can you carry on a dialogue with yourself? You do so through **brainstorming.** Here you list on a piece of paper as many possible solutions as you can. List unbelievable, ridiculous, or even unacceptable solutions. Write any and all suggestions you can create, and try not to evaluate or edit any ideas until you've exhausted yourself on possible solutions. Brainstorming in this way releases you from tunnel vision and allows you to entertain ideas that could lead to a worthwhile and workable solution. Once you've completed your list, then you need to evaluate the information and add promising possibilities to your possible solutions worksheet. Evaluation questions appear in Table 8.4.

Many of the options you list on your worksheet will be unworkable because of the amount of money, time, or risk they involve. Eliminate these from your list. Doing so allows you to reduce a long list into a more manageable size.

Balance Sheet

According to Janis and Mann (1977), a balance sheet (see Table 8.5) of pluses and minuses helps you logically weigh your available options. Janis and Mann found that balance sheet users regretted their choices less often and were more likely to stick to their decisions. To create a balance sheet, you record projected gains and losses for yourself; projected gains and losses for others; projected self-approval or self-disapproval; and projected approval or disapproval of others.

Although the balance sheet gives you only your odds, it's value lies in making explicit the possible implications involved in the options you are weighing. What do you stand to gain? What might you lose in the bargain? The decision remains yours. You determine how much risk you're willing to take or the level of safety you want to maintain.

Criteria Matrix

Much like a balance sheet, a criteria matrix allows you to see options and evaluate them. Here, however, you identify beforehand the standards, or criteria, you will use for evaluation and the scale by which you will evaluate them. Criteria usually include those aspects of the decision that seem most important to you. For example, if you were deciding whether to purchase school insurance, you might use *cost, level of risk,* and *effect of illness on your coursework* as possible criteria. Scales for ratings include + or –; grades such as *A, B,* or *C* or *A, C,* or *F*; and numeric scales like 1 to 3, 1 to 5, or 1 to 10.

To complete a criteria matrix (see Table 8.6), you list possible solutions in the left-hand column of the matrix. Then you list criteria across the top; remember to abbreviate, if necessary. Next, rate your possibilities against each criteria. If you use a numeric scale, add each row to get the score for each possibility.

You can and you can't

You shall and you shan't;

You will and you won't

You'll be damned if you do,

And you'll be damned if you don't.

—Lorenzo Dow
Nineteenth century American evangelist

Table 8.4   Questions for Evaluating Brainstorming Activities

1. How does each possibility measure up?
2. Which possibility seems most workable and worthwhile?
3. What possibility has the best chance to succeed?
4. How risky is each possibility?
5. Which possibility seems most preferable?

SOURCE: Adapted from Pokras, S. (1995). *Team problem solving: Solving problems systematically.* Menlo Park, CA: Crisp Publications.

Table 8.5   Balance Sheet for Making a Decision

Projected Gains for Self	*Projected Losses for Self*
Projected Gains for Others	*Projected Losses for Others*
Projected Self-Approval	*Projected Self-Disapproval*
Projected Approval for Others	*Projected Disapproval from Others*

Table 8.6   Criteria Matrix

Rating Scale:

Problem to Be Solved/Decision to Be Made: _____

Alternative Solutions	*Evaluation Criteria*	*Summary Rating*

SOURCE: Adapted from Pokras, S. (1995). *Team problem solving: Solving problems systematically.* Menlo Park, CA: Crisp Publications.

Exercise 8.8   List a situation in which you need to make a decision. Assess the situation as objectively as possible. Then assess it from another point of view. (You can ask someone to provide this for you.) Generate and list three possible options. Then, on separate sheets of paper, create a balance sheet to explore each possibility. Using Table 8.5 as a template, identify the type of conflict each option involves, then choose the option you plan to pursue.

1. a. Situation: _____

_____

b. Your assessment _____

_____

_____

c. Second assessment: _____

_____

_____

d. Option 1: _____

e. Option 2: _____

f. Option 3: _____

g. Conflict in option 1: _____

h. Conflict in option 2: _____

i. Conflict in option 3: _____

j. Write balance sheets on separate sheets of paper.

k. Decision: _____

_____

You cannot choose your battlefield,

The gods do that for you,

But you can plant a standard

Where a standard never flew.

—Nathalia Crane

Twentieth century American poet and author

Enacting Your Decisions

Consider the role of the explorer. Explorers venture into the unknown—sometimes damned if they do, and sometimes damned if they don't. Enacting a decision requires the same sort of risk taking. It also mandates commitment and effort. Table 8.7 gives you some tips for putting your decisions into motion.

APPLYING STANDARDS TO THINKING

A **standard** is another word for a flag—a piece of colored fabric that serves as a symbol or signaling device. Flags express victory, honor, loyalty, hope, pride, and many other messages about a person or a group of people. The symbols a

Table 8.7   Tips for Enacting Decisions

1. Set a reasonable deadline for enacting your decision. Doing so gives you a target to aim for.

2. Think of your decision positively instead of negatively. You, like others, probably tend to think in major concepts. Sometimes your mind overlooks the small details. A decision *not* to score less than a C on any test in the semester sounds like a good one. However, instead of stating your goal negatively ("I do not want to score less than a C on any test in the semester"), a positive way to think about that choice would be to say "I intend to score a C or better on every test in the semester."

3. Make your decisions dependent on only you. Forming a study group the week before the final exam seems like a good goal . . . unless everyone gets sick or otherwise fails to show up. If you depend on others for success on the test, you might be disappointed with the results.

4. Use others for support. This seems like a contradiction of the previous suggestion; however, there is a difference. While not making a decision contingent on others, you should use others only for help and assistance. This kind of network provides you with information, advice, and friendship.

5. Visualize success. Once you make a choice, do you find yourself constantly doubting your decision? Do you picture the worst possible outcome? Most people tend to mentally replay their personal errors and mistakes until they've rehearsed them well enough that they happen again and again. If you tend to replay images of your past mistakes, you might also be rehearsing images of future mistakes. You can avoid some problems by visualizing and rehearsing the success of your decision rather than its failure.

6. Become aware of self-sabotage; instead, set yourself up for success. What do you do to shortchange your decisions? If you decide to study, do you put yourself in situations (dorm room, student center, kitchen, and so forth) in which you might be unable to concentrate? What could you do to set yourself up for success? Organize your study area? Choose a quiet location? Unplug the telephone?

---

person or country chooses to use on a flag tells a lot about how a person or country thinks and believes as well as what it values.

Standard is also another word for the criterion or rule against which you judge or measure success. Like the standard that is synonymous with flag, a standard expresses messages about what you think and what you value. To paraphrase Crane, you might not always get to choose the situations in which you must think critically, but you can set the standards by which you will judge your success in thinking in whatever situations you encounter. These standards help you focus, govern, and guide the thinking process. They provide benchmarks to assist you in assessing or evaluating the effectiveness of your thinking. Just as someone who paints as a hobby differs from an artist whose paintings hang in the Louvre, a thinker who thinks without standards differs from one who applies standards to evaluate thinking.

Although every standard theoretically applies to each aspect of thinking, the use or lack of use of some standards in conjunction with particular components affects the outcome of thinking more directly. For example,

```
                    Classroom Types
                     by Val Cheatham

  2×(4+3)      4×2      3+(4-2)      3×2      4×(3+2)
               ─               ─
               3               4

   3×4         2×3      2-(4+3)    3-(4+2)    4×(3-2)
   ─           ─
   2           4

  3-2×4        2+2        2×2      3+2-4       3-3
                          ─
                          3+3

   2+2        3×2+4      3×(2+4)     4-3        3+4
   ─                                ─          ─
   4                                2          2

   4-2        2×3+4      (2+2)=4     3-2        3+2
                                                ─
                                                4

                                    3×4
                                    ─
                                    2
```

*"Now that we all know how to set up the equation,
who can tell me the correct answer?"*

SOURCE: Reprinted by permission of Val Cheatham

clarity of information affects all aspects of thinking from your information to your analysis of your assumptions to your identification of implications and consequences. However, some standards are less applicable for other aspects of thinking. For instance, the standards of fairness and consistency affect question and purpose less than they affect point of view or information. Table 8.8 compares MIND components to applicable standards.

Clarity

If you've ever thought you understood a lecture, only to find out later that you were completely off base, you've experienced a lack of understanding. But what causes such misunderstandings? Was the professor unclear in giving information or was your thinking unclear? Whatever the case, **clarity,** or clearness, of thought forms the first standard against which you judge thinking. If you fail to express or understand a situation, idea, or assumption clearly, you cannot apply the other standards effectively. For example, although businesses spend billions of dollars on advertising each year, some

Table 8.8   **Comparison of MIND Components to Applicable Standards**

	Clarity	Accuracy Precision Specificity	Relevance Significance	Depth Breadth Completeness	Fair Consistency	Logic Justifiability
Materials						
information	X	X	X	X	X	X
assumptions	X				X	X
point of view	X			X	X	X
Inquiry						
purpose	X	X	X			X
questions	X	X	X		X	X
Introspection						
inferences/implications	X	X	X	X	X	X
Decision						
conclusions	X	X	X	X	X	X
implications	X	X	X	X	X	X
consequences	X	X	X	X	X	X

ads backfire as the result of lack of clarity in language. Translating American ad slogans into foreign languages is particularly tricky. When advertisers tried to translate Coca-Cola in phonetic Chinese symbols, they used the symbols for "Co" "Ca" "Co" "La." Unluckily, that means "Bite the wax tadpole." When General Motors introduced the Chevrolet Nova in Latin America, they discovered that the Spanish translation of nova is "doesn't go." In both cases, lack of clarity resulted in great misunderstandings. Clarity, then, forms the foundation for evaluation of thought because it assesses understanding. And without understanding, no further thinking can occur.

Although the concept of clarity—clearness or transparency of thought and language—seems obvious, applying the standard is often difficult. In situations where you can verbally discuss or question the clarity of information, you can paraphrase what you think you understand and ask for confirmation of meaning. For example, perhaps your math instructor says, "A convex n-gon is an n-sided polygon with the property that a straight line segment between any two points of the polygon is entirely within the polygon." Your response might be, "So, a triangle would be a convex n-gon because you can draw a line from any point to any other point inside the triangle and it remains in the triangle. But, a crescent is not a convex n-gon because a line from one tip to the other would be outside the shape." If your instructor agrees with your translation, you know that you clearly understand the information. In asking questions for clarity, you might try prefacing the information

ONLINE CLASS   **Web Exercise 8.1**

A variety of information related to the topics in this chapter is available on the World Wide Web. For this exercise, access one of the following Web sites (for the most up-to-date URLs go to http://csuccess.wadsworth.com):

Any article from Longview Community College's Critical Thinking Across the Curriculum Project:

http://www.kcmetro.cc.mo.us/longview/ctac/toc.htm

Critical Thinking: What It is and Why it Counts:

http://www.calpress.com/critical.html

Any article in Critical Thinking Library:

http://www.sonoma.edu/cthink/University/univlibrary/library.nclk

1. Which Web site did you choose? _____
   _____
   _____

2. How did the author of the article define critical thinking?_____
   _____
   _____

3. How did the information you selected relate to the discussion of critical thinking in Chapter 8? _____
   _____
   _____

4. How did the content of the article change your understanding of critical thinking?
   _____
   _____

you don't understand with information you do understand. For example, using the information on the convex *n*-gon, you might say, "I understand that an *n*-sided polygon can be called a convex *n*-gon, but I don't understand what you mean about the line segment property." Expressing information this way gives your instructor a place to start in clarifying information.

In analyzing information for clarity, you should look for one or more of the following: concrete examples, vocabulary and ideas that you understand, or metaphors or analogies. Although you can't always ask for confirmation, putting information in your own words—either in written or verbal form—often helps you attain clarity. You can also look words up in a dictionary or use a thesaurus for clarification of meaning. Finally, you can look for a variety of other resources on the topic, which might express the information in a way that is more clear to you.

Accuracy, Precision, and Specificity

What are you afraid of? Whatever it is, there is probably a term that exactly defines your fear. Such fears are called phobias, and research shows that the average person possesses three phobias. More than 150 words have been coined to express our fears. Do you faint at the sight of blood? Perhaps you have hematophobia, or fear of the sight of blood. Do you dislike confinement in small spaces? You might have claustrophobia, or fear of enclosed spaces. You could even suffer from dromophobia (fear of crossing streets), telephonophobia (fear of using the telephone), or even verbaphobia (fear of words). Whatever the case, there is a term that specifies the concept you fear in accurate and precise terms.

Once you satisfy the standard of clarity, you analyze your thoughts in terms, **accuracy, precision,** and **specificity.** Accuracy refers to correctness, whereas precision concerns exactness. Specificity suggests a limiting of details so that you exclude particulars to identify a single item. To further illustrate these concepts, imagine that you must take two science courses for your major, and you have to decide which course to take this term. You look in the catalog and notice that freshman-level science courses consist of two courses in each of the following: biology, chemistry, physics, and astronomy. At this point, any choice you make about science would be accurate. Reading the catalog more closely, however, you see that one science must be biological and one science must be physical. To follow the directions in the catalog precisely, you would not be able to take both courses in biology. You could, however, choose one biology and one chemistry. To make sure that you enter the beginning-level course for your first science class, you sign up for Biology 101. That is the specific course that you are choosing. You limited which course in biology you wanted to the first-semester freshman course and excluded the rest. There will be no doubt in the registrar's mind which biology course you want.

Relevance and Significance

Imagine that you went on a cruise that, unluckily, ran into an unexpected hurricane. Your ship begins to sink. Not knowing what will happen, you race around the ship gathering supplies. You find the following items: a flashlight and some batteries, a short-wave radio, a chest full of money, a case of canned food, ten gallons of water, a gun, another passenger, and a raincoat. You realize that you will only be able to carry three items on the two-person lifeboat. Which three will you choose? As you make your decisions, you face questions of **relevance** and **significance.**

Relevance, as indicated previously in this chapter, means to be connected to something else. Significance refers to importance. The distinction between them lies in the application of the terms. For example, suppose you and your roommate want to choose a cable TV package for this term. As an incentive for buying, one package offers an extra channel featuring children's programming for free if you enroll in the next week. If the programs on that channel fail to interest either of you, the free channel is not relevant to your decision. As you look at the other features and cost of the cable packages, you notice that the two packages under consideration differ by $10.00 a month or $120.00 a year. You choose the cheaper package. That information was not only relevant in your decision making, it became an important or significant factor in your decision.

Breadth, Depth, and Completeness

What do you see in the following figure? This image, called Necker's Cube, combines an unstable figure with an illusory figure. In an unstable figure, contradictory cues affect depth perception making it difficult to determine which part of the figure is closer to you. In this case, when you look once one side appears closer. Look again, and the other side appears closer. To be an illusory figure, you see things that are not actually there. In most figures, lines and

shapes form the image with paper and space forming the background. Here you see a complete geometric figure even though no lines form it. You used your background knowledge to "fill in" the spaces and create a full image.

In many ways, this figure depicts the roles of **breadth, depth,** and **completeness** in thinking. As you make decisions or think about issues, you must also consider the amount and quality of the information you have. Just as you can look at the image in more than one way, breadth suggests that you consider more than one viewpoint, kind of information, implication, or other aspect of thinking. Depth considers the level of complexity of the thought much like this three-dimensional image is more complex than a two-dimensional figure. Completeness requires that you have all the information to form a comprehensive picture either from the information itself or combined with your own background knowledge.

Choice of a particular college or university provides an example for examining these standards. For example, if you wanted to attend an institution that allows you to major in international business and gives you an opportunity to participate in an internship in South America, you would not want to consider just one institution and its program. That would not give you a broad base from which to make a decision. At the same time, reading just the catalog information about the courses would not afford the same depth that you would gain from visiting the institution and talking with the faculty. And finally, before you make a decision, you would need to have all the information about each college or university that you are considering to have information that is complete enough to make a decision.

Fairness and Consistency

The standards of **fairness** and **consistency** help you examine how thinking is done as well as the quality of the thinking. Comparisons help you determine fairness and consistency in information. A variety of different sources often provides a more balanced and fair view. Thus, if you have three treatments of the same information by three different individuals, similarities help you pinpoint consistencies and fair, unbiased coverage of the topic. Or, within a single document, you look for biased language or incompatible information to assess fairness and consistency.

For example, suppose you want your friend to be elected as student body president. But, as chairman of the group that schedules debates in the student union, you neglect to give information about the upcoming debate to the strongest opponent. You did not treat the information fairly and might have manipulated the outcome of the election. Consistency suggests that you apply the same criteria all the time. In the case of the election, if you gave each candidate ten minutes to speak, followed by five minutes for questions, you would have to treat each candidate in the same way to be both fair and consistent.

Logic and Justifiability

A professor at a local college was noted for his practical approach to life. He always insisted that there were logical and justifiable explanations for everything. Naturally, his friends were surprised to see that he carried a lucky rabbit's foot keychain. "Why do you use that?" one of them asked. "Surely you don't believe that old superstition that a rabbit's foot brings good luck." "Of course I don't believe it," growled the professor, "but I understand that it's supposed to work whether you believe it or not." "Just remember," said his friend, "it didn't bring much luck to the rabbit."

Logic and **justifiability** form two final standards against which to judge thought. Logic suggests that thinking or problem solving follows a line of reasoning that others can understand. In other words, it makes sense. You begin with a problem and, after looking at the information and your interpretation of it, you choose a decision that makes sense. The professor's decision to hang on to a rabbit's foot does not actually make sense. In fact, from the rabbit's point of view, it's not justifiable at all. Thus, beyond just knowing that something makes sense, you must be able to list the reasons so that others can follow your thought processes in decision making.

Exercise 8.9   Create a chart with the following headings at the top: High degree of comfort, Rationale, Low degree of comfort, Rationale, Strategies for change. List the standards for assessing components of MIND vertically on the left. Using your favorite course as the subject of your consideration, complete the chart as follows: In column 1, check the standards you feel most comfortable using in this subject. Describe why you feel comfortable using these in column 2. In column 3, check which of the standards you feel least comfortable using in this subject. Describe why you feel uncomfortable using these in column 4. For each standard checked in column 4, identify a strategy for increasing your level of comfort in column 5.

Create a second chart using your least favorite course as the subject of your consideration. What accounts for similarities and differences between the charts?

Exercise 8.10   Reread pages 508–513, "Women" in Sample Chapter 12, "Women and Ethnic Groups" at the back of this book. Then answer the following questions as a way of using MIND to identify information from a text.

1. What are your assumptions about aging women?

_____

_____

_____

_____

(continues)

Exercise 8.10 *Continued*

2. What is your point of view as you read/learn about older women?

_____

_____

_____

_____

3. What concepts pertaining to elderly women are discussed in this section? List them below, one concept per line.

_____

_____

_____

_____

_____

_____

_____

_____

_____

_____

4. Beside each concept listed in your answer to the preceding question, identify information to support it.

5. a.   What is the author's purpose for including this information?

_____

_____

   b.   What is your purpose for reading it?

_____

_____

_____

_____

6. a.   What is the question at issue for the author?

_____

   b.   What is the question at issue for you?

_____

_____

_____

_____

(continues)

Exercise 8.10 *Continued*

7. a.   What inferences can you make about the elderly women?

_____

_____

_____

_____

   b.   What inferences can you make about the topics discussed in this chapter?

_____

_____

_____

_____

8. What ultimate conclusion do you make about elderly women?

_____

_____

_____

_____

9. What are implications of that conclusion?

_____

_____

_____

_____

10. What consequences have resulted from having an increased population of elderly women?

_____

_____

_____

_____

Exercise 8.11   Read the article "It Seemed Like a Good Idea at the Time" found after Sample Chapter 12 on page 542 at the back of this book. Then answer the following questions:

1. From what point of view did Frank Gasparro design the coin?

_____

_____

_____

_____

_____

2. How does this point of view reflect information given in Sample Chapter 12 ("Women and Ethnic Groups")?

_____

_____

_____

_____

_____

3. What was the point of view of the New York Public Relations firm hired to promote the coin?

4. What was the point of view of the United States Department of Treasury in asking for the coin to be designed?

_____

_____

_____

_____

_____

5. What were the points of view of banks and businesses toward the coin?

_____

_____

_____

_____

6. Suppose the coin had been re-minted in a copper color (similar to a penny). What might have happened to public reaction at this point? What would explain this change, if any, in point of view?

(continues)

Exercise 8.11   *Continued*

_____

_____

_____

_____

_____

7. Identify three examples of bias in "It Seemed Like a Good Idea at the Time." What accounts for the bias in each of these examples?

_____

_____

_____

_____

_____

8. From what point of view does the author write this article? If the author had been an employee of the Treasury Department, what, if anything, would he have omitted from the article? Why?

_____

_____

_____

_____

_____

9. Identify three examples of euphemistic or loaded language in this article.

_____

_____

_____

_____

_____

10. Identify three concepts from this article. List them below, one per line. Then identify information to support each concept.

_____

_____

_____

_____

_____

CLASSIC CRITICAL THINKING

Read the following paragraph. Then answer the questions that follow on a separate sheet of paper or in your journal.

Marly Helmich did have a semester of college. What she remembered most clearly was how her freshman English teacher wrote the words "critical thinking" on the board, and then, after some discussion, during which all of the students, including Marly, expressed discomfort with the idea of "critical thinking," the teacher had written the phrase "Critical thinking is to a liberal education as faith is to religion." After the semester, Marly understood that the converse was true also—faith is to a liberal education as critical thinking is to religion—irrelevant and even damaging.

SOURCE: *Moo*, a novel by Jane Smiley.

1. What is critical thinking?
2. Why would students or people in general feel discomfort with the idea of critical thinking?
3. How is critical thinking to a liberal education as faith is to religion?
4. How is faith to a liberal education as critical thinking is to religion?
5. Why does Marly consider that faith to a liberal education and critical thinking to a religion are irrelevant and even damaging? Do you agree or disagree? Explain your answer.

GROUP LEARNING ACTIVITY   STEREOTYPES: DEBUNKING ARCHIE BUNKER

Archie Bunker, a character in TV's "All in the Family," was known for branding people and behavior. Uncritical thinkers—like Archie—often think in stereotypes. These are typical images or conceptions held by members of a specific group or applied to a person, group, or idea. Like Archie, you probably believe some form of stereotypes. That's because you've never examined these ideas to find why you hold them.

Application

What stereotypes do you hold? What stereotypes might apply to you? Determine how each person in your group defines each person in the following pairs. What does each one do? How would he/she or they act? What facts and opinions apply to each one? How does the concept of relevance apply to each one? Discuss your responses and conclusions with the group.

1. College Student/Retiree
2. Employer/Employee
3. American/Foreigner
4. Gang Member/Police
5. Priest/Atheist
6. Kindergarten Teacher/Professor
7. Two-Year-Old Child/Adult
8. Democrat/Republican
9. Men/Women
10. Vietnam Veteran/Desert Shield Veteran

Application

How do stereotypes impact your ability to think critically? What examples could debunk these stereotypes? How does this activity change the way you think about these groups and yourself?

CHAPTER SUMMARY

1. Critical thinking involves examining materials (information, concepts, assumptions, point of view), establishing purposes and asking questions through inquiry, using introspection to make inferences and interpretations, and making and enacting a decision (conclusion about the issue based on implications and consequences).

2. Evaluating information involves determining relevance, checking credibility, identifying facts, evaluating opinions, noting expert opinions, and recognizing propaganda and bias.

3. The critical thinker also must recognize the reader's as well as the author's purposes in both informational and persuasive writing.

4. Introspection concerns logical reasoning such as deductive and inductive processes and illogical reasoning identified by recognizing both fallacies in deductive reasoning and illogical inductive reasoning.

5. Decision-making procedures include informal dialogues, balance sheets, and criteria matrices.

6. Critical thinking mandates the application of standards such as clarity, accuracy, precision, specificity, relevance, significance, breadth, depth, completeness, fairness, consistency, logic, and justifiability.

Class*ACTION*

Respond to the following on a separate sheet of paper or in your journal. Combine the chapter map and chapter summary to form a synthesis map which reflects the main ideas and important details of this chapter. Personalize the map by indicating specific ways in which you plan to implement suggestions offered by this chapter.

CHAPTER REVIEW

1. List three of the courses in which you are now enrolled. For each course, what do you think it means for you to think like a professional in that field? For example, how would a mathematician think? How do assignments in each course contribute, or fail to contribute, to your ability to think like a professional in the field?

   _____

   _____

   _____

   _____

   _____

   _____

   _____

   _____

2. What does it mean to discipline and control your thinking? Is discipline and control the same for every subject or does it differ by topic? Explain your point of view.

   _____

   _____

   _____

   _____

   _____

   _____

   _____

3. Reread the section on introspection. Using the text from that section, identify one example of a concept and one example of information related to that concept.

   _____

   _____

   _____

   _____

   _____

   _____

   _____

KEY TERMS

Terms appear in the order in which they occurred in chapter.

critical thinking
MIND
information
concepts
assumptions
point of view
relevance
credibility
facts
primary sources
secondary sources
weasel words
opinions
definitional
   assumption
expert opinions
bias
propaganda
euphemisms
loaded words
purpose
questions
inferences
interpretations
conclusion
implications
consequences
informal dialogues
balance sheets
criteria matrices
brainstorming
standard
clarity
accuracy
precision
specificity
relevance
significance
breadth
depth
completeness
fairness
consistency
logic
justifiability

4. Imagine that you could discuss your ability to think critically with two of the following individuals: your parents or guardians, your best friend, your first-grade teacher, your employer, your favorite high school teacher, one of your current professors. For each individual that you choose, give two examples of each person's assumptions about you. How does each person's point of view affect those assumptions? Use the following chart as a guide and record your answers on a separate sheet of paper or in your journal.

Individual	*Perspective*	*Assumptions*

5. Consider one of your academic goals (for example, to complete an undergraduate degree, to make a 3.0 (B) average at the end of this term, to complete a lab assignment in chemistry). State your goal. Then describe how each step of MIND can help you achieve that goal.

Goal _____

M _____

I _____

N _____

D _____

6. You have a job in the Admissions Department at your college. One of your assignments is to call prospective students and provide them with information about your institution. What three concepts do you think are most important for a new student to know about postsecondary education? What one assumption might you have to refute about your institution? What question about your institution should new students ask?

Important Concepts _____

_____

Incorrect Assumptions _____

_____

Questions _____

_____

7. Choose one of your textbooks and turn to Chapter 3 in it. Respond to the following based on the content of that chapter: Identify three to five concepts that appear to be most important to understanding the content. How did you make this determination? What assumptions do you

have about the content of this chapter? What questions might you have about the content?

_____

_____

_____

_____

_____

8. It has been said that thinking is essentially interesting whereas memorization is essentially uninteresting. Why would this be so? How might using the MIND approach result in more interesting thinking about a topic?

_____

_____

_____

_____

_____

9. List three inferences you made about your college relative to your major. How do you interpret these inferences affecting your ability to get a job after you complete your coursework?

_____

_____

_____

_____

_____

10. Using a separate sheet of paper, respond to the following questionnaire on nutrition:

A. Identify the categories of food as described in the food pyramid. (See Chapter Three)

B. Describe how your eating habits and patterns have changed since entering college.

C. Describe a typical breakfast meal that you regularly eat.

D. Describe a typical lunch or dinner that you regularly eat.

E. Describe the snacks you regularly eat.

Using the questionnaire and your responses, identify three concepts important to the subject of nutrition. Identify two assumptions you make about nutrition. Define your point of view. Other than completion of an assignment, what might be your purpose for completing the questionnaire? What questions do you have as a result of your responses? How do you interpret the results of the questionnaire? How might those results impact a decision to maintain or alter current eating habits? In what ways could you assess your thinking process on this issue?

_____

_____

_____

_____

_____

11. How could you use the standards described in this chapter to evaluate your progress in a course?

_____

_____

_____

_____

12. Courts often hear cases in which homicide is said to be justified. How are the legal concepts of justice and justifiability alike? How are they different? What is an example of justifiable homicide? How would justice be served in this case?

_____

_____

_____

_____

_____

Answer for analysis figure

No. Because you are looking at concentric circles, *not* a spiral.

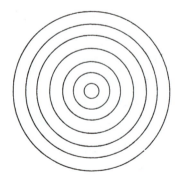

VOCABULARY DEVELOPMENT   Connotation: Know What It Means?

An elderly woman watched MTV for a long time. She turned to her son and asked, "But what does it all mean?" College coursework and life exposes you to a variety of situations, people, and ideas. Appearances are often deceiving, and things are not always what they seem. You, too, might find yourself wondering just what everything means. Postsecondary education helps you refine your ability to analyze and evaluate experience and find meaning. Words, too, represent a variety of situations, people, and ideas. Your ability to think critically about their meanings, both in connotation and denotation, helps you understand the courses you take, as well as life in general.

Vocabulary development is a constant analysis to discover the answer to "Know what it means?" in college coursework because words actually have two meanings. The first is the denotation—the literal, or dictionary definition. The second is the connotation. This includes the way a word is understood and used by the text or lecturer, as well as your own understanding of what a word means. You derive these implied meanings from hearing, reading, speaking, writing, and experiencing the word in everyday life. For example, a sociology class might study labor unions. The denotation of *labor union* would be "an organization of wage earners designed to improve the economic interests and general working conditions of its members." Your experiences might provide you with your own connotations. If your experiences were good, you might define a labor union as a benevolent group that works for the common good and supports its members. If your experiences were not favorable, (for example, your family's company was financially ruined by a union strike), you might think of a labor union as a ruthless group that destroys companies and the people associated with it.

The words an author or lecturer chooses and uses provide insights into what they really mean—both in literal meaning and implied connotations. The words you use in responding to class discussions or writing assignments similarly require the listener or reader to know what you mean. Vocabulary development occurs when you critically consider connotation as well as denotation in listening, reading, speaking, and writing.

Activity 1

For each of the following taken from an anthropology chapter entitled "Culture: The Ideas and Products People Adopt and Create," list your connotation for the boldface words or phrases. Then, using a dictionary, provide the word's denotation. Contrast your connotation and the word's definition.

Derek Freeman, another ethnographer who studied the Samoan culture between 1940 and 1967, reported evidence that contradicted Mean's findings (Freeman, 1983).

Contrary to Mead's report, the Samoan **adolescents** that Freeman describes are aggressive, **impulsive,** status-hungry, violent, and sexually "hung up."

1. adolescents

Connotation _____

_____

Denotation _____

_____

Contrast _____

_____

2. impulsive

Connotation _____

_____

Denotation _____

_____

Contrast _____

_____

In his inaugural address, George Bush suggested what he hoped to be the values of his Presidency," a **summons** back to the **patrician** values of restraint and responsibility.

3. summons

Connotation _____

_____

Denotation _____

_____

Contrast _____

_____

4. patrician

Connotation _____

_____

Denotation _____

_____

Contrast _____

_____

The youth movement of the 1960s, the Hare Krishna religious **sect,** and the **Amish** are examples of countercultures. The theme of the youth movement of the sixties was that success and materialism were misguided goals for individuals in society. Love, peace and sharing was the suggested alternative. The **"hippies"** (as they were called) who flourished in such communities as Haight-Ashbury in San Francisco and the East Village in New York have virtually disappeared.

5. sect

Connotation _____

_____

Denotation _____

_____

Contrast _____

_____

6. Amish

Connotation _____

_____

Denotation _____

_____

Contrast _____

_____

7. "hippies"

Connotation _____

_____

Denotation _____

_____

Contrast _____

_____

Activity 2

On a separate sheet of paper or in your journal, describe how the differences between your connotations and the word's denotation changed your understanding of the word's meaning? Give one example and explain.

Making Your Way Through the Maze: Library and Research Skills

Someone to Assist You:
The Librarian

A Thread to Guide You:
Library Organization

The Card
Catalog

The Computerized
Card Catalog

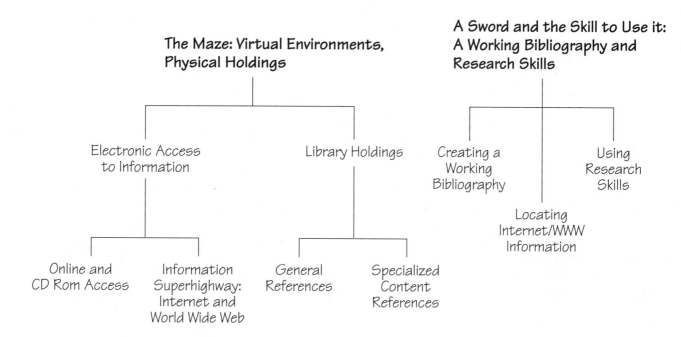

A Greek myth tells how the Minotaur, a creature with a man's body and a bull's head, was imprisoned in a maze by King Minos of Crete. The Minotaur, the strongest creature of the time, was fed seven young men and seven young women each year. A young prince named Theseus posed as one of the young men so he could kill the Minotaur. He took with him a sword given to him by his father. He also carried a ball of thread given to him by Ariadne, daughter of Minos. He used the thread to help him mark his way, found the Minotaur, and killed it with his sword. Then, using the thread as a guide, he returned to freedom.

If you have ever spent time trying to find information in a library or on the Internet, you probably know how Theseus felt. You, too, were trapped in a maze, facing what seemed to be dead ends. You needed what Theseus had— someone to assist you, a thread to help you find information and guide you through the maze of information, and a sword and the skill to use it.

SOMEONE TO ASSIST YOU: THE LIBRARIAN

The librarians of today, and it will be true still more of the librarians of tomorrow, are just fiery dragons interposed between the people of the books. They are useful public servants who manage libraries in the interest of the public.

—Sir William Osler
Twentieth century Canadian physician

If you feel confused by the maze of information in a library or on the Internet, you need the assistance of someone like Ariadne to help you find your way. That person is the librarian or librarian assistant.

A librarian or a librarian assistant is one of the most helpful people you can know on campus. The librarian knows what sources of information and services are available. The librarian can direct you to those sources you might overlook. Librarians also know about materials and services of other libraries. Often they can help you secure materials from them through an **interlibrary loan.**

You don't always have to go to the library in person to get assistance. If you need a quick answer to a simple question (for example, verification of a reference, correct spelling of a word, availability of a particular book), a phone call to the library often gets you the help you need. Some libraries also provide computerized reference assistance or responses by e-mail.

Complex questions require more time from both you and the librarian. Libraries, like other departments, often have peak time periods at which every student on campus appears to be working on papers or requiring other library assistance. To ensure a librarian has a block of time to devote to your needs, schedule a reference interview or appointment. This enables the librarian to provide you with undivided attention, and it gives you an opportunity to fully explain the requirements of your project (for example, the nature of your topic, your approach to the topic, the kinds of references you've already examined, suggestions from your instructor, and so on). This is a better approach than asking, "Do you have any books on . . . ?"

Librarians spend years learning about a wide variety of reference materials. Trained to aid students who are looking for specific information, librarians are much more than clerical people who keep up with the library's physical or virtual inventory. Librarians are more like travel agents who guide you in your library search. Perhaps the most valuable travel advice librarians offer concerns the way your campus library or computerized references are organized. Exercise 9.1 helps you locate the information you need from your librarian.

Exercise 9.1   Provide the following information about your campus library:

1. Library's hours.

_____

_____

_____

2. Policy on overdue books.

_____

_____

_____

3. Titles of five books found in the ready reference section.

_____

_____

_____

_____

(continues)

Exercise 9.1   *Continued*

    4.   Titles of three indices.

    _____

    _____

    _____

    5.   Titles of three computerized indices.

    _____

    _____

    _____

    6.   Location of current and bound periodicals.

    _____

    _____

    _____

    7.   Location of a map of the library holdings.

    _____

    _____

    _____

    8.   Location of the card catalog or computerized card catalog.

    _____

    _____

    _____

    9.   Location of the microfiche reader, computerized reference materials, or online access.

    _____

    _____

    _____

    10. Location of general collection books.

    _____

    _____

    _____

A Thread to Guide You:
Library Organization

The thread that marks your way through the maze of library information is the catalog. A library's catalog is stored either in files or in a computerized **database** (collections of information such as phone lists, bibliographic references, summaries of articles). The catalog is organized numerically according to either the **Library of Congress (LC)** or the **Dewey decimal** system. The **call numbers** in these systems identify the subject area of the material and indicate where the material is shelved.

Many large research and university libraries use the LC system. Its advantages over the Dewey decimal system include its precision and capability for expansion. A combination of capital letters and numbers classify and identify books. The first letter indicates the general topic (see Table 9.1). The

> 66 99
> **The closest you will ever come to an orderly universe is a good library.**
>
> —Ashleigh Brilliant
> *Twentieth century*
> *American author*
> *and artist*

Table 9.1   **Comparison of the Dewey Decimal and Library of Congress Systems**

Subject	Dewey Decimal	Library of Congress
General works	000	A
Philosophy and psychology	100	B
Religion	200	BL-BX
History	900	C-E
Geography	910	G
Social science	300	H
Political science	320, 350	J
Law	340	K
Education	370	L
Music	780	M
Fine arts	700	N
Language	400	P
Literature	800	P
Pure science	500	Q
Medicine	610	R
Agriculture	630	S
Applied science and technology	600	T
Military science	355	U
Naval science	359	V
Bibliography	010	Z

second letter represents a subject of the topic. The numbers further specify the subject. A second line identifies the book's author and edition.

Some libraries use an older but just as effective means of classifying materials called the Dewey decimal system. The method organizes materials into ten major categories (see Table 9.1). Its call numbers also are written in two lines. The top line is the Dewey decimal classification number (three digits with decimals indicating more specific classifications). The bottom line identifies the book's author and edition.

The Card Catalog

The catalogs of some libraries are stored physically in sets of drawers that contain cards, at least one for each book in the library. Drawers are labeled on the outside, much like encyclopedias, to tell you what they contain. Cards, filed alphabetically, help you find what you need. A traditional **card catalog** usually contains three cards for each **nonfiction** publication in the library: the **author card** or **main entry card,** the **subject card,** and the **title card.** Only title and author cards are used for **fiction.**

Each card provides information about the author, publisher, contents, and call number of the book. Author information includes the author's name (last name first) followed by the dates of the author's birth and death. Publishing facts tell who published the book as well as when and where it was published. Content information consists of the number of pages, if there are maps and illustrations, a brief description of the contents, and cross-references.

At the bottom of a card, there are two distinct kinds of cross references. Those numbered with Arabic numerals list the subjects of the book; these are subjects taken from the Library of Congress List of Subject Headings. A book can fall into several categories, and each of these will be listed.

Searching by subject is an effective way to locate information as long as you search by the right descriptors. The Library of Congress publishes a special book that lists the specific terms it uses to define subjects. Your librarian can help you locate this book and provide suggestions about its use.

References listed with uppercase Roman numerals are additional cards found in the author/title catalog. These tracings which are used for catalog maintenance—if a book is withdrawn from the collection, they help the librarian locate the complete card set for the item.

To save space, some libraries store their card listing on **microfiche.** Microfiche, one of the many types of **microforms,** is a piece of photographic film usually 4 by 6 inches. Such film is kept in files similar to those containing cards. However, one piece of film actually holds dozens of cards, greatly reduced in size. To read it, you enlarge the print with a machine

called a **microfiche reader.** Like other microforms, a microfiche card catalog saves space, is cheaper to produce, and can be updated quickly.

The Computerized Card Catalog

In many libraries, the card catalog has been replaced either partially or entirely by an online catalog accessible through a computer terminal. A computerized card catalog helps you find information more quickly because the
computer does the work for you. It searches all entries for the author, subject,
or title you need. Sometimes such a system uses specialized subject headings.
A list of these is kept in a manual near the computer terminals. Some libraries
develop their own catalog systems, but many others alter ready-made software to fit their collections. The examples in this text are from NOTIS, a
widely used system developed at Northwestern University.

The features and commands for differing online systems vary. The
commands are the symbols or terms that are used to access information
(see Table 9.2). Figures 9.1 through 9.3 show sample screens from the
NOTIS system.

If you aren't sure of a material's title or author, you can search by subject. As in online searching, keywords form the entry points for locating relevant materials. You must, however, search by the right descriptive terms for
the concepts you need. The Library of Congress publishes a special book that
lists the specific terms it uses to define subjects. Your librarian can help you
locate this book and provide suggestions about its use.

Table 9.2	Commands for Retrieving Information Using NOTIS
Author search	a = author's name; last name first
Title search	t = exact title of the publication; ignore *a*, *an*, and *the* if they are the first word in a title
Subject search	s = appropriate subject heading
Keyword search	k = important ideas or concepts

WRITE TO LEARN

A friend of yours is not in this class but is taking a course in which he
must write a term paper. On a separate sheet of paper or in your journal, explain to him how to use a card catalog or a computerized card
catalog database, whichever your college library has.

Figure 9.1   **Introductory Screen**

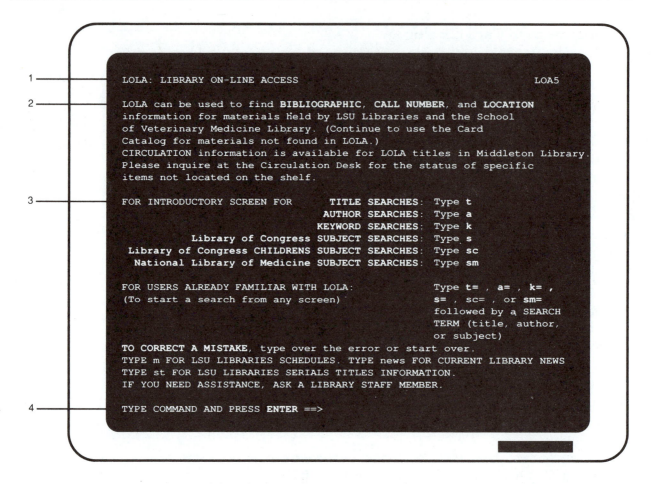

1. Acronym used for Library Online Access.

2. Introductory information provides general data about the system. This is necessarily brief, so libraries often provide more comprehensive written instructions.

3. List the kinds of searches available on the system and the commands needed to find materials by author, title, subject or keyword.

4. Information needed to access the database.

1. Figures 9.1–9.3 are screen reproductions from the NOTIS System currently being used in the Louisiana State University Libraries. (Copyright 1993 by NOTIS Systems. Inc. Material reproduced by permission of the copyright holder and the Louisiana State University Libraries.)

SOURCE: Figures 9.1, 9.2, and 9.3 are reprinted with permission from Bolner, et al.; *Library Research Skills Handbook*. Copyright © 1993 by Kendall/Hunt Publishing Company. Used with permission.

Figure 9.2   Subject and Title Index Screen

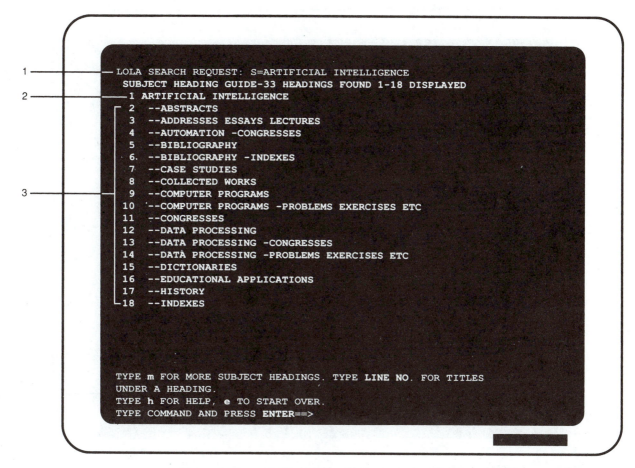

```
  1 ──────── LOLA SEARCH REQUEST: S=ARTIFICIAL INTELLIGENCE
                 SUBJECT HEADING GUIDE-33 HEADINGS FOUND 1-18 DISPLAYED
  2 ─────────── 1 ARTIFICIAL INTELLIGENCE
                   2  --ABSTRACTS
                   3  --ADDRESSES ESSAYS LECTURES
                   4  --AUTOMATION -CONGRESSES
                   5  --BIBLIOGRAPHY
                   6. --BIBLIOGRAPHY -INDEXES
                   7  --CASE STUDIES
                   8  --COLLECTED WORKS
  3 ───────────  9  --COMPUTER PROGRAMS
                  10  --COMPUTER PROGRAMS -PROBLEMS EXERCISES ETC
                  11  --CONGRESSES
                  12  --DATA PROCESSING
                  13  --DATA PROCESSING -CONGRESSES
                  14  --DATA PROCESSING -PROBLEMS EXERCISES ETC
                  15  --DICTIONARIES
                  16  --EDUCATIONAL APPLICATIONS
                  17  --HISTORY
                  18  --INDEXES


                 TYPE m FOR MORE SUBJECT HEADINGS. TYPE LINE NO. FOR TITLES
                 UNDER A HEADING.
                 TYPE h FOR HELP, e TO START OVER.
                 TYPE COMMAND AND PRESS ENTER==>
```

1. Number 1 entered to go from subject heading guide to the subject title index.

   Number 7 selected to go to the bibliographic record screen.

   Number 11 selected to go to the bibliographic record screen.

2. Example of a reference to a government publication. Call number is a SuDocs number. GP, dodd indicates that the book is in the documents collection.

3. Both MD and midl indicate that the book is in the Middleton Library.

Searching a computerized catalog helps you accomplish purposes that would be more difficult to achieve through a manual search. For example, a computerized search often allows you to link words and terms to include or exclude specific types of information. In addition, some searches are more thorough because they include computer indexes and abstracts as well as

Figure 9.3   Author and Title Index Screen

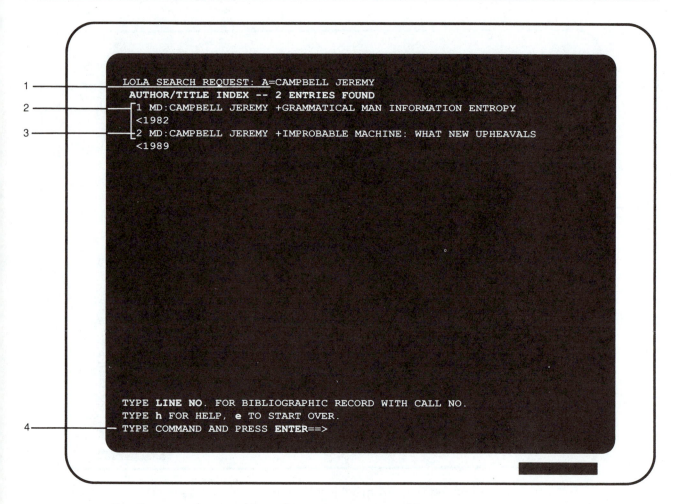

1. Command entered into the system to access this screen.
2. Numbers 1–2. List of book titles available in the database under the author's name.
3. Number entered to access the complete bibliographic record for the book. *The Improbable Machine* by Jeremy Campbell.
4. Instructions needed to enter the database.

subjects, authors, and titles. Exact spelling is essential although you may be able to abbreviate or omit some words. Table 9.3 lists rules for abbreviating reference titles. Finally, computerized searches can result in a quickly obtained printout of the sources you want to pursue. Exercise 9.2 gives you practice in finding materials in your library.

Table 9.3   Rules for Abbreviating Reference Titles

- Abbreviate from right to left, for example, *Dictionary of Recreational Education* becomes *Dictionary of Recreational Ed.*

- Use standard abbreviations, for example, *Psych* for psychology and *J* for journal.

- Omit the articles *a, an,* and *the* (and foreign language equivalents) from titles and begin the search command with the first word that follows the article.

- Enter initials, acronyms, abbreviations, numbers, and dates exactly as they appear in the title. For example, if you are looking for the book *100 Ways to Manage Time Better,* type *100 Ways to Manage Time Better,* not *One Hundred Ways to Manage Time Better.*

- Type two dashes between the primary subject heading and all subdivisions.

- To avoid confusion and save time in searches, avoid using common last names without first names or initials.

Exercise 9.2   Answer briefly.

1. Which of the following books are in your library? List call numbers and dates of publication for each one.

   The Mental Measurements Yearbook by Oscar K. Buros

   _____

   The Collected Papers of Albert Einstein by Albert Einstein

   _____

   The Making of the President, 1972 by T. H. White

   _____

   Davis's Drug Guide for Nurses by J. H. Deglin

   _____

   Travels by Michael Crichton

   _____

2. Who wrote *All the King's Men*?

   _____

3. List the call numbers for each of the following subjects: architecture, music, education, computer science, and psychology.

   _____

   _____

4. How many books does your library hold under the listing *dogs*? What type of books (that is, fiction, nonfiction, reference, and so on) are included under this listing?

   _____

   _____

(continues)

Exercise 9.2   *Continued*

5. List three books that your library has on or by Sherwood Anderson.

_____

_____

6. List three periodicals or journals that are found on microfiche, microfilm, CD-ROM, or on line in your library.

_____

_____

7. Photocopy or print the title page from one article found on microfiche, microfilm, CD-ROM, or on line.

8. Do your library holdings include ERIC documents? If so, what are they used for?

_____

_____

9. On separate sheets of paper or in your journal, copy one author, one title, and one subject card or screen and label their parts.

10. Identify three daily newspapers to which your library subscribes or makes available on line.

_____

_____

THE MAZE: VIRTUAL ENVIRONMENTS, PHYSICAL HOLDINGS

To many learners, the stacks in the library always resembled the Minotaur's maze. In the past, knowing your ways through the stacks was sufficient for doing library research. However, today's libraries reflect the ever-increasing influx of knowledge, both in the size and formats of their collections. Although you need to know your way around in your campus's library physically, you might also find that you can access what you need at a virtual library from the keyboard of your own computer.

Electronic Access to Information

In today's libraries, many references no longer physically exist within the library's walls. The use of stand-alone and online computers revolutionized access to information. Instead of painstakingly copying bibliographic information from information in a card catalog, you often can download the

*"Medieval history . . . on a bearing of N37°E
go 400 feet, then S15°E 175 feet."*

references you want and print the results. Instead of searching for a specific piece of information through mountains of books, you can search electronic texts. Instead of using the resources of only your library, you can use online access to search libraries and research facilities across the country and around the world.

Online and CD-ROM Access

Computers allow you to use and search information electronically. Online access provides you with information from another computer at a remote site—either somewhere else on your campus, within your college system, in another state, or even in another country. The information you search usually consists of a card catalog of database from which you can extract specific pieces.

Libraries subscribe to database services and provide online access to science, social science, and humanities databases. Such databases include indices and abstracts, full-text materials, collections of raw data, and directories to other information.

Although online searching has many advantages, it does have a few flaws. First, online searches often involve some expense, if you are charged for computer time. Thus, you must weigh the worth of your time against the amount of money you want to spend. Second, the logic of database searching sometimes fails because of the ambiguity of the English language. Thus, if you want to search for information on Apple computers and use only the key word *apple,* you'll probably get information about fruits as well as on computers. Your librarian can help you select key word and qualifiers (for example, *and, or, not)* so that you locate the information you need while excluding irrelevant topics. Third, although databases can provide the latest information, they often do not include older references and materials.

Databases are also available on stand-alone computers that use CD-ROM drives to access information. Because a CD stores much less data than mainframe computers, separate databases are stored on single CDs or, in some cases, collections of CDs. In addition to databases, CDs also store other types of information including visual and auditory data. With new information pressed on CDs all the time, the array of multimedia materials available in these formats ranges from three-dimensional models of molecules, which can be rotated to show different perspectives, to full texts of the classics of literature. Your librarian can show you what CDs are available at your library and instruct you in their use.

Information Superhighway: Internet and World Wide Web

During the 1960s, the U.S. Department of Defense created a special system of computers to connect key locations in case of nuclear or other disaster. What made the system special was that there really was no system. There was no hub, no central switching location, and no governing authority to administer the system. Instead, the computers formed an interconnected network through which information traveled, more or less independently, from sender to receiver. In the 1960s and 1970s, some colleges and universities, as well as government research labs, also joined the network. As time went on, other countries joined, making it an international network. During the mid 1980s, the National Science Foundation (NSF) built the data lines to form a backbone for the network, and in 1992, the NSF lifted commercial restrictions. This made the **Internet** available to virtually anyone with a computer and modem access and created an information superhighway with millions of users and a theoretically unlimited source of information.

The Internet continues to be a worldwide nonsystem. Nobody controls or owns the Internet. The only thing constant about it is its lack of constancy. Information on the Internet is in a constant state of change as knowledge expands and explodes. Information on the Internet, then, is more up-to-date than other sources that require commercial publication and distribution. You can access information on the Internet through your campus library, computer center or other department, or through a commercial online service. Your library or computer center can show you how to get on the information superhighway.

The World Wide Web (WWW) opened a new phase in the development of worldwide communication. In this subset of the Internet system, Web software integrates sound, video clips, fancy text markings, and other types of information through **hypertext** or **hypermedia links.** Hypertext links show up as highlighted key words on the computer screen. Like menus, these key words form doorways to additional text information. Hypermedia links provide multimedia information. For example, in accessing the text of a famous speech, you might also be able to watch a video clip of the speech being given. Your campus library or computer center can help you gain access to the Web, if you don't have a computer with modem access of your own. Exercise 9.3 provides you with an opportunity to find relevant information on the World Wide Web.

Exercise 9.3   Using any one of the sample chapters, identify five topics that you want to know more about and list them below. Go to your college library or use the Internet or World Wide Web and locate three references on each topic. Identify the title of the reference and the catalog number or URL.

SAMPLE CHAPTER _____

Topic 1 _____
Reference 1 _____
Reference 2 _____
Reference 3 _____

Topic 2 _____
Reference 1 _____
Reference 2 _____
Reference 3 _____

Topic 3 _____
Reference 1 _____
Reference 2 _____
Reference 3 _____

Topic 4 _____
Reference 1 _____
Reference 2 _____
Reference 3 _____

Topic 5 _____
Reference 1 _____
Reference 2 _____
Reference 3 _____

WRITE TO LEARN

Review your efforts to locate information on the topics you selected in Exercise 9.3. Respond to the following on a separate sheet of paper or in your journal. Which topics were most and least difficult to find? Why do you think that was so?

Library Holdings

In addition to the books you find in the stacks, your library contains a wealth of additional information for your use. General references help you specify your topic more clearly, locate the most current information about it, and identify background information on it. Specialized content references provide you with more in-depth information from experts in their fields.

General References

General references are vast in number and scope. Because of their utility to large numbers of students, they are available in both traditional print and virtual formats. Most libraries store print forms of general reference materials in **ready reference** or on **reserve**. Such materials can be used within the library, but not checked out for use outside of the library. You can also find many general references on the Internet or on the World Wide Web (See Table 9.4).

General **periodical indices** do for journals what the card catalog does for other materials. They help you locate articles according to authors, titles, and subjects. They also include cross-references. The *Reader's Guide to Periodical Literature* is a common index of general and nontechnical journals and magazines. An alphabetical listing includes authors and subjects of articles. Entries provide information for finding specific articles (See Figure 9.4).

Accurate research often depends on knowing exactly what is meant by the words that describe the topic. A library's holdings usually include two general sources about word meanings. The first source is the **unabridged dictionary,** the most comprehensive general dictionary found in a library. It lists all words used in the English language, including obsolete words, scientific terms, and proper names. Definitions include word histories, quotations, related terms, and other information. A **thesaurus** provides a second general source for finding words. It identifies synonyms, antonyms, and related words for specific headings. Like a dictionary, this aids you in finding other key words that identify your topic. Dictionaries and thesauruses are available in computerized forms as well as at numerous sites on the World Wide Web (See Table 9.4).

Accurate research often must reflect the most current information available. The most logical source of such information are daily or weekly newspapers. Current issues of local, state, and national papers are usually shelved or displayed on racks at the library. Some libraries also carry newspapers from other countries. A variety of newspapers, including other college papers (See Table 9.3) are also available on the Internet. Newspapers might or might not be indexed. This causes no problems, however. If you find the date of a particular event in any **newspaper index**, other papers probably carried reports of that event the same day. Examples of such indices include *Facts on File* (weekly summaries of world news), the *New York Times Index* (summaries of New York Times articles), and the *Wall Street Journal Today* (a yearly list of its financial and business articles).

Figure 9.4   Examples of Reader's Guide Entry

POLICE
See also
Policewomen
State Police
"911 . . . please hold". G. Witkin. ii *Reader's Digest* v10
p140-4 N '96
America's best suburban police forces. 1. Domanick, il
Good Housekeeping v223 p82-4+ N '96
Equipment

Article title ►Robocop's dream [military derived hardware used in police
surveillance] C. Parersti. il *The Nation* v264 p22-4 F 3 '97◄ Month/date/year
Public relations
See also
Community policing

Subject **►Retirement**
Mandatory retirement. H. B. Deets. il *Modern Maturity* v40◄ Volume number
p74 Ja/F '97
Surveillance operations
Robocop's dream [military derived hardware used in police
surveillance] C. Parenti. il *The Nation* v264 p22-4 F 3 '97
Training
A constabulary of thugs [Haiti's U.S.-trained police force]

Author ►T. Drummond. il *Time* v149 p62-3 F 17 '97
Alabama
See also
Birmingham (Ala.)—Police
California
See also
Los Angeles (Calif.)—Police
Canada
See also
Royai Canadian Mounted Police
Colorado
See also
Boulder (Colo.)—Police
Haiti
A constabulary of thugs [U.S.-trained police force] T.
Drummond, il *Time* v149 p62-3 F 17 '97
Louisiana
See also
New Orleans (La.)—Police
New York (State)
See also
Brookly (New York, N.Y.)—Police
New York (N.Y.)—Police
South Africa
Five ex-South African policemen seek amnesty for killing
Steve Biko. por *Jet* v91 p64 F 17 '97
Mrs. Biko's dilemma [editorial] M. Gevisser. *The Nation* ◄ Periodical title
v264 p6-7 Mr 3 '97The Palme murder planned in
Pretoria? E. Wiedemann. il pors *World Press Review* v44
p42-3 Ja '97
Requiem for a heavyweight [killing of S. Biko] D. Woods. il ◄ Illustrations
Newsweek v129 p43 F 10 '97
Unmasking a guilty past [killers of antiapartheid hero S.
Biko confess before South Africa's Truth Commission]
P. Hawthorne. il pors *Time* v149 p49 F 10 '97
Texas
See also
Dallas (Tex.)—Police
Washington (D.C.)

Cross reference ► *See* Washington (D.C.)—Police
West Bank
Taking care of business [Israeli soldiers and Palestinian
police in Hebron work together] M. Dennis. ii *Newsweek*
v129 p42 Ja 13 '97
POLICE CHIEFS
See also
Black police chiefs
POLICE CORRUPTION
Pennsylvania
See also
Philadelphia (Pa.)—Police corruption
POLICE HORSES
The real Spur Posse [Border Patrol] C. Dangaard. il *Los
Angeles* v41 p40-2 0 '96
POLICE INFORMERS *See* Informers
POLICE INTELLIGENCE UNITS
See also
Police—Surveillance opersilons
POLICE RACISM
See also
Simpson, 0. J.—Murder case, 1994—Racial aspects
POLICEWOMEN
Grace under fire [Los Angeles female police detective T.An-

Governments documents are materials published by municipal, state, and federal governmental agencies. They include detailed information about governmental policies and procedures as well as about almost any other topic. Writing to your representative or senator of the U.S. Government Printing Office aids in finding the proper department and publication you need. In addition, the *U.S. Government Organization Manual* and the *Monthly Catalog of the United States Publications* index federal government publications. Some universities are depositories for collections of government documents. In many cases, the information you need can be found on the Internet (See Table 9.4). The Library of Congress's Web site also includes historical collections and other documents in digital form.

If you want to compare information about the United States with that of other countries, **almanacs** and **yearbooks** include details about government, industry, politics, commerce, world events, sports, and a variety of other topics. Updated, they contain statistical, tabular, and general information. **Atlases** and **gazetteers**, available in both print, computerized, and WWW formats provide geographical information about the United States or other countries. An atlas contains a collection of topographical, climactic, geological, economic, and political maps. They often include gazetteers, which are general dictionaries of geographical names. A gazetteer lists names of places, seas, mountains, and so on. Entries cover pronunciation, classification, population, height, length, area, and points of interest.

Sometimes you need to find the definitive remark or outstanding comment from a famous person. Books of quotations, available in print and Internet formats, identify well-known or important statements by general topic and by their sources. You can find more information about important people in general biographical indices or biographical dictionaries. Facts include birth and death dates, nationality, profession, accomplishments, and other personal and professional information. Examples of such dictionaries include *Who's Who in America, Who Was Who in America,* and *Current Biography. Who's Who in America,* updated every other year, contains information about notable living Americans. *Who Was Who in America* provides information about important deceased Americans. *Current Biography* contains an illustrated description and a short biography about important world figures who are still living.

Most of the books you need are not classified as general references; however, when you find that the last copy was just checked out, you might wish that such books were as readily available as ready reference books. Luckily, more and more books—particularly those classics of literature and history—are available electronically in full-text form. These books can be downloaded to files or printed for your use. Table 9.4 shows the names of Web sites that provide such materials.

Table 9.4   General References on the WWW

For the most up-to-date URL addresses of these sites, go to http://csuccess.wadsworth.com.

Type	Online Example	Description
General references with multiple links	*My Virtual Reference Desk*	Provides links to a variety of sites including atlas, biographies, dictionaries, electronic texts, encyclopedias, U.S. government documents, thesaurus, quotations, and much more
Dictionary	*Oxford English Dictionary,* 2nd Edition	Search by entry, etymology, definition; look up quotes by author, work, date, and quoted text; find entries that have two or three words or phrases in close proximity to each other; locate bibliographic information for sources cited in the *Oxford English Dictionary*
	ARTFL Project: *Webster's Revised Unabridged Dictionary,* 1913 Edition	Search by entry or by substring match (for example, looking up *qualit* would find *qualitative, quality*); includes hypertext cross-references
	Hypertext Webster Gateway	Search by entry; includes hypertext links within definitions; provides substring match and spell correction feedback
	Merriam-Webster WWWebster Dictionary	Search by entry; also provides a "word of the day" page and archives and radio scripts for Word for the Wise, a 2-minutes show about etymology and other aspects of language
	American Sign Language Dictionary	Search key terms alphabetically to find how to translate to ASL
	Casey's Snow Day Reverse Dictionary	Enter definition to search for matching word
	Biography	Search by name or browse through alphabetical listing.
Thesaurus	*Roget's Thesaurus*	Search by key terms; supports Boolean searching (using *and* and *or*)
	Roget's Internet Thesaurus	Search by key terms; browse through alphabetical listing of entries; provides information about Roget's six main classes of words (abstract relations, space, matter, intellect, volition, and affection); links to other Internet language reference resources
	ARTFL Project: *ROGET's Thesaurus* Search	Search by keywords
Encyclopedia	*Free Internet Encyclopedia*	Provides searchable MacroReference of large areas of knowledge and MicroReference of shorts bits of information and references to specific subjects; includes MacroIndex
	My Virtual Encyclopedia	Search by keyword or browse through topics
	U.S. Census Bureau	Official Federal statistics for social, demographic, and economic information

(continues)

Table 9.4   *Continued*

Type	Online Example	Description
	National Archives and Records Administration	Historically valuable records of the three branches of government (executive, legislative, judicial); includes Federal Register, U.S. Government Manual, Public Laws, and a searchable database of pointers to NARA information resources
	U.S. House of Representatives Internet Law Library	Includes Federal laws, international laws, and information about other legal resources
Gazetteer	Alexandria Digital Library, *Gazetteer*	Search for geographical area by specific name; by specific county, state, providence, country, or region; or by specific class or type of feature; shows display on a map browser which can be modified to show different features or change views; provides longitude and latitude
Electronic Texts	*The Online Books Page*	Search over 5000 listings by title, author, or subject; provides complete text of work on line
	Alex: A Catalog of Electronic Texts on the Internet	Catalog of Internet-based electronic texts; contains over 2000 entries on gopher servers. Search by subject or browse contents
	Project Gutenberg	Electronic books which can be downloaded. Search by author or title or browse contents
Almanac	*The 1996 World Factbook*	Lists articles by country or region; includes reference maps and other related information
	Old Farmer's Almanac	Provides long-range weather forecasts; information about astronomical rise and set times
Quotations	*The Quotations Page*	Search for a quotation; provides quote of the day/week feature; random quotations; links to other quotations sites
	Project Bartleby, *Bartlett's Familiar Quotations*	Search by word; provides alphabetical index to all authors; chronological index of primary authors, bibliographic information
	Quotation Collections on the Internet	Links to other sources including *Bartlett's Famous Quotations*, quotes about libraries and librarians, mathematical quotations, TV and movie quotations, and much more
	Electronic Reference Quotations	Links to *Bartlett's ShepWeb Quotations*, Yahoo Reference quotations and other sites
Newspapers	*My Virtual Reference Desk, First Things First*	Include links to wire services, news services, daily almanac, stock quotes, quick references/research, and other features
	My Virtual Reference Desk, My Virtual Newspaper	Includes Weather Channel, *USA Today* weather, and other weather information; wire services and headlines by topic; U.S. newspapers by state; international newspapers by continent; news features; college newspapers; and worldwide and national news sites

(continues)

Table 9.4   *Continued*

Type	Online Example	Description
	Chicago Tribune	Online articles and features
	Los Angeles Times	Online articles and features
	The New York Times	Online articles and features
	San Jose Mercury News	Online articles and features
	USA Today	Online articles and features
Government Documents	Library of Congress	Includes historical collections in a digital library; access to information about bills under consideration, visual exhibitions, research tools, and links to other Internet and WWW collections

---

WRITE TO LEARN

On a separate sheet of paper or in your journal, identify the general reference that would be of most use to you in researching the sample chapter you used in Exercise 9.3.

Specialized Content References

Your interests, as well as the courses you take, often require you to research topics in subject-specific resources rather than in general references. Whereas general references direct you to further resources, subject area resources often contain the specific information you need. Your librarian can help you identify the subject area materials you need.

Because a published book can take anywhere from one to several years to progress from an author's initial idea for a text to publication, the material it contains is already somewhat dated by the time it reaches your library shelf. As a result, subject-area resources in the ready reference section, as well as materials in the stacks, provide more current general, historical, or background information. For timely information or research, consult periodicals—either professional journals or popular magazines. Periodicals are often available in microform or online versions as well as in traditional formats.

A Sword and the Skill to Use It:
A Working Bibliography and Research Skills

To reach his goal of killing the Minotaur, Theseus needed a weapon and the skill to use it. In meeting your goal of finding information within the library, you also need a weapon—a **working bibliography** or list of Internet information or Web sites—and the skill to use it—research skills.

Creating a Working Bibliography

A working bibliography consists of a list of materials found on a topic after a survey of the card catalog. To compile this list, you record or printout the titles, authors, dates of publication, and call numbers of materials that seem relevant to your topic and worth your consideration (see Table 9.5). Writing each item of this list on an index card provides a permanent record of possible references.

Another way to develop a working bibliography is through the use of a computer search of special databases. Such a search generally requires the assistance of the librarian or other staff member in identifying the most appropriate database and explaining necessary procedures for its use. The computer printout serves the same purpose as the self-made list of references. The computer search has two advantages over the self-prepared working bibliography. First, it identifies references you might overlook. Second, it takes you less time and effort to find possible sources of information. The major disadvantage of computer searches is cost. Unless you consider time equal to money, the self-made working bibliography is free compared with the fees often charged for computer searches. Rates vary from one database service to another. Rates also vary within services depending on the time of day or day of the week.

Locating Internet/WWW Information

As you surf the Net, crawl the Web, or otherwise look for what you need, you will often find numerous hits. How do you decide which are important and relevant to your topic? You make inferences about importance and relevance in one of two ways. First, when possible, you can specifically locate and search general and reliable sources of information such as online encyclopedias and other reference materials to help you make inferences about other sources. These sources will give you background information about a topic and help you to specify important concepts for further consideration or for additional searches. As you find other online materials, you can compare them with this basic standard to assess their value to your purpose and questions. Table 9.6 lists questions to use in comparing new materials with other sources.

Table 9.5   Checklist for Judging the Relevance of References

1. Who is the author? Do you know anything about the author's reputation?

2. If you cannot judge the author's qualifications or reputation, does the author have more than one publication on this topic?

3. If you cannot judge the author's qualifications, depth of writing experience, or reputation, what is the reputation of the publisher?

4. When was the material published? Is information of this time period relevant to your research?

5. Does the material contain a bibliography?

6. Does the material contain appendices?

7. Does the material contain illustrations?

8. Was this publication considered worthy of reprinting?

9. Have you seen other publications reference this publication?

10. If a book, has the information in it been updated through the publication of subsequent editions?

Table 9.6   Questions to Use in Comparing Online Sources

To determine the relationship between the new material and the old material, answer the following questions:

1. Does the new material present additional information?

2. Does the new material present contradictory information?

3. Does the new material provide more comprehensive information?

4. Does the new material provide more recent information?

Determining the strength of a hit when using a search engine forms a second way to assess worth. The list created by a search engine usually places the strongest match first (according to the limitations of that search engine) with additional matches in decreasing order of strength. This is not always the case, however. Sometimes the first few hits don't meet your needs at all. For example, in searching for information on *beaches,* many of the first few hits may be documents about rental properties at beaches or restaurants on the beach rather than information about beaches.

Depending on the specificity of your keyword, you can get thousands of matches. Examining the first 10 or so should give you an idea if you're on the right track concerning how well the information answers your purposes and questions. As you read through the materials and refine your purpose or questions, you might find that a later document meets your needs more exactly than the one that was first on the list. If the information doesn't seem to fit your needs, you could try a different synonym for the keyword or a more general or specific keyword.

You might be tempted to use the links in each document to jump to additional or related topics. Before making your way through any one of them, however, you should probably assess their initial value. As you compare materials and get a more complete understanding of the information, you increase your ability to judge a material's value to your purpose and questions. According to the World Wide Web Bible (Pfaffenberger, 1995), once you find one highly applicable link in your area of interest, you should explore the hyperlinks within it. As you read, avoid getting sidetracked by issues and concepts that are unrelated to your purpose and questions. Finally, set time limits for using a particular search engine or keyword. If you don't find something useful within the first ten or twenty hits, you probably need to rethink your keyword.

Using Research Skills

After acquiring your working bibliography, you are ready to begin searching for and evaluating materials. First, locate the references on the shelves. Then, survey the pertinent features of the material. Next, skim or scan these features to decide if the material fits your needs. Skimming and scanning speed the process of selecting or eliminating materials. Skimming is a means of quickly understanding what a publication is generally about, its main idea. Scanning helps you find specific details. In evaluating the relevance of material, you use your skimming and scanning skills at the same time (see Table 9.7). Finally, you note information or eliminate unsuitable materials.

When you evaluate online materials you often need to analyze information to a greater extent than you do with library books, journals, or compact disks. The content of these more traditional materials has usually be scrutinized by reviewers, editors, and other professionals associated with publication of the materials. Because no one owns and manages the Internet, however, and because virtually anyone with the right hardware and software can create at **home page** and put information online, just about anything and everything goes. Some materials, such as online journals and research, do undergo rigorous review, but others do not. The Internet serves as a great repository of valuable information, but it also hold a lot of junk and trash. How do you know which is which? Some of the suggestions for evaluating traditional materials (see Tables 9.6, 9.7, and 9.8) also apply to online materials. More serious treatments of a topic clearly identify the author or authors of the material and include bibliographic information. Professional affiliation also helps validate a source. Additional reading of related materials by other authors helps you maintain perspective and avoid bias. Finally, you can verify online information with what you find in more traditional library resources.

There are seventy million books in American libraries, but the one I want to read is always out.

Tom Masson
Nineteenth century editor and author

Table 9.7   Important Features to Survey in Evaluating Books

1. Survey the title page and copyright page (usually found on the book of the title page) to answer these questions:
   a. What is the complete title of this material?
   b. Who wrote the material?
   c. What is the author's title and professional affiliation?
   d. What occupation, position, titles, education, experience, and so forth qualifies this author to write on this topic?
   e. Is this material collected from other sources? If so, who edited the collection?
   f. Who is the publisher of the material?
   g. When and where was the material published?
   h. Have there been other editions or revisions?

2. Scan the table of contents to determine the following:
   a. How is the book organized?
   b. Are topics important to you covered and how many pages are devoted to them?
   c. How does the coverage in this material compare with other references?

3. Scan the preface or introduction to discover:
   a. What is the author's point of view?
   b. Why did the author write this material?
   c. What information is covered in the material?
   d. Does the author's experience and scholarship seem sufficient for a thorough discussion of the topic?

e. What method of research or data collection was used—personal opinion, personal experience, interviews, library research, surveys, clinical experiments, or other?
   f. To what audience is this material addressed?

4. Scan the bibliography, a listing of references used in the material, to answer these questions:
   a. Does the author give primary sources (the actual words of an identified person, a historical document, a literary work, and so on) rather than secondary sources (other authors' descriptions of the original events)?
   b. Does the length of the bibliography indicate the scholarship of the author?
   c. Does the bibliography contain references you can use to further research your topic?
   d. Does the bibliography include articles by other authorities in the field besides the author?

5. Scan the index (an alphabetical listing of important topics included in the material) to answer these questions:
   a. Are topics important to you covered?
   b. How many pages are devoted to them?

6. Scan, then skim, important terms in the materials' glossary (a small dictionary of terms used in the material) to decide the following:
   a. Do terms have specialized definitions?
   b. Are terms defined clearly and completely?
   c. Do the meanings of terms provide new insights into the topic?

After you decide what information you want for your paper, take notes or make photocopies of the information for later use. Whatever method you choose, it's important to reference your notes or photocopies with complete bibliographical information (title, author, publisher, place and date of publication, volume or issue number, and page numbers) for later identification.

If you only need a small amount of information, notetaking is sufficient (see Table 9.9). If you need a larger amount or complex graphics, photocopying might be more useful. Laws allow you to make a single copy of a small percentage of the total material for educational research.

Notes consist of two basic types: **direct quotes** and summaries or paraphrases of main ideas and specific details (see Figure 9.5). Direct quotes are

Table 9.8   Important Features to Survey in Evaluating Articles

1. Survey the introductory pages of the journal to answer the following:
   a. Who publishes this journal?
   b. What is the mission or purpose of the journal?
   c. Who is the editor, or who serves on the editorial board? What are their professional affiliations or credentials?
   d. Does the journal describe the criteria for submission of articles? If so, what kinds of articles does it accept? What kind of review process does it use?
   e. When was this particular edition of the journal published? How long has the journal been published (usually identified by volume number)?

2. Survey the journal's table of contents to answer the following:
   a. What kinds of articles does the journal include?
   b. What are the reputations of other authors in this journal? What are their professional affiliations?
   c. What is the complete title of the article in which you are interested?
   d. Who wrote the article?

3. Read the article to answer the following:
   a. What is the author's point of view in the article?
   b. Why did the author write this article?
   c. What information is covered in the article?

   How does the information relate to your purpose and questions?
   d. What is the author's title and professional affiliation?
   e. What occupation, position, titles, education, experience, and so forth, qualifies this author to write on this topic?
   f. Does the author's experience and scholarship seem sufficient for a thorough discussion of the topic?
   g. What method of research or data collection was used—personal opinions, personal experience, interviews, library research, surveys, clinical experiments, or other?
   h. To what audience is this material addressed?

4. Scan the references used in the material to answer the following:
   a. Does the author give primary sources (the actual words of an identified person, a historical account, a literary work, and so on) rather than secondary sources (other authors' descriptions of the original events)?
   b. Does the quantity and quality of the references indicate the scholarship of the author?
   c. Can you use any of the references to further research your topic?
   d. Do the references include articles by other authorities in the field beside the author?

Table 9.9   Steps in Taking Research Notes

1. Use note cards or regular-sized pieces of paper to record important information.

2. Write all notes about one topic on the same piece of paper or note card. If you need additional space, be sure to keep notes on the same topic together.

3. Write notes using a standard format.

4. If you are taking notes on large amounts of information, use the same shorthand system you use when taking notes in class (see Chapter 4).

5. Cross-reference information.

exactly what an author says about a topic. They leave no room for your opinion or thoughts. A **summary** or a **paraphrase**, likewise, contains an unbiased version of what the author said. This version, however, is written in your own words. It is your attempt to condense and clarify information.

Figure 9.5   Examples of Direct Quotes and Summaries or Paraphrases

---

Intact Text

Most messages are sent with signals. Animals use singing, growling, chirping, roaring, and other sounds to warn and attract others. Baboons display their huge canine teeth to threaten one another. Dogs and other animals raise their hackles to intimidate; some apes pound their chests. Animals also use gestures to attract mates. Dances, feather displays. and other signals convey mating intentions.

Sloshberg, W. and NesSmith, W. (1983). *Contemporary American Society: An Introduction to the Social Sciences* St. Paul, MN: West Publishers, p. 65.

Direct Quote

"Animals use singing, growling, chirping, roaring and other sounds to warn and attract others. Animals also use gestures to attract mates."

Sloshberg, W. and NesSmith, W. (1983). Contemporary American Society: An Introduction to the Social Sciences St. Paul, MN: West Publishers, p. 65.

Summary/Paraphrase

Animals use sounds and gestures as signals to warn and attract other animals

Sloshberg, W. and NesSmith, W. (1983). Contemporary American Society: An Introduction to the Social Sciences St. Paul, MN: West Publishers, p. 65.

You record a direct quote exactly as it is written and note its original source. You identify a direct quote as such by using quotation marks to set it apart from other statements. When a quote contains information that you think is unnecessary or unimportant, you can omit it only if you indicate that you are doing so. You show this omission by placing an **ellipsis,** three dots (...), where the missing information would appear.

Summaries or paraphrases state main ideas and supporting details or examples in your own words. They include specific details that are new or important points or concepts. Van Dijk and Kintch (1978) identified five basic rules essential to summarization. Table 9.10 lists these as steps—with slight variations—for you to follow in summarizing or paraphrasing information. Exercises 9.4 and 9.5 provide practice in summarizing and paraphrasing.

Table 9.10   Steps in Writing Summaries or Paraphrases

1. Delete unimportant information.
2. Delete repeated information.
3. Group similar objects and concepts; find an identifying word for this group. (For example, group *pears, bananas, apples,* and *peaches* as *fruit.*)
4. Write important details in your own words.
5. Locate the topic sentence of the passage.
6. Once you locate the topic sentence, restate it in your own words. If you cannot locate the topic sentence, compose your own.

Exercise 9.4   Use Sample Chapter 14, "Organizing Information" (at the back of this book) to identify two pieces of information that you could use as direct quotes. Then summarize or paraphrase this same information. Complete this exercise on a separate sheet of paper or in your journal.

Exercise 9.5   In the space provided below, use the rules in Table 9.10 to write a summary or paraphrase of the case study in Sample Chapter 13, "Concepts in Human Biology."

WRITE TO LEARN

On a separate sheet of paper or in your journal, compare and contrast the characteristics of a working bibliography and the bibliography that should be included with your final draft.

——— CLASSIC CRITICAL THINKING ———

You cannot always apply the information you use to evaluate print resources to Internet or World Wide Web sources. Access one of the following Web sites or one of the following printed resources. Using the information you locate, create your own list of suggestions for evaluating Internet and WWW information according to the standards of critical thinking (See Chapter 8).

Web Sites

For the most up-to-date URL addresses, go to
http://csuccess.wadsworth.com.

Evaluating World Wide Web Information:
http://thorplus.lib.purdue.edu/research/classes/gs175/3gs175/
evaluation.html

Thinking Critically about World Wide Web Resources:
http://www.library.ucla.edu/libraries/college/instruct/critical.htm

Evaluating Internet Resources (choose any site from *Internet Resources* section):
http://refserver.lib.vt.edu/libinst/evaluating.html

Print Resources

Bodi, Sonia (1995). Scholarship or propaganda: How can librarians help undergraduates tell the difference? *Journal of Academic Librarianship,* January: 21–25.

Brandt, Scott (1996). Evaluating information on the Internet (Techman's Tech Page). *Computers in Libraries,* 16(5, May): 44–47.

Collins, Boyd (1996). Beyond cruising: Reviewing. *Library Journal,* February 1: 32.

Miller, William (1997). Troubling myths about online information. *Chronicle of Higher Education,* 43(47, August 1): A44.

Oberman, Cerise (1991). Avoiding the cereal syndrome, or critical thinking in the electronic environment. *Library Trends,* 39(3, Winter): 189–202.

Web Exercise 9.1

A variety of information related to the topics in this chapter is available on the World Wide Web. For this exercise, access any three of the general reference Web sites found in Table 9.4. Using the Web site, locate the appropriate information for the site based any of the topics you identified in Exercise 9.3. Respond to the following questions for each site.

WEB SITE 1

1. What is the name and URL of the site? _____

   _____

2. Describe the ease with which you found the information you needed. _____

   _____

   _____

3. Use the list of suggestions you developed for the Classic Critical Thinking box of this chapter, evaluate the Web site on a separate sheet of paper or in your journal.

WEB SITE 2

1. What is the name and URL of the site? _____

   _____

2. Describe the ease with which you found the information you needed. _____

   _____

   _____

3. Use the list of suggestions you developed for the Classic Critical Thinking box of this chapter, evaluate the Web site on a separate sheet of paper or in your journal.

WEB SITE 3

1. What is the name and URL of the site? _____

   _____

2. Describe the ease with which you found the information you needed. _____

   _____

   _____

3. Use the list of suggestions you developed for the Classic Critical Thinking box of this chapter, evaluate the Web site on a separate sheet of paper or in your journal.

GROUP LEARNING ACTIVITY   APPROACHING LIBRARY RESEARCH

Just as you can take different routes to get to a specific location, you can use different routes to approach library research. These approaches do not have to be used exclusively. You can choose to use one as a starting point until you have enough information to try something else. The following eight standard approaches often are suggested (Morse, 1975).

Bibliographic. This approach is the most basic. A bibliography is a list of all materials consulted in your search for information. References all relate to the topic in some way, although those relationships can differ. Thus, the result of a bibliographic approach is an annotated list of books, articles, and other related materials.

Biographical. Biographies concern people—their lives and accomplishments. Thus, if a particular person is associated with a topic, the story of that person's life might be an appropriate starting point for the context of your paper. Although this approach is not suitable for all topics, it is appropriate for some.

Chronological. Chronological order concerns the timeline of events associated with your topic. This approach is particularly suitable for historical events, current events, and other topics that have a beginning, middle, and, sometimes, end.

Geographical. Sometimes you want to know where or in what places an event occurred. In this approach, you use a map to focus on specific areas, locations, or countries.

Linguistic. Linguistics refers to the study of language. This approach focuses on defining key words and ideas as the basis for beginning research. Other words or terms in the definition or the etymology of the word can be a springboard to other references. The meanings you find help you clarify your topic and the words you intend to research.

Practical. The sequence of order of a process can be the focus of your research. This method is particularly appropriate for "how to do it" topics that focus on the step-by-step progression of an action or idea.

Statistical. Some topics are best described by data. Here, you search for information that tells you how many, how much, who, where, and why in numerical terms. This collection of facts forms the basis for analysis and interpretation of information to form new conclusions.

Theoretical. Sometimes exact answers to life's questions are not available. In such cases, the theories that answer those questions suffice. These can be compared, contrasted, or related in other ways.

Application

As a group, complete the following activity and compare your results.

1. The group as a whole should select one of the following topics: AIDS research and treatment, automobiles, the brain, gymnastics, voting rights, or war veterans of the twentieth century.

2. Each group member should select one of the eight approaches described. No two group members should use the same approach.

3. Each group member should find and annotate five references for that topic and approach.

4. As a group, compare the information you located.

CHAPTER SUMMARY

1. The librarian assists your research by identifying appropriate sources and services.

2. Understanding the organizational system that your library uses helps you locate materials efficiently. The card catalog is a file or computerized database that indexes nonfiction library holdings by author, title, and subject, and fiction holdings by author and title. Two classification systems are used to identify library holdings: the numerically based Dewey decimal system and the alphabetically based Library of Congress system.

3. Modern libraries contain a variety of materials for general, content-specific, and computerized research purposes. General references include unabridged dictionaries, thesauruses, almanacs, yearbooks, atlases, gazetteers, biographies, books of quotations, government documents, and indices to magazines and newspapers. The specific subject references you need depend on your interests and coursework. You use indices to content-specific sources to find them. Computerized references can be found through online or CD-ROM sources or through Internet or World Wide Web access.

4. A working bibliography, created through a systematic search of the card catalog or a computer search, provides you with a list of possible research references. Searching, evaluating, and recording information from reference sources requires skills in skimming, scanning, and notetaking.

CLASSACTION

Respond to the following on a separate sheet of paper or in your journal. Combine the chapter map and chapter summary to form a synthesis map that reflects the main ideas and important details of this chapter. Personalize the map by indicating specific ways in which you plan to implement suggestions offered by this chapter.

CHAPTER REVIEW

Answer briefly but completely.

1. Compare and contrast the role of Ariadne with that of the librarian. Be specific.

   _____

   _____

   _____

   _____

2. What is the purpose of a call number?

   _____

   _____

   _____

   _____

3. Contrast the advantages of online or computerized material with their disadvantages.

   _____

   _____

   _____

   _____

4. You plan to write a research paper on music in the 1920s. List three key words you might use to access this information in your library's database.

   _____

   _____

   _____

   _____

5. Contrast the Dewey decimal system with the Library of Congress system. Which system does your library use?

   _____

   _____

   _____

6. When might you use direct quotes instead of summaries? Why?

   _____

   _____

   _____

   _____

TERMS

Terms appear in which they occurred in the chapter.

- interlibrary loan
- database
- Library of Congress (LC) system
- Dewey decimal system
- call numbers
- card catalog
- nonfiction
- author card
- main entry card
- subject card
- title card
- fiction
- call number
- microfiche
- microforms
- microfiche reader
- Internet
- hypertext
- hypermedia links
- ready reference
- reserve books
- periodical indices
- unabridged dictionary
- thesaurus
- newspaper index
- almanacs
- yearbooks
- atlases
- gazetteers
- working bibliography
- home page
- direct quotes
- summary
- paraphrase
- ellipsis

7. Using the microfiche or microfilm in your library, copy the front page of the *New York Times* on the day you were born.

8. How do skimming and scanning aid you in researching a paper?

   _____

   _____

   _____

   _____

9. Identify two of each of the following found in your library:

   a. general references and their call numbers

   _____

   _____

   b. general biographical indices

   _____

   _____

10. Compare and contrast the use of a library's physical holdings with that of the World Wide Web or Internet.

   _____

   _____

   _____

   _____

VOCABULARY DEVELOPMENT   Ready References for Words: Dictionary, Glossary, and Thesaurus

"...98, 99, 100! Here I come, ready, prepared, anticipated, girded, on the alert, provide for—or not."

SOURCE: Reprinted by permission of Frank Hauser

Like Roget, you, too, need to be ready, prepared, apt, and all set to seek whatever your college coursework has hidden. Luckily for you, three references found in all libraries—the dictionary, the glossary, and the thesaurus—are ready for your use in learning the meaning of unfamiliar terms.

Using the Dictionary

What do you do when you see a word you don't know? Most students define words by looking them up in the dictionary. After all, for years parents and teachers have said, "You don't know how to spell that word? You don't know what it means? Well, look it up!" Using the dictionary, then, becomes second nature to you. This often-used method works best when you know how to use the dictionary effectively.

To find word entries quickly in the dictionary, use the **guide words** at the top of each page. They indicate the words that appear between them. Arranged in alphabetical order, definitions contain much more than correct spellings, pronunciations, and meanings.

Example V9.1   Example of a Dictionary Entry

---

library (lī'brer'ē) *n., pl.* -ies[<L. *liber.*book] 1. a collection of books, etc.
2. a room or building for, or an institution in charge of, such a collection

---

A dictionary **entry** follows a general format (see Example V9.1). First, the word is spelled and divided into syllables. Second, the word's phonetic pronunciation is given. (A key to phonetic symbols usually appears at the bottom of the page.) Next appears an abbreviation of the word's part of speech followed by its **etymology.** This is the word's origin or history and tells how or why the word became a word. The word's definition comes after the etymology. Usually the longest and most often used part of the entry, the definition is the word's meaning(s). If the word has several different and distinct meanings, these are numbered separately. Some entries also include **synonyms** (words with the same meaning) and/or **antonyms** (words with the opposite meaning). Finally, the entry shows the **derivations** of the word and their parts of speech. Derivations are words formed from the entry word. Although entry formats vary slightly from one dictionary to another, their general consistency allows you to use a variety of dictionaries easily.

Resorting to a dictionary is not always the best solution. First, because many words have specialized meanings, you might have difficulty locating the meaning you need. By the time you find the one you need, you might forget why you needed it. This break in concentration leads to a loss of understanding. This increases study time and decreases study efficiency. Glossary usage, context, and structural analysis are alternatives for understanding.

Using a Glossary

When a glossary is included in a textbook, it is your greatest resource in understanding the language of the course. An entry in this dictionary-like listing of words generally consists of only the term and its course-specific definition. Examining the glossary before the beginning of a course provides you with an introduction to the language of the course. Referring to the glossary during reading requires less time than using a dictionary. It also assures that you get the correct meaning for the content of the course.

Using a Thesaurus

Once you have a sense of what a word means, using a thesaurus provides you with other words with similar meanings (synonyms). First compiled by Peter Mark Roget in 1852, a thesaurus is a collection of words that enhances vocabulary development.

Example V9.2 Examples of Various Thesaurus Entries

Gratitude

Nouns—gratitude, grateful, thankfulness; indebtedness; acknowledgment, recognition, thanksgiving; thanks, praise; paean. *Te Deum,* WORSHIP, grace; thank-offering; requital.

Verbs—be grateful, thank; give, render, return, offer, or tender thanks; acknowledge, require; thank or bless one's [lucky] starts.

Adjectives—grateful, thankful, appreciative, obliged, beholden, indebted to, under obligation.

Interjections—thanks! much obliged! thank you! thank Heaven! Heaven be praised! thanks a million! *gracias! merci!*

Antonyms, see INGRATITUDE.

---

rumble, *n.* roll, hollow roar, reverberation. See LOUDNESS.

---

rumble, *v.* boom, thunder, roll (RESONANCE, LOUDNESS).

---

rumble *verb*

1. To make a continuous deep, reverberating sound: *heard the convey rumbling in the distance.* **Syns:** boom, growl, grumble, roll.

2. MUTTER

rumble *noun* MUTTER.

As in a dictionary, the information found in a thesaurus entry varies (see Example VD 9.2). A thesaurus entry is less complicated than a dictionary entry. It omits a word's pronunciation, etymology, and derivations. Consistently, however, entries contain a word's part of speech, synonyms and related words or phrases, and cross-references. Some also include antonyms.

Thesauruses use the same labels for parts of speech as dictionaries. Again, these labels tell how a word functions in language. Because many words can be used as more than one part of speech, a thesaurus lists synonyms for each function. Thus, when looking for words in a thesaurus, you need to know how a word is to be used in a sentence.

Because it would be redundant to reprint every term associated with each entry, an entry sometimes includes cross-references. Found at the end of an entry, these either begin with the words "See also" or are written in all caps. Cross-references direct you to other entries that contain additional synonyms or to antonyms.

Choosing Ready References

A glossary is your first and best choice for determining the meaning of the terms you encounter because their meanings are specific to your course of study. Nonetheless, a personal dictionary and thesaurus are imperative for continued vocabulary development. Contrary to popular opinion, all dictionaries and thesauruses are not alike. Most are abridged versions containing a limited number of entries. When determining what to purchase, you should base your choice on more than size alone. Indeed, large unabridged dictionaries would be inappropriate for everyday use but would be the best choice for an extensive etymology search. How, then, do you decide which reference book you need? Table V9.1 provides guidelines for your selection.

Table V9.1   Guidelines for Purchasing a Dictionary and Thesaurus

---

Dictionary

1. What size is the dictionary? Will you use it at home or in class? If you plan to use the dictionary at home, it can be larger than if you will be carrying it to class each day.

2. How many total entries are included? Within the limits of size manageability, the more entries, the better.

3. What is the copyright date of the dictionary? More up-to-date dictionaries contain new words that older dictionaries do not contain.

4. What is the quality of the entries given? Contrast the entries of several dictionaries to determine which would best fit your needs.

5. Is the type clear and easy to read?

6. Does the dictionary include a clear guide to aid you in using information contained in it? Skim it to determine how easy it is to use.

7. What additional information is included in the dictionary? Many contain such features as a periodic table, sections on punctuation and language usage, lists of foreign words or spellings, and a table of weights and measures. The components you need depend on how you plan to use your dictionary.

(continues)

Table V9.1   *Continued*

Thesaurus

1. Are entries listed alphabetically or by subject? Thesauruses with an alphabetical format are easier to use.

2. How many total entries are included? Within the limits of size manageability, the more entries, the better.

3. Are cross-references included? Cross-references help you locate the exact synonym you need.

4. Does the entry include antonyms when possible? Thesauruses with antonyms are helpful because sometimes you need a word that means the opposite of a word you know.

5. Is the type clear and easy to read?

6. Does the thesaurus include a clear guide to aid you in using information contained in it? Skim it to determine how easy it is to use.

Activity

I. Define each of the following words using a dictionary. Then define them using the glossary found in Activity 1 of the Vocabulary Development Section in Chapter Two. Using a thesaurus, find three to five words that would generally be considered synonyms of these words. Compare the glossary, dictionary, and thesaurus meanings. What differences do you find?

1. *affiliates*

   Dictionary: _____

   _____

   Glossary: _____

   _____

   Thesaurus: _____

   _____

   Comparison: _____

   _____

   _____

   _____

   _____

   _____

2. *accreditation*

Dictionary: _____

_____

Glossary: _____

_____

Thesaurus: _____

_____

Comparison: _____

_____

_____

_____

3. *channel*

Dictionary: _____

_____

Glossary: _____

_____

Thesaurus: _____

_____

Comparison: _____

_____

_____

_____

4. *content*

Dictionary: _____

_____

Glossary: _____

_____

Thesaurus: _____

_____

Comparison: _____

_____

_____

_____

5. *interactive*

Dictionary: _____

_____

Glossary: _____

_____

Thesaurus: _____

_____

Comparison: _____

_____

_____

_____

II. How does using these references as combined sources affect your vocabulary development?

_____

_____

_____

_____

_____

_____

_____

_____

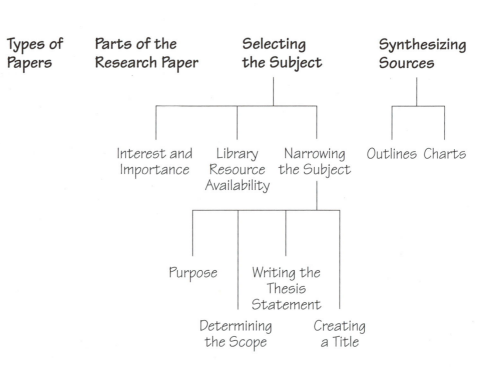

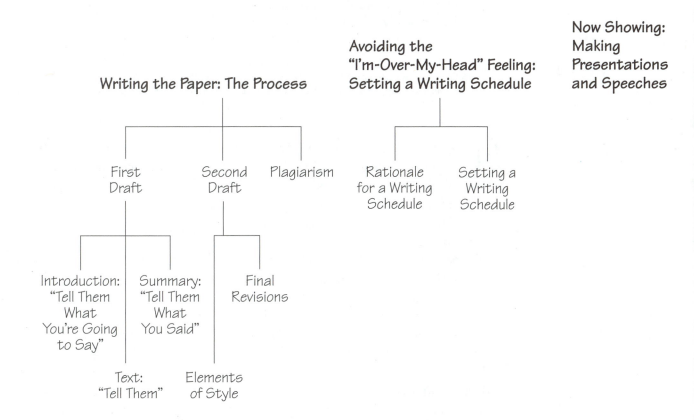

Writing the Paper: The Process

First Draft

Second Draft

Plagiarism

Introduction: "Tell Them What You're Going to Say"

Summary: "Tell Them What You Said"

Final Revisions

Text: "Tell Them"

Elements of Style

Avoiding the "I'm-Over-My-Head" Feeling: Setting a Writing Schedule

Rationale for a Writing Schedule

Setting a Writing Schedule

Now Showing: Making Presentations and Speeches

The deadline would strike in exactly twenty-one days. I had to start writing. The next morning, a beauteous one in June, I woke up, washed my face and brushed my teeth in a hurry, made a pot of coffee, tightened the sash on my bathrobe, snapped my typewriter out of its case, carefully placed it on the kitchen table, unwrapped the pack of bond paper I had purchased the day before, retrieved my notes from the floor where they were stacked tidily in manila folders . . . opened the first folder, put the top sheet of paper in the typewriter, looked at it, put my head on the keys, wrapped my arms around its base, and cried. If I had known then how many times, during the next fifteen years, I would have the same feeling—the I'm-over-my-head-and-this-time-they're-going-to-catch-me feeling–I might have become a receptionist in a carpeted law office and married the first partner in a three-piece suit who asked me. But I didn't know. I thought, if I get through this, it'll be over.

—Betty Rollin

SOURCE: *Am I Getting Paid for This?* by Betty Rollin. Little, Brown and Company, Publishers. Copyright © 1982 by Betty Rollin and Ida Rollin. Reprinted by permission of William Morris Agency, Inc. on behalf of the Author.

No matter if your assignment comes from an editor or an instructor, the "I'm-over-my-head-and-this-time-they're-going-to-catch-me feeling" often prevails. Unlike Betty Rollin, you might have no clear idea of what's involved in researching and writing a paper. Perhaps the writing process confuses and frustrates you. If so, you—like Betty Rollin—probably feel like crying.

Writing a paper is much like cooking. If a chef follows the recipe, everything goes as planned. If the chef leaves something out or fails to follow directions, the recipe is ruined. A paper has a recipe, too. As with cooking, leaving out a part of the paper or a step in the writing process results in a paper that's not all you hoped it would be.

The recipe for your paper depends on the type of paper you need to write and the parts you plan to include. It also consists of other key ingredients and steps for you to follow. These help you find where you are in the process and what you need to do next. You complete four steps when writing a paper: selecting a topic, narrowing your subject, gathering information, and actually writing the paper.

TYPES OF PAPERS

There are almost as many types of papers as there are types of food. Instructors often assign **themes** or **essays, reports,** and **research papers** or **term papers.** Themes require little or no research. Somewhat short in length, they usually contain your personal opinions about a single topic. Other kinds of papers vary in length and purpose. Reports narrate or describe something that you have experienced firsthand. They sometimes include information that you derive from the accounts of others. Research papers are required assignments, written as a culmination or synthesis of a course's content. They often require supporting research. Called term papers by some instructors, research papers involve much library work. They focus on either part or all of a course's content or a related topic.

PARTS OF THE RESEARCH PAPER

Regardless of the purpose or topic, all research papers include the same basic parts: the title page, body of the paper, and **bibliography,** in that order. In addition, research papers often contain a table of contents, an **abstract,** and **appendices** (see Figure 10.1).

The title page lists the paper's title, your name, the course and the instructor for whom the paper is written, and the date. Second is the body of the paper, which contains the topic introduction, synthesis of information, and summary or conclusions. Third, your paper includes a list of references, sometimes called a bibliography.

Whether or not your paper contains additional information depends on the options your instructor wants and the scope of the paper. The first optional item is a table of contents, often used in papers that are lengthy or segmented. An abstract—a second optional element—briefly summarizes the content of your paper. Both the table of contents and abstract follow the title page. A final optional element consists of appendices that contain supplementary material (for example, illustrations, figures, charts). These are placed at the end of your paper.

"A fill-in-the-blank research paper is a unique idea, but . . ."

Figure 10.1   Parts of a Research Paper

TITLE

The State of Education:
Comparisons between Louisiana and Maryland

Henry Brandt

Professor Miles Jeffrey
Education 4443
Trends in Education
Spring 1994

SAMPLE PAGE FROM BODY

Population Characteristics

The population of Maryland is comparable to that of Louisiana (4,265,000 vs. 4,362,000), although Maryland is much more densely populated than Louisiana (431.2 persons per square mile vs. 97.1 per square mile). Louisiana is 68.7% urban as compared to Maryland's urban population of 80.3%. Louisiana's racial make-up is 69.2% white, 29.4% black, and 1.4% other. Only two other states have black populations higher than Louisiana. The racial make-up of Maryland is 74.9% white, 22.7% black, and 2.4% other. (Feist, 1983; American Almanac, 1983).

Maryland's physical density and urban atmosphere would seem to be advantageous for its residents. This would facilitate accessibility to formal educational resources (i.e. libraries and schools). In addition, opportunities for participating in non-school educational/cultural activities (i.e., museums, plays, concerts, exhibitions, etc.) would be increased.

History

Louisiana was first visited by Spanish explorers in 1530 but was claimed for France in 1682. French control of the state

ABSTRACT

ABSTRACT

The State of Education:
Comparisons between Louisiana
and Maryland

Henry Brandt

The purpose of thin paper is to provide a descriptive examination of factors relating to education in the states of Louisiana and Maryland.

The context of the situation in each state will be developed through a discussion of population characteristics, state history, political history, economic trends, and readership data.

The scope of this paper focuses on the following aspects of the educational system in each state: enrollment, public elementary and secondary schools, private elementary and secondary schools, teachers, adult literacy, and post-secondary institutions.

APPENDIX

APPENDIX A. Readership Data

	LOUISIANA	MARYLAND
Newsweek 07/30/83)		
Subscriptions	55,025	60,000
Single Copy Sales	2,933	4,535
Total	57,958	65,535
Time (7/30/83)		
Subscriptions	53,700	79,036
Single Copy Sales	3,542	3,216
Total	56,242	82,252
U.S. News and World Report (7/30/83)		
Subscriptions	39,162	44,775
Single Copy Sales	924	1,644
Total	40,086	46,419
Sports Illustrated (7/30/83)		
Subscriptions	62,741	58,149
Single Copy Sales	1,391	2,126
Total	64,132	60,275
House Beautiful (7/30/83)		
Subscriptions	18,725	19,048
Single Copy Sales	4,600	5,016
Total	23,326	24,064
Reader's Digest (6/30/83)		
Subscriptions	244,603	286,333
Single Copy Sales	15,235	10,333
Total	232,538	296,666

(continues)

Figure 10.1   *Continued*

| TABLE OF CONTENTS | REFERENCES |

BIBLIOGRAPHY

Ashworth, J., (1980). *Education in Louisia*na. Baton Rouge, Louisiana; University Press.

Craig, F. J. (ed.). (1983). American Almanac Boston: Ginn Co.

Feist, J. T., (1983). *General Education Facts and Figures* New York: Holt.

Jones, E. M. (1982). "Maryland's Push for Better Education." *Journal of General Educa*tion, *21,* pp. 192–193.

Stoll, E. P., & Bradley, A. C. (1984). *Readership Data for Popular Magazines.* New York: Hill & Smith.

SELECTING THE SUBJECT

A chef's library contains many specialized cookbooks. The choice of a specific recipe depends on the ingredients on hand, the amount of preparation time involved, the number to be served, and so on. The subject of your paper, much like a specialized cookbook, is the general area that you plan to research. Your instructor sometimes assigns specific topics. If this is the case, your job is to find information on that topic and write about it. If not, your job is more difficult. You then choose a subject from either a list of subjects supplied by the instructor or from your own research. Subject selection depends on your interest, the importance of the subject, and the availability of resources.

Interest and Importance

The subject you choose needs to be one of interest or importance to you, the course content, and your audience. Because writing a paper requires much work, you stand a better chance of doing a good job if you care about the subject that you select. The subject of your paper also should be relevant to the course. Finally, the content of your paper needs to meet the demands of your audience, whether that be your instructor, your peers, or others.

Finding a subject that relates to you, the course, and your audience requires effort. By scanning your text's index or table of contents, you can identify topics that interest you or appeal to your audience. Skimming your notes or class handouts also helps you pinpoint likely subjects. Talking with your instructor or classmates is a third means of finding possible areas of research. Finally, subject areas surface through vicarious and direct experiences. These include books, magazines, television, Web sites, newspaper accounts, travel, and work.

Library Resource Availability

The availability of library resources is a second consideration in subject selection. Consulting the card catalog helps you determine if your library owns books or other references on your subject. Computer access to on-line information on the topic also can be an option. If your library contains limited information or if on-line information is not readily available, choosing another subject might be advisable. In addition, checking the location of such resources helps you determine the availability of those references to you. If the ones you want are checked out or are otherwise unavailable, you might have to find another subject.

Narrowing the Subject

Narrowing your subject into a manageable topic is much like a chef deciding what kind of cake to bake. Because you can't write about every aspect of a subject, you need to decide specifically what you plan to cover. The narrower the topic, the better your chance of covering it.

Purpose

Establishing the purpose of a paper aids you in narrowing the subject. Purposes are sometimes set by instructors; however, you often must set them yourself. Determining the purpose helps you identify the type of information you need to collect (see Table 10.1).

To establish your purpose, you ask questions about the subject. Asking "Who?" elicits information describing a person or a group. Asking "What?" requires you to find information defining a process, an event, a place, or an object. Asking "Why?" involves your finding information that explains the importance of the person or group, a process, an event, a place, an object, or the relationships among these. Asking "When?" helps you pinpoint the time frame you want to cover. Asking "How?" helps you focus on process.

Table 10.1   **Identifying Research Purposes**

If Your Purpose is to . . .	You Collect . . .
analyze,	factors or elements that comprise the totality of the topic.
chronicle,	sequence, process, or history.
compare or contrast,	similarities and differences.
define or describe,	details, characteristics, features, qualities, relationships.
explain or interpret,	reasons, causes, effects, data.
infer,	evidence to make predictions or conclusions.
persuade,	facts that support or refute an argument.
relate,	logical, spatial or geographical associations or patterns.

*"I don't think that's what your instructor meant
by reducing the scope of your paper."*

Determining the Scope

Once you identify your purpose, you determine the **scope** of your paper. This refers to the general size and specification of your topic. The scope of your topic needs to be neither too broad nor too specific but "just right." Your paper reflects its scope. Its contents, too, must be neither too broad nor too specific but "just right."

Scope involves setting limits on the amount of information covered and the number of details included. It also depends on your expertise, the amount

Figure 10.2   Example of Progressively Limiting a Subject's Scope

of time you have to spend on the topic, and the type of paper you are writing. Once you determine your scope, you refrain from exceeding these limits. You set these limits by progressively narrowing your topic until it becomes a manageable size (see Figure 10.2). In doing so, you move from general to specific. Encyclopedias and textbooks do this when they divide information into sections or chapters. You can use these as guides when setting the scope of your paper. You can practice narrowing the scope of a topic in Exercise 10.1.

Writing the Thesis Statement

The scope of a paper's contents often determines the **thesis statement.** Because it defines the limits of your research, the thesis statement guides and controls your research, your writing, and—later—your audience. The thesis statement of your paper is much like a topic sentence in a paragraph. It states your paper's purpose and your major assertions or conclusions. You write your thesis statement in the form of a complete, declarative sentence. It restates your title or topic, states major assertions or conclusions (not minor details, illustrations, quotations), and establishes the purpose of your research.

For example, suppose you are researching the topic "Rising Health Care Costs for Big Businesses" to analyze results of increases in the cost of health care. You assert that the rising cost of health care results in lower dividends for stockholders. Based on this, your topic sentence could be this: "The rising cost of health care for employees threatens to wipe out many companies' profits."

Creating a Title

Like the thesis statement, your title identifies the contents of your paper. Also, the title needs to appeal to your readers, spark their interest in your topic, and motivate them to read your paper. Often, your narrowed topic serves as the title of your paper. On the other hand, composing the thesis statement sometimes helps you form a more appropriate title. Such titles are precise and state your topic in a few key words. Wordy, overly cute, or fancy titles often detract from the seriousness of your research. Finally, it really

A good title should be like a good metaphor; it should intrigue without being too baffling or too obvious.

—Walker Percy
Twentieth century American author

Exercise 10.1   Go to your campus library and locate two additional sources that pertain to one of the following broad topics or another related topic of your choice from Sample Chapter 11 or 12. Skim the references to help you narrow the scope to a workable topic.

1. Crimes Against the Aging Population
2. Crime and Women
3. Crime and Ethnicity

Subject _____

Subtopic _____

Subtopic _____

Subtopic _____

Workable topic _____

> **The title comes last.**
> —Tennessee Williams
> *Twentieth century*
> *American author*

doesn't matter if you title your paper before or after you write it. Sometimes you find through research or **synthesis** (concise, unified compilation of ideas) a title that perfectly fits your paper. Until then, your thesis statement serves as your composition guide. A good title is worth the wait.

Exercise 10.2 helps you construct thesis statements.

SYNTHESIZING SOURCES

It's a great feeling. You have completed your research. You have taken your last note. No more searching through books, articles, and computer screens for information. You have everything you need. All you have to do is combine the information and write the paper.

For some people, the moment of elation over completing their research turns to one of dread. Like Betty Rollin, they suddenly have that "I'm-over-my-head-and-this-time-they're-going-to-catch-me" feeling. You, too, might experience these "what-do-I-do-now" feelings when you begin the actual writing process.

As in identifying and collecting research information, your thesis statement guides the process of writing your paper. It reminds you of the original purpose of your research and the limits you set for its scope. Knowing your purpose and limits helps you organize the information you've collected. Outlining and charting major sections provide you with the means of establishing the framework for the development of your topic.

Exercise 10.2 Given the following topics, major assertions or conclusions, and purposes of research, construct a thesis statement for each topic.

1. *Topic:* The American Presidential Election of 1864

   Major assertions: Out of their desire for an end to the Civil War, many leading Republicans refused to support Abraham Lincoln in his bid for renomination to the presidency.

   Purpose of research: To analyze the political scene.

   Thesis statement: _____

   _____

2. *Topic:* Choosing a Personal Computer

   Major assertions: Choosing a personal computer is based on the software you want to use, the amount of money you have to spend, and the recommendations you receive from other users.

   Purpose of research: To compare and contrast features of Macintosh and IBM personal computers.

   Thesis statement: _____

   _____

3. *Topic:* Increasing Unemployment Rates in Urban Poverty Areas

   Major assertions: Rising unemployment rates in urban poverty areas have increased in the past five years.

   Purpose of research: To analyze reasons for the increase in unemployment rates in urban poverty areas.

   Thesis statement: _____

   _____

4. *Topic:* Quality of Health Care in Public Health Facilities

   Major assertions: Patient care in public health facilities is of a lower standard than that in private facilities.

   Purpose of research: To compare health care in public and private institutions.

   Thesis statement: _____

   _____

5. *Topic:* The Origin of the Universe

   Major assertions: One of the fundamental problems in astronomy is to develop a theory describing the origin of the universe.

   Purpose of research: To analyze various theories describing how the universe was formed.

   Thesis statement: _____

   _____

(continues)

Exercise 10.2   *Continued*

6. *Topic:* U.S. Space Program's Unmanned Interplanetary Missions

    Major assertions: Unmanned interplanetary missions are a major component of the U.S. space program. This is based on the fact that they began with the program's inception and continue today.

    Purpose of research: To chronicle the history of the U.S. space program's unmanned interplanetary missions.

    Thesis statement: _____

    _____

7. *Topic:* Comparing the Netherlands and My Home State

    Major assertions: The terrain of the Netherlands varies from low and flat to hilly.

    Purpose of research: To compare the Netherlands with my state.

    Thesis statement: _____

    _____

8. *Topic:* Cable Television: The Pros and Cons

    Major assertions: The local cable television company celebrated its tenth anniversary with the usual insincere promises of expansions and breakthroughs.

    Purpose of research: To analyze propaganda techniques used in advertisements to persuade people to subscribe to cable television.

    Thesis statement: _____

    _____

9. *Topic:* Rebuilding the Statue of Liberty

    Major assertions: The rebuilding of the Statue of Liberty was financed through contributions of patriotic Americans.

    Purpose of research: To list the sources of contributions for the refurbishing of the Statue of Liberty

    Thesis statement: _____

    _____

10. *Topic:* UFOs: Sightings as Proof

    Major assertions: Since 1947, reports of UFOs have been increasing. Large numbers of sightings in varied locations prove their existence.

    Purpose of research: To persuade the reader to believe in UFOs.

    Thesis statement: _____

    _____

Outlines

Outlining—organizing information in a sequence—is the first step in synthesis. Because research usually is collected from a variety of sources at different times, information can seem disjointed and isolated. Thus, in completing an outline, you first review your notes. This helps you become familiar with what they contain.

The second stage of outlining—determining relevance—depends on how well you know what your references contain. Now you judge their importance to your paper. One way to do this is to randomly list important terms and concepts necessary to the understanding of your topic. Next, determine the relative importance of each term and concept. You do this by making inferences about the relationships between common themes found in your research and your paper's purpose. These themes become the main headings or subheadings of your outline, depending on their complexity. If the remaining terms and concepts further develop your topic, they become supporting details. Omit unnecessary information. You probably won't need all the information you collected in your research. That doesn't mean that you wasted your time. The information you gathered helped you refine your understanding to define the limits of relevance.

The third stage of outlining begins the charting process in synthesis. Once you identify the main headings and subheadings you want to include, search for information on these themes in your different sources.

Charts

As discussed in Chapter 6, charts help you identify and categorize information. As you write your research paper, they aid you in comparing themes from various sources.

To construct a synthesis chart for writing (see Figures 10.3 through 10.6), first list horizontally the sources you plan to use as references. Then, list vertically the themes you've identified. Third, construct a grid by drawing lines between each theme and each source. Fourth, determine if the source contains information about a specific theme and briefly note that information. Fifth, look at your chart to categorize sources based on likenesses and differences of information contained in them. This helps you to see patterns and relationships. Finally, use the chart to write your paper.

Figure 10.3   Example Synthesis Chart, Source 1

INTRODUCTION

The hardware of the computer is the physical devices that comprise the computer system: the central processing unit, the input devices, the output devices, and the storage devices. Basically, hardware includes all parts of the computer that are tangible. Hardware is not operating systems, concepts, or programs (these are software). Hardware consists of only those parts of the computer that one could reach out and touch.

THE CENTRAL PROCESSING UNIT

The **central processing unit,** or **CPU,** is the essence of the computer's hardware. It is the "brain" of the computer. It tells the other parts of the computer what to do; it decides what to do with the instructions that the programmer gives it; and it ensures that the tasks assigned to it are properly carried out.

The CPU is composed of three separate units—the control unit, the arithmetic/logic unit, and the primary storage unit (Figure 21). The **control unit** is, quite literally, in control of the operations. It reads the actual instructions and tells the other computer parts what to do. The control unit directs the appropriate input device to send the necessary data. It keeps track of what parts of the program have already been executed and which ones are left to be done. Finally, it controls the execution of the specific instructions, collects the output, and sends the output to the designated output device.

The **arithmetic/logic unit (ALU)** is the computer's own personal mathematician. It executes all arithmetic and logic statements. Logic statements aren't quite so straightforward as arithmetic statements, but they are equally easy to understand. A logic statement is a statement that makes a comparison and then does something based on the result. For example, if today is Friday, then pick up paycheck and go to the bank; if not, don't. Obviously, this isn't quite the type of logic statement that the computer would work with, but the idea is the same. More likely, the computer would want to know: If this is the end of the input data, then make the calculations and output the results. If not, read the rest of the input. Arithmetic and logic operations are the only type of instructions that the ALU can execute. But when you think about it, you will realize that almost everything you want the computer to do is either an arithmetic or logic problem. The only noticeable exceptions are reading input and printing output. (These are controlled by the control unit.)

The **primary storage unit** is in charge of storing data and programs in the computer's internal memory. It is very important to distinguish this internal memory, called primary

CENTRAL PROCESSING UNIT (CPU)

Acts as the "brain" of the computer.

CONTROL UNIT

Controls the execution of programs.

ARITHMETIC/LOGIC UNIT (ALU)

Executes mathematical and logic statements.

PRIMARY STORAGE UNIT

The computer's internal memory.

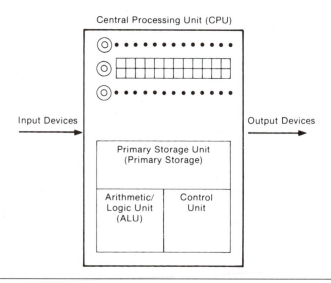

Figure 2-1.
Computer System Components

Figure 10.3   *Continued*

storage, from external memory, called auxiliary storage. The primary storage unit is a part of the actual internal hardware of the computer. Without the primary storage unit, the computer could not work because it would not be able to store the programs. Auxiliary storage is not necessary for the computer to function; it is not part of its internal hardware. The CPU can access only primary storage; information between primary and auxiliary storage is transferred through electrical lines.

Most current primary storage hardware consists of **semiconductors** which have their memory circuitry on silicon chips. The data are stored in **bit cells,** located on the chips, which can be in either an "on" or an "'off" state. Each cell holds a Binary digit (bit). The cells are arranged so that they can be written to or read from as needed.

Basically, the primary storage unit holds the program that is being executed, as well as its input, output, and intermediate results of any calculations. When a program is entered into the computer, the control unit sends the program to the primary storage unit. The control unit then retrieves one line at a time from the primary storage unit. Therefore, the primary storage unit acts somewhat like a shelf upon which statements, instructions, and results are placed when they aren't being read by the control unit.

All three parts of the central processing unit work together to enable the computer to function. Together they are often called the "computer proper" because in some micro-computers, they are the computer. In any computer, the CPU is the central core.

Computers derive most of their amazing power from three features; speed, accuracy, and memory. Generally, computer speed is expressed as the time required to perform one operation. The following units of time apply:

UNIT	SYMBOL	FRACTIONS OF A SECOND	
Millisecond	ms	one-thousandth	(1/1,000)
Microsecond	μs	one-millionth	(1/1,000,000)
Nanosecond	ns	one-billionth	(1/1,000,000,000)
Picosecond	ps	one-trillionth	(1/1,000,000,000,000)

Today's computers can complete computations in a matter of **nanoseconds.**

A nanosecond is one-billionth of a second. The best way to comprehend just how small a nanosecond is to compare it visually with one second. In the computer, computations are made electrically. The speed of electricity is approximately the speed of light. Thus, in one second the electricity used for computations will travel 186,000 miles. In one nanosecond that electricity will travel 11.8 inches.

MORE ON INTERNAL STORAGE

Storage Locations and Addresses

When the CPU stores programs, input data, and output, it does not do so randomly. These items are stored in specific memory locations that can then be accessed by their addresses to retrieve their contents.

To process information, the CPU's control unit must first locate in storage each instruction and piece of data. Computer storage can be compared with a large array of mailboxes. Each mailbox is a specific location and can hold one item of information. Since each location in storage has a distinct address, stored program instructions can locate particular items by giving their addresses.

Suppose, for instance, the computer is instructed to calculate an employee's salary by subtracting TOTAL TAX from his or her GROSS PAY.

SEMICONDUCTOR
A type of primary storage that stores data in bit cells located on silicon chips.

BIT CELL
Used in semiconductors; stores data by designating each cell as "on" or "off."

NANOSECOND
One-billionth of a second.

SOURCE 1: Reprinted with permission from *Understanding Computers,* by Hopper and Mandell. © 1984 by West Publishing Company. All rights reserved.

Figure 10.4   Example Synthesis Chart, Source 2

The Central Processing Unit

The central processing unit is *the* essential component of a computer because it is the part that executes the program. Other components—such as auxiliary memory, input and output devices, or even main memory—can sometimes be omitted. But without a central processor, there is no computer.

Not surprisingly, in view of the job it has to do, the central processor is the most complex part of a computer. This is why the development of the microprocessor, a central processor on a single silicon chip, was such an important advance. Microprocessors make it possible to buy the complex central processor as a single, inexpensive component, instead of having to build it out of thousands of individual transistors and integrated circuits.

The central processor is itself made up of two components—the *arithmetic-logic unit*, which does the calculations, and the *control unit*, which coordinates the activities of the entire computer.

The arithmetic-logic unit

The arithmetic-logic unit performs the same jobs for a computer that a pocket calculator performs for a human being. It can perform arithmetical operations, comparisons, and logical operations.

Arithmetical operations. The arithmetic-logic unit adds, subtracts, multiplies, and divides. On some computers, only addition and subtraction are built into the arithmetic-logic unit. Such machines need programs to tell them how to multiply and divide.

Comparisons. The arithmetic-logic unit can determine such things as whether two alphabetic characters are the same or whether one number is less than, equal to, or greater than another. The results of these comparisons are made available to the control unit, which can use them to determine which instruction to execute next. Under the control of its program, the computer can "decide" what action to take next depending on the input it has received and on the outcome of previous calculations.

This decision-making capability allows a computer to be far more responsive to its user's requests than is possible with most other machines. Indeed, one reason computers are often installed in machines such as household appliances is to endow these machines with some of the computer's flexibility and responsiveness.

Logical operations. Sometimes we want to use complicated criteria to determine the action a computer will take. For example, we may ask a computer to print the names of every employee of a company who has been with the company more than ten years *and* who makes less than twenty thousand dollars *and* who has not had a raise in the last three years.

In general, such criteria consist of simple conditions (such as "the employee has been with the company more than ten years") joined by *and, or,* or *not.* Given whether each of the simple conditions is true or false for a particular individual, the program must calculate whether or not the overall criterion is satisfied. To simplify this kind of calculation, the arithmetic/logic unit provides *logical operations,* which correspond to the English words *and, or,* and *not.*

The control unit

The control unit fetches instructions one by one from main memory. Like everything stored in memory, instructions are represented by binary codes. The control unit decodes each instruction, then sends the necessary control signals to other units (such as the arithmetic-logic unit or a peripheral device) to get the instruction carried out.

The control unit is said to work in a *fetch-execute cycle* because it fetches each instruction from main memory and then executes the instruction. When an instruction has been executed, the control unit fetches the next instruction, executes it, and so on. (To speed things up, some computers fetch the next instruction while the previous instruction is being executed.)

It's important to realize that no matter how complex or subtle the job is that the program is doing, the control unit is still working in a simple, repetitive cycle—fetching and executing instructions, one after another. Herein lies the real power of programming A machine that works in a very simple, repetitive cycle can nevertheless exhibit very complicated behavior by following suitable instructions. People who sneer that a computer can only do what it is told to do completely miss this point.

Computer Memory

Memory is the part of the computer that stores information for later use. Most computers have both *main memory* and *auxiliary memory.* Main memory is sometimes referred to as *main storage, primary memory,* or *primary storage.* In the past, because of the widespread use of the now-obsolete magnetic-core technology, main memory was often called *core.* Auxiliary memory is sometimes referred to as *auxiliary storage, secondary memory, secondary storage,* or *mass storage.*

Figure 10.5   Example Synthesis Chart, Source 3

The Central Processing Unit

The **central processing unit (CPU)** is the heart of the computer system. It is composed of three units: the control unit, the arithmetic/logic unit (ALU), and the primary storage unit. Each unit performs its own unique functions.

CENTRAL PROCESSING UNIT
The heart of a Computer system. Consisting of three components.

The **control unit,** as its name implies, controls what is happening in the CPU. It does not process or store data; rather, it directs the sequence of operations. The control unit retrieves one instruction at a time from the storage unit. It interprets the instruction and sends the necessary signals to the ALU and storage unit for the instruction to be carried out. This process is repeated until all the instructions have been executed.

CONTROL UNIT
The part of the CPU that directs operations.

Another function of the control unit is to communicate with the input device in order to transfer program instructions and data into storage. Similarly, it communicates with the output device to transfer results from storage to the output device.

The **arithmetic/logic unit** *(ALU)* handles the execution of all arithmetic computations. It does not store data; it merely performs the necessary calculations. Functions performed by the ALU include arithmetic operations (addition, subtraction, multiplication, and division) and comparisons. Since the bulk of computer processing involves calculations or comparisons, the capabilities of a computer often depend upon the capabilities of the ALU.

ARITHMETIC/ LOGIC UNIT
The part of the CPU that executes arithmetic computations and comparisons.

The **primary storage unit (internal storage or main storage)** holds all the instructions and data necessary for processing. These are transferred from an input device to the primary storage unit, where they are held until needed for processing. Data that are being processed and intermediate results from ALU calculations are also held in primary storage. After all processing is completed, the control unit directs the final results to be transferred to an output device.

PRIMARY STORAGE
Part of storage inside the CPU.

A **microprocessor** is the CPU of a microcomputer. It performs arithmetic operations and control functions, much as the CPU of a large computer does; however, a microprocessor fits on a single silicon chip the size of a nailhead.

The CPU in Operation

Let us examine a simple problem. Assume we want the computer to add two numbers and print the result. The following series of steps demonstrates the flow of program instructions and data through the CPU.

Step A: The control unit directs an input device to transfer program instructions to primary storage. (As will be shown later, some data and instructions may be stored outside of the CPU and transferred to primary storage when needed.) Since this is a simple problem, there maybe only two instructions—one to add and one to print.

Step B: The control unit examines the first instruction and interprets it as addition.

Step C: The control unit sends an electronic signal for the data (the two numbers) to be brought Into primary storage from an input device, or for data already in primary storage to be transferred to the ALU.

Step D: The ALU performs the necessary calculation (addition).

Step E: The results are transferred back to the primary storage unit.

Steps B through E: These steps are repeated until all instructions are executed. (In this simplified example, steps B through E are not repeated.)

Step F: The control unit signals the primary storage unit to transfer the results to an output device to be printed.

Source 3: Reprinted with permission from Introduction to Computers and BASIC Programming, by Brenan and Mandell. © 1984 by West Publishing Company. All rights reserved.

Figure 10.6   Example Synthesis Chart and Resulting Paper

SYNTHESIS CHART:

Topic: Central Processing Unit

	BRENAN/MANDELL	HOPPER/MANDELL	GRAHAM
CONTROL UNIT			
DIRECTS PROCESSES	X	X	X
Retrieves instructions	X	X	X
Interprets instructions	X	X	X
Sends instructions	X	X	X
COMMUNICATES W/INPUT & OUTPUT	X		
Reads input		X	
Prints output		X	
DECISION-MAKING CAPABILITY			X
USES BINARY CODES			X
EXECUTES "FETCH, EXECUTE CYCLES"			X
ARITHMETIC LOGIC UNIT			
PERFORMS ARITHMETICAL CALCULATIONS	X	X	X
COMPARES INFORMATION	X		X
<,>,=			X
CARRIES OUT LOGICAL OPERATIONS		X	X
"and," "or," "not"			X
DEFINITION OF LOGIC STATEMENT		X	
PRIMARY STORAGE			
SAME AS INTERNAL OR MAIN STORAGE	X	X	
FUNCTIONS OF PRIMARY STORAGE	X	X	
Holds program being executed	X	X	
Holds results	X	X	
PRIMARY STORAGE HARDWARE		X	

PAPER:

The Central Processing Unit:
A Model as Old as Time

Although computers have significantly advanced in the last decade, research indicates that their basic processing unit is fundamental. A computer's central processing unit consists of three components: the control unit, the arithmetic logic unit, and primary storage.

In general the control unit directs the computer's processes by retrieving instructions from storage. interpreting and sending instructions back to storage (Brenan and Mandell, 1984; Graham, 1983; and Hopper and Mandell, 1984). These form "fetch-execute" cycles (Graham 1983). It also communicates with input and output devices by reading input and printing output (Hopper and Mandell, 1984). The control unit utilizes binary codes and has decision-making capability (Graham, 1983).

The second component of the central processing unit is the arithmetic logic unit (ALU). As its name suggests, the ALU performs arithmetical calculations (Brenan and Mandell, 1984; Graham, 1983; and Hopper and Mandell, 1984). It also compares information (Brenan and Mandell, 1984; Graham, 1983) by determining if one piece of information is equal to, greater than, or less than another piece of information (Graham, 1983). The ALU also carries out logical operations (Graham, 1983; Hopper and Mandell, 1984). A logic statement is "a statement that makes a comparison and then does something about it based on the results" (Hopper and Mandell, 1984).

Primary storage (also called Internal or main storage) is a final component of the central processing unit. It holds both the program being executed and the results of processing (Brenan and Mandell, 1984; Hopper and Mandell, 1984). Here data is stored as binary digits (bits) in the computer's hardware (Hopper and Mandell, 1984).

WRITING THE PAPER: THE PROCESS

> **What is written without effort is, in general, read without pleasure.**
>
> —Samuel Johnson
> *Eighteenth century*
> *English author*

The effort you put into writing a research paper shows in the quality of what you've written. Often *how* you write your paper is graded as much as *what* you write in your paper. It pays, then, to spend whatever effort and time is necessary to master the two main steps of the writing process: writing the first draft and revising it in the second draft. Your final version, the product of your effort, will deserve the grade it receives.

First Draft

Your first writing effort is often called a **rough draft,** and with good reason. Its goal is simply to get your ideas on paper. As Jackie Collins once said, "If you want to be a writer, stop talking about it and sit down and write!" No one reads your first draft but you. To some extent, you write without worrying about neatness. However, writing only on the front of your paper or using a word processor aids you in later constructing your second draft.

The flow of words forms your most important consideration. Because your objective is to sketch your paper, you might try following the advice given to speakers. In the introductory paragraph, "Tell them what you're going to say." In the text, "Tell them." And, in the summary, "Tell them what you said." Although this seems redundant, most papers take this form.

Although you should keep the basic format of introduction-body-summary in mind, many writers find starting and completing a paper to be the hardest parts. Because your thesis statement guides your writing, sections need not be written in a set order. As you write the body of your paper, you might think of the perfect beginning or ending for it. Otherwise, you might stare at a blank page for a very long time.

Introduction: "Tell Them What You're Going to Say"

In telling your audience what you're going to say, you set the stage for the rest of your paper. The introduction informs readers of your paper's general content and tells them why they will want to read your paper. The introduction lets you be creative, an important trait in capturing an audience's attention. A new approach, perfect example, or clever phrase won't always come easily. You need to keep an open mind and a patient outlook in searching for ideas.

By getting your readers' interest, you motivate them to continue reading. Briefly summarizing your most important sources provides a background for your specific subject. The reader then sees how your paper relates to a larger context of information. Interest also can be elicited by focusing the reader's attention on a particularly relevant or surprising aspect of your topic. This could be a question, generalization, viewpoint, definition, quotation, problem, conflict, or other pertinent factor. A related way to motivate the reader is to note the significance of your research. Here you tell the contribution (answers to questions, facts that support a generalization or viewpoint, new insights) that your paper proposes to make.

In telling your readers what you're going to say, you want to familiarize them with your topic. Your thesis statement tells them your purpose and plan for your paper. A summary of the main headings to be discussed in the paper expands the thesis statement. It provides a preview of important ideas.

Text: "Tell Them"

The bulk of your paper consists of the text. Here you provide a detailed synthesis of your information. When you synthesize information, you identify patterns and relationships among supporting details found through charting. Thus, the end result of your research is a concise, unified combination of ideas, rather than a summary or collection of facts.

Your most important consideration in writing the text of your paper is its organization. How you order the points you make in your text depends on your purpose and the research you collect. Several patterns of organization are possible (see Table 10.2). Once again, you rely on your inferential skills to determine which pattern best fits your paper. Following an organizational pattern helps you include all the information you've identified for a specific point. It also makes corrections in the second draft easier.

No matter what your topic and organizational pattern are, your paper needs to conform to a research paper format, which includes footnotes or endnotes with an accompanying bibliography or parenthetical references with an accompanying list of references. Rules for making these notations depend on the style that your instructor requires or that you choose. Specific

---

Table 10.2   Organizational Patterns

Alphabetical

Categorization

Cause-Effect

Chronological (time order)

Comparison or Contrast

Hierarchical (most to least or least to most)

Inductive or Deductive (specific to general or general to specific)

Part to Whole or Whole to Part

Problem-Solution

Sequential (process order)

Spatial (top to bottom, left to right)

---

books describe and provide examples for your reference. Table 10.3 identifies some of the most common **style manuals** for different content areas.

Summary: "Tell Them What You Said"

The summary paragraphs provides closure for the text of your paper. It is especially important in lengthy papers. In the summary paragraphs, you restate your thesis and the purpose of the research. In addition, you highlight the major points that supported your topic. You indicate the relationship between headings and how these proved the points you've made. You also identify the need for further research. You raise new questions or speculate on information or conclusions in your paper.

Second Draft

Have you ever talked with a friend, left, and then thought of a forgotten detail, an omitted point, or a perfect example, and thought, "I wish I'd said that." Your second draft gives you that chance. Allowing some time between writing the first draft and starting the second lets your ideas gel. Thus, when you begin to revise your paper, you have a fresh perspective.

One way to revise your first draft involves scissors and tape. Instead of rewriting, you simply cut apart sentences, paragraphs, or sections, and tape them in the order you desire. This patchwork manuscript forms the basis for writing your final draft.

Using a personal computer for writing your rough draft decreases the time it takes for revisions. Word processing programs allow you to change sentence or paragraph order, style, spelling, and punctuation without having to retype the entire manuscript. Some programs even check your grammar and writing style.

Two drawbacks hinder the use of word processing programs. Luckily, they are not insurmountable ones. First, using a word processor takes some skill. Learning a word processing program involves time and practice. When planning to use a word processor, you need to allow time for learning the program. Second, word processing requires access to personal computers. If you do not own a computer, one may be available through local computer rental agencies or your institution's computer center.

Elements of Style

Regardless of the subject of your research, to write a well-organized, readable paper, you must remember the three elements of style: conciseness, clarity, and cohesion. Each is easier if you consider order when compiling your first draft. These elements demand much of your writing ability.

First, conciseness demands brevity. If you've got something to say, you need to say it clearly and quickly without omitting important details. Adding extra details detracts from the quality of your paper. Undue padding contributes nothing to your topic.

Table 10.3   Style Manuals for Various Content Areas

American Institute of Physics, *AIP Style Manual*. 4th ed. (1990). New York: American Institute of Physics.

Atlas, Michael C. (1996). *Author's handbook of styles for life sciences journals.*. Boca Raton, FL: CRC.

American Mathematical Society. (1990). *A manual for authors of mathematical papers,* 7th ed. Providence, RI: American Mathematical Society.

American Psychological Association. (1994). *Publication manual of the American Psychological Association,* 4th ed. Washington, DC: American Psychological Association.

Bellquist, John Eric. *A guide to grammar and usage for psychology and elated fields.* (1996). Mahuan, NJ: Lawrence Erlbaum.

Council of Biology Editors. Style Manual Committee. (1994). *CBE Style manual: A guide for authors, editors, and publishers in the biological sciences.* Bethesda, MD: Council of Biology Editors.

Day, Robert A. (1988). *How to write and publish a scientific paper,* 3rd ed. Phoenix, AZ.: Oryx.

Dodd, Janet S., ed. (1986). *The ACS style guide: A manual for authors and editors.* Washington, DC: American Chemical Society.

Hicks, Wynford (1998). *English for journalists.* New York: Routledge.

Gibaldi, Joseph, and Achtert, Walter S. (1995). *MLA handbook for writers of research papers,* 4th ed. New York: Modern Language Association.

Harvard Law Review Association. (1991). *A Uniform System of Citation.* 13th ed. Cambridge, MA: Harvard Law Review Association.

Huth, Edward J., M.D. (1990). *How to write and publish papers in the medical sciences.* 2nd ed. Baltimore: Wilkins & Williams.

Iverson, C. Flanagin, A., Fontanarosa, P. B. (1997). *AMA manual of style.* Baltimore: Williams & Wilkins.

Kessler, Lauren, and McDonald, Duncan. (1995). *When words collide: A media writer's guide to grammar and style.* Belmont, CA: Wadsworth.

Li, X., & Crane, N. (1993). *Electronic style: A guide to citing electronic information.* Westport, CT: Meckler.

Lynch, P. (1995, February). *Yale WWW Style Manual.* New Haven: Yale Center for Advanced Instructional Media [on line]. http://info.med.yale.edu/caim/StyleManual.

Martin, Paul R. *The Wall Street Journal Stylebook.* New York: Dow Jones.

McIntosh, William A. (1994). Guide to effective military writing. Mechanicsburg, PA: Stackpole.

Michaelson, Herbert B. (1986). *How to write and publish engineering papers and reports,* 2nd ed. Philadelphia: ISI.

Ritter, R. M., ed. (1998). *The Oxford Guide to Style for Writers and Editors.* Oxford, England: Oxford University Press.

Rosnow, R. L., & Rosnow, M. (1992). *Papers in psychology.* Belmont, CA: Wadsworth.

Steffens, H. J. & Dickerson, M. J. (1987.) *Writers Guide: History.* Lexington, MA: DC Heath.

Zeigler, Mimi (1991). *Essentials of writing biomedical research papers.* New York: McGraw Hill.

> I think of being a child in my family at the dinner table, with seven kids and hubbub and parents distracted by worries and responsibilities. Before I would say anything at the table, before I would approach my parents, I would plan what I wanted to say. I'd map out the narrative, sharpen the details, add color, plan momentum. This way I could hold their attention. This way I became a writer.
>
> —Peggy Noonan
> *Twentieth century American author*

Second, clarity means writing clearly and logically to clarify vague or complex information. It also involves rewriting stilted sentences and omitting trite expressions.

Clarity relates to coherence, or cohesion, the "glue" that holds your paper together. The topic and summary sentences of paragraphs or sections and transition words build coherence. They help the parts of your paper "stick together."

Writing a research paper, or any paper, is difficult. Some students choose to take composition courses to improve their skills. Others use style manuals to develop better writing styles. Table 10.4 lists such manuals on writing style.

Table 10.4   Guide to Manuals of Writing Style

Ballenger, Bruce. (1997). The curious researcher: A guide to writing research papers, 2nd ed. Boston: Allyn & Bacon.

Campbell, William G. (1990) *Form and style: Theses, reports, term papers.* Boston: Houghton Mifflin.

Chicago manual of style. (1993). 14th ed. Chicago: University of Chicago Press.

Hairston, Maxine (1996). *Scott, Foresman handbook for writers,* 4th ed. New York: HarperCollins College.

Harnack, Andrew (1997). *Writing research papers: A student guide for use with opposing viewpoints,* 2nd ed. San Diego: Greenhaven.

Hodges, J. C., and Whitten, M. E. (1995). *Harbrace college handbook,* 12th ed. New York: Harcourt Brace Jovanovich.

Kramer, M. S. (1995). *Prentice-Hall handbook for writers,* 8th ed. Englewood Cliffs, NJ: Prentice-Hall.

Lester, James D. (11996). *Writing research papers: A complete guide.* New York: HarperCollins College Division.

Meyer, Michael. (1994). *The Little, Brown guide to writing research papers.* New York: HarperCollins College Division.

Ramage, John D., Bean, John C. (1996). *Macmillan Guide to Writing: Brief Edition.* New York: Allyn & Bacon.

Strunk, W. Jr., and White, E. B. (1995). *The elements of style.* New York: Macmillan.

Veit, Richard. (1997). *Research: The student's guide to writing research papers.* New York: Macmillan College Division.

Walker, Melissa. (1997). *Writing research papers: A Norton guide.* New York: Norton.

Weidenhorner, Sharon, and Caruso, Domenick. *Writing research papers: A guide to process Vol 1.* New York: St. Martin's.

Final Revisions

Final revisions consist of editing, rewriting, and polishing your second draft into the final draft. You reread, looking for both structural and grammatical errors. You check the paper's structure by looking at organization and transition. You look at your choice of words and use of details and examples. To check for grammatical errors, you inspect words, sentences, and paragraphs for mistakes in spelling, punctuation, and so forth.

When you select a book to read, does its cover affect your choice? What about the size of the print? Do you consider how well it's packaged? Just as these external factors color your perception about a book, they affect the way your instructor perceives your paper. Your final draft needs to be a revised copy, as error-free as possible. Papers that are neatly written in ink or neatly formatted and printed out receive higher grades than those typed without care. Margins should be wide enough for your instructor's comments. However, they should not be so wide that your instructor suspects that you're padding your work. Your final draft should include a title page, body, references, and any other elements required by your instructor. Table 10.5 is a checklist for locating errors that need correcting. Now, practice your writing skills in Exercises 10.3, 10.4, and 10.5.

WRITE TO LEARN

On a separate sheet of paper or in your journal, explain how the old saying, "Making a silk purse out of a sow's ear" is analogous to writing a research paper.

Table 10.5   Checklist for Revisions

	Revise	Leave as is
1. Structure		
a. Appropriate title	_____	_____
b. Thesis statement	_____	_____
• Purpose		
• Audience appeal		
c. Introductory paragraph(s)	_____	_____
d. Logically organized text	_____	_____
e. Supporting research and examples	_____	_____
f. Summary or concluding paragraph(s)	_____	_____
2. Grammar		
a. Spelling	_____	_____
b. Sentences (complete? run-ons?)	_____	_____
c. Punctuation	_____	_____
d. Paragraphs (indented? topic and summary sentences?)	_____	_____
e. Tense (past, present, future)	_____	_____
f. Subject-verb agreement	_____	_____
3. Style		
a. Conciseness	_____	_____
b. Clarify	_____	_____
c. Cohesion (transition)	_____	_____
d. Word choice	_____	_____
e. Format of footnotes and bibliography (as required by style book of choice)	_____	_____
4. References		
a. Identification of direct quotes or other referenced information	_____	_____
b. Complete citations	_____	_____
c. Relevancy	_____	_____
d. Objectivity	_____	_____
e. Author's qualifications	_____	_____
f. Primary sources	_____	_____
g. Secondary sources	_____	_____
h. Adequate number of references	_____	_____
i. References from a variety of sources	_____	_____
5. Form		
a. Title page	_____	_____
b. Table of contents	_____	_____
c. Abstract	_____	_____
d. Bibliography of references	_____	_____
e. Appendices	_____	_____

Exercise 10.3   On a separate sheet of paper, revise the following paper according to the standard indicated in the checklist in Table 10.5.

COUNTRIES AND THEIR CONSTITUTIONS

A constitution is a statement which outlines the basic principals of formal organizations. Such organizations include countries, political associations, and private groups. A constitution can be written or unwritten. It sets up the way the organization will function in terms of rules and purposes, etc.

The first kind of American Constitution was a document called the Articles of Confederation. It granted freedoms to each state, but this document was inadequate for governing the country. The new country of America faced many problems left unresolved by the Articles. The document did not contain means for getting states to work together. It lacked provisions for an executive branch and a national court system. The Articles of Confederation made no allowances for regulating trade among states. No means for getting taxes.

At first statesman such as George Washington and Alexander Hamilton planned to meet to rewrite the Articles into a stronger document but then they decided to write the Constitution of the United States. A Constitutional Convention got together in 1787. Twelve of the thirteen colonies attended. Only Rhode Island didn't. George Washington was president of the convention.

Fifty-five men attended the convention, but only thirty-nine signed the Constitution. The ones that did not sign disagreed with some of the things it said. But just because these men signed it, it did not represent the wishes of American yet. It had to be voted on and approved by nine states. This kind of approval was called ratification. People who liked the Constitution and supported it were called Federalists. Those that opposed it were Anti-Federalists. These groups formed the basis of the first political parties in the U.S.

The Constitution consist of the preamble, seven articles, and twenty-six amendments. The preamble a short introduction which explains the overall purposes of the Constitution. The Constitution established a federal government which divided power between the states and the national government.

The first three articles establish the branches of the government. So there are three branches of the national government. Including the executive, legislative, and the judicial. The executive branch enforces the laws made by the legislative branch which are explained by the judicial branch. The fifth article provides for future amendments or changes in the Constitution The sixth article concerns the national debt. The fourth article tell how states will relate to each other. The last article tells how the constitution was to be ratified.

After the Constitution was ratified. It was amended by a document called the Bill of Rights. These were the first ten amendments to the Constitution. They protect citizens from unfair governmental acts. In all there have been twenty-six additions or amendments to the Constitutions covering everything from individual freedoms to voting procedures. Everyone agrees that the American Constitution is the best document for running a country.

Exercise 10.4 On a separate sheet of paper, construct a synthesis chart and write a paper comparing and contrasting information found in the four following sources.

Source 1: Education

Television Violence and Behavior: A Research Summary
by Marilyn E. Smith
ERIC/IT Digest, 1993. ED 366 329

Introduction

The National Association for the Education of Young Children (NAEYC) position statement on media violence and children (1990) reports that violence in the media has increased since 1980 and continues to increase, particularly since the Federal Communication Commission's decision to deregulate children's commercial television in 1982. The NAEYC statement cites the following examples:

- Air time for war cartoons increased from 1.5 hours per week in 1982 to 43 hours per week in 1986.
- In 1980, children's programs featured 18.6 violent acts per hour and now have about 26.4 violent acts each hour.

According to an American Psychological Association task force report on television and American society (Huston, et al., 1992), by the time the average child (i.e., one who watches two to four hours of television daily) leaves elementary school, he or she will have witnessed at least 8,000 murders and more than 100,000 other assorted acts of violence on television.

Indicating growing concern regarding the issue of television violence, recent commentaries in the Washington Post (Harwood, 1993; Will, 1993; "Televiolence," 1993) highlight

- a paper by Centerwall (1993) that examines several studies and argues that television violence increases violent and aggressive tendencies in young people and contributes to the growth of violent crime in the United States;
- and a Times Mirror poll, reported in March 1993, that found that the majority of Americans feels that "entertainment television is too violent . . . that this is harmful to society . . . that we as a society have become desensitized to violence."

This digest describes the overall pattern of the results of research on television violence and behavior.

Several variables in the relationship between television violence and aggression related to characteristics of the viewers and to the portrayal of violence are identified. Finally, concerns regarding the effects of television violence are summarized.

Research Findings

The overall pattern of research findings indicates a positive association between television violence and aggressive behavior. A Washington Post article (Oldenburg, 1992), states that "the preponderance of evidence from more than 3,000 research studies over two decades shows that the violence portrayed on television influences the attitudes and behavior of children who watch it." Signorielli (1991) finds that: "Most of the scientific evidence . . . reveals a relationship between television and aggressive behavior. While few would say that there is absolute proof that watching television caused aggressive behavior, the overall cumulative weight of all the studies gives credence to the position that they are related. Essentially, television violence is one of the things that may lead to aggressive, antisocial, or criminal behavior; it does, however, usually work in conjunction with other factors. As aptly put by Don and Kovaric (1980), television violence may influence 'some of the people some of the time'" (pp. 94-95).

Characteristics of Viewers

The following characteristics of viewers, summarized by Clapp (1988), have been shown to affect the influence of television violence on behavior.

- *Age.* "A relationship between television violence and aggression has been observed in children as young as 3 (Singer & Singer, 1981). Longitudinal data suggest that the relationship is much more consistent and substantial for children in middle childhood than at earlier ages (Eron and Huesmann, 1986). Aggression in early adulthood is also related to the amount of violence watched in middle childhood, although it is not related to the amount

(continues)

Exercise 10.4   *Continued*

watched in early adulthood (Eron, Huesmann, Lefkowitz, & Walder, 1972). It has been proposed that there is a sensitive period between ages 8 and 12 during which children are particularly susceptible to the influence of television violence (Eron & Huesmann, 1986)" (pp. 64-65).

- *Amount of television watched* "Aggressive behavior is related to the total amount of television watched, not only to the amount of violent television watched. Aggressive behavior can be stimulated also by frenetic, hectic programming that creates a high level of arousal in children (Eron & Huesmann, 1986; Wright & Huston, 1983)" (p. 65).

- *Identification with television personalities.* "Especially for boys, identification with a character substantially increases the likelihood that the character's aggressive behavior will be modeled (Huesmann & Eron, 1986; Huesmann, Lagerspetz, & Eron, 1984)" (p. 65).

- *Belief that television violence is realistic.* "Significant relationships have been found between children's belief that television violence is realistic, their aggressive behavior, and the amount of violence that they watch (Huesmann, 1986; Huesmann & Eron, 1986)" (p. 65).

- *Intellectual achievement* "Children of lower intellectual achievement generally (1) watch more television, (2) watch more violent television, (3) believe violent television reflects real life, and (4) behave more aggressively (Huesmann, 1986)" (p. 65).

Comstock and Paik (1987, 1991) also identify the following factors that may increase the likelihood of television influence:

- Viewers who are in a state of anger or provocation before seeing a violent portrayal.

- Viewers who are in a state of frustration after viewing a violent portrayal, whether from an extraneous source or as a consequence of viewing the portrayal.

Portrayal of Violence

The following are factors related to how the violence is portrayed which may heighten the likelihood of television influence. Research on these factors is summarized by Comstock and Paik (1987, 1991):

- Reward or lack of punishment for the portrayed perpetrator of violence.

- Portrayal of the violence as justified.

- Cues in the portrayal of violence that resemble those likely to be encountered in real life. For example, a victim in the portrayal with the same name or characteristics as someone towards whom the viewer holds animosity.

- Portrayal of the perpetrator of violence as similar to the viewer.

- Violence portrayed so that its consequences do not stir distaste or arouse inhibitions.

- Violence portrayed as real events rather than events concocted for a fictional film.

- Portrayed violence that is not the subject of critical or disparaging commentary.

- Portrayals of violent acts that please the viewer

- Portrayals in which violence is not interrupted by violence in a light or humorous vein.

- Portrayed abuse that includes physical violence and aggression instead of or in addition to verbal abuse

- Portrayals, violent or otherwise, that leave the viewer in a state of unresolved excitement.

Comstock and Paik (1991) argue that "these contingencies represent four dimensions: (a) efficacy (reward or lack of punishment); (b) normativeness (justified, consequenceless, intentionally hurtful, physical violence); (c) pertinence (commonality of cues, similarity to the viewer, absence of humorous violence); and (d) susceptibility (pleasure, anger, frustration, absence of criticism)" (pp. 255–256).

Concerns

Three major areas of concern regarding the effects of television violence are identified and discussed by the National Association for the Education of Young Children (1990):

1. Children may become less sensitive to the pain and suffering of others.

2. They may be more likely to behave in aggressive or harmful ways toward others.

3. They may become more fearful of the world around them.

Of these, Signorielli (1991) considers the third scenario to be the most insidious: "Research...has revealed that violence on television plays an important role in communicating the social order and in leading to

(continues)

Exercise 10.4 *Continued*

perceptions of the world as a mean and dangerous place. Symbolic victimization on television and real world fear among women and minorities, even if contrary to the facts, are highly related (Morgan, 1983). Analysis also reveals that in most subgroups those who watch more television tend to express a heightened sense of living in a mean world of danger and mistrust as well as alienation and gloom" (p. 96).

Another concern addressed by the National Association for the Education of Young Children (1990) is the negative effect on children's play of viewing violent television: "In short, children who are frequent viewers of media violence learn that aggression is a successful and acceptable way to achieve goals and solve problems; they are less likely to benefit from creative, imaginative play as the natural means to express feelings, overcome anger, and gain self-control" (p. 19).

References

Centerwall, B. S. (1993). Television and violent crime. *The Public Interest*, 111, pp. 56-77.

Clapp, G. (1988). *Child Study Research: Current Perspectives and Applications*. Lexington, MA: Lexington.

Comstock, G. & Paik, H. (1987). *Television and Children: A Review of Recent Research*. Syracuse, NY: ERIC Clearinghouse on Information Resources. (ED 292 466).

Comstock, G. & Pink, H. (1991). *Television and the American Child*. San Diego, CA: Academic.

Dorr, A. & Kovaric, P. (1980). Some of the people some of the time—But which people? In E. L. Palmer & A. Dorr (eds.), *Children and the Faces of Television: Teaching, Violence, Selling* (pp. 183-199). New York: Academic.

Eron, L. D. & Huesmann, L. R. (1986). The role of television in the development of prosocial and antisocial behavior. In D. Olweus, J. Block, & M. Radke-Yarrow (eds.), *The Development of Antisocial and Prosocial Behavior: Research, Theories, and Issues*. New York: Academic.

Eron, L. D., Huesmann, L. R., Lefkowitz, M. M., & Walder, L. D. (1972). Does television violence cause aggression? *American Psychologist*, 27, 253-63.

Harwood, R. (1993, April 17). Is TV to blame for violence? *Washington Post*, p. A23.

Huesmann, L. R. (1986). Psychological processes promoting the relation between exposure to media violence and aggressive behavior by the viewer. *Journal of Social Issues*, 42, 125-139. (EJ 355 099)

Huesmann, L. R. & Eron, L. D. (1986). *Television and the Aggressive Child: A Cross-National Comparison*. Hillsdale, NJ: Erlbaum.

Huesmann, L. R., Lagerspetz, K., & Eron, L. D. (1984). Intervening variables in the TV violence-aggression relation: Evidence from two countries. *Developmental Psychology*, 20(5), 746-777. (EJ 308 850)

Huston, A. C., Donnerstein, E., Fairchild, H., Fashbach, N. D., Katz, P. A., Murray, J. P., Rubinstein, E. A., Wilcox, B. L., Zuckerman, D., (1992). *Big World, Small Screen: The Role of Television in American Society*. Lincoln, NE: University of Nebraska.

Morgan, M. (1983). Symbolic victimization and real-world fear. *Human Communication Research*, 9(2), 146-157. (EJ 272 383)

National Association for the Education of Young Children. (1990). NAEYC position statement on media violence in children's lives. *Young Children*, 45(5), 18-21. (EJ 415 397)

Oldenburg, D. (1992, April 7). Primal screen-kids: TV violence and real-life behavior. *Washington Post* p. E5.

Signorielli, N. (1991). *A Sourcebook on Children and Television*. New York: Greenwood.

Singer, J. L., & Singer, D. G. (1981). *Television, Imagination and Aggression: A Study of Preschoolers*. Hillsdale, NJ: Erlbaum.

Televiolence. (1993, April 17). *Washington Post* p. A22.

Will, G. F. (1993, April 8). Yes, blame TV. *Washington Post*, p. A21.

Wright, J. C. & Huston, A. C. (1983). A matter of form: Potentials of television for young viewers. *American Psychologist*, 38, 835- 843. (EJ 283 455).

SOURCE: Marilyn E. Smith is Database Coordinator, ERIC Clearinghouse on Information & Technology, Syracuse University. December 1993. ERIC Digests are in the public domain and may be freely reproduced and disseminated. This publication was prepared with funding from the Office of Educational Research and Improvement, U.S. Department of Education, under contract no. RI88062008. The opinions expressed in this report do not necessarily reflect the positions or policies of OERI or ED. ERIC Clearinghouse on Information & Technology, Syracuse University, 4-194 Center for Science and Technology, Syracuse, NY 13244-4100, (800) 464-9107, ericir@ericir.syr.edu.

(continues)

Exercise 10.4 *Continued*

Source 2 : Psychology

The Tube as Teacher?

Focus: Does television promote observational learning

The impact of TV can be found in these figures: By the time the average person has graduated from high school, she or he will have viewed some 15,000 hours of TV, compared with only 11,000 hours spent in the classroom. In that time, such viewers will have seen some 18,000 murders and countless acts of robbery, arson, bombing, torture, and beatings. It's true that TV programming in the United States has improved somewhat during the last decade. Overall. however, violent acts. dynamite blasts, gun battles, high-speed car wrecks, stereotypes, and sexism still prevail (Kubey & Csikszentmihaly, 1990). Children watching Saturday morning cartoons see a chilling 26 or more violent acts each hour (Pogatchnik, 1990). Teenage mutant ninja turtles, indeed!

Life after TV

What effect does the North American penchant for TV watching have on behavior? To answer this question, a team of researchers found a town in northwestern Canada that did not receive TV broadcasts. Discovering that time town was about to get TV, the team seized a rare opportunity. Tannis Williams and her colleagues carefully tested residents of time town just before TV arrived and again 2 years later. This natural experiment *revealed* that after the tube came to town:

- Reading development among children declined (Corteen & Williams, 1986).
- Children's scores on tests of creativity dropped (Harrison & Williams, 1986).
- Children's perceptions of sex roles became more stereotyped (Kimball, 1986).
- There was a significant increase in both verbal and physical aggression.

This occurred for both boys and girls, and it applied equally to children who were high or low in aggression before they began watching TV (Joy et al., 1986).

Televised Aggression. The last finding comes as no surprise. At this point, hundreds of studies involving well over 10,000 children, have been completed. The vast majority point to the same conclusion: "If large groups of children watch a great deal of televised violence, they will be more prone to behave aggressively" (Heath, Bresolin, & Rinaldi, 1989; Joy et al., 1986; Levinger, 1986; National Institute of Mental Health, 1982). Inn other words, not all children will become more aggressive, but many will. Incidentally, the same conclusion applies to violent video games (Schutte et al., 1988).

Is it fair to say, then, that televised violence causes aggression inn viewers, especially children? Fortunately, that would be an exaggeration. Televised violence can make aggression more *likely,* but it does not invariably "cause" it to occur (Freedman, 1984; Levinger, 1986). Many other factors affect the chances that hostile thoughts will be turned into actions (Berkowitz, 1984). Among children, one such factor is the extent to which a child *identifies* with aggressive characters (Huesmann et al., 1983). That's why it is so sad to find TV *heroes* behaving aggressively, as well as villains.

A recent study investigated the effects on children's aggressive behavior of a popular children's TV program, *The Mighty Morphin Power Rangers.* In each episode, the "Power Rangers" "morph" into super-heroes who use karate and other violent actions to conquer monsters. The study found that after watching an episode of the Power Rangers, a group of 7-year-old children committed 7 times more aggressive acts than a control group that did not watch the program. The aggressive children hit, kicked, and karate—chopped their peers, often directly imitating the "Power Rangers" (Boyatzis, Matillo, & Nesbitt, 1995).

Youngsters who believe that aggression is an acceptable way to solve problems, who believe that TV portrayals of violence are realistic, and who identify with TV characters are most likely to copy televised aggression (Eron, 1986). Inn view of such findings, t is understandable that Canada, Norway, and Switzerland have restricted the amount of permissible violence on television (Levinger, 1986). Should all countries do the same?

Conclusion. Watching televised violence does not directly cause aggression but it can increase the likelihood that a person will behave aggressively.

SOURCE: Coon, D. (1997). *Essentials of pyschology,* 7th ed. (pp. 312–313). Pacific Grove, CA: Brooks/Cole.

(continues)

Exercise 10.4   *Continued*

Source 3: Economics

Children's Advertising

Studies show that the role children play in consumer decision making in our economy is rapidly expanding. A 1994 estimate put the **discretionary spending** (spending for products that are not necessities) of the 52 million American children who were under age 14 at more than $15 billion a year. Additional discretionary spending by adults on products for these children pushed the total well over $100 billion. When the cost of necessary products like food, clothing, furniture, and education were included, the total reached over half a trillion dollars. Further, it was estimated that this type of spending was growing at about 8 percent a year, a rate much faster than for almost any other part of the American consumer products market.

It is hard to say exactly why spending on products intended for children is growing so rapidly. One possibility is that as we have more families where two parents work and more single-parent homes, children are staying by themselves more often. Parents may be giving their children more money and buying them more products to keep them busy or to try to make them feel better about being alone. Others are convinced that a good part of this growth is the result of more successful advertising that increases children's demand for products and preys on parents' insecurities or inadequacies (if you don't buy your child the latest toy, you must not love them enough).

Although most purchase decisions for children's products are made by adults, children almost always influence those choices. How often have you heard children demand particular brands of breakfast cereal or soft drinks in a grocery store? How often do their parents give in to such demands? The impact of children on consumer spending far exceeds the few billion dollars they spend themselves.

The fact that children are an important force in our economy has not been lost on businesses that manufacture and market products. In 1994 expenditures for advertising directed to children approached a total of $550 million.[1] These advertisements presented American consumers with important economic and ethical choices to make.

Why Businesses Advertise to Children

The most apparent reason for directing advertising to children is the influence they have over their parents' spending. For example, the average American consumed almost 12 pounds of ready-to-eat breakfast cereal in 1994. If we assume that every child tinder 14 ate this average amount of cereal, then we can estimate that these 52 million children consumed over 600 million pounds of cereal. The market value of this cereal alone was over $1.5 billion. It is not surprising that cereal producers direct much of their advertising to children. Other businesses direct advertising to children in an attempt to establish **brand loyalty** that they hope will last as the children mature. Their reasoning is that children who become accustomed to drinking a particular type of soda, or to wearing a special brand of shoes when they are young, will continue to purchase and use these products as adults. This is probably one reason why such a large portion of McDonald's advertising is directed toward young people. Ronald McDonald may appeal only to children, but people who get used to eating McDonald's food as children are likely to continue to purchase these products as adults.

There are even some firms that sell no products intended for children but still buy advertising directed to children. This may seem to be a contradiction, but marketing experts say it will pay off in the long run. Delta Air Lines, for example, has purchased advertising that is oriented to children's interests even though few children will purchase airline tickets until they are adults. The firm hopes to create an awareness of its business products in children that will let them fly Delta as adults. Hyatt Hotels also advertise to children apparently for the same reason. IBM and Apple Computers have provided free equipment to schools and directed advertising to children. Although few children are in a position to purchase the computers IBM and Apple manufacture, children can influence their parent's spending decisions and may develop a lasting desire for these brands of computers when they become adults.

---

1. Bryan Kim Junu, "For Kids, It's a Fast Spinning Real World," *Advertising Age*, February 14, 1994, pp. S-1 S—10.

(continues)

Exercise 10.4   *Continued*

Selling Children Adult Products

The most rapid growth in children's advertising in the early 1990s was children's versions of products that are more often consumed by adults. For example, Gregory's boys' cologne was marketed for $15.50 an ounce, using an advertisement that shows a 4-year-old splashing the product on his neck. Other brands of children's toiletries that have been marketed include Radical Hair Stuff (for $3.00), Environmental Protection Cream ($16.50), and Fun and Fresh deodorant (for $2.50). It is doubtful that children need any of these products.

Marketers also try to appeal to children's desire to be older when they advertise children's clothing. In 1994, market research expert James McNeal stated "One of the things children learn very quickly, by first grade, is they can buy and/or wear designer brands similar in name to those of adult brands and obtain some level of distinction." He remembers meeting with a group of fourth-graders and asking them to draw pictures of themselves shopping for clothing. Several of the children were aware enough of designer names to include them on the clothes in their drawings.

Much of children's clothing advertising is directed to parents. Marian Salzman, president of BKG Youth (a market research firm) said, "It's an adult market. Parents who are buying these fashions are parents who use department stores as a source of entertainment." A survey carried out by *Kids Fashion,* a fashion industry publication, indicated that 64 percent of parents believe it is important for their children to gain status from wearing brand-name clothing. The *cost* of such products to consumers can be seen in the success of products like $180 DKNY pea coats for preteens that sold out in the weeks just before Christmas in 1994.[2]

Another class of goods frequently promoted to children is electronic products. Sanyo markets a child-size "mini-vac" so kids can "clean up your mess by yourself." The Little Operator Easy Dialer Picture Phone sells for $50 and may be programmed to dial numbers by pushing the picture of a person children want to call. This product allows even two- or three-year-olds to use a telephone. Digital watches and hand-held electronic games add to the list of products children are encouraged to demand.

Advertisements often encourage children to demand products that are unnecessary or too expensive for their family's budgets. This raises an ethical question for society: Since children lack the knowledge and critical thinking skills to analyze advertisements and make rational consumer choices, should limitations be placed on the content or form of advertising that is directed toward them?

Increased Pressure and Adult Responsibilities

Many adults have expressed resentment to marketers and the government for the impact children's advertising has had on their lives. The more products that are advertised to children, the more often the parents are forced to say "no." Many adults believe that children's advertising encourages children to grow up too rapidly, to become materialistic, and to develop lifestyles and relationships better suited to adults. These are some of the reasons why some parents have pressured the government to limit the advertising that may be directed to children or placed on television shows watched primarily by young people.

Other people support children's advertising by saying it provides parents an opportunity to teach their children values and how to use buying strategies. Some people have gone so far as to suggest that parents should provide children with control over a share of their family's food or clothing budget so they may learn how to be responsible consumers. Although there is a value to teaching children good spending habits, many people believe these ideas are little more than rationalization by advertisers to justify their current practices.

In 1995 the typical American child watched nearly 26 hours of TV programming a week. During this time that child was exposed to an average of over 500 commercials, or a total of 4 hours and 10 minutes of advertising. This amount of advertising certainly affected the desires and judgment of many children. It probably made them want more products, and many of the products they were encouraged to want probably did not represent a good use for their family's limited income.

Parents faced with their children's demands for more, and often expensive, products of questionable value are left with essentially three choices. They may choose to give in and buy as many of the products as they can afford. They may simply ignore their children's demands and spend their money as they see fit. Or they can take the time to explain to their children why certain products are not

---

2. Adrienne Ward Fawcett, "Sunday Best Becoming More of a Daily Ritual," *Advertising Age,* February 14, 1994, p. S-10.

(continues)

Exercise 10.4   *Continued*

the best ways to spend the family income. Obviously, the last alternative involves the most time and effort.

Even young children can be taught to distinguish between reality and advertising hype. When questioned, a three-year-old will usually be able to explain that the plastic model that flies unaided through the air to destroy the invading slime people in a TV advertisement will need to be held in their hands when they use it at home. Children can be taught that phrases like "each part sold separately," "some assembly required," or "batteries not included," mean that what they see is not what they get. Sometimes it is worthwhile to show children how much of their favorite type of food could be purchased with the price of a single toy that they will use for a day and then discard. Many children can understand simple cost–benefit explanations.

Consumers Union has produced a videotape called "Buy Me That: A Kid's Survival Guide to TV Advertising" that may be borrowed from many libraries. This entertaining tape shows how TV commercials employ double meanings and special photography to mislead young consumers. *Zillions* is a worthwhile consumer magazine for children that is also published by the Consumers Union. At $16 a year it is not cheap, but if it saves a child from making one bad purchase a year it may pay for itself. A final strategy parents can use to help their children make better consumer decisions is to require them to give three logical reasons for buying a product they want. Statements like "I want it" would not be acceptable; the child would have to explain the product's value.

Government Intervention

Although federal government regulations do not satisfy many critics, steps have been taken to put some limitations on the amount of advertising directed to children. Congress passed a law in *1990* that directed the Federal Communications Commission (FCC) to draw up regulations for this type of advertising. In 1991, to comply with this law, the FCC announced that TV programming directed to children could contain no more than 12 minutes of advertising per hour on weekdays, and 10½ minutes on weekends. In addition, TV stations were required to summarize the advertising they aired directed to children in the applications for license renewals. At this time, members of the community served by the TV stations would have the right to make complaints. Although this law limited the amount of advertising that could he directed to children, it did nothing to control advertising content or the type of products that could be promoted.

Many people feel the time limits established under this law are inadequate. Other regulations that have been suggested but not implemented include eliminating advertisements for food products that contain large amounts of sugar or fats. Many people would stop programming that features commercial products based on characters like GI Joe and Power Rangers. There is even pressure from some organizations to adopt a policy similar to that of the French government that outlaws the use of children in any television advertising. It is likely, however, that for the foreseeable future, American children and their parents will be subjected to a continuing barrage of advertising that they will need to evaluate for themselves.

Children's TV and the Decision-Making Process

Many American families experience a running battle between parents and children over the amount of time the children may spend watching television. Many parents set rules that allow children a set amount of viewing time each week or each day. Other common rules involve not watching television until all homework or household chores are completed, or as a reward for some desired behavior. When parents' rules are broken, possible reactions range from a loss of TV privileges for a period of time, through loss of allowance, to getting rid of the cable service or even the television altogether. Surveys show that in most American families, children (at least those under 13) are not consulted when TV-watching rules are created. If you were the head of a family with several young children, how might you use the decision-making process presented in Chapter 3 to establish rules for watching television that your children would follow with a minimum of dissent and the least possible difficulty for you? Would your family's decision be influenced by the amount and kinds of children's advertising on television?

Terms

BRAND LOYALTY. A willingness by consumers to purchase a particular brand of product without seriously considering alternative brands.

DISCRETIONARY SPENDING. Spending for goods and services that are not necessities.

SOURCE: Miller, L. M., and Stafford, A. D. (1997). *Economic issues for consumers,* 8th ed. (pp. 116–118) Belmont, CA: Wadsworth.

(continues)

Exercise 10.4   *Continued*

Source 4: Journalism

Children's Viewing Habits

Many studies about children and television, such as the National Institute of Mental Health report, have concentrated on the effects of portrayals of violence. But in 1981, a California study suggested a link between television viewing and poor school performance.

The California Assessment Program (CAP), which tests academic achievement, included a new question on the achievement test: "On a typical weekday, about how many hours do you watch TV?" The students than were given a choice ranging from zero to 6 or more hours.

An analysis of the answers from more than 10,000 sixth graders to that question was matched with the children's scores on the achievement test. The results suggested a consistent relationship between viewing time and achievement. Students who said they watched a lot of television scored lower in reading, writing, and mathematics than students who didn't watch any television. The average scores for students who said they viewed 6 or more hours of television a day were 6 to 8 points lower than for those children who said they watched less than a half-hour of television a day.

Because the study didn't include information about the IQ score or income levels of these students, the results cannot be considered conclusive. The study simply may show that children who watch a lot of television aren't studying. But the results are particularly interesting because of the number of children who were included in the survey.

Further research could examine whether children are poor students because they watch a lot of television or whether children who watch a lot of television are poor students for other reasons.

SOURCE: Biagi, Shirley (1995). *Media/impact: An introduction to mass media,* 3rd ed. Belmont, CA: Wadsworth.

Exercise 10.5   Create a synthesis chart and write a paper addressing a topic of your choice that integrates the content of two or more sample chapters with references in your campus library.

Plagiarism

Plagiarism (see Chapter 1) is stealing another person's work and presenting it as your own. Plagiarism comes in two forms: unintentional and intentional. Unintentional, or accidental, plagiarism occurs through inaccurate notetaking or through incorrect citation of references. Intentional plagiarism is deliberate, premeditated theft of published information. Intentional plagiarism also includes getting a paper from a friend or "term paper service." The article reprinted in Excerpt 10.1 describes the hazards of buying term papers.

When you plagiarize, you run the risk of disciplinary action. You avoid plagiarism by carefully noting and documenting reference materials.

Excerpt 10.1   Buying a Term Paper Could Turn Out to Be the First Step to Academic Bankruptcy

Tired of typing? Is your research wretched? When term paper trauma sets in, call us! 15,483 papers to choose from. All subjects from Anthropology to Zoology. Call Researchers to the Rescue now! 555–3211.

The end of the semester. It's 3:00 in the morning. You've already gone through two pots of coffee and a box and a half of cookies. Your eyes are bloodshot. You've been staring at that blank sheet of paper so long you've memorized the number of lines.

Worst of all, you still don't know what you're going to write for your Econ paper.

When academic deadlines have you stressed out, an ad like the one above could have you dialing in desperation. But, beware! Before you send up an S.O.S. to "Researchers to the Rescue," consider what happened to Suzy B.

"I went to an organization that advertised in the classified section of the campus paper," she confessed. "Since I had a paper due on one of Shakespeare's plays, which is a pretty universal topic, I figured they could whip out a great essay. At $10 a page, it was worth its weight in gold for the amount of aggravation it saved me. It was worth gold until I showed it to a friend of mine who went to the same place last semester and found parts of her paper in mine!"

Although Suzy's lack of originality went unnoticed, her story points out one of the major hazards of buying a term paper. The biggest risk, of course, is getting caught at what clearly is cheating. We'll deal with that biggie in a moment, but it's not the only risk. Another is being accused of plagiarism.

For instance, let's say the one paper you choose out of the fifteen written on Shakespeare was submitted to your prof by another student last semester. Your professor might spot this repeat or even discover your paper contains a few lines of famous criticism copied verbatim.

Other things can go wrong. You always run the risk that the style of a purchased paper will clash with the rest of your semester's work. When you suddenly start sounding like Hemingway, your professor will notice. And you might find that you can do a better job yourself.

"Often the papers aren't that good," one student pointed out. "The companies that write these papers don't know the focus of the course or the teacher's expectations. I paid $120 for a 10-pager and only got a C+."

Which brings up another issue: cost. Any paper longer than a few pages is a costly investment for a questionable return. At $10–$12 a page, wouldn't it be better to do the research yourself and spend the money on the finer things in life?

The biggest hazard, of course, is getting caught. One university alone reported fifteen cases last year. If you do get caught, the price is a lot more than just a slap on the hand.

Robert Brooks, Associate Dean of Students at the University of Massachusetts, warns, "Not only is it in violation of our code of student conduct, but in Massachusetts it is a statutory offense to sell plagiarized goods, punishable by fine and imprisonment."

Care to know the procedure you'll go through if you're caught plagiarizing? Robert Mannes, Dean for Student Life at the University of Southern California, says that the faculty member who teaches the course the student is enrolled in makes the initial decision. "For a paper that doesn't count as a major portion of the course grade, the student will usually receive an *F* for the paper alone, particularly if it's a first offense. However, if the paper is more heavily weighted in the course, if it is a student's second offense or if the degree of plagiarism is severe, then the student will usually receive an F in the course and go before a review board."

Proving plagiarism, Mannes continues, can be tough. "If we're not sure if a paper has been plagiarized, we'll compare it to the catalog from one of these organizations. In one case, the student didn't even change the title of the paper!"

Okay, okay. So you're smart enough to change the title. What else can happen?

At the University of Arizona, a charge of plagiarism is also worked out as much as possible between faculty member and student. However, if the case does go through a formal committee hearing (profs and peers present), several things can happen.

According to Dean Glenn Smith, Administrator of the Code of Academic Integrity, "the student can be suspended for a semester or more, expelled from the university altogether, have an academic dishonesty clause placed on his transcripts or be refused a degree from that particular department."

While writing a paper on the imagery and style of Shakespearean tragedy might take a lot of effort on your

(continues)

Excerpt 10.1   *Continued*

part, the alternative of buying a paper can take a lot more out of you. Getting caught will not only contribute to the decline of that GPA you worked so hard for, but will cause a lot of embarrassment. It may also bias the teacher against the rest of the work you do in that class.

And, in the end, you have to live with the fact that you compromised your integrity by taking credit for someone else's work.

The risks are real. So, even if it takes two typewriter ribbons, three pots of coffee and forsaking your cherished sleep, work until you rip your hair out and write your own paper.

SOURCE: Reprinted with permission from "Buying Term Papers," by Gina Gross. Copyright © 1986 by *College Woman Magazine*.

CLASSIC CRITICAL THINKING

What is . . . and isn't . . . academic honesty? Consider each of the following situations. On a separate sheet of paper or in your journal, identify whether or not you believe each of the following situations to be a form of cheating and describe your rationale for your belief.

1. You are writing a research paper for a class. The staff of your college's writing center assists you with the development of the topic and questions of grammar.

2. You are taking a psychology course in which you must write a research paper on a topic of your choice. Luckily, you took a literature course last year in which you analyzed the characters of a play from psychological perspectives. With a little editing, you can use that paper for this semester's course.

3. A member of your study group broke an arm so you volunteered to type a paper for him. As you type, you find a number of

grammatical and spelling errors. Kindly, you make the corrections for him.

4. You are typing a research paper for yourself. You use your computer's spell-check and grammar-check features to correct your work.

5. You are taking several courses this semester that require you to write research papers and you are pressed for time. You find that the same research you are collecting for a paper in American history can also be used as the basis of a different paper in political science.

6. You are taking several courses this semester that require you to write research papers and you are pressed for time. You find that by titling your paper "The History of Political Parties in Nineteenth-Century America," you can use the same paper for your American History class and your political science class.

WRITE TO LEARN

Consider Excerpt 10.1. On a separate sheet of paper or in your journal, describe the hazards of buying term papers. Identify other implications of buying term papers.

Avoiding the "I'm-Over-My-Head" Feeling: Setting a Writing Schedule

All authors experience the "I'm-over-my-head-and-this-time-they're-going-to-catch-me" feeling. Knowing what's involved in writing a paper helps you avoid the writer's block that comes with this feeling. Table 10.6 outlines the writing process.

Once you know the process of writing a research paper, you realize that you cannot write a paper in a day or a week. Avoiding the "I'm-over-my-head-and-this-time-they're-going-to-catch-me" feeling involves scheduling enough time to complete the writing process. Setting specific objectives and completion dates helps you budget time and make the best use of resources.

Table 10.6   Steps in Writing a Research Paper

1 Identify type of paper
   a. Theme essay
   b. Report
   c. Term paper
   d. Research paper

2. Determine format of paper
   a. Title page
   b. Table of contents
   c. Abstract
   d. Body
   e. References
   f. Appendices

3. Select subject
   a. Identify interest and importance of topic
   b. Estimate availability of library resources

4. Narrow subject into management topic
   a. Establish purpose of paper
   b. Set scope of paper
      • *Write thesis statement*
      • *Select title*

5. Gather sources
   a. Library research
   b. Observation
   c. Interviews
   d. Personal experience
   e. Personal inferences

6. Evaluate sources
   a. Determine primary sources
   b. Judge relevancy
   c. Estimate objectivity and bias
   d. Evaluate author's qualifications

7. Avoid plagiarism

8. Synthesize sources
   a. Outline
   b. Chart
   c. Revise thesis statement and/or title

9. Write first (rough) draft
   a. Introduction
   b. Text
      • Determine organizational pattern
      • Select style manual
   c. Summary

10. Write second draft
    a. Check style
    b. Make final revisions

Rationale for a Writing Schedule

You need a writing schedule for several reasons. First, research takes time in what is probably a full schedule of academic, personal, and perhaps work commitments. Without a time line for beginning, continuing, and completing your research, your paper might not reflect the quality of work you wish.

Second, the resources you need might not be readily available. Interlibrary loans help you obtain materials that are not part of the library's holdings. If a book you need is checked out, you can ask the library to request that it be returned as soon as possible. Copy machines might be out of order, preventing you from obtaining information for later study. Whatever the case, you need to plan for such delays.

Finally, you need time to reflect on the information you gather. This time gives you opportunities to consider your information in different ways and get fresh perspectives. Such reflection helps you determine the commonalties of your ideas and your organizational structure.

Setting a Writing Schedule

Suppose that on the first day of class your instructor says that a research paper will be due at mid-term. Your first task in completing this assignment would be to set a writing schedule. Table 10.7 lists the steps in setting a schedule.

Table 10.7 Setting a Writing Schedule

Using your term calendar, mark the following dates:

1. Due date for the paper.
2. If the paper needs to be typed, identify a completion date for getting your final draft to a word processor, whether you or someone else is typing the paper. You might have to call a word processor and reserve time if your final due date is close to midterm, finals, or other busy times in the term. Determine how the length of your paper will affect the time it will take to be typed.
3. Your personal due date for the final draft. Leave ample time for typing or rewriting your draft.
4. Your personal due date for completing a rough draft. The rough draft should be completed approximately 10 days to two weeks before the final due date.
5. Due date for completing your research. Allow time to evaluate and synthesize your sources before beginning your rough draft. Your research should be completed approximately two-and-a-half to three weeks before the due date.
6. Due date for beginning your research. This should be the day the research paper is assigned. Within the first week, you should determine the type and format of the paper, select a subject, and narrow your subject into a manageable topic.

Modify the steps according to your own research and writing strengths or weaknesses. If you are familiar with your library's holdings and your subject, you might complete your task more quickly. If you lack such background information, your task will probably take more time. If writing comes easily to you, you might not require as much time. On the other hand, if writing is difficult for you, you need to budget extra time.

In most procedures, you begin at the beginning. Here you begin at both the beginning and the end. You begin at the beginning by setting your schedule as soon as a research paper is assigned. You begin at the end by plotting the activities you need to complete in relationship to the paper's final due date.

ONLINE CLASS   ## Web Exercise 10.1

A variety of information related to the topics in this chapter is available on the World Wide Web. For this exercise, access one of the following Web sites (go to http://csuccess.wadsworth.com for the most up-to-date URLs) and respond to the following:

Any article or resource from the Purdue University Writing Lab Writing-Related Resources: On Line Resources or Handouts on Writing Skills:

> http:owl.english.purdue.edu/writers/introduction.html

Any article or resource from any Writing Center Web Page from *Other Writing Center Web Pages* (University of Northern British Columbia):

> http://quarles.unbc.edu/lsc/other-handouts.html

Any article or resource from Roane State Community College Online Writing Lab:

> http://www2.rscc.cc.tn.us/~jordan_jj/OWL/owl.html

Any article or resource from Write Your Way to a Higher GPA: Indispensable Writing Resources (Stetson University):

> http://www.stetson.edu/~rhansen/writing.html

1. Which Web site did you choose? _____

2. Summarize the content of the Web site on a separate sheet of paper or in your journal.

3. Why did you choose the Web site? _____
_____

4. What new information did you learn about writing? _____
_____
_____

5. How can you apply that information to your next research paper?_____
_____
_____

Now Showing:
Making Presentations and Speeches

How do you feel about giving a speech or presentation in a class? If the idea of making a speech strikes a bit of fear in your heart, you're not alone. Most people rank giving speeches as being almost as frightening as being physically assaulted or as the prospect of surgery. Although the context of Roosevelt's statement was World War II, it applies to giving speeches today.

The content of your paper, with some modifications, forms the basis of your speech or presentation. As in any good paper, your speech should begin with an introduction that tells the audience what you intend to tell them. The text of your paper forms the body of your speech. Your summary and conclusions tell the audience what you said.

The careful work you invested in your research paper forms a solid foundation that allows you to make presentations and speeches with confidence. For most people, speechmaking is a learned skill that improves with practice. Developing a good speech, like developing a good paper, involves a number of steps, which require time and effort. If you follow the practical suggestions for making speeches and presentations listed in Table 10.8 you will have nothing to fear when you make your next speech in class. You can practice your skills in Exercises 10.6 and 10.7.

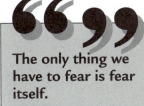

The only thing we have to fear is fear itself.

—Franklin Delano Roosevelt
Twentieth century American president

Table 10.8   Suggestions for Making Speeches and Presentations

Before giving a speech or presentation, you should . . .

1. **Identify with your audience.** Although the content of your paper dictates the content of your speech to some degree, the tone of your speech should match that of the audience in terms of vocabulary and background knowledge. Avoid using jargon, or specialized or technical vocabulary. Use examples you think apply to the audience or that bridge the gap between your knowledge level and theirs. As others in the class give their presentations, listen and watch carefully to determine how it feels to be in the audience, what appeals to members of the audience, and what fails to appeal to them. Consider involving the audience by asking a question or using a short activity.

2. **Structure your content.** The organization of a speech or presentation must be clear, obvious, and simple because the listening audience has no way to see the overall structure of information or visually review what you've said.

3. **Recreate your information.** Although you might have to turn in your speech for credit, you need to modify its form to facilitate presentation. At the very least, you might want to enlarge the print size of your speech, highlight important points, or note ideas to emphasize. Some people transfer main points of their speech to note cards or create concept maps to organize ideas graphically.

4. **Show them what you're going to tell them.** The saying "one picture is worth a thousand words," applies to presentations as well as art. Diagrams, photos, models, and actual items add interest because they give the audience something to see as well as hear. Some individuals use overhead transparencies so they can face the audience as they provide text and graphic information. Today's speechmakers often create electronic presentations with computer graphics and multimedia or presentation software. Your campus media center

(continues)

Table 10.8   *Continued*

or computer center can help you devise visuals to accompany your speeches and presentations. Whatever visuals you choose, they should be eye-catching as well as accurate, legible from the back of the room, clear, simple, and neat.

5. **Practice.** Although some people believe practice makes perfect, practice actually makes permanent. The way you rehearse contributes to your final performance; thus, visualize yourself doing well. Envisioning worst-case scenarios often becomes a self-fulfilling prophecy because you rehearse them so often and so well. As you begin rehearsing your speech, practice it aloud to check for inadvertent tongue twisters and other aspects of verbal style. Verbal rehearsals also help in timing because you read silently more quickly than you speak. Gain familiarity with the manuscript, but don't over-rehearse.

6. **Play it again.** If possible, videotape or audiotape your speech. Review and critique your performance. If equipment is unavailable, ask a supportive friend to listen to your speech—preferably in a location similar to the one in which you will give your presentation. Have that person sit in different areas of the room to check for volume of speech and visibility of visuals.

7. **Dress for the part.** Just as a neatly-printed paper makes a better impression than a handwritten copy, presentations made in appropriate attire set the tone for your speech. Your appearance should contribute to the effectiveness of your speech, not detract from it. Choose something a little more formal than you might normally wear to class. Select a "lucky" item of clothing or one that you enjoy wearing.

When giving a speech or presentation, you should . . .

1. **Wait a minute.** Don't start your speech until you reach the speaker's stand and feel ready.

Pause, survey your notes and mentally review your opening sentence. Take a deep breath. If the audience is quiet and prepared to listen, begin.

2. **Be yourself.** Don't affect an unnatural style. Show your interest and enthusiasm in your topic.

3. **Get a head start.** Learn your first sentence or two cold so you don't hesitate.

4. **Get a grip.** Attribute initial nervousness to eustress (positive adrenaline that gives you a boost to do your best) rather than distress (negative stress that leads to panic). Check your self-talk and replace it, if necessary, with positive affirmations. Take a deep breath. Speak slowly and at a volume loud enough to be heard. Keep in mind that the audience is with, not against, you. After all, one of them will be speaking next.

5. **Look 'em over.** Look directly at a person each time you make a point as if you were really talking to that individual. Make eye contact with individuals in the audience as you speak.

6. **Watch your watch.** End your speech in a timely manner.

7. **End it all.** Provide a finish for your speech. Summarize your main points, draw conclusions based on the content, use a particularly relevant quotation, or conclude your speech in some other definite manner.

After giving a speech or presentation, you should . . .

1. **Reward yourself.** You did it! Savor your successful conclusion. Mentally replay what went well. Congratulate yourself for your preparation, practice, and presentation.

2. **Critique your performance.** Critique, rather than criticize, your performance. Analyze what went right as well as what went wrong. Make written notes for future reference.

WRITE TO LEARN

On a separate sheet of paper or in your journal, describe how preparing for a presentation is like writing a research paper. How is it different?

Exercise 10.6   Convert one of the following into a format suitable for a two-minute presentation: "Countries and Their Constitutions" from Exercise 10.3; "Buying a Term Paper Could Turn Out to Be the First Step to Academic Bankruptcy" in Excerpt 10.1; or the paper you wrote in Exercise 10.4 or 10.5.

Exercise 10.7   Read the sample article, "It Seemed Like A Good Idea . . ." (at the back of this book, page 542). Find three books in your campus library about Susan B. Anthony. Create a synthesis chart that combines information from these books and information in this story. Then write a three-page biography of Anthony. Be prepared to present this information in class.

GROUP LEARNING ACTIVITY   NOTETAKING AS A CAUSE OF UNINTENTIONAL PLAGIARISM

Although the consequences of intentional and unintentional plagiarism are the same, their consequences differ greatly. Intentional plagiarism has deceit as its purpose. But could people accidentally copy information and plagiarize without realizing it? Yes, it is easier than you think. The following group exercise (Nienhuis, 1989) can be used to demonstrate how unintentional plagiarism might occur.

1. Divide the group into two parts.

2. Individually, group members should go to the campus library and observe other students taking notes. Observe the methods that students use most often in taking notes from reference materials.

3. Compare observations in the group. Did you see students looking back and forth between the references and their paper? Did they seem to look at the source, write, look at the source, and write again? Did it appear as if they were copying almost directly from the text?

4. Half of the study group should take notes from the "Case Study: The Scientific Method in Cancer Research" from Sample Chapter 13 (Concepts in Human Biology) as described in Step 3. The other half of

the group should take notes on the same material in the following manner. Put pencils and pens down and read without taking notes. Mentally summarize information that you think is important. Close the book and summarize on paper without looking back at the source. Open the book and check what you've written against the original source. Add quotation marks around direct quotes that you recalled. Note bibliographical citations.

Application

Compare the notes taken according to each of the two methods. Use the following questions as springboards for group discussion. What differences can you find? What do you think accounts for the differences? How would these differences change if the material were more difficult? Less difficult?

Application

The two subgroups in Step 4 should exchange notes. Underline any phrases or sentences in the notes that are uncited direct quotations from the passage. Compare results.

CHAPTER SUMMARY

1. Instructors usually assign themes or essays, reports, and research papers or term papers.

2. A research paper includes a title page, table of contents, abstract, body, references, and appendices.

3. Select the subject depending on your interest, the subject's importance, and the availability of library resources.

4. Narrow the subject by determining the purpose of the paper. The scope determines the thesis statement and title.

5. Use outlining and charting to organize information for synthesis.

6. The first draft of your paper includes an introduction, the text of the paper, and a summary.

7. Your second draft should follow an established style. Revisions occur until the paper is error-free.

8. To complete your paper, first set a writing schedule and then follow the steps in the writing process.

9. Effective presentations rely on principles of speech-making as well as well-written content.

Class*ACTION*

Respond to the following on a separate sheet of paper or in your journal. Combine the chapter map and chapter summary to form a synthesis map that reflects the main ideas and important details of this chapter. Personalize the map by indicating specific ways in which you plan to implement suggestions offered by this chapter.

CHAPTER REVIEW

Answer briefly but completely.

1. Complete the following analogy:
    reports : narration :: research papers : _____

2. On what factors do you base the decision to include a table of contents, abstract, or appendices?

    _____

    _____

    _____

3. Your instructor has asked you to write a paper on any aspect of environmental pollution. Identify a topic that would be of interest to you and your classmates. Explain the factors on which you based your topic selection. Then narrow this topic into one of suitable scope.

    _____

    _____

    _____

    _____

    _____

    _____

4. Complete the following analogy:
    topic sentence : _____ :: thesis statement : research paper

    _____

5. Contrast outlines and charts as methods for synthesizing sources of information. Which method do you prefer? Why?

    _____

    _____

    _____

6. Reread the quotation by Samuel Johnson on page 452. Use this quote to write the point you would make in an argument in favor of writing first and second drafts and for using word processing programs.

    _____

    _____

    _____

7. Complete the following analogy:
    plagiarism : _____ :: grand theft auto : cars

    _____

TERMS

Terms appear in the order in which they occurred in chapter.

themes
essays
reports
research papers
term papers
bibliography
abstract
appendices
scope
thesis statement
synthesis
rough draft
footnotes
endnotes
parenthetical references
style manuals
plagiarism

8. Examine Table 10.6. How would you modify the steps shown to accommodate your research and writing strengths and weaknesses?

   _____

   _____

   _____

9. How does a writing schedule help you avoid procrastination?

   _____

   _____

   _____

10. Review the specific suggestions for giving a speech or presentation found in Table 10.8. To what aspect of giving speeches do they relate?

    _____

    _____

    _____

VOCABULARY DEVELOPMENT   Figurative Language: Just Like Home

You can only analyze and measure knowledge and experience against what you already know. If you don't have prerequisite knowledge, you must get a sense of how an experience is like something else you already know. Because authors are well-acquainted with their subjects, they can draw comparisons between a subject's features and features of some other, more common, concept or process. Writers often use figurative speech to make such comparisons. In writing a paper, your role is that of an author. You must inform your reader—who might or might not be familiar with your subject. Figurative language helps you refine your own thoughts about a concept and facilitates communication with your reader.

Analogies, it is true, decide nothing,
but they can make one feel more at home.

—Sigmund Freud
Twentieth century psychologist

The problem with a new idea is often your unfamiliarity with it. You might not understand the processes involved. You might lack the terms to describe those processes. Everything seems strange. In short, you just don't know what the new idea is like. And that is the solution to your dilemma. To learn new information, you must link it to something you do know. You have to figure out what the new information is like.

The authors of your textbooks and the instructors in your classrooms also want you to know what new information is like. Thus, they often describe new and unfamiliar concepts by relating them to common items and processes with which you are familiar. Such comparisons often take the form of figures of speech: similes, metaphors, symbols, and analogies. Like Freud, these authors know that such comparisons can help you feel more at home with unfamiliar subject matter.

Similes and metaphors. Similes and metaphors are figures of speech that state or imply that two unlike ideas are comparable. At first glance, the two ideas might seem so totally different that they could have nothing in common. However, a closer look reveals a basic relationship between them.

The words *like* or *as* signal the use of a simile. For example, in describing an atom, you might describe the movement of electrons around a nucleus as being "like planets around the sun." Thus, if you know how a solar system moves, you know that the parts of an atom move in a similar fashion.

In a metaphor, one idea is described as if were another, but without the use of *like* or *as* to serve as a link between the disparate items. For example, a biology professor might describe glucose as the gasoline that powers the human engine. That means that glucose performs the same function in the body as gasoline performs in a car.

Symbols. Symbols are like metaphors and similes with one major difference. Similes and metaphors name both ideas being compared. In symbolism, the comparison between two ideas became so well-known that one part of the comparison is no longer used. Thus, you are given one idea. You must infer the other. For example, the sentence "A rainbow is like a promise of better times for the coalition" would be a simile. "A rainbow is a promise of better times" is a metaphor. A rainbow alone symbolizes a promise of better times.

Symbols are based on background knowledge and experiences. In general, they are universally understood because of years of association between the symbol and the object it represents; however, symbols mean different things in different cultures. The flag that inspires patriotism in one country evokes little sentiment in another. A symbol's meaning also varies according to context. Symbols in one time and place (for example, X as in "X marks the spot," "X-tra Savings," size XXXL, and so on) can have a different meaning in another time and place.

Analogies. An analogy is a kind of expanded simile. Instead of comparing items as a whole, analogies compare specific features of a concept, process, person, place, or thing. For example, suppose you need to understand the relationship between a secondary trait (a characteristic that affects personality only under certain conditions) and personality. You might think of this concept as being like a knock that you get in your engine when you forget to add oil. This comparison is clarified by an analogy: A secondary trait is to personality as a knock is to a car's engine. The order of the ideas expressed in the analogy is important. Analogies can show any kind of relationship. These include synonyms, antonyms, parts to whole, age or size, or object to use.

Using figurative language in writing. Just as authors and faculty use figurative language to make you feel at home with an idea, you, too, can use such language to help the reader feel at home with the concepts in your research paper.

Your own understanding of the topic increases as you think of clear and appropriate examples. The metaphor, simile, symbol, or analogy you choose should include the following characteristics described by Yelon and Massa (1990):

- **Accuracy.** The ideas being compared should be similar in definition, composition, function, or description. The comparison should be believable and realistic.

- **Clarity.** Whenever possible, use words, images, or actions that are observable and evoke sensory images. The connection between the example and the topic should be emphasized so that the reader easily grasps the relationship.

- **Brevity.** Examples need to be short enough so that their connection to the topic is not lost.

Activity

Following the guidelines presented in this section, use figurative language to create an example to explain each of the following paragraphs.

1. Simple sequence is one of the four major logic patterns in computer programming. In simple sequence, the computer executes one statement after the other in the order in which they are listed in the program.

Example _____

_____

_____

2. In exploitation, one person or party controls the "rules" for access to rewards while keeping the second party or person naive or helpless concerning such access.

Example _____

_____

_____

3. The vascular, or blood circulatory, system is a closed system of vessels through which blood flows continuously in a figure eight, with the heart serving as a pump at the crossover point. As the blood circulates through the system, it picks up and delivers materials as needed.

Example _____

_____

_____

4. Pinocytosis involves a large area of the cell membrane, which actively engulfs liquids and "swallows" them into the cell. Occasionally, an entire protein can enter the body this way.

Example _____

_____

_____

5. The concept of nuclear reactions emerged following research into atomic structure in the 1920s. In fusion reactions, nuclei merge to create a larger nucleus representing a new chemical element. In fission reactions, a single nucleus splits into two or more smaller nuclei.

Example _____

_____

_____

Sample Chapter 11

Organizing the Police Department

Reprinted by permission of Policing: *An Introduction of Law Enforcement* by Dempsey. Copyright 1994 by West Publishing Company. All rights reserved. Some figures and tables have been removed.

ORGANIZING THE POLICE DEPARTMENT

CHAPTER GOALS

▶ To acquaint you with the organizational and managerial concepts necessary to organize and operate a police department.

▶ To acquaint you with the complexities of modern police organizations.

▶ To show you how police departments are organized on the basis of personnel, area, time, and function.

▶ To introduce you to the major ranks in a police department and to the responsibilities connected with those ranks.

▶ To introduce you to the major units of a police department and the functions they perform.

This chapter deals with organizing a police department. In any organization, someone must do the work the organization is charged with doing; someone must supervise those doing the work; and someone must command the operation. Certain commonly accepted rules of management must be followed to accomplish the goals of the organization. This chapter will include the organization of the police department by personnel (rank), area, time, and function or purpose. It will look at the various ranks in a police department and examine the responsibilities of the people holding those ranks. Then it will discuss how a police department allocates or assigns its personnel by area, time, and function or purpose. This chapter is designed to give you an awareness of the complexities involved in policing seven days a week, twenty-four hours a day.

Not all police organizations are as complex as described here. In fact, most police departments in the United States are small. The intent of this chapter, however, is to cover as many complexities of the police organization as possible to give you the broadest possible view of policing in the United States.

ORGANIZING THE DEPARTMENT: MANAGERIAL CONCEPTS

Before discussing the organization of a police department, some managerial concepts common to most organizations should be understood. These concepts include division of labor; chain of command (hierarchy of authority); span of control; delegation of responsibility and authority; unity of command; and rules, regulations, and discipline.

Division of Labor

Obviously, all the varied tasks and duties that must be performed by an organization cannot be performed by one, a few, or even all of the members of the organization. The different tasks and duties an organization performs must be divided among its members in accordance with some logical plan.

In police departments, the tasks of the organization are divided according to personnel, area, time, and function or purpose. Work assignments must be designed so that similar (homogeneous) tasks, functions, and activities are given to a particular group for accomplishment. In a police department, patrol functions are separate from detective functions, which are separate from internal investigative functions. Geographic and time distinctions are also established, with certain officers' working certain times and areas. The best way to think of the division of labor in an organization is to ask the question, Who is going to do what, when, and where?

The division of labor should be reflected in an organization chart, a pictorial representation of reporting relationships in an organization. A good organizational chart is a snapshot of the organization. Workers can see exactly where they stand in the organization (what functions they perform, who they report to, and who reports to them).

Chain of Command (Hierarchy of Authority)

The managerial concept of chain of command (also called hierarchy of authority) involves the superior-subordinate or supervisor-worker relationships throughout the department, wherein each individual is supervised by one immediate supervisor or boss. Thus, the chain of command as pictured in the organizational chart shows workers which supervisor they report to; the chain of command also shows supervisors to whom they are accountable and for whom they are responsible. All members of the organization should follow the chain of command. For example, a patrol officer should report to his or her immediate sergeant, not to the captain. A captain should send his or her orders through the chain of command—to the lieutenant, who disseminates the directions to the sergeants, who disseminate the information to the patrol officers (see Figure 3–2). Chain of command may be violated, however, when an emergency exists or speed is necessary.

Span of Control

The number of officers or subordinates that a supervisor can supervise effectively is called

Figure 3–2 Chain of Command from Chief to Patrol Officer
Source: Permission granted by publisher, Anderson Publishing, Cincinnati, Ohio 45202. Robert Sheehan and Gary W. Cordner, *Introduction To Police Administration,* 2d ed. (Cincinnati; Anderson, 1989), p. 184.

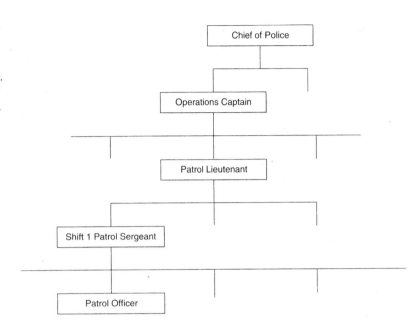

the span of control. Although no one can say exactly how many officers a sergeant can supervise or how many sergeants a lieutenant can supervise, most police management experts say the chain of command should be one supervisor to every six to ten officers of a lower rank. Nevertheless, it is best to keep the span of control as limited as possible so that the supervisor can more effectively supervise and control. The number of workers a supervisor can effectively supervise is affected by many factors, including distance, time, knowledge, personality, and the complexity of the work to be performed.

Delegation of Responsibility and Authority

Another important managerial concept in police organizations is delegation of responsibility and authority. Tasks, duties, and responsibilities are assigned to subordinates, along with the power or authority to control, command, make decisions, or otherwise act in order to complete the tasks that have been delegated or assigned to them.

Unity of Command

The concept of unity of command means that each individual in an organization is directly accountable to only one supervisor. The concept is important, because no one person can effectively serve two supervisors at one time. Unity of command may be violated in emergency situations.

Rules, Regulations, and Discipline

Most police organizations have a complex system of rules and regulations designed to control and direct the actions of officers. Most departments have operations manuals or rules and procedures designed to show officers what they must do in most situations they encounter.

Rule books are often complex and detailed. In the New York City Police Department, the police rule book is almost 1 foot thick.

Police departments have disciplinary standards that are similar to, but less stringent than, the military's. Violation of department standards in terms of dress, appearance, and conduct can lead to sanctions against officers in terms of reprimands, fines, or even dismissal from the department.

ORGANIZING BY PERSONNEL

A police department faces the same organizational challenges as any organization, and a major challenge is personnel. The civil service system plays a large role in police hiring. This section will describe that role, along with the quasi-military model of police, sworn versus nonsworn personnel, rank structure, and other personnel issues.

The Civil Service System

The **civil service system** is a method of hiring and managing government employees that is designed to eliminate political influence, favoritism, nepotism, and bias. Civil service rules govern the hiring, promoting, and terminating of government employees. The Pendleton Act created a civil service system for federal employees in 1883, in the wake of the assassination of President James Garfield, who was killed in 1881 by a person who had been rejected for appointment to a federal office. Eventually, many state and local governments adopted their own civil service systems.

Today, over 95 percent of all government employees at the federal, state, and local levels are covered by the civil service system. Civil service has reduced political interference and paved the way for merit employment, a system in which personal ability is stressed above all other considerations. However, some civil service systems seem to guarantee life tenure in the organization and provide an atmosphere of absolute employee protection instead of stressing the merit that the system was initially designed to emphasize.[2]

Most police departments, particularly larger departments, are governed by civil service regulations. Some complain that the civil service system creates many problems for police administrators, because a chief or commissioner cannot appoint or promote at will but must follow the civil service rules and appoint and promote according to civil service lists. Additionally, it is often difficult to demote or terminate employees under the civil service system.[4] Although many criticize civil service rules, it must be remembered that they help eliminate the autocratic power of a supervisor to hire, fire, or transfer employees on a whim.

Quasi-military Model of Police

As Chapter 1 indicated, the U.S. police are a civil, as opposed to a military, organization. Despite this, our police departments are **quasi-military organizations** (organizations similar to the military). Like the military, the police are organized along strict lines of authority and reporting relationships; they wear military-style, highly recognizable uniforms; they use military-style rank designations; they carry weapons; and they are authorized by law to use force. Like the military, police officers are trained to respond to orders immediately.

Despite similarities, however, the police are far different from the military. They are not trained as warriors to fight foreign enemies but instead are trained to maintain order, serve and protect the public, and enforce the criminal law. Most important, the power of the police is limited by state laws and by the Bill of Rights.

Sworn and Nonsworn (Civilian) Personnel

People who work for police departments fall under two major classifications: sworn members of the department, or police officers, and nonsworn members of the department, or civilians.

Sworn Members

Sworn members are those people in the police organization we usually think of as police officers, troopers, or deputy sheriffs. They are given traditional police powers by state and local laws, including penal or criminal laws and criminal procedure laws. Additionally, upon appointment, sworn members take an oath to abide by the U.S. Constitution and those sections of state and local law applicable to the exercise of police power.

The best example of police power is the power to arrest. Regular citizens also have the power to arrest (citizen's arrest). However, these powers differ.

As an example, the *Criminal Procedure Law* of New York State grants arrest powers to both police officers and ordinary citizens:

> Section 140.10. . . a police officer may arrest a person for:
>
> (a) Any offense when he has reasonable cause to believe that such person has committed such offense in his presence; and
>
> (b) A crime when he has reasonable cause to believe that such person has committed such crime, whether in his presence or otherwise. . . .
>
> Section 140.30 . . . any person (citizen) may arrest another person:
>
> (a) for a felony when the latter has in fact committed such felony: and
>
> (b) for any offense when the latter has in fact committed such offense in his presence.[5]

The law is quite specific. Police officers need only to have probable cause (not definite proof) to make arrests for any crimes committed in their presence or not. They can make arrests for any offenses (including minor infractions) committed in their presence.

Probable cause is a series of facts that would indicate to a "reasonable person" that a crime is being committed or was committed and that a certain person is committing, or did commit it. A good example of facts leading to probable cause follows:

1. At 3 A.M., screams from a female are heard in an alley.
2. An officer sees a man running from the alley.
3. Upon the officer's command, the man refuses to halt and rushes past the officer.

This gives the officer probable cause to stop the man, even though there is no "proof" yet of a crime. If it later turns out that no crime was committed, the officer has done nothing wrong, because he or she acted under probable cause.

Citizens, in contrast, cannot use probable cause, and the crimes must have actually happened. (In fact, this leaves citizens open for false arrest lawsuits.) Additionally, citizens can only arrest for offenses actually committed in their presence.

In addition to the power of arrest, the police officer has the power to stop temporarily and question people in public places, to stop vehicles and conduct inspections, and to search for weapons and other contraband. Additionally, the police officer has significantly more power to use physical force, including deadly physical force than does the citizen.

Nonsworn (Civilian) Members

Nonsworn (civilian) members of police departments are not given traditional police powers and can exercise only the very limited arrest power given to ordinary citizens. Thus, they are assigned to nonenforcement duties in the department. They serve in many different areas of a police organization and in many roles. When we think of nonsworn members, we usually think of typists, 911 operators, and police radio dispatchers. However nonsworn members serve in many other capacities as well, including clerical, technical, administrative, and managerial jobs. Their rank structure is generally not as vertical as is that of sworn officers.

Rank Structure

Sworn members generally have a highly organized rank structure (chain of command). The lowest sworn rank in the police organization is usually the police officer, although many organizations have lower-ranked sworn officers, such as cadets or trainees, who generally perform duties similar to nonsworn members or assist sworn members in performing nonenforcement duties. Many cadets or trainees aspire to an eventual sworn position or are in training for one. In most organizations, those in training at the police academy are known as recruits or cadets and generally have the same legal authority as regular officers except that they are generally not assigned to enforcement duties while still in training.

To say the police officer is the lowest rank in a police department may sound demeaning to the rank. However, it only refers to the relative rank in the organizational chart, not to the police officer's power or to the quality and importance of the service performed.

The following sections describe the various ranks in the police organization using generic terms. Most departments use the titles police officer, detective, sergeant, lieutenant, and captain. However, some organizations, such as state police departments and county sheriff's offices, use different terms to describe their members. In a state police force, the rank of trooper is almost identical to the rank of police officer. In a sheriff's office, the rank of deputy sheriff is synonymous with the rank of police officer.

The police officer/trooper/deputy sheriff is the most important person in the police organization. He or she is the person who is actually working on the streets, attempting to maintain order and enforce the law. A police agency is only as good as the quality of the men and women it employs.

Police Officer

Police officers serve as the workers in the police organization. The average police officer is assigned to patrol duties. (See Chapters 7 and 8 for a complete discussion of the activities of patrol officers.) Police officers perform the basic duties for which the police organization exists. They are under the control of supervisors, generally known as ranking officers or superior officers. Ranking officers are generally known as sergeants, lieutenants, and captains. At the highest level in most police organizations are inspectors and chiefs. In some state police organizations, military ranks such as major and colonel are used instead of inspector and chief. In federal law enforcement organizations, nonmilitary terms are used to reflect rank structure, such as agent, supervisor, manager, administrator, and director.

Corporal or Master Patrol Officer

Many police departments have established the corporal or master patrol officer rank as an intermediate rank between the police officer and the first-line supervisor, the sergeant. Often this rank is given to an officer as a reward for exemplary service or for additional services performed, such as training or technical functions.

Detective/Investigator

Some police officers in a department are designated as detectives, investigators, or inspectors. Their role is to investigate past crimes. (See Chapter 7 for a complete discussion of the role and activities of the detective.) Detectives exercise no supervisory role over police officers except at a crime scene (the location where a serious crime occurred and where possible evidence may be present), where they are in charge and make most major decisions.

The role of the detective is generally considered more prestigious than that of police officer. Detectives generally receive a higher salary and do not wear uniforms. They are usually designated detectives not through the typical civil service promotional examination but rather by appointment, generally for meritorious work. Often detectives do not possess civil service tenure and can be demoted back to the police officer rank without the strict civil service restrictions applicable to the other ranks in a police organization.

Sergeant

The first supervisor in the police chain of command is the sergeant. The sergeant is the first-line supervisor and, as many will say, the most important figure in the police supervisory and command hierarchy. The sergeant has two main responsibilities in police operations. First, the sergeant is the immediate supervisor of a number of officers assigned to his or her supervision. This group of officers is generally known as a squad. (Generally, six to ten officers make up a squad, and several squads may work on a particular tour of duty.) The sergeant is responsible for the activities and conduct of members of his or her squad. Second, the sergeant is responsible for decisions made at the scene of a police action until he or she is relieved by a higher-ranking officer.

The sergeant is responsible for getting the job done through the actions of people. Thus, he or she must possess numerous important personal qualities, such as intelligence, integrity, and dedication. The sergeant also draws on numerous organizational, motivational, and communication skills.

Lieutenant

Just above sergeant in the chain of command is the lieutenant. Whereas the sergeant is generally in charge of a squad of officers, the lieutenant is in charge of the entire **platoon**. The platoon consists of all of the people working on a particular tour (shift). Not only is the lieutenant in charge of employees; he or she also is in charge of all police operations occurring on a particular tour.

Captain

Next in the chain of command above the lieutenant is the captain. The captain is ultimately responsible for all personnel and all activities in a particular area, or for a particular unit, on a twenty-four hour-a-day basis. The captain must depend on the lieutenants and sergeants under his or her command to communicate his or her orders to the officers and to exercise discipline and control over the officers.

Ranks above Captain

Many larger municipal agencies have a hierarchy of ranks above the rank of captain. Inspectors generally have administrative control over several precincts or geographic areas, whereas assistant chiefs or chiefs have administrative control of major police units, such as personnel, patrol, or detectives.

Chief of Police/Police Commissioner

The head of the police agency is usually termed the chief of police or the police commissioner. Chiefs of police and police commissioners are generally appointed by the top official of a government (mayor, county executive, or governor) for a definite term of office. Generally, commissioners and chiefs do not have civil service tenure and may be replaced at any time.

One of the major exceptions to this lack of civil service tenure is the chief of the Los Angeles Police Department (LAPD). The LAPD chief of police is not subject to the direction of the Los Angeles mayor but rather to a board of officials called the Police Commission, who may remove the chief of police from duty, but only for cause.[6] This proved to be a complicating factor in the 1991 Rodney King case in that the Police Commission fired Chief Daryl Gates, who was then returned to his post by the Los Angeles City Council. Gates maintained his post, despite much pressure, during the 1992 Los Angeles riots.

Gates resigned after the riots and was replaced by former Philadelphia top cop Willie

Dempsey's Law

MAKING RANK

Professor Dempsey, how do you make rank in a police department? How do you get promoted?

All police departments are different. Would you like me to tell you how I made rank in the NYPD?

Sure, that would be great.

I was appointed to the rank of police officer in 1966, after passing all the entry examinations, which we will discuss when we get to Chapter 4. At that time, the entry-level rank in the NYPD was called *patrolman* instead of *police officer*. It was changed to *police officer* for reasons we will discuss when we get to chapter 11. I worked in the Forty-first Precinct, which was located in the South Bronx, until 1973, when I was transferred to the police academy as a recruit instructor. I was promoted to detective in 1973. There is no examination for the rank of detective; generally, officers make detective based on merit.

I was promoted to sergeant in 1974 and transferred to the Sixtieth Precinct in Coney Island, Brooklyn. Promotion to sergeant was based on a civil service examination and an assessment center. I spent my years as a sergeant in the 60 (Sixtieth Precinct) and the Organized Crime Control Bureau. Because of the city's financial crisis, there was no test for the next rank, lieutenant, until 1982.

I was promoted to lieutenant in 1983 and assigned to the 60 once again. Promotion to lieutenant involved a three-stage civil service examination, including administrative, operational, and oral exercises.

I was promoted to captain in 1985 and transferred to Patrol Borough Brooklyn North. Promotion to captain was also based on a three-stage civil service examination. I spent my years as a captain in Patrol Borough Brooklyn North; the Seventy-ninth Precinct in Bedford Stuyvesant, Brooklyn; the Civilian Complaint Review Board; and the Personnel Bureau.

Professor, you must have worked very hard to get all those promotions!

I sure did.

Was it worth it?

I would say so. My pension today and for the rest of my life is $40,000 a year, and I had a great time.

Williams. Williams was instrumental in planning strategy to deal with possible problems in the wake of the 1993 re-trial of the officers involved in the Rodney King case and was generally credited with maintaining order on Los Angeles streets during that time.

Other Personnel

Police departments are increasingly using nonsworn employees and civilians to perform tasks in the police department. This effort can increase both efficiency in the use of human resources and cut costs. Community service officers and police auxiliaries also help some departments operate more effectively.

Civilianization

The process of removing sworn officers from noncritical or nonenforcement tasks and replacing them with civilians or nonsworn employees is **civilianization.** Civilians with special training and qualifications have been hired to replace the officers who formerly did highly skilled nonenforcement jobs (traffic control, issuing parking tickets, taking past crime reports, and so on). Additionally, civilians with clerical skills have been hired to replace officers who were formerly assigned to desk jobs. In 1992, approximately one quarter of all local police department employees were civilians.[7]

The replacement of sworn officers by civilians in nonenforcement jobs is highly cost-effective for police departments, because civilian employees generally earn much less than sworn officers. This strategy also enables a department to have more sworn personnel available for patrol and other enforcement duties.

A study of civilianization programs found that managers and officers were favorably impressed with the use of civilians for nonenforcement duties. Many officers observed that civilians performed some tasks better than the sworn officers they replaced. Perhaps the civilians were not subject to rotation and emergency assignments and thus could concentrate better on their specific duties. Additionally, many officers tended to consider some of the non-civilianized jobs as confining, sedentary, a form of punishment, and not proper police work. Officers in the study felt that civilians want careers in police work, and a sizable number of officers recommended that more be hired.[8]

Community Service Officers

The President's Commission on Law Enforcement and Administration of Justice recommended that three distinct entry-level police personnel categories be established in large and medium-size police departments: (1) police agents, (2) police officers, and (3) community service officers.[9] Police agents would be the most knowledgeable and responsible entry-level position. They would be given the most difficult assignments and be allowed to exercise the greatest discretion. The commission suggested a requirement of at least two years of college and preferably a bachelor's degree in the liberal arts or social sciences. Some departments have adopted this recommendation and give these officers the title of corporal or master patrol officer.

Police officers would be the equivalent of the traditional and contemporary police officer. They would perform regular police duties, such as routine preventive patrol and providing emergency services. The commission recommended that a high school degree be required for this position.

Community service officers (CSOs) would be police apprentices, youths seventeen to twenty-one years of age, preferably from minority groups. They would have no general law enforcement powers and no weapons. The commission reasoned that because of their social background and greater understanding of inner-city problems, community service officers would be good police-community relations representatives. The commission suggested that the CSOs work with youths, investigate minor thefts, help the disabled, and provide community assistance. The commission also recommended that the lack of a high school diploma and the existence of a minor arrest record not bar the CSOs from employment. It also recommended that the CSOs be allowed to work their way up to become regular police officers.

In 1983, the Tulsa (Oklahoma) Police Department began a community service officer program. The CSOs received twelve weeks of training, compared with the sixteen weeks required for regular officers. A high school education is required for CSOs, whereas police officers need 108 hours of college. The salary also is lower. The community service program provides career opportunities for qualified young people who either cannot or prefer not to attend college. The CSOs in Tulsa are certified law enforcement officers; they carry guns, and they may arrest law violators.

The community service officers have provided excellent services in Tulsa. The system was designed to relieve some of the pressures on the time of other officers and to save the community money. The program supervisor said the program was designed "to relieve police officers of routine chores and place them back on field duty and to provide security at municipal facilities at a price less than what it would cost to use regular officers." The use of community service officers at the Tulsa airport alone saved $60,875 in one year.[10]

Police Auxiliaries

Personnel shortcomings in police departments may be perennial or seasonal, depending on the jurisdiction. Some resort communities face an influx of vacationers and tourists during a particular season that can more than double the normal size of the population. In response to this annual influx, some communities employ "summertime cops." One example is Cape May County, New Jersey, which has ten separate departments that hire summer officers, most of whom are students in college criminal justice programs.[11]

Police agencies in other communities employ part-time officers throughout the year. These men and women, sometimes referred to as reserve or auxiliary officers, either are unpaid volunteers or are paid less than full-time officers. In Illinois and North Carolina, for example, they are sworn officers who carry firearms. In Arizona, the highway patrol has used unpaid reserve officers for more than thirty years. These troopers are fully certified state law enforcement officers. Regarding the Arizona Highway Patrol reserve troopers, two researchers have written, "the only distinguishing element of their uniform is the word 'Reserve' written on the badge. The public sees reserve officers as Highway Patrol officers, which, by statute and training, they are. Reserves issue traffic citations, effect felony or misdemeanor arrests, investigate accidents and perform all the functions of a full time officer."[12]

In some cities, auxiliary officers are unpaid volunteers. Although they wear police-type uniforms and carry nightsticks, these auxiliaries are citizens with no police powers, and they do not carry firearms. They usually patrol their own communities, acting as a deterrent force and providing the police with extra eyes and ears. New York City has more than 8,000 of these unpaid volunteer auxiliary officers.

Some Personnel Issues

Like all organizations with employees, police departments have a distinct set of personnel issues. Some important issues are lateral transfers, police unions, and other police affiliations (for example, fraternal organizations and professional organizations).

Lateral Transfers

Lateral transfers, or lateral movement, in police departments can be defined as the ability and opportunity to transfer from one police department to another. Some states allow lateral transfers from one department in the state to another department and also allow lateral transfers from out-of-state departments. Some states allow only in-state lateral transfers, and some states do not allow lateral transfers at all. Table 3–1 lists some police departments that allow lateral transfers.

The major problem with lateral transfers is that many police pension systems are tied into the local government, and funds put into that fund cannot be transferred into other funds. Thus, lateral transfers in those departments can cause officers to lose all or some of their investments.

The President's Commission on Law Enforcement and Administration of Justice recommended developing a national police retirement system that would permit the transfer of personnel without the loss of benefits. A few experiments with portable police pensions have been tried.[13]

Police Unions

Police unionism has a long and colorful history. Police employee organizations first arose as fraternal associations to provide fellowship for

TABLE 3–1   Sample of Police Departments Allowing Lateral Transfers

Police Department	In-State Lateral	Out-of-State Lateral
Los Angeles County Sheriff's Department	✔	
Mesa (Arizona) Police Department	✔	
Alachua County (Florida) Sheriff's Office	✔	✔
Prince George County (Maryland) Police Department	✔	✔
Bethlehem (Pennsylvania) Police Department	✔	
Florence (South Carolina) Police Department	✔	
Salt Lake County (Utah) Sheriff's Office	✔	✔

Source: Adapted from material in *Law Enforcement Opportunities,* 1992. Published monthly by L.E.O. Publishing, P.O. Box 060010, Staten Island, N.Y. 10306.

officers, as well as welfare benefits (death benefits and insurance policies) to protect police families. In some cities, labor unions began to organize the police for the purpose of collective bargaining, and by 1919, thirty-seven locals had been chartered by the American Federation of Labor (AFL). The Boston Police Strike of 1919, as we saw in Chapter 1, was triggered by the refusal of the city of Boston to recognize the AFL-affiliated union. In response to the strike, Calvin Coolidge, the then governor of Massachusetts, fired all of the striking officers—almost the entire police department. Because of the Boston strike, the police union movement stalled until the 1960s, when it reemerged.[14]

Today, nearly 75 percent of all U.S. police officers are members of labor unions. About two-thirds of all the states have collective bargaining laws for public employees. In those states, the police union bargains with the locality over wages and other conditions of employment. In the states that do not have collective bargaining agreements, the police union serves a more informal role.[15]

Police unions are predominantly local organizations that bargain and communicate with the local police department and the mayor's or chief executive's office. Local unions often join into federations on a state or federal level to lobby state and federal legislative bodies. Some of the major national federations of local police unions are the International Union of Police Associations (IUPA), the Fraternal Order of Police (FOP), the International Conference of Police Associations (ICPA), and the International Brotherhood of Police Officers (IBPO). Some officers are also members of national federations of civil service workers, such as the American Federation of State, County, and Municipal Employees (AFSCME).

Unions exist in order to harness the individual power of each worker into one group, the union, which can then speak with one voice for all the members. The ultimate bargaining tool of the union has traditionally been the strike. Members of many organizations—the telephone company, the department store, the factory, and so on—strike to win labor concessions from their employers.

Should police officers be allowed to strike? Many feel that police officers are special employees and should not have the right to strike. In fact, most states have laws that specifically prohibit strikes by public employees. New York State has one of the toughest laws against strikes by public employees in the nation, the Taylor Law.

Despite the presence of the Taylor Law and similar laws, there have been strikes by police employees. In 1970, members of the New York City Police Department staged a wildcat strike, for which all officers were fined two days' pay for each day they participated in the strike. Police strikes have also been staged in Baltimore, San Francisco, and New Orleans.

To avoid the penalties involved in a formal police strike, police union members occasionally engage in informal job actions to protest working conditions or other grievances felt by the officers. These job actions include the **blue flu** (where officers call in on sick report) or a refusal to perform certain job functions, such as writing traffic summonses.

Other Police Affiliations

Police officers affiliate on levels other than unions. The two major types of affiliations are fraternal and professional.

Fraternal organizations generally focus on national origin, ethnic, or gender identification. In the New York City Police Department, some examples include the Emerald Society (Irish-American officers), the Columbian Society (Italian-American officers), the Guardians Association (African-American officers), the Schomrin Society (Jewish officers), the Policewoman's Endowment Society (female officers), and the Gay Officers Action League (gay and lesbian officers).

The two major professional organizations for police officers, designed as a forum to exchange professional information and provide training, are the International Association of Chiefs of Police (IACP) and the Police Executive Research Forum (PERF), a research-oriented organization.

ORGANIZING BY AREA

Police departments must be organized not only with regard to personnel but also with regard to the geographic area they serve. Each officer and group of officers must be responsible for a particular well-defined area. Geographic areas may be beats or posts, sectors or zones, and precincts. In very large police departments having numerous precincts, the precincts may be grouped together to form divisions. Figure 3–3 shows a map of a precinct divided into sectors.

Beats/Posts

The beat or post is the smallest geographic area that a single patrol unit—one or two people in a car or on foot—can patrol effectively. A beat may be a foot beat, radio car beat, mounted beat, motorcycle or scooter beat, or even bicycle beat. Obviously, radio car beats can be much larger than foot beats.

The beat officer ideally should know everyone living or doing business on his or her beat, as well as conditions and problems on the beat that require police assistance or concern. For this reason, a beat should be as geographically limited as possible without being so small that it is nonproductive or boring to the officer.

Sectors/Zones

A sector or zone is a number of individual beats grouped together. A radio car sector

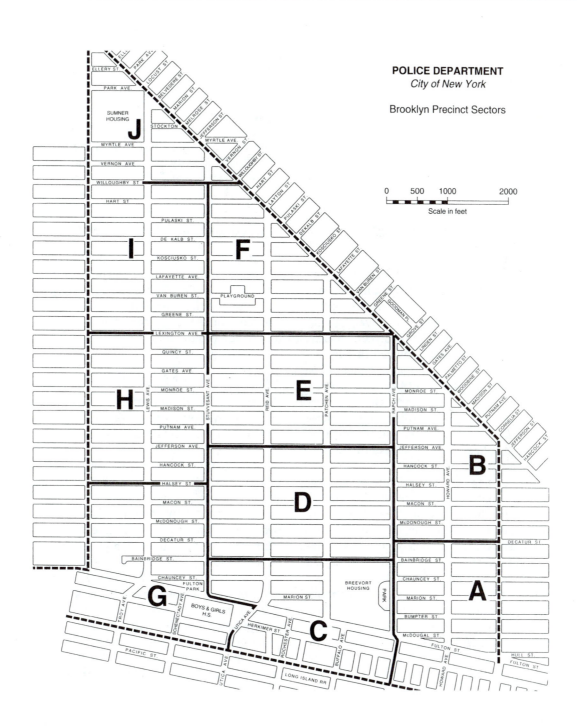

Figure 3-3   Map Dividing Precinct into Sectors

may patrol several foot beats. A supervisor's zone may include numerous foot beats and several auto sectors.

Precincts

A precinct is generally the entire collection of beats and sectors in a given geographic area. In a small department, generally only one precinct serves as the administrative head-quarters for the entire department. The Long Beach Police Department, in Nassau County, New York, which patrols a city of 35,000 people with 70 police officers, has one precinct. The Corning (Iowa) Police Department, which serves 2,100 people, has one precinct. The Suffolk County (New York) Police Department, which serves over 1.5 million people with about 2,000 officers, has six precincts geographically placed throughout the county. The city of Imperial Beach, California, policed by the San Diego County Sheriff's Office, has one precinct. The New York City Police Department, which serves over 8 million people with 27,000 officers, has seventy-five police precincts spread throughout the five boroughs of the city.

The building that serves as the administrative headquarters of a precinct is generally called a precinct house or station house. The station house usually contains detention cells for the temporary detention of prisoners awaiting a court appearance after an arrest, locker rooms in which officers can dress and store their uniforms and equipment, administrative offices, meeting rooms, and clerical offices.

The focus of the precinct or station house is the desk. The desk is usually an elevated platform near the entrance of the station house, where all major police business is carried on. Prisoners are booked at the desk, and officers are assigned to duty from it. A ranking officer, generally a sergeant or lieutenant, is assigned as the desk officer and supervises all activities in the station house. The desk officer is usually in charge of the police blotter, a record in chronological order, of all police activities occurring in a precinct each day. The blotter traditionally has been a large bound book in which all entries are handwritten by the desk officer. Although some departments still maintain the classic handwritten blotter, that term is now used more generically as the written record of all activity in a precinct. The blotter can include typed and computerized reports.

ORGANIZING BY TIME

In addition to being organized by personnel, and by area, a police department must organize its use of time. The following discussion will describe the tour system, including the common three-tour system, tour conditions, and steady (fixed) tours.

The Three-Tour System

Common sense dictates that police officers, like other workers, can work only a certain number of hours and days before fatigue sets in and they lose their effectiveness. Tradition and civil service rules have established the police officer's working tour (also called the *shift* or *platoon*) as eight hours. The traditional police organization separates each day or twenty-four-hour period into three tours: (1) a midnight or night tour, which generally falls between the hours of 12 midnight and 8 A.M.; a day tour, which generally falls between the hours of 8 A.M. and 4 P.M.; and an evening tour, which generally falls between the hours of 4 P.M. and 12 midnight. Shifts or tours do not necessarily have to fall between these exact hours; they can be between any hours, as long as all twenty-four hours of the day are covered. Some departments have shifts that last longer than eight hours, and they use the overlapping time as training time. Also, some departments use variations of the three-tour system, including two 12-hour tours a day or four 10-hour tours a week.

TABLE 3–2 Patrol Duty Chart

	1	2	3	4	5	6	7	8	9	10	11	12	13	14	15
					First Platoon Duty Schedule **243 Appearances**										
Squad No. 1	1	1	1	1	1			1	1	1	1	1			
Squad No. 2	1	1				1	1	1	1	1			1	1	1
Squad No. 3			1	1	1	1	1				1	1	1	1	1
January	13–28	14–29	15–30	1–16–31	2–17	3–18	4–19	5–20	6–21	7–22	8–23	9–24	10–25	11–26	12–27
February	12–27	13–28	14	15	1–16	2–17	3–18	4–19	5–20	6–21	7–22	8–23	9–24	10–25	11–26
March	14–29	15–30	1–16–31	2–17	3–18	4–19	5–20	6–21	7–22	8–23	9–24	10–25	11–26	12–27	13–28
April	13–28	14–29	15–30	1–16	2–17	3–18	4–19	5–20	6–21	7–22	8–23	9–24	10–25	11–26	12–27
May	13–28	14–29	15–30	1–16–31	2–17	3–18	4–19	5–20	6–21	7–22	8–23	9–24	10–25	11–26	12–27
June	12–27	13–28	14–29	15–30	1–16	2–17	3–18	4–19	5–20	6–21	7–22	8–23	9–24	10–25	11–26
July	12–27	13–28	14–29	15–30	1–16–31	2–17	3–18	4–19	5–20	6–21	7–22	8–23	9–24	10–25	11–26
August	11–26	12–27	13–28	14–29	15–30	1–16–31	2–17	3–18	4–19	5–20	6–21	7–22	8–23	9–24	10–25
September	10–25	11–26	12–27	13–28	14–29	15–30	1–16	2–17	3–18	4–19	5–20	6–21	7–22	8–23	9–24
October	10–25	11–26	12–27	13–28	14–29	15–30	1–16–31	2–17	3–18	4–19	5–20	6–21	7–22	8–23	9–24
November	9–24	10–25	11–26	12–27	13–28	14–29	15–30	1–16	2–17	3–18	4–19	5–20	6–21	7–22	8–23
December	9–24	10–25	11–26	12–27	13–28	14–29	15–30	1–16–31	2–17	3–18	4–19	5–20	6–21	7–22	8–23

Note: 1 = 0001 to 0800 hours. Each tour consists of 8 hours and 35 minutes, as described in Operations Order 105S78.
Source: Courtesy of New York City Police Department.

Table 3–2 shows a duty chart, a schedule of assigned working tours for the year 1993 for all members of the New York City Police Department who work steady midnight-to-8 A.M. tours (the first platoon). The chart is divided into the three squads that work that tour, Squads 1, 2, and 3.

By a quick glance, officers can tell if they are working or off for any day of the year. For example, an officer from Squad 1 or 2 knows he or she is working on January 13 and January 28, 1993 (the first box after the word *January*), whereas an officer from Squad 3 knows he or she is off duty. The number *1* in the box indicates the first platoon. If an administrator wants to know who is working January 1, 1993, he or she can immediately tell that Squads 1 and 3 are working and Squad 2 is off.

Officers take these charts very seriously, because they also affect their private lives. For example, Squad 3 has Christmas Day (December 25) off but must be back on duty at midnight after Christmas Day, at 0001 hours, December 26. Squad 3 members will consider themselves very fortunate in that they have the dreaded New Year's Eve off.

Using the traditional three-tour system, each day it takes three officers to cover each—one on the night tour, one on the day tour, and one on the evening tour. When days off, vacation time, and sick time are factored into the three-tour system, approximately five officers are required to cover each beat twenty-four hours a day, seven days a week, 365 days a year. (Formulas to allocate personnel are available in police organization and management texts.)

Historically, police officers have been allocated evenly during the three tours of duty each day, with equal numbers of officers assigned to each of the tours. However, the academic studies of the police beginning in the 1960s discovered that crime and other police problems do not fit neatly into the three-tour system. Studies indicated that the majority of crime and police problems in the United States occurred during the late evening and early morning hours. Many police departments began to change their methods of allocating police personnel. Most now assign their personnel according to the demand for police services, putting more officers on the street during those hours when crime and calls for police officers are highest.

Many departments now distribute patrol officers according to a work load formula based on reported crimes and calls for service. The Dallas Police Department, for example, assigns 43 percent of its officers to the tour from 4 P.M. to midnight, 25 percent to the tour from midnight to 8 A.M., and 32 percent to the tour from 8 A.M. to 4 P.M.[16]

However, a survey by the Police Executive Research Forum found that some cities still routinely distribute one-third of all patrol officers to each shift. Some also assign the highest percentage of officers to the day shift rather than to the evening one.[17]

Tour Conditions

Each of the three shifts in the three-tour system has its own characteristics, as any police officer will tell you.

The midnight tour is sometimes called the graveyard shift. Most people are sleeping during this time, although in some large cities a good deal of commerce and business occurs. The most common problems for police officers during this tour are disorderly and intoxicated people at home and on the street, disorderly tavern patrons, commercial burglaries, prostitution, and drug sales. In addition to handling these specific problems, the police provide their normal duties, such as routine patrol, response to emergency calls, aiding the sick and injured, and solving disputes. Generally, the least amount of police activity occurs on this tour, and the lowest number of officers are on duty.

The day tour occurs during the normal business hours in the United States. Stores and offices are open, highway and construction crews are working, and children are in school and at play. The most common activities for police officers during this tour are facilitating the traffic flow and ensuring the safety of those traveling to and from work by enforcing parking and moving violations, ensuring the safety of children walking to and from school and entering and leaving school

busses, preventing robberies and other property thefts in commercial areas, and providing other normal police services. Generally, the second highest amount of police activity occurs on this tour, and the second largest number of police officers are on duty.

The evening tour is generally the busiest for the police. The workday and school day are over; the sun goes down; and the hours of darkness are here. During the evening hours, normal adherence to acceptable ways of behavior often gives way to alcohol and drug abuse, fights, and disputes. The most common activities of the evening tour are facilitating traffic for the homeward-bound commuter; dealing with bar fights, violence at home, and violence on the streets; preventing and dealing with street and commercial robberies; and providing normal routine police services. The largest amount of police activity occurs on this tour, and the majority of officers are assigned to it.

Steady (Fixed) Tours

Traditionally, most police departments have assigned their officers to rotating tours of duty: one week of night tours, one week of day tours, and one week of evening tours. Officers' days off rotate to accommodate the three-tour system. This practice has caused tremendous problems for police officers in both their on-duty and off-duty lives. The strain of working a new shift every other week has a negative effect on eating, living, sleeping, and socializing. It creates tremendous levels of stress.

There has been a move in recent years, therefore, to place officers on steady, or fixed, tours of duty, much like most other workers in the United States. Today, officers in many jurisdictions are assigned to steady night tours, day tours, or evening tours based on seniority or the officer's own choice. Police administrators hope that these steady tours will make officers' on-duty and off-duty lives more normal, thus eliminating the many problems created by shift work.

ORGANIZING BY FUNCTION OR PURPOSE

The best way to organize a police department in this way is to place similar functions performed by the police into similar units. Thus, all members of the department performing general patrol duties are placed into a patrol division, whereas all officers performing detective duties are placed into a detective division.

Line and Staff (Support) Functions

Police departments, like all organizations, must be organized by function or purpose. The first and simplest grouping of units or divisions of a department differentiates between line functions and staff (support) functions. Line functions are those tasks that directly facilitate the accomplishment of organizational goals, whereas staff (support) functions are those tasks that supplement the line units in their task performance.[18]

One of the organizational goals of a police department is order maintenance. Thus, the patrol officers who actually patrol the streets to preserve order would be grouped under a patrol unit or patrol division. Another organizational goal of a department is to investigate past crime. Thus, the detectives charged with investigating past crimes would be grouped together under a detective unit or detective division. Patrol and detective units directly facilitate the accomplishment of the organizational goals of a police department; thus, they perform line functions.

Staff (support) functions are those functions of the police department that are not directly related to the organizational goals of the department but nevertheless are necessary to ensure the smooth running of the

department. Investigating candidates for police officers, performing clerical work, and handing out paychecks are examples of staff (support) functions.

Police Department Units

Robert Sheehan and Gary W. Cordner provide an excellent and comprehensive description of the basic tasks of a police department.[19] They describe thirty tasks or duties the police must perform to have an effective police department. They state that in very large police departments, separate units may be established to perform each task. In smaller departments, the tasks may be grouped together in various ways to be performed by certain units or people. Sheehan and Cordner divide the thirty tasks into three subsystems, which are similar to the previously mentioned division of line and staff functions. Their three task subsystems are operations, administration, and auxiliary services. Table 3–3 summarizes the Sheehan and Cordner system of organizing a police department by function or purpose.

TABLE 3–3 Organizing a Police Department by Function or Purpose

Operations	Administration	Auxiliary Services
Patrol	Personnel	Records
Traffic	Training	Communications
Criminal investigations	Planning and analysis	Property
Vice	Budget and finance	Laboratory
Organized crime	Legal assistance	Detention
Juvenile services	Public information	Identification
Community services	Clerical/secretarial	Alcohol testing
Crime prevention	Inspections	Facilities
Community relations	Internal affairs	Equipment
	Intelligence	Supply
		Maintenance

Source: Permission granted by publisher, Anderson Publishing, Cincinnati, Ohio 45202. Robert Sheehan and Gary W. Cordner, *Introduction to Police Administration*, 2d ed. (Cincinnati: Anderson, 1989), pp. 114–115.

You Are There!

WHAT COPS DO, AS TOLD BY COPS

The police department is a service organization, open for business twenty-four hours a day, seven days a week. Dial their number and somebody has to answer, no matter what it is you want. As one officer put it, "People'll (sic) call us for everything. If their toilet runs over, they call the police before they call the plumber." A police officer deals with the desperate, the disturbed and all those people out there who are just plain lonely in the middle of the night. His duties put him on intimate terms with the bizarre things people are doing to each other and to themselves behind all the closed doors and drawn shades in the community. While the rest of us look the other way, he carts away the societal offal we don't want to deal with—suicides, drunks, drug addicts and derelicts. We call it keeping the peace, but the policeman often thinks of himself as humanity's garbageman. Every smart cop carries a pair of rubber surgical gloves in his car for handling dirt, disease and death. He uses his gloves much more often than he uses his gun.

* * *

The woman who opened the door for me was just a medium-sized black female. The thing unique about her was that I could not see either one of her eyes. Her nose no longer existed. And she had a cavernous opening where there would have been a mouth and teeth. Her cheekbones were broken. In my entire career, I had never seen anybody who was so thoroughly battered. I asked her what the problem was and she said, "My husband beat me up." . . . I'm holding him by his left arm, escorting him down in handcuffs. As we stepped through the front door of the building, she tried to bury a twelve-inch butcher knife right between my shoulder blades. Kachunk! She hit me right in the old bulletproof vest. . . .

It's human nature. When I walked in there she was upset because he beat her up so bad. When she saw her true love going out the door with the big bad police hauling him off, then no longer is he the villain. The police is the villain. It just tears your mind up. In spite of all that damage he did to her, she still loved him so much that she wanted me dead as opposed to taking him away.

* * *

So it goes, each shift ticked off by one stomach-curdling cup of coffee after another, enlivened only by the knowledge that something hairy just might happen. In those dead hours on the underbelly of the night when the orange glare of streetlights slowly gives way to the dawn, when the worst bar brawler is home in bed or sleeping it off in a cell and the ugliest hooker has made her quota, the hardest part of the job is staying awake until quitting time. By then the cop is running on residual adrenaline alone, struggling to remember that the next wife beater might have a deer rifle, that the next empty warehouse might not be empty after all, that the next under-aged driver he stops for speeding might just be crazy enough to poke a pistol in a policeman's face and pull the trigger.

* * *

Police work is basically 99 percent pure bull____t, because there is just not that much going on. But it is punctuated by one percent of just sheer terror. And it happens just that quick. That's the reason a lot of policemen keel over from heart attacks, because of all that adrenaline pumping all of a sudden all of the time. Ulcers, too. You ride around for five or six shifts in utter boredom, worried to death about when the next time is going to happen.

Source: Adapted from Mark Baker, *COPS: Their Lives in Their Own Words* (New York: Simon & Shuster, 1985), pp. 41–44.

Operational Units

Operations are activities performed in direct assistance to the public. These are the duties most of us think about when we think of police departments, including crime fighting, crime detection, and providing service. Operational units include patrol, traffic, criminal investigations, vice, organized crime, juvenile services, community services, crime prevention, and community relations.

The patrol unit performs the basic mission of the police department: maintaining order, enforcing the law, responding to calls for assistance, and providing services to citizens. Patrol officers, who are usually on radio motor patrol or foot patrol, are the backbone of the police service. They are the most important people in police service. Police patrol will be the subject of Chapters 7 and 8.

The traffic unit performs traffic control at key intersections and in other heavily traveled areas, enforces the traffic laws, and investigates traffic accidents. The police traffic function will be covered in Chapter 7.

The criminal investigations unit investigates past crimes reported to the police in an effort to identify and apprehend the perpetrators of those crimes. Criminal investigations will be covered in Chapter 7 of this text.

The vice unit enforces laws related to illegal gambling, prostitution, narcotics, pornography, and illegal liquor sales.

The organized crime unit investigates and apprehends members of criminal syndicates who profit from continuing criminal enterprises, such as the vice crimes just mentioned, extortion, loan sharking, and numerous other crimes.

The juvenile services unit provides a multitude of services to juveniles, including advice and referral to appropriate social agencies designed to assist youth, particularly youthful offenders. This function also investigates cases of child abuse and child neglect.

The community services unit provides a multitude of services to the community, including dispute resolution, crime victim assistance, counseling, and other routine and emergency services. Relationships between the police and the community, including numerous partnership programs between the police and the community, will be covered in Chapter 9 of this text.

The police crime prevention unit attempts to organize and educate the public on methods people can take—alone and with the police—to make themselves at less risk to crime. Some techniques include target hardening, neighborhood watch programs, and operation identification programs. Crime prevention will be covered in Chapter 9.

The community relations unit attempts to improve relationships between the police and the public so that positive police-community partnerships can develop to decrease crime and improve the quality of life in U.S. neighborhoods. Community relations will be covered in Chapter 9.

Administrative Units

Administration in a police department is defined as those activities performed not in direct assistance to the public but for the benefit of the organization as a whole, usually from 9 A.M. to 5 P.M. five days a week. Administrative units include personnel, training, planning and analysis, budget and finance, legal assistance, public information, clerical/secretarial, inspections, internal affairs, and intelligence.

The personnel unit performs the duties generally associated with corporate personnel departments, including recruiting and selecting candidates for police positions and assigning, transferring, promoting, and terminating police personnel. The training unit provides entry-level training to newly hired recruits and in-service training for veteran officers. Police training is covered in Chapter 4 of this text.

The planning and analysis unit conducts crime analysis to determine when and where crimes occur in order to prevent them. This unit also conducts operational and administrative analysis to improve police operations and the delivery of police services.

The budget and finance unit of the police department is involved in the administration of department finances and budgetary matters, including payroll, purchasing, budgeting, billing, accounting, and auditing. The legal assistance unit provides legal advice to members of the department, including patrol officers.

The public information unit informs the public, through the news media, about police activities, including crime and arrests. This unit also informs the public about methods they can take to reduce their chances of becoming crime victims. The clerical/secretarial unit prepares the necessary reports and documents required to maintain police record keeping.

The inspections unit conducts internal quality control inspections to ensure that the department's policies, procedures, and rules and regulations are being followed. The internal affairs unit investigates corruption and misconduct by officers. Corruption, misconduct, and internal affairs will be covered in Chapter 10. Finally, the intelligence unit conducts analyses of radical, terrorist, and organized crime groups operating in a police department's jurisdiction.

Auxiliary Services Units

Auxiliary services are defined as activities that benefit other units within the police department, but on a more regular and frequent basis than do administrative activities. Auxiliary services functions are usually available to assist the police officer twenty-four hours a day. Auxiliary services units include records, communications, property, laboratory, detention, identification, alcohol testing, facilities, equipment, supply, and maintenance.

The records unit of a police department maintains department records, including records of crimes and arrests, statistics and patterns regarding criminal activity, and records of traffic accidents. The communications unit answers incoming calls to the department's 911 telephone lines and assigns police units to respond to emergencies and other requests for police services. Communications will be discussed in Chapter 13 of this book.

The property unit inventories and stores all property coming into the custody of the police, including evidence, recovered property, and towed and recovered vehicles. The laboratory unit examines and classifies seized evidence, including drugs, weapons, and evidence found at crime scenes (for example, fingerprints, fibers, and stains). The police laboratory will be discussed in Chapter 13.

The detention unit provides temporary detention for prisoners awaiting their appearance in court. The identification unit fingerprints and photographs criminals, classifies prints, and maintains identification files. The alcohol testing unit administers driving while intoxicated tests for court prosecution.

The facilities unit of a police department maintains buildings designed for police use, such as station houses, offices, and detention facilities. The equipment unit maintains the numerous types of equipment necessary for the department's effective operation. The numerous supplies necessary for the proper operation of the department are purchased by the supply unit. Finally, the maintenance unit keeps all facilities and equipment serviceable.

Table 3–4 shows the breakdown, by rank and assignment, of a police department. By reading the top line of the chart and following it down to the bottom line ("Total"), one can easily see that there are a total of 165 employees in this department, with 82 police officers, 19 ranking officers (1 chief, 2 captains, 6 lieutenants, and 10 sergeants), 5 civilians, 2 coordinators, and 57 crossing guards.

By reading the details under "Police Officers" from the top line down, one can see that fifty-nine of the officers are assigned to the Patrol Bureau (twenty-one to 8-A.M.-to-4 P.M. tours, twenty-three to 4 P.M.-to-midnight tours, and fifteen to midnight-to-8 A.M. tours); six to the Detective Bureau; three to the Juvenile Bureau; eight to the Traffic Bureau; two to the Prosecutions Unit; one to the Planning and

TABLE 3-4   Staffing of a Police Department by Function and Time

	Chief	Captain	Lieutenant	Sergeant	Police Officer	Civilian	Coordinators	Crossing Guards	Total
Office of the Chief	1					1			2
Operations Division		1				½			1½
Patrol Bureau									
8–4			1	3	21				25
4–Midnight			1	3	23				27
Midnight–8			1	3	15				19
Detective Bureau									
8–4			1		4				5
4–Midnight					1				1
6–2					1				1
Juvenile Bureau									
8–4			1		2				3
6–2					1				1
Traffic Bureau									
8–4				1	3		2	57	63
4–Midnight					3				3
Midnight–8					2				3
Prosecutions Unit					2				2
Fingerprint and Photography Unit				None full-time					
Administration and Services Division		1	1			½			2½
Planning and Records Bureau					1	2			3
Payroll, Billing, and Budget Unit					1				1
Community Services and Training Unit					2				2
Custodial Services						1			1
Total	1	2	6	10	82	5	2	57	165

Source: Permission granted by publisher, Anderson Publishing, Cincinnati, Ohio 45202. Robert Sheehan and Gary W. Cordner, *Introduction to Police Administration*, 2d ed. (Cincinnati: Anderson, 1989), p. 38.

Records Bureau; one to the Payroll, Billing, and Budget Unit; and two to the Community Services and Training Unit.

▼ CHAPTER SUMMARY

This chapter described the tremendous complexity involved in a police organization. The discussion covered managerial concepts relating to a police department, such as division of labor, chain of command, span of control, and delegation of responsibility and authority. The chapter described the civil service system, the quasi-military nature of the police, the police rank structure, civilianization, police auxiliaries, and police unions and other police affiliations.

The size of the geographic area many police agencies cover forces them to subdivide the area into beats (posts), sectors (zones), precincts, and sometimes divisions. Because of the responsibility of being available twenty-four hours a day, seven days a week, the police must employ a three-tour system.

The functions the police are charged with performing are complex and diverse. The primary responsibility of the police is to maintain order, enforce the law, and provide services to citizens. These functions are generally charged to a department's operational units—primarily patrol, criminal investigations, traffic, and community services units. The police also perform administrative duties and auxiliary services.

Learning Check

1. Identify the major managerial concepts that must be considered when organizing a police department.
2. Discuss how police departments exercise their quasi-military nature.
3. Name some ways in which civilianization can benefit a police department.
4. Discuss the special problems that must be dealt with in organizing a police department that operates seven days a week, twenty-four hours a day.
5. Differentiate among operational units, administrative units, and auxiliary services units.
6. Identify the backbone of the police department, and tell why this is the most important person in police service.

Review Exercise

You have been appointed the new commissioner of the Anycity Police Department. Anycity is a suburban city 60 miles from a major U.S. city; it has a population of 30,000 people and a police department of one hundred officers. The major police problems in Anycity are disorderly teens making unnecessary noise at night, parking and traffic problems in Anycity's commercial district during business hours, and daytime residential burglaries.

The former commissioner's assistant informs you that the department has no organizational chart, no written rules and procedures, and "has always done a great job in the past."

Any city's city manager, however, tells you that the former commissioner was incompetent and that the department is totally disorganized and ineffective. You review the department's personnel records and find that of the one hundred officers in the department, 30 percent are patrol officers, 30 percent are detectives, and 40 percent are supervisors.

Additionally, the entire department is divided evenly into the three tours of duty.

In view of what you learned in this chapter, would you reorganize the department? Why or why not? If you would reorganize, how would you do it?

Key Concepts

civil service system
quasi-military organization
sworn member
nonsworn (civilian) member
squad
platoon
civilianization
lateral transfers
the blue flu

Notes

1. Lawrence W. Sherman, *Scandal and Reform: Controlling Police Corruption* (Berkeley: University of California Press, 1978), p. 128.
2. Ronald J. Waldron, *The Criminal Justice System: An Introduction,* 4th ed. (New York: Harper & Row, 1989), pp. 174–175.
3. George W. Griesinger et al., *Civil Service Systems: Their Impact on Police Administration* (Washington, D.C.: U.S. Government Printing Office, 1979).
4. Dorothy Guyot, "Bending Granite: Attempts to Change the Rank Structure of American Police Departments," *Journal of Police Science and Administration* 7, no. 3 (1979), 253–284.
5. *Criminal Procedure Law of the State of New York,* Article 140, Sections 140.10, 140.30.
6. Leonard Ruchelman, *Who Rules the Police?* (New York: New York University Press, 1973).
7. Brian J. Reaves, *Census of State and Local Law Enforcement Agencies, 1992* (Washington, D.C.: U.S. Government Printing Office, July 1993).
8. National Institute of Law Enforcement and Criminal Justice, *Employing Civilians for Po-*

lice Work (Washington, D.C.: U.S. Government Printing Office, 1975), Preface.

9. President's Commission on Law Enforcement and Administration of Justice, *Task Force Report: The Police* (Washington, D.C.: U.S. Government Printing Office, 1967), p. 123.

10. "Tulsa Police Officials Praise Community Service Program," *Tulsa World,* 15 September 1985, p. 4-B.

11. William B. Donohue, "Summertime Cops," *FBI Law Enforcement Bulletin,* February 1982, p. 3.

12. L. I. Deitch and L. N. Thompson., "The Reserve Officer: One Alternative to the Need for Manpower," *Police Chief,* May 1985, pp. 59–61.

13. President's Commission on Law Enforcement and Administration of Justice, *The Challenge of Crime in a Free Society* (Washington, D.C.: U.S. Government Printing Office 1967), p. 112; and Geoffrey N. Calvert,

Portable Police Pensions—Improving Inter-Agency Transfers (Washington, D.C.: U.S. Government Printing Office, 1971).

14. Anthony V. Bouza, "Police Unions: How They Look from the Academic Side," in *Police Leadership in America,* ed. William A. Geller (New York: Praeger, 1975), p. 241.

15. Bouza, "Police Unions," p. 241.

16. Police Executive Research Forum, *Survey of Police Operational and Administrative Practice, 1981* (Washington, D.C.: Police Executive Research Forum, 1982), pp. 606–610.

17. Police Executive Research Forum, *Survey of Police Practice,* pp. 606–610.

18. Waldron, *Criminal Justice System,* p. 154.

19. For the section on police department units: Permission granted by publisher, Anderson Publishing, Cincinnati, Ohio 45202. Robert Sheehan and Gary W. Cordner, *Introduction to Police Administration,* 2d ed. (Cincinnati; Anderson, 1989), pp. 113–162.

Sample Chapter 12

Women and Ethnic Groups

Reprinted by permission of *Aging, the Individual, and Society* by Georgia M. Barrow. Copyright 1996 by West Publishing Company. All rights reserved. Some figures and tables have been removed.

13 Women and Ethnic Groups

*M*ulticulturalism has become a central focus of the social sciences. This focus corrects a past tendency to ignore the diversity and richness that ethnic groups have added to American life. Until recently the study of aging America was a study of the older white Americans who made up nearly 90 percent of America's elderly population; while the many ethnic groups were ignored. Generalizing from the population to all subcultures of elders is misleading, incorrect, and insensitive. As researchers become more aware of ethnic differences, more attention will be drawn to their unique situations and needs.

In future years there will be marked increases in the racial and ethnic diversity of those 65 and over. Presently the ethnic aged comprise 13 percent of all those 65 and over, but they will grow to 22 percent of all elders in 2020 and be 33 percent of the older population by the year 2050. Thus, with every passing year they become a larger component of aging America. The proportion of all elders who are African-American will increase slowly from 8 percent in 1990 to 10 percent by 2050. The American Indian population will increase from .1 million to .5 million in that time span. It is the Asian and Hispanic populations that will swell the ranks the most swiftly. Asians will increase from 1 percent to 8 percent of the elder population, and Hispanics from 4 percent to 16 percent of the elder population by 2050. Immigration is a big factor contributing to the rise in the elder population of these two later groups. Increases in all the groups are related to past fertility patterns and to increasing life expectancy *(National Institute on Aging, 1993)*.

The exploration of ethnic minorities must begin with basic definitions of what constitutes an ethnic group and what constitutes a minority. If an ethnic group has a shared identity based on language and cultural tradition, the Asian, Hispanic, or American Indian groups might each be defined as one ethnic group or many ethnic groups, depending on one's interpretation. And

African Americans, if they had no interest or knowledge of their African heritage, might not fit the definition of an ethnic group. Acknowledging the limitations of the "ethnic" concept, we consider here four groups: African Americans, Hispanics, Asian, and Native Americans. A minority elder is someone 65 or over who is discriminated against by the dominant group in a society. That person suffers from both ageism and racism. Women are not necessarily an ethnic minority, but they hold a lower status in our culture than men. Therefore, women, have been judged a minority group, not in terms of numbers, but in terms of status. Older women are considered first in this chapter and the section on ethnic minority elders follows.

☼ Women

The minority status of women is based on the sexism that pervades U.S. society. For older women sexism is compounded by ageism. Older women have trouble finding acceptance and equality in the work world, in politics, and in romance. Women are making progress in these areas; however, hundreds of years of established patterns cannot be changed overnight.

One advantage for women is their willingness to reach out and get help: from each other, from books and seminars, from re-entry programs at colleges, and from various counseling services. Models of positive aging such as Meryl Streep and Susan Sarandon, in their 40s; Jane Fonda, Erica Jong, in their 50s; and Gloria Steinhem, who turned 60 in 1994, are looked to for advice and inspiration. Dr. Ruth Jacobs (1993), a university professor and author of books for older women is also one who offers support to aging women. She recommends books such as hers and the following:

Be an Outrageous Older Woman (Jacobs, 1993)
I Am Becoming the Woman I've Wanted (Martz, ed., 1994)
Flying Solo: Single Women in Midlife (Anderson and Stewart, 1994)
Moving Beyond Words (Steinhem, 1994)
Going Strong (York, 1991)
Women, Aging and Ageism (Rosenthal, 1991)
Look Me in the Eye: Old Women, Aging and Ageism (Macdonald and Rich, 1991)
Old and Smart: Women and Aging (Nickerson, 1991)

suggest that the present generation of older women is receiving more attention and validation than previous generations. Roles for older women, which formerly have been narrowly constructed in the U.S., are broadening. According to Gail Sheehy (1993), American women are beginning to view the approach of menopause not as a marker to the end, but as a bridge to a new stage of adulthood. Increasingly, older women have more options to experience a rewarding and fulfilling later life. Two areas of struggle for older women are discussed in this section of the text: finances and the double standard of aging.

Financial Status

Some have called the high percentage of women and their children among the poor the "feminization of poverty." Just as for younger cohorts, poverty after age 65 is heavily concentrated among women. Of all individuals poor enough to receive Supplemental Security Income (SSI), two-thirds are women. Women comprise more than 70 percent of the older poor. Poverty rates have fallen more slowly over the last two decades among older women living alone than for older men or for older married couples.

MIDDLE-AGED DISPLACED HOMEMAKERS

Financial problems for women frequently originate in middle age, or even earlier. A typical displaced homemaker is middle-aged and has been a homemaker for most of her adult life, dependent on her husband for her income and security. She finds herself suddenly alone with little or no income and with limited marketable skills. In 1993, 30 percent of all women in the 45-to-64 age bracket were single, widowed, or divorced.

Most divorced women do not receive alimony. Many widows are left with few funds; they are ineligible for unemployment insurance because they have been engaged in unpaid labor in their homes. As more young women get educations and start careers before middle age, the displaced homemaker problem will become smaller.

The middle-aged woman who can save some money (or at least pay into Social Security) improves her chances for a fulfilling old age. Though middle-aged women are now in the workforce in large numbers, a pay gap persists for these women and for older women. They tend to be in low-paying "women's jobs," working as secretaries, sales clerks, waitresses, nurses, or teachers.

SINGLE, WIDOWED, AND DIVORCED OLDER WOMEN

Single Women

More than 25 percent of women 65 and older who live alone or with nonrelatives live below the poverty level (U.S. Bureau of the Census, 1993, 470, table 738). This percentage would almost double if the Federal Poverty Index were updated as experts recommend. In contrast, 8 percent of those living with their husbands are poor. Those married and living with their husbands have the benefits of another income. Those single women receiving Social Security receive lower

On Aging

■ *Maya Angelou*

When you see me sitting quietly,
Like a sack left on the shelf,
Don't think I need your chattering.
I'm listening to myself.
Hold! Stop! Don't pity me!
Hold! Stop your sympathy!
Understanding if you got it,
Otherwise I'll do without it!

When my bones are stiff and aching
And my feet won't climb the stair,
I will only ask one favor:
Don't bring me no rocking chair.

When you see me walking, stumbling,
Don't study and get it wrong
'Cause tired don't mean lazy
And every goodbye ain't gone.
I'm the same person I was back then,
A little less hair, a little less chin,
A lot less lungs and much less wind.
But ain't I lucky I can still breathe in.

From *And Still I Rise* by Maya Angelou. © Copyright 1978 by Maya Angelou. Reprinted by permission of Random House, Inc.

pensions than men because the earnings on which they contributed to the program tend to be lower than the earnings of men of their generation. Women who are 65 years old today are still paying for the wage and social discrimination they suffered in their earlier working years.

Widows

Widows constitute nearly one-half of all women 65 and over. Of women 65 and over who live alone, 85% are widows. Some widowed women depended on their husbands' incomes, and, when retired, on their husbands' private pension plans or Social Security. More often than not, private pension plans fall sharply when a retired spouse dies. The death of a spouse also lowers the amount of Social Security benefits. If this is the case, widows' low incomes expose them to greater social and economic risks than other segments of the elder population. Data from a national sample of widows of all ages found that widowhood decreased living standards by 18 percent and pushed into poverty 10 percent of women whose prewidowhood incomes were above the poverty line. Not surprisingly, economic status prior to widowhood is the strongest prediction of status during widowhood (Bound et al., 1991). A major social issue is how to meet the needs of older widows.

The opportunity for older widows to remarry is quite limited, due to the relatively small number of eligible males in their age group. Older females who are eligible for marriage outnumber eligible males by a ratio of three to one. In addition, males who marry after age 65 tend to marry women from younger age groups. The number of men aged 65 and older who marry during a given year is twice as high as the number of brides in that age category. Over half of the older grooms marry females under the age of 65.

Older couples tend to live by themselves. The death of a woman's spouse thus assumes great significance. More than 60 percent of widows continue to live alone. This can be expensive and isolating, even if it is a preferred lifestyle.

Divorcees

The socioeconomic well-being of divorcees is significantly below that of married or even widowed women. Given current statistics and expected trends in marriage, divorce, and widowhood, the numbers of married and widowed older women will decline, but the proportion of divorced older women will dramatically increase. Included in the increasing divorce rate are divorces involving women over age 40. And, although 7 percent of women over age 60 are divorced (and not remarried), this statistic is expected to increase. Viewed from another angle, 18 percent of all married women 40 and over (based on recent trends) will experience a divorce from their first marriage. From still another perspective, 11 percent of those who have been married for 20 years will divorce (Uhlenberg, 1990).

For women, the probability of remarriage after divorce declines steeply with age and is quite low after age 45. In 1990, for example, fewer than 5 out of every 100 divorced women between the ages of 45 and 64 remarried within the year. The remarriage rate for divorced women between 45 and 64 is only one-tenth of that for those under age 25. If current rates persist, few women who enter midlife divorced, or who divorce after midlife, will ever remarry. Remarriage rates have fallen dramatically since 1965; they have fallen by half for women between the ages of 45 and 64.

According to rough projections, by 2025 no more than 37 percent of women between the ages of 65 and 69 will be in their first marriage. Half will not be in any marriage; this figure could be considerably higher if the divorce rate after age 40 continues to increase and the remarriage rate continues to decline (Uhlenberg, 1990). There is good reason for public concern over these statistics. Older women living outside marriage, especially those who are divorced, have much lower standards of living than married women. Unless this fact changes, the economic well-being of older women will continue to deteriorate. The high divorce rates of adult children strains family resources as well. Divorced sons and daughters have more trouble finding time and money for their aging parents. Older divorced women, financially vulnerable, are often forced to look for work and to share residences. They must be creative to make ends meet.

Upgrading the Financial Status of Older Women

In our society, in spite of positive steps toward equality, women in the workforce and in politics remain in inferior positions. Their lower incomes reflect this fact. Inequalities in income for older women will not totally disappear until women achieve equality in the workplace from the beginning of their careers.

Today, women on their own and as a part of the women's movement are attempting to upgrade their status. As more women get good-paying jobs in their younger years, they acquire built-in protection for their older years by becoming entitled to their own Social Security at maximum benefits.

If women are homemakers or caretakers of children or elder parents during their working years, they suffer financially in old age. Being removed from the paid labor market reduces their Social Security benefits (Kingson and O'Grady-LeShane, 1993). They could be compensated in a number of ways. One way would be for women to receive full credit for their nonmarket labor in pension plans, including Social Security (Quadagno and Meyer, 1993). Another plan suggests combining the wage earner's 100 percent benefits with the dependent homemaker's 50 percent benefits. The wage earner and the homemaker could then divide the resulting 150 percent into equal shares of 75 percent that they would receive regardless of gender or family earning roles, and they could place the equal shares in separate accounts under their own names and Social Security numbers. The funds would thus remain unaffected by possible divorce or separation.

Some centers provide job counseling, training, placement services, legal counseling, and outreach and information services to middle-aged and older women. Policies that encourage work and insure adequate survivor benefits improve the financial status of older retired women.

DOUBLE STANDARD OF AGING

In 1972, Susan Sontag coined the term **double standard of aging.** By implication, the standard of aging for a woman progressively destroys her sense of beauty and self-worth, whereas the standard of aging for a man is much less wounding.

Society trains women from an early age to care in an exaggerated way about their physical beauty. As a result, women spend much more time and money on their appearance than men. They may disappear periodically at parties and other social gatherings to see that their makeup and hairstyle are still intact. Their role, society tells them, demands this behavior. Women must be more concerned about being "fat" or "ugly." Cosmetic and plastic surgery and face-lifts are performed more often on women than on men. Many women's exercise programs emphasize appearance rather than strength or endurance: In the self-help section at any local video store, note the number of cassettes that promise shapelier breasts, thighs, or buttocks. Or attend an aerobics class at a local health club and note the female clients' concerns about their exercise clothing.

The youth culture in our society exerts an intense social pressure for women to remain young. In a personal account of her own aging Ruth Thone, an activist from Lincoln, Nebraska, gave her reason for writing her book. It was the "subtle, deep, pervasive, unspoken distaste and derision" for old Americans in general and old women in particular (Thone, 1993, xi). She wrote of her own "internalized aging" in which she is filled with self loathing and anxiety about aging. She is also furious at being sexually invisible to men and being patronized by younger people. She is sensitive about any jokes putting down older women. She gave this account.

My husband found a joke in a magazine, that he added to his repertoire, about two women in a nursing home who decided to streak their fellow residents. Two startled old men looked up and one asked, "What was that?" "I don't know," the other replied, "but whatever they were wearing sure needs ironing." My husband did not understand how hurt I was by that joke, by that ridicule of women's aging skin and by the double standard that does not

....

words never spoken

■ *Doris Vanderlipp Manley*

walking through the city I saw the young girls
with bodies all silk from underthings to eyebrows
legs shaven
heels pumiced
nails glossed
hair lacquered
thighs taut
eyes clear
gladbreasted tittering girls

and I wondered how even for an hour
you could love a woman who has no silk
no silk
only burlap
and that
well worn
tattered
and frayed
with the effort of making a soul

Sandra Martz, ed., *When I Am an Old Woman I Shall Wear Purple* (Manhattan Beach, CA: Papier-Mache Press, 1987), p. 89. Reprinted by permission of the author.

....

make a mockery of men's aging skin. He insisted it was my feminism, not any ageism in him that kept me from knowing the joke was harmless. (Thone, 1993, 54)

She wondered, "Am I an object of scorn as my body ages?" She dealt with self-criticism, self-rejection, and self-hate, coming to terms with aging by writing in her journal, meditating, and becoming more spiritual. In a chapter on "The Grief of Aging" she described working through her sadness at the loss of her youth.

Not all women can confront their aging so directly and honestly. They buy into the idea that they must stay young and beautiful in appearance forever. According to researcher Goodman (1993), dieting programs have become a national obsession and cosmetic surgeries are greatly escalating in the 1990s. Older women in her study assigned more importance to their faces, and young women measured self-worth by body size—especially breast size. Older women were concerned with wrinkles, "saggy" jowls, and "droopy" eyelids. These concerns led to face- and neck-lifts and to chemical peels to "smooth" the skin. The successful exploitation of women's fears of growing older has been called **age terrorism.** Women are so frightened of being rejected or abandoned at home by romantic partners and in the workplace by their bosses that they will buy any product to prolong a youthful look (Pearlman, 1993). Pearlman speaks of **late midlife astonishment**—a developmental crisis in which women aged 50 to 60 work through society's devaluation of their physical appearance. Women suffer a loss of self-esteem, depression, and feelings of shame and self-consciousness. Feminist therapists believe that body image disturbances are not limited to eating-disordered clients and occur to women of all ages (Chrisler and Ghiz, 1993). One example is Helen Gurley Brown, former editor of Cosmopolitan Magazine, the "Cosmo Girl," who at age 71 referred to age as the great destroyer. She admits to silicone injections, cosmetic surgery, shrink sessions, endless dieting, and a 90-minute daily "killer" exercise regime. She says:

I'm afraid of losing my sexuality. I'm desperately afraid of retirement. I fear that with age, I'll cease being a woman, that I'll be neuter. I fear losing my looks and ending up looking like . . . like an old crumb. (quoted in an interview with Marian Christy, 1993)

The perception that only youthful women are beautiful perpetuates the older man-younger woman syndrome and isolates the older woman. Women who base their self-worth on signs of youthful beauty have problems aging. Some inroads have been made, for example, by older women who date and marry younger men. But the double standard still endures.

In terms of diet and exercise, our society emphasizes health and fitness like never before. In one sense this has been positive as older women join the trend and live healthier lives. But as long as society's definition of being beautiful sets expectations that are unrealistic, women will continue to suffer.

☼ African Americans

African Americans constitute the largest minority group in the United States, totaling 30 million in 1990 (U.S. Bureau of the Census, 1993, 32, table 33). About 2.5 million of these African Americans are 65 or over. They are a diverse group, yet, some overall pictures do emerge. A majority of elder African Americans (53 percent) live in the South. There are fewer males than females. Older men tend to be married; women tend to be divorced or widowed. African-American elders are less likely to be married than any other ethnic group, but all ethnic elderly, including African Americans, are more likely to live with other family members (not counting the spouse) than whites.

African Americans as a group differ widely in socioeconomic factors. As a result of the civil-rights movement, African Americans have gained a large middle class, a class having grown so greatly that it now outnumbers the African-American poor. As comparatively well-off African Americans move to better neighborhoods, they leave behind an African-American "underclass"—chronic welfare recipients, the unemployed, high-school dropouts, and single-parent families. Although many moved into the upper middle class in the 1980s, one-third remained locked in deprivation. There now exists a deep class division among African Americans (Frisby, 1991). Elders in inner cities are often left to cope with deteriorating neighborhoods, high crime rates, and the threat of violence.

INCOME AND HOUSING

Compared with Caucasian elders, **African-American elders** have less adequate income, and poorer quality housing. Although the income level for older African Americans has improved over the past 25 years, the improvement rate has not been as rapid as that for older whites. In 1959, 62.5 percent of African-American elders were living in poverty, double the percentage for whites. In 1992, 24.9 percent of African Americans aged 65 and over were living below the poverty level, a figure more than triple that of whites (see Figure 13.1). Unemployment rates for African Americans of all ages tend to be higher than those for whites, and have been for many years.

A small percentage of retired African Americans are from the upper class, having owned large businesses or real estate, headed large corporations, or worked in the highest levels of industry. Other retired African Americans are middle class, having been schoolteachers, owners of small businesses, or government employees. Still others are retired from manual labor or domestic service jobs. Overall, however, they have not paid as much into Social Security as whites have; therefore, they will be eligible for less in old age. They are also less likely to have accumulated savings, assets such as real estate, or pensions.

African-American elders are slightly more likely to be looking for work after age 65, due to inadequate retirement income. Older African-American men have higher unemployment rates than older white men. Elders in the

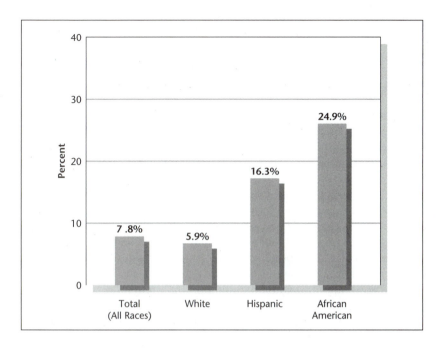

Figure 13.1

Percentage by Race of Persons Aged 65 and Older Living below the Poverty Level, 1992

SOURCE: U.S. Bureau of the Census, *Statistical Abstract of the United States.* 1994, 114th (Washington, DC: U.S. Bureau of the Census 1994), p. 478 (selected information from table 734).

lower socioeconomic groups, regardless of race, have a different understanding of retirement. Health permitting, they often must work at lower-paying jobs well beyond retirement age in order to meet basic expenses for food, medical care, and housing. Studies of work patterns among African Americans revealed a large group of "unretired retirees" aged 55 and over who need jobs but cannot find them. They do find occasional work well into old age—but this work is usually part-time and temporary. Those under age 62 are not eligible for Social Security or other pension programs and, therefore, without work, are more financially needy than those eligible for pensions.

Studies of African-American retirees aged 65 and over show that those who receive Social Security have relatively high morale—higher, in fact, than that of their counterparts who are still working. This finding is reversed for whites. One explanation for the high morale of retired African Americans is the undesirable work they often face should they remain employed (Gibson, 1993).

Older African Americans are more likely than older whites to reside within decaying central cities and to live in substandard housing. They are also more likely than whites to live in public housing. Those who work with minority elders must be able to advise them accurately on low-cost public housing, low-interest housing loans, and other forms of available property relief.

Older African Americans are admitted to nursing homes at between one-half and three-quarters of the rate of whites. This underutilization cannot be explained only with the statement that African Americans prefer to care for elders within their families. In many cases they cannot afford the long-term care they need. Thus, racial disparities in institutional care must be considered (Belgrave et al., 1993).

HEALTH CARE AND LIFE EXPECTANCY

Low-income African Americans tend to have health-care problems. They lack the money required for good health care, and this inadequate care results in a life expectancy rate that is much lower than that for whites. The average African American's life expectancy was 69.1 years in 1991, 7 years below the average of 76.1 years for whites (U.S. Bureau of the Census, 1994, 88, table 116). Given an average retirement age of 65, the average African-American *male*, whose life expectancy in 1991 was 64.5 years, cannot realistically expect to live long enough to collect benefits from Social Security and Medicare. The lower life expectancy does, however, equalize with whites at age 80 and after.

The differences in life expectancy between African and white Americans fade away if a number of social variables are held constant, these being marital status, income, education, and family size. (Marriage, high income and education, and small family size are correlated with longevity). Thus, longevity appears to be more socially than racially determined (Guralnik et al., 1993; Bryant and Rakowski, 1992).

Between 1986 and 1991, life expectancy for African Americans actually *dropped*. Though African Americans had been sharing in life expectancy increases over the decades, the trend reversed in the late 1980s. One major reason is the high number of African-American babies who die in their first year. But this is only one factor. Thousands of African Americans die in the prime of life from illnesses that could be cured or treated by routine medical care: appendicitis, pneumonia, hypertension, cervical cancer, tuberculosis, and influenza are examples. Given early detection and good treatment, all these illnesses are curable; nobody should be dying of these things (Hilts, 1990).

Older African Americans have endured a lifetime of "the color barrier." Operating under a theory that low social status generates repressed negative emotions and inner tensions, some gerontologists believe the high incidence of hypertension reflects the pressures of low social status. They believe that both physical and mental illness can result from the ongoing prejudicial attitudes and behavior of others. Others believe hypertension to be genetic.

Whatever the cause, the incidence of high blood pressure among African Americans is nearly two-and-a-half times that of whites, and the mortality rate from high blood pressure is higher for African Americans than for whites (U.S. Bureau of the Census, 1993, 25). Though yoga, aerobics, and biofeedback programs to reduce blood pressure have typically been attended by white, middle-class persons, African Americans are now joining these programs.

FAMILY AND SOCIAL RELATIONSHIPS

More than 40 percent of African-American women 65 and over live in poverty. The high mortality rate of African-American males and the high divorce rate alienate these women from a traditional family lifestyle. More effort needs to be directed toward unifying African-American women and channeling their efforts to improve their socioeconomic conditions. Consequently, political activists urge women to join organizations, such as the National Association for the Advancement of Colored People (NAACP) and the National Black Women's Political Caucus, that can speak and work effectively for them.

Despite racism and economic woes, African Americans have possessed a resolve to persevere. The solid family ties, which are one source of this strength, is indicated in the concept of **familism.** The notion of family often extends beyond the immediate household. Within the family network, roles are flexible and interchangeable. A young mother, an aunt, a grandfather, or an older couple may head a family. Grandmothers often help raise children while the parents work (Strom et al., 1993). The high divorce rate has encouraged reliance on older relatives. Families tend to value their elder members because they have survived in the face of hardship and because they play important roles within the family (Luckey, 1994). A study of 60 African-American grandmothers and grandfathers rearing their children's children as a consequence of the adult children's drug addiction showed that grandparents bore a large burden. It was emotionally rewarding but exacted many costs, psychological and financial (Burton, 1992). Similar findings were shown in grandmothers raising grandchildren in the crack cocaine epidemic (Minkler et al., 1992).

Religion has also been a resource of support (Nye, 1993; Walls, 1992). The African-American church has been a source of strength for coping with racial oppression and has played a vital role in the survival and advancement of African Americans. The church has provided a place of importance and belonging. Within the church, elders receive recognition as members, choir vocalists, deacons, and treasurers. A study of a Pennsylvania church, which revealed that church membership contributed to feelings of well-being among older African Americans, recommended that these churches act as a link between families and aging agencies. The church is a likely information and referral institution because so many older individuals are active participants (Walls and Zarit, 1991).

A spirit of survival has seen older African Americans through hard times. Thankful to have survived, they are more likely to appreciate aging; thus, they accept it more easily than those who have not experienced such hardship.

FUTURE OUTLOOK

Though data on the lives of African-American elders are becoming more available, our knowledge is still far from adequate. We are gaining knowledge about their lifestyles, roles, and adaptations to living environments, but the information on whites that pertains to these topics still far exceeds that about minorities.

Table 13.1

....

Social and Economic
Characteristics of
White and African-
American Population
(percent), 1992

Characteristic	Percent	
	White	*Black*
Age 65 and over	13.0	8.3
Homeowner	67.5	42.3
College, 4 years or more	22.1	11.9
Income of $50,000+	34.1	14.9
Unemployed	4.3	8.9
Person below poverty level	10.3	33.8

SOURCE: U.S. Bureau of the Census, *Statistical Abstract of the United States,* 1993, 113th (Washington, DC: Bureau of the Census, 1993), p. 46, table 49.

Studies of *fear* of crime and victimization show much higher rates of fear for African Americans than for whites; and, in fact, their rates of victimization are significantly higher than those for whites. The major reason is thought to be geographic locations—more of them compared with white American elders, live in high-crime areas such as the inner city and in or near public housing. And because feelings of alienation and mistrust of police may have existed from their youth, these elders are less likely than their white counterparts to reach out for help. Social policy experts suggest neighborhood watch programs to unite residents and also recommend age-segregated housing with more safety features (Barazan, 1994).

Despite recent affirmative action plans in the United States, the economic outlook for large numbers of older African Americans is bleak. Table 13.1 reflects some characteristics that are related to their economic inequality. African Americans and other minorities are still disproportionately clustered in peripheral industries that pay lower wages: agriculture, retail trade, nonunionized small businesses, and low-profit companies that pay minimum wage. In contrast, white Americans are still clustered in better-paying "core" industries, such as the automobile industry, construction, and other high-profit, unionized industries. Although some improvement can be expected by the twenty-first century, it will be small: Between 1982 and 1992, the ratio of African-American family income to white family income actually declined, from 62 to 56 percent. In 1992, the average income of whites was $37,783 a year; the African-American average was $21,548 (U.S. Bureau of the Census, 1993, 46, table 49). If young and middle-aged working African Americans cannot fare as well as whites, they will not compare much better in old age. Only through major economic changes that promote the hiring of minorities in major businesses and industries will they begin to achieve economic parity in middle and old age.

✹ Hispanic Americans

Older Hispanics, the "ancianos," are not a homogeneous group. Researchers are often unprepared for the cultural and socioeconomic diversity of the Hispanic community. One of the many obstacles preventing **Hispanic elders**

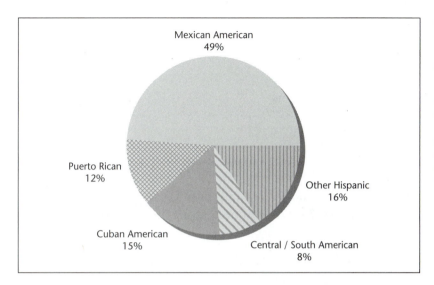

Figure 13.2

Hispanic Population by Nation of Origin

SOURCE: Data for Circle Graph from National Institute on Aging, "Profiles of America's Elderly," Washington, DC: U.S. Dept. of Health and Human Services, November 1993, p. 2.

from being understood and served is the lack of a clear-cut definition of who they are. Census counting often uses two inclusive terms that increase the problem: Spanish heritage (having Spanish blood or antecedents) and Spanish origin (having been born in a Spanish-speaking country or having antecedents who were). Theoretically, then, a person could be of Spanish origin but not of Spanish heritage and vice versa. The term *Hispanic* will be used here to mean Spanish people in a broad sense including either term.

DEMOGRAPHICS

In 1990, more than 22 million persons in the United States were of Hispanic origin. Of these, 5.5 percent were aged 65 or older, and this figure will rise to 7.2 percent by 2010 and 10.9 percent by 2025 (U.S. Bureau of the Census, 1993, 22, 25). Mexican Americans are the largest Hispanic group in the United States—more than half of all Hispanics combined. The percentage breakdown is shown in Figure 13.2.

The 1970 and 1980 censuses identified only four categories of Hispanics: Mexican, Puerto Rican, Cuban, and Other. The 1990 census, reflecting the large influx from still other countries, identifies 14 categories.

Mexico
Cuba
Puerto Rico
Dominican Republic
Central America
   El Salvador
   Guatemala

Nicaragua

Ecuador

Honduras

Panama

Other Central Americans

South America

Peru

Columbia

Other South Americans

The Hispanic population, one of the fastest-growing ethnic groups, is expected to be the largest U.S. minority group after the year 2000.

MINORITY STATUS

Several social factors indicate the minority status of Hispanic elders: (1) the high percentage that live below the poverty level; (2) the inadequate health care; (3) the second highest illiteracy rate among U.S. racial/ethnic groups—only the rate for Native American elders is higher; and (4) low occupational levels such as operatives, artisans, unskilled laborers, and farm workers. Because they receive fewer social services than whites, Hispanics tend to stay in the workforce longer than whites. Some Mexican-American elders are unlikely to seek social services support because they entered the country illegally; by seeking government help, they risk detection and expulsion.

MIGRATION PATTERNS

Most Hispanic immigrants are from Mexico, Cuba, and Puerto Rico. (Their portion totals 76 percent of all Hispanics.) The majority of Mexican Americans were born in this country, yet other Hispanic elders are more likely to be foreign born. The foreign-born Hispanics are not as acculturated as native-born citizens: They need more help in understanding and utilizing services. Further, programs developed for them must acknowledge the traditions and values they have retained.

Differing patterns of migration have brought Hispanics to various locations in the United States. Hispanic-American immigrants tend to live in urban areas. Immigrants from 6 of the 12 Hispanic nations identified in the 1990 census have more than 80 percent of their populations in the nation's 20 largest cities (New York, Los Angeles, Chicago, Miami, Washington, D.C., Boston, Philadelphia, and San Diego, for example), and three others have between 70 percent and 79 percent in the 20 largest cities. Because so many Mexican Americans are born in the U.S., they are not as extensively urbanized as other Hispanics. Some became citizens when the rural Mexican territory in the Southwest was incorporated into the United States. It is still very rural and heavily populated with Mexican Americans.

However, Hispanics who immigrate (including Mexican immigrants) tend to locate in urban areas. In Texas, for example, the older urban immigrants outnumber their rural counterparts by a ratio of five to one. San Antonio, Houston, and Dallas have large numbers of Mexican Americans who are foreign born.

Puerto Rican and Cuban elders are almost exclusively city dwellers. The Hispanic populations of Florida and the Northeast are more urbanized than those of the Southwest.

THE AMERICAN EXPERIENCE

Hispanic elders today are an ethnic composite that has suffered major linguistic and cultural barriers to assimilation and has occupied a low socioeconomic status. Forty-five percent of Hispanic elders are not proficient in English (Applewhite and Daley, 1988). In 1992, 16.3 percent of persons of Hispanic origin aged 65 and over lived below the poverty level (see Figure 13.1). A major reason for the financial disadvantages of older Hispanics is the lack of pension plan coverage during their working lives: Their coverage rates are lower than those for whites or African Americans. Health problems such as diabetes and obesity are more common among Hispanic elders than in the aged population as a whole.

UTILIZATION OF SERVICES

As a rule, Hispanic elders tend to be somewhat suspicious of governmental institutions and of service workers and researchers not of their culture. Their suspicion, along with a lack of education and money, results in isolation and nonutilization of available services. This underutilization tends to conceal their very real need. Further, because the census undercounts minorities, underutilization is even greater than is generally recognized. One example is in nursing home care, where Hispanic elders are greatly underrepresented (Mui and Burnette, 1994). Social program providers need to develop a sensitivity to, and communication skills with, Hispanic seniors. Popular beliefs characterize Mexican Americans as living in extended families and, in fact, Hispanic families do tend to be larger than white families in the United States. But that does not mean that the extended family system runs smoothly. Generally speaking, the more acculturated the family members, the less extensive the family interaction, and the more the breakdown of extended family. Traditionally, adult children provide a great deal of support to Hispanic parents in terms of chores such as laundry, housework, transportation, and shopping; both cultural values and economic need dictate these close family ties. Moreover, for those who do not speak English, adult children are needed to provide a link to American culture. But changes are eroding the extended family concept and replacing it with the nuclear family group (Lubben and Becerra, 1987).

STUDYING ETHNIC VARIATIONS

For all Hispanic groups, researchers are studying the types of ethnic communities and institutions that tend to develop in given localities and their impact on the lives of elders. Mexican Americans, for example, participate heavily in senior citizen clubs. Actually, the senior citizen culture is strong in the various representations of Hispanic community (Torres-Gill, 1988). Though minority elders tend to underutilize government and health services, high ethnic population density seems to correlate with higher rates of utilization. The status of the elders in the various Hispanic groups is better in large, fully developed ethnic communities than in small or scattered ones. Here are some statistics about high ethnic population density:

- Eighteen percent of all Hispanics live in Los Angeles.
- Twelve percent of all Hispanics live in New York.
- New York's Puerto Rican population is double that of San Juan, Puerto Rico.
- Seventy-seven percent of immigrants from the Dominican Republic live in urbanized New York.
- Laredo, Texas, is 94 percent Hispanic. The percentage is nearly that high in several other Texas border towns.
- Cubans are clustered in Miami and other cities of southeastern Florida.
- Panamanians are the most geographically diverse. Other groups cluster in enclaves of large cities, by national origin. (Winsberg, 1994)

Another area of research is the unique cultural traditions that are maintained in each Hispanic group. Cuban elders, for example, tend to be much more politically active than Mexican Americans. A professor from Miami describes some unique aspects of Cuban culture as they affect elders (Hernandez, 1992): Cuban culture is a blend of whites from the Iberian Peninsula and blacks from Africa. The Afro-Cuban culture emphasizes respect for elders, stemming from their folk healing beliefs and practices. "Familism" (adherence to strong family values) is strong in Cuban culture and evokes guilt when members do not fulfill expected roles. For example, adult children are filled with guilt if they do not care for aged parents. Cuban women tend to marry older men who care for them financially. Eventually the younger wife cares for the aged husband. Complete dependence on family members, such as adult children or spouses, is welcomed and encouraged by the culture and not interpreted as pathology.

Neglected areas of research are social stratification within ethnic groups, rate of return migration, and degree of cultural adaptation. Hispanic elders who lived most of their lives in their native countries and do not immigrate until late adulthood no doubt experience more culture shock and isolation, but this phenomena needs to be explored.

☼ Asian Americans

Asian American refers in the broadest sense to persons of Chinese, Korean, Japanese, Filipino, East Indian, Thai, Vietnamese, Burmese, Indonesian, Laotian, Malayan, and Cambodian descent who live in the United States. Most **Asian-American elders** are concentrated in California, Hawaii, New York, Illinois, Washington, and Massachusetts. The total U.S. population of Asians and Pacific Islanders was 7.5 million in 1991 (U.S. Bureau of the Census, 1993, 22). Of this number, 6.3 percent are aged 65 and over, or nearly .5 million persons. Of the Asian elders in 1990, about 30 percent were Chinese; 24 percent Japanese; 24 percent Filipino; 8 percent Korean; and 14 percent other Asians and Pacific Islanders.

A single description cannot encompass the Asian communities in the United States. Differences of culture, language, and religion make each group unique (see Table 13.2). Asians are alike, however, in the sense that they all have encountered language barriers and racism.

That Asian elders have nothing to worry about because Asians always care for their own is a misconception. The current generation of Asian Americans, which has been conditioned to our social and cultural folkways and mores, may regard their elders as an unwelcome burden, just as many middle-class white Americans seem to do. According to traditional culture in China, Japan, and Korea, the eldest son assumes responsibility of his elder parents. Filial piety is a custom demanding that family members respect and care for elders. Because of the high proportion of single Asian immigrants, this custom has weakened. Further, a considerable moral "generation gap" often exists between young Asian Americans and their elders. Older family members tend to hang on to traditions, especially those concerning moral propriety, whereas the young move away from them.

Because health and welfare agencies have few bilingual staff members, and because they therefore have difficulty publicizing their available services to the Asian community, outreach programs to Asian-American seniors have been limited in their success. These deficits, in addition to their socially conditioned reluctance to seek aid from their adopted land, result in neglect of Asian-American elders.

JAPANESE AMERICANS

Most of the Japanese who first came to the United States were single men, often younger sons who did not inherit any family wealth. The bulk of the Japanese immigration, which took place between 1870 and 1924, consisted primarily of men who wanted to have traditional families. Many waited until they could afford a wife, who was generally much younger, and then paid for one to come from Japan. This pattern reinforced traditional values of high status for men and elders. The survivors of that earliest immigration period, called *issei*, are now mostly women because the men, being much older, have died.

The first generation worked primarily on farms or as unskilled laborers or service workers. However, within 25 years of entering the United States, they showed great economic mobility. Though their internment during World War II was economically as well as morally devastating, Japanese Americans as a group rebounded remarkably. First-generation Japanese, the *issei*, learned to live socially segregated from American culture. The children of the *issei*, the *nissei*, generally born between 1910 and 1940, are more likely to be integrated into the American mainstream. Most *nissei* are now over 65 and doing well economically and socially.

Japanese-American elders, on the whole, have adequate savings or family support in their retirement years. Japanese Americans have largely replicated the traditional pattern of family care for elders; 46 percent live with an adult child in addition to or in lieu of a spouse. In traditional Japanese society, when retirement occurred, the retiree joined the ranks of elders and assumed religious duties in the community. This particular tradition is lacking in the United States (Markides and Mindel, 1987).

CHINESE AMERICANS

Because past restrictive immigration laws denied entry to wives or children, a disproportionate share of Chinese- and Filipino-American elders are men. Male immigrants have outnumbered females by at least three to one in census counts. These Asian men were valuable as cheap labor in U.S. mines, canneries, farms, and railroads, but their wives and children were neither needed nor wanted. Though we cannot fully assess the damage to the family life of the elderly Chinese American, such damage has no doubt been extensive, traumatic, and demoralizing.

The immigration law of 1924, which halted Asian immigration, forbade males of Chinese descent from bringing their foreign-born wives to the United States. As a result, many Chinese men in the United States could not marry. Although the men who originally came in the early 1900s are a rapidly vanishing group, a few can still be found, typically living in poverty and without close family ties.

Chinese Americans retain a tradition of respect for elders based on Confucian ethics. Traditionally, the Chinese family was embedded in a larger system of extended family and clans than was the Japanese family. Older family members held wealth and power, not only in their immediate family but all the way up the family hierarchy to the encompassing clan. Though this traditional structure has never been reproduced in the United States, respect for elders persists. The Chinese pattern is for adult children to bring a widowed parent into their household.

Chinese elders are increasingly second-generation. This generally means that they are more educated, more acculturated, and have a more comfortable financial situation. There is a vast difference between the lifestyles of those who are foreign born and who have never learned English and those who were born in the United States. The second generation is retiring with pensions and savings, reaping the harvest of their hard work in this country. Despite discrimination, Chinese Americans have achieved a high rate of occupational mobility; many have gone from restaurant and laundry businesses to educating children who have entered professional and technical occupations.

SOUTHEAST ASIAN AMERICANS

The settlement of Vietnamese, Cambodians, and Laotians in the United States has included a small percentage of elders, who enter a world alien in all facets of life, from language, dress, and eating habits to religious beliefs. Family ties are strong for most of these people. Traditionally, extended families are standard. Southeast Asians have a special respect for their elders, especially for fathers and grandfathers.

Though immigration procedure initially places Southeast Asians throughout the entire United States, once on their own, many have gradually migrated to areas where the weather is similar to their native countries. California has by far the largest number of Southeast Asians. Studies of Southeast Asian refugees show that, like other Asian groups, they adjust fairly well to U.S. culture. Older first-generation immigrants who have suffered, living near or below the poverty line, take pride in children or grandchildren who have achieved financial and other successes.

In Los Angeles, a study that interviewed 19 older Hmong refugees and their families clearly demonstrated the pain and culture shock of displacement (Hays, 1987). In Laos, they lived in extended families with households containing as many as 35 members. Order and authority were maintained through respect for age. The oldest male of each clan sat on a governing council that handled all problems. Both male and female elders experienced a high degree of status within the village.

The Hmong believed that they would be resettled in the United States in a large group, possibly on a reservation. It was a major blow to be scattered in cities. They were shocked to learn about American housing standards; they were unable to understand, for example, why a family of ten could not live in a two-bedroom apartment. One elder Hmong recalled, "When I found out that some of my children would not live with me, my life stopped." The older Hmong had had no formal education in Laos, and many could not face the rigors of learning English in an American classroom.

The role of elders in the Hmong family has changed. In Laos, the elders acted as counselors for adult children experiencing marital difficulties. In the United States, in contrast, they are more out of touch with young couples' marital problems; and they rarely act as advisers and mediators. The older women try to help with child care, but the men don't have much to do. Many would like a farm and animals to tend. Elderly Hmong have experienced loss of function, loss of mobility, loss of religious customs, and loss of status. Some are very depressed. Studies of Southeast Asian refugees find that, because of the language barrier and lack of communication with the larger society, displacement is more difficult for the elderly than for their young (Yee, 1993).

☀ Native Americans

Measured by numbers alone, **Native-American elders** constitute a small percentage of American society: In 1991, there were 1.8 million Native Americans, slightly more than 6 percent of whom were age 65 or over (U.S. Bureau of the Census, 1993, 22). By any social or economic indicator of living conditions, however, they are possibly the *most* deprived of all U.S. ethnic groups.

Many of the problems of Native-American elders are due to minority status rather than to age. American Indians on reservations and in rural areas experience extremely high unemployment rates. Few jobs exist on the reservations, and those who leave in search of work pay the high price of losing touch with family, lifestyle, and culture. Many houses on reservations are substandard, and, despite substantial improvements in health, disparities still exist, especially in sanitation and nutrition. More than 140 years of federal programs have done little to improve the lives of Native Americans.

CULTURAL UNIFORMITY AND DIVERSITY

Though Native Americans are a diverse group, they do share some values that set them apart generally from the larger society. Their lifestyle and spirituality dictate a deep reverence for the land, animals, and nature; and, generally, they believe in attaining harmony between human beings and nature.

Family structure, values, and norms among Native-American tribes are diverse. Generally speaking, Native Americans have close family ties. Though many family structures are patriarchal, a wide variety of descent systems exist. The largest tribe, the Navajo, follows a matrilineal structure. The position of the elderly varies from tribe to tribe, as does emphasis on peace versus war and many other values. And, although some tribes are rivals, there exists today an extensive pan-Indian network that promotes intertribal networking, visiting, and cooperation. Marriage between members of different tribes is also more common (Kitano, 1991). The United States has approximately 278 federally recognized reservations, more than 300 recognized tribes, and around 100 nonrecognized tribes (John, 1991). This includes Eskimo and Aleut populations.

POPULATION DATA

For many years, despite rapid growth in the population of the country as a whole, the Native-American population declined. At the time of the first European settlement in what is now the United States, the number of Indians is estimated to have been between 1 and 10 million. By 1800, the native population had declined to approximately 600,000; by 1850, it had shrunk to

250,000. This mortifying decrease, the result of malnutrition, disease, and an all-out military assault on Native Americans, was a unique occurrence in our national history. However, the population eventually stabilized and is now increasing (Kitano, 1991, 173). Because of early childbearing, it is common for Native Americans to become grandparents in their mid to late thirties. By comparison, grandparenthood usually comes to whites in their mid fifties.

Many older Native Americans live on reservations, tending to stay behind while the young seek work in the city. Young or old, those who go to the city often expect to return to rural reservations to retire. Although the American population as a whole is more urban than rural, the reverse is largely true for the Native-American population. Native Americans are the most rural of any ethnic group in the country. Fifty-three percent live in nonmetropolitan areas; 22 percent live in central cities; and the rest live in suburban areas outside central cities (Schick and Schick, 1994).

Life expectancy among Native Americans is substantially lower than that for whites. The Native-American population is largely young; in 1991 nearly 50 percent were under the age of 25 (U.S. Bureau of the Census, 1993, 21, table 22). Elders constitute slightly more than 6 percent of the total Native-American population; by comparison, they represent 12 percent of the total U.S. population. As in the white population, Native-American women live longer than Native-American men.

Native Americans who leave the reservations are usually scattered throughout urban areas, rather than forming ethnic enclaves. Over 48,000 Native Americans, for example, live throughout the Los Angeles area. San Francisco, Tulsa, Denver, New York City, Seattle, Minneapolis, Chicago, and Phoenix all have sizable Native-American populations; Minneapolis has a Native-American enclave. Although a multitude of tribes are scattered throughout the United States, 44 percent of all Native Americans reside in California, Oklahoma, Arizona, and New Mexico (Kitano, 1991). Findings for one tribe cannot be generalized to include all others; values and behavior vary greatly. Specific patterns of aging need to be examined in each tribe.

EDUCATION, EMPLOYMENT, AND INCOME

The educational attainment of Native Americans today is behind that of whites. A sizable percentage of unemployed Navajo adults, for example, cannot speak English; nor can they read or write it. Among Native-American youths, the school dropout rate is twice the national average. Because education has been a traditional means of social advancement in the United States, these data suggest that future generations of Native-American elders may continue to suffer from functional illiteracy. A high percentage of Native-American elders have graduated neither from elementary nor from high school.

Unemployment creates a problem in the Native-American community. An extremely high percentage of the Native-American workforce is unemployed, and most of those who work hold menial jobs with low pay and few, if any, fringe benefits. Because they have often paid only small amounts into

Social Security, retirement for Native Americans is a great hardship. White Americans often associate major difficulties of growing old with retirement from the workforce. Native Americans usually have no work from which to retire. For most over 65, old age merely continues a state of poverty and joblessness that has lasted a lifetime.

HEALTH CHARACTERISTICS

Native-American elders are more likely to suffer from chronic illnesses and disabilities than any other ethnic aged group, and they have the lowest life expectancy. However, though the mortality rates for younger Navajos are relatively high, mortality rates among elder Navajos are lower than those for non-Indians of the same age. This paradox represents an instance of the mortality "crossover" (Kunitz and Levy, 1989, 216). Native Americans are more likely than the general population to die from diabetes, alcoholism, influenza, pneumonia, suicide, and homicide ("The Health of America's Native Tribes," 1990). Lack of finances leads to poor nutrition and health care. Further, the Native-American accident rate is high. Native Americans are more likely than the general population to be killed in motor-vehicle accidents; and death from other types of accidents is also more likely. And, although research is underway to study the high rates of alcoholism, minority status is thought to be a major cause. Health problems are compounded by the alien nature of the dominant health-care system to the traditional culture of Native Americans.

Older Native Americans remain an enormously needy group. Today, Native Americans suffer both from dependency on the federal government and from the impact of conflicting federal policies. They are sometimes denied assistance from various government agencies under the excuse that the Bureau of Indian Affairs (BIA) is responsible for providing the denied service. According to the *United States Government Manual 1989/90*, the principal objectives of the BIA are to "actively encourage and train Indian and Alaska Native people to manage their own affairs under the trust relationship to the Federal Government; to facilitate, with maximum involvement of Indian and Alaska Native people, full development of their human and natural resource potential; to mobilize all public and private aids to the advancement of Indian and Alaska Native people for use by them; and to utilize the skill and capabilities of Indian and Alaska Native people in the direction and management of programs for their benefit." The BIA has 12 area offices in the United States, so that the distance between the service provider, the work site, and the reservation (place of residence) compounds the difficulties of eligibility and availability of assistance.

☼ Improving the Status of Ethnic Elders

A large number of minority elders spend their last years lacking income, adequate housing, decent medical care, and needed services. Aging accentuates the factors that have contributed to a lifetime of social, economic, and psychological struggle. Rather than achieving comfort and respect with age, minority persons may get pushed further aside.

Upgrading the status of ethnic elders in the short term requires, first, recognition of the various factors that prevent them from utilizing services and, second, outreach programs designed to overcome those factors. The object should be to expand present programs, to develop more self-help programs, to increase the **bilingual** abilities of social service staffs, and to recruit staff members from the ethnic groups they serve.

With these goals in mind, the Administration of Aging (AOA) has funded four national organizations to improve the well-being of minority elders.

1. The National Caucus and Center on Black Aged (NCCBA) in Washington, D.C.
2. The National Indian Council on Aging (NICOA) in Albuquerque, New Mexico.
3. Asociación Nacional Pro Personas Mayores (National Association for Hispanic Elderly) in Los Angeles, California.
4. National Pacific/Asian Resource Center on Aging (NP/ARCA) in Seattle, Washington.

These centers educate the general public and advocate for their groups.

Ultimately, though, spending a bit of extra money and adding a few services will not solve the real problem. The disadvantages tend to derive from economic marginality that has lasted a lifetime. One's work history is a central factor in how one fares in later life. A work history that allows for a good pension or maximum Social Security benefits is a big step toward economic security in old age. Also, those who have made good salaries have had a chance to save money for their retirement years—a safety net not possible for low wage earners. Until members of minority groups are from birth accorded full participation in the goods and services our society offers, they will continue to suffer throughout their lives. The critical perspective in sociology calls for addressing these basic inequalities and taking major steps toward making all citizens equal.

Chapter Summary

Women, including older ones, in the United States, are in a minority status. They do not participate equally in the political and economic structures. Older women are victims of the double standard of aging—a standard that judges them more harshly as they age. A large percentage of elders in poverty are female.

Ethnic elders suffer from inequality in the United States. Older blacks are poorer than older whites and have a lower life expectancy, poorer health, more inferior housing, and less material comforts. Although some older

African Americans are well-to-do, others are impoverished. Family ties, religion, and a resolve to persevere are special strengths. Hispanic elders are not a homogeneous group. About half of all Hispanic elders are Mexican Americans; others come from Cuba, Puerto Rico, and various Central and South American countries. Hispanic elders have suffered major linguistic and cultural barriers to assimilation and have occupied low socioeconomic status. Asian-American elders come from many countries, also. They, too, have encountered racial hatred, language barriers, and discrimination. Native-American elders are a small group. But by any social or economic indicator, they are, possibly, the most deprived group in the United States. More efforts need to be directed at correcting inequities for ethnic minorities and women.

Key Terms

African-American elders	ethnic group
age terrorism	Hispanic elders
Asian-American elders	late midlife astonishment
bilingual	minority elder
familism	Native-American elders
double standard of aging	

Questions for Discussion

1. What special problems do older women experience? Older African Americans? Hispanics? Asian Americans? Native Americans?

2. What generation-gap problems exist between the young and the old of each minority group?

Fieldwork Suggestion

1. Interview an older person from a racial minority. Note carefully the person's lifestyle and outlook on life. What past and present discrimination has he or she experienced?

References

Applewhite, S., an R. Daley, "Cross-Cultural Understand-ing for Social Work Practice with the Hispanic Elderly." In *Hispanic Elderly in Transition,* edited by S. Applewhite, 3–16. New York: Greenwood Press, 1988.

Barazan, M. "Fear of Crime and Its Consequences Among Urban Elderly Individuals." *International Journal of Aging and Human Development* 38:2 (March, 1994): 99–116.

Belgrave, L. L. et al. "Health, Double Jeopardy, and Culture. The Use of Institutional-ization by African-Americans." *Gerontologist* 33:3 (June 1993): 379–385.

Bound, J. et al. "Poverty Dynamics in Widowhood." *Journal of Gerontology* 46:3 (May 1991) 115–124.

Bryant, S., and W. Rakowski. "Predictors of Morality Among Elderly African-Ameri-cans." *Research on Aging* 14:1 (March 1992): 50–58.

Burton, L. "Black Grandparents Rearing Children of Drug Addicted Parents." *Geron-tologist* 32:6 (December 1992): 774–751.

Chrisler, J., and L. Ghiz. "Body Image Issues of Older Women." In *Faces of Women and Aging,* edited by N. Davis et al. Binghamton, NY: Haworth Press, 1993.

Christy, M. "At 71 She's Still a Cosmo Girl." *Santa Rosa Press Democrat* (15 April 1993): D1.

Current Population Reports, Series P-20, No. 444, Table 1, 1990.

Fowler, M., and P. McCutcheon, eds. *Songs of Experience: An Anthology of Literature on Growing Old.* New York, NY: Ballantine, 1991.

Frisby, M. "Gap Among Blacks Widening." *The Boston Globe* (9 August 1991): 1.

Gibson R. "Reconceptualizing Retirement for Black Americans." In *Worlds of Differ-ence,* edited by E. Stoller, and R. Gibson. Thousand Oaks, CA: Pine Forge Press, 1993.

Goodman, M. "Culture, Cohort, and Self-Worth in Women." A paper presented at the 46th Annual Meeting of the Gerontological Society, New Orleans, November 1993.

Guralnick, J., et al. "Educational Status and Active Life Expectancy Among Older Blacks and Whites." *The New England Journal of Medicine* 329:2 (8 July 1993): pp. 110–117.

Hays, C. D. "Two Worlds in Conflict: The Elderly Hmong in the United States." In *Ethnic Dimensions of Aging,* edited by D. Gelfard and C. Barresi. New York: Springer, 1987.

"The Health of America's Native Tribes," *Washington Post Health Section* (13 February 1990): 5.

Hernandez, G. "The Family and Its Aged Members: The Cuban Experience." In *His-panic Aged Mental Health,* edited by T. Brink, Binghamton, NY: Haworth Press, 1992, pp. 45–58.

Hilts, P. "Life Expectancy for U.S. Blacks Drops Again," *San Francisco Chronicle* (29 November 1990): A14.

Jacobs, R. *Be An Outrageous Older Woman*, Manchester, CN: Knowledge Ideas, & Trends, 1993.

John, R. "The State of Research on American Indian Elders." In *Minority Elders*. 38–50. Washington, D.C.: Gerontological Society of America, 1991.

Kingson, E. and R. O'Grady-LeShane. "The Effects of Caregiving on Women's Social Security Benefits," *Gerontologist* 33:2 (April 1993): 230–239.

Kitano, H. *Race Relations.* Englewood Cliffs, NJ: Prentice-Hall, 1991.

Kunitz, S. and J. Levy. "Aging and Health Among Navajo Indians." In *Aging and Health: Pespectives on Gender, Race, Ethnicity and Class,* edited by K. Markides 211–245. Newbury Park, CA: Sage, 1989.

Lifshitz, L. *Only Morning in Her Shoes: Poems About Old Women,* Logan, UT: Utah State Univ. Press, 1990.

Lubben, J. E., and R. M. Becerra. "Social Support Among Black, Mexican, and Chi-nese Elderly." In *Ethnic Dimensions of Aging,* edited by D. Gelfand and C. Barresi. New York: Springer, 1987.

Luckey, I. "African American Elders: The Support Network of Generational Kin." *Families in Society: The Journal of Contemporary Human Services* 75:2 (February 1994): 82–90.

Markides, Kuriakos S., and Charles H. Mindel. *Aging and Ethnicity.* Newbury Park, CA: Sage, 1987.

Minkler, M., et al. "Raising Grandchildren in the Crack Cocaine Epidemic." *Gerontologist* 32:6 (December 1992): 752–761.

Mui, A., and D. Burnette. "Long-term Care Service Used by Frail Elders: Is Ethnicity a Factor?" *Gerontologist* 34:2 (April 1994): 190–198.

National Institute on Aging, "Profiles of America's Elderly: Racial and Ethnic Diversity," Washington, D.C.: U.S. Dept. of Health and Human Services, November, 1993.

Nickerson, B. *Old and Smart: Women and Aging,* Eugene, OR: All About Us, 1991.

Nye, W. "Amazing Grace: Religion and Identity Among Elderly Black Individuals. *International Journal of Aging and Human Development* 36:2 (March 1993): 103–105.

Pearlman, S. "Late Mid-Life Astonishment: Disruptions to Identity and Self-Esteem." In *Faces of Women and Aging,* edited by N. David, et al. Binghamton, NY: Haworth Press, 1993.

Porcino, J. *Growing Older, Getting Better,* Redding, MA: Addison-Wesley, 1983.

Quadagno, J. and M. Meyer. "Gender and Public Policy." In *Worlds of Difference,* edited by E. Stoller and R. Gibson. Thousand Oaks, CA: Pine Forge Press, 1993.

Rosenthal, E., ed. *Women, Aging and Ageism.* Binghamton, New York: Harrington Park Press, 1991.

Schick, F. and R. Schick, eds. *Statistical Handbook on Aging Americans.* Phoenix, AZ: Oryx Press, 1994.

Sheehy, G. *Preface Women on the Front Lines,* edited by J. Allen and A. Pifer. Washington, D.C.: The Urban Institute Press, 1993.

Sontag, S. "The Double Standard of Aging" *Saturday Review* (23 September 1972).

"Special Report: Black and White in America." *Newsweek* (7 March 1988): 18–45.

Strom, R. et al. "Strengths and Needs of Black Grandparents." *International Journal of Aging and Human Development* 36:4 (May/June 1993) 255–259.

Taylor, R., and L. M. Chatters. "Correlates of Education, Income, and Poverty Among Aged Blacks." *Gerontologist* 28 (August 1988): 435–444.

Thone, R. *Women and Aging: Celebrating Ourselves,* Binghamton, NY: Haworth Press, 1993.

Torres-Gill, F. "Interest Group Politics: Empowerment of the 'Ancianos.'" In *Hispanic Elderly in Transition,* edited by S. Applewhite, 75–94. New York: Greenwood Press, 1988.

Troll, I. "Issues in the Study of Older Women." In *Health and Economic Status of Older Women,* edited by A. Herzog, K. Holden, and M. Seltzer. Amityville, NY: Baywood Publishing, 1989.

Uhlenberg, P. "Divorce for Women After Midlife." In *Journal of Gerontology* 45:1 (January 1990): 53–61.

U.S. Bureau of the Census. *Statistical Abstract of the United States, 1993,* 113th ed. Washington, D.C.: U.S. Department of Congress, Census Bureau, 1993.

Walls, C. "The Role of Church and Family Support in the Lives of Older African Americans." *Generations* (Summer 1992) 16:3, 33–37.

Walls, C., and S. Zarit. "Informal Support from Black Churches and the Well-Being of Elderly Blacks." *Gerontologist* 31:4 (August 1991): 490–495.

Winsberg, M. "*Special Hispanics.*" American Demographics, February, 1994, pp. 44–53.

Yee, B. K. W. "Elders in Southeast Asian Refugee Families." In *Worlds of Difference,* edited by E. Stoller and R. Gibson. Thousand Oaks, CA: Pine Forge Press, 1993.

York, P. *Going Strong,* New York, NY: Arcade Pub. Inc., 1991.

Further Readings

Banner, L. *In Full Flower: Aging Women, Power, and Sexuality.* New York: Random House, 1993.

Blakemore, K. and Boneham, M. *Age, Race and Ethnicity.* Buckingham, England: Open University Press, 1994.

Gelfand, D. *Aging and Ethnicity: Knowledge and Services.* New York: Springer Publishing, 1993.

Holden, K. "Continuing Limits of Productive Aging: The Lesser Rewards for Working Women." *Achieving a Productive Aging Society,* ed. by Bass, S. et al. Westport: Auburn House, 1993, pp. 269–284.

Holstein, M. "Women's Lives, Women's Work: Productivity, Gender, and Aging," *Achieving a Productive Aging Society,* ed. by Bass, S. et al. Westport: Auburn House, 1993, pp. 235–244.

Narduzzi, J. *Mental Health Among Elderly Native Americans.* New York: Garland Pub. Inc., 1994.

Savishinsky, J., ed. Special issue on ethnicity and aging, *Ethnic Groups* 8:3 (1990): 143–214.

Sample Short Story

"Mother"
from *Winesburg, Ohio*

by Sherwood Anderson

Elizabeth Willard, the mother of George Willard, was tall and gaunt and her face was marked with smallpox scars. Although she was but forty-five, some obscure disease had taken the fire out of her figure. Listlessly she went about the disorderly old hotel looking at the faded wallpaper and the ragged carpets and, when she was able to be about, doing the work of a chambermaid among beds soiled by the slumbers of fat traveling men. Her husband, Tom Willard, a slender, graceful man with square shoulders, a quick military step, and a black mustache trained to turn sharply up at the ends, tried to put the wife out of his mind. The presence of the tall ghostly figure, moving slowly through the halls, he took as a reproach to himself. When he thought of her he grew angry and swore. The hotel was unprofitable and forever on the edge of failure and he wished himself out of it. He thought of the old house and the woman who lived there with him as things defeated and done for. The hotel in which he had begun life so hopefully was now a mere ghost of what a hotel should be. As he went spruce and business-like through the streets of Winesburg, he sometimes stopped and turned quickly about as though fearing that the spirit of the hotel and of the woman would follow him even into the streets. "Damn such a life, damn it!" he sputtered aimlessly.

Tom Willard had a passion for village politics and for years had been the leading Democrat in a strongly Republican community. Some day, he told himself, the fide of things political will turn in my favor and the years of ineffectual service count big in the bestowal of rewards. He dreamed of going to Congress and even of becoming governor. Once when a younger member of the party arose at a political conference and began to boast of his faithful service, Tom Willard grew white with fury. "Shut up, you," he roared, glaring about. "What do you know of service? What are you but a boy? Look at what I've done here! I was a Democrat here in Winesburg when it was a crime to be a Democrat. In the old days they fairly hunted us with guns."

Between Elizabeth and her one son George there was a deep unexpressed bond of sympathy, based on a girlhood dream that had long ago died. In the son's presence she was timid and reserved, but sometimes while he hurried about town intent upon his duties as a reporter, she went into his room and closing the door knelt by a little desk, made of a kitchen table, that sat near a window. In the room by the desk she went through a ceremony that was half a prayer, half a demand, addressed to the skies. In the boyish figure she yearned to see something half forgotten that had once been a part of herself recreated. The prayer concerned that. "Even though I die, I will in some way keep defeat from you," she cried, and so deep was her determination that her whole body shook. Her eyes glowed and she clenched her fists. "If I am dead and see him becoming a meaningless drab figure like myself, I will come back," she declared. "I ask God now to give me that privilege. I demand it. I will pay for it. God may beat me with his fists. I will take any blow that may befall if but this my boy be allowed to express something for us both." Pausing uncertainly, the woman stared about the boy's room. "And do not let him become smart and successful either," she added vaguely.

The communion between George Willard and his mother was outwardly a formal thing without meaning. When she was ill and sat by the window in her room he sometimes went in the evening to make her a visit. They sat by a window that looked over the roof of a small frame building into Main Street. By turning their heads they could see through another window, along an alleyway that ran behind the Main Street stores and into the back door of Abner Groff's bakery. Sometimes as they sat thus a picture of village life presented itself to them. At the back door of his shop appeared Abner Groff with a stick or an empty milk bottle in his hand. For a long time there was a feud between the baker and a grey cat that belonged to Sylvester West, the druggist. The boy and his mother saw the cat creep into the door of the bakery and presently emerge followed by the baker, who swore and waved his arms about. The baker's eyes were small and red and his black hair and beard were filled with flour dust. Sometimes he was so angry that, although the cat had disappeared, he hurled sticks, bits of broken glass, and even some of the tools of his trade about. Once he broke a window at the back of Sinning's Hardware Store. In the alley the grey cat crouched behind barrels filled with torn paper and broken bottles above which flew a black swarm of flies. Once when she was alone, and after watching a prolonged and ineffectual outburst on the part of the baker, Elizabeth Willard put her head down on her long white hands and wept. After that she did not look along the alleyway any more, but tried to forget the contest between the bearded man and the cat. It seemed like a rehearsal of her own life, terrible in its vividness.

In the evening when the son sat in the room with his mother, the silence made them both feel awkward. Darkness came on and the evening train came in at the station. In the street below feet tramped up and down upon a board sidewalk. In the station yard, after the evening train had gone, there was a heavy silence. Perhaps Skinner Leason, the express agent, moved a truck the length of the station platform. Over on Main Street sounded a man's voice, laughing. The door of the express office banged. George Willard arose and crossing the room fumbled for the doorknob. Sometimes he knocked against a chair, making it scrape along the floor. By the window sat the sick woman, perfectly still, listless. Her long hands, white and bloodless, could be seen drooping over the ends of the arms of the chair. "I think you had better be out among the boys. You are too much indoors," she said, striving to relieve the embarrassment of the departure. "I thought I would take a walk," replied George Willard, who felt awkward and confused.

One evening in July, when the transient guests who made the New Willard House their temporary home had become scarce, and the hallways, lighted only by kerosene lamps turned low, were plunged in gloom, Elizabeth Willard had an adventure. She had been ill in bed for several days and her son had not come to visit her. She was alarmed. The feeble blaze of life that remained in her body was blown into a flame by her anxiety and she crept out of bed, dressed and hurried along the hallway toward her son's room, shaking with exaggerated fears. As she went along she steadied herself with her hand, slipped along the papered walls of the hall and breathed with difficulty. The air whistled through her teeth. As she hurried forward she thought how foolish she was. "He is concerned with boyish affairs," she told herself. "Perhaps he has now begun to walk about in the evening with girls."

Elizabeth Willard had a dread of being seen by guests in the hotel that had once belonged to her father and the ownership of which still stood recorded in her name in the county courthouse. The hotel was continually losing patronage because of its shabbiness and she thought of herself as also shabby. Her own room was in an obscure corner and when she felt able to work she voluntarily worked among the beds, preferring the labor that could be done when the guests were abroad seeking trade among the merchants of Winesburg.

By the door of her son's room the mother knelt upon the floor and listened for some sound from within. When she heard the boy moving about and talking in low tones a smile came to her lips. George Willard had a habit of talking aloud to himself and to hear him doing so had always given his mother a peculiar pleasure. The habit in him, she felt, strengthened the secret bond that existed between them. A thousand times she had whispered to herself of the matter. "He is groping about, trying to find himself," she thought. "He is not a dull clod, all words and smartness. Within him there is a secret something that is striving to grow. It is the thing I let be killed in myself."

In the darkness in the hallway by the door the sick woman arose and started again toward her own room. She was afraid that the door would open and the boy come upon her. When she had reached a safe distance and was about to turn a corner into a second hallway she stopped and bracing herself with her hands waited, thinking to shake off a trembling fit of weakness that had come upon her. The presence of the boy in the room had made her happy. In her bed, during the long hours alone, the little fears that had visited her had become giants. Now they were all gone. "When I get back to my room I shall sleep," she murmured gratefully.

But Elizabeth Willard was not to return to her bed and to sleep. As she stood trembling in the darkness the door of her son's room opened and the boy's father, Tom Willard, stepped out. In the light that steamed out at the door he stood with the knob in his hand and talked. What he said infuriated the woman.

Tom Willard was ambitious for his son. He had always thought of himself as a successful man, although nothing he had ever done had turned out successfully. However, when he was out of sight of the New Willard House and had no fear of coming upon his wife, he swaggered and began to dramatize himself as one of the chief men of the town. He wanted his son to succeed. He it was who had secured for the boy the position on the Winesburg Eagle. Now, with a ring of earnestness in his voice, he was advising concerning some course of conduct. "I tell you what, George, you've got to wake up," he said sharply. "Will Henderson has spoken to me three times concerning the matter. He says you go along for hours not hearing when you are spoken to and acting like a gawky girl. What ails you?" Tom Willard laughed good-naturedly. "Well, I guess you'll get over it," he said. "I told Will that. You're not a fool and you're not a woman. You're Tom Willard's son and you'll wake up. I'm not afraid. What you say clears things up. If being a newspaper man had put the notion of becoming a writer into your mind that's all right. Only I guess you'll have to wake up to do that too, eh?"

Tom Willard went briskly along the hallway and down a flight of stairs to the office. The woman in the darkness could hear him laughing and talking with a guest who was striving to wear away a dull evening by dozing in a chair by the office door. She returned to the door of her son's room. The weakness had passed from her body as by a miracle and she stepped boldly along. A thousand ideas raced through her head. When she heard the scraping of a chair and the sound of a pen scratching upon paper, she again turned and went back along the hallway to her own room.

A definite determination had come into the mind of the defeated wife of the Winesburg hotel keeper. The determination was the result of long years of quiet and rather ineffectual thinking. "Now," she told herself, "I will act. There is something threatening my boy and I will ward it off." The fact that the conversation between Tom Willard and his son had been rather quiet and natural, as though an understanding existed between them, maddened her. Although for years she had hated her husband, her hatred had always before been a quite impersonal thing. He had been merely a part of something else that she hated. Now, and by the few words at the door, he had become the thing personified. In the darkness of her own room she clenched her fists and glared about. Going to a cloth bag that hung on a nail by the wall she took out a long pair of sewing scissors and held them in her hand like a dagger. "I will stab him," she said aloud. "He has chosen to be the voice of evil and I will kill him. When I have killed him something will snap within myself and I will die also. It will be a release for all of us."

In her girlhood and before her marriage with Tom Willard, Elizabeth had borne a somewhat shaky reputation in Winesburg. For years she had been what is called "stage-struck" and had paraded through the streets with traveling men guests at her father's hotel, wearing loud clothes and urging them to tell her of life in the cities out of which they had come. Once she startled the town by putting on men's clothes and riding a bicycle down Main Street.

In her own mind the tall dark girl had been in those days much confused. A great restlessness was in her and it expressed itself in two ways. First there was an uneasy desire for change, for some big definite movement to her life. It was this feeling that had turned her mind to the stage. She dreamed of joining some company and wandering over the world, seeing always new faces and giving something out of herself to all people. Sometimes at night she was quite beside herself with the thought, but when she tried to talk of the matter to the members of the theatrical companies that came to Winesburg and stopped at her father's hotel, she got nowhere. They did not seem to know what she meant, or if she did get something of her passion expressed, they only laughed. "It's not like that," they said. "It's as dull and uninteresting as this here. Nothing comes of it."

With the traveling men when she walked about with them, and later with Tom Willard, it was quite different. Always they seemed to understand and sympathize with her. On the side streets of the village, in the darkness under the trees, they took hold of her hand and she thought that something unexpressed in herself came forth and became a part of an unexpressed something in them.

And then there was the second expression of her restlessness. When that came she felt for a time released and happy. She did not blame the men who walked with her and later she did not blame Tom Willard. It was always the same, beginning with kisses and ending, after strange wild emotions, with peace and then sobbing repentance. When she sobbed she put her hand upon the face of the man and had always the same thought. Even though he were large and bearded she thought he had become suddenly a little boy. She wondered why he did not sob also.

In her room, tucked away in a corner of the old Willard House, Elizabeth Willard lighted a lamp and put it on a dressing table that stood by the door. A thought had come into her mind and she went to a closet and brought out a small square box and set it on the table. The box contained material for makeup and had been left with other things by a theatrical company that had once been stranded in Winesburg. Elizabeth Willard had decided that she would be beautiful. Her hair was still black and there was a great mass of it braided and coiled about her head. The scene that was to take place in the office below began to grow in her mind. No ghostly worn-out figure should confront Tom Willard, but something quite unexpected and startling. Tall and with dusky cheeks and hair that fell in a mass from her shoulders, a figure should come striding down the stairway before the startled loungers in the hotel office. The figure would be silent—it would be swift and terrible. As a tigress whose cub had been threatened would she appear, coming out of the shadows, stealing noiselessly along and holding the long wicked scissors in her hand.

With a little broken sob in her throat, Elizabeth Willard blew out the light that stood upon the table and stood weak and trembling in the darkness. The strength that had been as a miracle in her body left and she half reeled across the floor, clutching at the back of the chair in which she had spent so many long days staring out over the tin roofs into the main street of Winesburg. In the hallway there was the sound of footsteps and George Willard came in at the door. Sitting in a chair beside his mother he began to talk. "I'm going to get out of here," he said. "I don't know where I shall go or what I shall do but I am going away."

The woman in the chair waited and trembled. An impulse came to her. "I suppose you had better wake up," she said. "You think that? You will go to the city and make money, eh? It will be better for you, you think, to be a business man, to be brisk and smart and alive?" She waited and trembled.

The son shook his head. "I suppose I can't make you understand, but oh, I wish I could," he said earnestly. "I can't even talk to father about it. I don't try. There isn't any use. I don't know what I shall do. I just want to go away and look at people and think."

Silence fell upon the room where the boy and woman sat together. Again, as on the other evenings, they were embarrassed. After a time the boy tried again to talk. "I suppose it won't be for a year or two but I've been thinking about it," he said, rising and going toward the door. "Something father said makes it sure that I shall have to go away." He fumbled with the doorknob. In the room the silence became unbearable to the woman. She wanted to cry out with joy because of the words that had come from the lips of her son, but the expression of joy had become impossible to her. "I think you had better go out among the boys. You are too much indoors," she said. "I thought I would go for a little walk," replied the son stepping awkwardly out of the room and closing the door.

Sample Article

It Seemed Like a Good Idea at the Time

What if they minted a coin and no one would use it? That's what happened with the Susan B. Anthony dollar.

From *Uncle John's 7th Bathroom Reader* by The Bathroom Readers' Institute

The Bathroom Reader's Institute
1400 Shattuck Ave., #25
Berkeley, CA 94709

Background

In the mid-1970s, the demand for dollar bills was increasing at a rate of about 10% a year. Each bill cost the government a few cents to make . . . but only lasted about 18 months. Treasury officials figured they could save taxpayers about $50 million a year if they replaced the $1 bill with a $1 coin-which would last about 14 years and only cost 3¢ to make. They were confident that the American public would make the change.

Beauty and the Beast

Responding to the political currents of the mid-'70s, U.S. Mint officials told chief designer Frank Gasparro to draw a portrait of a woman for the proposed new dollar coin. "I decided to draw Miss Liberty," he says, "but they told me they didn't want Miss Liberty. It had to be Susan B. Anthony." Gasparro had no idea what Anthony, an activist for women's rights in the late 1800s, looked like. So he went down to the local newspaper and looked at the photograph files. They contained two portraits of Anthony: one taken at the age of 28, and the other at age 84. "I chose the younger one," he recalls. "She was a very attractive woman at 28."

But feminists complained that it was "too pretty." So Gasparro drew a new portrait of Anthony, trying to approximate what she looked like in middle age. He gave her a square jaw, a hooked nose, heavy browline, and a drooping right eye. Though he succeeded his task (hardly anyone accuses the Susan B. Anthony dollar of being "too pretty" anymore), he had reservations about the final design. But the U.S. Treasury approved it.

Damsel in Distress

Introduced on July 2, 1979, the Susan B. Anthony dollar was an instant failure. Everybody hated it—people said it was too small to be a dollar and too ugly to represent the United States.

But the biggest problem with the coin was that it looked and felt like a quarter. Many businesses refused to accept them, fearing that cashiers would mistake them for quarters and give them away as change.

Stopgap Measures

Government officials fought hard to keep the coin alive, spending more than $600,000 on a nationwide campaign to increase public acceptance. Then they brought in a New York public relations firm to help—the first time in history that a coin had to be promoted. But it was hopeless. "Our job was to get the good story out about the coin," said a spokesman for the PR firm,

> But we made a false assumption. We assumed that there would be good stories to get out. There weren't. We were looking for any little piece of good news about the coin, so we could feed it to the networks and the wire services. The stories didn't have to come from big cities; we were looking for the little town that decided to pay everyone in Susan B. Anthony coins—that kind of thing. We'd take anything. Spokane, San Luis Obispo, Dover-Foxcroft, Mobile . . . our feeling was that as soon as something good happened, we could start to build a success. But nothing good ever happened. Anywhere.

Femme Fatal

By the time production was halted in the spring of 1980, more than 840 million coins had been minted . . . but only 315 million had made it into circulation. "There is an extraordinary amount of resistance to this coin," a U.S. Mint official admitted. "As far as I can tell, it isn't being accepted anywhere."

Esquire magazine reported in April 1981 that, "Most Americans refuse to carry the coins. Bank tellers and cashiers in stores have learned not to even try to give them out as change; people won't take them. People . . . don't even like to touch them."

The Treasury department suspended production in 1981, estimating they had enough of them on hand to last 40-50 years.

"I think we will just let sleeping dogs lie," the Secretary of the Treasury said.

Sample Chapter 13

Introduction: Concepts in Human Biology

Reprinted by permission of *Human Biology,*
2nd edition by Cecie Starr and Beverly
McMillan. Copyright 1997 by Wadsworth
Publishing Company. All rights reserved.

Some figures have been removed.

Introduction CONCEPTS IN HUMAN BIOLOGY

Human Biology Revisited

Buried somewhere in your brain are memories of discovering your own hands and feet, your family, the change of seasons, the smell of grass. The memories include early introductions to a great disorganized parade of insects, flowers, frogs, and furred things—mostly living, sometimes dead. There are memories of questions: "What is life?" and "Where do I fit in the world around me?" There are memories of answers, some satisfying, others less so.

By observing, asking questions, and accumulating answers, you have built up a store of knowledge about the world of life (Figure I.1). Experience and education have been refining your questions, and no doubt some answers are difficult to come by. Think of a young man whose brain is functionally dead as a result of a motorcycle accident. If breathing and other basic functions proceed only as long as he remains hooked up to mechanical support systems, is he "alive"? Think of an embryo, a cluster of cells growing inside a pregnant woman. At what point in its development is it a definably "human" life? If questions like these cross your mind, your thoughts about life obviously run deep.

The point is, this book isn't your introduction to human biology, for you have been studying yourself and the world around you ever since information began penetrating your brain. This book simply is human biology *revisited*, in ways that may help carry your thoughts to more organized levels.

To biologists, the question "What is life?" opens up a story that has been unfolding for several billion years. "Life" is an outcome of ancient events by which nonliving materials became assembled into the first living cells. With the emergence of living cells came biological **evolution**—change in details of the body plan and functions of organisms through successive generations. In the course of evolution, broad groups of life forms, including animals, emerged.

Humans, apes, and some other closely related animal species are primates. As primates we are also mammals, and all mammals, including humans, are **vertebrates**—animals with "backbones." We share our planet with millions of other animal species, as well as with plants, fungi, bacteria, and other organisms. Figure I.2 provides a general picture of the place our human species, **Homo sapiens,** occupies in the living world.

"Life" is also a way of capturing and using energy and materials. "Life" is a way of sensing and responding to specific changes in the environment. "Life" is a capacity to grow, develop, and reproduce. In fact, much of this text explores aspects of anatomy and functioning through which your body maintains the living state. A partial list of those life-support systems includes your brain and an elaborate network of nerve cells, a digestive system that can extract nutrients from thousands of foods, respiratory and circulatory systems that keep your body supplied with oxygen, a urinary system, an immune system, a hormone-based communication system, a skeleton and muscles for support and movement, and organs for reproduction.

This chapter introduces some basic concepts that provide a foundation for understanding the material to come. Here, too, we introduce several themes that are cornerstones of the study of human biology. One theme is our evolutionary heritage, which includes cultural as well as biological evolution. Another is the state of internal constancy called *homeostasis*. Living cells can function properly only within narrow environmental limits, and each

Figure I.2   FIVE KINGDOMS OF LIFE

Human beings are only one species among millions inhabiting the earth. Our species, *Homo sapiens*, is a subgroup of the class Mammalia, which in turn is classified as a subgroup of the phylum Chordata, which includes vertebrates. The vast majority of animals on earth are not vertebrates; they are invertebrates, such as insects, and lack a "backbone." Among the organisms with which we share our world are at least 1 million species of insects, more than 400,000 species of plants, and vast numbers of single-celled organisms, including amoebas (Protistans) and bacteria (Monerans).

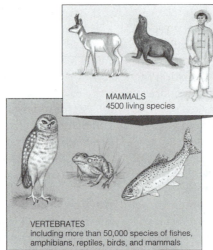

MAMMALS
4500 living species

VERTEBRATES
including more than 50,000 species of fishes,
amphibians, reptiles, birds, and mammals

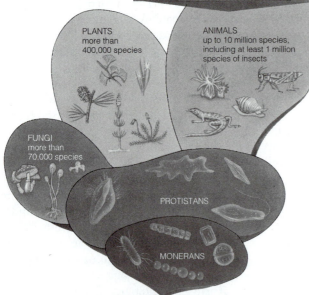

PLANTS
more than
400,000 species

ANIMALS
up to 10 million species,
including at least 1 million
species of insects

FUNGI
more than
70,000 species

PROTISTANS

MONERANS

KEY CONCEPTS

1. Humans exhibit basic characteristics of life. First, the structural organization and functions of the human body depend on certain properties of matter and energy. Second, humans obtain and use energy and materials from their environment. Third, they make controlled responses to changing conditions. Fourth, they grow and reproduce, based on instructions contained in DNA.

2. Life processes depend on a stable internal state called homeostasis.

3. Human anatomy, physiology, and possibly some aspects of behavior have been shaped by processes of evolution.

4. Biology, like other branches of science, is based on systematic observations, hypotheses, predictions, and relentless testing. The external world, not internal conviction, is the testing ground for scientific theories.

of the life-support systems we will study makes an essential contribution to maintaining a constant internal environment. Finally, throughout the text you will also find *Focus* and *Choices* features that relate basic biological concepts to health topics, environmental concerns, and social issues.

Energy and DNA

Picture a climber on a rock face, inching cautiously toward the safety of the top (Figure I.3). Without even thinking about it, you know the climber is alive and the rock is not. Yet the climber, the rock, and all other things are composed of the same particles (protons, electrons, and neutrons). The particles are organized into atoms according to fundamental physical laws. At the heart of those laws is something called **energy**—a capacity to make things happen, to do work. Energetic interactions bind atom to atom in predictable patterns, giving rise to the structured bits of matter we call molecules. Energetic interactions among molecules hold a rock together—and they hold a human together.

It takes a special molecule called deoxyribonucleic acid, or **DNA**, to set living things apart from the nonliving world. No chunk of granite or quartz has it. DNA molecules in sperm and eggs contain the instructions for assembling each new human being from carbon, hydrogen, and a few other kinds of "lifeless" substances. By analogy, with proper instructions and a little effort, you can turn a disordered heap of ceramic tiles—even just two kinds of tile—into ordered patterns such as these:

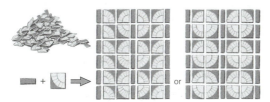

Similarly, life emerges from lifeless matter with DNA's "directions," raw materials, and energy inputs.

Levels of Biological Organization

Look carefully at Figure I.4, which outlines the levels of organization in nature. The properties of life emerge at the level of the cell. A **cell** is an organized unit that has the capacity to survive and reproduce on its own, given DNA instructions and appropriate sources of energy and raw materials. In other words, the cell is the basic *living* unit.

Figure I.4 also shows more inclusive levels of organization, from populations on through communities, eco-systems, and the biosphere. (*Biosphere* refers to all regions of the earth's waters, crust, and atmosphere in which organisms live.) We will return to each of these concepts later in the book, when we consider some basic principles of ecology and human impacts on ecosystems.

Interdependency Among Organisms

With a few exceptions, a flow of energy from the sun maintains the pattern of organization in nature. Plants and some other organisms that capture solar energy through photosynthesis are the entry point for this flow. They are food producers for the living world. Animals, including humans, are consumers; directly or indirectly, they feed on energy stored in plant parts. Thus you tap directly into the stored energy when you eat a banana, and you tap into it indirectly when you eat hamburger made from a steer that fed on grass or grain. Bacteria and fungi are decomposers. When they feed on tissues or remains of other organisms, they break down sugars and other biological molecules to simple raw materials, which can be recycled back to producers.

The point here is, every part of the living world is ultimately linked to every other part. Organisms, including humans, are interdependent. There is a one-way flow of energy through them and a cycling of materials among them (Figure I.5). Interactions among

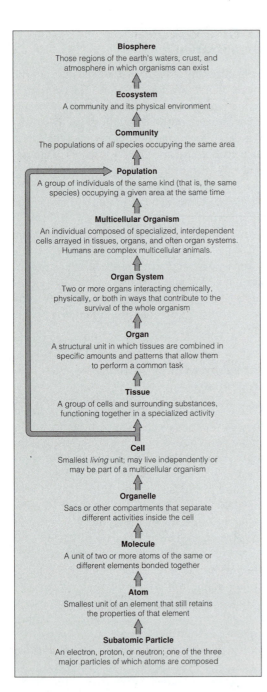

Figure I.4 Levels of organization in nature, starting with the subatomic particles that serve as the fundamental building blocks of all organisms, including human beings.

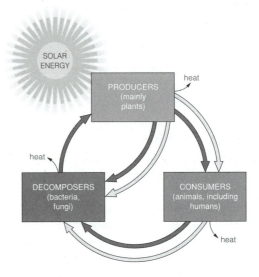

Figure I.5 Energy flow and the cycling of materials in the bio-sphere. Humans are consumers and are inextricably linked with both producers and decomposers.

organisms influence the cycling of carbon and other substances on a global scale; such interactions even influence the earth's energy "budget." Understand the extent of these interactions—and how they are affected by the activities of more than 5.6 billion human beings—and you will gain insight into the thinning of the ozone layer, acid rain, and many other modern-day problems.

The structure and organization of nonliving and living things arise from the properties of matter and energy.

The structure and organization unique to living things begin with instructions contained in DNA molecules.

Levels of organization in the living world begin with sub-atomic particles, atoms, and molecules. Cells, multicellular organisms, and whole ecosystems are part of this continuum of increasing complexity.

All organisms, including humans, are part of webs of organization in nature, in that they depend directly or indirectly on one another for energy and raw materials.

I.2   METABOLISM AND MAINTAINING HOMEOSTASIS

Metabolism

The basic characteristics of life also include metabolism, a feat that only living cells can accomplish. **Metabolism** refers to the cell's capacity to (l) extract and convert energy from its surroundings and (2) use energy to maintain itself, grow, and reproduce. Molecules of **ATP**, an "energy carrier," transfer energy to other molecules that either perform metabolic work (enzymes), serve as building blocks, or serve as energy reserves. In humans (Figure I.6), as in most animals and plants, stored energy is released and transferred to ATP by way of metabolic processes we will consider in Chapter 2.

Homeostasis: Sensing and Responding to Change

Cells of the human body can sense changes in the environment and make controlled responses to such changes. They manage this monitoring task with the help of receptors, which are molecules and structures that can detect specific information about the environment. When cells receive signals from receptors, they adjust their activities in ways that bring about an appropriate response.

For example, your body can withstand only so much heat or cold. It must rid itself of harmful substances, and certain nutrients must be available in certain amounts. Yet temperatures shift, harmful substances are sometimes encountered, and nearly everyone occasionally gorges on junk food or fruit or skips a meal entirely.

Suppose you skip breakfast, then lunch, and the level of the sugar glucose in your blood—"blood sugar"—falls. A hormone then signals liver cells to dig into their stores of energy-rich molecules. Those complex molecules are broken down to glucose, which is released into the bloodstream, and your blood-sugar level returns to normal.

After you eat, glucose enters your bloodstream, blood sugar rises, and pancreas cells step up their secretion of another hormone, insulin. Most cells in your body have receptors for insulin, which induces them to take up glucose. With so many cells taking up glucose, the blood-sugar level returns to normal.

Blood is part of the "internal environment," the fluid environment bathing your cells. Usually, the internal environment of your body is kept fairly constant. When the internal environment is maintained within tolerable ranges, a state called **homeostasis** exists.

Living things show metabolic activity. Their cells acquire and use energy to stockpile, tear down, and eliminate materials in ways that promote survival and reproduction.

Cells sense and respond to changes in the environment. The responses help maintain the stable internal state called homeostasis.

Homeostasis results in favorable operating conditions inside the cell or the body as a whole.

I.3   REPRODUCTION AND INHERITANCE

We humans tend to think we enter the world rather abruptly and are destined to leave it the same way. Yet we and all other organisms are part of an immense, ongoing journey that began billions of years ago. Think of the first cell produced when a human egg and sperm join. The cell would not even exist if the sperm and egg had not formed earlier according to DNA instructions that were passed down through countless generations. With the time-tested instructions in DNA, a new human body develops in ways that will prepare it, ultimately, for helping to produce individuals of a new generation. With **reproduction**—that is, the production of offspring by parents—the journey of life continues.

Inheritance and Variation

Reproduction involves **inheritance** (Figure I.7). The word means that parents transmit to their offspring instructions for duplicating their body form and other traits. DNA molecules contain the required instructions.

DNA instructions assure that offspring will resemble parents, and they also permit *variations* in the details of traits. For example, although having five fingers on each hand is a human trait, some humans are born with six fingers on each hand. Variations in traits arise through **mutations**, which are heritable changes in the structure or number of DNA molecules.

Most mutations are harmful, for the separate bits of information in DNA are part of a coordinated whole. For example, a single mutation in human DNA may lead to hemophilia, a genetic disorder in which blood cannot clot properly after the body is cut or bruised (Chapter 18).

Adaptation

Some mutations may prove harmless, or even beneficial, under prevailing conditions. For example, the disease sickle-cell anemia is caused by a DNA change that results in a defective form of the blood protein hemoglobin. The sickle-cell trait is most prevalent in parts of the world where malaria is common. People who inherit the mutation from both parents suffer the debilitating disease. But, for complex reasons, people who inherit the mutation from only one parent are resistant to malaria. For them, the mutation is adaptive; it increases their chances of survival.

An **adaptive trait** helps an organism survive and reproduce under a given set of environmental conditions. In the long course of human evolution, countless DNA mutations, tested in the environments of our ancestors, have given rise to an elaborate nervous system, efficient mechanisms for taking in and distributing oxygen and food molecules, and other characteristics that enable each of us to live the biologically complex life of a human being. Later in the book we will consider the actual mechanisms by which evolution occurs.

DNA is the molecule of inheritance. Its instructions for reproducing traits are passed on from parents to offspring.

Mutations introduce variations in heritable traits.

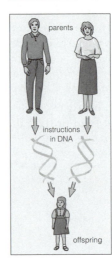

Figure I.7   Reproduction is a life characteristic. Instructions in DNA assure that offspring will resemble parents—and they also permit variations in the details of traits, as the photograph demonstrates.

I.4   SCIENTIFIC METHODS

Biology, like science generally, is an ongoing record of discoveries arising from methodical inquiries into the natural world. Human biology focuses, naturally enough, on the workings of the human body and closely related topics.

Our fascination with ourselves is probably as ancient as our species' beginnings. Thinkers such as Hippocrates, Leonardo da Vinci, and Charles Darwin pursued their curiosity under the umbrella of "natural history." Modern biologists are just as curious, if not more so, but they now investigate complex topics ranging from the molecular structure of HIV, the virus responsible for AIDS, to the impact on human health of a hole in the stratospheric ozone. In fact, the range of possible specialization within "human biology" is so broad that no single "scientific method" can be used to approach all the relevant topics and issues.

Even so, scientists everywhere still have practices in common. *Scientists ask questions, make educated guesses about possible answers, and then devise ways to test their predictions, which will hold true if their guesses are good ones.* The following list describes the steps scientists generally follow when they proceed with an investigation:

1.   Ask a question or identify a problem.

2.   Develop a **hypothesis**, a testable idea or guess, about what the answer (or solution) might be. This might involve sorting through what has been learned already about related phenomena.

3.   With a hypothesis as a guide, make a **prediction**—that is, a statement of what you should be able to observe, if you were to go looking for it. This is often called the "if-then" process. (*If* something in cigarette smoke is a cancer-causing agent in human lungs, *then* we should be able to detect a higher rate of lung cancer among smokers than among nonsmokers.)

4.   Devise ways to test the accuracy of predictions. You might do this by making observations, developing models, and doing experiments. By definition, an **experiment** is a test in which some phenomenon in the natural world is manipulated in controlled ways to gain insight into its function, structure, operation, or behavior. An essential step in any experiment is establishing a **control group**. Control groups are used to evaluate possible side effects of a test being performed on an experimental group. If an experiment involves laboratory rats, then the control group will be rats; if it involves college students, the controls will be students, and so on. Ideally, members of a control group should be identical to those of an experimental group in every respect—except for the key factor, or **variable**, under study. Both groups also must be large enough so the results won't be due to chance alone. Generally, experiments are devised to disprove a hypothesis. Why? It is impossible to prove beyond a shadow of a doubt that a hypothesis is correct, for it takes an infinite number of experiments to demonstrate that it holds under all possible conditions.

5.   If the test results are not as expected, check for what might have gone wrong. A procedure may have been perfomed improperly, something might have been overlooked, or the hypothesis may not be a good one.

6.   Repeat or devise new tests—the more the better. Hypotheses supported by many different tests are more likely to be correct.

7.   Objectively report the test results and conclusions drawn from them.

In broad outline, a scientific approach to studying nature is that simple. Figure I.8 diagrams the steps. You can use this approach to pick your way logically through environmental, medical, and social issues of the sort

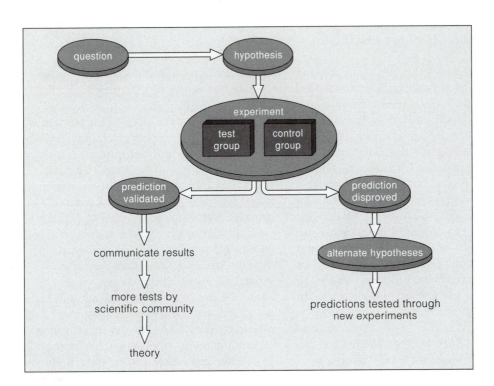

Figure I.8   Example of a scientific method.

described later in the book. And understanding how good science operates will help you evaluate media accounts of discoveries, advances, and research in progress. Section I.5 gives one example of a common scientific method used in actual research.

About the Word "Theory"

What is the difference between a hypothesis and a the·ory? In science, a **theory** is a set of hypotheses which, taken together, form a broad-ranging, testable explanation about some fundamental aspect of the natural world. A scientific theory differs from a scientific hypothesis in its *breadth of application*. Charles Darwin's theory about the evolution of species fits this description: It is a broad, encompassing "Aha!" explanation that, in a few intellectual strokes, makes sense of a huge number of observable phenomena.

Ultimately, no theory can be an "absolute truth" in science. Why? It would be impossible to perform the infinite number of tests required to show that a theory holds true under *all* possible conditions. Objective scientists say only that they are *relatively* certain that a theory is correct.

Such "relative certainty" can be extremely impressive. Especially after exhaustive tests by many scientists, a theory may be as close to the "truth" as we can get with the evidence at hand. After more than a century's worth of thousands of different tests, Darwin's theory still stands, with only minor modification. Most biologists accept the theory although they still keep their eyes open for contradictory evidence.

Scientists must keep asking themselves "Will some other evidence show my hypothesis to be incorrect?" They are expected to put aside pride or bias by testing their hypothesis. If an individual doesn't (or won't) do this, *others will*—for science is conducted in a community that is both cooperative and competitive. Ideas are shared and examined with the understanding that it is just as important to expose errors as it is to applaud insights. Individuals can change their mind when presented with new evidence—and this is a strength of science, not a weakness.

The Limits of Science

The call for objective testing strengthens the theories that emerge from scientific studies. Yet it also puts limits on the kinds of studies scientists can carry out. Beyond the realm of scientific analysis, some events remain unexplained. Why do we exist, for what purpose? Why does any one of us have to die at a particular moment and not another? Should one person aid another incurably ill person in the act of suicide? Answers to such questions are subjective. This means they come from within us, as an outcome of all the experiences and mental connections that shape our consciousness. Because people differ so enormously in this regard, subjective answers do not readily lend themselves to scientific analysis. The *Choices* essay on page 11 considers some wrenching personal and societal dilemmas in which scientific information is only a limited part of a more complex decision-making process.

Outside the scientific arena, subjective answers can have great value. For example, no human society can function without a shared commitment to standards for making judgments, even if the judgments are subjective. Moral, aesthetic, economic, and philosophical standards vary from one society to the next. But all guide their members in deciding what is important and good and what is not. All attempt to give meaning to what we do.

Every so often, scientists stir up controversy when they question or explain part of the world that was considered beyond natural explanation—that is, belonging to the supernatural. On occasion, a new, natural explanation runs counter to supernatural belief or to some other widely held, nonscientific view. This doesn't mean the scientists who raise the questions are any less moral, less law-abiding, less sensitive, or less caring than anyone else. It simply means one more standard guides their work: *The external world, not internal conviction, must be the testing ground for scientific beliefs.*

A scientific theory is a testable explanation about the cause or causes of a broad range of related phenomena. As is true of hypotheses, theories are open to testing, revision, and tentative acceptance or rejection.

Systematic observations, hypotheses, predictions, tests—in all these ways science differs from systems of belief that are based on faith, force, or simple consensus.

I.5 CASE STUDY: THE SCIENTIFIC METHOD IN CANCER RESEARCH

To get a feel for how researchers use a common scientific method, put yourself in the shoes of Michael Pariza, a biochemist who is probing the effects of different forms of linoleic acid (LA) on cancer (Figure I.9). LA is a "Jekyll-and-Hyde" substance: The human body requires it in small amounts as a building block for fats, but studies on mice and rats show that in large doses it is associated with the development of certain types of cancer. There is also an alternate form of the compound, called CLA—and here the plot thickens. When you paint CLA on the skin of mice that have been exposed to a potent carcinogen (cancer-causing agent), those mice develop only half as many skin cancers as mice painted with LA. A second experiment shows that force-feeding CLA to mice a few days before administering a carcinogen inhibits cancerous stomach tumors. Now you are getting excited, because you know that CLA occurs in some common human foods, including grilled ground beef and some cheese products. Could CLA inhibit cancer when it is consumed as an additive to food?

Moving from Hypothesis to Prediction

Pariza, Clement Ip, and several colleagues agreed on a hypothesis: Based on their existing knowledge, they reasoned that CLA consumed as a regular part of the diet could help prevent certain cancerous tumors from developing. Notice that at least one alternative hypothesis would also have been reasonable; for example, they might have proposed that CLA exerts its effects only when it is administered immediately before exposure to a carcinogen. In science, alternative hypotheses are the rule, not the exception.

The researchers then made a prediction they (and other scientists) could readily test—that rats fed certain doses of CLA would develop fewer cancers than rats in a control group, when all the rats were exposed to a carcinogen known to cause tumors in mammary glands.

Testing a Prediction by Experimentation

Some hypotheses can be tested by direct observation. (You can watch birds visiting a feeder to see whether one type of bird feeds more aggressively, for example.) In this instance, Pariza and his coworkers conducted a series of experiments, using the experimental method described in the previous section. They began with five groups of 30 healthy rats. One group, the control, received a normal diet; the other four groups were fed the same diet, except that each group's food contained a certain amount of CLA, which was added for several weeks before all the animals were exposed to the carcinogen. What was the outcome? The team reported in the prestigious journal *Cancer Research* that, under the conditions of their experiments, regular feeding of CLA in the diet "is effective in cancer prevention."

Pariza, Ip, and the rest of the team are now investigating exactly how CLA deters cancer. Based on knowledge they and others have gained, one hypothesis is that CLA may interfere with steps in a pathway that promotes the runaway multiplication of cancer cells (Chapter 20). No one yet knows whether the results of these experiments will apply to humans. If it turns out that they do, a CLA-like substance could become a routine additive to some human foods.

Commonly, scientists develop alternative hypotheses as possible answers to a particular question about the natural world.

Hypotheses often are tested by experimentation. Proper methods, including the uses of controls, are essential to obtaining reliable results.

I.6   Choices: Biology and Society

DEFINING DEATH

In an austere hospital room, a young mother and father face the most anguished moment of their lives. Their baby has been born with no brain, except for a small portion of brain **stem**. For this child, none of the qualities that we associate with human life—the potential to think, feel joy or pain, learn, or speak—will ever be possible. For the moment, however, that **bit** of brain tissue controls lung and heart functions, so the heart beats sporadically and the lungs occasionally take in air. Within hours or days, even those halting functions will cease.

In the United States, about one baby in a thousand is born with this condition, called *anencephaly*. For parents and physicians alike, the situation is agonizing. During the short period while the heart and lungs minimally function, other organs (such as the liver and kidneys) receive enough oxygen-carrying blood to keep them reasonably healthy. If the child is declared legally dead during that time, those organs can be transplanted and can bring the gift of life to others. If doctors wait until the nubbin of brain stem gives out, potentially transplantable organs will be irreversibly damaged by lack of oxygen and will be useless.

If this were your child, what **course** would you follow? You might not have a choice, if the matter went to court. In recent years many states have **adopted** a strict legal standard for such cases. A person may be declared legally dead only if *all* of the brain, including the brain stem, no longer functions. Some ethicists prefer this approach because it does not put society in the position of determining that some parts of the brain—but not others—make a person human and truly alive. Other people disagree strongly in cases in which the patient is in a "persistent vegetative state" (that is, has no higher brain function) and there is no hope of recovery. In particular, advocates for a less **strict** definition of brain death point to the serious shortage of organs for transplants and the potential for saving other lives.

As individuals, we deal with this kind of issue in many ways. Some people hold religious beliefs that require that individuals receive care as long as the heart can **beat** (Figure I.10). Others draw up "living wills" designed to convey their wishes that life-support equipment, such as respirators, heart-bypass **pumps**, and other high-tech machinery, not be used to prolong life artificially. Many people ignore the issue altogether, hoping that they or their loved ones will never have to **grapple** with it. Unfortunately life and death are not always so simple.

SUMMARY

1. As living organisms, humans have the following characteristics:

a. Their structure, organization, and interactions arise from the basic properties of matter and energy.

b. Processes of metabolism and homeostasis maintain the living state.

c. They have the capacity for growth, development, and reproduction, based on instructions contained in their DNA.

2. Diversity in features and characteristics arises through mutation. Mutations introduce changes in the DNA. The changes may lead to variations in the form, functioning, or behavior of individual offspring.

3. Individuals vary in their heritable traits (the traits that parents transmit to offspring). Such variations influence an organism's ability to survive and reproduce. Under prevailing conditions, some varieties of a given trait may be more adaptive than others; such traits will be "selected," whereas others will be eliminated through successive generations. Thus the population changes over time; it evolves. These points are central to the theory of evolution by natural selection.

4. There are many specialized scientific methods, corresponding to many different fields of inquiry. The following key terms are important in all of those fields:

a. Theory: an explanation of a broad range of related phenomena. An example is the theory of evolution by natural selection.

b. Hypothesis: a possible explanation of a specific phenomenon; sometimes called an "educated guess."

c. Prediction: a claim about what an observer can expect to see in nature if a theory or hypothesis is correct.

d. Test: an effort to gather actual observations that may (or may not) match predicted or expected observations.

e. Conclusion: a statement about whether a hypothesis (or theory) should be accepted, rejected, or modified, based on tests of the predictions derived from it.

5. Scientific theories are based on systematic observations, hypotheses, predictions, and tests. The external world, not internal conviction, is the testing ground for scientific theories.

Review Questions

1. For this and subsequent chapters, make a list of the boldface terms that occur in the text. Write a definition next to each, and then check it against the one in the text.

2. Why is it difficult to give a simple definition of life? (For this and subsequent chapters, *italic numbers* following review questions indicate the pages on which the answers may be found.) *2*

3. As living organisms, what characteristics do humans exhibit? *4*

4. What is energy? What is DNA? *4*

5. Define metabolic activity; briefly describe a metabolic event. *6*

6. Describe the one-way flow of energy and the cycling of materials through the biosphere. *4–5*

7. What is mutation? What role does it play in evolution? *7*

Critical Thinking: You Decide *(Key in Appendix V)*

1. Witnesses in a court of law are asked to swear "to tell the truth, the whole truth, and nothing but the truth." What are some of the problems inherent in the question? Can you think of a better alternative?

2. Design a test (or series of tests) to support or refute the following hypothesis: A diet high in salt is associated with hypertension (high blood pressure), but hypertension is more common in people who have a family history of the condition.

Self-Quiz *(Answers in Appendix IV)*

1. The complex patterns of structural organization characteristic of life are based on instructions contained in _____.

2. _____ is the ability of cells to extract and transform energy from the environment and use it to maintain themselves, grow, and reproduce.

3. _____ is a state in which the body's internal environment is being maintained within a tolerable range. This state depends on _____, which are cells or structures that detect specific aspects of the environment.

4. Diverse structural, functional, and behavioral traits are con-sidered to be _____ to changing conditions in the environment.

5. The capacity to evolve is based on variations in traits, which originally arise through _____.

6. Each of us has some number of traits that also were present in our great-great-great-great-grandmothers and grandfathers. This is an example of _____.
a. metabolism   c. a control group
b. homeostasis   d. inheritance

7. A scientific approach to explaining some aspect of the natural world includes all of the following except _____.

a. hypothesis   c. faith and simple consensus
b. testing   d. systematic observations

8. A related set of hypotheses that collectively explain some aspect of the natural world is a scientific _____.

a. prediction   d. authority
b. test   e. observation
c. theory

Selected Key Terms

adaptive trait 7   hypothesis 8
ATP 6   inheritance 7
cell 4   metabolism 6
control group 8   mutation 7
DNA 4   prediction 8
energy 4   reproduction 7
evolution 2   theory 8
experiment 8   variable 8
homeostasis 6

Readings

Alberts, B., and K. Shine. December 4, 1994. "Scientists and the Integrity of Research." *Science.*

Committee on the Conduct of Science. 1989. *On Being a Scientist.* Washington, D.C.: National Academy of Sciences. Paperback.

Larkin, Tim. June 1985. "Evidence vs. Nonsense: A Guide to the Scientific Method." *FDA Consumer.*

Raloff, J. February 15, 1992. "Cancer-Fighting Food Additives." *Science News.*

Rosenthal, Elizabeth. October 1992. "Dead Complicated." *Discover.* Is a person with no functional brain, maintained by life-support machinery, alive or dead? The author, a physician, discusses this and other questions society faces as a result of modern, high-technology medical practices.

Sample Chapter 14

Organization of Information

Reprinted by permission of *Technical Communication*, 4th edition by Rebecca E. Burnett. Copyright 1996 by Wadsworth Publishing Company. All rights reserved.

The purpose of a document is to communicate information to readers; thus, making your document understandable is critical. As you initially explore a topic, you may outline and then draft a *writer-based document,* one that helps you examine and organize the information. A writer-based document may be helpful in your preliminary investigations because it uses your point of view, focus, and organization. However, it doesn't consider whether they'll be effective for your readers. Your end goal should be to create a *reader-based document,* one that considers the needs and reactions of your readers and organizes information so that they can understand the issues.

Outlining

You may decide to outline your information simply because changing an outline is usually easier than changing the draft of a text. Any outline you develop should be flexible and easy to change as you arrange and rearrange ideas, add new information, and delete unnecessary material. Outlines are not intended to restrict you; rather, they are tools to help you manage the material for a document. Think of them as document blueprints that show overall structure and primary features. As with buildings that exist only on paper, changes in documents are easier to make before drafting.

Outlines can help you arrange and examine collected information. They do not have to be formal, complete-sentence outlines. Initially, you can just jot down information and then rethink, rearrange, and reorganize it in an outline. For example, the following list is simply a series of unorganized points for a paper reporting a Harvard ethnobotanist's attempts to explain the zombies of traditional Haitian voodoo:[1]

- *Natives believe in zombies (walking dead); fertile ground for mind control*

- *Natives believe in power of a bocor, malevolent voodoo priest*

- *Zombies created by a bocor, sophisticated knowledge of pharmacology and psychology*

- *Poisons from puffer fish contain powerful neurotoxin, tetrodotoxin*

- *Initially produces hypothermia, nausea, respiratory difficulties, hypertension, hypotension, paralysis*

- *Long-term control maintained with hallucinogenic plant containing daturas; causes disorientation, amnesia*

- *Bocor have variety of poisons, all with same main ingredient*

- *Tetrodotoxin reduces metabolic functions to deathlike state*

Figure 7.1 shows a computer screen of an outline that was developed from this preliminary list. Outlining is an option with most word processing software. An online outline offers you a different *view* of your document rather than creating a separate document. The online changes you make in the outline automatically become part of the document, and vice versa. You can easily switch back and forth between an *outline view* of your document and a full *text view*.

The writer could examine the online outline in Figure 7.1 to determine whether the information is complete and parallel—equivalent in importance, sequence, and wording. In this case, this first outline has incomplete information, needs reordering, and isn't parallel. But without the outline (whether online or on paper), the writer might not see these inadequacies.

Figure 7.2 shows a revised online outline in which the writer has corrected the problems. The changes are more than cosmetic. First, expressing ideas in parallel structure demonstrates that the writer intends to treat them equally, as shown in the revision of the sections. Next, the sequence of entries must be logical, as shown in the revision in the order of entries. Here, indicating native susceptibility logically comes first; instances of their beliefs resulting from this susceptibility follow. Finally, essential information must not be inadvertently omitted, as shown by the omission of the type of poison in the first section. In each case, changing the outline is easier than changing the draft of the paper.

The original and revised outlines about zombies (Figures 7.1 and 7.2) show how helpful outlines can be to organize and reorganize information before starting to draft a document. These outlines identified gaps in data, inconsistencies in the relative importance of various segments, and problems in sequencing information. If you use outlines as tools for planning and revision, you may save yourself a great deal of frustration and time.

As you plan your material, you can ask yourself the questions in Figure 7.3 to check whether your outline is likely to result in a successful document. If you can answer yes to all the questions in Figure 7.3, your outline will probably be useful in planning, organizing, and drafting your document.

Figure 7.1 ■ *Online Outline Showing Problems in the Completeness, Organization, and Parallelism*

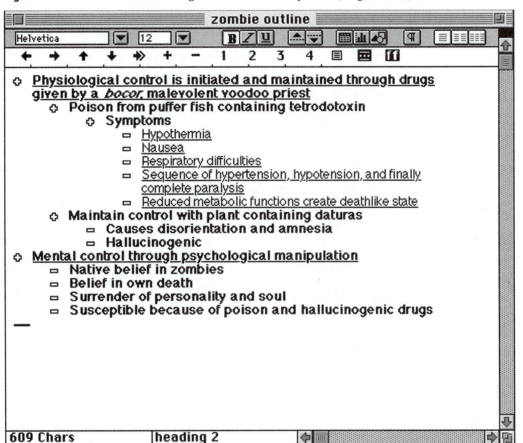

Outlines have additional uses besides help in planning and revising. In a long document, an outline's main headings can provide ready-made headings for the document itself. Outlines can also be modified for use as a table of contents. And sometimes outlines actually form the body of a document, as in the excerpt in Figure 7.4 from "External and Internal Parasites—Causes, Symptoms, Treatment, and Control," which appeared in a professional journal for farmers.[2] Using an outline for the body of a document can make it easy for readers to skim the document to locate main points.

■ *Online Outline Showing Revisions*

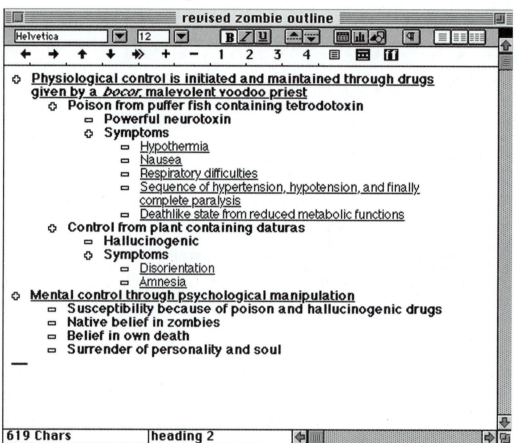

Organizing Information

The way the information in a document is organized affects the meaning that readers construct. Once you've decided how to organize your information, you can help readers by using signals that identify that organization. Two tools are helpful for signaling: topic sentences and transitions.

■ A *topic sentence* identifies both the content and organization of a paragraph so that readers have definite signals about what a paragraph is about and how the information is organized.

Figure 7.3 ■ *Questions to Ask About Your Outline*

Content and context	◆ Is all important information included and all unnecessary information omitted?
	◆ Are contextual factors that will influence the document's interpretation acknowledged?
Audience	◆ Do the headings give readers an accurate overview of the document?
	◆ Is the level of detail appropriate for the purpose and audience?
Purpose and key points	◆ Are the main headings and subheadings logically arranged?
	◆ Is the organization in the outline appropriate to the content, purpose, audience, and genre?
Organization	◆ Is all information in the outline in the appropriate places—both in the main sections and the subsections?
Professional standards	◆ Do the details in each subsection reflect the emphasis for that heading?
	◆ Are main headings in the outline written in parallel grammatical form (so that you can use them as headings in the document)?

■ *Transitions* are words and phrases that act as the glue connecting ideas and sentences within a single paragraph, linking one paragraph to another and relating one section of a document to the next section.

Technical communicators organize information to make it clear and accessible to readers. Some common ways to organize information are presenting parts/whole organization, chronological order, spatial order, ascending/descending order, comparison/contrast, and cause and effect.

No communicator settles down to write and says, "I'm about to begin a document using chronological order." Instead, the communicator may ask questions like these: "What's the situation or problem this document is responding to?" "What's my purpose?" "Who's the audience, and what are their expectations?" "How can I help my readers understand this information?" "What's the appropriate genre?" And then the communicator may ask, "What's the most appropriate way to organize the information—given the situation, purpose, audience, and genre?" In organizing the information, technical communicators use topic sentences and transitions to help make the information more accessible and appealing to readers.

Figure 7.4 ■ *Outline Forming the Body of a Document*

INTRODUCTION

Dairy goats, like other animals, wild or domestic, have their share of parasites (both external and internal) and effective parasitic treatment, prevention and control play an integral part in milk and meat production . . .

There are two main types of parasites in most domestic animals including the dairy goat. In this article, basic information will be presented on the common signs and symptoms of the most prevalent external and internal parasites along with their treatment, prevention and control.

1. EXTERNAL PARASITES

A. Lice

Lice are the most common external parasites of dairy goats. The two primary types of lice which affect goats are:

1. Biting louse—Bovicola caprae
2. Sucking louse—Linognathus stenopsis

The biting louse, red in color, feeds on the skin and burrows into the hair follicles causing severe itching. The blood-sucking louse, blue in color, is larger and more visible. It pierces the skin to feed and is prevalent on the sides of the neck, underline and around the udder.

Symptoms

a. Excessive scratching against the sides of the barn, fence post and wire
b. Weight loss
c. Decreased milk production
d. The appearance of dry, crusty or scabby areas on the back, side of the face and underside of the neck

Treatment and Control

The best time to control and treat lice is in the fall. Dipping or spraying using "Coral" (coumaphos) is the drug of choice even in lactating animals. Good control is obtained if spraying is repeated once or twice at least 10-14 days apart

to kill all the lice which hatch from eggs. Lice must live on their host to survive, thus neither barns nor bedding need be treated.

B. Mange

Two types of mange are common in dairy goats:

1. Sarcoptes scabei, var. caprae
2. Demodectic spp

Sarcoptic mange, Sarcoptes scabei var. caprae is seen mostly around the neck, the underline, and face, while demodex is generalized but can be commonly found in the flank and udder areas. Demodex, the more prevalent of the two, is caused by Demodex caprae. The mites which burrow into the hair follicles leave blebs (or small raised welts) which are mainly detected by shaving the hair close, or passing the hand over the areas involved.

Symptoms

a. In addition to excessive scratching, sarcoptic mange exhibits a relative thickening of the (epidermal) layer of skin in the areas of irritation.
b. With demodex, when the hair is shaved, the blebs or subcutaneous swellings laden with mites are seen. These swellings or nodules, ranging in size from pin head to hazel-nut, contain thick grayish material of waxy consistency, which can be easily expressed. Numerous demodectic mites are found in this material.

Treatment

Frequent dips with an insecticide are necessary, and "Coral" (coumaphos) does an effective job even with lactating animals.

C. Ear Mites

Ear mite infestation in the dairy goat is a common problem and is easy to misdiagnose. The infestation is caused by a mite of the genus Psoroptes spp.

Does every paragraph in a document have a topic sentence? Not necessarily. Some paragraphs are transitional, connecting one main paragraph or section to the next. Occasionally, an excessively long paragraph is separated into two or more to make the paragraph easier to read and give readers a chance to breathe. Usually, however, most of the paragraphs in a well-constructed document have clear topic sentences, which can be separated from the document and listed together as a summary. If the message from this topic sentence summary is clear and logical, then the document is probably well constructed.

Parts/Whole Organization

A document that uses parts/whole organization presents readers with a relationship between the *whole* (whether an idea, object, or entire system) and *parts* of that whole (whether on a micro level or a macro level). Sometimes this parts/whole organization involves separating a single item into individual components. At other times, it involves identifying related types of an item. It may also involve identifying the broad category to which something belongs.

A parts/whole organization to present the categories of integrated circuits is shown in Figure 7.5. The paragraph shows the relationship between the whole (the category of devices called integrated circuits) and the parts of that whole (three types of circuits: programmable devices, memory devices, and linear devices). This example (and those that follow related to integrated circuits) were written by the supervisor of a testing line in an inspection group of a plant that manufactured and assembled integrated circuits. This supervisor was required to train the unskilled entry-level workers assigned to her area. She decided to

Figure 7.5 ■ *Part/Whole Organization of Information*

Whole: integrated circuits

Parts:
first type
second type
third type

Integrated circuits are divided into three categories, depending on their function and capability in the final product. (See the diagram below.) The first type is a programmable integrated circuit, a multifunctional component designed to be programmed by the supplier or by in-house technicians. The second type of integrated circuit is the memory device, used to store memory in an end product. The third type is a linear device designed to do many specific predetermined functions and used in conjunction with other components to operate computers.

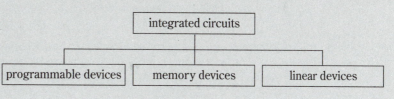

provide these workers with short, easy-to-read explanations about the inspection process. She believed that helping them understand how their specific job fit into the larger process would increase the quality of their work.

Chronological Order

Chronological order presents readers with material arranged by sequence or order of occurrence. When the purpose is to give instructions, describe processes, or trace the development of objects or ideas, chronology is appropriate. For example, chronologically organized information about computer disks might include a description identifying each step of the manufacturing process or an explanation of the historical development of electronic storage media, from paper tape to mylar disks. Information can be presented chronologically in visual forms, as shown in Figure 7.6, which also lists an example of each form.

A topic sentence conveying chronology includes words or phrases that indicate a process or a sequence of actions, as illustrated in the following sentences:

EXAMPLES

Seven operations are necessary to fabricate sheet metal. . . .

Most poultry farms are vertically integrated, from breeding to egg to packaged product. . . .

Readers can justifiably expect the paragraph that follows the first topic sentence to identify and explain the seven steps of sheet-metal fabrication. The paragraph that

Figure 7.6   ■   *Visual Forms for Chronological Order*

Form	Example
Flow chart	Sequence of manufacturing process
Time line	Development of synthetics for medical use
Genealogy chart	History of family with Huntington's disease
Sequential photos	Embryo development
Sequential drawings	Steps in resuscitation of drowning victim
Story board	Public service ad urging water conservation
Time-lapse photos	Emergence of butterfly from cocoon
Line graph	Increase in restlessness during REM sleep
Calendar	Production schedule for new product
Chart	Stratification of rock layers according to geologic periods

follows the second topic sentence should identify each stage in the process of poultry production.

Transitions in chronological paragraphs can indicate the sequence of events or the passage of time. Figure 7.7 presents an example that explains the *chronology* of incoming inspection that integrated circuits go through. The reader easily follows the process because the chronological transitions highlight each step of the five-step process.

Figure 7.7 ■ *Information Organized Using Chronological Order*

Chronological transitions:

the first stage

then

Next

After this

The final step

Integrated circuits received at incoming inspection go through a five-step process. As the flowchart shows, the first stage of inspection ensures that the parts have been purchased from a predetermined qualified vendor list. The parts are then prioritized according to daily back-order quantities and/or line shortages assigned by the production floor. Next the parts are moved into the test area where a determination is made as to which lots will be tested at 100 percent and which will be sample tested. After this, the parts are electrically tested for specific continuity and direct current parameters using MCT handlers. The final step of incoming inspection is distributing the parts according to need on the production floor.

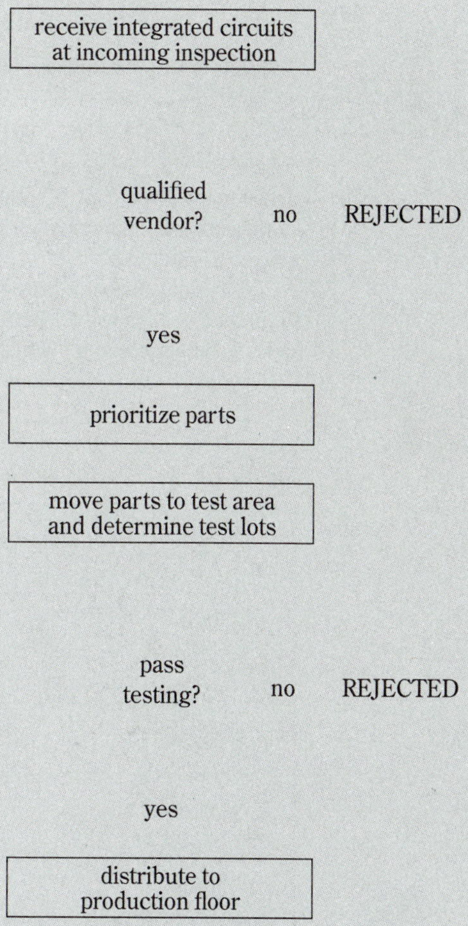

receive integrated circuits at incoming inspection

qualified vendor?   no   REJECTED

yes

prioritize parts

move parts to test area and determine test lots

pass testing?   no   REJECTED

yes

distribute to production floor

Spatial Order

Spatial order—arrangement by relative physical location—describes for readers the physical parts of nearly anything, from cellular structures to the orbital path of a satellite. Spatial organization could explain parts of a computer disk or the location of the disk drives in relation to the other parts of the computer. Figure 7.8 presents examples of several visual forms. You may find visual presentations are particularly effective for spatially arranged material because they help your readers see the actual physical relationships.

Because spatial arrangement deals with the relative physical location of objects, the topic sentence suggests their placement, as seen in these examples.

EXAMPLES

Unnecessary or damaged inventory that is scheduled to be scrapped is placed on skids in one of six bin locations in the Defective Stockroom. . . .

Sound is a ripple of molecules and atoms in the air that travels from its source to our ears. . . .

Readers of the first sentence anticipate the identification of each bin's location according to type of scrap material. The second topic sentence indicates to readers that the paragraph will track the sound as it moves through the air from source to listener.

Transitions in spatial paragraphs suggest the relative physical location of components or objects. Figure 7.9 presents an example that uses *spatial order* to describe the incoming inspection of an integrated circuit.

Figure 7.8 ■ *Visual Forms for Spatial Order*

Form	Example
Map	Identification of migration stopovers
Blueprint	Specification of dimensions for machined part
Navigational chart	Location of sand bars and buoys
Celestial chart	Sequence of moons around Jupiter
Exploded view	Assembly of disk brake
Cutaway view	Interior components of pool filter
Wiring diagram	Wiring of alarm system
Floor plan	Workflow in busy area
Set design	Arrangement of furniture/props for *Hamlet*
Architectural drawing	Appearance of building with solar modifications

Figure 7.9 ■ *Information Organized Using Spatial Order*

Spatial transitions:
through the test area from the supplier into a removable channel within a clear tube in the same direction into the MCT handler in the upper left through a slot to the manufacturing area to another engineering station

The movement of the IC (integrated circuit) chip through the test area is very efficient. The chips arrive from the supplier, already set—24 at a time—into a removable channel within a clear tube. The chips are aligned in the same direction within the tube. This tube is inserted by the operator into the MCT handler so that pin 1 of the first chip, marked by a small dot, is in the upper left. The tube slides through a slot, into the testing compartment, where each chip is tested individually. Automatically, the good chips are placed in one channel, the rejects in another. The channels are moved so the operator can slip on the protective tubes. The good chips are sent to the manufacturing area; the rejects are sent to another engineering station for further testing.

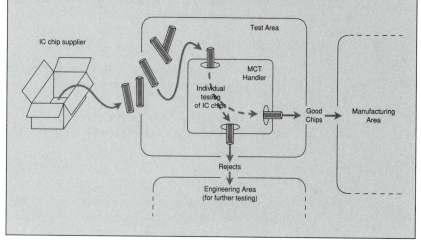

Ascending/Descending Order

Ascending and descending orders present readers with information according to quantifiable criteria.

appeal	durability
authority	ease of manufacture, operation, repair
benefit	frequency
cost	importance
delivery	size

Descending order uses a most-to-least-important order; ascending order, a least-to-most. Descending order is found in workplace writing more frequently than ascending order because most readers want to know the most important points first. In business and industry, readers generally form opinions and make decisions based on what they read initially; they expect descending order in nearly all technical documents. Descending or ascending order would be appropriate for organizing the relative convenience of various forms of electronic data storage or for identifying the disk specifications in various price ranges. If you wanted to arrange information visually, one of the forms illustrated in Figure 7.10 would work.

Unlike topic sentences for paragraphs organized in other ways, those beginning descending or ascending paragraphs do not give an immediate clue about the subsequent organization. The reader understands that the paragraph will present a series of related ideas, but the specific relationship is not clear until the second sentence. The topic sentence in the next example begins a paragraph about the master satellite station in Beijing, presenting the characteristics of the Beijing antenna in descending order of importance.

EXAMPLE

The largest earth station in China is a 15-to-18-meter-diameter dish antenna in Beijing for domestic satellite communications.

A paragraph using a descending organization to identify the various sized antennas in China begins with a general statement before going on to identify each type of station.

EXAMPLE

Three types of earth stations are planned for domestic satellite communication in China. The largest is a 15-to-18-meter-diameter dish antenna of the master station in Beijing. . . . Regional stations are equipped with a 10-to-13-meter-diameter antenna. . . .[3]

Figure 7.10 ■ *Visual Forms for Ascending/Descending Order*

Form	Example
Numbered list	Priority of options for treating breast cancer
Bull's-eye chart	Population affected by nuclear explosion
Percent graph	Percent of different economic groups receiving balanced nutrition
Pareto diagram	Productivity using different methods (bar graph arranged in descending order)
Line graph	Increasing success for breeding endangered species in captivity over twenty-year period

Readers would expect the remainder of the paragraph to identify a series of satellite dish antennas, arranged by size, from largest to smallest.

Transitions in ascending/descending paragraphs indicate the relative priority of points in the paragraph or document. Figure 7.11 uses *descending order* to identify the priorities for testing circuits.

Figure 7.11 ■ *Information Organized Using Descending Order*

Integrated circuits received at incoming inspection are processed according to priorities. As the following figure shows, the most important integrated circuits are those that fill line shortages on the production floor. These parts take first priority at incoming inspection and are handled according to frequency of use and critical demand. These priority parts are further separated according to how fast they can be accurately tested and sent to the production floor. All other integrated circuits are then prioritized by back-order demand and the availability of open test equipment.

INSPECTION PRIORITIES

1   Fill line shortages

2   Determine speed of testing

3   Determine back-order demand and equipment availability

Comparison/Contrast

Comparison and contrast tell readers about similarities and differences. Comparison identifies the similarities of various ideas, objects, or situations; contrast, the differences. A comparison or contrast organization could present the advantages and disadvantages of certified versus uncertified computer disks or the ease or difficulty of various methods of storing electronic data. Any of the techniques in Figure 7.12 could visually present information that you want to compare and contrast.

Readers expect comparison and contrast topic sentences to present ideas dealing with similarities and differences, or both, as illustrated by the following two sentences:

EXAMPLES

The Honey Bee Lens, with three telescopic lenses for each eye, is patterned after the compound eye of a bee. . . .

Figure 7.12 ■ *Visual Forms for Comparison and Contrast*

Form	Example
Paired photos or drawings	Before/after of patient treated for scoliosis
Multiple or paired bar graphs	Expenditures for utilities for each quarter of the fiscal year
Multiple or paired percent graphs	Utilization of nutrients with and without coconut oil to increase absorption
Line graph	Changes in toxicity of emissions since installation of scrubbers
Multiple or paired gauges	Illustration of danger/no-danger in training manual for pilots
Table	Data collected on species size of bats according to age, sex, and location
Dichotomous key	Distinction of edible wild plants
Pareto diagram	Distinction between major and minor causes of shipping delays
Histogram	Women, grouped by age, affected by lung cancer
Columned chart	Physical symptoms of substance abuse

Computers can now analyze measurable differences between the cries of healthy newborns and high-risk infants. . . .

The first sentence introduces a paragraph that compares new lenses to the compound eyes of bees. The second sentence leads readers to expect the paragraph to deal with characteristics that differentiate cries of healthy and high-risk infants.

Transitions in comparison and contrast paragraphs identify various similarities and differences. Figures 7.13 and 7.14 use *comparison and contrast* to differentiate the responsibilities of incoming inspection and in-process inspection of integrated circuits. Figure 7.13 shifts back and forth between incoming inspection and in-process inspection, explaining how each deals with specific responsibilities.

Figure 7.14 takes the same paragraph and rearranges it to present all the information about incoming inspection first and then discusses the in-process inspection.

Figure 7.13 ■ *Information Organized Using Comparison and Contrast*

Organization of information:
incoming inspection

in-process inspection

incoming inspection

in-process inspection

mutual goal

Integrated circuits are inspected and/or tested by two separate quality control departments: incoming quality control and in-process quality control. Incoming quality control is responsible for ensuring that all integrated circuits sent to the production floor meet all electrical standards set by the Component Engineering Department. In-process quality control is only responsible for ensuring that the parts are properly mounted on the printed circuit board. Incoming quality control also has to verify the markings on the integrated circuits in order to do proper testing and make certain that the company has purchased a qualified product. In contrast, in-process quality control only has to do random inspections of the circuit markings to ensure that qualified parts are being used in the manufacturing process. Although incoming and in-process inspection are two different areas, they do share the same goal of building a quality product. The following lists summarize each department's responsibilities.

Component Engineering Department responsible for IN-COMING INSPECTION	Quality Control Department responsible for IN-PROCESS INSPECTION

- verify parts meet standards
- verify IC markings
- confirm qualified vendors

- ensure proper mounting
- do random inspections

Cause and Effect

The cause-and-effect organization of information focuses on precipitating factors and results. You can move from cause to effect or from effect to cause. For example, you could carry the disk through an electronic surveillance scanner and then trace the effects—the various disk errors that appear. Or beginning with the effect—a damaged disk—you could investigate the causes of the damage. Figure 7.15 identifies and illustrates various visuals that are effective for presenting cause-and-effect relationships.

One type of cause and effect—*inductive reasoning*—moves from specific instances to broad generalizations, forming the basis for the *scientific method* used in much research and experimentation. You begin by collecting data in support of an unproved hypothesis. After you have organized and examined a sufficient body of data, you draw a conclusion. When your conclusion proves consistently to be valid, it is considered a generalization. Most scientific principles and theories are based on this method of inquiry.

Because there is no way to test every instance, induction has a certain risk, and researchers must be careful to avoid basing their reasoning on invalid assumptions.

Figure 7.14 ■ *Information Organized Using Comparison and Contrast*

Organization of information:

incoming inspection

incoming inspection

in-process inspection

in-process inspection

mutual goal

Integrated circuits are inspected and/or tested by two separate quality control departments: incoming quality control and in-process quality control, as shown in the lists below. Incoming quality control is responsible for ensuring that all integrated circuits sent to the production floor meet all electrical standards set by the Component Engineering Department. Incoming quality control also has to verify the markings on the integrated circuits in order to do proper testing and make certain that the company has purchased a qualified product. In-process quality control is only responsible for ensuring that the parts are properly mounted on the printed circuit board. In-process quality control only has to do random inspections of the circuit markings to ensure that qualified parts are being used in the manufacturing process. Although incoming and in-process inspection are two different areas, they do share the same goal of building a quality product.

Component Engineering Department responsible for IN-COMING INSPECTION	Quality Control Department responsible for IN-PROCESS INSPECTION
• verify parts meet standards • verify IC markings • confirm qualified vendors	• ensure proper mounting • do random inspections

Figure 7.15 ■ *Visual Forms for Cause and Effect*

Form	Example
Paired photos or drawings	Effects of two different treatments for removing facial birth marks
Weather map	Impact of cold front on majority of Midwest
Bar graph	Efficiency of various methods for harvesting cranberries
Line graph	Destruction of American chestnut by blight during this century
Cause-and-effect diagram	Identification of multiple contributing factors to contamination of drinking water
Pareto diagram	Identification of major causes in low birth weight

They must not assume chronology is the same as causality, and they must examine a large sample before drawing a conclusion.

The first of these problems, equating chronology with causality, represents an error in reasoning. Just because B follows A does not mean that A causes B. Because inductive reasoning moves from specifics to a generalization, an investigator should not assume that sequence of events alone causes the effect. (Such an error in reasoning is called *post hoc, ergo propter hoc,* Latin for "after this, therefore because of this.") For example, a donor may become ill the day after donating blood to the Red Cross, but he cannot logically conclude that donating blood caused him to become ill. Guard against fallacious reasoning by examining all possible causes.

You also need to examine a large number of instances before drawing a conclusion. For example, before a new drug is allowed on the market, the Food and Drug Administration requires extensive tests with a broad segment of the target population. As a result of testing, a powerful painkiller such as propoxyphene, when taken according to directions and under a physician's care, is certified as safe even though all propoxyphene tablets and capsules have not been individually tested. Unfortunately, errors occur, although rarely, causing some people to suspect all inductive reasoning. So make sure your methodology is sound, your sample large, and your analysis free from bias or distortion.

When a generalization is widely accepted, you can use it as a base from which to predict the likelihood of specific instances occurring. This process is called *deductive reasoning*—moving from general premises to specific causes. A patient taking propoxyphene trusts that the pills are safe even though those particular ones have not been tested.

In paragraphs that show cause and effect, both should be identified in the topic sentence, as seen in the next examples.

EXAMPLES

One hypothesis about the formation of mineral-rich marine nodules suggests that marine bacteria break down organic material into free-floating minerals that eventually collect to form nodules. . . .

The Zephinie Escape Chute (ZEC) can rapidly evacuate people from 10-story burning buildings because of its unique construction. . . .

Readers of the first sentence expect the information in the paragraph to explain how minerals form marine nodules. The second sentence develops a paragraph that explains how the ZEC's unique construction aids rapid evacuation.

Transitions in cause-and-effect paragraphs signal the relationship between an action and its result. The example in Figure 7.16 uses *cause and effect* to organize information about IC testing. In this example, the cause-and-effect transitions indicate the descending order of the reasons an IC chip can be rejected.

Figure 7.16 ■ *Information Organized Using Cause and Effect*

Causal transitions:
because
therefore
so

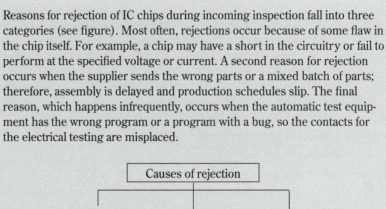

Reasons for rejection of IC chips during incoming inspection fall into three categories (see figure). Most often, rejections occur because of some flaw in the chip itself. For example, a chip may have a short in the circuitry or fail to perform at the specified voltage or current. A second reason for rejection occurs when the supplier sends the wrong parts or a mixed batch of parts; therefore, assembly is delayed and production schedules slip. The final reason, which happens infrequently, occurs when the automatic test equipment has the wrong program or a program with a bug, so the contacts for the electrical testing are misplaced.

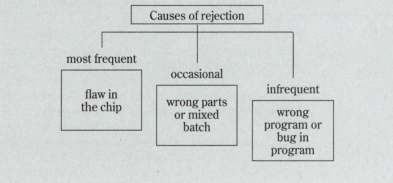

Using Organization

These ways of organizing information are frequently used in technical documents—as short, self-contained segments (like the examples about integrated circuits) and also combined in longer pieces of writing.

You can make a paragraph or document more understandable, as well as overcome some of the noise that interferes with readers' acceptance or comprehension of information, by organizing information so that it meets the needs of the content, purpose, and audience. For example, processes, procedures, and directions are best organized chronologically for all audiences. Descriptions of physical objects, mechanisms, organisms, and locations frequently make the most sense to readers if the information is organized spatially. Reasons and explanations are usually presented in descending order so that the audience reads the most important information first. Explanations of problems and their solutions often make the most sense to readers if the information is organized using comparison/contrast and cause and effect.

You can also use organization of information to adapt your material to readers' attitudes. Specifically, you can take advantage of what you know about induction (specific to general) and deduction (general to specific). If you think readers might be reluctant to accept your conclusions or recommendations, you can organize the material inductively, moving from various specifics to your conclusion. Thus, readers can follow your line of reasoning and, perhaps, be persuaded by your analysis. If you think readers will agree with your conclusions, you can organize the information deductively, presenting the conclusion initially and then following it with the specifics that led to it. Deductive organization is more common in technical documents.

End-of-Chapter Review

Recommendations for Technical Communicators

1. Prepare *reader-based documents* that consider the needs and reactions of your readers.

2. Use a working outline to help you arrange and rearrange ideas, add new information, and delete unnecessary material.

3. Decide whether information is better presented verbally or visually given your purpose and audience.

4. Organize your document so that the information is clear to your readers and helps you accomplish your purpose. Consider these standard ways to organize information verbally or visually:
   - Parts/whole organization
   - Chronological order
   - Spatial order
   - Ascending/descending order
   - Comparison/contrast
   - Cause and effect

5. Use topic sentences to identify both the content and organization of a paragraph.

6. Use transitions as one way to achieve coherence in a document.

Inquiries and Applications

Discussion Questions

1. In what ways do topic sentences make technical information easier to read?

2. For a reader who is an expert in the subject, why are transitions necessary? Won't an expert understand the relationships among the ideas?

3. Biological researcher Lance Stewart is preparing a report about the results of his work during the past six months. He wants his readers to follow the progress of his experiments step by step, not knowing the results until they read the conclusions and recommendations at the end of the report. He says he worked hard to get the results; he wants the readers to appreciate all of his work. What is wrong with Lance's reason for placing conclusions and recommendations at the end? What would you say to persuade him to reconsider his plan?

4. Identify the expectations about the paragraph's organization readers might have if they read these topic sentences. What content would readers expect in each paragraph? One example is provided.

EXAMPLE

The use of a sulfur-asphalt mixture for repaving the highway will result in several specific benefits.

ANALYSIS

The sentence presents a cause-and-effect relationship between using a sulfur-asphalt mixture and specific benefits. The paragraph will identify these benefits.

a. The CAT scan creates an image resembling a "slice" that clearly visualizes anatomical structures within the body.

b. The fetus is in the birth position by the ninth month of a normal pregnancy.

c. The routine use of drugs in labor and delivery sometimes has adverse effects on otherwise healthy, normal infants.

d. The stages of normal labor and delivery begin at term when the fetus reaches maturity and end with the expulsion of the placenta.

e. Two major forms of leukemia—chronic myelocytic and acute myelocytic—have distinct differences.

f. Improper downstroke and follow-through can cause the golf ball to either hook and fade to the left or slice and fade to the right.

g. Three main types of parachutes are used for sky diving. The most widely used parachute has a round, domelike canopy. . . .

h. A square parachute provides more maneuverability and a better overall ride than does a conventional round parachute.

i. Two methods of disinfecting treated wastewater are chlorination and ozonation.

j. The chlorinator room contains the evaporators, chlorinators, and injectors, three of each. The evaporators are used only when liquid chlorine is being drawn from the containers. . . .

Individual and Collaborative Exercises

1. Revise the memo in Figure 7.17 so that the subject line in the heading, the topic sentences, and the paragraphs are unified and coherent. The intended readers are interested in information that will help decrease rejects during manufacturing. They are not particularly concerned with personnel or cost.

Figure 7.17 ■ *Memo That Needs Revision*

Stanford Engineering, Inc.

February 14, 19

To: Quality Control Supervision
From: T. R. Hood, Engineer
Subject: Increased scrap and customer rejects

The Engineering Department is recommending the purchase of an International glue line inspection system to strengthen standard visual inspection. Machine operators will not be slowed down by the addition of this new glue line inspection system. The system will detect breaks in the glue line and eject a carton from the run before it reaches shipping. If the system detects more than five consecutive rejects, it will automatically stop the machine.

Purchasing this International system is a better solution than purchasing a new glue pot for $6,500. The savings in purchasing the $4,000 International system will allow us to rebuild the existing glue pot.

2. Revise the following paragraphs by adding topic sentences:

PARAGRAPH 1

Buss bars, the smallest of the parts the Sheet Metal Fabrication Shop produces, are made of grade A copper and are tin-plated before being used for internal grounding. Paper deflectors, used in printers, are made of stainless steel and do not require any plating or painting. Deflectors guide the paper through the printer and usually measure 4" in width and 15" in length, depending on the size of the printer. A larger box-like structure, made of aluminum and requiring plating in the enclosure chassis, is designed to hold a variety of electronic devices within an even larger computer main frame. A steel door panel requiring cosmetic plating and painting is the largest of the parts produced by the Sheet Metal Fabrication Shop.

PARAGRAPH 2

The fetal causes for abortion are infectious agents: protozoa bacteria, viruses, particularly rubella virus. Drugs such as thalidomide cause fetal abnormalities. When radiation is given in therapeutic doses to the mother in the first few months of pregnancy, malformation or death of the fetus may result.

Assignments

1. Select a topic, and use it as the topic for five separate paragraphs.

- Identify the specific audience.
- Whenever possible and appropriate, use parallel visual figures to supplement the verbal information. (Refer to these figures in the paragraph.)
- Use a different way of organizing the information in each paragraph.
- Use topic sentences that reflect the organization and content of each paragraph.
- Use transitions that signal the organization of each paragraph.

You may approach the assignment in one of two different ways:

a. Use the same information (or as close as possible) for all five paragraphs so that you gain experience in writing about the same aspect of a subject in a variety of ways. The five paragraphs will not form a unified, cohesive paper, but will serve as a rigorous exercise.

b. Use the same subject for all five paragraphs, but select material so that the paragraphs form a unified, coherent paper.

Notes

1. Modified from Nick Jordon, "What's in a Zombie," Review of *The Serpent and the Rainbow,* by Wade Davis, *Psychology Today* (May 1984): 6.
2. A. B. Watkins, "External and Internal Parasites—Causes, Symptoms, Treatment, and Control," *Dairy Goat Journal* 61 (August 1983): 14, 16. Reprinted with permission of the publisher.
3. Modified from Jeffrey M. Lenorovitz, "China Plans Upgraded Satellite Network," *Aviation Week & Space Technology* 119 (21 November 1983): 71–75.

Glossary

A

abilities   power to do some special thing; skill

abstract   a brief statement of main ideas of an article, book, and so on; a summary

academic action   suspension from the university after a period of extended probation

academic code of student conduct   the academic standards for your university

academic probation   goes into effect if a student's cumulative grade average is ten quality points below a 2.0 or C average

accuracy   refers to correctness

acronyms   words created from the first letter or the first few letters of the items on a list

acrostics   phrases or sentences created from the first letter or first few letters of items on a list

active listening   conscious control of the listening process through preplanned strategies

adult   one of the three inner dialogue voices; the one who thinks analytically and solves problems rationally

almanacs   annual publications which include calendars, weather forecasts, and other useful tabular information

analysis   a stage of critical thinking that requires an examination of information by breaking it into parts

antonym   a word that has the opposite meaning of another

appeals   the right to contest academic disciplinary actions

appendices   additions at the end of a book or document; supplements

application   a stage of critical thinking that requires using information concerning the process, idea, and theory, and so on, appropriately to accomplish what is required

aptitude test   an examination which predicts future performance in a given activity

aptitudes   natural tendencies or talents

assumption   an inference made with the use of given facts and global knowledge

atlas   a book of maps

auditory practice   repeating aloud information that you are trying to remember or discussing it with another student

aural   acquiring information through listening

author card   a catalog card filed under the author's last name which contains other bibliographical information

B

background knowledge   what you know about a topic

balance sheets   a mechanism that helps you logically weigh your available options

bar graphs   graphics in which bars indicate the frequency of data; shows quantitative comparisons; histograms

behavior modification   a technique to change behavior by systematically rewarding desirable behavior and either ignoring or punishing undesirable behavior

bias   an opinion before there is a reason for it; prejudice

bibliography   a list of books or articles consulted or referred to by an author in the preparation of a manuscript

brain dominance the side of your brain that influences your thinking the most

brainstorming a method of dialoging with yourself in which you list as many possible solutions as you can

breadth suggests that you look at more than one viewpoint, kind of information, implication, or other aspect of thinking

burnout physical or mental exhaustion of a person's supply of energy, ambition, or ideas

C

call number a classification number assigned to library material to indicate its location in the library

card catalog an alphabetical listing with one or more cards for each item

cartographer one who draws maps or charts; a mapmaker

cause/effect in a communication, a stated or implied association between some outcome and the condition which brought it about

chapter maps provide verbal information in the context of a visual arrangement of ideas; show relationships among concepts and express an author's patterns of thought

charts information arranged by rows and columns; also called tables

child one of the three inner dialogue voices; the part of you that wants to have fun

chronology arrangement of data according to group features

chunks groups of information that are clustered together to help you remember through association

circle graphs graphics that show how a whole unit is divided into parts

clarity clearness of thought; the first standard against which you judge thinking

closure the condition of being ended, finished, or concluded; the process by which incomplete figures, ideas, or situations tend to be completed mentally or perceived as complete

college catalog a book describing the services, curricula, courses, faculty, and other information pertaining to a post-secondary institution

comparison/contrast the organization of information for placing like or unlike ideas, situations, or characters together

completeness requires that you have all of the information to form a comprehensive picture

comprehensive tests examinations that cover all materials presented in class over the course of an entire term

concept map a method of notetaking or processing notes; a diagram, similar to a flow chart, which shows relationships between and among concepts

concepts connected and organized networks or webs of information

conclusions decisions, judgments, or opinions reached by reasoning or inferring

consequences a series of given outcomes

consistency reliability of information in both spoken and written forms

coping strategies strategies that help you manage stress more effectively

cramming studying rapidly under pressure for an examination; usually done at the last minute instead of over time

creativity ultimate form of synthesis; taking all available information, creating hypotheses, drawing conclusions, and coming up with a new idea or product

credibility evaluating whether or not information is fact or opinion

credit hour the quantitative measure of recognition given to a course, usually based on the number of times a course meets in one week of a regular semester

criteria matrices mechanisms that allow you to see options and evaluate them

critical thinking thinking logically about information, people, and choices in order to make reasonable, informed decisions about learning, relationships, and life

critic   one of three inner dialogue voices; the part of you that denounces you

cross-references   information which refers from one item, passage, or text to another

curricula   the total program of studies of a school

curve of forgetting   a line diagram which shows the relationship between recall of information without review and the amount of time since the material's presentation; also called the Ebbinghaus Curve

D

data base   collection of data arranged for ease of retrieval, especially by a computer

definition   a type of context clue in which punctuation marks that indicate that the meaning of an unknown word follows directly

definitional assumption   concluding that everyone defines qualitative words the same way you do

denial   a defense mechanism that involves pretending that a problem doesn't exist or isn't important

depth   consideration of the level of complexity of the thought

derivations   the use of affixes to build new words from a root or base word, often with a change in the part of speech of the word

Dewey decimal system   library classification scheme which divides all knowledge into ten major groups by subject, each of which can be subdivided infinitely

diagrams   plans, drawings, figures, or combination thereof made to show clearly a thing or how it works

direct quote   showing a person's exact words

distractions   diversions which cause a turning away from the focus of attention

distress   a type of stress that hurts your performance

distributed   practice a method of developing a skill by setting task or time limits (practicing a specified amount of time or information each day) rather than attempting to cram much practice into a small period of time; spaced study

disuse   release of information that is seldom used from memory

E

ellipsis   the omission of a word or phrase shown by a series of marks (. . .)

endnotes   a form of footnotes which occurs at the end of a book or document

(dictionary) entry   a term listed alphabetically, usually in boldface, in a dictionary

enumeration/sequence   placement of information in a systematic organizational pattern according to time or rank

ESL students   students whose native languages aren't English and who are enrolled in a program for learning English language skills (English as a Second Language) .

essay   a brief paper expressing opinion about a single topic; theme etymology the study of the origins of words

euphemisms   words or phrases used to soften the reality of negative statements or to disguise the truth

eustress   the type of stress that energizes you and drives you to be your best

evaluation   judgement, the highest level of thinking; requires being able to recall, translate, interpret, apply, analyze, and synthesize to judge and evaluate effectively

expert opinions   judgments of those who have knowledge and skill in particular subjects

exploration   evaluation of oneself and one's career possibilities

external motivation   behavior directed toward satisfaction through anticipated rewards or punishment

F

fact   information based on direct evidence, a statement of truth

fairness   unbiased coverage of a topic

fantasy   belief that one can have any career; unrealistic expectation

feature analysis table   a table analyzing characteristics rather than amounts; a quality table

fiction   one of two types of writing; not fact or truth; written to entertain

flowcharts   drawings that show the steps in a complicated process

footnotes   notes at the bottom of a page about something on the page

free elective   a course which is not specified in a degree
program

full-time student   student carrying enough credit
hours during a term to be considered as having a
complete load of coursework

G

gazetteer   dictionary or index of geographical terms

general reference maps   maps that give general geographic information

government documents   library holdings consisting of
material published by U.S. government agencies

grade point average (GPA)   average of numerical values assigned to course grades

graphics   drawings or reproductions of drawings,
maps, pictures, graphs

graphs   diagrams or charts in which various data is
presented through differing lengths of bars (bar
graphs), dots connected to form lines (line
graphs), or pie-shaped wedges to form circles (pie
or circle graphs; symbolic representations of information that show quantitative comparisons between two or more kinds of information

guide words   words that appear at the top of each page
in a dictionary to aid in locating entries quickly

H

histogram   a graphic in which bars indicate the frequency of data; shows quantitative comparisons; a
bar graph

home page   preset Internet Web page to which your
Web Browser opens

hypermedia links   key words to multimedia information

hypertext   like menus; key words that form doorways
to additional text information

hypothesis   an educated guess; an idea of what will
happen next in a particular situation or of what
the consequences of a given action will be

I

idea or concept map   a method of notetaking or processing notes; a diagram, similar to a flow chart,
which shows relationships between and among
concepts

implications   a series of possible outcomes

inductive outline   a process in which you reduce information from major concepts to specific main ideas

inferences   statements or predictions about the unknown based on the known

informal dialogues   conversations which allow you to
explore new points of view, acquire new information, and hear what others see as the implications
of various issues

information   knowledge which comes from the data
you acquire from life—what you see, hear, smell,
taste, touch, feel, read, or experience

information matrices   tables, pictures, or diagrams of
information; charts

interest inventory   an informal checklist for exploring
preferences for a given activity

interests   feelings of wanting to know, see, do, own,
share in, or take part in

interference   memory loss caused by the process of
conflicting information

interlibrary loan   a method by which one library bor-
rows an item from the holdings of another library

interpretations   your translations of concepts and
information

internal motivation   self-directed incentives for behavior interpretation the ability to explain events
through a knowledge of the connections that exist
among ideas

Internet   a collection of computer networks that facilitates the exchange of information; includes the
World Wide Web

intramural sports   athletic events other than varsity
competition involving members of the same
school, college, or organization

introduction/summary   placement of information for
the purpose of initiating or ending a discussion of
a topic

J

justifiability   a rationale based on a list of logically supportive reasons

K

key   a list of words or phrases giving an explanation of symbols or abbreviations used on a map; a legend

kinesthetic   acquiring information through the use of physical experiences

kinesthetic perception   the drawings made from words or phrases that appeal to the senses; physical imagery; mnemonigraphs

L

lecture patterns   the organizational pattern of a lecture (similar to text patterns)

left brain   cognitive processing of information in sequential, linear, logical ways

legend   a list of words or phrases giving an explanation of symbols or abbreviations used on a map

Library of Congress (LC) system   a method of classifying publications using letters and numerals which allows for infinite expansion

line graphs   graphics used to show quantitative trends for one or more items over time

loaded words   words or phrases that make people, issues, and things appear worse than they might really be

logic   a form of thinking or problem solving that follows a line of reasoning that others can understand

logical inference   a conclusion that cannot be avoided; for example, if a=b and b=c, then a=c

long-term goal   an objective which requires a lengthy time committment

long-term memory   permanent memory; last stage of memory processing

M

main entry card   the full catalog record of an item in the library's collection, often the author card

mantras   relaxing words repeated in a meditative manner

maps   two-dimensional graphics of a specific location

meditation   a form of relaxation, it involves narrowing your conscious mind until anxiety wanes

microfiche   a microfilm sheet containing rows of written or printed pages in reduced form

microfiche reader   a device that makes any microform large enough to be easily read

microforms   consist of microfiche, microfilm, ultrafiche; reduced forms of books, journals, articles, and so on

MIND   an acronym that helps you systematically work through the process of critical thinking

mnemonigraph   the drawings made from words or phrases that appeal to the senses; kinesthetic perception; physical imagery

multisensory   the combination of two or more senses (sensory preferences)

Myers-Briggs Type Indicator (MBTI)   an evaluation of personality types, based on the work of Carl Jung

N

need   something that is thought necessary or desired

newspaper index   an index to selected daily/weekly published newspapers

noncomprehensive   describes examinations that do not cover all materials presented in class over the course of an entire term; examinations covering only a specific amount of material

nonfiction   prose based upon fact; written to explain, argue, or describe rather than to entertain

note-taking outline   outline made before reading a chapter as preview for the lecture

O

objective test   a type of test in which a student selects an answer from several choices provided by the instructor; included among these are multiple choice, true/false, matching and some fill-in-the-blank

opinion   a judgement or viewpoint

outlining   a formal or informal pattern of ideas

overlearning   overlapping study of information to reinforce initial learning

P

paraphrase   a summary; contains an unbiased version of what the author said

parenthetical references   statements which help explain or qualify information

parody   copy of series works or phrases through satire or burlesque

part-time student   student carrying less than the minimum number of credit hours to be considered full-time

peer pressure   a controlling mechanism that regulates group membership through conformity and loss of personal freedom

perception   reception of information that is understood in memory

periodical indicies   alphabetical listings, journals and magazines that list the authors, titles, and subjects of articles in periodicals

personality   your personal preferences based on the Myers-Briggs Type Indicator or other instrument

perspective   point of view

pictorial graphs   graphics that use symbols to show quantitative amounts; symbol graphs

plagiarism   an idea, expression, plot, and so forth, taken from another and used as one's own

point of view   the position from which one looks at something

precision   refers to exactness

previewing   surveying to get the main idea about something that will be read later

primary source   original documents or first-person accounts of an event

prime study time   the time of day or night when a student is most mentally alert for learning and remembering information

procrastination   the act or habit of putting tasks off until later

projection   defense mechanism in which the blame for a problem is placed on someone or something else

propaganda   tells only one side of an issue to make you believe only that particular viewpoint

psychoactive drugs   drugs that lead to psychological dependence, the feeling that you need a drug to stay "normal" or "happy"

puns   use of words or phrases to suggest more than one meaning

purpose   intention for reading

Q

quality points   numerical value assigned to each letter grade from "A" to "F" when given as the final grade in a course; used to calculate grade point average

quality table   a table analyzing characteristics rather than amounts; a feature analysis table

questions   ways to set purpose in thinking and reading

R

rationalize   defense mechanism which offers acceptable excuses in place of the real ones

ready reference   books held in reserve by a library for patrons to use only while they remain in the library

realistic period   career development stage consisting of exploration, crystallization, and specification

recall   the lowest level of understanding; requires little more than auditory or visual memory skills

reception   receiving information into short-term memory without understanding

recitation   silent, oral, or written repetition of information to increase recall

registration   the part of memory consisting of reception, perception, and selection; first stage of memory processing

relevance; relevancy   the state of being applicable, appropriate, pertinent, useful

report   a formal written presentation of facts

repression   defense mechanism in which the cause of stress is blocked from memory

research paper   a lengthy, well documented written presentation

reserve books   books held in a special area of the library that can be checked out only for designated periods of time

rewards   recompense for something that you do or say

right brain   cognitive processing which synthesizes rather than analyzes, it uses holistic, perceptual understanding

rough draft   an author's first attempt at writing a particular manuscript

S

scale of distance   a representation of size or space on maps; indicates the relationship between the distance of one place shown on a map and this distance in actuality

scan   reading quickly to find specific information; reading for specific answers

schedule   a written or printed statement of fixed times or appointments; a timetable

scope   range of application

secondary source   second-person accounts of an event

selection   a deliberate processing of information into memory or a deliberate disregard of it

self-talk   the dialogue inside your mind as your think to yourself about how to act or feel about a situation

semantic practice   writing or diagraming information that you are trying to remember

sensory preferences   concern the way or ways in which you like to acquire information

short-term goals   an objective which requires a brief time commitment

short-term memory   immediate or brief memory; second stage of memory processing

significance   refers to importance

skim   reading quickly to find main ideas

spaced study   a method of learning which requires setting task or time limits (practicing a specified amount of time or information each day) rather than attempting to cram much practice into a small period of time; distributed practice

special purpose maps   maps which highlight some specific natural or man-made feature; a thematic map

specification period   final career decision

specificity   a limiting of details so that you exclude particulars to identify a single item

stacks   shelves in the library for holding books and journals

standard   the criteria against which you judge thinking

stress   a physical or emotional factor that causes tension; anxiety

style   the mix of attributes that defines you

style manual   reference for the preparation of a manuscript

subject card   filed under the subject of the material, this card contains the full catalog record of an item in the library's collection

subject development   the organization of information for discussing a topic and its related details

subjective   describes tests that require you to supply the answers in your own words

subjective tests   type of exam in which students must provide an original written answer; included among these are essay and some fill-in-the-blank questions

summary   a condensed statement or paragraph that contains only the essential ideas of a longer statement, paragraph, or passage

symbol graphs   graphics which uses symbols to show quantitative amounts; pictorial graphs

symbols   an idea or concept that stands for or suggests another idea or concept by means of association or relationship

synonym   a word which has a similar meaning to that of another word

synthesis   the combination of parts or elements into a whole

T

tables   systematic listings of information in rows and columns

tentative period   one's realization that some careers are inappropriate goals while others are more appropriate goals

term papers   lengthy, well documented written presentations of information

terms specialized or technical vocabulary in a specific subject

test an examination; a way of evaluating how well a student has mastered the material presented in class or in the textbook. These examinations can be comprehensive or non-comprehensive. There are two types of questions that may appear on a test, objective and subjective.

text labeling strategy that helps you identify relationships and summarize information

text marking strategy that involves finding important information and highlighting or underlining it

text structure the way in which a written text is presented (outline, headings, sub-headings, and so on)

thematic maps maps that highlight some specific natural or manmade feature; special purpose maps

theme a brief paper expressing opinion about a single topic; essay

thesaurus book of synonyms and sometimes antonyms

thesis statement similar to a topic sentence, this sentence contains the main idea to be covered in a paper

time lines graphic outlines of sequenced information; a chronology of important dates or events

time management a system for scheduling commitments efficiently

title card filed under the title of the material, this card contains the full catalog record of an item in the library's collection

transition words terms that signal the identity and flow of a lecture's pattern

translation the ability to convert information into your own words while retaining the essence of the idea

trends changes in direction over time

U

unabridged dictionary a dictionary whose number of entries have not been limited or reduced

V

values that which is of worth/importance to an individual

verbatim information information that you must remember word for word—exactly as it was written or said

vertical file clipping file; source of print materials which have not been published in book form

visual acquiring information through the use of visual perception; practice silently reading information that you are trying to remember

visualization uses imagination to put positive messages into action

W

weasel words words that show the possibility of other options and that lack exactness

working bibliography a list of the books or articles consulted or referred to by an author as the rough draft is written

working memory part of memory where information is processed; limited in size; third stage of memory processing

Y

yearbooks published yearly, this book contains a summary or review of facts

References

Anderson, R. C., & J. W. Pichert (1978). Recall of previously unrecallable information following a shift in perspective. *Journal of Verbal Learning and Verbal Behavior,* 17: 1–12.

Benson, H. (1975). *The relaxation response.* New York: Morrow.

Berne, E. (1966). *Principles of group treatment.* New York: Simon & Schuster (2nd ed.).

Bower, G. H. (1970). Analysis of a mnemonic device. *American Scientist* 58: 496.

Brown, S. A. (1985). Expectancies versus background in the prediction of college drinking patterns. *Journal of Consulting and Clinical Psychology,* 53:123–130.

Brunvand, J. H. (1989). *Curses! Broiled again!* New York: Norton.

Bryson, B. (1990). *The mother tongue and how it got that way.* New York: Morrow.

Carmen, R. & W. R. Adams (1985). *Study skills: a student's guide for survival.* New York: Wiley.

Corvey, S. A. R. Merrill, & R. R. Merrill (1994). *First things first.* New York: Simon and Schuster.

Dale, E. (1958). How to know more wonderful words. *Good Housekeeping,* 147, 17+.

Geiselman, R. E., R. P. Fisher, D. P. MacKinnon, & H. L. Holland (1986). Eyewitness memory enhancement with cognitive interview. *American Journal of Psychology,* 99: 385–401.

Howe, M. J. (1970). Notetaking strategy, review and long-term relationships between notetaking variables and achievement measures. *Journal of Educational Research,* 63: 285.

Janis, I. L., & L. Mann (1977). *Decision-Making.* New York: Free Press.

Kiewra, K. A. (1985). Investigating notetaking and review: a depth of processing alternative. *Educational Psychologist* 20(l): 23–32.

Knox, D. (1990). *Sociology.* St. Paul, Minn.: West.

Larson, C. O., & D. E. Dansereau (1986). Cooperative learning in dyads. *Journal of Reading* 29: 516–520.

Lawrence, G. (1987). *Personality types and tiger stripes* Gainesville, FL.: Center for Applications of Psychological Types.

Light, R. J. (1990). *The Harvard assessment seminars: first report.* Harvard University Graduate School of Education and Kennedy School of Government: Cambridge, Mass.

Light, R. J. (1992). *The Harvard assessment seminars: second report.* Harvard University Graduate School of Education and Kennedy School of Government: Cambridge, Mass.

Maslow, A. H. (1954). *Motivation and personality.* New York: Harper & Row.

Miller, G. A. (1956). The magical number seven, plus or minus two: some limits on our capacity for processing information. *Psychological Review* 63: 81–97.

Morse, G. W. (1975). *Concise guide to library research,* 2nd ed. New York: Fleet Academic Editions.

Nienhuis, T. (1989). Curing plagiarism with a note-taking exercise. *College Teaching* 37(3): 100.

Owen, D. (1990). The best teacher I ever had. *Life* 13: 70.

Palkovitz, R. J. & R. K. Lore (1980). Notetaking and note review: why student fail questions based on lecture material. *Teaching of Pyschology,* 7: 159–160.

Pauk, W. (1984). *How to study in college.* Boston: Houghton Mifflin, 127–129.

Paul, R. W. (1990). *Critical thinking: What every person needs to survive in a rapidly changing world.* Rohnert Park: Center for Critical Thinking and Moral Critique.

Peper, R. J., & R. E. Mayer (1978). Notetaking as a generative activity. *Journal of Educational Psychology* 70(4): 514–522.

Psaffenberger, B. (1995). Worldwide Bible. NY: Mis: Press.

Sarros, J. C., & I. L. Densten (1989). Undergraduate student stress and coping strategies. *Higher Education Research and Development* 8: 1.

Scott, G. G. (1994). *The empowered mind.* Englewood Cliffs, NJ: Prentice Hall.

Shanker, A. (1988, Fall). Strength in numbers. *Academic Connections,* 12.

Sher, B. (1994). *I could do anything if I only knew what it was.* New York: Delacourte.

Simpson, M. L. (1986). PORPE: A writing strategy for studying and learning in the content areas. *Journal of Reading* 29: 407–414.

Tenney, J. (1986, March). Keyword notetaking system. Paper presented at the nineteenth annual meeting of the Western College Reading Association, Los Angeles.

Tomlinson, L.M. (1997). A coding system for notetaking in literature: Preparation for journal writing, class participation and essay tests. *Journal of Adolescent and Adult Literacy* 40: 468-473.

Van Dijk, T. A., & W. Kintch (1978). Cognitive psychology and discourse: recalling and summarizing stories. In *Trends in text linguistics,* edited by W. V. Dressler. New York: DeGruyter.

von Oech, R. (1986). A *Kick in the seat of the pants.* New York: Harper and Row.

Williams, T. H. (1969). *Huey Long.* New York: Alfred A. Knopf, 262–263.

Wittrock, M. C. (1977). The generative processes of memory. In *The Human Brain,* edited by M. C. Wittrock. Englewood Cliffs, NJ: Prentice-Hall.

Yelon, S., & M. Massa (1990). Heuristics for creating examples. In *Teaching college: Collected readings for the new instructor,* edited by R. A. Neff and M. Weimer. Madison, WI: Magna Publications.

Index